Manual S

Residential Equipment Selection

Second Edition, Version 1.00

ANSI/ACCA 3 Manual S — 2014

ISBN # 978-1892765-58-1

*The Second Edition of ACCA **Manual S** ® is the*
Air Conditioning Contractors of America
procedure for selecting and sizing heating and cooling equipment for
single family homes, and low-rise multi-family dwellings.

To comment on the content of this manual or for information pertaining to technical content respond to:

Glenn Hourahan or Hank Rutkowski

ACCA
2800 Shirlington Road, Suite 300
Arlington, VA 22206
Voice: 703-575-4477

Copyright and Disclaimer

This publication and all earlier working/review drafts of this publication are protected by copyright. By making this publication available for use, ACCA does not waive any rights in copyright to this publication. No part of this publication or earlier working/review drafts of this publication may be reproduced, stored in a retrieval system, or transmitted in any form by any technology, without written permission from ACCA. Address requests to reproduce, store, or transmit to: Chris Hoelzel at the ACCA offices in Arlington, Virginia.

© 2014, Air Conditioning Contractors of America
2800 Shirlington Road, Suite 300
Arlington, VA 22206
www.acca.org

Adoption by Reference
Public authorities and others are encouraged to reference this document in laws, ordinances, regulations, administrative orders, or similar instruments. Any deletions, additions, and changes desired by the adopting authority must be noted separately. The term "adoption by reference" means references shall be limited to citing of title, version, date and source of publication.

Disclaimer and Legal Notice
Diligence has been exercised in the production of this publication. The content is based on an industry consensus of recognized good practices drawn from published handbooks, manuals, journals, standards, codes, technical papers, research papers, magazine articles, textbooks used for engineering curriculums, and on information presented during conferences and symposiums. ACCA has made no attempt to question, investigate or validate this information, and ACCA expressly disclaims any duty to do so. The commentary, discussion, and procedures provided by this publication do not constitute a warranty, guarantee, or endorsement of any concept, observation, recommendation, procedure, process, formula, data-set, product, or service. ACCA, members of the *Manual S* Review Committee, and the document reviewers do not warrant or guarantee that the information contained in this publication is free of errors, omissions, misinterpretations, or that it will not be modified or invalidated by additional scrutiny, analysis, or investigation. The entire risk associated with the use of the information provided by this standard is assumed by the user.

ACCA does not take any position with respect to the validity of any patent or copyright rights asserted in connection with any items, process, procedures, or apparatus which are mentioned in or are the subject of this document, and ACCA disclaims liability of the infringement of any patent resulting from the use of or reliance on this document. Users of this document are expressly advised that determination of the validity of any such patent or copyright, and the risk of infringement of such rights, is entirely their own responsibility. Users of this document should consult applicable federal, state, and local laws and regulations. ACCA does not, by the publication of this document, intend to urge action that is not in compliance with applicable laws, and this document may not be construed as doing so. Nothing in this manual should be construed as providing legal advice, and the content is not a substitute for obtaining legal counsel from the reader's own lawyer in the appropriate jurisdiction or state.

Acknowledgments

The author, Hank Rutkowski, P.E., ACCA Technical Consultant, gratefully acknowledges the diverse expertise embodied in the membership of the ACCA *Manual S* Advisory Committee:

Manual S, Second Edition, Reviewers and Advisors:

Mechanical Contractors

Dan Foley, Foley Mechanical Inc.; Lorton, VA

Ellis G. Guiles, Jr. P.E., TAG Mechanical Systems, Inc.; Syracuse, NY

Jolene O. Methvin, Bay Area Air Conditioning & Heating; Crystal River, FL

John D. Sedine, Engineered Heating and Cooling, Inc.; Walker, MI

Daryl F. Senica, Senica Air Corporation, Inc.; Spring Hill, FL

Kenneth B. Watson, Roscoe Brown, Inc.; Murfreesboro, TN

Instructors

Jack Bartell, Virginia Air Distributors, Inc.; Midlothian, VA

John "Pete" Jackson, Alabama Power Company; Mobile, AL

Arthur T. Miller, Community College of Allegheny County; Oakdale, PA

Fred G. Paepke, Fitzenrider, Inc.; Defiance, OH

John F. Parker, J. Parker Consulting Services; Clanton, AL

Thomas A. Robertson, Baker Distributing Company, Inc.; New Haven, MO

David E. Swett, Omaha Public Power District; Omaha, NE

Original Equipment Manufacturer's

Pamela Androff, Mitsubishi Electric Cooling & Heating; Suwanee, GA

Tom Fesenmyer, Emerson Climate Technologies, AC Division; Sidney, OH

Raymond A. Granderson, Rheem Manufacturing Company–A/C Division; Fort Smith, AR

J. Kelly Hearnsberger, Goodman Manufacturing Company; Houston, TX

Tom Johnson, Lennox Industries Inc.; Dallas, TX

Eric Weiss, The Trane Company; Tyler, TX

Robert Lambert, Carrier Residential and Commercial Systems; Indianapolis, IN

Consultants

Charles S. Barnaby, Wrightsoft Inc.; Lexington, MA

Stan Johnson, Consultant; Austin, TX

Michael Lubliner, Washington State University–Extension Energy Program; Olympia, WA

Jack Rise, Jack Rise HVAC Technical Training; Tampa, FL

Henry T. Rutkowski, P.E., HTR Consulting, Inc.; Dover, OH

William W. Smith, Elite Software, Inc.; College Station, TX

Brent Ursenbach, Salt Lake County Planning & Development; Salt Lake City, UT

Richard F. Welguisz, HVAC Consultant; Tyler, TX

Jon Winkler, National Renewable Energy Laboratory (NREL); Golden, CO

Association and Other Participants
Timothy M. Donovan, Sheet Metal Workers Local 265; Carol Stream, IL

Glenn C. Hourahan, P.E., Air Conditioning Contractors of America (ACCA); Arlington, VA

Edward Janowiak, Eastern Heating & Cooling Council (EHCC); Mt Laurel, NJ

Warren B. Lupson, Air-Conditioning, Heating and Refrigeration Institute (AHRI); Arlington, VA

Patrick L. Murphy, Refrigeration Service Engineers Society (RSES); Des Plaines, IL

Extended Reviewers to the Committee
Ron Bladen, ACCA Staff, Fairfax, VA

Jeff Hammond, Geo-Flo Products Corp.; Bedford, IN

Dean Gamble, U.S. Environmental Protection Agency; Washington, DC

Special Thanks and Appreciation
John D. Sedine for his guidance and leadership as the Committee Chair

Staff Liaison — Technical
Glenn C. Hourahan, P.E., ACCA; Arlington, VA

Staff Liaison — Production, Publishing, and Editing
Christopher N. Hoelzel, ACCA; Arlington, VA

Publishing Consultant
Page layout and electronic publishing provided by Carol Lovelady, Lovelady Consulting; Roswell, GA

Dedication

Personal Dedication

The author offers a personal thank-you to equipment manufacturers that provide, by varius media, comprehensive (expanded) performance data for their products.

Professional Dedication

The author greatly appreciates Ron Bladen's (ACCA Staff, Arlington, VA) efforts to improve the quality and integrity of code enforcement work.

This overview is not part of the this standard. It is merely informative and does not contain requirements necessary for conformance to the standard. It has not been processed according to the ANSI requirements for a standard, and may contain material that has not been subject to public review or a consensus process. Unresolved objectors on informative material are not offered the right to appeal at ACCA or ANSI.

Overview

This manual provides procedures for selecting and sizing residential cooling equipment, heat pumps, electric heating coils, furnaces, boilers, ancillary dehumidification equipment, humidification equipment, equipment tested and rated according to retail appliance standards, and direct evaporative cooling equipment. These procedures emphasize the importance of using performance data that correlates sensible and latent cooling capacity with all the variables that affect performance. Similar principles apply to heat pump selection and sizing, and to furnace and boiler selection and sizing. All procedures produce installed, design condition capacity that is appropriate for the applicable building load(s), but is less than, or equal to, the over sizing limit allowed for a given type of equipment.

This manual has been divided into two parts—a 'normative' portion and an 'informative' portion. The three, up-front normative sections provide all the equipment selection and equipment sizing criteria necessary to implement the standard's requirements (there are no additional selection requirements or sizing requirements in the balance of the document):

Section N1 – Definitions and General Requirements
Section N2 – Equipment Size Limits
Section N3 – OEM Verification Path

The informative sections and informative appendices in the balance of this document provide discussion and instruction related to procedure intent and use; includes example problems that detail application of the procedure. These informative presentations are provided to augment practitioner understanding and application of the normative material:

Sections 1 to 4 – Basic Concepts and Issues
Sections 5 to 10 – Central Ducted System and Hydronic Heating Examples
Sections 11 to 13 – Ductless Air-Air Equipment
Appendixes 1 to 5 – Implementation Issues and Procedures
Appendixes 6 to 15 – Related Information
Appendix 16 to 22 – Ancillary Pages

Commentary on Over-Size Limits for Cooling-Only Equipment and Heat Pumps

For *Manual S* procedures, the sizing value for equipment size is 100% (1.00 factor) of the smallest defensible value for the *Manual J* total cooling load (sensible load plus latent load). When indoor humidity control for the entire cooling season (the summer design condition, and all part-load conditions) is an issue, total cooling capacity must be as close as possible to the sizing value on the high side, or total cooling capacity may be a little less than the sizing value (0.90 is the absolute minimum factor). Normative Section N2, Tables N2-1 and N2-2 provide upper and lower limits for the installed cooling capacity of various types of cooling-only equipment and heat pump equipment.

When cooling season humidity control is not an issue, and when heating season energy use is an issue, the over-size limit for heat pump equipment cooling capacity is equal to the Manual J total cooling load plus 15,000 Btuh. This reduces winter energy use because it increases the amount of seasonal heat provided by the compressor, and reduces the amount of seasonal heat provided by an electric heating coil. Normative Section N2, Table N2-2 shows this procedure.

There is no energy use benefit for over sizing cooling-only equipment, regardless of the summer humidity control issue, or the cold winter weather issue. In other words, the 15,000 Btuh exemption does not apply to any type of cooling-only equipment. Even when there is no latent cooling load, summer comfort is improved by adequate room air motion, so the equipment must run as much a possible. As far as energy use is concerned, compressor cycling degrades seasonal efficiency, so the equipment must be as small as possible.

There is no energy use benefit for over sizing heat pump equipment installed in a location that has a mild winter climate. This is because electric coil heat is not an issue when the thermal balance point for equipment that has little or no excess cooling capacity is below, at, or slightly above, the *Manual J* winter design temperature for outdoor air. Therefore, the plus 15,000 Btuh limit does not apply to any type of heat pump equipment installed in a location that has mild winter weather. Also note that on-off cycling degrades seasonal heating efficiency when the outdoor air temperature is above the thermal balance point, and on-off cycling degrades seasonal cooling efficiency, so excess cooling capacity increases annual energy use. Even when there is no latent cooling load, summer comfort is improved by adequate room air motion, so the equipment must run as much a possible.

Standard Size Issues

Residential HVAC equipment is mass produced for economies of scale. Cooling-only equipment and heat pumps have significant jumps in nominal size. The over-size limits specified in Table N2-1 and Table N2-2 allow for substantial deviation from the sizing value because of the realties of the market place.

- For central ducted equipment, the nominal condenser capacity for single compressor speed equipment may start at 1½ tons, and typically increases in ½ ton steps, but there tends to be a 1 ton jump from 4-tons to 5-tons. Some OEMs do not have a 1½ ton product (2 tons is the smallest size).

    Effective total cooling capacity may be increased or reduced by a mismatch for nominal condenser-evaporator tonnage values, but this is generally a 2,000 Btuh adjustment, more or less.

    *The primary reason for mismatching condenser-evaporator tonnage values is to obtain correspondence between the evaporator coil sensible heat ratio and the **Manual J** sensible heat ratio.*

    OEM expanded performance data may not be readily available for condenser-evaporator combinations that deviate from the basic matched-size product.

    Product availability and delivery time depends on what is commonly purchased vs. what may possibly be purchased.

- For ducted equipment, the nominal condenser-side capacity for a multi-speed or variable-speed compressor typically increases in 1-ton steps.

    This type of equipment will cycle or modulate between low and high compressor speed for a large number of part-load hours. There is significant latent capacity for this mode of operation, so the undesirable effect of excess cooling capacity, as far as indoor humidity control is concerned, is somewhat less than what it would be for single-speed equipment.

    However, there is a low-limit to equipment cooling capacity. When the cooling load is below this limit, the compressor cycles on and off. So for these part-load hours, indoor humidity control is similar to the control provided by single-speed equipment. In other words, excess cooling capacity is an important issue for a significant number of part-load hours.

- Ductless equipment may be as small as one-ton (or less), and may have ½ ton steps (or less) to 5 tons. However, a duct system is required to distribute capacity among a group of rooms that are not part of a common open space.

    Room cooling loads typically range from less than 1,000 Btuh to less than 4,000 Btuh.

    Indoor air motion occurs in the space that is near the indoor coil, and less so for a common space that is beyond the throw of the indoor coil's grille, and not at all for remote spaces that have partition walls (with or without partition doors).

    Some indoor coils are designed to serve a duct system. However, the available static pressure of the equipment's blower, and the type of duct fittings, establishes the distribution limits (distances) of the duct runs.

Efficiency Issue

In general, high SEER values are at the expense of latent capacity and indoor humidity control. Excess cooling capacity, is a bigger issue for contemporary high SEER equipment than it was for older, lower SEER equipment.

Job Economics and Practitioner Talent

Proper use of expanded performance data (or the software equivalent) does not require much time, and is relatively simple, providing the data is readily available. However, practitioner access to this data may be limited to products produced by one OEM, or a few OEM's. In addition, expanded performance data may not be readily available for various condenser-evaporator size matches.

- Business issues typically limit practitioner access to the entire collection of available products.
- Time-is-money issues limit the scope of the available equipment capacity investigation.
- Price-point issues may eliminate classes of equipment that have preferred attributes, as far as excess capacity and humidity control are concerned.
- Fine-tuning equipment selection by blower Cfm adjustments, and/or condenser-evaporator size matching, takes time and skill.

Conclusion

The possibility of a comfort problem, humidity problem, or mold-mildew problem increases with the amount of excess cooling capacity. The equipment sizing goal is to have no excess total cooling capacity. Tolerance for upside deviation depends on the *Manual J* sensible heat ratio (JSHR). For example, a 1.18 over-size factor is more compatible with an 0.90 JSHR, and less compatible with an 0.75 JSHR.

Overview of Size Limits for Residential HVAC Equipment

Equipment [a] Tested and Rated by the AHRI	Attributes of Local Climate Notes b, c	Issue	Minimum (deficient) and Maximum (excessive) Capacity Factors. [d]					
		Cooling Capacity (Btuh)	Single-Speed Compressor			Multi- and Variable-Speed Compressor		
			Air-Air	GLHP [e]	GWHP [f]	Air-Air	GLHP [e]	GWHP [f]
Air-Air and Water-Air Cooling-Only & Heat Pump	Mild Winter **or** Has a Latent Cooling Load	Total	0.90 to 1.15	1.25		0.90 to 1.20_{multi} or $1.30_{variable}$		1.30_m or 1.35_v
		Latent	Minimum = 1.00. Preferred maximum = 1.50 (may exceed 1.5 if no reasonable alternative).					
		Sensible	Minimum = 0.90. Maximum determined by total and latent capacities.					
Air-Air and Water-Air Heat Pump Only	Cold Winter **and** No Latent Cooling load	Total	Maximum capacity = *Manual J* total cooling load plus 15,000 Btuh; Minimum factor = 0.90					
		Latent	Latent capacity for summer cooling is not an issue.					
		Sensible	Not an issue (determined by the limits for total cooling capacity).					

a) Central ducted; ductless single-split; ductless multi-split equipment. AHRI: Air Conditioning, Heating and Refrigeration Institute.
b) Mild winter: Heating degree days for base 65°F divided by cooling degree days for base 50°F less than 2.0. Cold winter = 2.0 or more.
c) Latent cooling load: *Manual J* sensible load divided by *Manual J* total load less than 0.95. No latent load = 0.95 or more.
d) Minimum and maximum capacity factors operate on the total, latent, and sensible capacity values produced by an accurate *Manual J* load calculation (per Section 2 of the Eighth Edition of *Manual J*, version 2.0 or later). Multiply a size factor by 100 to convert to a percentage. For example, 1.15 excess capacity = 115% excess capacity.
e) GLHP: Ground loop heat pump (water in buried closed pipe loop).
f) GWHP: Ground water heat pump (ground water from well, pond, lake, river, etc., flows though equipment and is discarded).

Electric Heating Coils	Furnaces; Heat Pump supplement; emergency	Load (Btuh)	Maximum KW	Minimum Capacity Factor	Maximum Capacity Factor
		≤ 15,000	5.0	Satisfy Load	See Maximum KW
		> 15,000	See Min and Max	0.95	1.75

Minimum and maximum capacity factors operate on the heating load produced by an accurate *Manual J* load calculation. Multiply a size factor by 100 to convert to a percentage.

Natural Gas, Oil, Propane Furnaces	Duty	Minimum Output Capacity	Maximum Output Capacity
	Heating-only	1.00	1.40
	Heating-Cooling Preferred		1.40
	Heating-Cooling Allowed		2.00

Minimum and maximum capacity factors operate on the heating load produced by an accurate *Manual J* load calculation. Multiply a size factor by 100 to convert to a percentage. For heating-cooling duty, blower performance must be compatible with the cooling equipment.

Electric, and Fossil Fuel Water Boilers	Duty	Minimum Output Capacity	Maximum Output Capacity
	Gravity or forced convection terminals in the space, water coil in duct or air-handler.	1.00	1.40

Minimum and maximum capacity factors operate on the heating load produced by an accurate *Manual J* load calculation. Multiply a size factor by 100 to convert to a percentage. Refer to OEM guidance when a boiler is used for potable water heat, or snow melting.

Hot Water Coils	Duty	Minimum Factor	Maximum Factor	
			Two-position 1.25	Throttling 1.50
	Gravity or forced convection terminals in the space.	1.00		
	Water coil in duct or air-handler.			

Minimum and maximum capacity factors operate on the heating load produced by an accurate *Manual J* load calculation. Multiply a size factor by 100 to convert to a percentage. Two-position= open-close valve; Throttling = Full modulating 2-way or 3-way valve.

Electric and Fossil Fuel Water Heaters	The space heating load is the *Manual J* load. The total load is the space heating load plus the potable water load. Refer to OEM guidance for selection and sizing guidance.
Dual Fuel Systems	Heat pump sizing rules apply, heating equipment sizing rules apply, see Section N2-11.
Ancillary Dehumidification	See Section N2-12. May allow +15,000 Btuh excess cooling capacity for cold winter climate.
Humidifiers (Section N2-13)	Minimum capacity ≥ humidification load, excess capacity dependent on smallest size available.
AHAM Cooling and Heat Pump Equipment	See Section N2-14 for sizing rules.
Direct Evaporative Cooling Equipment	See Section N2-15 for sizing rules.

This section is not part of the this standard. It is merely informative and does not contain requirements necessary for conformance to the standard. It has not been processed according to the ANSI requirements for a standard, and may contain material that has not been subject to public review or a consensus process. Unresolved objectors on informative material are not offered the right to appeal at ACCA or ANSI.

Prerequisites and Learned Skills

Manual S assumes the practitioner is familiar with residential comfort conditioning systems and equipment, load calculations, procedures for selecting and sizing air distribution hardware, and duct design and airway sizing procedures. The prerequisites for using *Manual S* procedures are summarized here:

- A general understanding of the concepts, components, arrangements, procedures, requirements and terminology that pertain to residential building construction and residential comfort systems.
- Experience with designing residential heating and cooling systems for comfort applications.
- Mastery of residential load calculation methods and procedures (the full version of ACCA *Manual J*, Eighth Edition).
- Mastery of air distribution principles, and experience with using manufacturer's performance data to select and size supply air hardware and return air hardware, and associated devices (ACCA *Manual T*).
- Mastery of duct design principles, and experience with designing duct systems (ACCA *Manual D*, Third Edition).
- A general understanding of HVAC operating and safety controls, control strategies, and control cycles.
- Experience with designing HVAC systems that adjust performance to maintain space temperature set-points at full-load conditions, and at all part-load conditions (i.e., mastery of capacity control issues and strategies).
- Installing and commissioning refrigerant-cycle equipment and fuel burning equipment, and related power supplies, controls and vents.
- Installing and commissioning HVAC systems and components (per the ACCA HVAC Quality Installation Specification).

Table of Contents One

Copyright and Disclaimer ii
Acknowledgements iii
Dedication v
Overview vii
Limit Summary xi
Prerequisites and Learned Skills xiii

Section N1

Definitions and General Requirements

N1-1   Definitions. N1
N1-2   Rounding N3
N1-3   Equipment Selection and Sizing Procedure. N3
N1-4   Load Calculation N3
N1-5   Heat Pump Sizing Condition N3
N1-6   OEM Performance Data Requirements . . N4
N1-7   Blower Cfm N5
N1-8   Entering Air Condition for Equipment
       Selection and Sizing N5
N1-9   Water Pump Gpm and Entering Water
       Temperature for Water-Air Heat Pumps . N6
N1-10 Extract Capacity Values from OEM
       Performance Data N6
N1-11 Altitude N7
N1-12 Interpolation and Extrapolation. N7
N1-13 Equipment Sizing Limits N7
N1-14 Documentation Requirements N7

Section N2

Equipment Size Limits

N2-1   Scope N11
N2-2   Compliance with Sizing Limits N11
N2-3   Climate N11
N2-4   Equipment Sizing Metrics N11
N2-5   Sizing Limits for AHRI-Certified
       Cooling-Only Equipment N12
N2-6   Sizing Limits for AHRI-Certified
       Heat Pump Equipment N13
N2-7   Sizing Limits for Electric Heating Coils . . N14
N2-8   Sizing Limits for Fossil Fuel Furnaces . . N15
N2-9   Sizing Limits for Water Boilers N15
N2-10 Sizing Limits for a Water Heater
       Used for Space Heat N15
N2-11 Sizing Limits for Dual Fuel Systems . . . N16
N2-12 Sizing Limits for Ancillary
       Dehumidification Equipment N16
N2-13 Humidification Equipment Sizing N17
N2-14 AHAM Appliance Sizing N18
N2-15 Sizing Direct Evaporative
       Cooling Equipment N19

Section N3

OEM Verification Path

N3-1   OEM Certification Document N21
N3-2   Designer Input N21
N3-3   OEM Output N21
N3-4   Compliance N22

Part 1: Informative Material Pertaining to Basic Concepts and Issues

Section 1

Equipment Size Issues and Limits

1-1   Momentary Loads 2
1-2   Excess Capacity Vs. Performance 3
1-3   Indoor Humidity Issues 5
1-4   Summer Dehumidification 5
1-5   OEM Performance Data 6
1-6   Equipment Sizing Methods 8
1-7   Summary of Sizing Procedure 8
1-8   Cooling-Only Equipment Size 8
1-9   Heat Pump Equipment Size 9
1-10   Interpolation 10
1-11   Application Compatibility Caveats 10
1-12   Electric Heating Coil Size 11
1-13   Fossil Fuel Furnace Size 13
1-14   Dual Fuel Systems 13
1-15   Water Boilers and Water Heaters 13
1-16   AHAM Appliances 14
1-17   Ancillary Dehumidification Equipment . . . 15
1-18   Humidification Equipment 15
1-19   Direct Evaporative Cooling Equipment . . . 15
1-20   Over Sizing Authority for Heat Pumps . . . 15
1-21   Power Disruptions 16
1-22   Set-Up and Set-Back 17
1-23   Performance Expectations 17
1-24   Energy and Operating Cost Calculations . . 19

Section 2

Cooling-Only and Heat Pump Equipment Selection

2-1   Load Calculation 21
2-2   Entering Air Condition 22
2-3   Equipment Operating Limits 23
2-4   Seasonal Efficiency Rating 23
2-5   Expanded Performance Data 23
2-6   Sizing Cooling Equipment 24
2-7   Sizing Heat Pumps 28
2-8   Thermal Balance Point Diagram 30
2-9   Thermal Balance Point Manipulation 32
2-10   Thermal Balance Point Use 33

2-11	Supplemental Heat	34
2-12	Emergency Heat	34
2-13	Auxiliary Heat	35
2-14	High-Limit Temperature for Heating Coils	35
2-15	Design Blower Cfm for Cooling	36
2-16	Design Blower Cfm for Heating	36
2-17	Design Blower Cfm for Duct Sizing	36
2-18	Blower Data	36
2-19	Component Pressure Drop Data	37
2-20	Operating and Safety Controls	37
2-21	System Start-Up and Set-Point Recovery	38
2-22	Air Zoning Controls	39
2-23	Ductless Split Controls	39

Section 3

Furnace and Water Boiler Selection

3-1	Load Calculation	41
3-2	Equipment Operating Limits	41
3-3	Seasonal Efficiency Rating	41
3-4	Performance Data	41
3-5	Furnace Temperature Limit Calculations	42
3-6	Water Temperature Limit Calculations	43
3-7	Design Value for Furnace Blower Cfm	43
3-8	Furnace Blower Data	44
3-9	Component Pressure Drop Data	44
3-10	Adequate Blower Pressure	44
3-11	Equipment Sizing	44
3-12	Fuel Burning and Combustion Venting	46
3-13	Operating and Safety Controls	46
3-14	Air Zoning Controls	47
3-15	System Start-Up and Set-Point Recovery	47

Section 4

Humidity Control and Evaporative Cooling Equipment

4-1	Ancillary Dehumidification	49
4-2	Whole-House Dehumidifier Examples	51
4-3	Ventilation Dehumidifier Examples	53
4-4	Direct Evaporative Cooling	54
4-5	Winter Humidification Equipment	57

Part 2: Informative Material Pertaining to Central Ducted System Examples and Hydronic Heating Examples

Section 5

Central Ducted Air-Air Cooling Examples

5-1	Latent Cooling Load Issues	61
5-2	Sensible Heat Ratio Issues	61
5-3	Maximum Capacity for Cooling-Only Equipment	61
5-4	Maximum Cooling Capacity for Heat Pump Equipment	62
5-5	Minimum Cooling Capacity	62
5-6	Total Cooling Capacity Value	62
5-7	Latent and Sensible Capacity Values	63
5-8	Equipment Selection Examples	63
5-9	Attributes of the Example Dwelling	63
5-10	Balanced Climate Humid Summer Example	64
5-11	Hot-Humid Climate Example	66
5-12	Dry Summer Cold Winter Example	68
5-13	Moderate Latent Load Applications	70
5-14	Multi-Speed Equipment Performance	70
5-15	Variable-Speed Equipment Performance	70
5-16	Product Comparison Study	71
5-17	Compare Fayetteville Equipment	72
5-18	Compare Brunswick Equipment	73
5-19	Compare Boise Equipment	74

Section 6

Central Ducted Air–Air Heat Pump Heating Examples

6-1	Balance Point Diagram	77
6-2	Electric Coil Heat	78
6-3	Heating Performance Examples	78
6-4	Balanced Climate Example	78
6-5	Hot-Humid Climate Example	79
6-6	Dry Summer Cold Winter Example	80
6-7	Multi-Speed and Variable-Speed Selection	82
6-8	Heating Performance for Two-Speed Equipment	82
6-9	Heating Performance for Variable-Speed Equipment	83
6-10	Entering Air Temperature and Heating Capacity Depend on Blower Cfm	85
6-11	Use of Minimum Compressor Speed Data	85

Section 7

Central Ducted Furnace Examples

7-1	Heating Load	87
7-2	Maximum Heating Capacity	87
7-3	Minimum Heating Capacity	87
7-4	Blower Cfm	87
7-5	Air Temperature Limits	87
7-6	Equipment Selection Examples	87
7-7	Attributes of the Example Dwelling	87
7-8	Balanced Climate Humid Summer Example	88
7-9	Hot-Humid Climate Example	90
7-10	Dry Summer Cold Winter Example	92
7-11	Oil or Propane Furnace	94
7-12	Electric Furnace	94

Section 8
Dual Fuel Heating Procedures and Examples
8-1	Economic Question	95
8-2	Heat Pump Outputs and Energy Inputs	95
8-3	Furnace Outputs and Energy inputs	95
8-4	Economic Balance Point	95
8-5	Break-Even COP	96
8-6	Water-Air Heat Pump	97
8-7	Return on Investment	97
8-8	Furnace Sizing	97
8-9	Heat Pump Sizing	97
8-10	Retrofit Application	98
8-11	Economic Balance Points – Fayetteville	98
8-12	Economic Balance Points – Brunswick	98
8-13	Economic Balance Points – Boise	99

Section 9
Central Ducted Water–Air Heat Pump Examples
9-1	Redundant Instructions	101
9-2	Entering Water Temperature	101
9-3	Balanced Climate Humid Summer Example	102
9-4	Hot-Humid Climate Example	107
9-5	Dry Summer Cold Winter Example	112
9-6	Multi-Speed Performance	118
9-7	Variable-Speed Performance	118

Section 10
Hydronic Heating Equipment Examples
10-1	Hot Water Heating System Design	119
10-2	Space Heating Load	119
10-3	Maximum Space Heating Capacity	119
10-4	Minimum Space Heating Capacity	119
10-5	Water Temperature Limits	119
10-6	Equipment Selection Examples	119
10-7	Attributes of the Example Dwelling	120
10-8	Cold Winter Example	120
10-9	Mild Winter Humid Climate Example	122
10-10	Hydronic Air Handler	123
10-11	Engineered Ventilation	125
10-12	Freeze Protection	125

Part 3: Informative Material Pertaining to Ductless Air-Air Equipment

Section 11
Ductless Single-Split Equipment
11-1	Applications	129
11-2	Design Goals	129
11-3	Outdoor Equipment	130
11-4	Indoor Equipment	130
11-5	Performance Data and Data Use	131
11-6	Expanded Performance Data	132
11-7	Air Distribution	133
11-8	Blower Data	134
11-9	Duct System Design	134
11-10	Equipment Selection and Sizing	135

Section 12
Ductless Multi-Split Systems
12-1	Applications	137
12-2	Design Goals	138
12-3	Outdoor Equipment	138
12-4	Indoor Equipment	139
12-5	Performance Data and Design Procedures	139
12-6	Expanded Performance Data for Cooling	141
12-7	Expanded Performance Data for Heating	144
12-8	Air Distribution	146
12-9	Blower Data	147
12-10	Duct System Design	147
12-11	Equipment Selection and Sizing	147

Section 13
Single-Package Equipment
13-1	Applications	151
13-2	Design Goals	152
13-3	Equipment Attributes	153
13-4	PTAC and PTHP Rating Data	153
13-5	Home Appliance Rating Data	153
13-6	Expanded Performance Data for Cooling	154
13-7	Expanded Performance Data for Heating	154
13-8	Air Distribution and Noise	154
13-9	Equipment Size	155
13-10	Heating Performance	155

Part 4: Informative Material Pertaining to Implementation

Appendix 1
Basic Concepts for Air System Equipment
A1-1	Load Calculations	159
A1-2	Operating Conditions for Cooling Equipment	159
A1-3	Operating Conditions for Heat Pump Heating	164
A1-4	Operating Conditions for Forced Air Furnaces	167
A1-5	Design Values for Supply Air Cfm	167
A1-6	Sensible Heat Ratio	168
A1-7	Cooling Cfm Determined by Design	169
A1-8	Prerequisites for Equipment Selection	171
A1-9	Expanded Performance Data	171
A1-10	Blower Performance Data	176
A1-11	Component Pressure Drop Data	177
A1-12	Performance Data Formats	178
A1-13	Standard Formats	180

A1-14	Alternative to Published Data	180
A1-15	AHRI-Certification Data	181
A1-16	Degree Day Data	182

Appendix 2

Entering Air Calculations

A2-1	Summary of Procedure	183
A2-2	Dry-Bulb and Wet-Bulb at the Return Grille	183
A2-3	Return Duct Loads	183
A2-4	Dry-Bulb and Wet-Bulb at the Exit of the Return Duct	184
A2-5	Outdoor Air Fraction	185
A2-6	Entering Dry-Bulb and Wet-Bulb Temperatures for Raw Air Ventilation	185
A2-7	Entering Dry-Bulb and Wet-Bulb Temperatures for Heat Recovery Ventilation	186
A2-8	Comprehensive Example	187
A2-9	Entering Air Worksheet for Cooling	189
A2-10	Entering Air Worksheet for Heating	189
A2-11	Entering Air Worksheet Psychrometrics	189

Appendix 3

Searching OEM Data for Candidate Equipment

A3-1	Total Capacity Method	191
A3-2	Ballpark Cfm Method	191
A3-3	Ballpark Cfm Calculation	192

Appendix 4

Requirements for Expanded Performance Data

A4-1	Cooling Capacity Values	193
A4-2	Compressor Heating Capacity Values	193
A4-3	Temperature Range for Air-Air Cooling	193
A4-4	Temperature Range for Water-Air Cooling	193
A4-5	Temperature Range for Air-Air Heating	194
A4-6	Temperature Range for Water-Air Heating	194
A4-7	Compressor Speed for Expanded Cooling Data	194
A4-8	Compressor Speed for Expanded Heating Data	194
A4-9	Indoor Blower Speed for Expanded Data	195
A4-10	Interpolation	195
A4-11	Additional Reporting Requirements	195

Appendix 5

Altitude Effects

A5-1	Psychrometric Calculations	197
A5-2	Altitude Affects Equipment Performance	197
A5-3	Air-Air Cooling Equipment	198
A5-4	Water-Air Cooling Equipment	199
A5-5	Hot Water Coil or Chilled Water Coil	199
A5-6	Electric Heating Coil	199
A5-7	Gas Burner	200
A5-8	Oil Burner	200
A5-9	Hot-Gas Coil	200
A5-10	Heat Pump Heating	201
A5-11	Blower Performance	201
A5-12	Duct System Performance	201
A5-13	Duct System Design	201
A5-14	Effect on Duct System Operating Point	201
A5-15	Air-to-Air Heat Exchangers and Desiccant Wheels	202

Part 5: Informative Related Information

Appendix 6

Energy and Op-Cost Calculations

A6-1	Heat Pump Heating—Reducing Use of Electric Coil Heat	205
A6-2	Intuitive Indicator	206
A6-3	Simplified Indicator	208
A6-4	Alternative to the Degree Day Ratio Method	208
A6-5	Basic Bin-Hour Calculation	209
A6-6	Advanced Methods	211
A6-7	Weather Data for Energy Modeling	212
A6-8	Proximity Issues for Weather Data Use	213

Appendix 7

Moisture and Condensation Issues

A7-1	Design Values for Indoor Humidity	215
A7-2	Moisture Issues for Winter	215
A7-3	Moisture Issues for Summer	215

Appendix 8

Condensation Calculations

A8-1	Condensation on Surfaces	219
A8-2	Dew-Point Temperature	219
A8-3	Condensation Models	219
A8-4	Minimum Surface Temperature	219
A8-5	Minimum R-Value	219
A8-6	Condensation on Interior Surfaces	220
A8-7	Condensation on Exterior Glass	220
A8-8	Winter Condensation in Structural Panels	221
A8-9	Summer Condensation in Structural Panels	222
A8-10	Condensation Inside of Duct Runs	222
A8-11	Condensation Outside of Duct Runs	223
A8-12	Condensation Software	225
A8-13	Consequences of Humidity	225
A8-14	Consequences of Condensation	225
A8-15	Building Science Software	226

Appendix 9
Water-Loop Issues for Water-Air Heat Pumps
- A9-1 Once-Through Water 227
- A9-2 Earth-Loop Water 227
- A9-3 Buried Water-Loop Design 227
- A9-4 Piping Geometry 228
- A9-5 Length of Buried Pipe 228
- A9-6 Summary of Design Issues 229
- A9-7 Other Issues 229
- A9-8 Energy Calculations 229
- A9-9 Comprehensive Instructions and Software . 229

Appendix 10
Ductless Multi-Split Piping
- A10-1 Pipe Names 231
- A10-2 Basic Two-Pipe System 231
- A10-3 Two-Pipe Recovery System 231
- A10-4 Three-Pipe Recovery System 232

Appendix 11
Furnace or Water Boiler Cycling Efficiency
- A11-1 Part-Load Efficiency Curves 233
- A11-2 Part-Load Efficiency Equations 233
- A11-3 Energy Use and Furnace Over Sizing . . . 234

Appendix 12
Matching Evaporators and Condensing Units
- A12-1 Evaporator Performance 235
- A12-2 Condensing Unit Performance 235
- A12-3 Refrigerant-Side Operating Point . . . 235
- A12-4 Optimum Refrigerant-Side Balance Point . 235

Appendix 13
Performance Models for Cooling-Only and Heat Pump Equipment
- A13-1 Performance Model Use 237
- A13-2 Altitude Effects — General Solution . . . 238
- A13-3 Air-Air Cooling Model 238
- A13-4 Modeling an Exhibit of Air-Air Data . . . 239
- A13-5 Data Presentation Adjustment 240
- A13-6 Air-Air Heating Model 241
- A13-7 Water-Air Cooling Model 242
- A13-8 Deficient Format for Cooling Data . . . 243
- A13-9 Modeling an Exhibit of Water-Air Data . 243
- A13-10 Error Check 245
- A13-11 Water-Air Equation Set Use 245
- A13-12 Water-Air Cooling Example 245
- A13-13 Water-Air Heating Model 246
- A13-14 OEM Data Format Issues 247
- A13-15 Modeling Issues and Caveats 247
- A13-16 Accuracy of OEM Data 247

Appendix 14
Air-Air Heat Pump Supply Air Temperature
- A14-1 Balance-point Diagram 249
- A14-2 Supply Air Temperatures 249
- A14-3 Supplemental KW Run Fraction 250
- A14-4 Two Stages Improve Performance . . . 250
- A14-5 Sizing Supplemental Heat 252
- A14-6 Staging Supplemental Heat 252

Appendix 15
Whole-House Dehumidifier Performance
- A15-1 Latent Load Vs. Month of Year 254
- A15-2 Expanded Capacity Data 254
- A15-3 Dehumidifier Performance Equations . . . 255

Part 6: Informative Ancillary Pages

Appendix 16
Glossary 259

Appendix 17
Symbols, Acronyms and Abbreviations . 271

Appendix 18
Summary of Equations 277

Appendix 19
Supporting Detail for Equipment Sizing Examples
- A19-1 Dwelling Performance and Attributes . . . 281
- A19-2 Balanced Climate with Summer Humidity . 281
- A19-3 Warm and Very Humid Climate 283
- A19-4 Cold Winter Hot Dry Summer Climate . . . 283
- A19-5 Moderate Climate with Some Humidity . . 283
- A19-6 Cold Winter Hot Humid Summer 283
- A19-7 Hot Dry Climate 283
- A19-8 Bin Weather Data 283

Appendix 20
Rationale for Section N2 Sizing Limits
- A20-1 Prescriptive vs. Performance Procedure . 287
- A20-2 Dry-Bulb Temperature Control 287
- A20-3 Indoor Humidity Control for Cooling . . . 288
- A20-4 Sizing for Heat Pump Energy Use 291
- A20-5 Performance Modeling for Cooling Equipment and Heat Pumps 293
- A20-6 Performance Method for Sizing Multi- and Variable-Speed Heat Pump Equipment . 296
- A20-7 Furnace and Boiler Sizing 301

Appendix 21
Related Resources 303

Appendix 22
Blank Forms
A22-1 Revised Version of *Manual J* Worksheet G . 309
A22-2 Entering Air Condition 309
A22-3 Friction Rate Worksheet 309

Index 313

This section is part of the requirements for this standard.

Section N1

Definitions and General Requirements

This section defines terminology that is unique to the standard. It also summarizes mandatory requirements and procedures that apply to equipment selection and sizing. Application specific requirements in Section N2 supersede the general requirements found in Section N1.

N1-1 Definitions

Terminology directly relevant to equipment sizing procedures is defined below.

AHAM Appliances

Original equipment manufacturer (OEM) air conditioning and heat pump products that are certified by the Association of Home Appliance Manufacturers (AHAM).

AHRI-Certified Equipment

OEM air conditioning and heat pump products certified by the Air-Conditioning, Heating, and Refrigeration Institute (AHRI).

AHRI Rating Speed

That compressor speed which OEMs use for rating residential HVAC equipment heating and cooling capacity per the AHRI rating test.

Note: For variable-speed equipment, the AHRI rating speed is the full compressor speed used to produce the advertised value for total cooling Btuh. The AHRI rating speed for equipment that operates at two or more compressor speeds is it's maximum (high) compressor speed. The unique compressor speed for single-speed equipment is it's AHRI rating speed.

AHRI Rating Test for Cooling

For air-air equipment, the Cooling-A test is for 95°F DB outdoor air and 80°FDB/67°FWB entering air (per ANSI/AHRI Standard 210/240). For water-air equipment using ground water, the cooling test is for 59°F water with 80.6°FDB/66.2°FWB entering air, or for water-air equipment using buried pipe loop water, the test is for 77°F water with 80.6°FDB/66.2°FWB entering air (per AHRI/ASHRAE/ISO Standard 13256-1).

AHRI Rating Test for Compressor Heating

For air-air equipment, the compressor heating test is for 47°F outdoor air and 70°F entering air (per ANSI/AHRI Standard 210/240). For water-air equipment using ground water, the compressor heating test is for 50°F water with 68°FDB/59°FWB entering air, or for water-air heating using buried pipe loop water, the test is for 32°F water with 68°FDB/59°FWB entering air (per AHRI/ASHRAE/ISO Standard 13256-1).

Applied Capacity

Applied capacity is the amount of equipment cooling or compressor heating capacity for the operating circumstances produced by the summer design condition, or the winter design condition, respectively.

- Applied cooling capacity is for the full compressor speed.
- Applied compressor heating capacity is for the compressor speed used for the AHRI rating test for heating. For variable-speed equipment, the applied compressor heating capacity is for the enhanced compressor speed, only when this enhanced speed is continuously available for an unlimited amount of time.

Economic Balance Point

For heat pump heating, the outdoor temperature that produces equality for refrigerant cycle heating cost (compressor heat) and fossil fuel heating cost.

Excess Latent Capacity

Excess latent capacity equals the latent capacity value indicated by an OEM's expanded cooling performance data minus the load calculation's latent load for the summer design conditions. Both values are for the operating circumstances that apply to the summer design conditions used to compute the cooling loads.

Expanded Performance Data

Cooling or heating performance data that correlates sensible and latent cooling capacity, or heating capacity, with all the operating variables that affect the capacity values. Original equipment manufacturers (OEMs) provide this data in electronic or hard-copy form, or as an interactive computer model. Expanded performance data is also widely known within the HVAC industry as "OEM Performance Data," as well as "Engineering Performance Data."

Enhanced Compressor Speed

For variable-speed equipment, a compressor speed that exceeds the compressor speed used for the AHRI rating test for heating capacity. Used for heat pump balance point diagrams and supplemental electric coil sizing.

Extreme Temperature

For water-air heat pumps that have an earth-coupled water-loop, extreme outdoor air temperatures for winter and summer shall be used as default values preliminary buried water-loop design. Use the following source of extreme temperature data:

Climatic design information provided by a CD-ROM in back of the in the 2009 ASHRAE Handbook of Fundamentals (or the latest version of this database).

- *Refer to the Extreme Annual Design Condition data.*
- *Use the dry-bulb temperature values for n = 50 years.*

Full Capacity

For single-speed equipment, full capacity refers to operation at the only available compressor speed. For staged equipment, full capacity refers to operation at the maximum available compressor speed. For variable-speed equipment, full capacity refers to performance when the compressor operates at the AHRI rating test speed for cooling, or the AHRI rating test speed for heating.

Full Compressor Speed

For single-speed equipment, full compressor speed is the only available compressor speed. For staged equipment, full compressor speed is the maximum available compressor speed. For variable-speed equipment, full compressor speed is the AHRI rating speed (see AHRI Rating Speed).

Heating Load

For equipment sizing, the *Manual J* heating load for the winter design condition.

Load Calculation

An ANSI-Standard procedure for calculating the rate of sensible and latent heat flow (Btuh units, or metric equivalent) from the outdoor environment to an indoor comfort-conditioned space (for summer cooling), and from an indoor comfort-conditioned space to the outdoor environment (for winter heating). The procedure also calculates sensible and latent heat flows caused by the dwelling's HVAC system (which may be for indoor blower heat, duct runs, pipe runs, and engineered ventilation). The purpose of the procedure is to provide sizing values for comfort conditioning equipment.

Maximum and Minimum Capacity

For staged equipment and variable-speed equipment, maximum and minimum capacity refers to the highest and lowest compressor speeds allowed by the OEM's design. For some variable-speed equipment, maximum compressor speed may exceed the full-capacity speed (see Enhanced Compressor Speed).

Over-Size Factor

The over-size factor (OSF) equals the applied equipment capacity value divided by the sizing value.

OSF = Applied capacity value / Sizing value

Over-Size Limit

The over-size limit (OSL) is the acceptable amount of deficient or excess applied capacity, as it relates to the sizing value. The over-size factor shall be within the boundaries of the over-size limit.

Minimum OSL ≤ OSF ≤ Maximum OSL
Section N2 provides OSL values.

Sizing Value

For cooling-only equipment and heat pump equipment, the sizing value is the *Manual J* total cooling load for the summer design condition, for the space served by the equipment. For furnaces and water boilers, the sizing value is the *Manual J* heating load for the winter design condition, for the space served by the equipment. A balance point diagram provides the sizing value for an electric heating coil installed in a heat pump. The sizing value for ancillary dehumidification equipment is 85 percent (0.85 factor) of the latent cooling load for the rooms and spaces served by the dehumidification equipment. The sizing value for winter humidification equipment is the *Manual J* humidification load for the winter design condition. The sizing value for direct evaporative cooling equipment is 100% (1.00 factor) of the value for the sensible cooling load.

Thermal Balance Point

For heat pump heating, the outdoor temperature that produces equality for the heating load and compressor heating capacity.

Thermal Balance Point Diagram

A graph that shows how compressor heating capacity (Btuh) and envelope heating load (Btuh) are affected by outdoor dry-bulb temperature. See informative Section 2-8.

Total Cooling Load

For equipment sizing, the sum of the *Manual J* sensible and latent cooling loads for the summer design condition.

Ventilation Dehumidifier

Ancillary dehumidification equipment that is designed to process indoor air and outdoor air (the cabinet has inlets for indoor air and outdoor air, and an outlet for discharge air). The dehumidifier will have a duct run to outdoor air, plus duct runs that interface with the primary equipment's duct system. It's purpose is to provide a high-limit (55% RH) for indoor humidity when the momentary sensible load is significantly less than the design (summer condition) load, and the momentary latent load is relatively large; about equal to, or greater than the summer design load.

Whole-House Dehumidifier

Ancillary dehumidification equipment that is designed to process indoor air (the cabinet has an inlet for indoor air, and an outlet for discharge air). It's purpose is to provide a high-limit (55% RH) for indoor humidity when the momentary sensible load is significantly less than the design (summer condition) load, and the momentary latent load is relatively large, about equal to, or greater than the summer design load. The equipment shall have access to the air in the entire volume of the conditioned space (a duct system shall provide connectivity when one or more interior partition doors separate the space that has the dehumidifier from other rooms and spaces). When outdoor air and indoor air are mixed in a duct tee and used as input to a whole-house dehumidifier, the dehumidifier is a ventilation dehumidifier, as far as equipment selection and sizing procedure are concerned.

N1-2 Rounding

There will be occasions where the OSF value is slightly different than the OSL value; a 1.201 to 1.209 OSF vs. a 1.20 limit, or a 0.891 to 0.899 OSF vs. a 0.90 limit, for example. For the purpose of comparing the over-size factor to the over-size limit, ignore everything after the third decimal place, and round up or down to the second decimal place. For example:

```
0.891 to 0.894 = 0.89
0.895 to 0.899 = 0.90
1.201 to 1.204 = 1.20
1.205 to 1.209 = 1.21
```

N1-3 Equipment Selection and Sizing Procedure

The following steps shall be used to select and size equipment.

Step 1) Produce a load calculation (see Section N1-4).

Step 2) When heat pump equipment is used, determine the heat pump sizing condition (see Section N1-5).

Step 3) Procure OEM performance data (see Section N1-6).

Step 4) Determine blower Cfm values for cooling and heating (see Section N1-7)

Step 5) Evaluate the entering air condition for cooling, and for heating (see Section N1-8).

Step 6) For water-air equipment, determine entering water temperature values and water pump Gpm values for cooling and heating (see Section N1-9),

Step 7) Extract capacity values from OEM performance data (see Section N1-10). As needed, adjust sea level capacity values for altitudes above 2,500 feet (see Section N1-11), and/or interpolate OEM capacity values for the operating circumstances that apply to the equipment (see Section N1-12).

Step 8) Select equipment that conforms to the sizing limits that apply to the project (see SectionsN1-13).

Step 9) Produce a project file that documents the design decisions (see Section N1-14).

N1-4 Load Calculation

A *Manual J* load calculation is the basis for equipment sizing values. This calculation shall conform to the *Manual J*, Section 2 guidance for making an accurate load calculation.

When ancillary dehumidification equipment supplements the primary cooling equipment, the load calculation for sizing primary equipment is not adjusted for dehumidifier use. For primary equipment, all sensible and latent loads, including the engineered ventilation load, shall be calculated in the normal manner.

N1-5 Heat Pump Sizing Condition

Air-air and water-air heat pumps shall be sized for the operating condition that applies to project circumstances.

Condition A (for cooling season humidity control): The *Manual J* sensible heat ratio (sensible cooling load divided by total cooling load) is less than 0.95, OR the local heating degree day (base 65°F) to cooling degree day (base 50°F) ratio is less than 2.0 (complies with either requirement).

Condition B (for heating season efficiency): The *Manual J* sensible heat ratio (sensible cooling load divided by total cooling load) is 0.95 or greater, AND the local heating degree day (base 65°F) to cooling degree day (base 50°F) ratio is 2.0 or greater (shall comply with both requirements).

- Appendix 20 provides the rationale for the procedure.
- Table N2-2 (next section) determines maximum and minimum cooling capacity values for heat pump equipment.

The Condition B evaluation shall be based on one of the following sources of degree-day data. When using this data, the practitioner shall:

- Consider the location (latitude, longitude and elevation) of the building site.
- Select the source document that is the most compatible with the attributes of the building site. (This is not an issue when there is no difference in available locations).

- Consider the attributes of the locations offered by the source document and select the most compatible location for extracting data from the source document.
- Use the extracted HDD-65 value, CDD-50 value, and the corresponding degree day ratio value to declare Condition A or Condition B.

ASHRAE Weather Data

Climatic design information (including degree day data) for 5,564 locations, as provided by a CD-ROM in back of the in the 2009 ASHRAE Handbook of Fundamentals (or the latest version of this database).

NOAA Degree Day Data

Heating and cooling degree day values for various base temperatures are provided by the following NOAA document:

Annual Degree Days to Selected Bases, 1971-2000; Climatography of the United States No. 81; Supplement No. 2; National Climate Data Center, Asheville N.C. See: http://cdo.ncdc.noaa.gov/climatenormals/clim81_supp/CLIM81_Sup_02.pdf.

N1-6 OEM Performance Data Requirements

Expanded cooling performance data shall correlate total capacity and sensible capacity (or sensible heat ratio) with outdoor air temperature, or entering water temperature, indoor coil (blower) Cfm, entering air wet-bulb temperature, and entering air dry-bulb temperature.

Expanded heat pump heating performance data shall correlate compressor heating capacity with outdoor air temperature, or entering water temperature, indoor coil (blower) Cfm, and entering air dry-bulb temperature, plus a defrost cycle adjustment for air-air heat pumps.

- There is no standard presentation format for these correlations. The blanket requirement is that the OEM's presentation satisfies the requirements for expanded cooling data and expanded heat pump heating data.
- When refrigeration cycle equipment has two or more indoor coils, the expanded performance data shall be for the configuration that will be installed (a given set of indoor units served by an outdoor unit), when the compressor is operating at the AHRI rating speed.

Detailed performance data requirements for cooling-only equipment, heat pumps, electric heating coils, fossil fuel furnaces, indoor air blowers, and water boilers are provided here.

Performance Data for AHRI-Certified Cooling-Only Equipment and Heat Pumps

Operating limit data, and expanded performance data shall be used to select and size cooling-only and heat pump equipment. This shall include, but is not limited to, the following (where applicable for the specific design application):

- The maximum and minimum operating values for outdoor air temperature (air-air equipment), or maximum and minimum operating values for entering water temperature (water-air equipment).

  Note: This applies to operating limit values for cooling, and where applicable, operating limit values for compressor heating.

  Note: This applies to operating limit values for each compressor speed used to present performance data.

- The compressor speed for expanded cooling performance data, and where applicable, the compressor speed for expanded compressor-heating performance data

  Note: Not required for single-speed equipment.

- Total cooling capacity values.
- Sensible cooling capacity values, or sensible heat ratio values.
- Indoor blower Cfm for cooling capacity values.
- Outdoor air dry-bulb temperatures, or entering water temperatures for a matrix of circumstantial cooling capacity values.
- Entering air wet-bulb and dry-bulb temperatures for cooling capacity values for a matrix of circumstantial cooling capacity values.
- Indoor blower Cfm for heating capacity values.
- Outdoor air dry-bulb temperatures, or entering water temperatures for a matrix of circumstantial compressor heating capacity values.
- Entering air dry-bulb temperatures for a matrix of circumstantial compressor heating capacity values.
- Blower data requirements also apply. These are provided below, after the fossil fuel furnace requirements.

Performance Data for Electric Heating Coils

Operating limit data and heating performance data shall be used to select and size electric heating coils used for supplemental, and/or emergency heat pump heat, or electric furnace heat. This shall include, but is not limited to, the following (where applicable for the specific design application):

- Maximum leaving air temperature value.

- Input KW for each stage of heat (e.g., the total KW value for the active stages). For modulating control, minimum input KW and maximum input KW.
- Blower data requirements also apply. These are provided below, after the fossil fuel furnace requirements.

Performance Data for Fossil Fuel Furnaces

Operating limit data and heating performance data shall be used to select and size fossil fuel furnaces. This shall include, but is not limited to, the following (where applicable for the specific design application):

- Minimum entering air temperature and maximum leaving air temperature values.
- Minimum and maximum air temperature rise values.
- Input and output Btuh for each stage of heat (e.g., the total Btuh value for the active stages). For modulating control, minimum input and output Btuh values, and maximum input and output Btuh values.
- The following blower data requirements also apply.

Performance Data for Indoor Air Blowers

OEM performance data (e.g., blower Cfm vs. external static pressure) is required in the design of the distribution system, per *Manual D*.

- Blower data is required for each PSC blower speed, or for each ECM blower speed setting.
- The blower data shall include guidance (typically blower table notes) that identifies the air-side components that are accounted for, as far as the published external static pressure values are concerned.
- The external static pressure value from the blower table shall be adjusted for any pressure drop, or pressure drops, produced by air side components that are external to the blower data.

Performance Data for Water Boilers

Operating limit data, and heating performance data shall be used to select and size water boilers. This shall include, but is not limited to, the following (where applicable for the specific design application):

- Minimum entering water temperature and maximum leaving water temperature values.
- Gross input and output Btuh for each stage of heat (e.g., the total Btuh value for the active stages). For modulating control, minimum input and output Btuh values, and maximum input and output Btuh values.

OEM Verification Path

The OEM Verification Path (per Section N3) shall apply as an alternative compliance path when:

- Published expanded performance data is not available to an OEM-authorized audience, or
- Available expanded performance data is incomplete for intended equipment use, or
- An authorized party needs help with, and/or confirmation of, available data use.

N1-7 Blower Cfm

Blower Cfm is determined when OEM engineering data is used to select and size equipment. The blower Cfm used to extract capacity values from OEM data shall be one of the blower Cfm values authorized by the OEM's performance data. There may be one Cfm value for heating and cooling, or there may be a heating Cfm and a cooling Cfm.

Note: Bear in mind that equipment sizing and selection decisions shall carry forward to air distribution system design. In this regard, the blower Cfm value, or values for equipment selection shall be used to design the air distribution system (i.e., to select and size supply air outlets and returns, and for duct airway sizing).

N1-8 Entering Air Condition for Equipment Selection and Sizing

Equipment selection and sizing shall be based on the entering air condition that applies to the project. For cooling, this requirement applies to all types of cooling-only equipment, and to all types of heat pump equipment that provides cooling. For heating, this requirement applies to all types of heat pump equipment, to all types of furnaces, and to electric heating coils.

Entering Air Condition for Cooling

The dry-bulb and wet-bulb temperatures of the air that enters cooling equipment shall be equal to the dry-bulb/wet-bulb temperatures of the comfort space air, plus or minus dry-bulb and wet-bulb changes caused by a return air duct, plus or minus the dry-bulb and wet-bulb changes caused by mixing outdoor air with return air.

Entering Air Condition for Heating

The dry-bulb temperature of the air that enters heating equipment shall be equal to the dry-bulb temperature of the comfort space air, plus or minus dry-bulb temperature change caused by a return air duct, plus or minus the dry-bulb temperature change caused by mixing outdoor air with return air.

N1-9 Water Pump Gpm and Entering Water Temperature for Water-Air Heat Pumps

The practitioner shall comply with OEM requirements for water flow rate for the heat pump equipment. In this regard, OEM expanded performance data provides an approved set or range of Gpm values. These Gpm values apply to open-pipe systems and to closed-loop systems.

Note: Pump Gpm is an issue for closed water-loop design. This standard does not address water-loop design, but instead defers to guidance by other authority. See informative Appendix 9 for summary information on water-loop design.

Note: Water pumps shall be sized and selected for the required flow rate and flow resistance. Water-air equipment manufacturer, and pump manufacturer guidance, shall be used to select and size water pumps.

Entering Water Temperature for Open Water Systems

For open water systems (water used and discarded), the entering water temperature equals the source (well, pond, lake, river) temperature.

Entering Water Temperature for Closed-Loop Systems

For heat pumps that have a buried closed-loop water system, the following default equations for entering water temperature shall be used for preliminary indoor equipment selection and sizing:

For determining cooling capacity values:
Maximum Entering Water Temperature (°F) = WTH
WTH = Extreme summer outdoor temperature - 10°F

For determining compressor heating capacity values:
Minimum Entering Water Temperature (°F) = WTL
WTL = Extreme winter temperature + 40°F
Low-limit for WTL = 25°F

Final selection and sizing shall be based on the specific details of the water-loop design.

Note: This standard does not address ground water-loop design. See informative Section 9 for example problems that use default values for WTH and WTL, and see informative Appendix 9 for summary information on water-loop design.

N1-10 Extract Capacity Values from OEM Performance Data

Cooling capacity values extracted from OEM expanded performance data shall be for the operating conditions that occur on a summer design day. Heating capacity values extracted from OEM expanded performance data shall be for the operating conditions that occur on a winter design day.

- Operating conditions for a summer design day shall be based on the outdoor air conditions used for the cooling load calculation, and the indoor air dry-bulb temperature and relative humidity value used for the cooling load calculation.

- Operating conditions for a winter design day shall be based on the outdoor air temperature used for the heating load calculation, and the indoor air dry-bulb temperature used for the heating load calculation.

Cooling Capacity Values for Air-Air Equipment

For air-air equipment, blower Cfm shall be for one of the options provided by OEM expanded performance data. Outdoor air temperature shall be equal to the summer design value. Indoor air temperature and relative humidity shall be the summer design values. Entering air wet-bulb and dry-bulb temperatures shall be adjusted for the psychrometric processes that affect the condition of the entering air, per Section N1-8.

Compressor Heating Capacity Values for Air-Air Equipment

For air-air equipment, blower Cfm shall be for one of the options provided by OEM expanded performance data. Outdoor air temperature shall be equal to the winter design value. Indoor air temperature shall be the winter design value. Entering air dry-bulb temperature shall be adjusted for the psychrometric processes that affect the temperature of the entering air, per Section N1-8.

Cooling Capacity Values for Water-Air Equipment

For water-air equipment, blower Cfm shall be for one of the options provided by OEM expanded performance data. Water pump Gpm shall be for one of the options provided by OEM expanded performance data. Entering water temperature shall be equal to the warmest temperature for the cooling season. Indoor air temperature and relative humidity shall be the summer design values. Entering air wet-bulb and dry-bulb temperatures shall be adjusted for the psychrometric processes that affect the condition of the entering air, per Section N1-8. Entering water temperature and water pump Gpm values for cooling shall be for the circumstances that apply to the project, per Section N1-8.

Heating Capacity Values for Water-Air Equipment

For water-air equipment, blower Cfm shall be for one of the options provided by OEM expanded performance data. Water pump Gpm shall be for one of the options provided by OEM expanded performance data. Entering water temperature shall be equal to the coldest temperature for the cooling season. Indoor air temperature shall be the winter design value. Entering air dry-bulb temperature shall be adjusted for the psychrometric processes that affect the temperature of the entering air, per Section N1-8. Entering water temperature and water pump Gpm values for heating shall be for the circumstances that apply to the project, per Section N1-9.

Electric Coils, Furnaces and Water Boilers

Observe OEM limits pertaining to entering air/water temperature, temperature rise, and leaving air/water temperature.

N1-11 Altitude

The practitioner shall adjust equipment performance data for altitudes above 2,500 feet, unless specific OEM instructions pertaining to the equipment installation at altitude state otherwise.

Note: Where OEM literature does not provide specific guidance for product use at higher elevations, see informative Appendix 5 for an approved adjustment method.

N1-12 Interpolation and Extrapolation

The practitioner shall fully interpolate across the set of relevant variables in order to extract the equipment capacity from OEM engineering performance data. The practitioner shall fully conform to OEM guidance pertaining to extrapolation.

N1-13 Equipment Sizing Limits

The equipment sizing value and equipment sizing rules determine the minimum and maximum limits for total (sensible plus latent) cooling capacity. Equipment selected for a particular application shall have a total cooling capacity that falls within this range. There are also lower and upper limits for latent cooling capacity, for sensible cooling capacity, and for electric coil heating capacity; the equipment shall comply with these limits as well.

Central cooling systems shall not be over-sized for load spikes that are caused by occasional periods of unusually high loads for a room/space, or as an attempt to solve a zoning problem. Heat pump equipment shall not be sized for the design day heating load, or for an arbitrary thermal balance point. See Section N2 for application-specific sizing rules.

N1-14 Documentation Requirements

The practitioner shall produce and maintain electronic and/or hard-copy documentation. General requirements for common types of equipment are listed here.

Documentation for Load Calculations

Archive load calculation input and output. This shall be the survey data collected prior to performing a load calculation, plus software reports that show computer input decisions and input values for envelope loads and system loads, plus software output reports that show the line item loads for the block load calculation, and the line item totals for the block load calculation.

Save a summary report that shows, as applicable, the final values for the sensible heating load, winter humidification load, sensible cooling load, and latent cooling load. Also document the following items:

- The location's elevation and latitude.
- For heating, the winter 99% dry-bulb temperature for outdoor air, the indoor air dry-bulb temperature for the sensible heating load, and when winter humidification is provided, the design value for indoor relative humidity.
- For cooling, the summer 1% dry-bulb temperature and coincident wet-bulb temperature for outdoor air, the indoor air dry-bulb temperature for the sensible cooling load, the design value for indoor relative humidity, the difference between the humidity ratio of the outdoor air and the indoor air (i.e., the Design Grains value from MJ8 Table 1A or Table 1B, or equivalent), and the daily range.
- Show the MJ8 AED curve for fenestration.
- Document the location(s) of the duct runs. For each unconditioned location, document the supply-side and return-side surface area values, the R-value for duct wall insulation, and the duct leakage classification per Figure N1-1 (next page).

  Duct surface area values may be as specified by the practitioner, or may be defaults from a hard copy or software version of MJ8, Table 7.

- When engineered ventilation routes outdoor air to the return-side of the equipment, document the outdoor air Cfm for heating and cooling. When heat recovery equipment is used, document the sensible effectiveness rating for heating and cooling. When the recovery equipment is the enthalpy type, also document the latent effectiveness rating for cooling.
- For hot water piping in an unheated space, document the water-air temperature difference for a winter design day, pipe diameter, pipe material, and the R-value for pipe insulation.

Documentation for Cooling-Only Equipment and Heat Pumps Certified by the AHRI

For cooling-only equipment and heat pumps, save a copy of the OEM's expanded performance data for cooling. For heat pumps, save a copy of the OEM's data for compressor heating; and when applicable, save a copy of the OEM's adjustment/correction factors for the basic expanded performance data. Save a copy of the OEM's summary of the equipment's AHRI-rated performance for cooling, and when applicable, for heating. Save a copy of the OEM's operating condition limits. Also save a list of the operating and safety controls for the installation.

For water-air heat pumps, save a copy of the calculations that produce design values for the entering water temperature for heating, and for cooling. Document the water pump Gpm used for heating, and for cooling. When applicable, document the type of antifreeze, and the percentage used for the water-antifreeze mixture.

Save a copy of the OEM's blower table, and when applicable, save copies of OEM pressure drop vs. Cfm data for air-side components that were not in place during the test that produced the blower table values. Document the design value for the blower Cfm or blower speed setting, and show that this is in the range allowed by the OEM.

Save a copy of the entering air calculations for cooling, and when applicable, for heating. This shall show the entering air dry-bulb and wet bulb temperatures used to select cooling equipment, and when applicable, the entering air dry-bulb temperature used to determine compressor heating capacity values.

Save a copy of the calculations that show the design condition cooling capacities are in the acceptable range for the total, latent and sensible loads, per Section N2 limits. This shall show fully interpolated values for total, latent and sensible capacity, and when applicable, the adjustment for excess latent capacity. Also show the design value for outdoor air temperature for air-air equipment, or the design value for entering water temperature for water-air equipment. Also show the design values for indoor air dry-bulb temperature and relative humidity, the design value for blower Cfm, the design values for the entering air dry-bulb and wet-bulb temperatures, the minimum and maximum over-size limit values for cooling, the sizing value for cooling, and the over-size factor for cooling.

Additional Documentation for Heat Pump Heating (Equipment Certified by the AHRI)

To document compliance with the heat pump sizing procedure, show the *Manual* J sensible heat ratio (JSHR) calculation for cooling and show how this value relates to the 0.95 rule (load calculation sensible heat ratio equal to, or greater than 0.95 for Condition B). Also show the heating-cooling degree day ratio calculation (identify the source of the degree day data, document the location used to extract degree day values, show that the degree day values are for the correct base temperature, document the degree day ratio value), and show how this value relates to the 2.00 rule (degree day ratio equal to, or greater than 2.00 for Condition B).

Duct Leakage Options for MJ8 Calculations			
Leakage Cfm per 100 SqFt of Duct Surface Area			
Tightness	Supply	Return	MJ8 Table 7 Values
Default Not Sealed	35	70	0.35 / 0.70
Partially Sealed	24	47	0.24 / 0.47
Default Sealed	12	24	0.12 / 0.24
Notably Sealed	9	15	0.09 / 0.15
Extremely Sealed	6	6	0.06 / 0.06

Figure N1-1

Save a copy of the thermal balance point diagram for heating. Document the thermal balance point (i.e., the default outdoor air temperature for activating supplemental coil heat). For dual-fuel heating, show the details of the economic balance point calculation, and document the economic balance point value.

When the heat pump is equipped with an electric heating coil, save and a copy of the calculations for the supplemental heating load in Btuh and KW units, and for the emergency heating load in Btuh and KW units. When supplemental heat is staged, document the number of stages and the total KW input and Btuh output for each stage, and document the outdoor air temperature set-points for staging action, or state that such decisions are made by automated intelligent controls. The documentation requirements for electric coil heat (below) also apply.

Documentation for Fossil Fuel and Electric Furnaces

Save a copy of the OEM's engineering performance data that shows steady state values for output heating capacity in Btuh units, and energy rate input in Btuh or KW units. Save a copy of the OEM's summary of the equipment's AHRI-rated performance. Document the minimum and maximum over-size limit values for heating, the sizing value for heating, and the over-size factor for heating. Save a copy of the OEM's operating condition limits. Also save a list of the operating and safety controls for the installation.

- For a fossil fuel furnace, save a copy of the OEM's limits for entering air temperature, the minimum and maximum limits for the air temperature rise through the heat exchanger, a copy of the calculations that show the air temperature entering and leaving the heat exchanger are within the limits allowed by the OEM.

- For an electric coil furnace, document the OEM's high temperature limit for leaving air, and save a copy of the calculations that show the worst-case for the air temperature leaving the electric coil is within the limit allowed by the OEM.

- When applicable, document the staging options and the associated set-points for staging controls, or state that such decisions are made by automated intelligent controls.

Save a copy of the OEM's blower table, and when applicable, save copies of OEM pressure drop vs. Cfm data for air-side components that were not in place during the test that produced the blower table values. Document the design value for the blower Cfm or blower speed setting, and show that this is in the range allowed by the OEM.

Documentation for Electric Heating Coils

Save a copy of the OEM's engineering performance data (heating Btuh output, input KW, staging options, high-limit for leaving air temperature, and electric coil pressure drop vs. Cfm). Document the minimum and maximum over-size limit values for heating, the sizing value for heating, and the over-size factor for heating. Save a copy of the calculations that show the worst-case for the air temperature leaving the electric coil is within the limit allowed by the OEM. When applicable, save a record of the staging options and the associated set-points for staging controls, or state that such decisions are made by automated intelligent controls. Save a list of the operating and safety controls for the heating coil.

Documentation for Water Boilers and Coils

Save a copy of the OEM's boiler performance data that shows steady state values for output heating capacity in Btuh units, and energy rate input in Btuh or KW units. Save a copy of the OEM's summary of the boiler's rated performance. Document the minimum and maximum over-size limit values for heating, the sizing value for heating, and the over-size factor for heating. Document the boiler's entering and leaving water temperature limits, and save a copy of the calculations that show conformance to these limits. Also save a list of the boiler's operating and safety controls.

For duct or air handler water coils, save a copy of the OEM's engineering data that correlates heating capacity with operating circumstances. Document the minimum and maximum over-size limit values for heating and the sizing value for heating. Save a copy of the air-side and water-side calculations for water coil performance (document water-side Gpm, entering water temperature, leaving water temperature, air-side Cfm, entering air temperature, leaving air temperature, and heating capacity). Document the over-size factor for heating. Document the coil's entering and leaving water temperature limits, and save a copy of the calculations that show conformance to these limits. Also save a list of the coil's operating and safety controls.

Documentation for Ancillary Dehumidification Equipment

Save a copy of the information, exhibits, and design calculations that were used to select and size the dehumidification equipment, per these requirements:

- Conform to the Section N1-14 documentation requirements for the load calculation.
- When a dehumidifier allows Condition B heat pump sizing rules for a Condition A application (per Section N2-12), document the HDD-65 and CDD-50 values for the location, and show that the degree day ratio is 2.0 or more.

    The documentation of the degree day values used for this calculation shall conform to Section N1-14 requirements, per the sub-section titled "Additional Documentation for Heat Pump Heating."

- Save a copy of the dehumidifier manufacturer's performance data (rated moisture removal value, energy factor value, input power value, and blower Cfm vs. external static pressure values), and the associated engineering information, exhibits and examples provided by the OEM. Also save a list of the operating and safety controls.
- Document the outdoor air dry-bulb and wet-bulb temperature values, and the indoor dry-bulb temperature and relative humidity values used to select an size equipment.
- When the dehumidifier processes outdoor air, document the values for outdoor air Cfm and indoor air Cfm, and show that the outdoor air fraction is 0.30, or less; also document the values for mixed air dry-bulb temperature and relative humidity.
- Save a copy of the latent load calculation for dehumidifier sizing.
- Document the calculations that show the sizing value for applied dehumidifier capacity complies with the dehumidifier sizing limits for moisture removal.
- When the dehumidifier has ductwork, document the external static pressure value for duct system resistance (as produced by air-side components eternal to the blower table, straight runs and fittings), and a dehumidifier blower Cfm value for this amount of external airflow resistance. Save a copy of the OEM's blower data.

Documentation for Humidification Equipment

Save a copy of the information, exhibits, and design calculations that were used to select and size the humidification equipment, per these requirements:

- Conform to the Section N1-14 documentation requirements for the load calculation.

This is typically the heating load and winter humidification load, possibly (for a dry climate) a sensible cooling load and a summer humidification load.

- Save a copy of the OEM's performance data and engineering information for the product used, and the size used.
- Save a copy of the calculations that show how dehumidifier capacity relates to the sizing value, and to the sizing limits

Documentation for AHAM Appliances

Save a copy of the information, exhibits, and design calculations that were used to select and size AHAM appliances, per these requirements:

- Conform to the Section N1-14 documentation requirements for the load calculation.
- Save a copy of the OEM's summary of the equipment's AHAM-rated performance for cooling, and when applicable, for heating. Save a copy of the OEM's operating condition limits. Also save a list of the operating and safety controls for the installation.
- Save a copy of the calculations that show how the rated total cooling capacity value relates to the sizing value, and to the sizing limits.
- For heat pumps, save a copy of the thermal balance point diagram for heating. Document the thermal balance point (i.e., the default outdoor air temperature for activating supplemental coil heat).
- Save a copy of the calculations that determine the supplemental heat requirement for the winter design condition, or show that supplemental heat is not required for the winter design condition.

Documentation for Direct Evaporative Cooling Equipment

Save a copy of the information, exhibits, and design calculations that were used to select and size the direct evaporative cooling equipment, per these requirements:

- Conform to the Section N1-14 documentation requirements for the cooling load calculation.
- Save a copy of the manufacturer's equipment performance data, the associated engineering information, and related exhibits and examples provided by the OEM. Save a list of the operating and safety controls for the installation.
- Document the direct saturation effectiveness value for the application, the entering and leaving dry-bulb temperatures for evaporative cooling, the altitude correction factor for the psychrometric sensible heat equation, and the corresponding blower Cfm value for satisfying the sensible cooling load.
- Save a copy of excess capacity calculation for the summer design condition.
- Save a copy of the manufacturer's blower data, plus a record of the design value for the blower Cfm or blower speed setting for evaporative cooling, and show that these values are in the range allowed by the OEM.

Note: Where applicable, copies of OEM pressure drop vs. Cfm data for air-side components that were not in place during the test that produced blower table values.

This section is part of the requirements for this standard.

Section N2

Equipment Size Limits

This section provides sizing limits for the following equipment:

- AHRI-certified cooling-only equipment
- AHRI-certified heat pump equipment
- Electric heating coils
- Fossil fuel furnaces
- Hot water boilers and water heaters
- Dual fuel systems
- Ancillary dehumidification equipment
- Winter humidification equipment
- AHAM certified appliances
- Direct evaporative cooling equipment

N2-1 Scope

This section specifies minimum and maximum sizing limits for total cooling capacity, sensible cooling capacity, latent cooling capacity, and heating capacity, where applicable to various types of residential comfort system equipment.

Note: See informative Sections 5 through 13 for application guidance and example problems.

N2-2 Compliance with Sizing Limits

For refrigeration cycle equipment, acceptable size is demonstrated by showing that a capacity value extracted from OEM expanded performance data is in a limited range when compared to the sizing value. The data that shall be used for equipment sizing is specified here:

ECM Step and Variable Blower Speed Equipment

The technology used to control indoor blower speed and outdoor fan speed for air-air equipment does not affect the equipment sizing procedures in this standard. Only compressor speed control shall affect the sizing procedures.

Single Compressor Speed Equipment

For single-speed equipment, expanded cooling performance data for the only possible compressor speed shall be used for equipment sizing.

Multi Compressor Speed Equipment

For two or more distinct compressor speeds, expanded cooling performance data for high-speed (full compressor capacity) shall be used for equipment sizing.

Variable Compressor Speed Equipment

The expanded cooling performance data for the compressor speed used for the AHRI rating test that produces the advertised value for AHRI total cooling capacity (the full compressor speed, as defined in Section N1-1) shall be used for equipment sizing.

Performance Data

Per Section N1-6, the use of expanded performance data for full-cooling capacity is a mandatory requirement for equipment selection and sizing. This applies to equipment that operates at a single compressor speed, two or more compressor speeds, and to equipment that has the variable-speed feature.

N2-3 Climate

The over-size limit (OSL) for cooling-only equipment and heating-only equipment shall not depend on the type of climate. Per Section N1-5, the over-size limit for heat pump cooling capacity shall depend on the type of climate (informative Section 1-9, and informative Appendix 20 provides rationale).

N2-4 Equipment Sizing Metrics

For cooling-only and heat pump equipment, expanded performance data provides equipment capacity values. For fossil fuel heating equipment and for electric heating coils, OEM engineering performance data provides heating capacity values.

Where applicable, dry-bulb and wet-bulb temperature values for the condition of the outdoor air, the condition of the indoor air, and the condition of the air that enters the equipment shall be used for equipment selection.

Entering water temperature values for heating and cooling are required for water-air equipment.

- Use the local ground water temperature for an open-pipe well-water system.
- Section N1-9 applies to the water temperature in a buried closed-loop system.
- Informative Section 9 provides water-air equipment examples.

For Cooling and Heat Pump Equipment:

Cooling-only equipment and heat pumps shall be sized for cooling. Expanded cooling performance data shall be used for equipment selection and sizing. Equipment performance shall be evaluated for the actual operating circumstances for the summer design conditions.

- Heat pump size shall not be based on the heating load, or an arbitrary balance point goal.
- The AHRI rating value for total cooling capacity for air-air or water-air equipment shall not be used for excess capacity calculations, or for equipment sizing and selection.

  Note: This is explained by informative Appendix 4, informative Appendix 5, informative Appendix 9, and informative Appendix 13. See also, informative Figure A1-22, and informative Figures A1-26 through A1-32.

- Equipment selection shall not be based on standard sizes, as implied by OEM model number nomenclature.
- Equipment selection and sizing requires values for total and latent cooling capacity for the equipment operating conditions caused by the summer design conditions for outdoor air and indoor air; and where applicable, the effect of return duct loads, and/or engineered ventilation loads; plus an entering water temperature for water-air equipment.
- For heat pumps, expanded performance data for heating shall determine compressor heating capacity for the relevant range of outdoor air temperatures, or the winter design value for entering water temperature. This data shall be used to draw a balance point diagram, which shall be used to size the supplemental heat device.

For Furnaces and Electric Heating Coils:

OEM engineering performance data that provides input Btuh or KW values, and output Btuh values, shall be used for equipment selection and sizing.

The air temperature value for mixing ventilation air (where applicable) with occupied space return air shall be the equipment entering air temperature for verifying compliance with a leaving air temperature limit.

For all Equipment:

Selection and sizing shall conform to the OEM's engineering guidance pertaining to operating limits for design issues such as blower Cfm, OAT, EWT, EDB, EWB, LAT, etc. Selection and sizing shall conform to the efficiency rating requirement (SEER, HSPF, AFUE, EER, or COP value) mandated by local codes and regulations.

Size Limits for Cooling-Only Equipment			
Equipment Type	Single Speed	Two Speed	Variable Speed See Note 8
	Ducted or Ductless Total Cooling Capacity		
Air-Air	Max = 1.15 Min = 0.90	Max = 1.20 Min = 0.90 FS	Max = 1.30 Min = 0.90 RS
Water-Air pipe loop system	Max = 1.15 Min = 0.90	Max = 1.20 Min = 0.90 FS	Max = 1.30 Min = 0.90 RS
Water-Air open-piping system	Max = 1.25 Min = 0.90	Max = 1.30 Min = 0.90 FS	Max = 1.35 Min = 0.90 RS
Zone Damper Systems	To minimize excess air issues, zone damper systems shall have as little excess cooling capacity as possible when full-cooling capacity is compared to the *Manual J* block load for the space served.		

1) This table applies to central ducted equipment, ductless 1:1 split equipment, ductless multi-split equipment, and packaged terminal air conditioning (PTAC) equipment.
2) FS = Full compressor speed; RS = The compressor speed used for the AHRI rating test for advertising total cooling Btuh.
3) OEM expanded performance data for continuous operation, and the operating conditions for a summer design day, determine total cooling capacity, latent capacity, and sensible capacity.
4) Sizing value = MJ8 block load (sensible Btuh plus latent Btuh) for the space served by the equipment.
5) Maximum total cooling capacity = Maximum limit x Sizing value.
   Minimum total cooling capacity = Minimum limit x Sizing value.
6) The latent capacity value extracted from OEM data shall be equal to, or greater than, the latent load, and should not be more than 150% of the latent load (1.00 to 1.50 factor).
7) Applied sensible capacity (after adjustment for excess latent capacity, where applicable) shall not be less than 90% (0.90 factor) of the sensible load.
8) Maximum equipment size may be determined by the OEM verification path (see Section N3).

Table N2-1

N2-5 Sizing Limits for AHRI-Certified Cooling-Only Equipment

For cooling-only equipment, there are size limit values for total cooling capacity, latent cooling capacity, and sensible cooling capacity.

Sizing Value for Total Cooling Capacity

The *sizing value* (as defined by Section N1-1) shall be used for selecting and sizing cooling equipment.

Size Limit Values for Total Cooling Capacity

Table N2-1 (previous page) determines maximum and minimum total capacity values for cooling-only equipment. The equipment shall be single-package ducted, or split-system ducted with the indoor coil in an air handler, or added to a furnace, or ductless split equipment with one or more indoor coils, or a packaged terminal air conditioner (PTAC).

Water-air equipment shall be evaluated as pipe-loop system equipment, or open-piping system equipment. Each application has a specific maximum size limit based on entering water temperature.

Latent Capacity Limits for Cooling Equipment

After sizing for total capacity, the corresponding latent capacity value extracted from OEM expanded performance data shall be equal to, or greater than, the latent load, but shall not be more than 150% of the latent load (1.00 to 1.50 over-size factor for latent capacity).

Low-Limit for Sensible Cooling Capacity

After sizing for total capacity and qualifying latent capacity, the sensible capacity shall be calculated by adding half of the excess latent capacity indicated by the OEM expanded performance data to the sensible capacity, where applicable. The adjusted sensible capacity shall not be less than 90% of the sensible load (0.90 over-size factor).

Note: The OEM's latent capacity value also is adjusted by subtracting half of the excess latent capacity from the OEM's latent capacity value. This reduces the amount of excess latent capacity by half.

Documentation of Selection Procedure

The practitioner shall produce and save a hard copy and/or electronic file of the information, exhibits, and design calculations that were used to select and size the cooling equipment, per Section N1-14 requirements.

N2-6 Sizing Limits for AHRI-Certified Heat Pump Equipment

Heat pump equipment is sized for cooling. Size limits depend on the type of climate.

Sizing Value for Total Cooling Capacity

The *sizing value* (as defined by Section N1-1) shall be used for selecting and sizing cooling equipment.

Size Limit Values for Total Cooling Capacity

Air-air and water-air heat pumps shall be sized for Condition A or Condition B, as defined by Section N1-5. Table N2-2 determines maximum and minimum cooling capacity values for heat pump equipment. The equipment shall be single-package ducted, or split-system

Size Limits for Condition A Heat Pumps
JSHR < 0.95; or HDD / CDD < 2.0

Equipment Type	Single Speed	Two Speed	Variable Speed
Ducted or Ductless Total Cooling Capacity			
Air-Air	Max = 1.15 Min = 0.90	Max = 1.20 Min = 0.90 FS	Max = 1.30 Min = 0.90 RS
Water-Air pipe loop system	Max = 1.15 Min = 0.90	Max = 1.20 Min = 0.90 FS	Max = 1.30 Min = 0.90 RS
Water-Air open-pipe system	Max = 1.25 Min = 0.90	Max = 1.30 Min = 0.90 FS	Max = 1.35 Min = 0.90 RS

a) Condition A limits are identical to the Table N2-1 limits.
b) Table N2-1 notes 1 through 8 apply to Condition A heat pumps.

Total Cooling Limits for Condition B Heat Pumps
JSHR = 0.95 or greater; and HDD / CDD = 2.0 or greater

Equipment Type	Single Speed	Two Speed	Variable Speed
Air-Air Ducted or Ductless	Max = +15,000 Min = 0.90	Max = +15,000 Min = 0.90 FS	Max = +15,000 Min = 0.90 RS
Water-Air pipe loop system	Max = +15,000 Min = 0.90	Max = +15,000 Min = 0.90 FS	Max = +15,000 Min = 0.90 RS
Water-Air open-pipe system	Max = +15,000 Min = 0.90	Max = +15,000 Min = 0.90 FS	Max = +15,000 Min = 0.90 RS

1) Condition B limits apply to central ducted equipment, ductless 1:1 split equipment, ductless multi-split equipment, and packaged terminal heat pump (PTHP) equipment.
2) JSHR = Sensible cooling load / Total cooling load.
   HDD = Heating degree days (65°F).
   CDD = Cooling degree days (50°F).
   FS = Full-speed; RS = The compressor speed used for the AHRI rating test for advertising total cooling Btuh.
3) OEM expanded performance data and the operating conditions for a summer design day determine total cooling capacity.
4) Sizing value = MJ8 block load (sensible Btuh plus latent Btuh) for space served by the equipment.
5) Maximum total cooling capacity = Sizing value + 15,000 Btuh.
   Minimum total cooling capacity = 0.90 x Sizing value.
6) Maximum equipment size may be determined by the OEM verification path (see Section N3).

Applies to Condition A and Condition B Applications

a) To minimize excess air issues when zone dampers close, zone damper systems shall have the minimum possible amount of excess cooling capacity when full capacity is compared to the MJ8 block load; and the minimum possible amount of supplemental (electric coil) heating KW when full KW capacity is compared to the supplemental heat load for the balance point diagram.
b) A performance method may be used for multi-speed and variable-speed heat pump sizing. Informative Section A20-6 provides related guidance.

Table N2-2

ducted, or ductless split equipment with one or more indoor coils, or a packaged terminal heat pump (PTHP).

Latent Capacity Limits for Heat Pumps

The latent capacity limits for cooling-only equipment shall apply to Condition A heat pumps. Latent capacity limits do not apply to Condition B heat pumps.

Sensible Capacity Limits for Heat Pumps

The sensible capacity limits for cooling-only equipment shall apply to Condition A heat pumps. Sensible capacity limits do not apply to Condition B heat pumps.

Documentation of Selection Procedure

The practitioner shall produce and save a hard copy and/or electronic file of the information, exhibits, and design calculations that were used to select and size the heat pump equipment, and when applicable, to select and size the electric heating coil, per Section N1-14 requirements.

N2-7 Sizing Limits for Electric Heating Coils

Electric heating coils used for supplemental heat, or as the only source of space heat, shall conform to local codes and utility regulations.

Sizing Value for Supplemental Heat

For air-air heat pumps and water-air heat pumps, a thermal balance point diagram shall provide the sizing value for sizing a supplemental heat coil.

- For air-air equipment, the OEM's expanded performance data for heating, with a defrost knee, shall determine conditional compressor heating capacity for the thermal balance point diagram.

- For water-air equipment, the OEM's expanded performance data for heating and the lowest entering water temperature for the year shall determine conditional compressor heating capacity for the thermal balance point diagram.

Note: Where heating performance data for sustained enhanced compressor speed is available, it is permitted to use this data to draw the heating capacity curve for the balance point diagram, even though equipment size for cooling has been determined for a slower compressor speed.

Note: Informative Section 2-8 provides detailed instructions for balance point diagram construction and use.

Sizing Value for Emergency Heat

For air-air heat pumps and water-air heat pumps, the target value for emergency heating capacity shall be 85% of the design value for the winter heating load. This 85% rule is superseded by local code or regulation.

Size Limits for Electric Heating Coils				
Heat Pump Supplemental Heat				
A balance point diagram determines the maximum amount of electric coil heat required (sizing value) when refrigeration cycle heat is active and functioning properly.				
Sizing Value	Max KW	Max Factor	Min Factor	
15,000 Btuh or less	5.0	na	na	
More than 15,000 Btuh	na	1.75	0.95	
Heat Pump Emergency Heat				
When refrigeration cycle heat is not available, the sizing value for emergency heat is 85 percent of the design heating load value, or use the sizing value for supplemental heat when the supplemental heat value is larger than the emergency heat value.				
Sizing Value	Max KW	Max Factor	Min Factor	
15,000 Btuh or less	5.0	na	na	
More than 15,000 Btuh	na	1.75	0.95	
Sole Source of Heat • Electric furnace • Electric coil in air handler cabinet, duct plenum, or duct run				
The design value for the heating load determines the sizing value for electric coil heat.				
Sizing Value	Max KW	Max Factor	Min Factor	
15,000 Btuh or less	5.0	na	na	
More than 15,000 Btuh	na	1.75	0.95	
Zone Damper Systems				
Zone damper systems shall have as little excess heating capacity as possible for any non-emergency operating condition.				
• Stage heat pump supplemental heat. • Stage electric coils that are the only source of heat.				
1) Maximum and minimum capacity factors are applied to the sizing value. 2) Electric coils that have a total capacity of 10 KW or more should be staged. Use 2-1/2 to 7-1/2 KW increments, depending on what is possible for the available coil circuiting options (5 KW steps are the desired goal). 3) When staging is available, the maximum number of active stages should be enough to satisfy the minimum heating requirement (95% of the sizing value). Keep additional stages off line.				

Table N2-3

Sizing Value for Heating-Only Equipment

For electric furnaces, and for electric coils that are the only source of heat, the sizing value for coil size shall be the design value for the winter heating load for the rooms and spaces served by the equipment.

Size Limit Values

Table N2-3 provides size limit values for electric heating coils used for supplemental heat, and/or emergency heat, or as the only source of space heat.

- A coil using 10 KW or more shall be staged.

- Electric coil staging shall be implemented for coils that are the sole source of heat (electric furnaces and electric coils added to cooling-only systems).

Documentation of Selection Procedure

The practitioner shall produce and save a hard copy and/or electronic file of the information, exhibits, and design calculations that were used to select and size the electric heating coil, or electric coil furnace, per Section N1-14 requirements.

N2-8 Sizing Limits for Fossil Fuel Furnaces

Furnaces have a burner size value, and a burner size limit for output heating capacity.

Sizing Value

For fossil fuel furnaces, the sizing value for burner output capacity is the design value for the winter heating load for the rooms and spaces served by the equipment.

Size Limit Values

Table N2-4 provides size limit values for fossil fuel furnaces.

Documentation of Selection Procedure

The practitioner shall produce and save a hard copy and/or electronic file of the information, exhibits, and design calculations that were used to select and size the furnace, per Section N1-14 requirements.

N2-9 Sizing Limits for Water Boilers

Size limits for water boilers that are used for space heat only are provided here:

- When a boiler provides space heat plus water heating, or snow melting, or both, the practitioner shall refer to code, to sizing guidance provided by the equipment manufacturer, and to related trade association guidance.

- When a water boiler provides radiant heat, the practitioner shall refer to code, and to design and sizing guidance provided by the radiant heating industry.

Sizing Value

The sizing value for space heating capacity is the design value for the winter heating load for the rooms and spaces served by the equipment.

Size Limit Values

Table N2-5 (next page) provides size limit values for water boilers that only provide space heat (no domestic water heating, no snow melting, no radiant heating coils).

Size Limits for Fossil Fuel Furnaces			
Output Capacity for Heating-Only	Single Stage	Multi Stage	Modulate Burner
	Sizing value to 1.4 x sizing value	Sizing value to 1.4 x sizing value at full capacity	Sizing value to 1.4 x sizing value at full capacity
Preferred [3] Output Capacity for Heating and Cooling	Sizing value to 1.4 x sizing value	Sizing value to 1.4 x sizing value at full capacity	Sizing value to 1.4 x sizing value at full capacity
Maximum [4] Output Capacity for Heating and Cooling	Sizing value to 2.0 x sizing value	Sizing value to 2.0 x sizing value at full capacity	Sizing value to 2.0 x sizing value at full capacity
Zone Damper Systems	Zone damper systems should have as little excess capacity as possible when full capacity is compared to the *Manual J* block load for the space served.		

1) Applies to natural gas, propane, and oil furnaces.
2) Sizing value = MJ8 block load (heating Btuh) for the space served by the equipment.
3) The 2.0 limit applies when the sizing value is 25,000 Btuh or less, but a need to use this limit indicates that a furnace is incompatible with the application. Consider a furnace that has a staged or modulating burner. Consider a heat pump, or a heating coil in a cooling equipment cabinet or duct, or baseboard heat, or radiant heat.
4) The excess output capacity factor shall range from 1.0 to 1.4 when furnace blower performance is adequate for cooling.
5) The excess output capacity factor may be as high as 2.0 when a larger furnace is the only way to obtain the necessary blower power for cooling.
  - This option is exercised after the practitioner has investigated the performance of commonly available products, and found that exceeding the 1.4 limit is necessary and defensible.
  - Consider a furnace that has a staged or modulating burner.
  - Other solutions may be more compatible with the application. Consider a heat pump, or a heating coil in a cooling equipment cabinet or duct, or baseboard heat, or radiant heat, for example.
6) Minimum capacity = Sizing value

Table N2-4

Documentation of Selection Procedure

The practitioner shall produce and save a hard copy and/or electronic file of the information, exhibits, and design calculations that were used to select and size the boiler, per Section N1-14 requirements.

N2-10 Sizing Limits for a Water Heater Used for Space Heat

Potable water heaters used for space heating shall be listed and labeled for this application, and shall be sized and installed in accordance with the manufacturer's installation instructions, and adopted national plumbing codes.

N2-11 Sizing Limits for Dual Fuel Systems

When a comfort system has an indoor heat pump coil installed in a fossil fuel furnace plenum, Section N2-6 applies to the heat pump and Section N2-8 applies to the furnace.

Section N2-6 also applies to a dual fuel system that is one engineered package (for this design, the outdoor unit has a fossil fuel burner that heats the outdoor coil, so the heat delivered to the space is entirely compressor heat).

N2-12 Sizing Limits for Ancillary Dehumidification Equipment

Ancillary dehumidification equipment shall be one of two types of equipment:

- A whole-house dehumidifier (equipment that processes indoor air only), or
- A ventilation dehumidifier (equipment that processes a mixture of indoor air and outdoor air).

Whole-House Dehumidifier (WDH) and Ventilation Dehumidifier (VDH)

Per this procedure, the dehumidifier shall be sized to maintain indoor humidity levels at or below 55% RH.

Humidity Control for New Equipment

For new construction, and for replacement of existing equipment, ancillary dehumidification equipment shall not be used to control indoor moisture when the primary equipment is subjected to the summer design condition for the cooling load calculation.

Note: Primary cooling equipment shall have adequate latent and sensible capacity for summer design condition per Table N2-1 or Table N2-2. An exception is allowed when dehumidification equipment is part of an engineered comfort system, per the following guidance (see, Energy Saving Measure for a Cold Climate that has a Latent Cooling Load).

Energy Saving Measure for a Cold Climate that has a Latent Cooling Load

The use of ancillary dehumidification equipment allows the use of Condition B heat pump sizing limits for a Condition A application, where the following requirements are met:

- The dehumidifier shall be part of an engineered system.
- The local degree day ratio shall be 2.0 or more.
- The Authority Having Jurisdiction (local or regional rule-making authority) does not provide different guidance.

Size Limits for Water Boilers Used for Space Heating-Only			
The sizing value is for the load on gravity or forced convection terminals in the space, and / or hot water coils in an air distribution system.	Single Stage	Multi Stage	Modulating Output
	Sizing value to 1.4 x Sizing value	Sizing value to 1.4 x Sizing value at full capacity	Sizing value to 1.4 x sizing value at full capacity

Size Limits for Duct or Air Handler Water Coils		
The sizing value is for the load on a hot water coil in an air distribution system.	Two-Position Valve	Throttling Value
	Sizing value to 1.25 x Sizing value	Sizing value to 1.5 x Sizing value

Size Limits for Water Heaters Used for Space Heat
A water heater that provides closed-circuit space heat shall also provide potable water heat. Section N2-10 summarizes code requirements. Also refer to design and sizing guidance proved by the equipment manufacturer.
1) Applies to natural gas, propane, oil, and electric heat. 2) When the boiler or water heater provides potable water heat and/or snow melting heat, in addition to space heat, refer to code guidance, OEM guidance, and trade association guidance that pertains to such applications. 3) Sizing value = MJ8 block load (heating Btuh) for the space served by the equipment. 4) Minimum capacity = Sizing value.

Table N2-5

Sizing Value

The sizing value for dehumidifier size shall be 85 percent (0.85 factor) of the latent cooling load for the rooms and spaces served by the dehumidification equipment.

Conversion Factors

The latent Btuh load shall be converted to the units of the dehumidifier's listed capacity (either Pints per Day or Liters per Day) by using the following equations:

Pint per hour load = Latent load (Btuh) / 1,054
Pint per day load = 24 x Pint per hour load
Liter / Day load = (Pint / Day) / 2.113

Where:
1,054 Btu per pint of phase change.
1 Day = 24 hours
1 Liter = 2.113 Pints

Applied Capacity

The dehumidifier's performance data shall be adjusted for the design air EDB and RH by using Figure N2-1 capacity adjustment factors.

Note: Rated dehumidifier performance data is at 80°F dry-bulb and 60% RH air entering the equipment (a single point rating condition).

Whole-House Dehumidifier Adjustment

The entering air condition for whole-house dehumidifier sizing is 75°F dry-bulb and 55% RH. The rated capacity value (pints/day or liters/day) shall be adjusted for this operating condition, per Figure N2-1. the default moisture removal adjustment (MRA) is 0.76.

WHD sizing capacity = 0.76 x Rated capacity

Ventilation Dehumidifier Adjustment

The entering air dry-bulb temperature and relative humidity for a ventilation dehumidifier shall be calculated, based on the psychrometric solution for mixing indoor air with outdoor air. Figure N2-1 shall determine the moisture removal adjustment for equipment sizing.

Note: Figure N2-2 (next page) provides default moisture removal factors for mixed air (per packaged psychrometrics).

Size Limits for Moisture Removal

The applied dehumidifier capacity (for 75°F dry-bulb and 55% RH entering air) shall be equal to, or greater than, the sizing value (85 percent of the latent cooling load the summer design condition).

Applied capacity ≥ 0.85 x Latent cooling load for 55% indoor RH in pints / day or liters / day units

For a sizing value of 50 pints/day, or less, the upper limit for dehumidifier size shall be 200% (2.00 factor) of the sizing value. For a sizing value that exceeds 50 pints/day, the upper limit for dehumidifier size shall be 150% (1.50 factor) of the sizing value.

Minimum Size for Processing Outdoor Air

For a ventilation dehumidifier, the outdoor air fraction (OAF) shall be 0.30 or less, based on the maximum dehumidifier Cfm for 0.0 IWC external static pressure.

OAF = Outdoor air Cfm / Dehumidifier Cfm ≤ 0.30

Documentation of Selection Procedure

The practitioner shall produce and save a hard copy and/or electronic file of the information, exhibits, and design calculations that were used to select and size the ancillary dehumidification equipment, per Section N1-14 requirements.

N2-13 Humidification Equipment Sizing

Humidification equipment is optional. When used, there is a sizing value and a size limit.

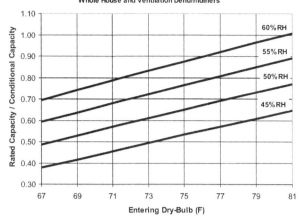

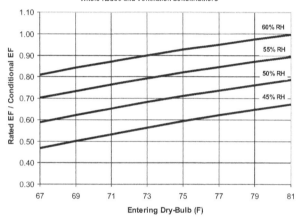

1) Based on research performed by Jon Winkler, Ph.D., Dane Christensen, Ph.D., and Jeff Tomerlin; National Renewable Energy Laboratory. The report is at: http://www.nrel.gov/docs/fy12osti/52791.pdf
2) Section A15-3 provides the equations for these curves.
3) The applied performance data for a specific product may be close to, or somewhat different than, this generic model. However, this model is compatible with the accuracy requirements of the equipment sizing procedure, considering steps in standard sizes, and the option to use a lower relative humidity set-point as excess dehumidifier capacity increases.
4) OEM data provides moisture removal rate values for entering air at 80°F dry-bulb and 60% RH. Based on the graph above, the default capacity adjustment for 75°F and 55% RH is 0.79; and the default capacity adjustment for 75°F and 50% RH is 0.65.
5) A 75°F and 50% RH set-point is used for dehumidifier sizing.

Figure N2-1

Sizing Value

The sizing value for equipment sizing is the *Manual J* humidification load for the winter design condition.

Size Limit Values

Humidifier capacity shall be equal to, or greater than, the sizing value. Excess capacity depends on the smallest available size that satisfies the sizing value.

Documentation of Selection Procedure

The practitioner shall produce and save a hard copy and/or electronic file of the information, exhibits, and design calculations that were used to select and size the humidification equipment, per Section N1-14 requirements.

N2-14 AHAM Appliance Sizing

Window and thru-the-wall cooling and heat pump equipment are classified as home appliances.

Sizing Value

The sizing value for cooling equipment and heat pump equipment is the total cooling load (sensible load plus latent load) for the rooms and spaces served by the equipment. For heat pump heating, the design value for the heating load is the load for the rooms and spaces served by the equipment.

The practitioner shall not use a simplified load calculation method to determine equipment size.

Size Limit Values

Because these units are essentially plug-in appliances, expanded performance data is not available.

Cooling Limits

When the load calculation sensible heat ratio is less than 0.95, the rated capacity of cooling-only equipment and heat pump equipment shall range from 90% to 115% (0.90 to 1.15 factor) of the total cooling load. When a product in this size range is not available, use the smallest available size that is larger than the total cooling load.

Heating Limits

When the load calculation sensible heat ratio is 0.95 or more, and the HDD/CDD ratio is 2.0 or more, it is permitted that the rated cooling capacity of heat pump equipment can exceed the total cooling load by a factor of 1.50 for improved heating capacity.

Note: This does not guarantee that compressor heating capacity will be adequate for the winter design condition.

The practitioner shall use the following equations to gauge the compressor heating capacity:

Default Adjustment Factors for Ventilation Dehumidifiers				
Capacity Adjustment				
Outdoor Air Fraction [2]	Grains Difference for 55% RH Indoors [1]			
	60	50	45	40 or less
0.10	0.83	0.81	0.80	0.78
0.15	0.84	0.82	0.80	0.78
0.20	0.89	0.86	0.83	0.79
0.25	0.92	0.88	0.84	0.80
0.30	0.94	0.89	0.85	0.81
Energy Factor Adjustment				
Outdoor Air Fraction [2]	Grains Difference for 55% RH Indoors [1]			
	60	50	45	40 or less
0.10	0.87	0.86	0.84	0.83
0.15	0.88	0.86	0.84	0.83
0.20	0.91	0.89	0.86	0.83
0.25	0.93	0.90	0.86	0.83
0.30	0.94	0.91	0.87	0.84

1) **Manual J**, Eighth Edition, Tables 1A and 1B provide grains difference values for USA and Canadian locations. The grains difference for any location is determined by plotting outdoor air and indoor air state-points on a physical or electronic psychrometric chart, and calculating the difference in absolute humidity, in grains of moisture per pound of water units.
2) Outdoor air fraction = Outdoor air Cfm / Dehumidifier Cfm.
3) Per Section N2-12 procedures, the outdoor air fraction shall not exceed 0.30.

Figure N2-2

Heating capacity (Btuh) for 47°F outdoors = HC_{47}
  HC_{47} = AHAM rating value
Winter design temperature (°F) = Manual J 99%DB
Air temperature difference (°F) = ATD
  ATD = 47 − 99% DB
Adjusted heating capacity (Btuh) = AHC
  AHC = HC_{47} − 0.5 × ATD
Design heating load (Btuh) = HL
  HL = Manual J value for 99% DB outdoors
Excess heating capacity (Btuh) = XHC
  XHC = HL − AHC

When excess heating capacity is negative, the practitioner shall provide a source of heat, or use a different type of equipment.

Documentation of Selection Procedure

The practitioner shall produce and save a hard copy and/or electronic file of the information, exhibits, and design calculations that were used to select and size the AHAM appliance, per Section N1-14 requirements.

N2-15 Sizing Direct Evaporative Cooling Equipment

The practitioner shall use appropriate psychrometric calculations to select and size direct evaporative cooling equipment. The practitioner shall not use a rule of thumb, such as capacity vs. square feet of floor area, to size equipment.

Note: Informative Section 4-4 provides guidance.

Sizing Value

The sizing value for direct evaporative cooling equipment is 100% (1.00 factor) of the value for the sensible cooling load. Sensible cooling capacity when the outdoor air dry-bulb and wet-bulb temperatures are equal to the load calculation values shall be equal to, or greater than, the sensible cooling load.

Over-Size Limit

The practitioner shall use the smallest size that has a capacity that is equal to, or greater than the sizing value.

Documentation of Selection Procedure

The practitioner shall produce and save a hard copy and/or electronic file of the information, exhibits, and design calculations that were used to select and size the direct evaporative cooling equipment, per Section N1-14 requirements.

This section is part of the requirements for this standard.

Section N3

OEM Verification Path

When comprehensive performance data is not available, or when the data is incomplete, per Section N1-6, it is an acceptable alternative that the OEM processes information provided by the system designer, and that the OEM returns values for total, sensible and latent cooling capacity; and for heating capacity, where applicable.

Note: This service can be applicable to condenser-evaporator matches that are not supported by published data, to equipment that uses advanced technology (such as variable compressor and blower speed, refrigerant management devices and controls, multiple indoor units for one outdoor unit, and other advanced features), to equipment that has limited production runs, or for special OEM equipment component matches that have no expanded performance data.

N3-1 OEM Certification Document

Based on information provided, the OEM shall provide, under it's official (trademark) letterhead, equipment identification numbers, and the related expanded performance data for cooling, and where applicable, the expanded performance data for heating (for one product/configuration, or for more than one product/configuration).

N3-2 Designer Input

The system designer shall provide the OEM with the following:

- Values for the sensible and latent cooling loads, and for the heating load, where applicable.
- Values (or local code values) for outdoor air dry-bulb and wet-bulb temperature for the summer design condition; and where applicable, the value (or local code value) for the winter design dry-bulb temperature.
- Values (or local code values) for indoor dry-bulb temperature and relative humidity for cooling; and for indoor dry-bulb temperature for heating, where applicable.
- Values for entering air dry-bulb and wet-bulb temperature for cooling, and for entering dry-bulb temperature for heating.
- For water-air equipment, design values for entering water temperature for cooling; and entering water temperature for heating, where applicable.

The practitioner shall specify the identification numbers for the equipment of interest, or shall ask the OEM to select the equipment.

N3-3 OEM Output

When equipment identification numbers are specified by the practitioner (or stakeholder), the OEM shall provide total, sensible, and latent capacity values, based on practitioner input. When the configuration and indoor and outdoor equipment is selected by the OEM, the OEM shall specify equipment identification numbers, and shall provide total, sensible, and latent capacity values, based on practitioner input.

- The OEM's report shall summarize equipment behavior (compressor speed, blower speed or blower Cfm setting for the indoor unit or units), plus information on control settings that affect cooling capacity.
- For heat pump equipment, the OEM's report shall provide compressor heating capacity values for balance point diagram construction. This requirement applies to the compressor speed used for the heating capacity tests for the AHRI 47°F rating, or for higher compressor speeds where applicable.

  The OEM shall provide heating capacity values for heat source temperatures that range from the coldest heat source temperature approved by the OEM to 70°F for air-air equipment, or to 80°F for water-air equipment, or to the warmest heat source temperature approved by the OEM.

  For air-air heat pump equipment, expanded heating capacity data shall include a defrost knee, or a warning that the data is not adjusted for defrost cycles.

- For heat pump equipment, the report shall provide information pertaining to available electric coil heating capacity, or a reminder that the equipment does not have an electric coil option.
- For air-air equipment, the report shall provide high-limit and low-limit values for heat sink/source dry-bulb/wet-bulb temperatures, and for entering air dry-bulb/wet-bulb temperatures for cooling and heating (where applicable).
- For water-air equipment, the report shall provide high-limit and low-limit values for heat sink/source water temperature, and for entering air dry-bulb/wet-bulb temperatures for cooling and heating (where applicable).

N3-4 Compliance

The practitioner, (or stakeholder) shall be responsible for verifying compliance to *Manual S* procedures. This is based on engineering performance data provided by the OEM.

Cooling-only equipment and heat pump equipment shall be approved for use when the OEM values for total cooling capacity, latent cooling capacity, and sensible cooling capacity comply with the *Manual S* sizing rules for cooling-only equipment and heat pump equipment (see Sections N2-6, N2-7, and Tables N2-1 and N2-2).

For the purpose of drawing a balance point diagram, OEM expanded performance data for compressor heating capacity vs. source temperature shall meet these requirements:

- Compressor heating capacity values shall start at the OEM's low-limit value for source temperature and run to the OEM's high-limit for source temperature.
- For air-to-air equipment, compressor heating capacity values shall include the OEM's defrost knee.
- The OEM shall show a default blower Cfm value for the expanded compressor heating capacity data, and provide adjustment factors for alternative blower Cfm values that are specified by the OEM.

For heat pumps that are the only source of heat, there shall be electric coil heat for supplemental heat and emergency heat, where required.

- Electric coil heating capacity shall be equal to, or greater than, the sizing value determined from the thermal balance point diagram.
- Electric coil heating capacity shall be equal to, or greater than, the emergency heat requirement.
- Table N2-3 determines size limits.
- Electric coil heat that is part of the heat pump equipment package provided by the OEM, or ancillary equipment (duct coil or baseboard heat, for example) provided by the practitioner is permitted.

For dual fuel heating systems, the source of fossil fuel heat for the winter design condition shall comply with Table N2-4, or Table N2-5 requirements.

Informative Material Pertaining to Basic Concepts and Issues

Section 1 – Equipment Size Issues and Limits

Section 2 – Cooling-Only and Heat Pump Equipment Selection

Section 3 – Furnace and Water Boiler Selection

Section 4 – Humidity Control and Evaporative Cooling Equipment

This section is not part of the this standard. It is merely informative and does not contain requirements necessary for conformance to the standard. It has not been processed according to the ANSI requirements for a standard, and may contain material that has not been subject to public review or a consensus process. Unresolved objectors on informative material are not offered the right to appeal at ACCA or ANSI.

Section 1

Equipment Size Issues and Limits

Cooling season and heating season comfort may be affected by equipment over sizing. For wet-coil cooling, the primary issue is indoor humidity control, but this is not an issue for dry-coil cooling.

Space air movement is a year-round issue. Over sizing reduces air distribution effectiveness when blower operation coincides with compressor, or burner operation. Continuous blower operation improves air distribution effectiveness, increases energy use, decreases system efficiency, and may increase the indoor humidity for summer cooling.

For heat pumps, excess compressor capacity reduces cooling season efficiency, and reduces heating efficiency when the outdoor air temperature is above the thermal balance point. However, this penalty may be more than offset by the improvement in heating efficiency when the outdoor air temperature is below the thermal balance point (less supplemental KWH for the heating season).

Comfort and efficiency compete for sizing limit priority. In other words, how much efficiency can comfort afford? This depends on the climate, the type of equipment, and the industry's knowledge of over sizing consequences.

- For wet-coil cooling, the HVAC industry knows that considerable excess cooling capacity has an unacceptable effect on indoor humidity control. Since indoor humidity control is a primary issue for applications that have a significant latent load, comfort has priority over efficiency.

- Indoor humidity control is an issue for single-stage, multi-stage, and variable-capacity equipment. The OEM's expanded performance data must show that the equipment configuration for design day cooling has adequate latent capacity for the *Manual J* latent load.

- Minimum or no excess cooling capacity reduces indoor humidity excursions when cooling equipment cycles, and increases blower operating hours for air distribution effectiveness.

- Blower operating minutes per hour affects space air distribution effectiveness and humidity control. Blower down time on a design day is undesirable because this increases blower down time for thousands of part-load hours.

*Per Year 2014, there is no HVAC industry model for calculating minimum blower runtime for adequate air mixing (as it affects the occupant's perception of comfort). Therefore, there is no **Manual S** requirement for blower run fraction for any operating condition.*

Continuous blower operation improves air mixing, but this may significantly increase energy use, and may have an adverse effect on indoor humidity control when coil/pan moisture evaporates to supply air when the compressor is off.

- The over sizing limit for cooling capacity may defer to heating efficiency concerns when the climate has no latent load, or a small latent load, at the cost of reduced air distribution effectiveness.

Air Distribution Issues

For ducted equipment, supply air grille type and size should provide at least 75 Fpm of air velocity at the end of the throw distance.

- The supply grille sizing Cfm is the room/space air balancing Cfm.

- The air balancing Cfm for a room or space may be the *Manual D* heating Cfm value, cooling Cfm value, or the average of the heating Cfm and cooling Cfm values multiplied by a normalization factor (NF) where:

  NF = Blower Cfm / The sum of average Cfms for the rooms served by the blower.

Minimum supply grille size (maximum face velocity) is limited by the threshold for objectionable noise. This is an experience issue:

- Noise depends on the product, the supply air Cfm, the product's size, and on the installation details (damper, boot, neck, extractor, etc.) that affect the behavior of approaching air.

- OEM performance data may not provide noise criteria (NC) values. The 700 Fpm, or less, face velocity rule may be conservative, or excessive, for a given product/installation scenario.

- For ductless equipment, interior partition(s) must not isolate a supply air grille from the space that it must serve (a grille in one room cannot affect air motion in an isolated room).

Section 1

Per year 2014, the HVAC industry has no standard model for predicting the over sizing effect on annual energy efficiency for a particular dwelling and location, served by a specific type of heating/cooling equipment and distribution system.

1-1 Momentary Loads

In general, comfort and efficiency are maximized when the momentary equipment capacity exactly matches the momentary heating load, or the momentary cooling loads (sensible and latent). However, steady-state operation is an abnormal condition because momentary loads range from a winter or summer design day value, to zero.

Design Condition Loads

Manual J design loads occur for 1% of the year. This is about 87 hours per year, on average, based on 20 years of hourly weather data.

Circumstantial Cooling Loads

Reduced cooling load occurs for thousands of hours per year, as demonstrated by Figure 1-1.

- Outdoor dry-bulb temperature is constantly changing.
- Solar loads for fenestration and opaque surfaces heated by beam radiation go from a design day maximum to zero, depending on month of year, hour of day, and momentary cloud cover.
- Internal sensible loads and fenestration loads depend on momentary occupant behavior and window shade adjustment.
- The latent cooling load for infiltration and engineered ventilation (where applicable), and indoor plants, fish tanks and hobbies (where applicable) may be as large, or larger, than the *Manual J* design day latent load when the momentary sensible cooling load is smaller, or much smaller, than the design day sensible load.
- The 1% dry-bulb and coincident wet-bulb condition used for comfort cooling load calculations is not the worst-case scenario for the latent load.

Wet or humid conditions are common when the outdoor temperature is in the 70s or 80s. The dew point for this type of outdoor air may be equal to, or greater than, the dew point for summer design condition air.

When indoor humidity control is the primary issue (HVAC for swimming pools and spas), load calculations are made for the 1% wet-bulb value and it's coincident dry-bulb temperature (see Manual SPS).

- The sensible heat ratio for momentary cooling loads can be much less than the design day sensible heat

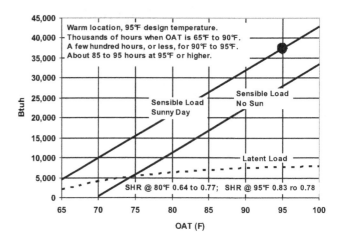

Figure 1-1

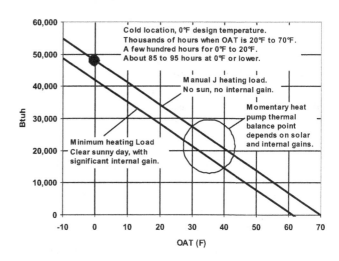

Figure 1-2

ratio (moderate sensible load, with a design day latent load).

Circumstantial Heating Loads

A reduced heating load occurs for thousands of hours per year, as demonstrated by Figure 1-2. For heat pumps, the momentary thermal balance point for a properly installed and commissioned system depends on solar loads and internal loads.

- Heating load calculations do not take credit for solar loads and internal loads (these effects may be minimal for significant periods of time, so this practice is conservative).

- The momentary thermal balance point will normally be lower than the system design balance point (which falls on the default load-line for the design day heating load), because of the heating effect of solar and internal gains (as processed by interior thermal mass, and shell thermal mass).

1-2 Excess Capacity Vs. Performance

The equipment runtime fraction (RTF) is defined below. For a sensible heat control, and given operating condition, the runtime fraction is roughly equal to the momentary sensible load divided by the momentary sensible capacity (start-up transients cause runtimes to be somewhat longer than indicated by a steady-state model).

RTF = Operating minutes per hour / 60
Approximate RTF = Sensible load / Sensible capacity

Excess Cooling Capacity

Figure 1-3 shows momentary cooling loads for a dwelling that has a 9,500 Btuh fenestration load for a summer design day. It also shows the momentary sensible capacity for equipment that has no excess total capacity, and for equipment that has 12,000 Btuh of excess total capacity.

- Note that properly sized equipment runs 100% of the time during summer design conditions, and 75% of the time when there is no solar load. It also shows that the design day runtimes are 80% and 60% for equipment that is excessively over-sized.
- Note that properly sized equipment runs 55% of the time when it is 80°F and sunny outdoors, and 30% of the time for 80°F with no sun. It also shows that the 80°F runtimes are 42% and 23% for equipment that is excessively over-sized.
- A 9,500 Btuh fenestration load is robust, but not uncommon, and larger values are possible.
- The difference between a with-sun run fraction and a no-sun run fraction decreases with less solar load, and vice versa.
- Figure 1-3 demonstrates typical behavior, so it is generic in this regard.
- The details of the Figure 1-3 graph, and the resulting performance values are not generic (each installation has it's own version of Figure 1-3).

Heat Pump Heat Vs. Excess Cooling Capacity

Figure 1-4 shows a balance point diagram for an air-air heat pump. It compares equipment that has no excess cooling capacity with equipment that has 12,000 Btuh of excess total cooling capacity.

- The compressor cycles when the outdoor temperature is above the thermal balance point. Runtimes

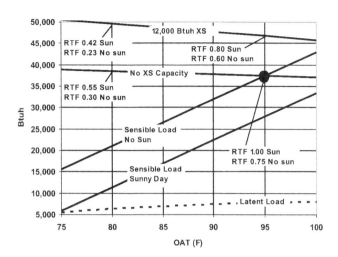

Figure 1-3

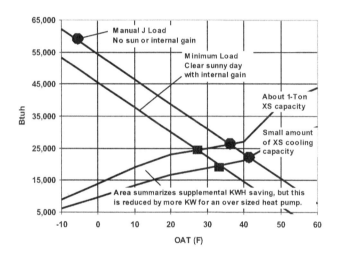

Figure 1-4

are somewhat shorter for larger equipment, but this not a primary energy-use issue.

- The larger unit has a lower heating load balance point (41°F to 42°F for the small unit vs. 36°F to 37°F for a unit that is 12,000 Btuh larger).
- The design supplemental heating load equals the difference between the *Manual J* heating load and the compressor heat when the outdoor air temperature is at the *Manual J* 99% dry-bulb value. For this example, the reduction in supplemental heating capacity is about 1.0 KW for -6°F outdoors.
- The reduction in the supplemental heating load gets a little larger as the outdoor air temperature increases, about 1.76 KW at 35°F, for this example.

Section 1

- The reduction in supplemental KW and KWH is offset by an increase in heat pump KW and KWH (a larger heat pump uses more power and has larger cycling losses).

  The blower Cfm for the smaller unit tends to be less than the blower Cfm for the larger unit.

  A larger unit operating at a higher blower Cfm uses more compressor power, and more blower power.

- The reduction in supplemental KWH for an outdoor air temperature bin equals the KW reduction for the bin, multiplied by the number of bin-hours.

- The increase in compressor KWH for an outdoor air temperature bin equals the KW increase for the bin, multiplied by the number of bin-hours, multiplied by the compressor runtime fraction for the bin (continuous compressor operation below the thermal balance point, compressor cycling penalty above the thermal balance point).

- When continuous blower is used to improve air distribution effectiveness for heating, the seasonal KWH penalty (for one blower speed) equals the blower KW multiplied by the number of additional operating hours (total bin heating hours above the thermal balance point, minus compressor heating hours above the thermal balance point).

- When the equipment is grossly over-sized, it may be that continuous blower is needed for cooling comfort. The seasonal KWH penalty (for one blower speed) equals the blower KW multiplied by the number of additional operating hours (total bin-hours for cooling, minus compressor operating hours for cooling).

  The total KWH saving for the heating season equals the sum of the bin KWH savings for supplemental heat, minus the sum of the bin KWH penalty for a larger compressor; minus the KWH penalty for continuous blower during heating, where applicable.

- Equipment cycling due to excess cooling capacity increases the cooling season KWH. The bin KWH penalty for cooling must be subtracted from the heating season savings. Also subtract the KWH penalty for continuous blower during cooling, where applicable.

- Figure 1-4 demonstrates typical behavior, so it is generic in this regard.

- The details of the Figure 1-4 graph, and the resulting performance values are not generic (each installation has it's own version of Figure 1-4).

- The concept of using a balance point diagram to evaluate the energy effects of equipment over sizing also applies to water-air heat pumps.

Air-Air Heat Pump Energy Use (KWH)						
Blower Cycles with Compressor			Add Continuous Blower at 500 Watts			
OEM 1	Heating Season	Cooling Season	Total Year	Heating Season	Cooling Season	Total Year
AHRI 2.0 Ton	20,110	1,650	21,760	~	~	~
AHRI 3.0 Ton	18,680	1,740	20,420	580	1,330	1,910
KWH Savings	1,430	-90	1,340	-580	-1,330	-1,910
OEM 2	Heating Season	Cooling Season	Total Year	Heating Season	Cooling Season	Total Year
AHRI 2.0 Ton	21,450	1,630	23,080	~	~	~
AHRI 3.0 Ton	18,930	1,740	20,670	580	1,290	1,870
KWH Savings	2,520	-110	2,410	580	1,290	-1,870

1) Smith House, Boise, ID, 2,700 SqFt. See MJ8 Section 12, for construction details. The loads for the Boise location are:
   Heating = 47,500 Btuh; Sensible cooling = 24,900 Btuh
   No latent load; Total cooling = 24,900 Btuh
2) OEM 1 ratings: TC = 26.0 MBtuh, SEER = 13.0; HC / COP at 47°F = 23.4 MBtuh / 3.79; 17°F = 12.2 MBtuh / 2.12
   TC = 36.0 MBtuh, SEER = 13.0; HC / COP at 47°F = 31.6 MBtuh / 3.78; 17°F = 18.4 MBtuh / 2.24
3) OEM 2 ratings: TC = 24.4 MBtuh, SEER = 13.0; HC / COP at 47°F = 21.8 MBtuh / 3.40; 17°F = 11.0 MBtuh / 2.00
   TC = 35.0 MBtuh, SEER = 13.0; HC / COP at 47°F = 32.0 MBtuh / 3.30; 17°F = 18.9 MBtuh / 2.20
4) Bin weather data for Boise, ID.
5) Days are divided into five hour groups, each group has it's own annual bin-hours, and internal loads.
6) Solar loads are adjusted for season of year, and discounted for seasonal cloud cover.
7) Load-lines (similar to Figure 1-4), provide bin heating load values and bin cooling load values.
8) Expanded OEM performance data provides cooling-heating capacity values for equipment selection and sizing. A nominal 2.0 AHRI ton unit is a close match to the 24,9000 Btuh load capacity.
9) Expanded OEM performance data provides bin cooling-heating capacity values (performance maps) for a nominal 2.0 AHRI ton unit, and a nominal 3.0 AHRI ton unit.
10) Defrost knees for demand defrost are adjusted for the frosting conditions at Boise, ID.
11) 500 blower watts is a ballpark value for a wet cooling coil, a 0.10 IWC filter, a 0.10 IWC electric coil, a hand damper, a supply grille, a return grille, and duct runs sized per **Manual D** procedures. Each installation has it's own blower watt value.

Figure 1-5

Example of Heating KWH Savings

Section 12 of *Manual J*, Eighth Edition provides construction details for an Ames, IA, home that has living space above, and in, a walk-in basement (the Smith Residence). For this example, the location is changed to Boise, Idaho, which has a 9°F winter design temperature, a 94°F summer design temperature, and no latent load. A nominal two ton heat pump (AHRI rating) provides a close match to the total cooling load for the Boise location. Bin calculations evaluate the energy use benefit of a heat pump that has 12,000 Btuh of excess cooling capacity. Figure 1-5 (previous page) summarizes the findings.

- When the blower cycles with the compressor, 12,000 Btuh of excess cooling capacity provides a significant reduction in heating season KWH, and annual KWH.

- The heating Btuh and COP values for 47°F and 17°F are an issue. Notice that for 2-ton units, the OEM 2 product uses more energy because it is less efficient than OEM 1 product. However, energy use for the 3-Ton units are similar, so the savings for using a larger OEM 2 unit, is more than the savings for using a larger OEM 1 unit.

- KWH savings for heating are significantly reduced when continuous blower is used for the entire heating season, and the penalty for continuous blower for the entire cooling season is much larger.

Blower KW depends on blower Cfm, on cabinet components not in place during the blower test, and on the air-side components, fittings, and straight runs in the critical circulation path.

*500 watts is a ballpark value for a wet cooling coil, a 0.10 IWC filter, a 0.10 IWC electric coil, a hand damper, a supply grille, a return grille, and duct runs sized per **Manual D** procedures.*

*The blower power value for a **Manual D** installation may vary by 200 Watts, or more, depending on blower performance and system airflow resistance. Blower power can approach 1,000 watts for a duct system that has an ECM blower motor, and under-sized ducts.*

- The bin model that produced the Figure 1-5 estimates has sensitivity to primary issues (see Figure 1-5 notes 5 through 11). Appendix 6 discusses modeling capabilities and sensitivities in more detail).

- Figure 1-5 is a plausible scenario that shows tendencies, so Figure 1-5 is generic in this regard.

- The Figure 1-5 values are not generic (each installation has it's own version of Figure 1-5).

1-3 Indoor Humidity Issues

The optimum range for space humidity is 40% RH to 60% RH for health and comfort (see Figure A7-1). People tend to object when the relative humidity is too high, but they feel cooler when humidity is low (a possible benefit for cooling, and a possible liability for heating).

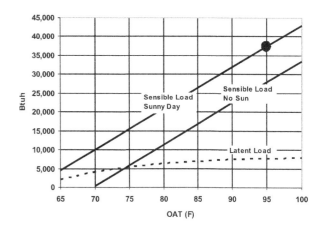

Figure1-6

High humidity may cause mold and mildew blooms and/or condensation on visible and/or concealed surfaces. High or low humidity may affect building materials and furnishings (see Appendices 7 and 8).

The concern is how a system controls space humidity during a summer design day, or a winter design day. In this regard, performance depends on system capability.

- For cooling, latent capacity (dehumidification) must be compatible with the latent cooling load.

- Controlling indoor humidity for a few summer design day hours is relatively easy (make accurate load calculations, and use correct equipment selection/sizing procedures).

- Controlling relative humidity for thousands of part-load cooling hours is a challenge because common residential system controls are designed to control space temperature, not space humidity.

- When winter humidification is desired, moisture may be introduced at a point in the supply-trunk (whole-house humidifier), or locally (self-contained room humidifier).

- Humidifier capacity must be compatible with the winter humidification load.

1-4 Summer Dehumidification

For summer cooling, space relative humidity depends on the amount of excess sensible capacity, and the effective latent capacity of the cooling coil as compressor cycles on and off to satisfy a dry-bulb thermostat. Indoor humidity may drift out of control when there is a significant latent load for a reduced sensible load.

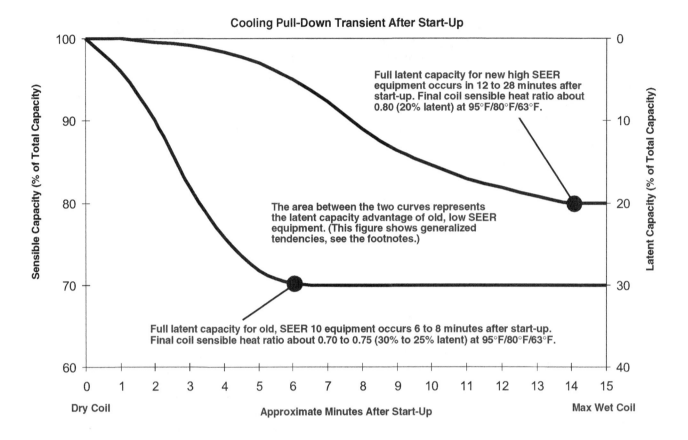

Figure 1-7

- For cooling, the momentary latent load can be close to, or even larger than the *Manual J* design load when the sensible load is much less than the *Manual J* design load. Figure 1-6 (previous page) summarizes this behavior.

- Space moisture is not removed when the compressor is shut-down, so latent capacity in Btuh terms is deficient when the compressor cycles on and off during an hour of time.

  The latent load is a steady load for a full hour, so the necessary rate of moisture removal is a constant value (latent capacity must be available for the entire hour).

  When the compressor cycles, latent capacity is not available for part of the hour, and this deficiency is significantly greater than indicated by the runtime fraction, as explained by the next bullet.

- After cooling equipment starts up, it can take from six to more than twenty minutes for the equipment to achieve it's full moisture wringing capability. So latent capacity in Btuh terms is further reduced by the system pull-down transient. This is demonstrated by Figure 1-7.

When the coil and drip pan are wet at start-up, moisture is added to supply air for the first few minutes of operation after start-up.

OEM's have control strategies for improved humidity control at part-load. For example, run the compressor for a short time before starting the indoor blower; a minimum runtime setting allows equipment to overcool indoor air dry-bulb by a few degrees; a humidistat reduces blower Cfm. See Figure 2-11.

Staged compressor capacity and variable compressor capacity improve the situation because there is reduced latent capacity vs. no latent capacity for many hours per season. However, there still are many hours when multi-speed and variable-speed equipment cycles on and off because the sensible load is less than the minimum capacity of the equipment.

1-5 OEM Performance Data

Comprehensive (expanded) OEM performance data shall be used to select and size equipment, and to design the air distribution system. Appendix 4 summarizes the performance data requirements for determining applied capacity. Related commentary and exhibits appear at various places in the informative sections of this document, and in the example problem sections.

- Cooling capacity may be reported as total capacity and sensible capacity, or as total capacity with a coil sensible heat ratio.
- OEM data provides sensible heating capacity values for compressor heat, furnace heat, boiler heat, water heater heat, electric coil heat, and water-coil heat.
- OEM data provides, as applicable, operating range limits for ambient air temperature, for entering air or water temperature, for leaving air or water temperature, for air or water temperature rise, and for air or water temperature drop.
- When applicable, a complete set of blower Cfm vs. external static pressure data is required for air distribution system design. Air-side components that were in place (produced a pressure drop) during the blower test must be identified by the OEM. Air-side components that are not identified as being in-place for the blower test (by blower table footnotes, or by an OEM letterhead response to a stakeholder request for information), must be treated as a source of external airflow resistance.
- For air distribution system design, air-side pressure drop data is required for any type of coil, filter, or air-side component that produces air flow resistance that is not accounted for by the OEM's blower data.
- Refrigeration cycle equipment, fossil fuel heating equipment, electrical resistance heating equipment, and hydronic heating equipment that is selected and sized without the aid of adequate performance data, is not in compliance with *Manual S* procedures.
- When adequate performance data is not available to authorized stakeholders, or when the available data is incomplete, the OEM must process design information provided by a stakeholder (typically a practitioner), and return values for total, sensible and latent cooling capacity; for compressor heating capacity; or for fossil fuel, electrical resistance, or hydronic equipment heating capacity, as applicable. When applicable, also provide operating range limits, temperature rise limits, and temperature drop limits.

Sensitivity to Heat Sink and Heat Source Temperature

OEM performance data for air-air equipment shows that refrigeration equipment capacity depends on the temperature of the outdoor air. For cooling, this is the design outdoor air temperature used for the cooling load calculation. For compressor heating, this is the design outdoor air temperature used for the heating load calculation.

OEM performance data for water-air equipment shows that equipment capacity depends on the temperature of the water entering the equipment. For cooling, this is the warmest temperature expected for the cooling season (the local ground water temperature, or a much warmer temperature for a buried, closed-loop system). For compressor heating, this is the coldest temperature expected for the heating season (the local ground water temperature, or a much cooler temperature for a buried, closed-loop system).

For buried, closed-loop (GLHP) systems, maximum and minimum water temperatures depend on a multitude of variables that affect the water-loop design. Water-loop design requires relevant expertise and software. Section 9-2 provides default procedures for maximum and minimum water temperature, see also Appendix 9.

- For this standard, the default procedures for producing entering water temperature values are used for example problems.
- The default procedures for producing entering water temperature values may be used for preliminary equipment selection and sizing.
- Final selection and sizing decisions must be based on the specific details of the water-loop design.
- This standard defers to water-loop design procedures provided by other authorities (local code, industry guidance, OEM guidance, for example).

Sensitivity to Blower Cfm

OEM performance data for cooling-only and heat pump equipment shows that cooling performance, and compressor heating performance, depend on blower Cfm. Any blower Cfm listed in the OEM's performance data may be used for equipment selection, but it is best to use a mid-range value in case a minor performance adjustment is required after the equipment is installed.

Hot water coil heating capacity depends, in part, on airflow Cfm through the coil. This may, or may not, be equal to the blower Cfm, depending on the location of the coil.

The temperature rise through a furnace heat exchanger, electric resistance coil, or hot water heating coil depends on the Cfm flowing through the device.

Sensitivity to Water GPM

OEM performance data for water-air refrigeration cycle equipment shows that cooling performance, and compressor heating performance, depend on the water flow rate (Gpm). The OEM may require a water flow rate for an open (once though water system), and a different flow rate for a water-loop system.

Hot water coil performance depends on coil Gpm. Water flow rate is a water temperature rise issue for boilers and water heaters.

Sensitivity to Entering Air Condition

OEM performance data for cooling-only and heat pump equipment shows that total, sensible and latent capacity depends on the condition of the entering air. OEM performance data for hot water coils shows that heating capacity depends on the dry-bulb temperature of the entering air.

- For wet-coil cooling, the total, sensible, and latent capacity values for size limit calculations must be based on the entering air wet-bulb and dry-bulb temperatures for the summer design condition.

- For dry-coil cooling (higher elevations, or a dry climate at a lower elevation), the total and sensible capacity values for size limit calculations must be based on the entering air wet-bulb temperature for the summer design condition.

  OEM data must show a wet-bulb temperature for dry-coil cooling, which may be 59°F, or lower. When the coil is dry, the entering dry-bulb temperature has no effect on the coil sensible heat ratio (which is 1.00).

- For compressor or water-coil heating, equipment capacity depends on the entering dry-bulb temperature for the winter design condition.

- The entering air temperature (typically dry-bulb, possibly dry-bulb and wet-bulb) for the summer design condition, or the winter design condition, must comply with OEM limits for entering air temperature, and for leaving air temperature.

- The condition of the air entering the equipment may be the same as the condition of the room air (no return duct or engineered ventilation load).

- The condition of the air entering the equipment may just depend on the sensible and latent return duct loads (no engineered ventilation loads).

- The condition of the air entering the equipment may just depend on the sensible and latent engineered ventilation loads (no return duct loads).

- The condition of the air entering the equipment may depend on the return duct loads and the engineered ventilation loads.

1-6 Equipment Sizing Methods

Cooling-only equipment and heat pump equipment may be (normally is) sized by the OEM data method, or by the OEM verification path method.

- The OEM data method requires practitioner (or stake holder) use of expanded performance data that is routinely published and distributed by an OEM, and Table N2-1 or Table N2-2 provides equipment sizing rules.

- The OEM verification path method applies the OEM's resources to load and operating condition information provided by the practitioner (or stake holder), and returns equipment capacity and performance information to the practitioner (or stake holder), and Table N2-1 or Table N2-2 provides equipment sizing rules.

- Section N3 provides procedures for OEM verification path use.

1-7 Summary of Sizing Procedure

The sizing procedure for refrigeration cycle equipment, fossil fuel heating equipment, and electric heating equipment is summarized here. See Sections 2, 3, and 4, for detailed instructions.

- Aggressive use of *Manual J* procedures (no fudging, no safety factors), applied to data from a competent survey provide sizing values for load matching.

- *Manual J* procedures (or code) determine the condition of the outdoor air, and the condition of the indoor air, for winter and summer.

- *Manual S*, Appendix 1 and Appendix 2 procedures determine the condition of the air entering the heating equipment, or cooling equipment.

- Expanded OEM performance data provides capacity values for the operating conditions that apply to the project.

- The practitioner matches conditional capacity values to the *Manual J* loads, subject to the over sizing limit for the application, per Section N2.

1-8 Cooling-Only Equipment Size

There is no economic benefit for over sizing cooling-only equipment. Excess cooling capacity degrades indoor humidity control (when needed), and air distribution effectiveness. Therefore, cooling-only equipment must not have excessive cooling capacity, and may be somewhat undersized.

Sizing Value

The total cooling load (sensible Btuh plus latent Btuh) provides the sizing value for calculating the over-size factor. This is the block cooling load for the rooms and spaces served by the equipment (see Section 2-1).

- The sizing value and equipment sizing rules determine the minimum and maximum limits for total (sensible plus latent) cooling capacity.

- There also are lower and upper limits for latent cooling capacity and for sensible cooling capacity.

- Section N2 provides related procedures and limit values.

Over-Size Factor

The over-size factor (OSF) equals the equipment's total cooling capacity (Btuh), when operating at the summer design conditions used for the load calculation, divided by the sizing value.

OSF = Total cooling capacity / Sizing value

Minimum-Maximum Capacity Limits

Table N2-1 provides minimum and maximum capacity limits for air-air equipment and water-air equipment. The product may be central ducted equipment, ductless 1:1 split equipment, ductless multi-split equipment, or packaged terminal air conditioning (PTAC) equipment. The product may be single-speed equipment, multi-speed equipment or variable-speed equipment.

Cooling Capacity Values

Total, latent and sensible cooling capacity values are extracted from the OEM's expanded performance data. For equipment that has capacity control, the OEM may provide data for full capacity, and for reduced capacity.

The range of the data, as defined by the available choice of operating variables (compressor speed, blower Cfm, outdoor air temperature, entering water temperature, entering air wet-bulb temperature, entering air dry-bulb temperature, for example) shall be compatible with the summer design conditions used for the cooling load calculation.

- Single compressor speed equipment has one set of expanded cooling performance data.
- Staged equipment may have (usually has) data for reduced compressor speed, and for full compressor speed. Use the expanded performance data for full compressor speed.
- Variable-speed equipment may have data for two to more compressor speeds. Use the expanded performance data for the compressor speed used for the advertised values for AHRI total cooling capacity (the AHRI rating speed).

  It may be that a variable-speed compressor can operate at speeds that exceed the speed used for the AHRI rating test for cooling, but cooling performance for this speed, or speeds, is not used for equipment sizing.

- Knowledge of the actual compressor speed value (Rpm, for example) for the AHRI rating test for cooling is not required for equipment sizing.

Cooling capacity values extracted from expanded performance data are for the operating conditions for a summer design day.

- Indoor blower Cfm, or indoor head Cfm for ductless spit coil equipment, must be the value, or one of the values, listed in the OEM's data set.

- *Manual J* Table 1A or 1B (or the local code value) provides an outdoor air dry-bulb temperature value for air-air equipment, or use the maximum entering water temperature value expected for the cooling season for water-air equipment.
- Values for entering air wet-bulb and dry-bulb temperature may be calculated per Appendix 2 procedures, or use Appendix 1 defaults.

1-9 Heat Pump Equipment Size

Heat pump size limits depend on the *Manual J* sensible heat ratio for cooling, and the type of climate. The issues are summer humidity control and winter heating energy.

Condition A Heat Pump

When indoor humidity control for cooling is an issue, the over-size limit for total cooling capacity, per Table N2-2, ranges from 90% to 135% of the total cooling load (0.90 to 1.35 factor), depending on the type of equipment (air-air; or water-air with a closed, earth-coupled piping loop, or an open-piping loop from/to a well, pond, lake, etc.). These limits also apply when the need for winter heating energy is relatively small, whether or not summer humidity control is an issue. Condition A, applies when:

- The *Manual J* sensible heat ratio is less than 0.95, regardless of harshness of the winter climate.
- The ratio of local heating degree days (HDD to base 65°F) to cooling degree days (CDD to base 50°F) is less than 2.0, regardless of the *Manual J* sensible heat ratio value.
- Note that the Table N2-2 limits for Condition A heat pumps are exactly the same as the Table N2-1 limits for cooling-only equipment.

Condition B Heat Pump

When indoor humidity control for cooling is not an issue, and when the winter heating energy requirement is an issue, air-air and water-air heat pumps may have, per Table N2-2, up to 15,000 Btuh of excess total cooling capacity, (compared to the total cooling load). Condition B applies when both of the following circumstances simultaneously occur:

- The *Manual J* sensible heat ratio is equal to, or greater than 0.95.
- The ratio of local heating degree days (HDD to base 65°F) to cooling degree days (CDD to base 50°F) is equal to, or greater than 2.0.

Sizing Value

Per Section 1-8, the *Manual J* total cooling load (sensible Btuh plus latent Btuh) provides the sizing value for calculating an over-size factor for Condition A equipment, or a maximum total cooling capacity value for Condition B equipment. This is the block cooling load for the rooms and spaces served by the equipment (per Section 2-1).

Over-Size Factor

The over-size factor (OSF) for Condition A equipment equals the equipment's total cooling capacity (Btuh), when operating at the summer design conditions used for the load calculation, divided by the sizing value. For Condition B equipment, there is a high-limit for total cooling capacity in Btuh units, as noted below:

OSF = Total cooling capacity / Sizing Value

Minimum-Maximum Capacity Limits

Table N2-2 provides minimum-maximum capacity limits for Condition A and Condition B. These limits apply to air-air equipment and water-air equipment. The product may be central ducted equipment, ductless 1:1 split equipment, ductless multi-split equipment, or packaged terminal air conditioning (PTAC) equipment. The product may be single-speed equipment, multi-speed equipment or variable-speed equipment.

Capacity Values

Total, latent and sensible cooling capacity values, and compressor heating values are extracted from the OEM's expanded performance data. Compressor heating capacity values are not used for equipment sizing, but expanded heating performance data is used to draw a balance point diagram, and to size supplemental heat. The OEM may provide data for full capacity, and for reduced capacity.

The range of the compressor heating data, as defined by the available choice of operating variables (compressor speed, blower Cfm, outdoor air temperature, entering water temperature, entering dry-bulb temperature, for example), shall be compatible with the winter design conditions used for the heating load calculation.

- Single compressor speed equipment has one set of data.
- Staged equipment may have (usually has) data for reduced compressor speed, and for full compressor speed. Use the data for full compressor speed.
- Variable-speed equipment may have (should have) data for more than one compressor speed. Use the data for the compressor speed used to advertise AHRI total cooling Btuh (the AHRI rating speed).

Applied Operating Conditions

Cooling capacity values extracted from expanded performance data are for the operating conditions for a summer design day.

- Indoor blower Cfm, or indoor head Cfm for ductless spit coil equipment, must be the value, or one of the values, listed in the OEM's data set.
- *Manual J* Table 1A or 1B (or the local code value) provides an outdoor air dry-bulb temperature value for air-air equipment, or use the maximum entering water temperature value expected for the cooling season for water-air equipment.
- Values for entering air wet-bulb and dry-bulb temperature may be calculated per Appendix 2 procedures, or use Appendix 1 defaults.

Efficiency Benefits

The practitioner should quantify the over sizing benefits for annual energy use and annual operating cost. When this is investigated, the information must be generated by a bin-hour calculation or hourly simulation that is compatible with Appendix 6 procedures.

1-10 Interpolation

Total cooling capacity, latent cooling capacity and sensible cooling capacity values, and compressor heating capacity values (where applicable) must be fully interpolated when the actual operating conditions do not exactly match the values that appear on the OEM's expanded performance data. Interpolate the:

- Heat sink temperature for cooling, or heat source temperature for compressor heating.
- Entering wet-bulb temperature for cooling.
- Entering dry-bulb for cooling, or for compressor heating.
- The blower Cfm equals the value, or one of the values, offered by the OEM's performance data.

1-11 Application Compatibility Caveats

Total cooling capacity for cooling-only equipment, and for Condition A heat pumps, must be compatible with the minimum and maximum limits specified by Table N2-1 or Table N2-2. However, this does not guarantee that the corresponding latent cooling capacity or/and sensible cooling capacity is/are optimized for the application.

Latent Capacity Limits

The applied latent capacity (the fully interpolated value) must not be less than the latent cooling load (1.00 factor), and should not exceed the latent load by more than 50% (1.50 ratio).

- Designing for 45% RH indoors reduces excess latent capacity.
- A larger blower Cfm value reduces excess latent capacity.

- An evaporator coil that is designed to operate at a warmer temperature for a given condenser package size (nominal condensing unit tons) reduces excess latent capacity.
- For more detail, see the excess latent capacity sidebar on this page (continued on the next page).

Sensible Capacity Limit

The applied sensible capacity (the fully interpolated value plus one-half of the excess latent capacity) must not be less than 90% (0.90 ratio) of the sensible cooling load.

- For humid climates, less sensible capacity for the summer design condition improves indoor humidity control and comfort for thousands of part-load hours.
- The summer design condition only occurs for a few days per season, and only for a few hours per day.
- The lower limit for sensible capacity is compatible with outdoor conditions for almost all of the cooling season hours, or possibly all of the cooling season hours.

  A load calculation procedure is an engineering model. Engineering models appropriately use conservative assumptions and defaults to simplify complex physical principles, and the related mathematics.

- For occupant comfort, the desire for a cooler indoor dry-bulb temperature decreases as indoor relative humidity decreases.

1-12 Electric Heating Coil Size

An electric heating coil may provide supplemental heat, emergency heat and defrost cycle heat for an air-air heat pump, or supplemental heat and emergency heat for a water-air heat pump. A cooling-only system is converted to a cooling and heating system by installing an electric coil in an equipment cabinet, plenum, or trunk duct. An electric heating coil in a branch trunk duct, or run out duct, creates a zone. Heat may be provided by an electric furnace, which may, or may not, have a cooling coil.

There is no economic benefit for over sizing an electric heating coil as far as energy use (KWH) is concerned, and this has an undesirable effect on KW demand, and on air distribution effectiveness. Therefore, electric heating coils should have little or no excess capacity, and should be staged when the installed size is 10 KW, or more.

- For home construction cost, the minimum ratings and cost for electrical system components tend to increase with increasing KW.
- For homeowner use, annual energy cost may increase when the utility bill includes a demand charge.

Excess Latent Capacity

For cooling comfort, there are two climate types. A dry climate has no latent load during a summer design day. A humid climate has a latent load during a summer design day. There are large differences in humid climate moisture, as shown by the grains difference values in Tables 1A and 1B, *Manual J*.

The latent cooling load mostly depends on infiltration Cfm, duct leakage to an unconditioned space, and engineered ventilation Cfm, which depend on the grains difference values in *Manual J*, Table 1A or 1B. So the latent load for a given dwelling that has a given set of attributes, increases as the climate becomes more humid (see Figure A1-17).

For humidity control, the indoor coil construction details and refrigerant metering device must be compatible with the latent load. So a high latent capacity design is compatible with a relatively large latent load (low sensible heat ratio), and a low latent capacity design is compatible with a relatively small latent load (high sensible heat ratio), or zero latent load.

Nominal cooling tons equals total cooling capacity at the AHRI rating condition (95°F/80°F/67°F) divided by 12,000. The condensing equipment has a ton value, and evaporating equipment that has orifice or cap-tube metering has a ton value. The apparatus dew point for a cooling coil decreases when nominal evaporator tons is less than nominal compressor-condenser tons, and vice versa.

So for a given outdoor unit size (nominal tons), the indoor unit size for orifice or cap-tube metering can be a half-ton larger for a dry climate, the same ton value for a normal wet climate, and a half-ton smaller for a very wet climate (the half-ton value is a ballpark number). Some OEM's provide expanded performance data for all three scenarios; some only provide data for a ton-to-ton match. In general, nominal Cfm/Ton values may be:

- Low range (350 to 425) for a smaller indoor unit.
- Mid-range (425 to 500) for an indoor-outdoor match.
- High range (500 to 600) for a larger indoor unit.

The indoor vs. outdoor ton concept does not apply to expansion valve metering. The indoor coil Cfm value and the action of the metering device determines the latent capacity of a given indoor coil design (face area, rows, circuiting, and fins per inch).

When the indoor-outdoor set is the correct match for the *Manual J* sensible heat ratio, the OEM's expanded

- Excess electric coil KW in a large number of homes may have an undesirable affect on the aggregate demand on the local power grid. This depends on the diversity factors for the hours of the year, which depend on the aggregate set-back strategy for the community served by the grid. Community start-up after a wide spread power outage is a related issue. Investigate the thinking and policy of the local utility.
- Excessive KW for the momentary heating load causes an unnecessarily high supply air temperature for a short period of time.

  Hot supply air tends to stagnate under ceilings.

  Air distribution effectiveness depends on blower operating time.
- Excessive KW during a defrost cycle is inefficient (space heat added at a COP of 1.0 is heat that is not provided at a higher COP when the system switches back to the heating mode), but this is a minor issue.

Sizing Value

The sizing value for electric coil size depends on the application. Related procedures are summarized here:

- For heat pump supplemental heat, a balance point diagram determines the maximum KW required for operation on a winter design day. Section 2-11 and Section N2-7 provide detailed instructions.
- For heat pump emergency heat, the sizing value depends on local code.

  Per Section N2-7 and Section 2-12, the sizing value is 85% (0.85 factor) of the Manual J heating load for a winter design day.

  Manual S procedures are superseded by local code. Use the code value when it is different than the Manual S value.
- For an electric furnace, or a central electric coil that converts a cooling-only air distribution system to a cooling and heating system, the sizing value is the *Manual J* heating load for a winter design day, for the rooms and spaces served by the equipment.
- For an electric coil in a duct run that serves a zone, room or space, the sizing value is the winter design day heating load for the zone, room, or space.

Over-Size Factor

The over-size factor (OSF) equals the maximum heating capacity (Btuh), divided by the total heating load (Btuh) for the rooms and spaces served by the electric heating coil (the sizing value).

OSF = Maximum heating capacity / Sizing Value

---

performance data will show that the coil sensible heat ratio is compatible with the *Manual J* value, so there will not be a large amount of excess latent capacity. When the indoor unit is too small for the *Manual J* sensible heat ratio, the OEM's expanded performance data will show that the coil sensible heat ratio is significantly less than the *Manual J* value, so there will be a large amount of excess latent capacity.

Phase change heat transfer is much more powerful than sensible heat transfer, so the first priority for a cooling coil is to extract moisture from the entering air. When there is excessive latent capacity for the design day load, the relative humidity of the indoor air gets dryer than the value used for the *Manual J* load calculation. This causes a reduction in the entering wet-bulb temperature.

For continuous operation, decreasing entering wet-bulb temperature causes decreasing latent capacity, but dryer air in the conditioned space causes an increase in the latent load. So, there is a balance point for the moisture flows.

An iterative psychrometric investigation shows that the house-equipment system balances out after a few return air passes through the cooling coil. When operating conditions stabilize, the indoor humidity will be somewhat lower than the design value (say, one to three points of relative humidity), the coil sensible heat ratio will be somewhat higher than indicated by the OEM's performance data. The latent capacity will equal the latent load, and there will be more sensible capacity than indicated by the OEM's data.

When psychrometric calculations are performed for a few scenarios, the tendency is for about one half of the excess latent capacity (latent Btuh from OEM data minus *Manual J* latent Btuh) to be available as sensible capacity (the applied EWB is less, so the applied CSHR and sensible capacity increase). As noted above, the other half of the excess latent capacity causes the indoor relative humidity to be somewhat less than the value used for the *Manual J* calculation.

Or, to look at it another way, when the *Manual J* calculation is based on an indoor humidity that is low enough, the latent load increases accordingly. This forces parity for the *Manual J* sensible heat ratio and the sensible heat ratio from the OEM's data. The result is that there is no excess latent capacity when the latent load is compared to the latent capacity.

So, excess latent capacity is self correcting with desirable consequences (lower indoor humidity). However, deficient latent capacity is a serious problem because it is not self correcting, and has undesirable consequences (higher indoor humidity).

- Table N2-3 provides size limit values for electric heating coils.
- Heating capacity values are extracted from OEM performance data for full KW input.

1-13 Fossil Fuel Furnace Size

Excessive heating capacity reduces seasonal heating efficiency, but this effect is not a significant issue for contemporary equipment (see Appendix 11). However, excessive heating capacity causes short operating cycles, which reduce air distribution effectiveness, increase the stress and strain on equipment, and may cause a vent condensation problem. Therefore, natural gas, propane and oil furnaces should have little or no excess heating capacity.

Sizing Value

The *Manual J* heating load provides the sizing value for calculating the over-size factor. This is the block heating load for the rooms and spaces served by the equipment (per Section 2-1).

Factor

The over-size factor (OSF) equals the equipment's full heating capacity (maximum burner Btuh), divided by the total heating load (Btuh) for the rooms and spaces served by the equipment (the sizing value).

OSF = Full heating capacity / Sizing value

- Table N2-4 provides size limit values for fossil fuel furnaces.
- Heating capacity values for full burner input are extracted from OEM performance data.
- Furnace blower power is an important issue when the cooling load is large relative to the heating load. A furnace that is the correct size for heating may have deficient blower power for cooling.

  The design Cfm value for cooling may be substantially larger than the appropriate value for heating.

  A cooling coil has a relatively large pressure drop. This is normally external to OEM blower data (not in place when the furnace's blower was tested).

  The pressure drop for air-side components that are external to the OEM's blower table must be subtracted from the external static pressure read from the blower table.

- The furnace blower must have enough power to move supply air and return air through all the external air-side components, fittings, and straight runs in the critical circulation path (the path of maximum airflow resistance).

- Table N2-4 relaxes the over-size limit for designs that use a larger furnace to obtain the necessary blower power for cooling.
- Use of the relaxed sizing limit is not the preferred solution for deficient blower performance.

  Some OEMs install powerful blowers in furnaces that have relatively small burners. This equipment is recommended when the design cooling load dominates the design heating load.

  Use a heat pump.

  Use a water potable heater that serves a hot water coil in the air distribution system for cooling (installed in an equipment cabinet, plenum, or supply trunk).

  Install radiant heat.

  Install an electric heating coil in the air distribution system for cooling, or use baseboard heat (when electric resistance heat is allowed by local code).

1-14 Dual Fuel Systems

The over-size limits for heat pumps (Table N2-2) and furnaces (Table N2-4) apply to dual fuel systems. An economic balance point (EBP) calculation provides information pertaining to control strategy, and the potential economic benefit from using two fuels. Section N2-11 provides additional sizing commentary; Section 8 discusses economic balance point calculations.

1-15 Water Boilers and Water Heaters

Water heating equipment may use a fossil fuel or electricity. Excess heating capacity for fossil fuel equipment has a small to insignificant affect on seasonal efficiency (see Appendix 11). Short-cycling increases equipment stress and wear, and may cause a vent condensation problem.

Cold start transients are an exceptional event, so a shorter warm-up time for an abnormal condition does not justify excessive capacity. A programmable thermostat should be able to manage set-back recovery for normal occupancy schedules, so excessive capacity for set-back recovery is not needed.

- An accurate heating load calculation has an implicit factor of safety, due to standard modeling assumptions, defaults, and fixed values.
- Complete set-point recovery will occur when momentary capacity is equal to, or more than, the momentary load.

  This is consistently true, when the equipment has no excess heating capacity, based on an accurate load calculation. The possible exception being when outdoor conditions are abnormally harsh (much worse than the winter design condition for the load calculation).

Section 1

Per Table N2-4, the equipment may have up to 40% excess heating capacity based on an accurate load calculation. This is more than enough for unusual weather.

- Set-back physics and economics is a complicated issue (see the sidebar on this page). Measures that satisfactory recovery from a five degree set-back, may not apply to significantly larger set-back values.

Sizing Value

Water boilers may be exclusively used for space heat; or, one piece of equipment may be used for space heat and potable water heat; or, one piece of equipment may be used for space heat and snow melting; or for space heat, water heat, and snow melting.

- For space heating boilers, the *Manual J* load provides the sizing value for calculating the over-size factor. This is the block load for the rooms and spaces served by the equipment (see Section N2-10, and Section 2-1).

- For multi-purpose boilers, for boilers used for radiant heat, and for water heaters used for space heat, refer to equipment use, selection, and sizing guidance provided by code, OEM literature, and trade associations.

Over-Size Factor

The over-size factor (OSF) equals the boiler's full heating capacity (maximum burner Btuh, or maximum electric element KW), divided by the total heating load (Btuh) for the rooms and spaces served by the equipment (the sizing value).

OSF = Full heating capacity / Sizing value

- Table N2-5 provides size limit values for water boilers.
- Heating capacity values for full burner input are extracted from OEM performance data.

1-16 AHAM Appliances

Window units and thru-the-wall equipment are home appliances. The Association of Home Appliance Manufacturers (AHAM) specifies the testing and performance data reporting requirements for this type of equipment.

An AHAM appliance be the only conditioning equipment for a room or space (a bonus room or ancillary space, for example), or may supplement local conditioning provided by a central system (to neutralize a cooling load spike cause by entertaining a large number of people, for example). Section N2-14 provides more commentary on appropriate use.

The performance data for this type of equipment is limited to the rating data (expanded performance data is not commonly available). The extent of this information is summarized here:

> **Set-Back Issues for Hot Water Heat**
>
> *Correlating recovery time (with reasonable accuracy) at the thermostat(s), and for the air in the rooms and spaces that do not have a thermostat, with input heating capacity, is a complex heat transfer problem. This depends, in part, on the set-back value, the set-back time, the thermal attributes of the structure, the floor plan, the use or non-use of forced convection and / or ceiling fans, the locations and attributes of the terminal heating equipment, the attributes of the hydronic heating equipment, the attributes of the distribution piping, and the outdoor air temperature and wind velocity during the recovery period (ignoring solar gain and internal gain for the worst-case scenario).*
>
> *Set-back is used to save energy and to reduce heating cost. The related cost-benefit calculations are complex. Knowledge gained by observing behavior for one set of architectural and climatological circumstances does not necessarily apply to other sets of circumstances.*

- For cooling, a total capacity value is provided, but there is no sensible capacity value, or sensible heat ratio value.

- The total capacity value is for a 95°F outdoor dry-bulb temperature, a 80°F entering dry-bulb temperature, and a 67°F entering wet-bulb temperature.

- For compressor heating, there is one capacity value for a 47°F outdoor dry-bulb temperature, and a 70°F entering dry-bulb temperature.

- OEM literature may not say that the compressor heating capacity is for 47°F outdoors, and may not provide heating capacity values for colder temperatures. Section N2-14 provides procedures that deal with this issue.

Sizing Value

For cooling equipment and heat pump equipment, the *Manual J* total cooling load (sensible Btuh plus latent Btuh) provides the sizing value for calculating the over-size factor. This is the block or zone cooling load for the rooms and spaces served by the equipment (per Section 2-1).

Over-Size Factor

The over-size factor (OSF) equals the equipment's total cooling capacity (Btuh) for the AHAM rating conditions, divided by the total cooling load (Btuh) for the rooms and spaces served by the equipment (the sizing value).

OSF = Total cooling capacity / Sizing value

- Section N2-14 provides size limit values for cooling-only equipment, and for heat pump equipment.

- For heat pumps, the size limit is relaxed when the *Manual J* sensible heat ratio is 0.95, or greater, and the HDD/CDD ratio is 2.0 or greater.

1-17 Ancillary Dehumidification Equipment

The primary comfort system may be supplemented by ancillary dehumidification equipment, which may be a whole-house dehumidifier, or a ventilation air dehumidifier. Section N2-12 procedures are summarized here:

Sizing Value for Dehumidification Equipment

For dehumidifier sizing, the sizing value for latent capacity is 85% (0.85 factor) of the latent cooling load, in pints per day units, for the outdoor summer design condition, and for 75°F and 55% RH indoors.

Applied Capacity

Dehumidifier rated capacity in pints per day units is for 80°F and 60% RH entering air. Figure N2-1 provides capacity adjustment factors for other entering air conditions. Applied capacity equals rated capacity multiplied by the appropriate capacity adjustment factor.

Size Limits for Dehumidification Equipment

The over-size factor for an ancillary dehumidifier ranges from the sizing value to the smallest available product that has an adjusted capacity that is greater than the full latent load for 75°F, 55% RH indoors.

Effect on Primary Equipment Size

The load calculation for new or replacement primary cooling-only equipment or heat pump equipment sizing is not affected by the use of ancillary dehumidification equipment. The primary equipment is sized (per Table N2-1 or N2-2 rules) to handle all the sensible and latent loads, including the engineered ventilation load (where applicable), for the summer design condition.

- Per *Manual J* procedures, the default load calculation value for indoor air is 75°F and 50% RH, but 75°F and 55% RH may be used for harsh circumstances.
- The load calculation is not adjusted for the moisture removed by the dehumidifier.
- The load calculation is not adjusted for the sensible heat added by the dehumidifier.

1-18 Humidification Equipment

Humidification equipment is commonly used for winter comfort, and may be used for summer comfort in dry climates. The humidification load is computed for the air-coupled space served by the equipment. Section 4 provides related procedures; air-coupled space is defined in the glossary.

Sizing Value

The sizing value for equipment sizing is the *Manual J* humidification load for winter or summer. When the equipment is used during winter and summer, the sizing value is the larger of the two humidification load values.

Over-Size Factor

The over-size factor (OSF) equals equipment humidification capacity (latent Btuh), when operating at the winter or summer design condition used for the *Manual J* load calculation, divided by the humidification load for the air-coupled rooms and spaces served by the equipment (the sizing value).

Application and Installation Issues

Calculating a humidification load for equipment sizing is not equivalent to designing a humidification system. Humidification equipment must not cause visible or concealed condensation, and/or mold and mildew on any structural surface, or any comfort system surface that is supposed to be dry during normal operation. See Appendix 7 and Appendix 8 for more discussion of this issue, and for condensation calculation procedures.

1-19 Direct Evaporative Cooling Equipment

Direct evaporative cooling equipment may be used for summer cooling when the moisture content of the outdoor air is compatible with evaporative cooling psychrometrics. Section 4 provides additional detail and procedures.

Sizing Value

For evaporative cooling, the latent cooling load must be zero for the summer design condition, so the total cooling load and the sensible cooling load are equal. The sizing value for equipment sizing is the *Manual J* sensible cooling load for the summer design condition (per Section 2-1).

Over-Size Factor

The over-size factor (OSF) equals the equipment's sensible cooling capacity, when operating at the summer design condition used for the *Manual J* load calculation, divided by the sensible cooling load from the *Manual J* calculation.

1-20 Over Sizing Authority for Heat Pumps

When the owner and practitioner are not bound by a local code or regulation, the owner may decide to use the sizing rule for a Condition B heat pump after reviewing and discussing indoor humidity control for summer cooling, the estimated energy and op-cost savings, and the additional installation cost for larger equipment, with the practitioner.

When use of the Condition B heat pump sizing rule is socialized by a local code or regulation, Manual S recommends that the code guidance for implementing excess cooling capacity be based on the actual variables and consequences that apply to each particular dwelling.

- Cooling and heating loads per an accurate *Manual J* calculation.
- Equipment capacity values extracted from comprehensive expanded performance data (as described in Sections 2-5 and A1-9).
- Industry research and/or mathematical modeling indicates acceptable indoor humidity control for summer cooling.
- A bin calculation or hourly simulation for energy use and op-cost based on local weather data (or data for the closest location at a similar elevation, and a similar proximity to a large body of water).
- Expanded performance data for heating and cooling provides conditional values for output Btuh and input KW for a bin calculation or hourly simulation (SEER, HSPF and AFUE equations are not acceptable).
- First year op-cost savings estimate based on the current rates for the local utility.
- A practitioner's estimate for the installed cost of larger equipment.
- Provide a rule for continuous blower operation.
- The criteria for converting this information to a yes (over-size) or no (do not over-size) decision is specified by the local authority.

1-21 Power Disruptions

Manual J load calculation procedures and *Manual S* equipment selection/sizing procedures are based on the premise that the heating-cooling equipment is continuously on line, and ready to respond to the beck and call of one or more space thermostats. These procedures do not apply when HVAC equipment is purposely turned off for a period of time by an occupant, owner, or owner representative. These procedures do not apply when HVAC equipment is inoperable due to a utility engineered disruption in power feed, based on it's contract agreement with the person, or organization, that pays the building's utility bill.

Start-Up Load

Shutting equipment off creates an undocumented start-up load for sensible capacity. For wet-coil cooling, this creates an undocumented start-up load for latent cooling. There is no industry approved standard for calculating these loads on a case-by case basis.

- Sensible heat absorbed by, or lost by, interior thermal mass must be restored after the equipment comes back on line.

- For wet-coil cooling, moisture absorbed by hygroscopic materials must be removed after the equipment comes back on line (the situation is acerbated when windows are open when the equipment is off line).
- For wet-coil cooling, latent capacity increases at the expense of sensible capacity during recovery (the coil sensible heat ratio is relatively low when the entering dry-bulb temperature is relatively high).

Equipment Size for Recovery Vs. Normal Operation

Excessive cooling capacity or heating capacity for faster dry-bulb recovery violates the Section N2 sizing rules, and is contrary to the rationale for these limits. There is no industry approved standard that correlates equipment capacity with recovery time on a case-by-case basis.

- When equipment is over-sized, the runtime for normal operation decreases. This has an adverse affect on comfort when design conditions apply, and this degrades part-load comfort for thousands of hours per year.
- For wet-coil cooling, indoor humidity control for normal operation may be seriously degraded when equipment is significantly over-sized.

Energy

Sensible and latent heat absorbed, or lost, by interior mass when the equipment is off line must be removed, or replaced, when the equipment comes back on line. The related amount of energy must be subtracted from the energy saved by taking the equipment off line. In addition, the recovery load may affect equipment efficiency during recovery. Then, excess capacity for recovery may affect equipment efficiency during normal operation.

- Momentary cooling efficiency depends on momentary operating conditions (entering dry-bulb and wet-bulb temperature, the cycling degradation coefficient, and the Btuh output vs. KW input consequences of steps in equipment size).
- Momentary heat pump heating efficiency depends on momentary operating conditions (use of electric coil heat, entering dry-bulb temperature, the cycling degradation coefficient, and the Btuh output vs. KW input consequences of steps in equipment size).
- Furnace efficiency is somewhat effected by cycling when runtimes are short, but this is a relatively minor issue.
- In general, energy savings increase with a longer shut-down time (the start-up penalty is less of an issue as the shut-down benefit increases).
- For humid climates, a prolonged lack of cooling may cause mold and mildew on interior surfaces.

1-22 Set-Up and Set-Back

Set-up and set-back may be used in an attempt to reduce the energy load (KWH or Btu), but this has nothing to do with equipment sizing. *Manual J* load calculation procedures and *Manual S* equipment selection/sizing procedures are based on the premise that the air in the conditioned space is continuously maintained at the summer or winter design condition.

- Set-up or set-back with a programmable thermostat is an acceptable practice.
- Initiate recovery before using the comfort space.
- Smart programmable thermostats continuously monitor circumstances and calculate the optimum time for starting the recovery cycle.
- For wet-coil cooling, indoor humidity control may be seriously degraded when cooling-only equipment, or heat pump equipment, is significantly over-sized in a misguided attempt to reduce the dry-bulb pull-down time for space air temperature.
- In some cases, a step up in system capability improves the situation (such as, zoning, staged or variable-speed equipment, or ancillary dehumidification equipment).

1-23 Performance Expectations

Dry-bulb temperature variations within a dwelling are caused by changes in local solar gain, internal gains, by differences in the density (buoyancy) of indoor air, and by significant differences in ceiling, wall and floor loads.

For example, variations in solar gain can cause east-facing rooms to overheat in the morning, and to be somewhat cool in the afternoon. Conversely, west-facing rooms may be too cold in the morning, and a little warm in the afternoon. For multi-level dwellings, cooler air tends to accumulate in the lower levels as warmer air tends to migrate to the upper levels.

Room-to-room temperature variations on one level depend on the openness of the floor plan. When two or more rooms share the same air, or when there are large openings between adjacent rooms, indoor air circulates through the aggregate space, so room-to-room temperature differences are minimized. Conversely, objectionable temperature differences may occur when rooms are isolated from the room or space that has the thermostat.

When objectionable room-to-room temperature variations occur, continuous blower operation may mitigate the problem, but this raises other issues:

- Continuous blower increases operating cost.
- Space humidity may increase when the blower operates with the compressor off (when cooling coil and drip pan moisture evaporate to supply air).
- Oversized cooling equipment acerbates the problem.

Single-Zone Performance

Figure 1-8 (next page) shows typical values for indoor design conditions (winter humidification is optional). When there is one central thermostat, remote rooms may have temperature swings.

- When properly designed and installed, single-zone systems maintain the desired temperature only for the space that has the thermostat.
- It may be that the desired temperature is maintained in adjacent spaces when they share air with the space that has the thermostat.
- It may be that the desired temperature is maintained in spaces that are isolated from the space that has the thermostat, providing they have hourly and/or seasonal load patterns that are similar to the space that has the thermostat.
- The desired temperature will not be maintained in spaces that are isolated from the space that has the thermostat when their hourly and/or seasonal load patterns are not compatible with the space that has the thermostat.
- During spring and fall, some rooms/spaces may need heat while other rooms/spaces need cooling. Conventional single-zone systems do not provide simultaneous heating and cooling.
- At any given time, room temperature swings may go in different directions, so a room-to-room temperature difference can be twice as large as room temperature swing.
- In general, a single-zone system cannot maintain the desired temperature for all the rooms and spaces in a dwelling. (Thoughtful architectural design may moderate, or eliminate, this problem.)

Multi-Zone Performance

Zoning provides more points of temperature control. Local thermostats respond to changes in room or space load and adjust local heating or cooling capacity accordingly.

- With local thermostats or temperature sensors, individual occupants can control the temperature of their personal space.
- The desired number of independent comfort zones depends on the architectural attributes of the dwelling, it's floor plans, it's construction details, and the use of it's rooms and spaces.

Residential Single-Zone and Multi-Zone Systems Temperature and Humidity Goals for Comfort and Safety [1]		
Temperature and Humidity Performance	**Heating Season**	**Cooling Season**
Thermostat set-point (**Manual J** default)	70°F	75°F
Relative humidity (RH) design values (**Manual J** default) [2]	20% to 30% typical	45% to 55%
Acceptable operating range for relative humidity [3]	Below 20% to 30% or higher	Below 45% to 60%
Single-Zone Multi-Space System Operating at Manual J Design Conditions		
Dry-bulb swing at the central thermostat	69°F to 71°F	74°F to 78°F [4]
Dry-bulb temperature swing for conventional rooms	67°F to 73°F	72°F to 78°F
Dry-bulb temperature swing for a bonus room [5]	No guideline (± 2 °F with zoning)	No guideline (± 2 °F with zoning)
Room-to-room temperature differences (same level)	67°F to 73°F	72°F to 78°F
Floor-to-floor temperature differences (any two rooms)	No guideline (± 2 °F with zoning)	No guideline (± 2 °F with zoning)
Single-Zone Multi-Space System Operating at Part-Load Conditions [6]		
Room-to-room temperature differences (same level)	No guideline (±2 °F with zoning)	No guideline (±2 °F with zoning)
Floor-to-floor temperature differences (any two rooms)		
Multi-Zone System Performance for Manual J Design Conditions [7, 11]		
Dry-bulb swing at any zone thermostat [8]	69°F to 71°F	74°F to 76°F [4]
Dry-bulb temperature swing for any room in a zone [9]	68°F to 72°F	73°F to 77°F
Dry-bulb temperature swing for a zoned bonus room [9]	68°F to 72°F	73°F to 77°F
Room-to-room temperature differences (same level)	68°F to 72°F	73°F to 77°F
Floor-to-floor temperature differences	68°F to 72°F	73°F to 77°F
Multi-Zone System Performance for Part-Load Conditions [10, 11]		
Room-to-room temperature differences (same level)	68°F to 72°F	73°F to 77°F
Floor-to-floor temperature differences	68°F to 72°F	73°F to 77°F

1) Condensation and/or mold and mildew is a health and safety issue.
2) For heating, winter humidification shall not cause visible or concealed condensation. (Maximum RH tends to decrease as the climate gets colder). For cooling, achievable RH depends on outdoor humidity. Use 45% RH for a dry climate, 50% RH is desired for all humid climates, 55% RH is acceptable for a very humid climate (such as New Orleans, LA; Houston, TX; Charleston, SC).
3) 50% RH is ideal for health and comfort. For heating, there is no lower limit when humidification is not provided. When provided, the maximum value is determined by condensation calculations (see MJ8, Section 27). For dry-climate cooling, indoor humidity may be less than 45% RH. For humid climate cooling, indoor humidity drifts at part-load; 55% to 60% RH is within the boundaries of the ASHRAE comfort chart; 60% RH is the threshold for discomfort and for mold and mildew blooms.
4) For dwellings, the average solar gain for daytime hours is used to calculate the block sensible cooling load for equipment sizing. This gain is normally less than the peak-hour gain. Therefore, a quality system that has no excess cooling capacity could have a + 3 °F swing at the thermostat when the outdoor condition mimics the summer design condition. However, it is known that an accurate load calculation has an embedded safety factor that reduces or eliminates the swing. In other words, the standard for minimum performance is dictated by a caveat in a design procedure, but installed performance is expected to be much better than the minimum requirement. (More information on this issue is provided in the glossary, see *temperature swing*).
5) A bonus room may be a below-grade room, an attic room, a room over a garage, etc. Such spaces may be thermally decoupled and/or incompatible with the primary conditioned space. The temperature in such a space has no effect on the thermostat for the primary space.
6) Single-zone, constant-volume systems cannot adjust for significant changes in solar gain and internal gain when equipment cycles at part-load. Nor do they adjust for different supply air Cfm requirements for heating and cooling.
7) Temperature swing may be larger than the listed values when heating-cooling capacity distribution is affected by equipment operating limits and/or system operating limits (i.e., the full amount of zone heating-cooling capacity must be available when design conditions apply).
8) Applies when one piece of central equipment serves two or more zones. Applies when one piece of equipment serves one zone.
9) Use ± 1 °F when the zone thermostat is in the subject room.
10) Temperature differences may be larger than the listed values when heating-cooling capacity distribution is affected by equipment operating limits and/or system operating limits. Listed values assume no restrictions on heating-cooling capacity distribution when part-load conditions apply.
11) The listed values apply to applications that are properly zoned (compatible load patterns for all rooms/spaces in a given zone). There is no protocol or procedure for a design that has incompatible rooms/spaces in the same zone.

Figure 1-8

- The number of installed zones may depend on the type of system (usually two zones to eight zones, some methods provide a larger number of zones).
- When all set-points are the same, local thermostats reduce room temperature swings and room-to-room temperature differences (see Figure 1-8).
- For ideal circumstances, room temperature swing depends on thermostat differential. This may range from ± 0.5 °F to ± 1.0 °F.
- For air zoning, room temperature swing may be larger than the thermostat differential when heating-cooling capacity distribution is affected by equipment operating limits, and/or system operating limits (low Cfm through equipment, high or low air temperature at equipment, fan stall, refrigerant pressures and/or flows out of range, etc.).
- During spring and fall, some zones may need heat while other zones need cooling.
- A zoned system may not provide simultaneous heating and cooling (for example, any piece of central air-handling equipment that is the only source of heating or cooling for two or more zones).
- When an all-air system cannot provide simultaneous heating and cooling, the zoning controls may choose the best operating mode for current conditions. Since zone loads and temperatures change with time, the operating mode will cycle between heating and cooling (providing this does not cause an unacceptable operating condition, or excessive humidity in one or more zones).
- Multi-split systems have a single condensing unit, multiple indoor coils, and a refrigerant management system. The maximum number of zones is determined by the number of indoor coils (one zone may have two or more coils). Through early 2014, simultaneous heating and cooling is not a common option for residential equipment.

Commercial three-phase equipment has this feature for sizes as small as three nominal tons. It may be that some residential products have this feature now, or will have it at some future time (ask the OEM).

- A central heating-cooling system that is supplemented with independent sources of zone heat can provide simultaneous heating and cooling (zone heat adjusts for deficient heating capacity, and/or excessive cooling capacity).
- Multiple systems can provide simultaneous heating and cooling (use one piece of heating-cooling equipment per zone).

When there is significant air exchange between floors, an upstairs system that is operating in the cooling mode will fight a downstairs system that is operating in the heating mode. Both systems will operate longer, energy use will increase, and operating cost will increase.

The air-side of each comfort system must be self-contained (provide a dedicated return air path for each system, do not use a common return).

1-24 Energy and Operating Cost Calculations

Per Year 2014, there is no HVAC industry approved standard for making residential energy and op-cost calculations. However, a defensible model should have certain capabilities and sensitivities. See Appendix 6 for more information.

This section is not part of the this standard. It is merely informative and does not contain requirements necessary for conformance to the standard. It has not been processed according to the ANSI requirements for a standard, and may contain material that has not been subject to public review or a consensus process. Unresolved objectors on informative material are not offered the right to appeal at ACCA or ANSI.

Section 2

Cooling-Only and Heat Pump Equipment Selection

For cooling, one procedure is used to select and size any type of air-air equipment, or water-air equipment. For heat pump heating, one selection and sizing procedure applies to any type of air-air equipment, or water-air equipment. Depending on the local climate, the heat pump sizing limit may favor enhanced heating performance. There also are performance tables for blowers and air-side components (coils and filters, for example).

2-1 Load Calculation

An accurate *Manual J* load calculation shall determine the sizing values for the total, sensible and latent cooling loads, the heating load, and where applicable, the humidification load. There shall be no implicit safety factor (fudging input data) applied to any step of the load calculation procedure. There shall be no explicit safety factor applied to any step of the load calculation procedure, or to the final value.

- The load calculation shall be based on information and details obtained by a careful and accurate survey of plans and drawings, or a site inspection.

- The load calculation shall be unique, in that it applies to a specific floor plan and it's construction details, and to the attributes of the actual HVAC equipment and distribution system that will be installed in the dwelling.

- A load calculation for a home-industry product, as identified by the home-builder's model name, and as described by the home-builder's plans and specifications for the product, shall be for the actual direction the front door of product faces when the product is installed on a building site.

- The load calculation shall be for the summer and winter design conditions for the actual location of the dwelling.

- As applicable, the load calculation shall account for the sensible and latent loads produced by occupants, appliances and plants, exposed duct runs, and engineered ventilation; and the sensible loads for blower heat and water piping; and the latent loads for moisture migration and winter humidification.

- The load calculation shall have altitude sensitivity.

  The state-point properties of outdoor air and indoor air depend on altitude.

  Infiltration loads and ventilation loads depend on air density (i.e., altitude).

Load Calculation Tools

The ANSI standard for performing a residential load calculation is the latest unabridged version of *Manual J*, Eighth Edition. An alternative load calculation method must have similar capabilities and sensitivities, and defensible procedures (as explained below).

The abridged version of *Manual J* may, or may not, be an alternative method. MJ8AE may be used when the attributes of the dwelling's construction and comfort system comply with the Abridged Edition Check List in front of the MJ8AE manual.

Capabilities, Sensitivities and Defaults

Capability relates to mathematical modeling. For example, load calculation procedures use mathematical models for fenestration loads, structural surface loads, duct loads and engineered ventilation loads. A credible procedure has a model for outdoor conditions, and for every load producing item associated with the structure, and it's comfort system. Equipment performance data provides an other example of a mathematical model.

Sensitivity relates to the variables in a mathematical model. For example, a fenestration model may only apply to clear, single pane, wood frame assemblies, or it may apply to any product listed in the NFRC directory. The credibility of the model depends on how it's sensitivities match up with the valuables that affect the fenestration load. An equipment performance model has it's own set of sensitivities.

Fixed defaults are standard inputs for sensitivity values. For example, the *Manual J* leakage values for a sealed duct system are 0.12 Cfm/SqFt for supply runs and 0.24 Cfm/SqFt for return runs (this is one of five leakage options). Fixed defaults must be technically defensible (based on physical and/or theoretical research). Using one, worst-case compass direction for the front door of a production home is a blatant example of improper use of a fixed default.

Adjustable defaults simplify model use for common occurrences. For example, when day-to-day work typically relates to dwellings that have clear, double pane, wood frame fenestration, the practitioner may use a form, or software setting, that is designed, or set-up, to solve this particular problem. The danger is that such forms and settings are used when they do not apply to the project at hand. (*End of this side bar.*)

Section 2

Manual J weather data and air-related procedures have altitude sensitivity.

The load calculations for the example problems in the informative sections of this document are adjusted for altitudes above sea level, even when the effect is small.

Altitude also affects equipment performance, see Section N1-11.

The load calculation also provides:

- Dry-bulb temperature values for outdoor air and indoor air for the winter and summer design conditions per the *Manual J* Figure 3-1 defaults, or comply with the values specified by a local code or utility regulation.
- Summer design condition values for outdoor wet-bulb temperature, and indoor relative humidity (45%, 50%, or 55% RH), and the option to select an indoor relative humidity value for winter humidification (or comply with a value specified by a code or utility regulation).

2-2 Entering Air Condition

For cooling equipment and heat pumps operating in the cooling mode, total capacity, and the total-capacity sensible-capacity split (coil sensible heat ratio) depend on the wet-bulb and dry-bulb temperature of the air that enters the indoor coil. For heat pumps, compressor heating performance depends on the dry-bulb temperature of the air that enters the indoor coil.

The dry-bulb and wet-bulb values for the air that flows through the return grille(s) are the starting point for determining values for the entering air dry-bulb and wet-bulb temperatures for equipment selection and sizing.

- If the possibility of space air stratification is ignored, the return air condition defaults to the dry-bulb and relative humidity design values for the air in the conditioned space.
- The wet-bulb temperature for a given dry-bulb temperature value and relative humidity value depends on altitude (i.e., use altitude sensitive psychrometric software for all state-point calculations).
- Per Section N1-8, adjust the dry-bulb and wet-bulb temperatures at the return grille(s) for the sensible and latent return duct loads and/or engineered ventilation loads.
- The sidebar on this page (continued on the next two pages) summarizes the issues and procedures. See also, Section A1-2 and Section A1-3 for related guidance.

Return Duct Load Effect

A sensible duct load affects the dry-bulb and wet-bulb temperatures of the entering air. A latent duct load affects the wet-bulb temperature of the entering air.

- The condition (dry-bulb and wet-bulb temperatures) of the air entering the return duct is the condition of the air at the return grille (the indoor air design condition used for the load calculation).
- For cooling, the condition of the air leaving the return duct depends on the sensible and latent loads for the return duct.
- For heating, the dry-bulb temperature of the air leaving the return duct depends on the sensible return duct load.

Implementation

Appendix 1 provides tables of default values that may be used to estimate the condition of the air leaving the return duct (the simplest method). Section A2-3 shows how a version of *Manual J* Worksheet G is used to evaluate return duct loads (the most accurate method). Appendix 2 also has procedures and equations that provide mathematical solutions to specific problems. The main issues are summarized here:

- The psychrometric equations for duct loads depend on an altitude correction factor (ACF).

  Sensible Btuh = 1.1 x ACF x Cfm x Temp. Difference
  Latent Btuh = 0.68 x ACF x Cfm x Grains Difference
  Figure A5-1 provides ACF values.

- Altitude sensitive psychrometrics determine the relationship between dry-bulb temperature, wet-bulb temperature, relative humidity, and humidity ratio.
- For consistency, the procedures and examples in this document have altitude sensitivity, even when the effect is small.

Related Forms and Software Tools

Appendix 22 provides a blank Worksheet G form, and forms for implementing Appendix 2 procedures. Some *Manual J* software products have an altitude sensitive psychrometrics module. Other sources for psychrometric software are available. These software tools are relatively simple to use.

Engineered Ventilation Load Effect

For indoor air quality, a relatively small amount of outdoor air may be mixed with a much larger amount of return air before it enters the comfort system equipment. A sensible ventilation load affects the dry-bulb and wet-bulb temperatures of the entering air. A latent

2-3 Equipment Operating Limits

OEM engineering guidance specifies equipment operating limits. Relevant limits must be compatible with intended use, or the design work cannot proceed to the next step. This is especially important for air-zoned systems because discharge air temperatures must not violate the OEM's limits as zone dampers open and close.

- For cooling, an OEM may specify a low and/or high-limit for the heat sink temperature (outdoor air dry-bulb, or entering water temperature), and there may be accessory components that allow operation at a colder heat sink temperature. There may be a low-limit for blower Cfm, and a low-limit for discharge air temperature. There may be limits for the condition of the entering air.

- For compressor heating, an OEM may specify a low and/or high-limit for the heat source temperature (outdoor air dry-bulb, or entering water temperature), and there may be accessory components that allow operation at a colder heat source temperature. There may be a low-limit for blower Cfm, and a high-limit for discharge air temperature. There may be limits for the condition of the entering air.

- There is a high-limit temperature for the air that leaves an electric resistance heating coil.

- For air-zoning, *Manual Zr* procedures for managing excess air demonstrates the benefit of a colder discharge air temperature for cooling, and a warmer discharge air temperature for heating.

2-4 Seasonal Efficiency Rating

A code, utility regulation, practitioner preference, or owner request may set a minimum value for the AHRI seasonal energy efficiency rating (SEER), and/or the heating season performance factor (HSPF). Investigate makes and models that have the desired rating(s).

2-5 Expanded Performance Data

Expanded performance data must be used to select and size equipment. For refrigeration cycle equipment, there is cooling data, and heat pump compressor heating data. For cooling, the performance data and it's use are conceptually the same for cooling-only equipment and for heat pumps (one procedure for both applications). For cooling and for compressor heating, the performance data and it's use are conceptually the same for air-air equipment and for water-air equipment (one procedure for both types of equipment). Electric heating coil capacity data and staging options are an issue for heat pump systems.

ventilation load affects the wet-bulb temperature of the entering air.

- If there are no return duct loads, the return air dry-bulb and wet-bulb temperatures depend on the dry-bulb and wet-bulb temperatures at the return grille.

- The procedures for the return duct effect (per the first part of this sidebar) determine the condition of the return air when the return duct is in an unconditioned space.

- The outdoor air dry-bulb and wet-bulb temperatures for cooling are the summer design values for the load calculation. The outdoor air dry-bulb temperature for heating is the winter design value for the load calculation.

- The condition of the mixed air depends on the outdoor air cfm and the return air Cfm. At the air handler, outdoor air Cfm plus return air Cfm equals blower Cfm.

- The condition of the outdoor air that is mixed with return air may depend on the use and effectiveness of heat recovery equipment (sensible only, or sensible and latent recovery).

Implementation

Appendix 1 provides tables of default values that may be used to estimate the condition of the air leaving the return duct, and the condition of mixed air (the simplest method). Appendix 2 has procedures and equations that provide mathematical solutions to specific problems (the most accurate method). The main issues are summarized here:

- For a given location, an outdoor air Cfm value, or a procedure to determine an outdoor air Cfm value, is specified by a local code or governing authority, or local authority may be silent on this issue.

- A fresh air Cfm value per an industry standard, such as ASHRAE 62.2, may be used when engineered ventilation is not locally mandated by a code or authority.

- Mixed air psychrometrics determine the relationship between outdoor air Cfm, return air Cfm; and the associated dry-bulb temperatures, wet-bulb temperatures, and humidity ratios.

- Altitude sensitive psychrometrics determine the relationship between dry-bulb temperature, wet-bulb temperature, relative humidity, and humidity ratio.

Altitude Effect

The output capacity of refrigeration cycle equipment, and fossil fuel heating equipment is affected by altitude. For example, OEM equipment performance data is for sea level air density, so cooling capacity, or furnace heating capacity, is less than indicated by the OEM's performance data when the equipment operates at 5,000 feet of elevation. Altitude also affects blower and fan mass flow rate, and electric power input.

The procedures in this manual apply to any altitude, providing that equipment selection and sizing decisions are based on altitude-adjusted performance data, per this protocol:

- The HVAC industry traditionally ignores altitude effects for altitudes of 2,500 Feet, or less. The procedures in this standard defer to this practice, for those who decide to use it.
- Sea level capacity data must be adjusted when the installation's altitude exceeds 2,500 feet.
- Appendix 5 procedures and derate factors apply when OEM literature does not provide specific guidance for product use at higher elevations.
- Appendix 5 guidance is superseded by specific OEM instructions pertaining to installation at altitude.
- The examples in this manual normally adjust for altitude, regardless of elevation. This demonstrates procedure.

Cooling Data

Exhibits of cooling data are provided by Figure A1-22 (central ducted air-air equipment), Figure A1-26 (central ducted water-air equipment), Figures A1-27 and A1-28 (ductless multi-split equipment), Figure 5-9 (two-speed equipment) and Figure 5-10 (variable-speed equipment). Note that these exhibits show the same set of mandatory sensitivities, which are sensible capacity and coincident latent capacity, vs. blower Cfm, heat sink temperature (outdoor dry-bulb temperature or entering water temperature), entering air wet-bulb temperature and entering air dry-bulb temperature. There should be two or more sets of data when capacity is staged or modulated. This concept also applies to ductless one-one or multi-split equipment, PTAC units and PTHP units.

Compressor Heating Data

Exhibits of heat pump heating data are provided by Figure A1-23 (central ducted air-air equipment), Figure A1-26 (central ducted water-air equipment), Figure A1-29 (ductless multi-split equipment), Figure 6-9 (two-speed equipment) and Figure 6-11 (variable-speed equipment). Note that these exhibits show the same set of mandatory

> - For consistency, the procedures and examples in this document have altitude sensitivity, even when the effect is small.
>
> ### Related Forms and Software Tools
>
> Appendix 22 provides forms for implementing Appendix 2 procedures. Some *Manual J* software products have an altitude sensitive psychrometrics module. Other sources for psychrometric software are available. These software tools are simple to use.

sensitivities, which are compressor heating capacity, vs. blower Cfm, heat source temperature (outdoor dry-bulb temperature or entering water temperature), and entering air dry-bulb temperature. There should be two or more sets of data when capacity is staged or modulated. This concept also applies to ductless one-one or multi-split equipment, PTAC units and PTHP units.

Special Rules for AHAM Appliances

Window and through-the-wall units do not have expanded performance data because they are a different class of equipment. These products are subject to requirements promulgated by the Association of Home Appliance Manufacturers (AHAM). All one can do is size for total cooling capacity and accept the resulting humidity control. Since compressor heating data may consist of one value for 47°F outdoors, a balance point diagram (with no defrost knee) requires an OEM value (or guess) for compressor heating capacity when it is the 17°F outdoors. For some types of equipment, the low-limit for outdoor temperature may be an issue of concern. Sections N2-15, 1-16, 2-5, 4-1, 4-2, 13-3, and 13-5 discuss AHAM appliances.

Electric Heating Coils

The performance data for electric resistance coils is simple and non-conditional. There is an input KW value and an output Btuh value for the heat that is added to the air that passes through the coil, and there is a high-limit for air temperature leaving the coil. There should be two or more sets of input-output data when installed capacity is staged or modulated.

2-6 Sizing Cooling Equipment

Cooling may be provided by cooling-only equipment, or a heat pump. For either case, equipment selection begins with a search for equipment that has adequate and appropriate cooling performance. The procedure provided here is summarized by Figure 2-1 (next page). Sections 5, 9, 11, and 13 provide application examples.

Section 2

Cooling Equipment Sizing Procedure

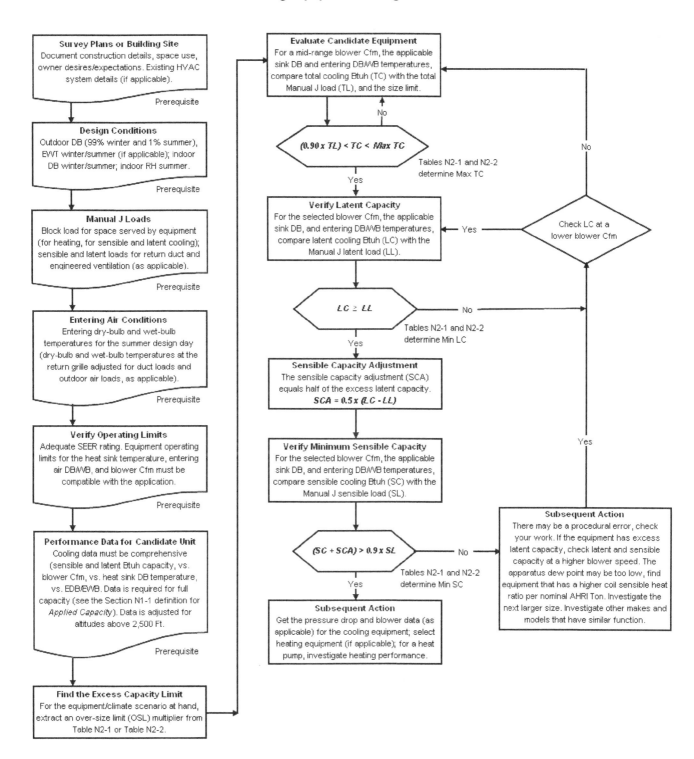

Figure 2-1

Step 1: Per Section 2-1, produce a proper load calculation for cooling.

- Requires construction survey data extracted from plans, or observed during a site inspection.

- Determine outdoor and indoor design conditions for cooling (local code, or *Manual J* defaults).

25

Section 2

Step 2: Per Sections 2-3 and 2-4, study the engineering data for the product of interest and verify that it's seasonal operating limits and efficiency rating are compatible with the application.

- For air-air equipment, use the outdoor air temperature for the summer design condition, adjusted for a hostile environment, where applicable (a condensing unit on a roof, for example).
- For water-air equipment use the warmest entering water temperature for the year.
- Use the entering wet-bulb temperature and the entering dry-bulb temperature for the summer design condition (per Appendix 1 defaults, or values from Appendix 2 procedures).
- Proceed to Step 3, when the equipment's operating limits are acceptable.
- When the operating limits are not compatible with the application, find equipment that has the required performance attributes, and proceed to Step 3.

Step 3: Per Section 2-5, get the cooling expanded performance data for the product (make and model) of interest.

- The product may have all components in one cabinet, may be a spit system, or may be an outdoor unit and an indoor coil for a furnace.
- The performance data for a given model normally covers many pages because products tend to be manufactured in a range of sizes.

  In general, equipment sizes range from one and one-half nominal AHRI tons, or two nominal AHRI tons, to five nominal AHRI tons.

  Ductless split equipment may be available in sizes that are less than one and one-half tons.

- Each model size will have it's own set of expanded performance data. When the equipment has staged or modulating capacity, there may be two or more sets of expanded data (for full or maximum capacity, and for reduced or minimum capacity).

  OEM performance data may be presented as table matrix that correlates total capacity and sensible capacity (or sensible heat ratio) values with sets of operating conditions (as demonstrated by Figures A1-22, A1-26 and A1-28).

  Expanded performance data may be OEM or third party software that returns capacity values for a specific set of operating conditions.

- The OEM's equipment capacity values must be sensitive to all the variables that effect total, sensible and latent cooling capacity.

Applied Capacity Notes

Applied capacity values shall be extracted from expanded performance data provided by an OEM (see Section N1-6 through Section N1-12).

- Sensible, latent, and total cooling capacity values depend on the blower Cfm, and the summer design condition values for outdoor air temperature or entering water temperature, entering air wet-bulb temperature, and entering air dry-bulb temperature.
- Heat pump compressor heating capacity depends on blower Cfm, and the winter design condition values for outdoor air temperature or entering water temperature, and entering air dry-bulb temperature.
- Applied capacity values must be for the entering air condition that is caused by load calculation circumstances.

  Entering air dry-bulb and wet-bulb temperature values depend on the load calculation values for the indoor air dry-bulb temperature and relative humidity (i.e., dry-bulb and wet-bulb temperature), the sensible and latent duct loads, and the sensible and latent engineered ventilation loads (see Section N1-8, Section N1-10 and Appendix 2)

- Applied capacity values cooling and heating shall be fully interpolated when equipment manufacturer's data conditions do not exactly match the operating conditions for the summer or winter design condition (per Section N1-12).
- For elevations above 2,500 Feet, applied capacity values for cooling and heating shall be adjusted for altitude, or follow OEM guidance when an adjustment is required for 2,500 feet, or less (per Section N1-11).

- Proceed to Step 4, when there is a proper exhibit of expanded performance data for full capacity. (For multi- or variable-speed equipment, reduced capacity data is desirable, but not mandatory.)
- When the expanded performance data is deficient in it's sensitivities, find equipment that has proper data, and proceed to Step 4.

Step 4: Find candidate equipment. Applied capacity values shall be used to search for candidate equipment (see the Section N1-1 definition of applied capacity, and see the side-bar on this page). A product's data set normally includes models that are obviously too small or too large, but some will appear to be the appropriate size.

- Per Appendix 3, the search for a likely candidate may be based on total cooling capacity, or a ballpark value for blower Cfm.
- The total capacity method is simpler because it does not require a speculative calculation (ballpark Cfm value).

  The total capacity method works for condenser-evaporator packages that are equally matched in nominal size, and for evaporators that are a size larger, or smaller, than the condenser package.

  There are a lot of total capacity values on a data sheet. The value of interest is the one that correlates with the application's heat sink temperature (outdoor dry-bulb, or entering water temperature), and the entering air wet-bulb temperature. Use a mid-range blower Cfm for the initial search.

- The ballpark Cfm method works best when the OEM has different evaporator size options for given condenser package size.

  A model's condensing side and evaporator side may be the same nominal size, sister models will have a smaller or larger evaporator.

  Blower Cfm per nominal AHRI ton tends to increase with evaporator size. The ballpark Cfm method is sensitive to this behavior.

- The total capacity method is generally compatible with the family of OEM condenser-evaporator sets, and the corresponding blower Cfm per nominal AHRI ton values.
- Practitioners tend to be more comfortable with the total capacity method, but either method will lead to a correct result, per Steps 5, 6, 7, and 8.

Step 5: Produce a target range for total cooling capacity, then use this range to evaluate a candidate unit.

- The sizing value (bull's-eye) for total cooling capacity equals the total **Manual J** cooling load (sensible plus latent) for the summer design condition.
- Section N2 provides lower and upper limits for total cooling capacity. These limits depend on equipment type (cooling-only unit, or heat pump). For a heat pump, the limits depend on the local heating and cooling degree day values, and on the load calculation sensible heat ratio for the summer design loads.

  Table N2-1 applies to cooling-only equipment.

  Table N2-2 applies to heat pump equipment.

- The total cooling capacity of a candidate unit must be within the range allowed by Table N2-1 or Table N2-2, where applicable.

  A total cooling capacity multiplier applies to cooling-only equipment, and to Condition A heat pumps.

  Up to 15,000 Btuh of excess cooling capacity is allowed for Condition B heat pumps.

Step 6: To validate size, compare the total cooling capacity for the candidate unit with the target range.

- Use a mid range blower speed (this makes higher and lower speeds available for fine-tuning after the equipment is installed).
- Use the summer design condition value for the outdoor air dry-bulb temperature, or the outdoor air dry-bulb adjusted for a harsh location (on a roof, or partially surrounded by hot masonry surfaces), or the cooling season design value for entering water temperature per Appendix 9 procedures.
- Use a defensible value for entering air wet-bulb temperature.

  As explained by Appendix 1 and Appendix 2, the entering wet-bulb temperature and dry-bulb temperature depend on the condition of the air at the return grille(s), the return duct loads (where applicable), and the outdoor air loads (where applicable), evaluated at altitude.

  For applications that have a dry cooling coil on a summer design day, use a wet-bulb value that is compatible with a dry cooling coil.

- When the data table value for total cooling capacity is within the target range, proceed to Step 7.
- When the data table value for total cooling capacity is outside the target range, find a candidate that has acceptable total capacity, and then proceed to Step 7.

Step 7: Compare the latent cooling capacity for the candidate unit with the latent cooling load.

- Latent capacity validation is based on the blower speed that was used to justify total capacity, for the same heat sink temperature, and the same entering air wet-bulb and dry-bulb temperatures
- When latent capacity is adequate (equal to, or greater than the latent load), subtract the latent load from the latent capacity, save the value, and proceed to Step 8.
- When latent capacity is deficient, it may be adequate at a lower blower speed. When this is true, subtract the latent load from the latent capacity, save the value, and proceed to Step 8.

  The practitioner has the option (not a mandate) to search for another candidate that has acceptable total capacity and adequate latent capacity at a mid-range blower speed, and then proceed to Step 8.

- When latent capacity is deficient, it may be adequate for a higher design value for indoor humidity. When this is true at a mid-range blower speed (or lower), subtract the latent load from the latent capacity, save the value, and proceed to Step 8.

    *The practitioner has the option (not a mandate) to reevaluate the **Manual J** latent load for a higher design value for indoor humidity, but the new indoor humidity value must not exceed 55% RH*

    Using a higher indoor humidity value challenges the limits of the design procedure, so latent capacity is evaluated for a mid-range blower speed.

- When latent capacity is still deficient, find a candidate that has acceptable total capacity and adequate latent capacity, then subtract the latent load from the latent capacity, save the value, and proceed to for Step 8.

- There may be cases when a ventilation dehumidifier, or a whole-house dehumidifier, is required for acceptable indoor humidity.

    Dehumidifier equipment is justified when equipment that has adequate latent capacity cannot be found after reasonable efforts have been made to minimize the latent load due to infiltration, duct leakage, and outdoor air (Figure A1-17 demonstrates the sensible heat ratio consequences of these effects.)

Step 8: Compare the sensible cooling capacity of the candidate unit with the sensible cooling load.

- Sensible capacity validation is based on the blower speed that was used to justify latent capacity, for the same heat sink temperature, and the same entering air wet-bulb and dry-bulb temperatures.

- Take one half of the excess latent capacity value from Step 7 and add it to the sensible capacity value from the data table.

- When the adjusted sensible capacity value is adequate (equal to, or greater than 90% of the sensible load), the equipment is certified for use.

- When sensible capacity is deficient, find equipment that has acceptable total capacity, adequate latent capacity, and adequate sensible capacity.

    Sensible capacity must not be less than 90% (0.90 factor) of the sensible load.

    There may be a procedural error, check your work.

    When there is excess latent capacity, check latent capacity and sensible capacity at a higher blower speed

    When there is excess latent capacity, the apparatus dew point may be too low for the application, find an evaporator-condenser combination that operates at a higher coil sensible heat ratio per nominal AHRI ton.

Investigate the performance of other makes and models that have similar function.

2-7 Sizing Heat Pumps

Air-air heat pumps and water-air heat pumps are sized for cooling, per Section 2-6, Steps 1 through 8. However, these steps are modified when the equipment provides year-round comfort. Then additional steps evaluate heating performance. The procedure provided here is summarized by Figure 2-2 (next page). Sections 5, 6, and 9 provide application examples.

Step 1: Section 2-6 procedures are modified. For heat pump applications, produce a proper load calculation for cooling, and for heating.

Note that the block load space is normally the same for cooling and heating, but the heated space could be smaller or larger when one or more rooms have there own source of heat or cooling (controls require some thought).

Step 2: Section 2-6 procedures are modified. For heat pump equipment, verify that cooling season and heating season operating limits are compatible with the application.

- For air-air equipment, use the outdoor air temperature for the summer design condition, and the winter design condition.

- For water-air equipment use the warmest entering water temperature for the year and the coldest entering water temperature for the year.

- Use the entering wet-bulb temperature and the entering dry-bulb temperature for the summer design condition, and the entering dry-bulb temperature for the winter design condition (per Appendix 1 defaults, or values from Appendix 2 procedures).

- Proceed to Step 3, when the equipment's operating limits are acceptable.

- When the operating limits are not compatible with the application, find equipment that has the required performance attributes, and proceed to Step 3.

Step 3: Section 2-6 procedures are modified. For heat pumps, get expanded performance data for cooling, and for compressor heating.

- Each model size will have it's own set of expanded performance data. When the equipment has staged or modulating capacity, there may be two or more sets of expanded data (for full or maximum capacity, and for reduced or minimum capacity).

    OEM performance data may be presented as table matrix that correlates total capacity and sensible capacity (or sensible heat ratio) values with sets of operating conditions (as demonstrated by Figures A1-22, A1-23, A1-26, A1-28, and A1-29).

Section 2

Heat Pump Sizing Procedure

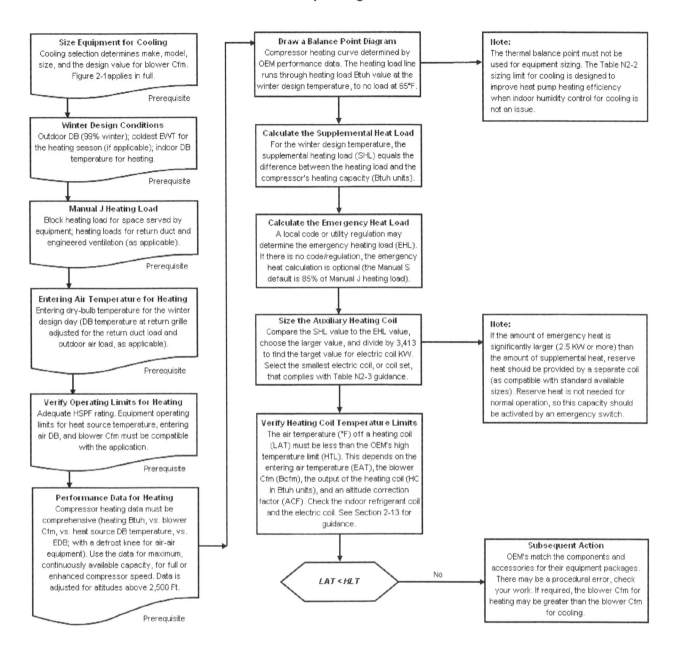

Figure 2-2

Expanded performance data may be OEM or third party software that returns capacity values for a specific set of operating conditions.

- The OEM's equipment capacity values must be sensitive to all the variables that effect total, sensible and latent cooling capacity, and compressor heating capacity.
- Proceed to Step 4, when there is a proper exhibit of expanded performance data for full capacity. (For multi- or variable-speed equipment, reduced capacity data is desirable, but not mandatory.)
- When the expanded performance data is deficient in it's sensitivities, find equipment that has proper data, and proceed to Step 4.

Step 4: Heat pumps are sized for cooling. Steps 4, 5, 6, 7, and 8 from Section 2-6 apply, but the design procedure will loop back to Step 4 when the heating performance of the candidate unit is deficient. When cooling requirements are satisfied, proceed to Step 9.

Section 2

Step 9: Draw a thermal balance point diagram for heating, per Section 2-8 procedures.

- Figure 2-3 provides an air-air example, and Figure 2-4 shows a water-air example.
- When the thermal balance point value is acceptable, proceed to Step 10.
- When the thermal balance point value is not in an appropriate range, go back to Step 4 (use larger equipment for a lower balance point).

   There are limits to balance point manipulation, and reasons why it is not an equipment sizing tool. See the Section 2-9 and Section 2-10 procedures.

   Heat pump equipment must not be sized for an arbitrary thermal balance point value. Balance point manipulation is subject to Table N2-2 sizing rules.

Step 10: Determine the supplemental heating load (Btuh), per Section 2-11 procedures.

Step 11: Determine the emergency heating load (Btuh), per Section 2-12 procedures.

Step 12: Determine the size (KW rating) of the auxiliary heating coil, per Section 2-13 procedures.

Step 13: Make sure that the air temperatures off the refrigerant and electric coils are in the range specified by the OEM, per Section 2-14 procedures.

2-8 Thermal Balance Point Diagram

Produce a graph that shows how compressor heating capacity (Btuh) and envelope heating load (Btuh) are affected by outdoor air dry-bulb temperature. The default value for the thermal balance point is at the intersection of the heating capacity curve and the load-line.

Compressor Heating Capacity Line

The details of the compressor heating capacity curve depend on compressor speed. This is not an issue for single-speed equipment. For staged capacity equipment use the full (final stage) speed. For variable-speed equipment, use the maximum, continuously available, compressor speed (this speed may exceed the speed used for the AHRI rating test for heating capacity).

Compressor heating capacity also depends on entering air temperature. Per Section A1-3 and Appendix 2, the entering dry-bulb temperature for the winter design day depends on the dry-bulb temperature at the return grille(s), and the dry-bulb temperature adjustments for a return duct load and/or an engineered ventilation load, where applicable.

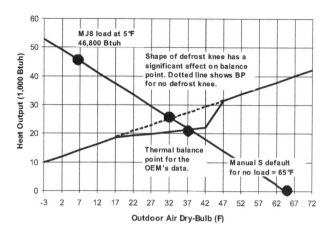

Figure 2-3

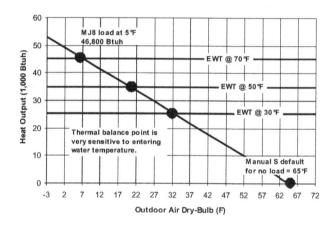

Figure 2-4

Note that the entering air temperature may increase incrementally as the outdoor air temperature moves from the winter design value toward 70°F. This is because duct and engineered ventilation loads diminish with increasing outdoor air temperature.

Defrost Knee Issues

For air-air heat pumps, the thermal balance point depends on the shape of the defrost knee that is embedded in the OEM's heating data. Figure 2-3 shows the balance point diagram for the Figure A1-23 heat pump data applied to a 46,800 Btuh heating load for a 5°F winter design temperature. Note that the default balance point is 37°F for the OEM's defrost knee, and 32°F for no knee.

- The shape of the momentary defrost knee depends on the momentary local weather (see Figure A1-25), and the reaction of the heat pump equipment.

There is no standard for determining the default (seasonal average) defrost conditions for load calculation towns and cities.

Even when average defrost load models were available, OEMs do not (and probably cannot) publish heating performance data for a comprehensive set of defrost load scenarios.

- There is a default defrost load model for the AHRI rating test (see Figure A1-25).
- The defrost knee in published OEM data, may be for the AHRI defrost load (used to compute rating HSPF), or for some other defrost load, or there may be no defrost knee at all.
- When OEM data shows a defrost knee, the default balance point (per the procedures in this document) is based on the OEM's defrost knee.
- When OEM data has no defrost knee, ask the OEM to provide adequate performance data, or investigate alternative products.
- For a given installation, the seasonal average defrost knee may be similar to the OEM's knee, or may be quite different than the OEM's knee.
- The shape of the defrost knee has a significant affect on the default thermal balance point value, as demonstrated by Figure 2-3.
- One OEM uses the term integrated heating capacity. This means that the compressor heating curve has a defrost knee.

Heating Load-Line

The default heating load model is a straight line that runs from the heating load for the winter design temperature to the no heating load condition for 65°F outdoors. Figures 2-3 and 2-4 show examples.

- This load model takes no credit for heat provided by solar and internal gains when the outdoor air temperature is at the winter design temperature (worst-case scenario for supplemental heat).
- This load model takes incrementally increasing credit for solar and internal loads as the outdoor air temperature moves from the winter design temperature to the no-load temperature.

The intent is to provide an approximate value for the average thermal balance point.

A rigorous solution for the average balance point for the entire heating season requires a set of hourly heating loads, a set of hourly balance point diagrams, a set of hourly balance point values, and the average of the hourly balance point values.

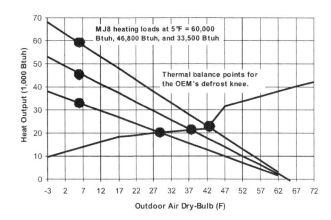

Figure 2-5

Outdoor Temperature for No Heating Load

The heating load depends on outdoor air temperature. When the indoor air temperature for the load calculation is 70°F, the heating load may be zero when the outdoor temperature is 70°F. However, the actual no-load temperature may range from about 70°F to less than 60°F, depending on momentary internal loads and solar loads.

The *Manual S* default for no heating load (cooling-heating change-over) is 65°F outdoors. This is used to draw a default (ballpark) balance point diagram.

- The actual (momentary) balance point moves a few degrees lower or higher, as internal loads and solar loads change.
- Balance point sensitivity to the no-load temperature is demonstrated by drawing a worst-case line (no solar or internal loads) from the design heating load condition to 70°F at zero load, then add parallel lines that intersect the zero load axis at cooler outdoor air temperatures (depending on the size of the solar and internal loads).

Heating-Cooling Load Ratio Issues

Dwellings that have similar cooling loads can have very different heating loads. Figure 2-5 shows how the design heating load affects the default value for the thermal balance point.

- The accuracy of the thermal balance point value depends on the accuracy of the heating load calculation.
- Measures that reduce the *Manual J* heating load are the proper way to lower the thermal balance point, whatever the actual balance point value may be.

Water-Air Heat Pump Issues

For water-air equipment, heating capacity is sensitive to entering water temperature. Figure 2-3 shows the balance point diagram for the Figure A1-26 heat pump data applied to a 46,800 Btuh load for a 5°F winter design temperature. Note that the default balance point is 32°F for 30°F water, 20°F for 50°F water, and 6°F for 70°F water.

- One water temperature applies to the whole heating season when ground water passes through the equipment on it's way to the point of disposal. The default water temperature for the balance point diagram is the local ground water temperature.
- A range of water temperatures apply to buried piping loop water. The default water temperature for the balance point diagram is the coldest water temperature for the year (see Appendix 9).

Heating Season Energy Issues

For a balance point diagram, the area to the left of the balance point, from the heating load-line to the heating capacity line, represents seasonal supplemental heating energy. For this model, each temperature bin has a set of supplemental KW values that depend on momentary values for solar load, internal load, and compressor heating capacity. Then, these momentary KW loads are correlated with a corresponding set of bin-hours values.

- Solar loads depend on month of year, time of day and cloud cover.
- Internal loads depend on time of day, but the inventory of load producing appliances and their use schedule depend on the life style of the occupants.
- A set-back schedule adds complexity to the model, and raises questions about the momentary source of recovery heat (compressor only, or a compressor aided by the electric coil).

The rating HSPF for air-air equipment is adjusted for supplemental heat. Looking at Figure 2-5, this HSPF value is compatible with the lower of the three load-lines, and this is for weather that is similar to Pittsburgh, PA.

- In other words, the rating HSPF value does not apply to a given application, except by coincidence.
- Computing an applied HSPF for a particular application (location, construction attributes and type of equipment) is a simple task for a credible energy calculation tool.

For a water-air heat pump, the area to the left of the balance point, from the load-line to the heating capacity line, represents seasonal supplemental heating energy. The caveats pertaining to solar and internal loads still apply. Compressor heat may be relatively constant for the whole heating season, or may vary from the beginning of the season to the end of the season.

- One heating capacity line applies to the whole heating season when ground water passes through the equipment on it's way to the point of disposal.
- For buried-loop systems, there is a balance point diagram for each entering water temperature value experienced during the heating season (with corresponding bin-hour sets).
- Water-air equipment does not have an HSPF rating (COP applies), but computing an applied HSPF for a particular application is a simple task for a credible energy calculation tool.

2-9 Thermal Balance Point Manipulation

A lower balance point does not automatically produce a significant reduction in energy use and operating cost, and may actually reduce efficiency and increase cost. This depends on the climate.

Ballpark values for the benefit provided by an additional half-ton of nominal AHRI cooling capacity are provided by Figure 2-6 (next page). In general:

- Excess cooling capacity must be as close to zero as possible when there is a significant latent load for summer cooling (significant means the load calculation sensible heat ratio less than 0.95).
- Per Table N2-2, excess cooling capacity may be used to force a lower thermal balance point when the load calculation sensible heat ratio 0.95 or greater, providing the heating degree day to cooling degree day ratio is 2.0 or more.
- Forcing a lower thermal balance point produces an annual efficiency benefit for heating dominate climates, but the reward may be modest.
- The key issue is the number of bin-hours for outdoor air temperatures that are below the thermal balance point (the colder the climate, the larger the reward).
- Conditioned basements significantly increase the heating load, and have no affect, or a small affect, on the cooling load. Everything else being equal, the efficiency benefit for a dwelling with a basement will be larger than for the same dwelling with no basement.

There is a larger lesson to be learned here. Measures that improve the thermal efficiency of the dwelling (tightness and component R-values), and measures that reduce system loads (duct efficiency and heat recovery for outdoor air, where applicable), are the proper way to lower the thermal balance point.

- The ratio of total cooling capacity (Btuh units) vs. total input KW of a given make/model may be relatively constant as model size increases or decreases, or may increase with increasing size, or may decrease with increasing size. An increasing or decreasing ratio can have a significant affect on annual cooling cost. (Figure 2-6 sensitivity is for a constant ratio.)

- An equipment cycling penalty (cycling degradation coefficient or C_d) applies to all cooling bins, and to the heating bins that are to the right of the thermal balance point. Lowering the balance point increases equipment size, which increases the cycling penalty, but the effect is modest.

The AHRI efficiency rating values (SEER and HSPF) may be based on an 0.25 default value for the cycling degradation coefficient, but the actual Cd value may be smaller. If so, the SEER and HSPF values for AHRI conditions will be a little larger than published.

After equipment is installed, momentary C_d values for cooling and heating are positively, or negatively, effected by variations in the outdoor air condition, the entering air condition, the amount of refrigerant charge, and the blower Cfm (vs. AHRI test conditions).

- The shape of the defrost knee for the local climate, and type of defrost control (demand defrost vs. time-temperature defrost) affects heating energy use. The effect is large enough to be of interest and concern.

For time-temperature, defrost cycles can be excessive when the cycle time is too short for the climate.

For time-temperature, defrost may be initiated when it is colder than 17°F outdoors.

- The amount of electric coil heat (KW) that is active during a defrost cycle affects heat pump efficiency.

The equipment is in the cooling mode, so supply air is relatively cool. This is a comfort issue. Electric coil heat makes supply air warmer. When too much KW is activated, supply air can be warmer than room air, which means that electric coil heat is heating the space during the defrost cycle.

- Air distribution effectiveness is reduced by shorter runs times. The energy saving benefit of a balance point manipulation may be destroyed when the owner decides to use continuous blower (perhaps recommended by the practitioner that installed the system, or services the system).

2-10 Thermal Balance Point Use

A thermal balance point diagram is useful for obtaining a ballpark outdoor temperature value for locking out supplemental heat (subject to field adjustment after installation). A thermal balance point diagram is not an equipment selection and sizing tool.

Consequences of Balance Point Manipulation

Akron, OH, at $ 0.10 $ / KHW					
Nominal Tons	Excess Capacity	TBP (°F)	$ Heat	$ Cool	$ Total
2.6	1.19	34	1,865	305	2,171
3.1	1.42	31	1,778	309	2,087

Atlanta, GA, at $ 0.10 $ / KHW					
Nominal Tons	Excess Capacity	TBP (°F)	$ Heat	$ Cool	$ Total
2.6	1.11	33	662	767	1,429
3.1	1.33	31	665	787	1,453

Minneapolis, MN, at $ 0.10 $ / KHW					
Nominal Tons	Excess Capacity	TBP (°F)	$ Heat	$ Cool	$ Total
2.6	1.18	36	2,707	320	3,027
3.1	1.42	33	2,623	327	2,950

Tacoma, WA, at $ 0.10 $ / KHW					
Nominal Tons	Excess Capacity	TBP (°F)	$ Heat	$ Cool	$ Total
2.3	1.24	37	1,325	152	1,477
2.8	1.52	34	1,320	157	1,477

1) TBP = Thermal Balance Point; TC = Total Capacity
2) Nominal tons = Rated total capacity / 12,000
3) Excess capacity = TC for site conditions / Total load
4) Seasonal and total KWH = 10 x Operation cost

Two story house over a basement with additional space on grade. The two story foot print is 676 SqFt. The on-grade foot print is 308 SqFt. The total above grade floor area is 1,660 SqFt. The basement floor area is 676 SqFt. Normal amount of double pane, clear, fenestration. Common insulation R-values. No engineered ventilation. The duct load factor for heating and cooling is 0.05. Bin weather data partitioned to five hour groups per day. Seasonally adjusted solar loads, and internal loads, assigned to each hour group. Air-air heat pump with electric coil heat. Compressor heating and cooling capacity vary with outdoor air temperature, per entering air conditions. Compressor operates for all temperature bins below the thermal balance point. Intermittent blower. Equipment cooling Btuh to input KW ratio is relatively constant vs. model size. Defrost knee computed for local climate, for demand defrost. Crank case heat applies. No set-up or set-back. All hours at $ 0.10/ KWH.

Figure 2-6

- A lower thermal balance point is desirable for a winter peaking utility, but a mandatory balance point goal may not be compatible with the climate.

Excess cooling capacity degrades summer humidity control.

The annual energy savings in KWH terms or dollars may be modest or insignificant (see Figure 2-6).

Larger equipment costs more to install.

It is possible for the utility to benefit from reduced demand on it's system at homeowner expense.

Rebate programs may, or may not, adequately compensate homeowners for the benefit to the utility (this depends on who gets the rebate money).

These caveats apply to air-air equipment, to water-air equipment, and to dual-fuel systems.

- A maximum thermal balance point mandate ignores the heating-load, cooling-load ratio issue. (see Figure 2-5)

- A maximum thermal balance point for air-air equipment ignores the defrost knee issue, and the defrost control issue.

The shape of the defrost knee has an affect on the thermal balance point (see Figures 2-3 and 2-5).

The seasonal average shape of the defrost knee for any particular application is not known.

- A maximum thermal balance point for water-air equipment that has buried-loop piping ignores the momentary water temperature issue.

- In general, efforts to specify a maximum thermal balance point value assume that a unique, predictable balance point value applies to the whole heating season. The preceding discussions show that this is not true.

- The Section N2 over sizing factors for heat pump cooling improve heat pump heating efficiency when heating energy is an issue, providing summer humidity control is not an issue.

2-11 Supplemental Heat

The supplemental heating load equals the difference between the *Manual J* heating load and the compressor heating capacity when the outdoor air is at the winter design temperature, as demonstrated by Figure 2-7.

- There is only one compressor heating capacity value for an air-air heat pump, which may, or may not, be effected by the shape of the defrost knee, depending on the design value for outdoor temperature.

- Since the performance of water-air equipment does not depend on outdoor air temperature, there is a compressor heating capacity value for once-through water, or a range of possible values for a buried piping loop. The default water temperature for evaluating compressor heating capacity is the coldest water temperature for the year.

- When the supplemental heating load is greater than the emergency heating load (per Section 2-12), the supplemental heating load is the sizing value for electric coil selection.

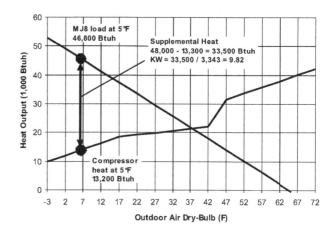

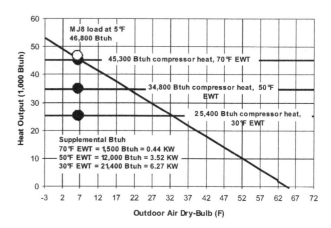

Figure 2-7

- To convert a supplemental heat Btuh value to a KW value, divide the Btuh value by 3,413.

- Depending on the situation, the KW requirement for supplemental heat may range from a few KW to more than 20 KW.

- Because of standard KW sizes, the installed electric heating coil capacity may exceed the sizing value. See the Section 2-13 procedures.

- The desired heat pump equipment may not provide electric coil heat. When needed, it must be provided by a separate system or device (electric duct coil, or baseboard heat, for example).

2-12 Emergency Heat

The local code authority or utility may have a rule for emergency heat. When so, the sizing value for the Btuh capacity of the electric coil may be equal to the design heating load, or may be some fraction of this load. When the local code/utility is silent on the issue, the use of emergency heat may be a practitioner practice, or owner preference.

- *Manual S* does not mandate emergency heat. When used, the *Manual S* value for emergency heat is 85 percent of the heating load for the winter design condition.
- When the emergency heating load is greater than the supplemental heating load (per Section 2-11), the emergency heating load is the sizing value for electric coil selection.
- To convert an emergency heat Btuh value to a KW value, divide the Btuh value by 3,413.
- Emergency heat power may range from less than 6 KW to more than 30 KW, depending on the winter heating load, and the sizing rule.
- Because of standard KW sizes, the installed emergency heating capacity may exceed the sizing value. See the Section 2-13 procedures.
- The desired heat pump equipment may not provide electric coil heat. When needed, it must be provided by a separate system or device (electric duct coil, or baseboard heat, for example).

2-13 Auxiliary Heat

Auxiliary heat is the total amount of installed electric coil heat. Auxiliary heat KW may be equal to the installed emergency heat KW, or the installed supplemental heat KW, depending on which is larger.

- There may be no emergency heat.
- When the design value for emergency heat is a fraction of the *Manual J* heating load, supplemental KW may be larger than the emergency KW.
- See Table N2-3 for sizing rules and size limits.

Lock-out Electric Coil Heat

For normal (non-emergency operation), controls must lock out electric coil heat when the outdoor air temperature is above the thermal balance point value. The lock out temperature for a manual set-point control is determined by a balance point diagram, or it may be conditionally determined by an intelligent control.

Reserve Heat

Reserve heat is the difference between the emergency heat value and a smaller supplemental heat value. Reserve heat is not needed for normal operation.

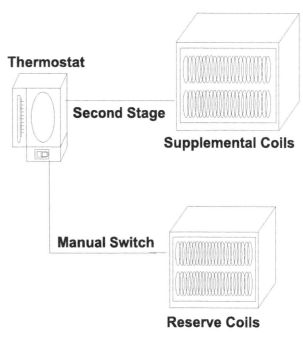

Figure 2-8

- When the amount of emergency heat is significantly larger (say, 2.5 KW or more) than the amount of supplemental heat, reserve heat should be provided by a separate coil or a capacity step (as compatible with standard sizes).
- Reserve heat should be activated by a manual switch (see Figure 2-8).

Capacity Control

Staged capacity control for supplemental heat is recommended when the installed electric coil capacity is 10 KW or more.

- OEM data for electric heating coils may show capacity steps (see Figure 2-9, next page).
- Or, use controls that modulate electric coil capacity.

2-14 High-Limit Temperature for Heating Coils

Indoor refrigerant coils and electric heating coils have a high-limit for leaving air temperature. The maximum leaving air temperature value is specified by the OEM (when the value is not in the engineering literature, ask the OEM for the information). Use these equations to see when heating coil Cfm is compatible with it's heating capacity.

Section 2

$HP_{lat} = HP_{eat} + HC / (1.1 \times ACF \times Cfm)$
$EAT_{coil} = LAT_{hp}$
$LAT_{coil} = EAT_{coil} + (3,413 \times KW) / (1.1 \times ACF \times Cfm)$

Where:
HP_{lat} = Air temperature leaving the refrigerant coil (°F).
HP_{eat} = Air temperature entering the refrigerant coil (°F).
HC = Maximum compressor heating capacity (Btuh).
 – The electric coil is locked out when the outdoor air temperature is warmer than the thermal balance point.
 – For air-air equipment, use the heating capacity for a 65°F outdoor air temperature for the refrigerant coil, and use the heating capacity for the thermal balance point temperature for the electric coil.
 – For water-air equipment, use the heating capacity for the warmest entering water temperature for the heating season for both coils.
ACF = Altitude correction factor (see Figure A5-1).
Cfm = The air flow rate through the equipment.
EAT_{coil} is the air temperature into the electric coil (°F).
LAT_{coil} is the air temperature off the electric coil (°F).
KW is the capacity of the electric heating coil.

Note: Excessive leaving air temperature should not be an issue when all the equipment is part of an engineered package supplied by one OEM, providing the equipment operates in the OEM's approved blower Cfm range. Investigate leaving air temperature when zone dampers affect system airflow (see **Manual Zr** procedures).

Electric Heating Coil Performance				
Model	BTUH	KW	Stages	CFM*
EHC-50	17,000	5.0	1	350
EHC-75	25,600	7.5	1	525
EHC-100-2	34,100	5.0 / 10.0	2	700
EHC-125-1	42,700	12.5	1	900
EHC-125-2	42,700	7.5 / 12.5	2	900
* Minimum CFM required to prevent over-heating				

Figure 2-9

2-15 Design Blower Cfm for Cooling

The design value for blower Cfm for cooling is determined when cooling equipment size is validated by comparing the conditional capacity values from expanded performance data with the *Manual J* cooling loads. See Section 2-6, steps 3 through 8.

- The design blower Cfm value for cooling must be compatible with the OEM's low-limit values for minimum blower Cfm, and leaving air temperature. For single zone systems, this occurs by default when the blower Cfm value comes from proper use of the OEM's expanded performance data (OEM data matches cooling capacity values to approved blower Cfm values).

- Blower Cfm values for undocumented operating conditions must be compatible with the OEM's low-limit values for cooling. This is a fundamental issue for equipment that serves a zone damper system (see ACCA *Manual Zr*).

2-16 Design Blower Cfm for Heating

For heating, the design value for blower Cfm is the Cfm that was used to extract compressor heating capacity values from OEM performance data. In other words, the blower Cfm that correlates with the heating capacity line on the balance point diagram.

- The design blower Cfm value for heating must be compatible with the OEM's limit values for blower Cfm, and the leaving air temperatures at the refrigerant coil and the electric heating coil (where applicable). For single zone systems, this occurs by default when the blower Cfm value comes from proper use of the OEM's expanded performance data (OEM data matches heating capacity values to approved blower Cfm values).

- Blower Cfm values for undocumented operating conditions must be compatible with the OEM's limit values for heating. This is a fundamental issue for equipment that serves a zone damper system (see ACCA *Manual Zr*).

2-17 Design Blower Cfm for Duct Sizing

Manual D uses the block heating and cooling loads, the room heating and cooling loads, and the blower Cfm for heating and cooling to produce a set of room Cfm values for heating, and a second set for cooling. Then heating Cfm is compared to cooling Cfm for points in the duct system, and the larger value is used for airway sizing. In other words, *Manual D* procedure accommodates different blower Cfm values for heating and cooling.

2-18 Blower Data

After expanded performance data is used to select and size equipment, the corresponding blower table is required for *Manual D* calculations. This data must be readily available (preferably a published supplement to the expanded performance data, vs. having to ask for it), and it must be comprehensive.

- The operating range (blower wheel speeds or blower Cfm set-points, blower Cfm values, and the corresponding external static pressure values) may be summarized by a table or graph.

- Table footnotes should (but may not) list all pressure dissipating components that affect the external static pressure values in the blower data (wet, or dry cooling coil, filter or not, electric resistance coil or not, or whatever).

- Pressure dissipating components that are not relevant to the blower data, may be part of the desired equipment package. These items reduce the available static pressure for duct airway sizing.

- Some blower tables do not have adequate footnotes, or may have no footnotes. A practitioner may be in for a nasty surprise when he or she mistakenly assumes that the blower data has been adjusted for necessary items such as a cooling coil, electric heating coil, or filter.

- Figure A1-31 provides an example of adequate blower data for a wheel driven by a PSC motor (comprehensive data, complete footnotes). Figure A1-32 provides an example of inadequate blower data for a wheel driven by a ECM motor (comprehensive data, deficient footnotes).

- When there is any question about what the blower data actually means, the practitioner is advised to raise the issue with the OEM.

2-19 Component Pressure Drop Data

The pressure drops for necessary, or desired, air-side components that are not relevant to the blower data must be subtracted from the external static pressure values read from a blower table, or graph. Component pressure drop values are read from tables or graphs published by the OEM. Such data must be readily available (preferably a published as part of the OEM's engineering data, vs. having to ask for it). An example of component pressure drop data is provided by Figure 2-10.

2-20 Operating and Safety Controls

OEM cooling and heat pump packages have a variety of standard controls and devices, and optional controls, devices, and features. The practitioner must specify adequate and appropriate operating and safety controls.

Additional operating and safety controls may be part of a zone damper kit provided by the OEM, or a zoning equipment vendor. Ductless split-coil zoning equipment has refrigerant distribution devices and controls.

Control functions and features may be strictly electrical-mechanical, or may involve proprietary programming (with or without embedded options and ports), or open-system programming. A list of common controls and devices is provided below. See OEM engineering literature for the features and options attached to a particular product.

Coil Resistance (IWC)		
Cfm	Dry	Wet
1,000	0.11	0.18
1,200	0.15	0.26
1,400	0.22	0.35
1,600	0.28	0.46

Electronic Filter Resistance	
Cfm	IWC
1,000	0.06
1,200	0.08
1,400	0.12
1,600	0.15

Heater Resistance	
Cfm	IWC
1,000	0.09
1,200	0.13
1,400	0.18

Figure 2-10

Operating Controls and Devices

Products that are similar in form and function may be differentiated by their operating controls and related devices. There usually is a set of standard items and a set of optional items. A partial list of operating controls and devices is provided here:

- Select operation mode switch (heating, cooling, fan-only, off).

- Space temperature sensor/control (simple set-point control, or set-up/set-back scheduling).

- Space or return air humidity sensor/control.

- Compressor controls and interlocks (on-off, or capacity staging, or variable-speed).

- Indoor blower and outdoor fan controls, and interlocks (on-off, possible speed change).

- Possible advance or delay for blower start/stop vs. compressor start/stop (see Figure 2-11).

- Refrigerant flow may be controlled by an orifice, cap-tube, thermostatic expansion valve (TXV), or electronic expansion valve (EEV).

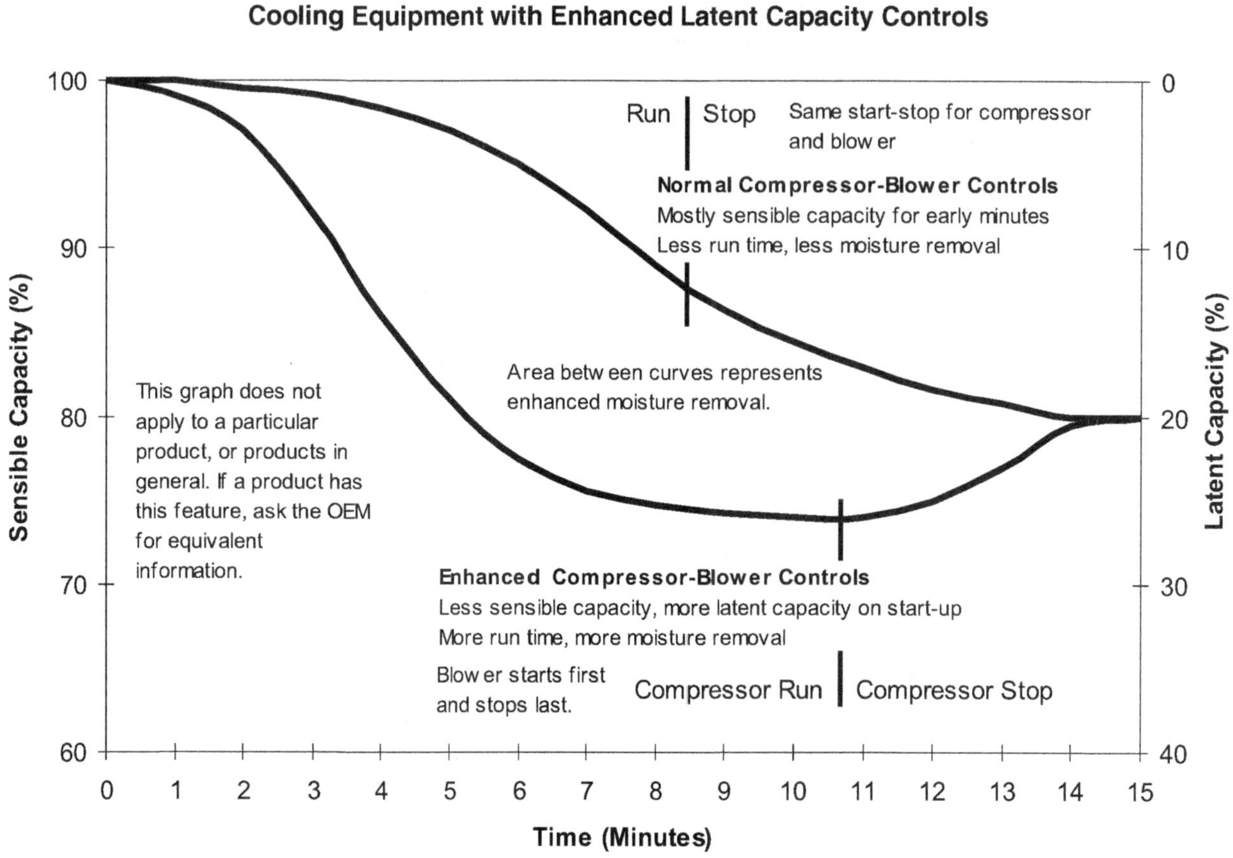

Cooling Equipment with Enhanced Latent Capacity Controls

Figure 2-11

- Refrigerant management devices and controls for ductless, multi-split equipment.
- Heat pump reverse cycle control.
- Heat pump defrost cycle control options.
- Hard start kit.
- Low ambient kit (to run cooling equipment when it is somewhat cold outdoors).
- Electric resistance heating coil controls and interlocks (on-off, staging, modulated capacity).
- Furnace interlock for dual-fuel system.

Safety Controls

Products that are similar in form and function may be differentiated by their safety controls and devices. There usually is a set of standard items and a set of optional items. A partial list of safety controls and devices is provided here:

- Low airflow sensor.
- Refrigerant coil freeze stat (monitor leaving air temperature).
- Refrigerant pressure switches (high-limit and low-limit).
- Anti-short cycle relay.
- Motor protection.
- High-limit for an electric coil in an airflow path.
- Duel fuel furnace high-limit (standard); low-limit (possible).

2-21 System Start-Up and Set-Point Recovery

Excess capacity for system start-up, and/or recovery from set-up/set-back, must not exceed Section N2 values. Use a properly adjusted programmable thermostat for recovery from set-up/set-back.

- Extra capacity for system start-up is not needed because this is an abnormal and rare event for systems that are designed, installed, and operated to a proper standard of care.

Heating may be set-back, but it is rarely shut off during the heating season.

Shutting cooling down on a day-to-day basis is not recommended because recovery times can be extensive, especially when there is a large moisture removal load.

Shutting cooling down and opening windows is an extremely bad idea when the humidity ratio of the outdoor air is significantly higher than the humidity ratio for the desired indoor DB/RH values. When the system starts, the evaporator coil will extract moisture from the indoor air, the carpet, the drapes, the furniture, and all other absorbent materials. This will cause the cooling coil sensible heat ratio to be relatively low (say 0.5 to 0.7) for a substantial period of time. A low sensible heat ratio reduces sensible capacity, and increases dry-bulb recovery time. Extracting abnormal amounts of moisture from the conditioned space on a frequent basis reduces seasonal efficiency, increases seasonal operating cost, and degrades comfort recovery.

- There is a significant difference between indoor air recovery and thermal mass recovery. For example, when one gets into a closed automobile on a hot sunny day, and turns the AC to it's maximum value, the air in the car is tolerable well before one can comfortably use the steering wheel.

For a dwelling, duplicating automobile HVAC performance would require a large amount of excess compressor capacity and wind tunnel air distribution (as defined by blower Cfm per square foot of floor area, and outlet throw strength).

- Even when there is almost no excess capacity for the summer design condition, there usually is plenty of excess capacity for most of the seasonal operating hours (see Figure 1-1).
- The physics for predicting the amount of excess capacity needed to satisfy a desired recovery time are conditional and complex (a rule of thumb cannot have sensitivity to all the issues).
- When a comprehensive model was available, the physics for predicting the amount of excess capacity needed to satisfy a desired recovery time may show that the desired recovery time is not practical (excess capacity reduces part-load comfort and efficiency, and increases installed cost).
- The physics for predicting the efficiency and operation cost benefit for set-up/set-back are conditional and complex (rules of thumb based on a few case studies are not equivalent to comprehensive knowledge).
- In general, the longer the set-up/set-back period, the larger the reward. The difficulty of modeling the issue for a specific dwelling, in a specific location, with specific equipment and controls has been noted above.
- The set-back period is especially important when recovery requires compressor heat, plus electric coil heat. There are scenarios when set-back reduces seasonal efficiency, and increases seasonal operating cost.
- For a climate that produces a significant latent load, set-up increases indoor moisture during the set-up period. As previously noted, the excess moisture held by the indoor air, and all absorbent materials, must be removed during recovery, at the expense of sensible capacity.
- Staged and variable-speed equipment adds another level of complexity to recovery physics, efficiency calculations, and op-cost calculations.

2-22 Air Zoning Controls

Air zoning controls may be provided by a single source (OEM turnkey system), or they may be a combination of OEM controls (for heating-cooling equipment) and zone equipment vendor (ZEV) controls. When zone damper controls are provided by a ZEV, it is most likely that their effect will be superimposed on the OEM's control logic (the result would be two compatible control systems that do not interact with each other). See *Manual Zr* for more information.

2-23 Ductless Split Controls

Ductless split equipment controls are similar to central ducted equipment controls in general, but for multi-split systems, each OEM has it's own strategy for refrigerant management. For variable-speed equipment, the compressor may operate at it's rated speed, at less than it's rated speed, and for some cases, at more than it's rated speed. OEM engineering literature provides information pertaining to standard and optional features.

This section is not part of the this standard. It is merely informative and does not contain requirements necessary for conformance to the standard. It has not been processed according to the ANSI requirements for a standard, and may contain material that has not been subject to public review or a consensus process. Unresolved objectors on informative material are not offered the right to appeal at ACCA or ANSI.

Section 3

Furnace and Water Boiler Selection

The performance data for a natural gas, propane, oil, or electric furnace, or boiler, is simple and non-conditional. There is an input Btuh, or KW value, for the fuel or power that flows to the equipment, and an output Btuh value for the heat that is added to the air or water that passes through the equipment.

For furnaces, there are temperature rise limits for the air that passes through the heat exchanger or electric coil, and a high temperature limit for discharge air. For boilers, there are water temperature rise limits, there is a water temperature set-point, a high water temperature safety, a high pressure safety, a water level safety, and there may be a low water temperature safety. Combustion equipment also has fuel train controls and safeties, and vent controls and safeties.

The design goal is to match heating capacity to the heating load per Section N2 procedures. This is based on output Btuh capacity data provided by the OEM. *Manual S* procedures are limited to equipment selection and sizing.

- For furnaces, use *Manual D* procedures for air distribution system design, and see OEM guidance for fuel piping, wiring, and venting requirements and details, and fuel train details.

- For hot water heat, use hydronic heat association and OEM guidance for water system design, and see OEM guidance pertaining to fuel piping, wiring, venting, and fuel train details.

3-1 Load Calculation

An accurate, no factor of safety anywhere, block load calculation for the heated space is used for equipment selection and sizing, with no allowance for a start-up or recovery load. This provides a heating load for normal system operation on a winter design day.

- For the guidance in this standard, boiler and water heater size is based on the space heating load. Refer to other procedures when the boiler or water heater provides heat for any other purpose (typically for potable water, perhaps for snow melting).

- The load calculation also provides a value for the outdoor dry-bulb temperature for the winter design condition (99% dry-bulb temperature), and it provides the design value for indoor dry-bulb temperature for heating (which may be a code or utility value, or the 70°F default from *Manual J*).

3-2 Equipment Operating Limits

OEM engineering guidance specifies equipment operating limits. These limits must be compatible with intended use, or the design work cannot proceed to the next step. This is especially important for furnaces that have air-zoned distribution, because discharge air temperature must not violate the OEM's limits as zone dampers operate (*Manual Zr* procedures for managing excess air show the benefit from using equipment that has a warmer limit for discharge air temperature).

- Fossil fuel furnaces have low- and high-limits for the air temperature rise through the heat exchanger, a high-limit value for discharge air temperature, and may have a low-limit for discharge air temperature.

- Electric furnaces and electric duct coils have a high-limit for discharge air temperature.

- A boiler has a high-limit temperature for leaving water, and there may be a low-limit for entering water temperature.

- Sections 3-5 and 3-6 deal with temperature calculations.

3-3 Seasonal Efficiency Rating

A code, utility regulation, practitioner preference, or owner request may set a minimum value for the annual fuel utilization Efficiency (AFUE), per AHRI test stand conditions. Investigate makes and models that have the desired efficiency rating.

3-4 Performance Data

Figure 3-1 (next page) provides examples of furnace performance data, and boiler performance data. OEM data sets typically show input capacity (Btuh or KW) and output capacity (Btuh), and an AFUE value. When the burner or electric coil is staged or modulated, at least two sets of input-output values are required to show performance for full capacity and reduced capacity.

- Furnace data also specifies minimum and maximum values for air temperature rise. The data may, or may not, provide a value for maximum discharge air, and/or minimum discharge air temperature (if not, ask for it).

- Boilers have a high-limit for leaving water temperature, a maximum value for water temperature rise, and there may be a low-limit for entering water temperature (if not stated, ask for it).

Section 3

- A duct load or water piping load is part of the total *Manual J* heating load (a line item on Form J1).
- Extra heating capacity for a system start-up load, or for a set-back recovery load, does not apply. The OEM's output heating capacity values must be gross capacity values (not adjusted for a distribution warm-up load, and/or space warm-up load).

Altitude Effect

Heating performance data is for sea level conditions. Sea level capacity values are adjusted when the installation's altitude exceeds 2,500 feet, or is at, or higher than, the elevation specified by the OEM.

- The procedures in this section apply at any altitude, providing that sizing decisions are based on adjusted performance data.
- Appendix 5 provides altitude adjustment procedures.

Steady-State Efficiency

Output capacity depends on input capacity and the efficiency for continuous burner operation at one firing rate, which is the steady-state efficiency (SS_{eff}). A steady-state efficiency value may not appear in the performance data. This equation determines steady-state efficiency:

SS_{eff} = Output Btuh / Input Btuh

3-5 Furnace Temperature Limit Calculations

The practitioner must verify that furnace use is compatible with OEM limits. There is an air temperature rise issue, a maximum leaving air temperature issue, and there may be a minimum entering air temperature issue.

Air Temperature Rise

The air temperature rise across the heat exchanger must be within the range specified by the OEM's performance data. The psychrometric equation for sensible heat is used for this calculation:

Rise (°F) = Output Btuh / (1.1 x ACF x Blower Cfm)

Where:
Output Btuh = Heat added to entering air
ACF = Altitude correction factor (see Figure A5-1)
Blower Cfm = The chosen air flow rate for heating, which may be the Cfm that was used to select cooling equipment, or a value that is compatible with the temperature rise limits. Per Section 3-11 Step 6, the blower must provide adequate external static pressure when delivering the desired Cfm.

Furnace Performance Data				
Model	F45	F70	F90	F110
Input Btuh	44,000	66,000	88,000	110,000
Output Btuh	36,000	54,100	72,100	90,200
Air Rise (°F)	35–65	40-70	40–70	50–80
AFUE	80%	80%	80%	80%

1) Sea level performance for the sea level configuration.
2) Maximum/minimum air temperature rise values.
3) Maximum discharge air temperature value.

Two-Stage Boiler Performance Data (Btuh)				
Model	B45	B70	B90	B110
Max Input	45,000	75,000	90,000	135,000
Gross Output	37,000	62,000	75,000	112,000
Net Output	32,000	54,000	65,000	97,000
AFUE	82.4%	82.4%	82.4%	82.4%
Min Input	23,000	38,000	45,000	68,000

1) Sea level performance for the sea level configuration.
2) Gross output: No deduction for piping and pick-up loads.
3) Net output: Default deduction for piping and pick-up loads.
4) See nameplate for high entering water temperature limit.
5) Water temperature rise: 10°F to 40°F; 20°F to 30°F typical.
6) Minimum entering water temperature: 140°F.

Figure 3-1

Leaving Air Temperature

Furnace leaving air temperature must not exceed the OEM's high-limit value. For this calculation, an air temperature rise value is added to entering air temperature.

- The worst-case is when the entering air temperature is at it's maximum value for the heating season, which occurs when there is no (or almost no) return duct load, and/or no (or almost no) load for mixing outdoor air with return air.
- For a high-limit investigation, the entering air temperature value equals the thermostat set-point for occupied comfort (the *Manual J* default for winter comfort is 70°F, or use the code value).
- When the furnace has a staged or modulating burner, investigate the worst-case (largest) temperature rise for the OEM's combinations of blower Cfm and output heat.

For minimum entering air temperature, the worst-case is when the return duct load (where applicable) is at it's maximum value, and when the load for mixing outdoor air with return air (where applicable) is at it's maximum value.

- *Manual J* calculations provide winter design condition values for a return duct load, and an outdoor air load (adjusted for heat recovery, where applicable).
- Appendix 2 procedures provide default temperature drop values for a return duct load and/or an air mixing load, or use Figures A1-14 and A1-15.
- For a low-limit investigation, the entering air temperature value equals the thermostat set-point value for night set-back, or for occupied comfort (where applicable), minus the temperature drop value for a return duct load, minus the temperature drop value for an outdoor air mixing load, where applicable.

3-6 Water Temperature Limit Calculations

For boilers and water heating equipment, the water temperature rise through the equipment is determined by this equation:

Water Rise (°F) = Output Btuh / (500 x Water Gpm)

Where:
Output Btuh = Heat added to entering water
Water Gpm = Water flow rate through the equipment

Entering water temperature and leaving water temperature must not exceed the limits specified by the OEM's engineering data. These calculations are performed by the person that is responsible for selecting the terminal heating equipment, and designing the piping system (per guidance provided by hydronic system design manuals and OEM literature).

3-7 Design Value for Furnace Blower Cfm

For a heating-only furnace, the design value for blower Cfm should be a mid-range value from the OEM's blower data (this makes higher and lower speeds available for air flow tuning after the equipment is installed).

For a heating/cooling furnace, the design value for cooling Cfm value is determined by Section 2 procedures. The design value for heating Cfm may be equal to the cooling Cfm value, or may be some other value that is compatible with furnace temperature rise limits. The heating/cooling equipment may be provided by one OEM, or it may come from different OEM's.

- The design blower Cfm value for heating must be compatible with the furnace manufacturer's limit value for minimum air flow rate, the temperature rise limits, and the high-limit value for discharge air.

Furnace Blower Performance
Cfm vs. System Resistance

Blower Speed	External Resistance (IWC)				
	0.20	0.30	0.40	0.50	0.60
Low	1,010	1,035	1,045	1,045	1,030
Med-Low	1,300	1,305	1,295	1,275	1,240
Med-High	1,470	1,460	1,440	1,410	1,370
High	1,875	1,805	1,735	1,660	1,580

Standard filter and heat exchanger in place for the blower test.

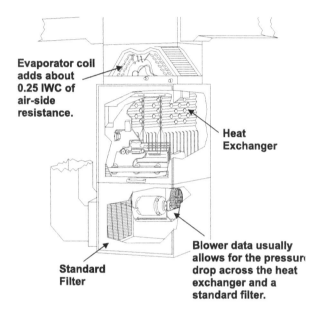

Figure 3-2

Compliance occurs by design, when the blower Cfm value comes from proper use of the OEM's performance data and temperature limit values.

- The design blower Cfm value for cooling must be compatible with the cooling equipment manufacturer's performance data, and the low-limit values for blower Cfm and leaving air temperature. For single zone systems, compliance occurs by design when the blower Cfm value comes from proper use of the OEM's engineering guidance and performance data.
- Blower Cfm values for any operating condition must be compatible with the OEM's temperature and blower Cfm limit values for heating and cooling. This is a fundamental issue for equipment that serves zone damper systems. (see ACCA *Manual Zr*).

Section 3

3-8 Furnace Blower Data

After OEM performance data is used to select and size equipment, the furnace's blower table is required for *Manual D* calculations. This data must be readily available (preferably a published supplement to the heating performance data, vs. having to ask for it), and it must be comprehensive.

- The operating range (blower wheel speeds or blower Cfm set-points, blower Cfm values, and the corresponding external static pressure values) may be summarized by a table or graph.
- Table footnotes must list all pressure dissipating components that were in place when the blower was tested (typically the heat exchanger and a standard filter). Verify this with the OEM.
- Some blower tables do not have adequate footnotes, or may have no footnotes. A practitioner may be in for a nasty surprise when he or she mistakenly assumes that the blower data has been discounted for necessary or desirable items such as a cooling coil or upscale filter.
- Figure 3-2 (previous page) provides an example of adequate blower data for a wheel driven by a PSC motor.
- When there is any question about what the blower data actually means, the practitioner is advised to raise the issue with the OEM.
- Pressure dissipating components that are not relevant to the furnace blower data reduce the available static pressure for duct airway sizing (a dry or wet cooling coil, an accessory filter, for example).

3-9 Component Pressure Drop Data

The pressure drops for necessary, or desired, air-side components that are not relevant to the blower data must be subtracted from the external static pressure values read from a blower table, or graph. Component pressure drop values are read from tables or graphs published by the product manufacturer. Such data must be readily available (preferably published as part of the OEM's engineering data, vs. having to ask for it). Figure 3-3 provides examples of pressure drop data for a cooling coil and an electronic filter.

3-10 Adequate Blower Pressure

Furnace blower data for a mid-range blower speed should provide 0.20 IWC of external static pressure (preliminary estimate) to circulate system air through straight duct runs and fittings, plus additional pressure (0.20 to 0.50 IWC, or more) for the air-side components that were not in place when the blower was tested (a cooling coil,

Coil Resistance (IWC)		
Cfm	Dry	Wet
1,000	0.11	0.18
1,200	0.15	0.26
1,400	0.22	0.35
1,600	0.28	0.46

Electronic Filter Resistance	
Cfm	IWC
1,000	0.06
1,200	0.08
1,400	0.12
1,600	0.15

Figure 3-3

supply grille, return grille, hand damper, accessory filter, for example).

- OEM blower data for a specific set of air-side components correlates Cfm and external static pressure for blower wheel speeds (PSC motor), or Cfm set-points (ECM motor).
- OEM performance data provides pressure drop values for air-side components that are external to the blower data (Figure 3-3 for example).
- Per *Manual D* calculations, one supply grille, one return grille, plus one hand damper defaults to 0.03 IWC each, or 0.09 IWC total.
- Everything else being equal, a furnace with a cooling coil needs 0.15 IWC to 0.60 IWC more external static pressure than a heating-only furnace (0.15 IWC to 0.30 IWC is common).
- The *Manual D* Friction Rate Worksheet shows when blower pressure is adequate, or deficient.
- When blower pressure is deficient, find a furnace that has a blower that is compatible with the design cooling Cfm value, and the *Manual D* Friction Rate Worksheet procedure. The selection also must be compatible with the Table N2-4 rules for excess heating capacity).

3-11 Equipment Sizing

Space heat may be provided by a furnace or water boiler. For all scenarios, equipment selection begins with a search for appropriate heating capacity. The procedure provided here is summarized by Figure 3-4. Sections 7 and 10 provide application examples.

Furnace Sizing Procedure

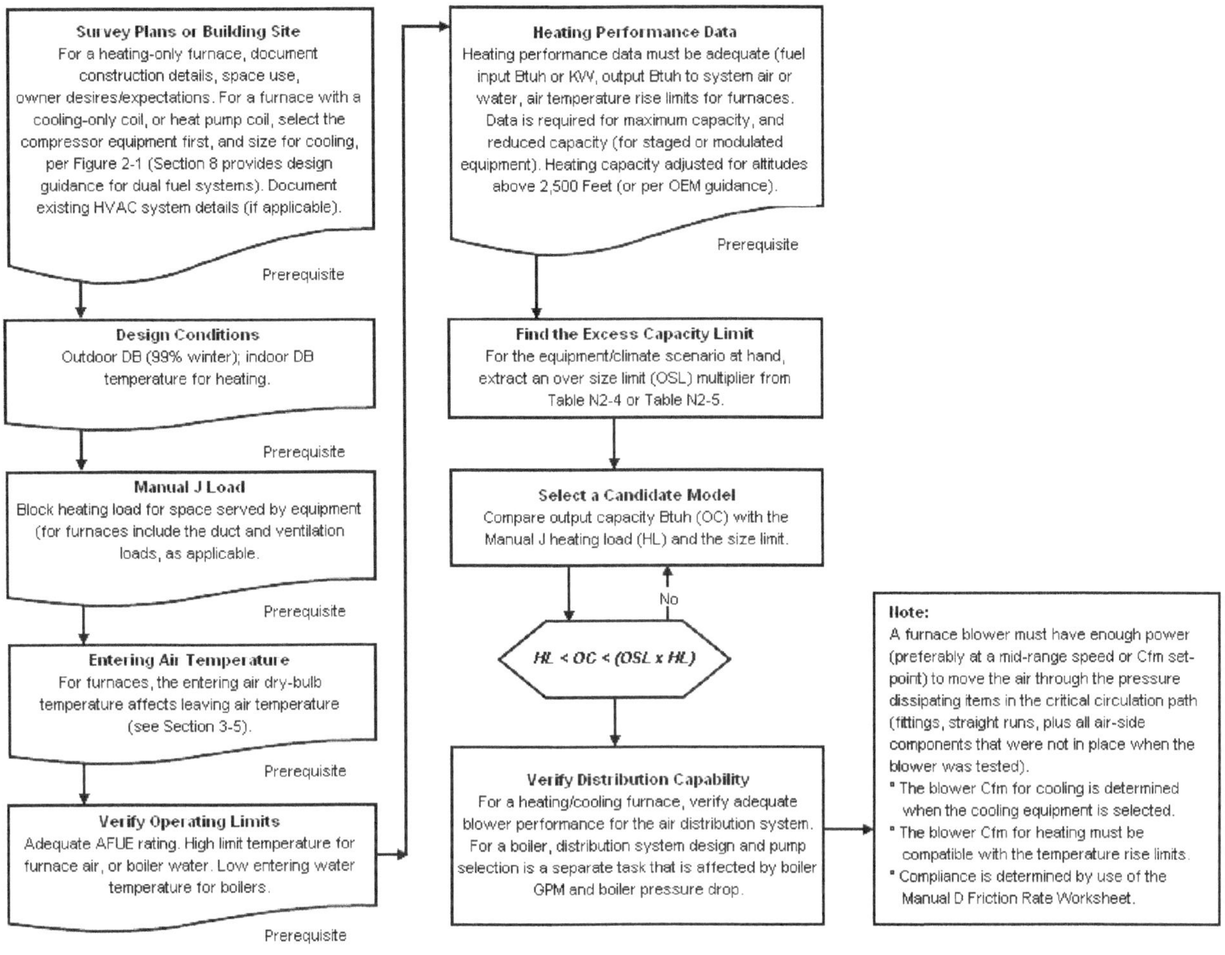

Survey Plans or Building Site
For a heating-only furnace, document construction details, space use, owner desires/expectations. For a furnace with a cooling-only coil, or heat pump coil, select the compressor equipment first, and size for cooling, per Figure 2-1 (Section 8 provides design guidance for dual fuel systems). Document existing HVAC system details (if applicable).

Prerequisite

Design Conditions
Outdoor DB (99% winter); indoor DB temperature for heating.

Prerequisite

Manual J Load
Block heating load for space served by equipment (for furnaces include the duct and ventilation loads, as applicable.

Prerequisite

Entering Air Temperature
For furnaces, the entering air dry-bulb temperature affects leaving air temperature (see Section 3-5).

Prerequisite

Verify Operating Limits
Adequate AFUE rating. High limit temperature for furnace air, or boiler water. Low entering water temperature for boilers.

Prerequisite

Heating Performance Data
Heating performance data must be adequate (fuel input Btuh or KW, output Btuh to system air or water, air temperature rise limits for furnaces. Data is required for maximum capacity, and reduced capacity (for staged or modulated equipment). Heating capacity adjusted for altitudes above 2,500 Feet (or per OEM guidance).

Prerequisite

Find the Excess Capacity Limit
For the equipment/climate scenario at hand, extract an over size limit (OSL) multiplier from Table N2-4 or Table N2-5.

Select a Candidate Model
Compare output capacity Btuh (OC) with the Manual J heating load (HL) and the size limit.

$HL < OC < (OSL \times HL)$

No → back to Heating Performance Data

Verify Distribution Capability
For a heating/cooling furnace, verify adequate blower performance for the air distribution system. For a boiler, distribution system design and pump selection is a separate task that is affected by boiler GPM and boiler pressure drop.

Note:
A furnace blower must have enough power (preferably at a mid-range speed or Cfm setpoint) to move the air through the pressure dissipating items in the critical circulation path (fittings, straight runs, plus all air-side components that were not in place when the blower was tested).
* The blower Cfm for cooling is determined when the cooling equipment is selected.
* The blower Cfm for heating must be compatible with the temperature rise limits.
* Compliance is determined by use of the Manual D Friction Rate Worksheet.

Figure 3-4

Step 1: Per Section 3-1, produce a proper load calculation for heating.

Step 2: Per Sections 3-2 and 3-3, study the engineering data for the product of interest and verify that it's seasonal operating limits are compatible with the application.

- Proceed to Step 3, when the equipment's operating limits are acceptable.
- When the operating limits are not compatible with the application, find equipment that has the required performance attributes, and proceed to Step 3.

Step 3: Per Section 3-4, get the heating performance data for the product (make and model) of interest.

- A product's data set normally includes models that are obviously too small or too large, but one or more should be roughly compatible with the heating load, when not, investigate other products.

- Each model size will have it's own performance data. When the equipment has staged or modulating capacity, there should be two or more sets of heating data (one for full capacity, and one or more for reduced capacity).

- Proceed to Step 4 when there is a proper exhibit of performance data for full capacity. Reduced capacity data is not used for equipment sizing, but is used for energy calculations.

- When the performance data is deficient in it's sensitivities (per Section 3-4), find equipment that has adequate performance data, and proceed to Step 4.

Step 4: Produce a target range for heating capacity, and then use this range to evaluate a candidate unit.

- The sizing value (bull's-eye) for heating capacity equals the heating load for the winter design condition.

- Table N2-4 (furnace heating) and Table N2-5 (hot water heating) provide lower and upper limits for excess heating capacity.

Step 5: Select a compliant product. To validate size, compare the heating capacity of the candidate unit with the target range.

- The search for a likely candidate is based on full heating capacity (maximum furnace output capacity, or gross boiler output capacity).

  Distribution loads must be embedded in the load calculation.

  No adjustment for a pick-up load or recovery load.

- For single-stage, staged, or modulating output, the target range applies to full (maximum) heating capacity.
- When the full heating capacity of the candidate unit is within the range allowed by Table N2-4 or Table N2-5, proceed to Step 6.
- When the heating capacity is outside the target range, find a candidate that has acceptable capacity, and proceed to Step 6.

Step 6: Verify distribution capability. A furnace blower must have adequate power for air distribution. For hot water heat, distribution depends on pump performance and pipe system design.

- The blower table for the furnace of interest should list the air-side components that were in place when the blower was tested. When this information is not part of the OEM's blower table, or when there is any doubt about the issue, ask the OEM to provide the information, or ask for data confirmation.
- Use pressure drop data for air-side components that are external to the blower data.
- Use the *Manual D* Friction Rate Worksheet to see when blower power is compatible with the design Cfm values for heating and cooling. When blower power is deficient, find a furnace product that has a more powerful blower (return to Step 5).

When the cooling load is large in comparison to the heating load, a significantly over-sized furnace may be used to obtain blower performance that is compatible with the size of the cooling coil, per the Table N2-4 limit.

Over sizing is not a fuel efficiency issue. Laboratory tests sponsored by the U.S. Department of Energy show that common furnaces and boilers can be over-sized by as much as 100 percent without causing a significant increase in the operating cost (Refer to Appendix 11 for more information.).

- A heat pump system, an electric resistance coil in a cold air duct or plenum, a water heater plus a hot water coil in a cold air duct or plenum, electric baseboard heat, or electric radiant heat may be preferable to an over-sized furnace or boiler when a home has a large cooling load, a small heating load for the winter design condition, and little or no heating load for most winter days.
- For boilers, the water pump is selected and sized by the person that designs the piping system (distribution system design is decoupled from equipment selection and sizing).

3-12 Fuel Burning and Combustion Venting

Make sure that the fuel train controls and combustion controls comply with all codes, regulations and OEM guidance. Make sure that a burner has an adequate supply of combustion air for any possible operating condition. Make sure that the venting system complies with all building codes, fuel gas codes, utility regulations, and OEM guidance.

- A possible operating condition may not be a safe operating condition. One or more combinations of active/inactive exhaust fans, appliance vents, duct leaks, and the momentary positions of interior doors may cause a negative pressure in the furnace/boiler space, and/or water heater space.
- The HVAC practitioner may not be responsible for a negative pressure problem, but can be the victim of work done by others. Sensitivity to the issue is required. When principled thought and/or a technical investigation finds a problem, or a potential problem, discuss the issue with the owner. Do not proceed until the issue is satisfactory resolved.
- For venting, the likelihood of a condensation problem increases in some proportion to the amount of excess heating capacity.

3-13 Operating and Safety Controls

OEM furnace/boiler packages have a variety of standard controls and devices, and optional controls, devices and features. The practitioner must specify appropriate and adequate operating and safety controls.

Control functions and features may be strictly electrical-mechanical, or may involve proprietary programming (with or without embedded options and ports), or open-system programming. Additional operating and safety controls may be part of a zone damper kit provided by the OEM, or a zoning equipment vendor.

A list of common controls and devices is provided below. See OEM engineering literature for the features and options attached to a particular product.

- Select operation mode switch (heating, cooling, continuous blower).
- Space temperature sensor/control (simple set-point control, or set-up/set-back scheduling).
- Indoor blower control, and cooling interlocks (on-off, and possible speed change).
- Low airflow sensor.
- Motor protection.
- Furnace high-limit for discharge air.
- Boiler water temperature control (on-off, possible capacity control; water temperature set-point may be scheduled by outdoor air temperature).
- Boiler high- and low-limits for water temperature.
- Boiler water level control and safety.
- Boiler pressure safety.
- Burner and fuel train controls/devices, with various interlocks (on-off, possible capacity control).
- Gas valve, gas pressure switch.
- Power vent controls, validation and interlocks.
- Ignition validation.
- Flame rollout and back draft switches.
- High altitude kit.
- Propane/LPG kit.
- Vent adaptor for masonry chimney.
- Heat pump interlock for dual-fuel system.
- Simultaneous operation of two furnaces/boilers.
- Space or return air humidity sensor/control for winter humidification where applicable).

3-14 Air Zoning Controls

Air zoning controls may be provided by a single source (OEM turnkey system), or they may be a combination of OEM controls (for heating-cooling equipment) and zone equipment vendor (ZEV) controls. When zone damper controls are provided by a ZEV, it is most likely that their effect will be superimposed on the OEM's control logic (the result would be two compatible control systems that do not interact with each other). See *Manual Zr* for more information.

3-15 System Start-Up and Set-Point Recovery

Excess capacity for system start-up, and/or recovery from set-up/set-back, must not exceed Section N2 values. Use a properly adjusted programmable thermostat for recovery from set-back.

- Even when there is no excess capacity for the winter design condition, there is plenty of excess capacity for 90% of the seasonal operating hours.
- Extra capacity for system start-up is not needed because this is an abnormal and rare event for systems that are designed, installed, and operated to a proper standard of care.

  Even when a winter design day (or colder) start-up is required, the indoor temperature will moderate within an hour or so, and a marginal level of comfort will be experienced within a few hours, and full comfort will eventually be restored, even when the furnace or boiler has no excess heating capacity.

- Heating may be set-back, but it is rarely shut off during the heating season.
- There is a significant difference between indoor air recovery and thermal mass recovery.

  The temperature of a sample of indoor air increases with each pass through the furnace. For a given air-change volume, a larger burner and blower will shorten the heat-up time for indoor air by five to ten minutes. Cold spots may linger when air distribution effectiveness is poor.

  The heat-up time for thermal mass (ceilings, walls, floors, furniture) depends on the surface convection coefficient, the mass of the solid material, the initial temperature distribution through the cold material, the thermal diffusivity of the solid material, and the temperature difference for nearby air and a solid surface.

  The convection coefficient depends on the rubbing velocity of air passing over a cold surface. This is relatively small for slow moving air. A larger blower has a negligible effect on the rubbing velocities at the various cold surfaces, and a negligible effect on materials recovery time.

  Materials recovery time also depends on the temperature difference for nearby air and a solid surface, but the benefit is small (when surface and space air temperatures start at 65°F, the air temperature is about 70°F in ten to twenty minutes, the initial temperature difference benefit is about 25%, but this decreases to zero as the surface warms up).

  In other words, the time that it takes to heat the floor, wall, and ceiling panels, and the furnishings, is not reduced in proportion to the amount of excess furnace capacity because the convective heat transfer that occurs at these points is not significantly affected by the size of the furnace or boiler.

- The physics for predicting the amount of excess capacity needed to satisfy a desired recovery time are extremely conditional and complex (a rule of thumb cannot have sensitivity to all the issues).

- When a comprehensive model was available, the physics for predicting the amount of excess capacity needed to satisfy a desired recovery time may show that the desired recovery time is not practical (excess capacity degrades air distribution effectiveness due to blower cycling and increases installed cost).
- The physics for predicting the efficiency and operation cost benefit for set-back are conditional and complex (rules of thumb based on a few case studies are not equivalent to comprehensive knowledge).
- In general, the longer the set-back period, the larger the energy-saving reward. The difficulty of modeling the issue for a specific dwelling, in a specific location, with specific equipment and controls has been noted above.
- Staged and variable-speed equipment adds another level of complexity to recovery physics, efficiency calculations, and op-cost calculations.

This section is not part of the this standard. It is merely informative and does not contain requirements necessary for conformance to the standard. It has not been processed according to the ANSI requirements for a standard, and may contain material that has not been subject to public review or a consensus process. Unresolved objectors on informative material are not offered the right to appeal at ACCA or ANSI.

Section 4

Humidity Control and Evaporative Cooling Equipment

This section provides procedures for selecting and sizing ancillary dehumidification equipment. There are procedures for selecting and sizing evaporative cooling equipment. There are procedures for selecting and sizing winter humidification equipment.

4-1 Ancillary Dehumidification

Ancillary dehumidification equipment may have a duct interface with the primary equipment's duct system, or may have it's own independent duct system, or may be an unducted, movable appliance.

- Figure 4-1 shows a whole-house dehumidifier (WHD) product that can be spliced into a comfort air distribution system. The figure also shows possible ducting arrangements.
- Some whole-house dehumidifiers are stand alone products with no duct system; or may have their own independent duct system, routed to two or more spaces.
- Figure 4-5 (page 53) shows a ventilation dehumidifier (VDH) product spliced into a comfort air distribution system.

The operating time (minutes per hour) of primary cooling equipment (cooling-only, or heat pump) is controlled, or is essentially controlled (ignoring OEM gadgetry), by indoor air dry-bulb temperature. Indoor air relative humidity excursions tend to increase as compressor runtime, or compressor capacity, decreases.

- Ancillary dehumidification may be used for improved indoor humidity control when the primary equipment's compressor cycles, or operates at reduced capacity.
- For heat pump sizing, Condition A rules apply when the load calculation sensible heat ratio is less than 0.95, regardless of the local degree day ratio value. Ancillary dehumidification allows use of Condition B sizing rules, providing the local degree day ratio is 2.0 or more
- Ancillary dehumidification may be used when cooling equipment cannot hold indoor humidity to 55% RH, or less, when the outdoor air is at the summer design condition.
- A dehumidifier may maintain a lower indoor humidity set-point when dehumidifier capacity exceeds the moisture load for 55% RH indoors.

Honeywell International, Inc. graphic

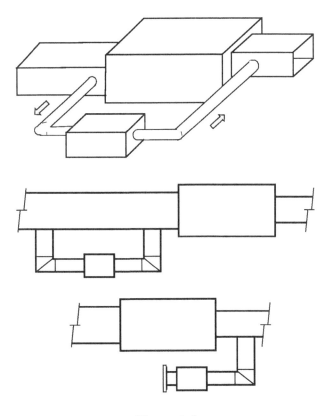

Figure 4-1

- Section N2-12 sizing procedures apply to these application scenarios.

Published Performance Data

OEM performance data is limited to a pints-per-day value for 80°F dry-bulb and 60% RH air entering the equipment. This is the capacity value from the AHAM rating test. Figure 4-2 shows some size options for residential products.

The maximum and minimum sizes shown are typical for 2014 products. Intermediate sizes may be somewhat different, depending on the OEM. Circumstances continuously change, investigate available product lines.

Entering Air Condition for Dehumidifier Sizing

A whole-house dehumidifier processes indoor air (no outdoor air component), therefore, the entering air condition is the indoor air condition. Per Section N2-12, the default entering air condition for dehumidifier sizing is 75°F dry-bulb and 55% RH.

A ventilation dehumidifier process a mixture of return air and outdoor air. Per Section N2-12, the default condition for return air is 75°F dry-bulb and 55% RH. The summer design condition determines the condition of the outdoor air. The two streams of airflow have an outdoor air fraction (outdoor air Cfm divided by total Cfm). Mixed air psychrometrics determines the entering air condition for ventilation dehumidifier sizing.

Dehumidifier Sizing Load

The equipment sizing load is the latent cooling load for the rooms and spaces served by the dehumidification equipment. This calculation must be for 75°F and 55% RH indoor air, and the summer design condition for outdoor air. Standard load calculation procedures apply. Section N1-14 specifies load calculation requirements..

Conversion Factors for Moisture Load

This equation converts a latent load in Btuh units to a moisture removal load in pints/day units.

Pints per day = 24 x Latent Btuh / 1,054

Adjusted Performance Data

Since dehumidifier performance data is for 80°F dry-bulb and 60% RH entering air, rated capacity is adjusted for the actual (applied) entering air condition. The Section N2-12 default for air entering a whole-house dehumidifier is 75°F dry-bulb and 55% RH, and the default adjustment factor for determining equipment capacity is 0.76.

WHD Capacity for 75°F/55%RH = 0.76 x Rated Capacity

Mixed air psychrometrics determines the entering air condition (EAC) for ventilation dehumidifier sizing. Figure N2-2 provides capacity adjustment curves or various entering air conditions, or Figure N2-2 provides default capacity adjustment factors for various entering air conditions.

VDH Capacity = EAC adjustment x Rated Capacity

\multicolumn{5}{c}{Example Performance Data For Ancillary Dehumidification Equipment}
Product	Removal Capacity Pints / Day	Energy Factor (EF) Pints / KWH	Rated Watts	Evaporator Cfm (Notes 2, 3)
A	25	2.54	410	~
B	30	2.96	422	~
C	45	3.17	591	103 / 91 / 81
D	65	3.80	713	195 / 175 / 155
E	70	5.01	582	170
F	105	8.80	497	145 to 250
G	150	7.87	794	415
H	183	5.50	1,386	540
I	205	5.70	1,499	460 to 525

1) Capacity and Watt values are for continuous operation with 80°F, 60%RH entering air.
2) Evaporator Cfm values may be for zero IWC external static pressure (used for the rating test, not suitable for a duct system), to 0.40 IWC (significant pressure is required for duct runs).
3) Cfm values for products F and I are for 0.0 IWC and 0.4 IWC. Cfm values for other products are for 0.0 IWC.

Figure 4-2

Dehumidifier Sizing Limits

Adjusted dehumidifier capacity must be equal to, or greater than, 85% (0.85 factor) of the latent cooling load for 75°F, 55% RH indoors. The upper limit for adjusted dehumidifier capacity is determined by the smallest available size that is compatible with the full latent cooling load for 75°F, 55% RH indoors.

Minimum capacity = 0.85 x Latent load
Maximum capacity = Smallest size ≥ Latent load

Dehumidifier Efficiency

An energy factor rating summarizes dehumidifier efficiency. Energy factors (EF) are expressed in pints per KWH units, or liters per KWH units.

1 pound of water = 1 Pint
2.113 Pints = 1 Liter

Energy factor ratings are for 80°F, 60% RH entering air. Per Section N2-12, the default efficiency adjustment factor for 75°F, 55% RH air entering a whole-house dehumidifier is 0.82.

WHD EF for 75°F/55%RH = 0.82 x Rated EF

Mixed air psychrometrics determines the entering air condition for a ventilation dehumidifier. Figure N2-1 provides efficiency adjustment curves or various entering air conditions, or Figure N2-2 provides default adjustment factors for various entering air conditions.

VDH EF = EAC adjustment x Rated EF

Load Calculation for Sizing Primary Equipment

For primary equipment sizing, the design value for indoor humidity is normally 50% RH. However, the design value for indoor humidity may be as high as 55% RH for harsh circumstances. Figure 4-3 provides the rationale for this caveat.

Per Section N1-4, the load calculation for sizing primary equipment is not adjusted for dehumidifier use. All sensible and latent loads, including the engineered ventilation load, are calculated in the normal manner, because the dehumidifier is logically inactive during peak summer conditions (the dehumidifier limits indoor humidity excursions for part-load cooling hours).

4-2 Whole-House Dehumidifier Examples

The following examples place the same dwelling in three different locations to show how whole-house dehumidifier size depends on the local climate. Section 4-3 provides a similar study for ventilation dehumidifiers.

Extremely Humid Climate Example

Brunswick, GA, weather (91°F dry-bulb, 79°F wet-bulb) provides a worst-case challenge for indoor humidity control (many gulf state locations compete for the trophy).

Indoor Design Condition for Sizing Primary Cooling Equipment

Per *Manual J* procedures for wet-coil applications, the default (recommended) values for indoor air are 75°F dry-bulb and 50% RH. However, the design value for indoor humidity may be as high as 55% RH when there is no commonly available product that has enough latent capacity for the 50% RH indoors. Use of the 55% RH option is subject to these caveats:

- The latent infiltration load is for envelope tightness, and vapor retarding membrane use, that complies with local code.
- The latent infiltration load is for duct system leakage that complies with local code.
- The design value for outdoor air Cfm, and the use of dedicated heat recovery equipment, complies with local code.

Figure 4-3

The example dwelling has 3,300 SqFt of floor area, and a sealed attic duct system (0.12 Cfm of leakage per SqFt of supply-side area, and 0.24 Cfm leakage per SqFt of return-side area), with 50 Cfm of raw outdoor air routed to the return air plenum. The indoor air condition for the dehumidifier sizing load is 75°F and 55% RH.

	McCoy Residence; Brunswick, GA Whole-House Dehumidifier Loads	91°F DB, 79°F WB; 75°F; 55% RH Indoors 62 Grains Difference			Sensible Btuh	Latent Btuh
12	Infiltration	Heat Loss ACH				
	SqFt cooling 3,300	Sensible Gain ACH = 0.150			1,452	
	CuFt cooling 33,000	Latent Gain ACH = 0.150				3,478
13	Internal Gains	a) Occupants at 230 and 200 Btuh			920	800
	Sens Btuh 5,073	b) Appliance Scenario		Default	1,200	
	Latent Btuh 800	c) Appliance Scenario Adjustments		See item d		
		d) Individual Appliances			2,953	
		e) Plants				
14	Sub Totals	For fenestration, walls, ceilings, floors, infiltration, and internal loads.			24,041	4,278
15	Duct Loss or Gain	EHLF and ESGF multipliers	0.125	0.196	4,712	
		ELG Btuh				812
16	Ventilation Loss or Gain	Vent Cfm = 50.0	Exh Cfm =	50.0	880	2,108
21	Load Totals	Note: The total latent load for 50% RH indoors is 8,801 Btuh.			29,633	7,198

Figure 4-4

Section 4

Latent Load and Sizing Value

Figure 4-4 (previous page) shows the latent cooling load is 7,198 Btuh, which converts to 163.9 pints/day. So, the sizing value for equipment sizing is 85% of the load, or 139.3 pints/day.

Pints / Day = 24 x (7,198 / 1,054) = 163.9
Target Pints / Day = 0.85 x 163.9 = 139.3

Dehumidifier Size

Figure 4-2 shows that Product H has 183 pints per day capacity for 80°F; 60% RH air. The adjusted capacity for 75°F; 55% RH air is 139.1 pints/day, which is essentially right on the 139.3 pints/day target.

Capacity adjustment for 75°F; 55% RH air = 0.76
Adjusted capacity = 0.76 x 183 = 139.1 Pints / Day
Target = 139.3 Pints / Day

Latent Load for Sizing Primary Equipment

The indoor humidity design value for sizing the primary cooling equipment may be equal to, or less than, 55% RH (the *Manual J* default is 50% RH). If 50% RH is used for the McCoy residence (Figure 4-4), the latent load on the primary cooling equipment is 8,801 Btuh, vs. the 7,198 Btuh value used for dehumidifier sizing.

Sensible Heat Ratio for Sizing Primary Equipment

The load calculation sensible heat ratio for the primary equipment should not be a problem for commonly available products, as demonstrated below. Therefore, dehumidifier operation is not required, or is marginal, when outdoor conditions are similar to summer design conditions.

Primary sensible load = 29,633 Btuh
Primary latent load for 50% RH = 8,801 Btuh
Load sensible heat ratio for 50% RH = 0.77
Primary latent load for 55% RH = 7,198 Btuh
Load sensible heat ratio for 55% RH = 0.80

Significantly Humid Climate Example

Fayetteville, AR, (93°F dry-bulb, 75°F wet-bulb) is humid, but not nearly as humid as Brunswick, GA, (91°F dry-bulb, 79°F wet-bulb). The attributes of the 3,300 SqFt dwelling and it's HVAC system are the same for both locations (attic duct with 0.12 Cfm/SqFt and 0.24 Cfm/SqFt leakage; 50 Cfm of raw outdoor air to the return plenum).

Latent Load and sizing value

For Fayetteville, the *Manual J*, Table 1A grains difference value for 55% RH indoors is 33 Grains (vs. 62 grains for Brunswick). The total latent cooling load for Fayetteville is 4,170 Btuh, which converts to 95 pints/day. So, the sizing value for equipment sizing is 85 percent of the load, or 80.7 pints/day.

Pints / Day = 24 x (4,170 / 1,054) = 95.0
Target Pints / Day = 0.85 x 95.0 = 80.7

Dehumidifier Size

Figure 4-2 shows that Product F has 105 pints per day capacity for 80°F; 60% RH air. The adjusted capacity for 75°F; 55% RH air is 79.8 pints/day, which is somewhat less than the 80.7 pints/day target, so Product F is not compatible with the size limit for minimum capacity.

Capacity adjustment for 75°F; 55% RH air = 0.76
Adjusted capacity = 0.76 x 105 = 79.8 Pints / Day
Target = 80.7 Pints / Day
The 105 size has deficient capacity.

Figure 4-2 shows that Product G has 150 pints per day capacity for 80°F; 60% RH air. The adjusted capacity for 75°F; 55% RH air is 114.0 pints/day, which is somewhat more than the full latent load (95 pints/day). So Product G is compatible with the equipment sizing rules.

Adjusted capacity = 0.76 x 150 = 114.0 Pints / Day
Target = 80.7 Pints / Day
The 150size has adequate capacity.

Note: Figure 4-2 provides a small inventory of available product sizes. It may be that there are products that have rated capacities in the 110 to 125 pints/day range.

Latent Load for Sizing Primary Equipment

The indoor humidity design value for sizing the primary cooling equipment is 50% RH, so the latent load on the primary cooling equipment is 4,908 Btuh, vs. the 4,170 Btuh value used for dehumidifier sizing.

Sensible Heat Ratio for Sizing Primary Equipment

The sensible load for Fayetteville is 30,085 Btuh. The load calculation sensible heat ratio for the primary equipment is relatively high, as demonstrated below. Therefore, dehumidifier operation is not required when outdoor conditions are similar to summer design conditions.

Primary sensible load = 30,085 Btuh
Primary latent load for 50% RH = 4,908 Btuh
Load sensible heat ratio for 50% RH = 0.86
Primary latent load for 55% RH = 4,170 Btuh
Load sensible heat ratio for 55% RH = 0.88

Humid Summer Cold Winter Example

The HDD-65 / CDD-50 ratio for Grand Rapids, MI; is more than 2.0 (about 2.5), so heating season efficiency will benefit from an over-sized heat pump. However, this location has significant summer humidity (*Manual J*, Table 1A shows 27 Grains difference for indoor air at

75°F, 50% RH), and the cooling load calculation for the example dwelling shows 27,352 Btuh sensible, 3,630 Btuh latent, for a 0.88 sensible heat ratio; so Condition A rules determine maximum heat pump size.

Condition B sizing rules may be used when a whole-house dehumidifier provides an upper limit for indoor humidity for summer cooling. Refer to the Section N2-12.

4-3 Ventilation Dehumidifier Examples

Figure 4-5 shows how the air-side of a ventilation dehumidifier (VDH) may interface with primary equipment ductwork. Outdoor air is routed directly to the dehumidifier, which may have an operating outdoor air damper (the outdoor air duct should have a balancing damper, regardless of dehumidifier features).

Indoor air at 75°F, 55% RH is used for dehumidifier sizing, but the design values for the condition of the entering air are provided by the psychrometric solution for mixing indoor air with outdoor air. Then the condition of the entering air determines the capacity adjustment factor, and the efficiency adjustment factor, per Figure N2-1 or Figure N2-2; or the Section A15-3 equation.

The default operating mode for the summer design condition is for the desired amount of outdoor air flowing through the dehumidifier with the dehumidifier compressor off. Therefore, the corresponding latent and sensible outdoor air loads appear as line items on the load calculation for sizing the primary cooling equipment, and there is no adjustment for the dehumidifier reheat effect.

The locations and circumstances for the whole-house dehumidifier examples are used here (details are provided in the previous section). The outdoor air flow rate for these examples is 50 Cfm.

Brunswick, GA, Example

Figure 4-4 shows the latent cooling load for 55% RH indoors is 7,198 Btuh, which converts to 163.9 pints/day. So, the sizing value for equipment sizing is 85% percent of the load, or 139.3 pints/day.

Pints / Day = 24 x (7,198 / 1,054) = 163.9
Target Pints / Day = 0.85 x 163.9 = 139.3

Capacity Adjustment Factors

Figure 4-2 shows that Product H has 183 pints per day capacity for 80°F; 60% RH air, and that 540 Cfm flows through the dehumidifier. The outdoor air flow rate is 50 Cfm. Brunswick is at 20 feet, with 91°F dry-bulb and 79°F wet-bulb, so, the solution for mixed air is 76.4°F dry-bulb and 56.2% RH. The moisture removal adjustment and efficiency factor adjustments for this condition are 0.82 and 0.86, per the Section A15-3 equation.

Honeywell International, Inc. graphic

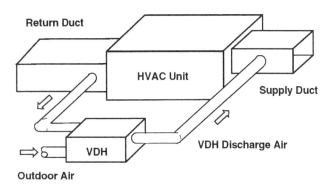

Figure 4-5

Condition of entering air = 76.4°F and 56.2% RH
MRA = 0.82; EFA = 0.86

Dehumidifier Size

The adjusted capacity for 76.9°F; 56.6% RH entering air is 126.0 pints/day, which is a little more than the 122.9 pints/day target.

Capacity adjustment for 76.4°F; 56.2% RH air = 0.82
Adjusted capacity = 0.82 x 183 = 150.1 Pints / Day
Target = 139.3 Pints / Day
The 183 size has adequate capacity.

Latent Load for Sizing Primary Equipment

The indoor humidity design value for sizing the primary cooling equipment is 50% RH, and the corresponding latent load on the primary cooling equipment is 8,801 Btuh (for all line items that produce a latent load, including the outdoor air load for 50% RH indoors).

Sensible Load for Sizing Primary Equipment

The base case sensible load on the primary cooling equipment is 29,633 Btuh (for all line items that produce a sensible load, including the outdoor air load for 91°F dry-bulb outdoors and 75°F dry-bulb indoors).

Fayetteville, AR, Example

The whole-house dehumidifier example for Fayetteville shows the total latent cooling load for 55% RH indoors is 4,170 Btuh, which converts to 95 pints/day. So, the sizing

Section 4

value for equipment sizing is 85 percent of this value, which is 80.8 pints/day.

Pints / Day = 24 x (4,170 / 1,054) = 95.0
Target Pints / Day = 0.85 x 95.0 = 80.7

Capacity Adjustment Factors

Figure 4-2 shows that Product G has 150 pints per day capacity for 80°F; 60% RH air, and that 415 Cfm flows through the dehumidifier. The outdoor air flow rate is 50 Cfm. Fayetteville is at 1,251 feet, with 93°F dry-bulb and 75°F wet-bulb, so the solution for mixed air is 77.1°F dry-bulb and 53.8% RH. The moisture removal adjustment and efficiency factor adjustments for this condition are 0.78 and 0.82, per the Section A15-3 equation.

Condition of entering air = 78.5°F and 53.1% RH
MRA = 0.78; EFA = 0.82

Dehumidifier Size

The adjusted capacity for 77.1°F; 53.8% RH entering air is 83.0 pints/day, which is a more than the 80.7 pints/day target.

Capacity adjustment for 77.1°F; 53.8% RH air = 0.78
Adjusted capacity = 0.78 x 150 = 117.0 Pints / Day
Target = 80.7 Pints / Day
The 150 size has adequate capacity for the full latent load.

Note: Figure 4-2 provides a small inventory of available product sizes. It may be that there are products that have rated capacities in the 115 to 135 pints/day range.

Latent Load for Sizing Primary Equipment

The indoor humidity design value for sizing the primary cooling equipment is 50% RH, and the corresponding latent load on the primary cooling equipment is 4,908 Btuh (for all line items that produce a latent load, including the outdoor air load for 50% RH indoors).

Sensible Load for Sizing Primary Equipment

The base case sensible load on the primary cooling equipment is 30,085 Btuh (for all line items that produce a sensible load, including the outdoor air load for 93°F dry-bulb outdoors and 75°F dry-bulb indoors).

4-4 Direct Evaporative Cooling

Evaporative cooling performance is at the mercy of the momentary weather condition. This is because the weather condition (outdoor air dry-bulb and wet-bulb temperatures, beam radiation, and cloud cover) simultaneously determine the sensible and latent cooling loads, and the sensible and latent cooling capacities. Appropriate use of evaporative equipment requires a dry climate, because the sensible cooling capacity provided by evaporation equipment adds moisture to the air in the conditioned space.

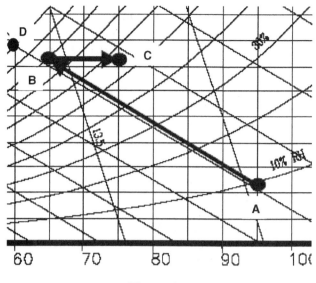

Figure 4-6

Altitude Psychrometrics

Evaporative cooling is a psychrometric process, so attitude is a factor that must not be ignored. An inspection of the weather data in *Manual J*, Table 1A or 1B shows that dry climate locations tend to be significantly above sea level. Therefore, altitude sensitive psychrometrics must be used for system design when a location is not relatively close to sea level.

Evaporative Equipment Performance

Direct (100 percent outdoor air) evaporative equipment may provide summer sensible cooling when the outdoor air condition is compatible with the application. Figure 4-6 summarizes the basic process for Truth or Consequences, NM, (elevation 4,858 feet, 1% dry-bulb is 95°F, coincident wet-bulb is 61°F).

- For the summer design load calculation condition, outdoor air enters the equipment at Point A (95°F DB; 61°F WB).
- The evaporation process follows the wet-bulb line, and moves toward the saturation line (Point D)
- For practical technical reasons, and for economic reasons, the evaporation equipment is not 100 percent efficient, so the relative humidity of the discharge air will be significantly less than 100% RH.

The properties of the discharge air depend on the saturation effectiveness of the equipment, as defined later in this discussion.

- For the Figure 4-6 example, the air leaves the equipment at about 65°F DB and 80% RH, as indicated by Point B.
- The supply air flows though the conditioned space, gains sensible heat, and exits the conditioned

space (exhausted to the outdoors) at 75°F DB and about 57% RH, as indicated by Point C.

- So the condition of the air in the conditioned space is 75°F db and somewhat less than 57% RH, depending on the size of the negative latent load caused by infiltration and duct leakage.
- Per Figure A7-2, indoor air at 75°F dry-bulb and 57% RH is acceptable for comfort.

Blower Cfm

The design Cfm for the evaporative equipment depends on the summer design value for the sensible cooling load. Figure 4-6 shows that supply air enters the space at about 65°F and leaves the space at 75°F, so the temperature difference for the sensible cooling effect is 10°F. For 4,858 feet the altitude correction factor (ACF) for the sensible heat equation is about 0.84 (per Figure A5-1). For this scenario, 3,118 Cfm is required for a 28,810 Btuh load.

Cfm = Sensible Btuh Load / (1.1 x ACF x ΔT)

Cfm = 28,810 / (1.1 x 0.84 x 10) = 3,118

Direct Saturation Efficiency

On Figure 4-6, the measured distance from Point A to Point B divided by the measured distance from Point A to Point D represents the direct saturation efficiency of the equipment. The following equation determines the direct saturation efficiency (DSE) of the equipment. For Figure 4-6, the DSE value is 88.2 percent.

DSE (%) = 100 x (DB$_{in}$ - DB$_{out}$) / (DB$_{in}$ - WB$_{in}$)

Where:
DB$_{in}$ = Air dry-bulb entering equipment
DB$_{out}$ = Air dry-bulb out of equipment
WB$_{in}$ = Air wet-bulb entering equipment
DSE (%) = 100 x (95 - 65) / (95 - 60) = 88.2

Dry-Bulb Temperature Out of the Equipment

For system design, OEM literature provides a direct saturation efficiency (DSE) value for the equipment, and the outdoor air condition determines the DB$_{in}$ and WB$_{in}$ values, so the DB$_{out}$ value is provided by this version of the direct saturation efficiency (DSE) equation.

DB$_{out}$ (°F) = DB$_{in}$ - DSE x (DB$_{in}$-WB$_{in}$) / 100

Temperature Difference Values for Cooling Cfm

As previously noted, the temperature difference for calculating blower Cfm equals the difference between the desired space temperature and the DB$_{out}$ value. Figure 4-7 provides temperature difference values that equal, or exceed 10°F, for various combinations of direct saturation efficiency, entering dry-bulb temperature, and entering wet-bulb temperature.

Supply Air TDs for a 75°F DB Space							
EWB (°F)	Entering Dry-Bulb (°F)						
	85	90	95	100	105	110	115
DSE = 75							
55	12.5	11.3	~	~	~	~	~
56	11.8	10.5	~	~	~	~	~
57	11.0	~	~	~	~	~	~
58	10.3	~	~	~	~	~	~
DSE = 80							
55	14.0	13.0	12.0	11.0	~	~	~
56	13.2	12.2	11.2	10.2	~	~	~
57	12.4	11.4	10.4	~	~	~	~
58	11.6	10.6	~	~	~	~	~
59	10.8	~	~	~	~	~	~
DSE = 85							
55	15.5	14.8	14.0	13.3	12.5	11.8	11.0
57	13.8	13.1	12.3	11.6	10.8	10.1	~
59	12.1	11.4	10.6	~	~	~	~
61	10.4	~	~	~	~	~	~
DSE = 90							
55	17.0	16.5	16.0	15.5	15.0	14.5	14.0
57	15.2	14.7	14.2	13.7	13.2	12.7	12.2
59	13.4	12.9	12.4	11.9	11.4	10.9	10.4
61	11.6	11.1	10.6	10.1	~	~	~
62	10.7	10.2	~	~	~	~	~

1) TD = 75°F for space - Dry-bulb °F out of equipment.
2) EWB (°F) = Entering wet-bulb = Outdoor air wet-bulb.
3) EDB (°F) = Entering dry-bulb = Outdoor air dry-bulb.
4) DSE = Direct Saturation Efficiency.
5) Blower Cfm = Sensible load / (1.1 x ACF x TD value).

Figure 4-7

For example, the summer design temperatures for Truth or Consequences, NM, are 95°F dry-bulb and 61°F wet-bulb. Therefore, direct equipment with a DSE value of 0.90 or more, is required for a sensible capacity temperature difference of 10°F or more (10.6°F for this example).

- Blower Cfm is proportional to the TD value.
- The TD for mechanical cooling in a dry climate may be about 18°F (57°F supply air), compared to a 10°F value for evaporative cooling.
- Therefore, blower Cfm for evaporative cooling will be substantial more than the Cfm for mechanical cooling.

Part-Load Performance Example										
Bin Dry-Bulb (°F)	DB_{out} (°F)	Air TD Load (Btuh)	Solar plus Internal (Btuh)	Total Load (Btuh)	Coincident Bin WB_{in} (°F)	Bin Hours	DSE % Value	LAT and SAT (°F)	ACF for 5,000 Feet	Blower Cfm for 75°F Indoors
70-80	75	0	16,512	16,512	55	1,389	88.2	57.4	0.84	1,013
80-90	85	6,473	16,512	22,985	59	863	88.2	62.1	0.84	1,924
90-100	95	12,945	16,512	29,457	61	265	88.2	65.0	0.84	3,192
100-110	105	19,418	16,512	35,930	62	57	88.2	67.1	0.84	4,906

1) Albuquerque, NM(5,311 Feet); bin data used for Truth and Consequences, NM (close enough for the purpose of this example).
2) Air TD Load = Transmission plus infiltration load. Approximately equal to the slope of the (Air TD load vs. OAT dry-bulb line) x (OAT – 75). Where the slope (M) = (Total MJ8 sensible load – Fenestration load – Internal load) / (MJ8 Design dry-bulb F – 75°F). For the Truth and Consequences dwelling: M = (28,810 – 11,439 – 5,073) / (94 – 75) = 647.263; so the Air TD load (Btuh) = M x (OAT – 75).
3) LAT (°F) = SAT (°F) = DB_{out} (°F) = DB_{in} – DSE x (DB_{in}-WB_{in}) / 100; where DBin is 75°F for this example.
4) Blower Cfm for full solar and internal loads = Total Load / (1.1 x ACF x (75 - SAT).

Figure 4-8

- Larger airways are required for evaporative cooling, per *Manual D* procedures. Adequate blower data is required for this calculation.
- Supply air outlet sizes increase with supply air Cfm, per *Manual T* procedures.
- Blower power draw depends on Cfm and the total (internal plus external) air flow resistance that the blower has to work against.

Part-Load Conditions and Performance

The outdoor air conditions used for the cooling load calculation, and for determining design day equipment performance (i.e., leaving dry-bulb air temperature per the equipment's DSE value, and the direct saturation efficiency equation), only occur for 1% of the hours in a year (88 hours per year on average). Different sets of outdoor dry-bulb and coincident wet-bulb values occur for thousands of cooling season hours.

Sensible Cooling Load

The momentary sensible cooling load depends on momentary beam radiation, momentary sensible internal load, and momentary outdoor dry-bulb temperature. Figure 4-8 shows how to estimate the worst-case load (largest sensible cooling load) for part-load conditions.

Outdoor and Indoor Conditions

Bin weather data provides outdoor air dry-bulb and coincident wet-bulb temperatures for part-load conditions, plus the associated hours of occurrence per year values. The indoor condition defaults to 75°F dry-bulb, or some other temperature may be used.

Momentary Leaving Air Temperature

Conditional leaving dry-bulb temperature (supply air temperature to the conditioned space) depends on the momentary values for outdoor air dry-bulb and wet-bulb temperatures, and the direct saturation efficiency of the equipment. The equation on the previous page provides this dry-bulb value.

Momentary Blower Cfm

The momentary blower Cfm depends on the momentary sensible load and the momentary leaving air temperature. The equipment has adequate capacity for a part-load condition when the momentary blower Cfm is equal to, or less than, the design value for blower Cfm. Figure 4-8 is an example of a part-load investigation.

Rainy Season or Unsuitable Outdoor Conditions

Some locations have a dry climate for most of the year, with a rainy season for a few weeks. When this is the case, evaporative cooling may be ineffective. Some locations have significant hours of the year when outdoor air is too humid for evaporative cooling.

- Use the ASHRAE 1% wet-bulb and coincident dry-bulb data to evaluate equipment performance for a rainy season scenario.
- It may be that sensible cooling is not an issue during the rainy season. (What is the sensible cooling load during the rainy season?).
- It may be that moisture removal is an issue during the rainy season. (Indoor humidity exceeds 60% RH for a significant amount of time.)
- Bin weather data or hourly weather data shows how outdoor air wet-bulb temperature correlates with dry-bulb temperature for the cooling season. Figure 4-9 demonstrates the concept.

Equipment Size Limits

Sensible cooling capacity for operating conditions that correlate with the summer design condition for the cooling load calculation must be equal to or greater than the sensible cooling load (the latent cooling load must be zero). Excess capacity is limited by the smallest standard size product that has adequate cooling capacity.

Heating

A climate that is compatible with evaporative cooling may have cold, long winters. Heating must be provided by a separate system, or a heating coil may be installed in the duct system. When a heating coil is used, the Cfm flowing through the coil must be compatible with the OEM's operating limits and installation guidance.

Operating Cost

Blower motor power may be more for evaporative cooling because the design value for blower Cfm is significantly more than for mechanical cooling, and pump power is required, but compressor power is not an issue. Heating cost depend on the type of heating system. Annual operating cost is the sum of the cooling cost and heating cost. The annual operating cost for a dwelling that has evaporating cooling and some type of heating system, should be compared to a competitive alternative, such as a heat pump equipment, or cooling-only and furnace equipment. A bin-hour calculation or hourly simulation that is compatible with Appendix 6 procedures should be used to evaluate economic benefits for a specific application (location, dwelling, equipment).

Air Balance for Conditioned Space

A large amount of supply air flows into the room. There must be a method for getting this air out of the conditioned space (i.e., exhaust Cfm equal to, or approximately equal to supply Cfm).

Media

Direct saturation efficiency depends on pad design. Also investigate pad cost, pad shrinkage, pad maintenance, pad life, pad blow-by, and air flow pressure drop.

Water Use

One thousand Btuh or sensible evaporative cooling roughly requires one pound of water (the latent heat of evaporation depends on altitude and temperature). So a 30,000 Btuh load requires 30 pounds of water per hour, which is 3.6 gallons per hour.

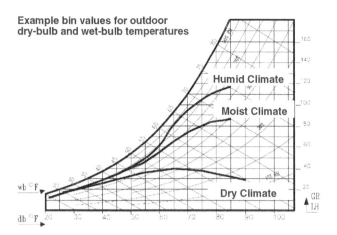

Figure 4-9

Additional water flow may be required for continuous equipment use and sump maintenance (bleed-off water, for example). A bin-hour calculation, or hourly simulation, provides the value for annual water use for a specific application (location, dwelling, equipment).

Water Issues

Water quality and water treatment must be suitable for the application. Scaling, mold, mildew; biological growth, and legionella are relevant issues. The water system requires correct design, plus scheduled maintenance and treatment. Moisture must not blow into duct runs. Discharge air velocity is an issue, eliminators may be required. Duct liner must not be used.

4-5 Winter Humidification Equipment

Winter humidification improves indoor comfort when outdoor air is very dry. Ideal relative humidity is in the 50% RH to 55% RH range, but the maximum indoor RH value for a given outdoor air temperature is determine by the thresholds for visible and concealed condensation, which depend on construction details, and outdoor air temperature. The current version of the Eighth Edition of *Manual J* provides a sizing procedure for humidifier use (the indoor relative humidity set-point must not cause condensation problems), and a procedure for calculating the winter humidification load in pints per day units.

Section N2-13 of this manual provides sizing limits. Appendix 7 of this manual provides procedures pertaining to moisture transfer and condensation. Appendix 8 of this manual provides procedures pertaining to condensation calculations.

Informative Material Pertaining to Central Ducted System Examples and Hydronic Heating Examples

Section 5 – Central Ducted Air-Air Cooling Examples

Section 6 – Central Ducted Air-Air Heat Pump Heating Examples

Section 7 – Central Ducted Furnace Examples

Section 8 – Dual Fuel Heating Procedures and Examples

Section 9 – Central Ducted Water-Air Heat Pump Examples

Section 10 – Hydronic Heating Equipment Examples

Section 5

Central Ducted Air-Air Cooling Examples

One selection/sizing procedure applies to all types of cooling-only equipment, and to heat pumps. This section shows how air-air equipment is sized for cooling. Section 6 shows how heat pump heating performance is evaluated after heat pump equipment has been sized for cooling. Appendix 19 provides supporting detail for the example problems in this section.

5-1 Latent Cooling Load Issues

The primary factor that affects the size of the latent cooling load is the local weather, as defined by a grains difference value extracted from *Manual J*, Table 1A or 1B. Latent load is not an issue (for normal internal loads) when the grains difference value is zero or negative. The latent load may not be an issue when the grains difference value is small (say 15 grains or less), but latent load consequences must be investigated for each particular application.

The size of the latent load always depends on the practitioner's design value for indoor relative humidity (45%, 50%, or 55% RH, per *Manual J* options), and on the latent infiltration load and the internal latent load. The size of the latent load also may depend on latent loads caused by duct leakage to/from an unconditioned space, and/or engineered ventilation.

- Normal internal latent loads are relatively small (per the default scenarios offered by Table 6, *Manual J*).
- Grains difference values from *Manual J*, Table 1A or Table 1B increase as the design value for indoor relative humidity decreases.
- When the *Manual J* Table 1A or 1B grains difference value is positive, the latent load increases with increasing leakage (building envelop and exposed duct surface area), and increasing ventilation Cfm, as demonstrated by Figure A1-17.
- The latent load also depends on moisture migration when a vapor retarding membrane, or portion thereof, is deficient or missing.
- *Manual J* procedures provide a latent load value for a specific set of circumstances.

5-2 Sensible Heat Ratio Issues

The *Manual J* sensible heat ratio (JSHR) value equals the *Manual J* sensible load divided by the *Manual J* total load. When this value is less than 0.80, the equipment's ability to satisfactorily control indoor humidity for the entire set of momentary operating conditions encountered during the cooling season is called into question. However, this 0.80 value is a rough guideline that flags concern, not a rule that guarantees a problem.

- In general, the probability of a summer humidity control problem decreases as the JSHR value moves toward 1.0, and vice-versa.
- *Manual S* procedures determine when the equipment has adequate latent capacity for any JSHR value (less likely when the JSHR value is less than 0.80, more likely when the JSHR value is 0.80 or more).
- The preferred way to deal with a low JSHR value is to apply measures that reduce the latent load (less infiltration, less duct leakage, reduce ventilation air Cfm, use enthalpy recovery).
- Some equipment makes and models have more latent capacity (lower coil sensible heat ratio) than others when operating continuously at full-speed during summer design conditions. Use equipment that is compatible with the local climate.
- For a given make/model, latent cooling capacity and coil sensible heat ratio is significantly affected by the nominal capacity of the condensing side vs. the nominal capacity of the evaporator side. A colder evaporator coil operating at a relatively low Cfm per ton of cooling is compatible with applications that have a low JSHR value.
- Ancillary dehumidification equipment may be used when efforts to minimize latent load, and to maximize latent capacity, are deficient.

5-3 Maximum Capacity for Cooling-Only Equipment

Over-sized cooling-only equipment causes compressor cycling (or throttling) on a summer design day, and reduces runtime for all part-load hours. This degrades indoor humidity control (see Section 1-4), and provides no efficiency or economic advantage.

- The latent capacity penalty for sort operating cycles is acerbated by the start-up transient (see Figure 1-7).
- Cycling penalties degrade seasonal efficiency somewhat (this is a secondary issue, as far as seasonal KWH is concerned).
- Size steps within a product line (make/model) may significantly affect the seasonal energy load (KWH) when the ratio of the output Btuh value vs. the corresponding input KW value (for compressor, blower and outdoor fan) varies with nominal size.

Inspect the Btuh/KW ratios for the sizes offered by a product line (make/model).

When the Btuh/KW ratio is relatively similar for all sizes, the seasonal energy load (KWH) is only affected by the cycling penalty.

When the Btuh/KW ratio significantly increases or decreases with size, seasonal KWH is affected by a change in equipment size, and the cycling penalty.

Different size units may have the same advertised SEER values, even though they have different Btuh/KW values. Compare EER values and ignore SEER values.

- Table N2-1 provides maximum capacity limits for cooling-only equipment based on aggressive use of *Manual J* procedures.

5-4 Maximum Cooling Capacity for Heat Pump Equipment

Indoor relative humidity is a primary comfort and health issue, so excess cooling capacity is important because over-sized heat pump equipment may degrade indoor humidity control for summer cooling. Therefore, the over sizing limit for air-air heat pumps depends on a threshold value for the *Manual J* sensible heat ratio (JSHR).

JSHR = Sensible load Btuh / Total Load Btuh

Where:
Threshold JSHR value = 0.95.
The capacity limit may increase when JSHR is 0.95, or more.
The load calculations must be as accurate as possible.

Excess cooling capacity is an efficiency and economic issue for heat pumps. When operating in the heating mode, larger equipment provides more compressor heat (COP greater than one), so use of electric coil heat (COP equals one) is reduced, and heating season efficiency is improved (the seasonal KWH advantage depends on case-by-case circumstances). Therefore, the over sizing limit for air-air heat pumps also depends on a threshold value for the severity of the winter climate, as indicated by the local degree day ratio (DDR) value.

DDR = HDD_{65} / CDD_{50}

Where:
Heating degree days (HDD) is to base 65°F.
Cooling degree days (CDD) is to base 50°F.
Threshold DDR value = 2.0.
The capacity limit may increase when DDR = or > 2.0.
See Section N1-5 for the source of degree day data.

Condition A Heat Pump

Condition A applies when the JSHR value is less than 0.95 for any HDD / CDD ratio, or when the HDD / CDD ratio is less than 2.0 for any JSRH value. Table N2-2 provides maximum capacity limits for Condition A equipment, based on aggressive use of *Manual J* procedures.

Condition B Heat Pump

Condition B applies when the JSHR value is 0.95 or greater, and the local HDD / CDD ratio is 2.0 or more. When the application passes both tests, heat pump total cooling capacity may exceed the *Manual J* total (sensible plus latent) cooling load by as much as 15,000 Btuh, per Table N2-2.

- Improved heating efficiency is desirable when the heating energy requirement is the dominate portion of the annual energy (KWH) requirement.
- The over-size benefit, as it pertains to annual energy savings and annual operation cost savings, may vary from minimal to substantial, depending on the local weather, building envelope details, HVAC system attributes, and local utility rates.
- Comprehensive energy and op-cost calculations should quantify the annual energy efficiency and economic benefits of excess cooling capacity (see Appendix 6).
- For acceptable pay-back criteria, *Manual S* defers to the judgment of the governing authority (homeowner preference, or local code/regulation).

5-5 Minimum Cooling Capacity

For cooling-only equipment, and for Condition A heat pumps, the minimum capacity vs. load ratio for total cooling capacity is 0.90 (90% of the total cooling load); the minimum capacity vs. load ratio for latent cooling capacity is 1.00 (100% of the latent cooling load); and the minimum capacity vs. load ratio for sensible cooling capacity is 0.90 (90% of the sensible cooling load after one half of the excess latent capacity has been added to the sensible capacity value listed in the OEM's data).

For Condition B heat pumps, the minimum capacity vs. load ratio for total cooling capacity is 0.90 (90% of the total cooling load). The purpose of the 0.90 rule is to widen the acceptance gate for standard equipment sizes. In general, excess total cooling capacity (OSF significantly more than 1.00) is preferred, because it reduces annual energy use.

5-6 Total Cooling Capacity Value

The total cooling capacity value for determining excess cooling capacity must be extracted from the OEM's expanded performance data (per Section A1-9). The total cooling capacity value must be for *Manual J* operating conditions at the building site (see Figure A1-21).

- The practitioner may choose from the blower Cfm or blower speed options offered by the OEM's data table. A mid-range selection is recommended. This leaves room for adjustment (when needed) after the equipment has been installed.

- The outdoor air dry-bulb temperature is the *Manual J* Table 1 value, or the local code value.
- The comprehensive procedures in Appendix 2 of this manual, or the Section A1-2 defaults, determine the entering air wet-bulb temperature.
- When the operating conditions are within the limits of the OEM's data table, the total capacity value is determined by exact interpolation.
- When one or more operating condition is outside the limits of the OEM's capacity data, ask the OEM for comprehensive data.

    Extrapolation of deficient data may, or may not, produce a usable value.

    Extrapolation may not be authorized by the OEM. Obtain permission and guidance from the OEM.

    Adjust cooling capacity for altitude (per Appendix 5) for locations above 2,500 feet.

5-7 Latent and Sensible Capacity Values

Latent and sensible capacity values must be extracted from the OEM's expanded performance data. These values are read from the OEM data table that provided the total capacity value for the same set of circumstances.

- The blower Cfm, outdoor air temperature, and entering wet-bulb temperature values used to determine total capacity are used to determine latent capacity and sensible capacity.
- Sensible capacity also depends on the entering dry-bulb temperature.
- The comprehensive procedures in Appendix 2 of this manual, or the Section A1-2 defaults, produce entering air wet-bulb and dry-bulb temperatures for total, latent and sensible capacity determination.
- OEM data may list total capacity and sensible capacity, or total capacity and a coil sensible heat ratio (CSHR). These equations apply:

    Total Btuh = Sensible Btuh + Latent Btuh
    Sensible Btuh = CSHR x Total Btuh

5-8 Equipment Selection Examples

The equipment selection examples in this section are for the cooling loads produced by a surrogate dwelling built in a warm humid location; a warm, very humid location; and a dry summer, cold winter location. The intent is to demonstrate an equipment sizing procedure that is sensitive to the latent cooling load, and to the attributes of the local winter and summer weather. However, the solution for an example problem is not a general solution for the housing stock in a given location, as explained here:

- The outdoor design condition for summer cooling, and the winter-summer degree day ratio, do not depend on dwelling's attributes and the HVAC system's attributes. So these values are common to the housing stock in a given location.
- The latent and sensible cooling loads for the summer design condition do depend on dwelling's features and attributes, and depend on the HVAC system loads for air distribution and engineered ventilation. So these values are not common to the housing stock in a given location.
- The *Manual J* sensible heat ratio depends on dwelling's attributes and the HVAC system's attributes when the local climate has a positive grains difference value in Table 1, *Manual J*. This is a case-by-case issue.
- For a given nominal size, expanded cooling performance data values may vary significantly for the same set of operating circumstances, depending on the brand name, the outdoor model and size, the indoor model and size, and the blower Cfm. This is case-by-case issue.
- Therefore, practitioners must apply *Manual J* and *Manual S* procedures to the actual dwelling in the actual location when selecting and sizing a specific piece of equipment.

5-9 Attributes of the Example Dwelling

The example dwelling is an attempt to define a common construction scenario that is sensitive to issues that affect the latent load. Envelope efficiency is good, but not exceptional. Glass area is modest. Attic ducts are insulated and sealed, but the workmanship is average. The dwelling has engineered ventilation with sensible heat recovery. Basic information is summarized below. Appendix 19 provides more detail.

- Slab on grade, one story, 3,300 SqFt (Figure A19-2 shows the floor plan).
- Two pane, clear glass, wood frame, tight fenestration. Fenestration area is 10.9 percent of the floor area. No AED excursion.
- Commonly used ceiling, wall and floor R-values.
- Average structural tightness.
- Attic ducts: R6 wall insulation, default sealed, (0.12/0.24 Cfm/SqFt leakage), installed in a vented attic under a white shingle roof (*Manual J*, Table 4, Construction 16C).
- Engineered ventilation: 75 Cfm of outdoor air and 75 Cfm of exhaust though a sensible heat exchanger.
- Heat recovery effectiveness: 0.50 for cooling and 0.55 for heating.

5-10 Balanced Climate Humid Summer Example

The over-size limit from Table N2-1 applies to cooling-only equipment. This procedure applies to all cooling-only equipment, regardless of the local degree day ratio and the application's JSHR value.

The over-size limit from Table N2-2 applies to heat pump equipment. Fayetteville, AR, has 4,166 heating degree days and 4,267 cooling degree days (NOAA data), so it's degree day ratio value is 0.98, which means that the over-size limit is for a Condition A heat pump. In addition, the *Manual J* sensible heat ratio for this example is much less than 0.95, so there are two reasons why this is a Condition A heat pump (either reason is sufficient).

Inspection of Table N2-1 and Table N2-2 shows that the size limit for total cooling capacity is the same for cooling-only equipment, and for Condition A heat pumps. Therefore, the following solution applies to both types of equipment.

Cooling Loads and Operating Conditions

Equipment size is based on the *Manual J* cooling loads and corresponding equipment operating conditions, as summarized below. Return duct loads and engineered ventilation details are important because they affect entering wet-bulb and entering dry-bulb temperatures. The 0.96 altitude adjustment factor for 1,251 feet applies to *Manual J* calculations and to psychrometric calculations for entering air temperature (the ACF adjustment is made for procedure consistency, even when the effect is small). Altitude also affects equipment performance (see Figure A5-3), but this effect may be ignored when the altitude is 2,500 Feet or less (per industry-wide default).

Sensible cooling load = 33,954 Btuh
Latent cooling load = 5,586 Btuh
Total cooling load = 39,540 Btuh
Manual J tons = 39,540 / 12,000 = 3.295
Floor area = 3,300 SqFt
SqFt floor area per Manual J ton = 3,300 / 3.29 = 1,002
Altitude = 1,251 Feet; Figure A5-1 ACF = 0.96
Outdoor conditions: 93°F db / 75°F wb
Indoor conditions: 75°F db and 50% RH
Sensible return duct load (Section A2-3) = 1,630 Btuh
Latent return duct load (Section A2-3) = 640 Btuh
Outdoor air = 75 Cfm; Sensible Eff. for cooling = 0.50
JSHR = 33,954 / 39,540 = 0.86
HDD / CDD = 3,935 / 4,368 = 0.90
OSL for cooling-only, or Condition A heat pump = 1.15

Data Search

Expanded performance data is searched for something close to 39,000 Btuh of total cooling capacity, for 95°F outdoors, using a preliminary value for the entering wet-bulb temperature. To get started, use the wet-bulb temperature for the indoor air.

048 Size -- OEM X					
Outdoor Air Dry-Bulb = 95°F					
Blower Cfm	Entering Wet-Bul °F	Total Btuh	Sensible Btuh		
			Entering Dry-Bulb °F		
			80	75	70
1,200	77	54.0	15.1	-	-
	72	49.6	22.9	17.2	-
	67	45.2	30.8	25.1	19.4
	62	41.4	37.3	31.6	25.9
	57	44.0	38.2	32.5	26.8
1,400	77	54.8	16.2	-	-
	72	50.3	24.7	18.0	-
	67	45.8	33.1	26.4	19.7
	62	42.1	40.2	33.4	26.7
	57	44.6	41.2	34.4	27.7
1,600	77	55.5	17.4	-	-
	72	51.0	26.5	18.7	-
	67	46.5	35.5	27.7	20.0
	62	42.7	43.1	35.3	27.5
	57	45.3	44.1	36.3	28.6
1,800	72	50.9	27.2	18.3	-
	67	46.4	36.5	27.6	18.8
	62	42.6	42.8	33.9	25.1
	57	45.2	44.6	35.8	26.9
2,000	72	50.8	27.9	17.9	-
	67	46.3	37.4	27.5	17.5
	62	42.5	42.5	32.6	22.6
	57	45.1	45.1	35.2	25.2

Figure 5-1

Condition of the indoor air = 75°F db and 50% RH
Indoor wb temperature at 1,251 feet = 62.35°F
Ballpark wb temperature value for search = 62°F to 63°F

Note: The actual entering wet-bulb temperature depends on the return duct load and the outdoor air load, but these adjustments require a blower Cfm value, which is not known until a candidate unit is selected.

Candidate Single-Speed Unit

The outdoor design temperature is 93°F. Figure 5-1 (previous page) shows actual cooling performance data for the 048 size when it is 95°F outdoors. This data was extracted from many pages of data for this product. Since 1,600 Cfm is a mid-range value, it is used to find a total cooling capacity value.

At 1,600 Cfm and 62°F wet-bulb, the single-speed unit has 42,700 Btuh of total cooling capacity. The excess total capacity factor is 1.08, so this unit is a candidate.

42,700 / 39,540 = 1.08

Entering Dry-Bulb and Wet-Bulb Values

Return duct loads and outdoor air loads increase the entering dry-bulb and wet-bulb temperatures. Per Section A2-3 procedures, the sensible return duct load is 1,630 Btuh and the latent return duct load is 640 Btuh.

When Sections A2-4 and A2-7 procedures are applied to the return duct loads and outdoor air loads (using altitude psychrometrics), the condition of the entering air is 76.4°F db and 63.3°F wb for 1,600 blower Cfm.

Altitude = 1,251 feet
Blower Cfm = 1,600; return Cfm = 1,525; OA Cfm = 75
Dry-bulb °F at return grille = 75.0
Wet-bulb °F at return grille = 62.347
Dry-bulb °F out of return duct = 75.964
Wet-bulb °F out of return duct = 62.802
Entering (mixed air) dry-bulb °F = 76.359 (76.4)
Entering (mixed air) wet-bulb °F = 63.308 (63.3)

Interpolated Cooling Capacity Values

The design value for blower Cfm is 1,600. The design value for outdoor dry-bulb temperature is 93°F. The design values for entering dry-bulb and entering wet-bulb are 76.4°F and 63.3°F. Preliminary cooling capacity values are interpolated from OEM performance data values (see Figure 5-2).

Total Btuh = 44,216
Sensible Btuh = 35,773
Latent Btuh = 8,443

Job Site Performance

The total cooling load is 39,540 Btuh, so the over-size factor is acceptable at 1.12. The latent cooling load is 5,586 Btuh, so the latent capacity to latent load ratio is 1.51, which is close to the recommended limit (1.50), so the equipment is suitable for the application in this regard. There is 2,857 Btuh of excess latent capacity. Half of the excess latent capacity is added to the sensible capacity, so the adjusted sensible capacity is 37,202 Btuh. The sensible cooling load is 33,954 Btuh, so the sensible capacity to sensible load ratio is 1.10, which is good. Therefore, the 048 unit complies with the Table N2-1 requirements for cooling-only equipment, or the Table N2-2 requirements for a Condition A heat pump

Total Capacity OSF = 44,216 / 39,540 = 1.12
Latent capacity / Latent load = 8,443 / 5,586 = 1.51
Excess latent = 8,443 - 5,586 = 2,857 Btuh
50% of excess latent = 0.5 x 2,857 = 1,429 Btuh
Adjusted sensible = 35,773 + 1,429 = 37,202 Btuh
Sens capacity / Sens load = 37,202 / 33,954 = 1.10

Square Feet per Ton Values

There is 3,300 SqFt or floor area, and the total cooling load is 39,540 Btuh, so there is 1,002 SqFt per *Manual J* ton. The

048 Size — OEM X			
Blower Cfm	Entering Wet-Bul °F	Total Btuh	Sensible Btuh
			Entering Dry-Bulb °F
			80	75
Outdoor Air Dry-Bulb = 85°F				
1,600	67	49.7	37.3	29.5
	62	45.1	44.7	37.0
Outdoor Air Dry-Bulb = 95°F				
1,600	67	46.5	35.5	27.7
	62	42.7	43.1	35.3

Figure 5-2

042 Size — OEM X			
Blower Cfm	Entering Wet-Bul °F	Total Btuh	Sensible Btuh
			Entering Dry-Bulb °F
			80	75
Outdoor Air Dry-Bulb = 85°F				
1,400	67	43.9	32.6	25.8
	62	40.0	39.8	33.0
Outdoor Air Dry-Bulb = 95°F				
1,400	67	41.0	31.4	24.6
	62	37.8	38.5	31.6

Figure 5-3

equipment's total capacity for *Manual J* conditions is 44,216 Btuh, so there is 896 SqFt per installed ton. The AHRI rating value for total capacity is 47,000 Btuh, so the there is 843 SqFt per AHRI rating ton.

Manual J SqFt per ton = 12,000 x 3,300 / 39,540 = 1,002
Applied SqFt per ton = 12,000 x 3,300 / 44,216 = 896
Rated SqFt per ton = 12,000 x 3,300 / 47,000 = 843

Check Smaller Equipment

The 048 size has 12% of excess total cooling capacity and excessive latent capacity. It may be that the 042 size is a better match. Figure 5-3 (previous page) provides capacity values for a performance evaluation. Interpolated performance values for *Manual J* operating conditions are provided here:

Blower Cfm = 1,400
Outdoor air temperature = 93°F
Entering db and wb temperature = 76.5°F and 63.4°F
Total capacity interpolated = 39,204 Btuh
Latent capacity interpolated = 7,231
Sensible capacity interpolated = 31,973 Btuh

Job Site Performance

The 042 size is the preferred size. The total capacity OSF is 0.99, the latent capacity to latent load ratio is 1.29 (vs. 1.51

Section 5

for the 048 size), and the sensible capacity to sensible load ratio is 0.97 (vs. 1.10 for the 048 size).

Total Capacity OSF = 39,204 / 39,540 = 0.99
Latent capacity / Latent load = 7,231 / 5,586 = 1.29
Excess latent = 7,231 - 5,586 = 1,645 Btuh
50% of excess latent = 0.5 x 1,645 = 823 Btuh
Adjusted sensible = 31,973 + 823 = 32,796 Btuh
Sens capacity / Sens load = 37,796 / 33,954 = 0.97

Square Feet per Ton Values

There is 1,002 SqFt per ton for *Manual J* load. The applied total capacity for *Manual J* conditions is 39,204 Btuh, so there is 1,010 SqFt per ton for the actual operating condition. The AHRI rating value for total capacity is 42,000 Btuh, so there is 943 SqFt per AHRI rating ton.

Manual J SqFt per ton = 12,000 x 3,300 / 39,540 = 1,002
Applied SqFt per ton = 12,000 x 3,300 / 39,204 = 1,010
Rated SqFt per ton = 12,000 x 3,300 / 42,000 = 943

5-11 Hot-Humid Climate Example

The over-size limit from Table N2-1 applies to cooling-only equipment. This procedure applies to all cooling-only equipment, regardless of the local degree day ratio and the application's JSHR value.

The over-size limit from Table N2-2 applies to heat pump equipment. Brunswick, GA, has 1,545 heating degree days and 6,765 cooling degree days (NOAA data), so it's degree day ratio value is 0.23, which means that the over-size limit is for a Condition A heat pump. In addition, the *Manual J* sensible heat ratio for this example is much less than 0.95, so there are two reasons why this is a Condition A heat pump (either reason is sufficient).

Tables N2-1 and N2-2 show that cooling-only equipment and Condition A heat pumps are subject to the same sizing rules. Therefore, the following solution applies to both types of equipment.

Cooling Loads and Operating Conditions

Equipment size is based on the *Manual J* cooling loads and corresponding equipment operating conditions, as summarized below. Return duct loads and engineered ventilation details are important because they affect entering wet-bulb and entering dry-bulb temperatures. Since Brunswick is 20 feet above sea level, there is no altitude adjustment (ACF = 1.0) for *Manual J* calculations or for the psychrometric calculations for entering air temperature, and there is no altitude adjustment for equipment performance.

Sensible cooling load = 29,413 Btuh
Latent cooling load = 8,801 Btuh
Total cooling load = 38,214 Btuh
***Manual J** tons = 38,214 / 12,000 = 3.18*
Floor area = 3,300 SqFt

048 Size — OEM X (Figure 5-3 abridged)						
Outdoor Air Dry-Bulb = 95°F						
Blower Cfm	Entering Wet-Bul °F	Total Btuh	Sensible Btuh			
			Entering Dry-Bulb °F		
			80	75	70
1,200	77	54.0	15.1	-	-
	72	49.6	22.9	17.2	-
	67	45.2	30.8	25.1	19.4
	62	41.4	37.3	31.6	25.9
	57	44.0	38.2	32.5	26.8
1,400	77	54.8	16.2	-	-
	72	50.3	24.7	18.0	-
	67	45.8	33.1	26.4	19.7
	62	42.1	40.2	33.4	26.7
	57	44.6	41.2	34.4	27.7
1,600	77	55.5	17.4	-	-
	72	51.0	26.5	18.7	-
	67	46.5	35.5	27.7	20.0
	62	42.7	43.1	35.3	27.5
	57	45.3	44.1	36.3	28.6
1,800	72	50.9	27.2	18.3	-
	67	46.4	36.5	27.6	18.8
	62	42.6	42.8	33.9	25.1
	57	45.2	44.6	35.8	26.9

Figure 5-4

*SqFt floor area per **Manual J** ton = 3,300 / 3.18 = 1,038*
Altitude = 20 Feet; Figure A5-1 ACF = 1.00
Outdoor conditions: 91°F db / 79°F wb
Indoor conditions: 75°F db and 50% RH
Sensible return duct load (Worksheet G) = 1,461 Btuh
Latent return duct load (Worksheet G) = 948 Btuh
Outdoor air = 75 Cfm; Sensible Eff. for cooling = 0.50
JSHR = 29,413 / 38,214 = 0.77
HDD / CDD = 1,523 / 6,676 = 0.23
OSL for cooling-only, or Condition A heat pump = 1.15

Data Search

Expanded performance data is searched for something close to 38,000 Btuh total cooling capacity, for 90°F outdoors, using a preliminary value for the entering wet-bulb temperature. To get started, use the wet-bulb temperature for the indoor air.

Condition of the indoor air = 75°F db and 50% RH
Indoor wb temperature at 20 feet = 62.54°F
Ballpark wb temperature value for search = 62°F to 63°F

Note: The actual entering wet-bulb temperature depends on the return duct load and the outdoor air load, but these adjustments require a blower Cfm value, which is not known until a candidate unit is selected.

Candidate Single-Speed Unit

The outdoor design temperature is 91°F. Figure 5-4 (previous page) shows actual cooling performance data for 048 size equipment when it is 95°F outdoors. This data was extracted from many pages of data for this product. Since 1,600 Cfm is a mid-range value, it is used to find a total cooling capacity value.

At 1,600 Cfm and 62°F wet-bulb, the unit has 42,700 Btuh of total cooling capacity. The excess total capacity factor is 1.12, so this unit is a candidate.

42,700 / 38,214 = 1.12

Entering Dry-Bulb and Wet-Bulb Values

Return duct loads and outdoor air loads increase the entering dry-bulb and wet-bulb temperatures. Per Section A2-3 procedures, the sensible return duct load is 1,461 Btuh and the latent return duct load is 948 Btuh.

When Sections A2-4 and A2-7 procedures are applied to the return duct loads and outdoor air loads (using sea level psychrometrics), the condition of the entering air is 76.2°F db and 63.8°F wb for 1,600 blower Cfm.

Altitude = 20 feet
Blower Cfm = 1,600; return Cfm = 1,525; OA Cfm = 75
Dry-bulb °F at return grille = 75.0
Wet-bulb °F at return grille = 62.543
Dry-bulb °F out of return duct = 75.830
Wet-bulb °F out of return duct = 63.017
Entering (mixed air) dry-bulb °F = 76.183 (76.2)
Entering (mixed air) wet-bulb °F = 63.769 (63.8)

Interpolated Cooling Capacity Values

The design value for blower Cfm is 1,600. The design value for outdoor dry-bulb temperature is 91°F. The design values for entering dry-bulb and entering wet-bulb are 76.2°F and 63.8°F. Preliminary cooling capacity values are interpolated from OEM performance data values (see Figure 5-5).

Total Btuh = 45,118
Sensible Btuh = 35,145
Latent Btuh = 9,973

Job Site Performance

The total cooling load is 38,214 Btuh, so the applied over-size factor for the 048 size is 1.18, which slightly exceeds the 1.15 limit. The performance of smaller equipment (in the 042 size) will provide a better match.

OSF = 45,118 / 38,214 = 1.18

048 Size — OEM X (Figure 5-2 repeated)			
Blower Cfm	Entering Wet-Bul °F	Total Btuh	Sensible Btuh
			Entering Dry-Bulb °F
			80 / 75
Outdoor Air Dry-Bulb = 85°F			
1,600	67	49.7	37.3 / 29.5
1,600	62	45.1	44.7 / 37.0
Outdoor Air Dry-Bulb = 95°F			
1,600	67	46.5	35.5 / 27.7
1,600	62	42.7	43.1 / 35.3

Figure 5-5

042 Size — OEM X (Figure 5-3 repeated)			
Blower Cfm	Entering Wet-Bul °F	Total Btuh	Sensible Btuh
			Entering Dry-Bulb °F
			80 / 75
Outdoor Air Dry-Bulb = 85°F			
1,400	67	43.9	32.6 / 25.8
1,400	62	40.0	39.8 / 33.0
Outdoor Air Dry-Bulb = 95°F			
1,400	67	41.0	31.4 / 24.6
1,400	62	37.8	38.5 / 31.6

Figure 5-6

Interpolated Capacity for Smaller Equipment

Figure 5-6 provides capacity values for the 042 size. Interpolated performance values for *Manual J* operating conditions are provided here:

Blower Cfm = 1,400
Outdoor air temperature = 91°F
Entering db and wb temperature = 76.3°F and 63.9°F
Total capacity interpolated = 40,030 Btuh
Latent capacity interpolated = 8,771
Sensible capacity interpolated = 31,259 Btuh

Job Site Performance

The 042 size is a very good match for this application. The total capacity OSF is 1.05, the latent capacity to latent load ratio is 1.00, and the sensible capacity to sensible load ratio is 1.06.

Total capacity OSF = 40,030 / 38,214 = 1.05
Latent capacity / Latent load = 8,771 / 8,801 = 1.00
Excess latent = 8,771 - 8,801 = -30 Btuh
50% of excess latent = zero if excess is zero or negative
Adjusted sensible = 31,259 + 0 = 31,259 Btuh
Sens capacity / Sens load = 31,259 / 29,413 = 1.06

Section 5

Square Feet per Ton Values

There is 1,036 SqFt per *Manual J* ton. The applied total capacity for *Manual J* conditions is 40,030 Btuh, so there is 1,010 SqFt per ton value for the actual operating condition. The AHRI rating value for total capacity is 42,000 Btuh, so the there is 943 SqFt per AHRI rating ton.

Manual J SqFt per ton = 12,000 x 3,300 / 38,214 = 1,036
Applied SqFt per ton = 12,000 x 3,300 / 40,030 = 989
Rated SqFt per ton = 12,000 x 3,300 / 42,000 = 943

5-12 Dry Summer Cold Winter Example

The over-size limit from Table N2-1 applies to cooling-only equipment. This procedure applies to all cooling-only equipment, regardless of the local degree day ratio and the application's JSHR value.

The over-size limit from Table N2-2 applies to heat pump equipment. Boise, ID, has 5,727 heating degree days and 2,856 cooling degree days (NOAA data), so it's degree day ratio value is 2.01, which means that the over-size limit is for a Condition B heat pump. Per *Manual J*, Table 1A; the Boise elevation is 2,838 feet, and the grains difference value for 45% RH indoors is -21 Grains, so the cooling coil will be dry. A JSHR value of 0.95, or more, is the second, and necessary, reason why this is a Condition B heat pump.

Table N2-2 procedures for a Condition B heat pump supersede Table N2-1 procedures for cooling-only equipment. Therefore, the solutions for cooling-only equipment and heat pump equipment are different.

Cooling Loads and Operating Conditions

Equipment size is based on the *Manual J* cooling loads and corresponding equipment operating conditions, as summarized below. The return duct load and engineered ventilation details are important because they affect entering dry-bulb temperature. The 0.88 altitude adjustment factor for 2,838 feet applies to *Manual J* calculations and to psychrometric calculations for entering air temperature. Altitude also affects equipment performance, per the adjustment factor from Figure A5-3.

Sensible cooling load = 30,145 Btuh
Latent cooling load = Negative (dry-coil)
Total cooling load = 30,145 Btuh
***Manual J** tons = 30,145 / 12,000 = 2.51*
Floor area = 3,300 SqFt
*SqFt floor area per **Manual J** ton = 3,300 / 2.51 = 1,315*
Altitude = 2,838 Feet; Figure A5-1 ACF = 0.88
Outdoor conditions: 94°F db / 63°F wb
Indoor conditions: 75°F db and less than 45% RH
Sensible return duct load (Worksheet G) = 1,346 Btuh
Latent return duct load (Worksheet G) = NA; dry-coil
Outdoor air = 75 Cfm; Sensible Eff. for cooling = 0.50

Humidistat Control for Cooling

Latent capacity is increased when the compressor operating cycle, blower operating cycle, and the dry-bulb set-point of the space thermostat depend on output from a space humidity control.

However, an effort to improve latent capacity for part-load conditions results in colder air through the duct runs, and colder air at supply air outlets.

- Condensation, mold and mildew must not occur on air distribution system surfaces, or on structural surfaces that are washed by cool supply air.
- The requirement for air distribution system insulation, sealing and use of a vapor retarding membrane depend on the temperature of the supply air.
- Appendices 7 and 8 provide related material.

JSHR = 30,145 / 30,145 = 1.00
OSL for cooling-only = 1.15
OSL for a Condition B heat pump = +15,000 Btuh TC

Select cooling-only Equipment

Expanded performance data is searched for something close to 30,000 Btu total cooling capacity, for 95°F outdoors, using a dry-coil value (or close to a dry-coil value) for entering wet-bulb temperature (typically 59°F or less).

Note: The lowest EWB temperature in OEM data may range from about 57°F to 63°F, depending on the OEM. The cooling coil is typically wet for a 63°F value. Dry-coil data is preferred, but a total capacity value for a 63°F wet-bulb temperature may be used for the search.

Candidate Single-Speed Cooling-Only Unit

Figure 5-7 shows actual performance data for a cooling-only product. The outdoor design temperature is 94°F, so the 95°F data is used for the search. Since 1,200 Cfm is a mid-range value, it is used to find a total cooling capacity value.

The unit has 31,300 Btuh of total cooling capacity for 95°F outdoors and 59°F EWB. The excess total capacity factor is less than 1.15, so this unit is a candidate.

31,300 / 30,145 = 1.04

Entering Dry-Bulb and Wet-Bulb Values

Return duct and outdoor air loads increase the entering dry-bulb temperature (wet-bulb temperature is not an issue for a dry climate). Per Section A2-3 procedures, the sensible return duct load is 1,346 Btuh.

When Sections A2-4 and A2-7 procedures are applied to the return duct load and outdoor air load (using altitude psychrometrics), the dry-bulb temperature of the entering air is 76.7°F for 1,200 Cfm.

Altitude = 2,838 feet
Blower Cfm = 1,200; return Cfm = 1,125; OA Cfm = 75
Dry-bulb °F at return grille = 75.0
Dry-bulb °F out of return duct = 76.159
Entering (mixed air) dry-bulb °F = 76.716 (76.7)

Interpolated Cooling Capacity Values

The design value for blower Cfm is 1,200. The design value for outdoor dry-bulb temperature is 94°F. The design value for entering dry-bulb temperature is 76.7°F. The total cooling capacity value is interpolated from OEM performance data values (see Figure 5-7).

Total Btuh = 31,420
Sensible Btuh = Equal to, or close to, total capacity.
Latent Btuh = Zero for a dry cooling coil.

Check Capacity at Altitude

The equipment has 31,420 Btuh of total cooling capacity at sea level (OEM data is for sea level). Per Figure A5-3, the altitude adjustment factor for 3,000 Feet is 0.95, so the adjusted total cooling capacity is about 29,849 Btuh. Since the coil is dry, the sensible capacity is about 29,849 Btuh.

TC at altitude = 31,420 x 0.95 = 29,849 Btuh
SC at altitude = 29,849 Btuh

Job Site Performance

The total cooling load is 30,145 Btuh, so the over-size factor for total capacity is 0.99. The latent capacity ratio is not relevant because the cooling coil is dry. The sensible cooling load is 30,145 Btuh, so the sensible capacity ratio is 0.99. The 036 size is an ideal solution for cooling-only equipment.

Total capacity OSF = 29,849 / 30,145 = 0.99
Latent capacity issues are not relevant
Sensible capacity = 29,849 Btuh
Sens capacity / Sens load = 29,849 / 30,145 = 0.99

Square Feet per Ton Values

There is 1,319 SqFt per *Manual J* ton. The applied total capacity at altitude for *Manual J* conditions is 29,849 Btuh, so there is 1,327 SqFt per ton value for the actual operating condition. The AHRI rating value for total capacity is 35,000 Btuh, so the there is 1,131 SqFt per AHRI rating ton.

Manual J *SqFt per ton = 12,000 x 3,300 / 30,015 = 1,319*
Applied SqFt per ton = 12,000 x 3,300 / 29,849 = 1,327
Rated SqFt per ton = 12,000 x 3,300 / 35,000 = 1,131

O36 Size at 1,200 Cfm — OEM Y					
OAT DB (°F)	EWB (°F)	TC (MBtuh)	SC (MBtuh) EDB (°F)		
			74	76	78
90	59	31.9	29.2	31.4	32.6*
	63	34.3	24.7	27.0	29.2
	67	36.8	19.8	22.0	24.3
95	59	31.3	28.9	31.1	32.1*
	63	33.6	24.4	26.7	28.9
	67	36.0	19.5	21.7	24.0

* Indicates a dry-coil, total capacity equals sensible capacity.

Figure 5-7

O48 Size at 1,600 Cfm — OEM Y					
OAT DB (°F)	EWB (°F)	TC (MBtuh)	SC (MBtuh) EDB (°F)		
			74	76	78
90	59	43.6	38.5	41.4	43.8*
	63	46.7	32.9	35.7	38.6
95	59	42.7	38.2	41.0	43.1*
	63	45.8	32.5	35.4	38.2

* Indicates a dry-coil, total capacity equals sensible capacity.

Figure 5-8

Select a Condition B Heat Pump

It has been demonstrated by the preceding cooling-only example that the total cooling capacity of a 036 size is close to the total cooling load. The 036 size plus 15,000 Btuh of total capacity points to a 048 size. Figure 5-8 (previous page) shows actual cooling performance data for a 048 heat pump.

Adjust Entering Dry-Bulb and Wet-Bulb Values

Return duct and outdoor air loads increase the entering dry-bulb temperature (wet-bulb temperature is not an issue for a dry climate). Per Section A2-3 procedures, the sensible return duct load is 1,346 Btuh.

When Section A2-4 procedures process the return duct load and the outdoor air load for 1,600 blower Cfm (using altitude sensitive psychrometric software), the dry-bulb temperature of the entering air is 76.3°F.

Altitude = 2,838 feet
Blower Cfm = 1,600; return Cfm = 1,525; OA Cfm = 75
Dry-bulb °F at return grille = 75.0
Dry-bulb °F out of return duct = 75.869
Entering (mixed air) dry-bulb °F = 76.289 (76.3)

Interpolated Cooling Capacity Values

The design value for blower Cfm is 1,600. The design value for outdoor dry-bulb temperature is 94°F. The design value for entering dry-bulb temperature is 76.3°F. The total cooling capacity value is interpolated from OEM performance data values (see Figure 5-8).

Total Btuh = 42,880
Sensible Btuh = Equal to, or close to, total capacity.
Latent Btuh = Zero for a dry cooling coil

Check for Adequate Capacity at Altitude

The equipment has 42,880 Btuh of total cooling capacity at sea level (OEM data is for sea level). Per Figure A5-3, the altitude adjustment factor for 3,000 Feet is 0.95, so the adjusted capacity is about 40,736 Btuh. Since the coil is dry, the sensible capacity is about 40,736 Btuh.

TC at altitude = 42,880 x 0.95 = 40,736 Btuh
SC at altitude = 40,736 Btuh

Job Site Performance

The total cooling load is 30,145 Btuh, so there is 10,591 Btuh of excess cooling capacity. The 048 size is an acceptable solution for heat pump equipment. The practitioner has the option to search for equipment that has more excess cooling capacity, subject to the 15,000 Btuh limit.

Square Feet per Ton Values

Square feet per ton values are a cooling issue. They are not relevant to heat equipment that is sized for more compressor heating capacity.

5-13 Moderate Latent Load Applications

A cooling-only, or a Condition A heat pump application may have a relatively high, to very high, *Manual J* sensible heat ratio (in the 0.85 to 0.94 range). This situation requires cooling equipment that has a compatible coil sensible heat ratio, when operating at summer design conditions.

- Blower speed setting options allow some manipulation of blower Cfm per job site ton, and coil sensible heat ratio.
- A larger nominal evaporator capacity, vs. the nominal condenser capacity, may produce a significant increase in the cooling coil sensible heat ratio.
- See Section A1-7 and Appendix 3.

5-14 Multi-Speed Equipment Performance

Figure 5-9 shows expanded cooling performance data for two-speed equipment. The data for full compressor speed, and the associated range of blower speeds, are used to select and size equipment. Therefore, the equipment section and sizing procedure for multi- speed equipment is identical to the procedure used for single-speed equipment.

| Two-Speed, 036 Size, Stage 2 at 1,200 Cfm ||||||
| OAT °F | EWB °F | Total Btuh | Sensible Btuh vs. EDB °F ||| Compr KW |
			74	76	78	
85	59	36.4	30.0	32.1	34.2	2.33
	63	38.8	25.7	27.8	29.9	2.36
	67	41.4	21.0	23.1	25.2	2.40
90	59	33.8	28.8	31.0	33.1	2.35
	63	36.2	24.6	26.7	28.8	2.39
	67	38.7	19.9	22.1	24.2	2.44
95	59	31.3	27.7	29.8	31.5	2.37
	63	33.6	23.5	25.6	27.8	2.42
	67	36.0	18.9	21.0	23.1	2.48
100	59	28.7	26.6	28.7	29.5	2.39
	63	30.9	22.4	24.6	26.7	2.45
	67	33.3	17.9	20.0	22.1	2.52

Net capacities (blower heat deducted)
Blower Cfm = 1,050; TC adjustment 0.99; SC adjustment = 0.95
Blower Cfm = 1,350; TC adjustment 1.01; SC adjustment = 1.05
Indoor blower 280 Watts; Outdoor fan 240 Watts

| Two-Speed, 036 Size, Stage 1 at 800 Cfm ||||||
| OAT °F | EWB °F | Total Btuh | Sensible Btuh vs. EDB °F ||| Compr KW |
			74	76	78	
85	59	20.0	18.3	19.7	20.4	1.09
	63	21.5	15.5	16.9	18.4	1.11
	67	23.0	12.5	13.9	15.3	1.13
90	59	18.8	17.8	18.9	19.4	1.15
	63	20.2	15.0	16.4	17.9	1.17
	67	21.7	12.0	13.4	14.8	1.19
95	59	17.5	17.3	17.9	18.4	1.21
	63	18.9	14.5	15.9	17.3	1.23
	67	20.4	11.5	12.9	14.3	1.26
100	59	16.3	16.5	16.9	17.4	1.27
	63	17.7	14.0	15.4	16.8	1.30
	67	19.1	11.0	12.4	13.8	1.33

Net capacities (blower heat deducted)
Blower Cfm = 1,050; TC adjustment 0.99; SC adjustment = 0.94
Blower Cfm = 1,350; TC adjustment 1.01; SC adjustment = 1.06
Indoor blower 80 Watts; Outdoor fan 230 Watts

Figure 5-9

For heat pumps, heating capacity for full compressor speed is used to draw the thermal balance point diagram.

5-15 Variable-Speed Equipment Performance

Figure 5-10 shows expanded cooling performance data for variable-speed equipment. Variable-speed equipment may operate at a maximum compressor speed, a minimum speed, or at any intermediate speed. The maximum and minimum compressor speeds are determined by the OEM's design and controls.

It may be that maximum compressor speed is the speed used for advertising the AHRI total cooling capacity value (full capacity), or the maximum speed may be higher than the speed used for advertising the AHRI total cooling capacity value (enhanced capacity). Expanded cooling performance data for full capacity (compressor operating at the AHRI rating speed), is used to select and size equipment. Therefore, the equipment section and sizing procedure for variable-speed equipment is identical to the procedure used for single-speed equipment.

Heat pump balance point diagrams, and supplemental electric coil size, are normally based on expanded heating performance data for the compressor speed that is used for the AHRI rating test that produces the advertised compressor heating capacity value for a 47°F outdoor air temperature, or a 70°F entering water temperature.

For single-speed equipment, there is only one compressor speed. The maximum available compressor speed applies to staged equipment. For variable-speed equipment, this may be the compressor speed for the AHRI rating test for heating, or the compressor may be able to operate at a higher speed (enhanced speed).

When applicable, expanded heating performance data for enhanced speed is used for balance point diagrams, and for supplemental electric coil sizing, providing that enhanced speed is continuously available for an unlimited amount of time.

5-16 Product Comparison Study

Sections 5-17, 5-18 and 5-19 compare the performance of single-speed equipment, two-speed equipment, and variable-speed equipment. These sections are an addendum to the example problems in Sections 5-10 through 5-12. A review of the application issues is provided here:

- Fayetteville has considerable summer humidity and moderate winter weather. The sizing limits for cooling-only equipment, and for a Condition A heat pump apply to this location (one rule for both types of equipment). An equipment capacity adjustment is not required for 1,251 feet of elevation.

- Brunswick has oppressive summer humidity and mild winter weather. The sizing limits for cooling-only equipment, and for a Condition A heat pump apply to this location (one rule for both types of equipment). An equipment capacity adjustment is not required for 20 feet of elevation.

- Boise has no latent cooling load and cold winter weather. The sizing limits for cooling-only equipment, and for a Condition B heat pump apply to this location (one rule for cooling-only equipment, and a different rule for heat pump equipment). An equipment capacity adjustment is required for 2,838 feet of elevation.

| Variable-Speed, 036 Size, Maximum; 1,240 to 1,120 Cfm ||||||
| OAT °F Cfm | EWB °F | Total Btuh | Sensible Btuh vs. EDB °F ||| System KW |
			72	75	78	
85 1,240	57	34.03	26.01	29.02	32.03	2.12
	63	34.19	24.81	27.82	30.83	2.12
	67	36.98	21.10	24.11	27.12	2.07
95 1,200	57	32.35	24.33	27.34	30.35	2.46
	63	32.33	23.62	26.63	39.64	2.46
	67	35.00	19.88	22.89	25.90	2.41
105 1,120	57	30.32	22.30	25.31	28.32	2.83
	63	30.31	21.96	24.97	28.98	2.83
	67	32.86	18.16	21.17	24.18	2.79

| Variable-Speed, 036 Size, Minimum; 500 Cfm ||||||
| OAT °F | EWB °F | Total Btuh | Sensible Btuh vs. EDB °F ||| System KW |
			72	75	78	
85	57	13.73	10.39	11.64	12.90	0.74
	63	13.68	10.09	11.34	12.59	0.74
	67	14.82	8.54	9.79	11.05	0.71
95	57	13.07	9.73	10.98	12.24	0.89
	63	12.89	9.76	11.01	12.26	0.90
	67	13.97	8.22	9.47	10.73	0.87
105	57	15.18	11.84	13.09	14.35	1.45
	63	15.56	10.91	12.16	13.41	1.44
	67	16.92	9.39	10.64	11.90	1.41

Net capacities (blower heat deducted)
System KW is for all indoor and outdoor components.
Interpolation is acceptable, extrapolation not allowed.

Figure 5-10

Performance Data for Reduced Speed

Entering Air Condition for Reduced Speed

When using low or minimum speed data, a blower Cfm value for low-capacity is used to calculate entering air dry-bulb and wet-bulb temperatures (when they are affected by a return duct load, and/or an outdoor air mixing load), and to determine the corresponding values for sensible and latent capacity.

Indoor Humidity Control

Expanded cooling performance data for less than full capacity is not used for equipment sizing, but this data is useful for comparing the latent cooling capacity for continuous operation at reduced speed with the *Manual J* latent load. This provides important, but incomplete evidence that two-speed and variable-speed equipment controls indoor humidity at part-load better than single-speed equipment. A complete investigation would consider runtime fractions and down time fractions for all part-load scenarios

- Equipment is sized for the same structure built in the noted locations (Figure A19-2 shows the construction details). Difference in the cooling loads and equipment size are due to the difference in summer design conditions.
- The load calculations for the example dwelling contain no buffers or factors of safety for any step of the procedure (see the square foot per *Manual J* ton values in Sections 5-10 through 5-12). This is important, because equipment sizing procedures must be applied to aggressive and accurate use of the *Manual J* load calculation procedures.

5-17 Compare Fayetteville Equipment

For Fayetteville, Figure 5-11 (next page) compares performance for three single-speed products of the same nominal size, for two-speed products in different sizes, and for a variable-speed product in three sizes. Related commentary is provided here.

Single-Speed Equipment

For single-speed equipment, products supplied by three different OEMs in the 042-042 size comply with equipment sizing requirements.

- Excess total cooling capacity for all three products is very close to 1.00, so total cooling capacity is right on target. All three units pass the excess total capacity test.
- All three units have more than adequate latent capacity for 50% RH indoors. The latent capacity vs. latent load ratios for OEMs A, B and C are 1.31, 1.29 and 1.11.
- The sensible capacity vs. sensible load ratios for OEMs A, B and C are 0.99, 0.97 and 1.00.
- OEM-C equipment would be the better choice for a less humid climate. Notice that it has less latent capacity and more sensible capacity than the OEM-A and OEM-B equipment.

Two-Speed Equipment

For two-speed equipment, OEM-D equipment in the 048-048 size; and OEM-E equipment in the 036-036, and 048-048-b sizes comply with equipment sizing requirements.

- OEM-D equipment in the 048-048 size has a 1.12 over-size factor, the latent capacity vs. latent load ratio is 1.52, and the sensible capacity vs. sensible load ratio is 1.10. All the ratios are in range, so this equipment is comparable with the application.
- OEM-E equipment in the 036-036 size has a 0.95 over-size factor, the latent capacity vs. latent load ratio is 1.12, and the sensible capacity vs. sensible load ratio is 0.93. All the ratios are in range, so this equipment is comparable with the application.

summarized by a bin-hour calculation or an hourly simulation, for various climates, for various construction practices.

- In general, latent capacity decreases at a lower compressor speed, but the latent cooling load may hold at, or near, the design load as the sensible load decreases (see Section 1-1).
- Single-stage equipment has no latent capacity when the compressor is off. Then when equipment cycles on, the effective latent capacity for the on-cycle is significantly degraded by the start-up transient (see Figure 1-7). This is also true when staged or variable-speed equipment cycles off.
- Staged or variable-speed equipment operates for more summer hours because it cycles or modulates between low and high capacity. The noted start-up transient penalty does not apply to this mode of operation.
- Practitioners can get a feel for moisture removal effectiveness at part-load by comparing latent capacity at low or minimum speed to the *Manual J* design value for latent load.

It is mathematically possible to compare indoor relative humidity drift for singe speed equipment with the drift for multi-speed or variable-speed equipment, but this goes beyond Manual S procedures.

Energy and Op-Cost Calculations

For multi-stage equipment, staged cooling capacity and KW maps may be used in a binary manner for bin-hour calculations, and for hourly simulations.

- The equipment cycles between stages when the load is equal to or greater than stage 1 capacity.
- Figure 1-7 behavior applies when the equipment cycles between stage 1 and off.

For modulating equipment, cooling capacity and KW maps for minimum speed and maximum speed may be used in an incremental manner for bin-hour calculations, and for hourly simulations.

- Btuh output and KW input can easily be estimated for intermediate compressor speeds when the performance vs. speed relation is approximately linear as compressor speed varies from minimum to maximum; ask the OEM about this.
- It may be that the OEM has performance vs. compressor speed curves or tables. When so, use this information (mandatory, when performance vs. speed is significantly non-linear).

Fayetteville, AR
Total load = 39,540 Btuh, Sensible load = 33,954 Btuh, Latent Load for 50% RH = 5,586 Btuh

OEM	Speed	Size and Mode	Blower Cfm	EWB / EDB (°F)	OSF	Excess Latent Btuh	Applied Capacity (Btuh) Total	Sensible	Latent	Applied Coil SHR
A	Single	042-042	1,400	63.4 / 76.5	1.01	1,735	39,934	32,613	7,321	0.84
B	Single	042-042	1,400	63.4 / 76.5	0.99	1,623	39,175	32,778	6,398	0.84
C	Single	042-042	1,400	63.4 / 76.5	1.01	589	39,925	34,044	5,881	0.85
D	Two	036-036 Hi	1,200	63.6 / 76.8	0.83	517	32,970	27,126	5,845	0.82
D	Two	048-048 Hi	1,400	63.4 / 76.5	1.12	2,918	44,279	37,235	7,045	0.84
E	Two	036 -036 Hi	1,400	63.6 / 76.5	0.95	665	37,500	31,582	5,918	0.84
E	Two	036-042 Hi	1,400	63.4 / 76.5	0.95	-1,063	37,560	33,037	4,523	0.88
E	Two	048-048-a Hi	1,600	63.3 / 76.4	1.24	3,473	49,225	41,902	7,323	0.85
E	Two	048-048-b Hi	1,380	63.4 / 76.5	1.19	4,563	47,250	39,383	7,867	0.83
F	Variable	036-036 Max	1,200	63.6 / 76.8	0.85	-1,214	33,589	29,216	4,372	0.87
F	Variable	048-048 Max	1,500	63.3 / 76.4	1.13	561	44,792	38,925	5,866	0.87
F	Variable	060-060 Max	1,850	63.2 / 76.2	1.33	2,916	52,632	45,588	7,044	0.87

1) For equipment size, the first number applies to the outdoor unit, and the second number applies to the indoor unit (042-042, for example).
2) Excess latent Btuh is for conditioned space at 50% RH. For applied capacity, half of the excess latent capacity is added to sensible capacity, the other half causes space humidity to be less than 50% RH, which causes the applied latent load to be more than 5,586 Btuh.
3) For two-speed and variable-speed equipment, size limits apply to expanded performance data for full capacity.

Figure 5-11

- OEM-E equipment in the 048-048-b size has a 1.19 over-size factor, the latent capacity vs. latent load ratio is 1.82, and the sensible capacity vs. sensible load ratio is 1.16. The total capacity and sensible capacity ratios are in range, but the latent capacity ratio is excessive, so the choice is between the other two products.

- The choice between OEM-D 048-048 and OEM-E 036-036 depends on the philosophy of the system designer.

  Some prefer equipment that is slightly undersized for improved part-load humidity control, some prefer a sensible capacity cushion.

  Both products are compatible with this application.

Variable-Speed Equipment

For variable-speed equipment, OEM-F equipment in the 048-048 size has a 1.13 over-size factor, the latent capacity vs. latent load ratio is 1.10, and the sensible capacity vs. sensible load ratio is 1.18. These are attractive ratios, so this equipment is comparable with the application.

5-18 Compare Brunswick Equipment

For Brunswick, Figure 5-12 compares performance for three single-speed products of the same nominal size, for two-speed products in different sizes, and for a variable-speed product in two sizes. Related commentary is provided here.

Single-Speed Equipment

For single-speed equipment, products supplied by three different OEMs in the 042-042 size comply with the equipment sizing requirements.

- Excess total cooling capacity ranges from 1.05 to 1.07, so all three units pass the total capacity test.

- OEM-A has just enough latent capacity for 50% RH indoors. Units B and C are short of latent capacity. The latent capacity vs. latent load ratios for OEMs A, B and C are 1.02, 0.80 and 0.88.

- The sensible capacity vs. sensible load ratios for OEMs A, B and C are 1.08 1.12 and 1.12

- OEM-A equipment is perfect for this application, based on 50% RH indoors. Units B and C may, or may not, qualify, when the *Manual J* design value for indoor humidity is increased to 55% RH.

Note that Manual J, Table 1A and Table 1B and related Manual J procedures support load calculations for 55% RH indoors. Therefore, equipment that fails the latent capacity test for 50% RH indoors may have adequate latent capacity when the Manual J latent load is recalculated for 55% RH indoors. It follows that excess latent capacity for a latent load based on 55% RH indoors will cause the indoor humidity to be less than 55% RH when the equipment operates continuously for summer design conditions. However, part-load humidity control for a 55% RH design will not be as good as

OEM	Speed	Size and Mode	Blower Cfm	EWB / EDB (°F)	OSF	Excess Latent Btuh	Applied Capacity (Btuh)			Applied Coil SHR
							Total	Sensible	Latent	
A	Single	042-042	1,400	63.9 / 76.3	1.06	152	40,646	31,768	8,877	0.78
B		042-042	1,400	63.9 / 76.3	1.05	-1,733	40,002	32,934	7,068	0.82
C		042-042	1,400	63.9 / 76.3	1.07	-1,047	40,740	32,986	7,754	0.81
D	Two	036-036 Hi	1,200	64.2 / 76.6	0.88	-1,326	33,714	26,239	7,475	0.78
		048-048 Hi	1,400	63.9 / 76.3	1.18	1,341	45,176	37,705	9,472	0.79
		048-048 Hi	1,200	64.2 / 76.6	1.15	2,758	44,114	33,934	10,180	0.77
E		036-036 Hi	1,260	64.2 / 76.6	0.99	-359	37,658	29,216	8,442	0.78
		036-042 Hi	1,400	63.9 / 76.3	1.00	-2,722	38,310	32,231	6,079	0.84
		036-042 Hi	1,200	64.2 / 76.6	0.97	-1,631	37,084	29,914	7,170	0.81
		048-048-a Hi	1,600	63.8 / 76.2	1.31	2,105	50,100	40,246	9,854	0.80
		048-048-b Hi	1,380	63.9 / 76.3	1.26	2,939	48,063	37,792	10,270	0.79
F	Variable	036-036 Max	1,200	64.2 / 76.6	0.90	-3,226	34,271	28,697	5,575	0.84
		048-048 Max	1,500	63.8 / 76.2	1.19	-293	45,664	37,156	8,508	0.81

Brunswick, GA
Total load = 38,212 Btuh, Sensible load = 29,413 Btuh, Latent Load for 50% RH = 8,801 Btuh

1) For equipment size, the first number applies to the outdoor unit, and the second number applies to the indoor unit (042-042, for example).
2) Excess latent Btuh is for conditioned space at 50% RH. For applied capacity, half of the excess latent capacity is added to sensible capacity, the other half causes space humidity to be less than 50% RH, which causes the applied latent load to be more than 5,586 Btuh.
3) For two-speed and variable-speed equipment, size limits apply to expanded performance data for full capacity.

Figure 5-12

the control provided by a 50% RH design; because, for a 60% RH limit, there is less room humidity drift when the design is based on 55% RH vs. 50% RH.)

Two-Speed Equipment

For two-speed equipment, OEM-D equipment in the 048-048 size operating at 1,400 Cfm or 1,200 Cfm, complies with equipment sizing requirements, as does the OEM-E equipment in the 036-036 size.

- OEM-D equipment in the 048-048 size operating at 1,400 Cfm just passes the total capacity test (1.18 excess vs. 1.20 limit), has excess latent capacity for 50% RH indoors. The latent capacity vs. latent load ratio is 1.15, and the sensible capacity vs. sensible load ratio is 1.21. This is an acceptable solution.

- OEM-D equipment in the 048-048 size operating at 1,200 Cfm has slightly better numbers. The OSF value is 1.15, the latent capacity vs. latent load ratio is 1.31, and the sensible capacity vs. sensible load ratio is 1.15. This is an acceptable solution.

- OEM-E equipment in the 036-036 size passes the total cooling capacity test (OSF = 0.99), and has adequate latent capacity for 50% RH indoors (the –359 Btuh deficiency is trivial). The latent capacity vs. latent load ratio is 0.96, and the sensible capacity vs. sensible load ratio is 0.99. This is an excellent solution.

- The other four examples of OEM E equipment either have deficient latent capacity for 50% RH indoors, or excessive total capacity.

Variable-Speed Equipment

OEM-F provides one exhibit of expanded performance data for outdoor and indoor units in the 036-036 sizes, and one exhibit for outdoor and indoor units in the 048-048 sizes. This data shows that both products have certain performance deficiencies or excesses.

- The 036-036 size barely passes the total capacity test with an OSF of 0.90. However, it does not have enough latent capacity for 50% RH indoors.

- The 048-048 size at maximum speed barely passes total capacity test with an OSF of 1.19, and it has enough latent capacity for 50% RH indoors (the –293 Btuh deficiency is trivial). The latent capacity vs. latent load ratio is 0.97, and the sensible capacity vs. sensible load ratio is 1.26. This is an acceptable solution.

5-19 Compare Boise Equipment

Latent capacity is not an issue for Boise, so Figure 5-13 compares performance for one single-speed product in four sizes, for two dual-speed products in two sizes, and for a variable-speed product in three sizes. Related commentary is provided here.

Section 5

OEM	Speed	Size and Mode	Blower Cfm	EWB / EDB (°F)	OSF	Excess Total Btuh	Applied Capacity (Btuh) at 3,000 Ft			Applied Coil SHR
							Total	Sensible	Latent	
A	Single	036-036	1,200	Use the total cooling capacity value. For a dry-coil. Sensible capacity equals total capacity. Latent capacity is zero.	0.99	-296	31,420	31,420	dry-coil	1.0
		042-042	1,400		1.16	4,819	36,880	26,880		
		048-048	1,600		1.35	10,591	42,880	42,880		
		060-060	2,000		1.66	19,749	52,520	52,520		
D	Two	036-036 Hi	1,200		1.00	-150	31,574	31,574		
		048-048 Hi	1,400		1.32	9,613	41,851	41,851		
E		036-036 Hi	1,260		1.09	2,644	32,789	32,789		
		048-048-a Hi	1,450		1.42	12,581	42,726	42,726		
F	Variable	036-036 Max	1,325		1.02	747	30,892	30,892		
		048-048 Max	1,550		1.36	10,913	41,058	41,058		
		060-060 Max	1,850		1.60	18,099	48,244	48,244		

Boise, ID (2,838 Feet)
Total load = 30,145 Btuh, Sensible load = 30,145, Btuh, Latent Load for 45% RH = Negative

1) For equipment size, the first number applies to the outdoor unit, and the second number applies to the indoor unit (042-042, for example).
2) For two-speed and variable-speed equipment, size limits apply to expanded performance data for full capacity.

Figure 5-13

Single-Speed Equipment

For single-speed, cooling-only equipment, the 036-036 size is almost a perfect match for the cooling load. This unit will provide the best air distribution effectiveness because blower operating hours are maximized. For heat pump equipment, the 048-048 size reduces annual energy use, and complies with the 15,000 Btuh limit on excess cooling capacity.

Two-Speed Equipment

For two-speed, cooling-only equipment, the OEM-D 036-036 size is a perfect match for the cooling load. This unit will provide the best air distribution effectiveness because blower operating hours are maximized. For cooling-only, the OEM-E equipment in the 036-036 size is almost as good (a 1.00 OSF for OEM-D equipment vs. the 1.09 OSF for the OEM-E equipment).

For heat pump equipment, the 048-048 sizes from OEM-D and OEM-E reduce annual energy use, and comply with the 15,000 Btuh limit on excess cooling capacity. Note that the OEM-E equipment should be a little more efficient than the OEM-D product (12,581 Btuh of excess capacity for OEM-E vs. 9,613 Btuh of excess capacity for OEM-D).

Variable-Speed Equipment

For variable-speed, cooling-only equipment, the 036-036 size is almost a perfect match for the cooling load. This unit will provide the best air distribution effectiveness because blower operating hours are maximized. For heat pump equipment, the 048-048 size reduces annual energy use, and complies with the 15,000 Btuh limit on excess cooling capacity.

Section 5

Section 6
Central Ducted Air-Air Heat Pump Heating Examples

Heat pump equipment is sized for cooling, as demonstrated by the Section 5 examples. After make, model and size have been determined, the OEM's expanded performance data for heating is used to evaluate heating performance, as explained and demonstrated here.

6-1 Balance Point Diagram

A thermal balance point diagram compares compressor heating capacity with the dwelling's heating load, as a function of outdoor air temperature. The thermal balance point (TBP) is the outdoor air temperature that produces equivalence between compressor heating capacity and building heating load. When the outdoor air temperature is at the winter design value (per *Manual J* procedures, or local code mandate), the difference between building heating load and compressor heating capacity determines the supplemental heat requirement. These concepts are summarized by Figure 6-1.

- The heating load is represented by a dot on the graph. The co-ordinates of the dot are determined by the *Manual J* heating load value and the winter design value for outdoor air temperature (about 56,000 Btuh at 13°F for this example).

- When the design value for indoor air temperature is 70°F, the default outdoor air temperature for no heating load is 65°F.

- Building performance is modeled by a straight line from the heating load dot to zero load at 65°F.

- The compressor heating capacity curve is produced by plotting the OEM's heating capacity vs. outdoor air temperature values.

- For variable-speed equipment, heating performance data for enhanced compressor speed may be used to draw the heating capacity curve, even when the equipment size for cooling has been determined for a slower compressor speed.

- Some OEMs provide compressor heating capacity graphs. When this is the case, the building performance line is conveniently superimposed on a copy of the OEM's graph.

- The compressor heating capacity curve should have a defrost knee. When it does, it may, or may not, be for the frosting condition produced by the local weather (see Figure A1-25).

- The thermal balance point depends on the shape of the defrost knee. The default balance point is for the OEM's defrost knee.

Thermal Balance Point Caveats

The default outdoor air temperature for no heating load simulates heat added by solar and/or internal loads when the outdoor temperature is warmer than the winter design temperature. The resulting thermal balance point may, or may not, approximate the average balance point value for the heating season.

When the design value for indoor air temperature is more or less than 70°F, the default outdoor air temperature for no heating load is more or less (by the same amount) than the 65°F default for no heating load.

Since the building heating load-line runs through the actual *Manual J* heating load, the supplemental heat calculation is for no heat added by solar effects and internal loads.

The actual outdoor air temperature for no heating load continuously varies, depending on the momentary values for the solar load and the internal load. For a 70°F indoor temperature, this may range from 70°F to less than 60°F, depending on combined size of the solar and internal loads. Momentary balance point values must be used for energy calculations (bin-hour method or hourly simulation).

Equipment must not be sized to obtain an arbitrary thermal balance point value. (There may be summer humidity control issues, and there is a return on investment question. A simplified rule of thumb cannot possibly apply to all local and regional housing stock, and it's equipment.)

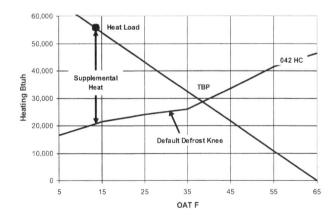

Figure 6-1

- Supplemental coil heat must be locked out when the outdoor air temperature is above the thermal balance point. For a control that monitors outdoor air temperature, the default thermal balance point may be used for this purpose.
- Microprocessor controls continually evaluate the momentary thermal balance point value and control the use of supplemental heat accordingly.
- Momentary balance point values that are sensitive to momentary solar and internal loads, and to momentary frosting conditions, must be used for energy calculations (bin-hour method or hourly simulation).

6-2 Electric Coil Heat

Supplemental electric coil heat is required when the outdoor air temperature is below the thermal balance point. The maximum amount of supplemental heat depends on information obtained from a thermal balance point diagram (see Figure 6-1).

Emergency heat is the total amount of electric coil heat. This may equal to, or greater than, the amount of supplemental heat, depending on local code/regulation, or practitioner-owner agreement when there is no code/regulation requirement.

The sizing value for emergency heating capacity is 85% of the design value for the winter heating load. This 85% rule is superseded by a local code or regulation that provides different guidance. When the balance point diagram value for supplemental heat is larger than the sizing value for emergency heat, the total capacity of the electric heating coil is determined by the supplemental heat requirement.

When the supplemental heat requirement is relatively large, electric coil heating capacity should be activated in stages. When the difference between the amount of emergency heat and the design value for supplemental heat is relatively large, the increment of heating capacity not needed for normal operation should be on a separate electrical circuit that is activated by a manual switch.

Electric heating coil capacity and staging decisions depend on standard sizes offered by the OEM. Table N2-3 and Appendix 14 provide relevant procedures.

6-3 Heating Performance Examples

The heating performance examples in this section are a continuation of the Section 5 equipment selection/sizing examples for a surrogate dwelling built in a warm humid location; a warm, very humid location; and a dry summer, cold winter location (see Sections 5-10, 5-11 and 5-12). The intent is to demonstrate the construction and use of thermal balance point diagrams. Therefore, the solution for an example problem is not a general solution for the housing stock in a given location, as explained here:

- The outdoor design condition for winter heating does not depend on the dwelling's attributes and the HVAC system's attributes. So this value is common to the housing stock in a given location.
- The sensible heating load for the winter design condition does depend on the dwelling's features and attributes, and depends on the HVAC system loads for air distribution and engineered ventilation. So this value is not common to the housing stock in a given location.
- For a given nominal size, expanded heating performance data values may vary significantly for the same set of operating circumstances, depending on the brand name, the outdoor model, the indoor model, and the blower Cfm. This is a case-by-case issue.
- Therefore, practitioners must apply *Manual J* and *Manual S* procedures to the actual dwelling in the actual location when selecting and sizing a specific piece of equipment.

6-4 Balanced Climate Example

Per Section 5-10, a Condition A heat pump in the 042 size is compatible with the *Manual J* cooling loads and the attributes of Fayetteville, AR, weather. Figure 6-2 (next page) shows the heating performance data for this equipment. The *Manual J* heating load and corresponding equipment operating conditions are summarized here:

Sensible heating load = 56,236 Btuh
Altitude = 1,251 Feet; Figure A5-1 ACF = 0.96
Outdoor air temperature = 13°F db
Indoor conditions: 70°F db, no humidification
Sensible return duct load (Section A2-3) = 2,272 Btuh
Outdoor air = 75 Cfm; Sensible Eff. for heating = 0.55

Entering Dry-Bulb Temperature

Return duct loads and outdoor air loads decrease the entering dry-bulb temperature. Per Section A2-3 procedures, the sensible return duct load is 2,272 Btuh.

When Sections A2-4 and A2-7 procedures are applied to the return duct load and outdoor air load (using altitude psychrometrics), the dry-bulb temperature of the entering air is 67.1°F for 1,400 blower Cfm.

Altitude = 1,251 feet
Blower Cfm = 1,400; return Cfm = 1,325; OA Cfm = 75
Dry-bulb °F at return grille = 70.0
Dry-bulb °F out of return duct = 68.463
Entering (mixed air) dry-bulb °F = 67.126 (67.1)

Interpolated Heating Capacity Values

The design value for blower Cfm is 1,400. The design value for entering air temperature is 67°F. Applied heating capacity values for 67°F are interpolated from OEM performance data values (see Figure 6-2).

Supplemental Heat

Figure 6-3 shows the balance point diagram for this application. The supplemental heat requirement is 35,536 Btuh. This is equivalent to 10.4 KW. A 10 KW coil is close enough, and it should be staged in 5 KW increments.

Default Thermal Balance Point

The default thermal balance point is about 37°F. Supplemental heat must be locked out when the outdoor air temperature is above 37°F. The balance point diagram shows that the second stage of supplemental heat should be locked out when the outdoor air temperature is above 26°F. Supplemental heating capacity may be activated by a simple outdoor air temperature sensor control that has manually adjusted set-points, or microprocessor control that evaluates the momentary need for electric coil heat.

Emergency Heat

The default value for emergency heat is 85% of the heating load. This is 47,701 Btuh, which is very close to 14 KW.

Auxiliary Heat

Because of standard sizes offered by this OEM, the total amount of electric coil heat is 15 KW. This is preferably split into two 5 KW coils (10 KW total) for supplemental heat, plus an additional 5 KW stage that should be activated by a manual switch.

6-5 Hot-Humid Climate Example

Per Section 5-11, a Condition A heat pump in the 042 size is compatible with the *Manual J* cooling loads and the attributes of Brunswick, GA, weather. Figure 6-2 shows the heating performance data for this equipment. The *Manual J* heating load and corresponding equipment operating conditions are summarized here:

Sensible heating load = 34,880 Btuh
Altitude = 20 Feet; Figure A5-1 ACF = 1.00
Outdoor air temperature = 34°F db
Indoor conditions: 70°F db, no humidification
Sensible return duct load (Section A2-3) = 1,155 Btuh
Outdoor air = 75 Cfm; Sensible Eff. for heating = 0.55

Entering Dry-Bulb Temperature

Return duct loads and outdoor air loads decrease the entering dry-bulb temperature. Per Section A2-3 procedures, the sensible return duct load is 1,155 Btuh.

When Sections A2-4 and A2-7 procedures are applied to the return duct load and outdoor air load (using altitude

Air-Air Heat Pump Heating Capacity (MBtuh) O42 Operating at 1.400 Cfm				
Outdoor Dry-Bulb (°F)	Entering Air Temperature (°F)			
	60	67	68.5	70
-3	12.8	12.6	12.5	12.5
2	15.4	15.1	15.1	15.0
7	18.0	17.7	17.6	17.5
12	20.6	20.2	20.1	20.0
17	23.2	22.7	22.6	22.5
22	24.2	23.7	23.6	23.5
27	25.2	24.6	24.5	24.4
32	26.2	25.6	25.5	25.4
37	27.2	26.6	26.5	26.4
42	28.2	27.6	27.5	27.4
47	38.6	37.8	37.7	37.5
52	41.2	40.4	40.2	40.0
57	43.8	42.3	42.7	42.5
62	46.4	45.4	45.2	45.0
67	48.9	47.9	47.7	47.5
Blower Cfm		1,225	1,400	1,575
Capacity adjustment		0.98	1.00	1.02

1) Heating values in the 17°F to 47°F range discounted for defrost cycles.
2) Heating values not adjusted (increased) for blower heat.

Figure 6-2

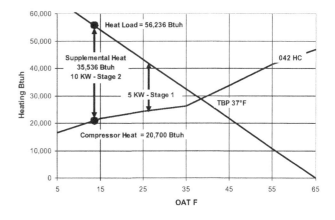

Figure 6-3

psychrometrics), the dry-bulb temperature of the entering air is 69.1°F for 1,400 blower Cfm.

Altitude = 1,251 feet
Blower Cfm = 1,400; return Cfm = 1,325; OA Cfm = 75
Dry-bulb °F at return grille = 70.0
Dry-bulb °F out of return duct = 69.250
Entering (mixed air) dry-bulb °F = 68.400 (68.4)

Section 6

Interpolated Heating Capacity Values

The design value for blower Cfm is 1,400. The design value for entering air temperature is 68.5°F. Applied heating capacity values for 68°F are interpolated from OEM performance data values (see Figure 6-2).

Supplemental Heat

Figure 6-4 shows the balance point diagram for this application. The supplemental heat requirement is 8,980 Btuh. This is equivalent to 2.6 KW. A 2.5 KW coil is close enough.

Default Thermal Balance Point

The default thermal balance point is about 41°F. Supplemental heat must be locked out when the outdoor air temperature is above 41°F. Supplemental heating capacity may be activated by a simple outdoor air temperature sensor control that has manually adjusted set-points, or microprocessor control that evaluates the momentary need for electric coil heat.

Emergency Heat

The default value for emergency heat is 85% of the heating load. This is 29,648 Btuh, which is about 8.7 KW.

Auxiliary Heat

Because of the OEM's standard sizes, the total amount of electric coil heat is 10 KW. This is preferably split into a 2.5 KW coil for supplemental heat, plus an additional 7.5 KW that should be activated by a manual switch.

6-6 Dry Summer Cold Winter Example

Per Section 5-12, a Condition B heat pump in the 048 size is compatible with the *Manual J* cooling loads and the attributes of Boise, ID, weather. Figure 6-5 shows the heating performance data for this equipment. The *Manual J* heating load and corresponding equipment operating conditions are summarized here:

Sensible heating load = 58,349 Btuh
Altitude = 2,838 Feet; Figure A5-1 ACF = 0.88
Outdoor air temperature = 9 °F db
Indoor conditions: 70°F db, no humidification
Sensible return duct load (Section A2-3) = 2,420 Btuh
Outdoor air = 75 Cfm; Sensible Eff. for heating = 0.55

Entering Dry-Bulb Temperature

Return duct loads and outdoor air loads decrease the entering dry-bulb temperature. Per Section A2-3 procedures, the sensible return duct load is 2,420 Btuh.

When Sections A2-4 and A2-7 procedures are applied to the return duct load and outdoor air load (using altitude psychrometrics), the dry-bulb temperature of the entering air is 69.1°F for 1,600 blower Cfm.

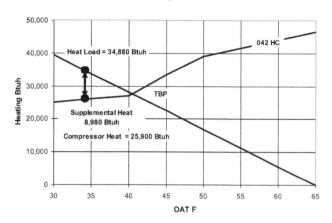

Figure 6-4

Air-Air Heat Pump Heating Capacity (MBtuh) O48 Operating at 1.600 Cfm				
Outdoor Dry-Bulb (°F)	Entering Air Temperature (°F)			
	60	67	70	75
-3	17.20	17.06	17.00	16.90
2	20.20	20.06	20.00	19.90
7	23.20	23.06	23.00	22.90
12	26.20	26.06	26.00	25.90
17	29.30	29.09	29.00	28.90
22	31.10	30.89	30.80	30.70
27	32.90	32.69	32.60	32.50
32	34.70	34.49	34.40	34.30
37	36.60	36.32	36.20	36.00
42	38.40	38.12	38.00	37.80
47	47.50	47.15	47.00	46.80
52	50.50	50.15	50.00	49.80
57	53.50	53.15	53.00	52.70
62	56.50	56.15	56.00	55.70
67	59.60	59.18	59.00	58.70
Blower Cfm		1,400	1,600	1,800
Capacity adjustment		0.98	1.00	1.02

1) Heating values in the 17°F to 47F range discounted for defrost cycles.
2) Heating values not adjusted (increased) for blower heat.

Figure 6-5

Altitude = 2,838 feet
Blower Cfm = 1,600; return Cfm = 1,525; OA Cfm = 75
Dry-bulb °F at return grille = 70.0
Dry-bulb °F out of return duct = 68.438
Entering (mixed air) dry-bulb °F = 67.184 (67.2)

Interpolated Heating Capacity Values

The design value for blower Cfm is 1,600. The design value for entering air temperature is 67°F. Applied heating capacity values for 67°F are interpolated from OEM performance data values (see Figure 6-5).

The defrost knee embedded in OEM data is for a default frosting potential. Since the Boise climate is very dry, the defrost knee for Boise is most likely less severe than the OEM's knee.

Altitude Adjustment

Heating performance data (Figure 6-5) is for sea level. Sea level capacity values must be adjusted when the installation's altitude exceeds 2,500 feet. Per Figure A5-1, the altitude adjustment factor for 3,000 Feet is 0.95,

Supplemental Heat

Figure 6-6 shows the balance point diagram for this application. The compressor heating capacity curve has been adjusted for altitude. The supplemental heat requirement is 35,338 Btuh. This is close to 10.0 KW, and it should be staged in 5 KW increments.

Default Thermal Balance Point

The default thermal balance point is about 33°F. Supplemental heat must be locked out when the outdoor air temperature is above 33°F. The balance point diagram shows that the second stage of supplemental heat should be locked out when the outdoor air temperature is above 21°F. Supplemental heating capacity may be activated by a simple outdoor air temperature sensor control that has manually adjusted set-points, or microprocessor control that evaluates the momentary need for electric coil heat.

The defrost knee embedded in OEM compressor heat data is for a default frosting potential. Since the Boise climate is very dry, the design thermal balance point value for Boise is most likely lower than indicated by OEM data.

Emergency Heat

The default value for emergency heat is 85% of the heating load. This is 49,597 Btuh, which about 14.5 KW.

Auxiliary Heat

Because of standard sizes offered by this OEM, the total amount of electric coil heat is 15 KW. This is preferably split into two 5 KW coils (10 KW total) for supplemental heat, plus an additional 5 KW stage that should be activated by a manual switch.

Compare 048 and 036 Sizes

Per Section 5-12, the 036 size was ideal for cooling, but the 048 size improves heating season efficiency for a

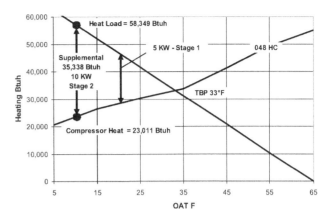

Figure 6-6

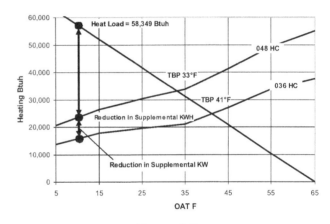

Figure 6-7

Condition B heat pump. Figure 6-7 compares the performance of the two sizes.

- The larger unit reduces the default thermal balance point by about 8°F.
- The larger unit reduces the design value for supplemental heat by about 2 KW.
- The graph area between the compressor heating curves, to the left of the heating load-line, represents the reduction in supplemental heat use. (Bin electric coil KWH equals bin KW times bin-hours; seasonal electric coil KWH equals the sum of the bin temperature KWH values.)
- The purpose of Figure 6-7 is to show tendencies. The magnitudes of noted benefit only apply to the particular dwelling and equipment used for the Boise, ID, example. The magnitudes of the noted benefit do not generally apply to Condition B housing stock. Each individual dwelling has it's own version of Figure 6-7.

Benefit of Excess Cooling Capacity

A crude bin-hour calculation provides a feel for the energy and operating cost benefit provided by the larger (048) unit. The output of this procedure is summarize by Figure 6-8 (Appendix 6 provides supporting detail). Accuracy is adequate for demonstrating concept viability, but for commercial purposes, a comprehensive bin-hour or hourly procedure should be used to estimate reductions in energy use and operating cost.

6-7 Multi-Speed and Variable-Speed Selection

The preceding examples show balance point diagrams and supplemental heat calculations for equipment that operates at one compressor speed. These concepts also apply to multi-speed equipment, and to variable-speed equipment. The design procedure requires:

- The heat pump equipment has been sized for cooling, and the amount of deficient, or excessive, cooling capacity fully complies with Section N2 procedures and limits, as demonstrated by Section 6 examples.

- Practitioner use of OEM expanded performance data for compressor heat, or a computerized calculation engine that generates equivalent information.

- For two-stage equipment, OEMs typically publish heating data for full capacity (stage 2 capacity), and for reduced capacity (stage 1 capacity).

- For variable-speed equipment, an OEM may publish heating data for the compressor speed used for the AHRI rating test for heating, and may provide heating data for enhanced compressor speed. There also may be heating data for low or minimum heating capacity.

- Expanded heating performance data for maximum, continuously available, compressor heat is used to draw the thermal balance point diagram.

Two-speed equipment has a full (stage-two) speed and a reduced (stage-one) speed. The heating performance data for full-speed is used for the balance point diagram.

Variable-speed equipment may have a minimum speed, and a full speed for the AHRI rating test. The heating performance data for full compressor speed is used for the balance point diagram.

A variable-speed compressor may operate at speeds that exceed value used for the AHRI rating test for heating. When this is the case, expanded heating performance data for enhanced compressor speed is used for the thermal balance point diagram, providing this feature is continuously available for an unlimited amount of time.

Benefit of Excess Capacity - Boise, ID, Example			
Nominal Size	Cooling KWH	Heating KWH	Annual KWH
036	3,239	26,197	29,436
048	4,066	20,351	24,417
Energy savings for larger size			5,019

1) Based on a crude bin-hour calculation (see Appendix 6).
2) Based on actual expanded performance data for a randomly selected OEM product. Published values for cooling and heating capacity were reduced by a factor of 0.95 to compensate for 3,000 feet of altitude.
3) For this product, total cooling Btuh per KW of input power was more for the 048 size, vs. the 036 size. Other products may have improved cooling efficiency for the larger size, or may have similar cooling efficiency for both sizes.
4) Indoor blower power is 500 Watts for both sizes. The blower cycles on-off with the compressor.
5) The KW for the 036 outdoor fan is 0.25, and 0.50 KW for the 048 outdoor fan.
6) KW inputs are for the compressor, indoor blower and outdoor fan. Cooling and heating capacity values are adjusted for the effect of the indoor blower.
7) The effect of conditional solar loads and internal gains for the heating and cooling seasons are crudely modeled by load vs. outdoor air temperature lines that run from the *Manual J* load for heating or cooling to zero load at 65°F outdoors.
8) Solar loads for temperature bins were not adjusted for cloud cover (Boise has about 43% sun for winter months, 65% sun for spring and fall, and 83% sun for summer months). This tends to reduce the bin cooling loads and increase the bin heating loads.
9) The *Manual J* internal loads were not scheduled for time of day. This tends to increase the bin cooling loads and decrease the bin heating loads.
10) The 036 size has 12.5 KW of supplemental heat, the 048 size has 10 KW of supplemental heat. Supplemental heat is locked out above the thermal balance point.
11) The AHRI SEER values for the 036 and 048 sizes are 13.0 and 13.5. The applied (bin calculation) values are 10.0 and 8.0.
12) The AHRI HSPF values for the 036 and 048 sizes are 7.7 and 8.0. The applied (bin calculation) values are 5.7 and 7.3.

Figure 6-8

- Heating performance values are for a blower Cfm listed in the OEM's expanded data table. The heating Cfm value (which may be the same as the cooling Cfm value) is used to determine entering air dry-bulb temperature when there is a return duct load, and/or an outdoor air mixing load, and it is used for duct sizing calculations.

6-8 Heating Performance for Two-Speed Equipment

Figure 6-9 (next page) shows a modified version of the OEM's compressor heating capacity data for two-speed equipment in the 048 size. For the Boise example, the 65°F and 70°F source data is interpolated for 69°F. The source data and the interpolated values are for sea level.

Section 6

Thermal Balance Points

Figure 6-10 shows the thermal balance point diagram for the 048 size equipment. For this diagram, compressor heating capacity is adjusted for altitude (0.95 capacity adjustment for Boise, ID, altitude).

Stage 1 capacity (low-speed) is adequate when the outdoor temperature is above 36°F, then the equipment cycles between stage 1 and stage 2 until the outdoor air temperature drops to 33°F, then stage 2 operates continuously when the outdoor air temperature is below 33°F.

The thermal balance point values for Figure 6-10 are approximate because the shape of the defrost knee for Boise, ID, weather will be different than the default knee embedded in the OEM's data.

Supplemental Heat

Stage two heating capacity is in effect when the outdoor air temperature is below 33°F. The size of the supplemental heat coil is based on the heating capacity curve for stage two.

6-9 Heating Performance for Variable-Speed Equipment

Figure 6-11 (next page) shows a portion of the OEM's compressor heating capacity data for variable-speed equipment in the 048 size. The 70°F data is for sea level.

Thermal Balance Points

Figure 6-12 (next page) shows compares the balance point diagram for variable-speed equipment in the 048 size with the balance point diagram for single-speed equipment in the 048 size (interpolated for 69°F, with a 0.95 capacity adjustment for Boise, ID, attitude). Note that the maximum available capacity curve for the variable-speed unit flattens out when the outdoor air temperature is less than 47°F, then starts to drop off below 15°F. This is because the compressor speeds up when the outdoor air temperature drops below 47°F, then maximum speed occurs when it is about 15°F outdoors.

Figure 6-13 (next page) shows heating capacity values for maximum and minimum compressor speed. Therefore, there is a thermal balance point for maximum speed, and a thermal balance point for minimum speed. When the outdoor air temperature is between these two balance points, compressor speed modulates so that momentary compressor heating capacity matches the momentary heating load, as demonstrated by Figure 6-13. Figure 6-13 also shows the behavior of a single-speed product in the 048 size.

- For single-speed equipment, heating capacity is what it is, depending on the outdoor air temperature. Capacity control is achieved by cycling the compressor when the outdoor air temperature is above the thermal balance point, then operation is continuous below the thermal balance point.

- Variable-speed equipment operates at minimum speed when the outdoor air temperature is above

Expanded Heating Performance Data Two-Speed Equipment — 048 Size Sea level; Entering dry-bulb temperature = 69°F				
OAT (°F)	1,600 Cfm		1,200 Cfm	
	High Btuh	High KW	Low Btuh	Low KW
-5	14,549	2.74	10,118	2.17
0	16,844	2.85	12,031	2.23
5	19,341	2.93	14,142	2.26
10	22,149	3.01	16,248	2.29
15	25,164	3.10	18,352	2.32
20	27,728	3.19	21,066	2.37
25	29,991	3.28	24,186	2.43
30	32,929	3.37	27,841	2.48
35	36,317	3.46	31,853	2.52
40	41,021	3.57	35,299	2.57
45	46,602	3.69	38,367	2.62
50	51,347	3.82	41,654	2.68
55	55,535	3.95	45,088	2.75
60	60,191	4.12	46,462	2.77
65	65,160	4.30	46,462	2.77

1) Sea level data interpolated for 69°F entering air temperature.
2) Heating capacity values include the effect of blower heat.
3) Heating capacity values adjusted for defrost cycle effect.
4) Blower heat and defrost adjustments are based on defaults that may, or may not, be appropriate for a specific application; therefore, the thermal balance point for an actual installation may be somewhat different than the value indicated by this data.
5) KW values are for compressor KW, indoor blower KW, and outdoor fan KW.
6) KW values do not include electric coil heat. Total system KW equals the listed KW value plus the KW for the electric coil.

Figure 6-9

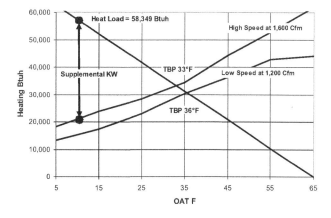

Figure 6-10

Section 6

Expanded Heating Performance Data Variable-Speed Equipment — 048 Size Sea level; Entering dry-bulb temperature = 70°F				
OAT (°F)	1,800 Cfm		600 to 800 Cfm	
	Max Btuh	Max KW	Min Btuh	Min KW
-10	21,735	3.08	13,893	2.09
-5	26,937	3.76	15,541	2.28
0	32,302	4.37	17,357	2.42
5	37,776	4.93	19,285	2.53
10	42,178	5.27	21,205	2.59
15	45,864	5.46	23,120	2.62
20	47,309	5.36	24,821	2.62
25	47,261	5.08	26,380	2.60
30	46,941	4.65	26,687	2.47
35	46,440	4.13	26,158	2.27
40	46,042	3.62	25,488	2.00
45	45,712	3.13	24,725	1.69
50	47,439	2.96	25,470	1.55
55	50,537	3.00	27,220	1.52
60	53,793	3.05	29,038	1.52
65	57,155	3.10	30,901	1.54
70	23,400	1.25	12,658	0.62

1) Use capacity adjustment factors (see ancillary data) for more or less blower Cfm, and/or for entering air other than 70°F.
2) Heating capacity values include the effect of blower heat.
3) Heating capacity values adjusted for defrost cycle effect.
4) Blower heat and defrost adjustments are based on defaults that may, or may not, be appropriate for a specific application; therefore, the thermal balance point for an actual installation may be somewhat different than the value indicated by this data.
5) KW values are for compressor KW, indoor blower KW, and outdoor fan KW.
6) KW values do not include electric coil heat. Total system KW equals the listed KW value plus the KW for the electric coil.
7) Interpolation is permitted, extrapolation is not recommended.

Figure 6-11

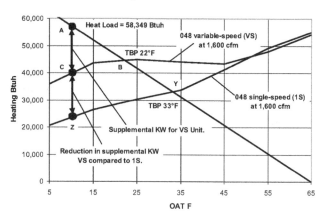

Figure 6-12

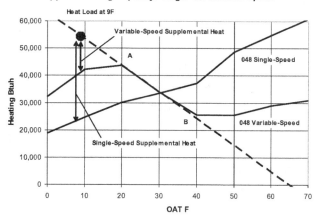

Figure 6-13

the thermal balance point for minimum speed. For this scenario, heating capacity is what it is, depending on the outdoor air temperature. Capacity control is achieved by cycling the compressor when the outdoor air temperature is above the thermal balance point for minimum speed (Figure 6-13, point B).

- The compressor starts to speed up when the outdoor air temperature drops below the thermal balance point for minimum speed, and compressor speed continuously increases as it gets colder outdoors. For this scenario, compressor heating capacity tracks the heating load (Figure 6-13, point B to point A.

- When it gets cold enough outdoors, the compressor is forced to operate continuously at maximum speed. Point A on Figure 6-13 is the thermal balance point for maximum speed.

- When outdoor air gets colder than the temperature that forces maximum compressor speed, compressor heating capacity starts to decrease as the outdoor air gets colder. The compressor operates continuously at maximum speed, and electric coil heat is required to maintain the desired space temperature.

Supplemental Heat

Figure 6-12 shows that he supplemental heat requirement (KW) for the variable-speed unit may be much smaller than for the single-speed unit. Also note that the variable-speed unit provides significant savings in electric coil energy (heating KWH for supplemental heat).

- Electric coil KWH for the variable-speed unit is related to the outdoor air temperature bin-hours associated with the ABC triangle.

- Electric coil KWH for the single-speed unit is related to the outdoor air temperature bin-hours associated with the AYZ triangle.
- Electric coil energy savings (KWH) is related to the difference in these triangles, which is obviously substantial for these particular products.
- However, total heating season KWH depends on compressor KWH plus electric coil KWH. So the sum of both of these bin-hour energy loads determines the heating season KWH used by a product.

6-10 Entering Air Temperature and Heating Capacity Depend on Blower Cfm

As indicated by Sections 6-7 through 6-9, compressor heating capacity depends on the heat sink temperature (outdoor air, for air-air equipment), blower Cfm, and entering dry-bulb temperature. However, blower Cfm for stage-one capacity, or for minimum variable-speed capacity, is typically much less than the blower Cfm for stage-two capacity, or maximum variable-speed capacity.

- Blower Cfm does not affect entering air temperature when there is no return duct load or outdoor air load because the entering dry-bulb temperature defaults to room temperature.
- Blower Cfm does affect entering air dry-bulb temperature when there is a return duct load, and/or an outdoor air mixing load, per Appendix 2 procedures.
- OEM data may show two or more blower speed options for a given compressor speed.
- When using maximum compressor speed data, a blower Cfm option for maximum compressor speed is used to calculate entering air temperature, and heating capacity.
- When using minimum compressor speed data, a blower Cfm option for minimum compressor speed is used to calculate entering air temperature, and heating capacity.

6-11 Use of Minimum Compressor Speed Data

As explained by Sections 6-8 and 6-9, heating performance data for stage 1 capacity, or for minimum variable-speed capacity, is not used to size supplemental heat. However, having maximum and minimum capacity lines on a balance point diagram is useful for making control decisions, and for energy calculations.

- The need for supplemental electric coil heat depends on the maximum compressor heating capacity line. For example, Figure 6-10 shows that electric coil heat must be locked out when the outdoor air temperature exceeds 33°F; and Figure 6-12 shows that electric coil heat must be locked out when the outdoor air temperature exceeds 22°F.
- For two-stage equipment, Figure 6-10 shows that the compressor cycles between stage 1 and stage 2 capacity when the outdoor air temperature is in the 33°F to 36°F range.
- For variable-speed equipment, Figure 6-13 shows that the compressor speed modulates between minim capacity and maximum capacity when the outdoor air temperature is in the 20°F to 40°F range.
- For two-stage equipment, stage 1 and stage 2 capacity maps for Btuh and KW are used in a binary (on-off) manner for bin-hour calculations, and for hourly simulations.
- For modulating equipment, minimum speed and maximum speed capacity maps for Btuh and KW are used in an incremental (graduated) manner for bin-hour calculations, and for hourly simulations.

This is relatively simple if compressor performance vs. compressor speed is relatively linear; if not, OEM data that relates performance to compressor speed is required.

Section 6

This section is not part of the this standard. It is merely informative and does not contain requirements necessary for conformance to the standard. It has not been processed according to the ANSI requirements for a standard, and may contain material that has not been subject to public review or a consensus process. Unresolved objectors on informative material are not offered the right to appeal at ACCA or ANSI.

Section 7

Central Ducted Furnace Examples

One selection/sizing procedure applies to all types of residential forced air furnaces. This section demonstrates procedure use.

7-1 Heating Load

The heating load for equipment selection/sizing is the block heating load for the rooms and spaces served by the equipment. This load is for the winter design temperature for outdoor air (per *Manual J* Table 1A or 1B, or code value), and the winter design temperature for indoor air (70°F per *Manual J*, or code value). Heat used for winter humidification is part of the block heating load when the furnace provides the heat for evaporation. The block heating load is not adjusted for internal gain, or for heat gain due to solar radiation.

7-2 Maximum Heating Capacity

Over-sized heating equipment causes equipment cycling (or throttling) on a winter design day, and reduces runtime for all part-load hours. This degrades air distribution effectiveness and occupant comfort, and provides no efficiency or economic advantage. Table N2-4 provides maximum heating capacity limits for furnaces, based on aggressive use of *Manual J* procedures (per Section N1-4).

7-3 Minimum Heating Capacity

Output heating capacity must be equal to, or greater than, the block heating load. For staged or modulating equipment, output heating capacity is for full capacity.

7-4 Blower Cfm

For heating-only, blower Cfm may be any value listed by the OEM's performance data (a mid-range value allows for field adjustment). For heating and cooling, the blower must be able to provide the design Cfm for cooling when it works against the airflow resistance produced by all the air-side components in the critical air circulation path (per the *Manual D*, Friction Rate Worksheet).

7-5 Air Temperature Limits

A cold entering air temperature, or low air temperature rise may cause condensation on equipment parts. Excessive air temperature rise may damage equipment parts (potentially deadly when the heat exchanger cracks). There is a high-limit for air temperature rise, and for discharge air temperature. The design must conform to OEM guidance pertaining to air temperature limits.

7-6 Equipment Selection Examples

The equipment selection examples in this section are for the heating and cooling loads produced by a surrogate dwelling built in warm, humid location; a warm, very humid location; and a dry summer, cold winter location. The intent is to demonstrate the equipment sizing procedure for furnaces. Therefore, the solution for an example problem is not a general solution for the housing stock in a given location or region, as explained here:

- The outdoor design condition for heating does not depend on dwelling's attributes and the HVAC system's attributes. So this value is common to the housing stock in a given location.

- The heating and cooling loads depend on dwelling's features and attributes, and the HVAC system loads for air distribution and engineered ventilation. So these values are not common to the housing stock in a given location.

- Dwellings with similar heating loads can have significantly different design values for cooling Cfm. So a furnace size for a given heating-cooling scenario does not apply to all of the housing stock in a given location.

- Furnace heating capacity vs. blower power may vary significantly from product to product. The limited amount of OEM data used for these examples does not represent the full range of possibilities.

- Therefore, practitioners must apply *Manual J* and *Manual S* procedures to the actual dwelling in the actual location when selecting and sizing equipment; and should consider the full range of products offered by OEMs.

7-7 Attributes of the Example Dwelling

The dwelling used for the cooling-only and heat pump examples (Sections 6 and 7) is used for these furnace heating, electric cooling examples. Envelope efficiency is good, but not exceptional. Glass area is modest. Attic ducts are insulated and sealed, but the workmanship is average. The dwelling has engineered ventilation with sensible heat recovery. Basic information is summarized below. Appendix 19 provides more detail.

- Slab on grade, one story, 3,300 SqFt (Figure A19-2 shows the floor plan).

- Two pane, clear glass, wood frame, tight fenestration. Fenestration area is 10.9 percent of the floor area. No AED excursion.

- Commonly used ceiling, wall and floor R-values.
- Average structural tightness.
- Attic ducts: R6, default sealed, 0.12/0.24 (Cfm/SqFt) in vented attic under a white shingle roof (*Manual J*, Table 4 Construction 16C).
- Engineered ventilation: 75 Cfm of outdoor air and 75 Cfm of exhaust though a sensible heat exchanger.
- Heat recovery effectiveness: 0.50 for cooling and 0.55 for heating.

7-8 Balanced Climate Humid Summer Example

The over-size limit from Table N2-4 applies to furnaces. When the furnace is equipped with a cooling coil, the over-size limit from Table N2-1 applies to cooling-only equipment. See Section 8 when dual fuel heating is provided by a furnace and a heat pump.

Heating Load and Operating Conditions

Furnace size is based on the *Manual J* heating load for Fayetteville, AR, as summarized below. Return duct loads and engineered ventilation details are relevant because they affect entering dry-bulb temperature, which affects leaving air temperature. The 0.96 altitude adjustment factor for 1,251 feet applies to *Manual J* calculations and to psychrometric calculations for entering air temperature (this adjustment is made for procedure consistency, even when the effect is small). Altitude also affects equipment performance (see Figure A5-3), but this effect is usually ignored for 2,500 Feet or less (an OEM may specify a different value for a particular product).

Altitude = 1,251 Feet; Figure A5-1 ACF = 0.96
Outdoor design temperature = 13°F
Indoor conditions: 70°F db; no humidification
Sensible heating load = 56,236 Btuh
Winter humidification load on furnace = None
Sensible return duct load (Section A2-3) = 2,272 Btuh
Outdoor air = 75 Cfm; Sensible eff. for heating = 0.55
Preferred furnace OSL = 1.40

Candidate XYZ Performance for Heating

Furnace performance data is searched for something close to 56,000 Btuh of output heating capacity for full burner capacity. Figure 7-1 shows actual heating performance data for a F80 size product that has one firing rate and three blower motor/wheel options. The 1.14 over-size factor complies with the 1.40 limit, and the temperature rise (TR) values for the models are acceptable, so all three products are tentatively acceptable for heating.

OSF = 64,000 / 56,236 = 1.14
TR (°F) = Output Btuh / (1.1 x ACF x Cfm)
Blower power must be adequate for the duct system.

Furnace Performance Data — OEM xyz			
Model	F80-OP1	F80-OP2	F80-OP3
Input Btuh	80,000	80,000	80,000
Output Btuh	64,000	64,000	64,000
Rise (°F)	50–80	30–60	25–55
AFUE	80%	80%	80%
Blower Watts	150	250	560
Wheel Size	9 × 7	10 × 7	11 × 10
Mid Cfm 0.50 IWC	681–809	1,008–1,147	1,674–1,933
Max Cfm 0.50 IWC	956	1,296	2,163
Max Cfm 0.70 IWC	803	1,189	2,026
Min Cfm 0.70 IWC	428	808	1,404

1) One-stage burner, PSC blower motor has 4 speed settings.
2) Blower data is for heat exchanger only, no filter, no AC coil.
3) Sea level performance.
4) Rise = Air temperature rise through heat exchanger.
5) Maximum discharge air temperature = 140°F.

Candidate Suitability			
Mid Cfm – Heating	809	1,147	1,674
Mid Cfm Rise (°F)	74.9 ok	52.8 ok	36.2 ok
Cool Cfm @ 0.70"	NA	NA	1,404
Cool Cfm Rise (°F)			43.2 ok
Available ESP for 1,404 Cfm (min blower speed)			0.70 IWC

F80-OP3 static pressure for 1,404 Cfm = 0.70 IWC. Deduct standard filter = 0.10; wet cooling coil = 0.25; supply grille, return grille and hand damper = 0.09. Net pressure for fittings and straight runs for critical circulation path = 0.70 - 0.44 = 0.26 IWC

Figure 7-1

Candidate XYZ Performance for Cooling

The Section 5 example for cooling equipment shows that the 042 size is appropriate for the Fayetteville location. The example also shows that the design air flow rate for the 042 unit is 1,400 Cfm. So, when the furnace blower is used for heating and cooling, it must be able to deliver 1,400 Cfm (or a little more, or less) when the equipment operates in the cooling mode. Figure 7-1 shows that the F80-OP3 furnace is the only choice for heating and cooling, because the other two models do not have enough blower power.

Manual D Compatibility

Figure 7-1 shows anemic blower watt values for two models, and a respectable blower watt value for the third model. Figure 7-2 shows that the OEM's blower performance data is for the airflow resistance produced by the heat exchanger, and nothing else. Therefore, the air-side performance of two models may, or may not, be adequate

Section 7

F80-V3 Blower Data									
Blower Speed	External Static Pressure (IWC)								
	0.1	0.2	0.3	0.4	0.5	0.6	0.7	0.8	0.9
Hi	2,308	2,281	2,254	2,209	2,163	2,095	2,026	1,950	1,873
Med-High	2,006	1,997	1,987	1,960	1,933	1,888	1,842	1,780	1,718
Med-Low	1,690	1,691	1,691	1,683	1,674	1,651	1,627	1,556	1,485
Low	1,437	1,437	1,437	1,434	1,431	1,418	1,404	1,369	1,334

1) Blower data is for no filter or cooling coil in place.
2) Heat exchanger pressure drop is accounted for.

Figure 7-2

for heating-only (depending on duct system resistance to airflow), and one model looks like it may be adequate for heating and cooling.

- The *Manual D* Friction Rate Worksheet is used to confirm adequate blower performance. A ballpark version of this calculation is provided by Figure 7-1. This shows that the F80-OP3 blower is adequate for cooling when the pressure drop for straight runs and fittings is 0.26 IWC, or less.

- The *Manual D* version of this calculation requires OEM pressure drop values for air-side components that are not factored into the OEM's blower data, plus a duct plan that shows duct system geometry, fitting identification numbers, straight run lengths; plus fitting equivalent length values from *Manual D*, Appendix 3.

Discharge Air Temperature

Discharge air temperature equals entering air temperature plus air temperature rise. The entering air temperature will be equal to, or less than, the thermostat set-point, depending on the return duct load, and outdoor air mixing load. The worst-case is for no duct load and no outdoor air load. So for this calculation, the default discharge air temperature equals the thermostat set-point value plus the temperature rise value for a given burner output value, and the corresponding blower Cfm value. The default discharge air temperature for this single-stage burner example is 113.3°F, which is safely less than the OEM's 140°F limit, as demonstrated here:

- The design Cfm for cooling is 1,400 Cfm, but the installed value may be somewhat more or less, depending on the actual duct system resistance and Figure 7-2 data for low blower speed. A 1,400 Cfm value is sufficient for this calculation.

- The following calculation shows that the heat exchanger temperature rise for 1,404 Cfm is in the acceptable range (43.3°F), so heating Cfm may be equal to cooling Cfm

> **Blower Power Vs. System Components**
>
> Blower compatibility for a given air distribution system depends on blower power vs. the air flow resistance for the critical circulation path. For the same filter and air distribution hardware, the airflow resistance for a heating and cooling system is substantially larger than heating-only resistance because there is a relatively large pressure drop (0.15 to 0.40 IWC; usually 0.20 IWC or more) across the cooling coil.
>
> The pressure drop across a new (clean) standard filter may be 0.10 IWC, or less. The pressure drop across a new (clean) optional (better efficiency rating) filter may be 0.20 IWC, or more.
>
> Blower power must be compatible with system components shipped by the OEM, and must be compatible with system components (cooling coil, hot water heating coil, filter upgrade, zone damper) added, or altered, after the system has been installed.
>
> This requirement applies to any ducted system, regardless of equipment function (heating-only, cooling-only, or heating and cooling).

- The 1,404 Cfm value is for low blower speed. Blower Cfm increases for the other speed options, so the air temperature rise and discharge air temperature values are less for other blower speeds.

Figure A5-1 ACF = 0.96
Thermostat set-point = 70°F
Burner output = 64,000 Btuh
Design value for blower Cfm = 1,404
Temperature rise (°F) = TR
TR (°F) = 64,000 / (1.1 x 0.96 x 1,404) = 43.3 OK
Discharge air temperature (°F) = 70 + 43.3 = 113.3 OK

Section 7

Entering Air Temperature

Normally, an entering air temperature value is not used for equipment selection. It may be an issue when the thermostat set-point is unusually low, and/or the net winter design condition value for the return duct load, and/or outdoor air load is unusually large. For this example, the Appendix 2 calculation procedure returns a 67.1°F value for entering air temperature, is demonstrated here:

Outdoor air temperature = 13°F
Temperature at return grille = 70°F
Figure A5-1 ACF = 0.96
Return duct load = 2,272 Btuh
Design value for blower Cfm for heating = 1,404
Outdoor air = 75 Cfm; Sensible eff = 0.55
Return Cfm = 1,404 – 75 = 1,329
Return duct temperature drop (°F) = TD
TD (°F) = 2,272 / (1.1 x 0.96 x 1,404) = 1.53
Return duct exit temperature (°F) = 70 – 1.53 = 68.47
Recovery exit temperature (°F) = RET
RET (°F) = 13 + 0.55 x (68.47 – 13) = 43.51
Mixed air temperature (°F) = MAT
MAT (°F) = (1,329 x 68.47 + 75 x 43.51) / 1,404 = 67.14
Entering air temperature (°F) = MAT = 67.14

7-9 Hot-Humid Climate Example

The over-size limit from Table N2-4 applies to furnaces. When the furnace is equipped with a cooling coil, the over-size limit from Table N2-1 applies to cooling-only equipment. See Section 8 when dual fuel heating is provided by a furnace and a heat pump.

Heating Load and Operating Conditions

Furnace size is based on the *Manual J* heating load for Brunswick, GA, as summarized below. Return duct loads and engineered ventilation details are relevant because they affect entering dry-bulb temperature, which affects leaving air temperature. Brunswick is close to sea level, so there is no altitude adjustment factor for *Manual J* calculations and psychrometric calculations. OEM equipment performance data is for sea level conditions.

Altitude = 20 Feet; Figure A5-1 ACF = 1.00
Outdoor design temperature = 34°F
Indoor conditions: 70°F db; no humidification
Sensible heating load = 34,880 Btuh
Winter humidification load on furnace = None
Sensible return duct load (Section A2-3) = 1,155 Btuh
Outdoor air = 75 Cfm; Sensible eff. for heating = 0.55
Preferred furnace OSL = 1.40

Candidate XYZ Performance for Heating

Furnace performance data is searched for something close to 35,000 Btuh of output heating capacity for full burner

---

> **Discharge Air Temperature for Air Zoning**
> A zone damper system must be designed and controlled so that the discharge air temperature does not exceed the OEM's temperature rise limit, and/or the high discharge air temperature. See *Manual Zr* for related procedures.

> **Coldest Entering Air Temperature for Heating**
> OEM's normally do not provide a low-limit value for entering air temperature, because it is not an issue for normal return duct loads and/or outdoor air mixing loads (entering air may be a few degrees colder than a normal thermostat set-point). When there is a need to investigate an abnormal situation, Appendix 2 procedures provide an entering air temperature value for the combined effect of a return duct load, and an outdoor air load.

Furnace Performance Data — OEM xyz			
Model	F40-OP-all	F60-OP2	F60-OP3
Input Btuh	40,000	60,000	60,000
Output Btuh	32,000	47,000	47,000
Rise (°F)	Deficient Output Capacity	30-60	30-60
AFUE		80%	80%
Blower Watts		250	250
Wheel Size		10 x 6	10 x 7
Mid Cfm 0.50 IWC		973-1,113	1,052-1,278
Max Cfm 0.50 IWC		1,236	1,412
Max Cfm 0.60 IWC		1,171	1,351

1) One-stage burner, PSC blower motor has 4 speed settings.
2) Blower data is for heat exchanger only, no filter, no AC coil.
3) Sea level performance.
4) Rise = Air temperature rise through heat exchanger.
5) Maximum discharge air temperature = 140°F.

Candidate Suitability			
Mid Cfm - Heating		1,113	1,278
Mid Cfm Rise (°F)	Deficient Output Capacity	38.4 ok	33.4 ok
Cool Cfm @ 0.50"		Deficient	1,412
Cool Cfm Rise (°F)			30.3 ok
Available ESP for 1,412 Cfm (max blower speed)			0.50 IWC

F60-OP3 static pressure for 1,4012 Cfm = 0.50 IWC max. Deduct standard filter = 0.10; wet cooling coil = 0.25; supply grille, return grille and hand damper = 0.09. Net pressure for fittings and straight runs for critical circulation path = 0.50 - 0.44 = 0.06 IWC.

Figure 7-3

capacity. Figure 7-3 (previous page) shows heating performance data for a product in the F40 size and the F60 size. This equipment has one firing rate, one anemic blower option (not shown), and two marginal blower options.

The F40 size is disqualified because it is deficient in output capacity. The over-size factor for the F60 size complies with the preferred 1.40 limit, and the temperature rise (TR) values are acceptable, so two F60 products are tentatively acceptable for heating.

$OSF = 47,000 / 34,880 = 1.35$
$TR (°F) = Output\ Btuh / (1.1 \times ACF \times Cfm)$
Blower power must be adequate for the duct system.

Candidate XYZ Performance for Cooling

The Section 5 example for cooling equipment shows that the 042 size is appropriate for the Brunswick location. The example also shows that the design air flow rate for the 042 unit is 1,400 Cfm. So, when the furnace blower is used for heating and cooling, it must be able to deliver 1,400 Cfm (or a little more, or less) when the equipment operates in the cooling mode. Figure 7-3 shows that the F60-OP3 furnace is questionable for cooling, because of deficient blower power, and because the temperature rise for 1,412 Cfm is close to the low-limit.

- When the pressure drop for a wet cooling coil turns out to be less than 0.25, the difference in component pressure drop is available for the straight runs and fittings.

- Designing for 1,351 cooling Cfm may be acceptable. When this proves to be true, there is an additional 0.10 IWC for the straight runs and fittings.

- Investigate other equipment when things are iffy.

Alternative PSC Candidates

Figure 7-4 shows heating performance data for a PSC blower-motor product in the F44 size and the F66 size. This equipment has a one-stage burner and two blower motor/wheel options (option 2 has the most blower power).

- The over-size factor for the F44 size complies with the preferred 1.40 limit, so it is a good choice for heating, but blower Cfm is deficient for cooling.

  $OSF = 35,900 / 34,880 = 1.03$
  Significantly less than 1,400 Cfm for cooling

- The F66 size has the correct blower Cfm for cooling for a medium-high blower speed, but the over-size factor exceeds the preferred 1.40 limit, so it is a good choice for cooling, but somewhat over-sized for heating. However, the excess heating capacity does not exceed the maximum (2.00) limit, so this product could be used for heating and cooling.

Furnace Performance Data — OEM psc & ecm			
Model	F44psc-OP2	F66psc-OP2	F44ecm
Input Btuh	44,000	66,000	44,000 Hi
Output Btuh	35,900	54,000	42,000 Hi
Rise (°F)	25-55	25-55	35-65 Hi
AFUE	80%	80%	95%
Blower Watts	150	375	375
Wheel Size	10 x 7	10 x 10	10 x 9
Mid Cfm 0.50 IWC	1,020-1,160	1,420-1,600	ECM
Max Cfm 0.50 IWC	1,265	1,740	1,370
Max Cfm 0.60 IWC	1,210	1,635	1,370
Max Cfm 0.70 IWC	1,135	1,545	1,370

1) PSC product has a one-stage burner, the PSC blower motor has four speed settings; the blower data is for heat exchanger and filter, no AC coil.
2) ECM product has a two-stage burner and an ECM motor; the blower data is for heat exchanger and filter, no AC coil.
3) Sea level performance.
4) Rise = Air temperature rise through heat exchanger.
5) Maximum discharge air temperature = 130°F and 135°F.

Candidate Suitability			
Heat Cfm @ 0.50IWC		1,420 @ ML	1,005 Set
Rise (°F)	Deficient Blower Power	34.6 ok	38.0 ok
Cool Cfm @ 0.70"		1,420 @ MH	1,370 Set
Cool Cfm Rise (°F)		34.6 ok	NA
Max pressure for fittings and runs		0.36 IWC	0.46 IWC

1) The F66psc blower, operating at medium-low speed, delivers 1,420 Cfm against 0.50 IWC of airflow resistance; when operating at medium-high speed, it delivers 1,420 Cfm against 0.70 IWC of airflow resistance.
2) For the F44ecm blower, maximum Cfm for stage 2 heating is 1,005 Cfm, and maximum Cfm for cooling is 1,370 Cfm. The blower motor holds 1,370 Cfm as airflow resistance varies from 0.10 IWC to 0.80 IWC.
3) Deduct wet cooling coil = 0.25; supply grille, return grille and hand damper = 0.09. Net pressure for fittings and straight runs for critical circulation path = Blower ESP - 0.34.

Figure 7-4

$OSF = 54,000 / 34,880 = 1.55$
$Max\ OSL\ per\ Table\ N2\text{-}4 = 2.00$
External static pressure is 0.70 IWC for 1,420 Cfm.
Passes all tests, but some other product may do better.

Alternative ECM Candidate

Figure 7-4 shows heating performance data for an ECM blower-motor product in the F44 size. This equipment has a two-stage burner and an ECM blower motor. This product is an excellent solution to the Brunswick heating-cooling problem.

$OSF = 42,000 / 34,880 = 1.20$

Section 7

- The over-size factor complies with the preferred 1.40 limit, so it is a good choice for heating.
- The ECM motor can be set for 1,370 Cfm for cooling, which is compatible with (close enough) the 1,400 Cfm requirement for cooling.
- Since 1,370 Cfm is maintained as the external static pressure varies from 0.50 IWC (actually down to 0.10 IWC) to 0.80 IWC, there should be more than enough pressure for duct system design.

Manual D Compatibility

The F66psc-OP2 blower can deliver 1,420 Cfm against 0.70 IWC of airflow resistance. The F44ecm blower can deliver 1,370 Cfm against 0.80 IWC of airflow resistance. Therefore, the air-side performance of both models should be adequate for cooling and heating.

- The *Manual D* Friction Rate Worksheet is used to confirm adequate blower performance. A ballpark version of this calculation is provided by Figure 7-4. This shows 0.36 IWC to 0.46 IWC may be available for the fittings and straight runs in the critical circulation path (this should be more than adequate).
- The *Manual D* version of this calculation requires OEM pressure drop values for air-side components that are not factored into the OEM's blower data, plus a duct plan that shows duct system geometry, fitting identification numbers, straight run lengths; plus fitting equivalent length values from *Manual D*, Appendix 3.

Discharge Air Temperature

As explained for the Fayetteville example, the default discharge air temperature value equals the thermostat set-point value, plus the temperature rise for a given burner output value, and the corresponding blower Cfm value. The default discharge air temperature for the F66psc-OP2 furnace is 104.6°F; and 108.0°F for the F44ecm furnace, as demonstrated here:

Figure A5-1 ACF = 1.00
Thermostat set-point = 70°F
Temperature rise (°F) = TR
F66 burner output = 54,000 Btuh
Design value for blower Cfm = 1,420
TR (°F) = 54,000 / (1.1 x 1.00 x 1,420) = 34.6 OK
Discharge air temperature (°F) = 70 + 34.6 = 104.6 OK

F44 burner output = 42,000 Btuh
Design value for blower Cfm = 1,005
TR (°F) = 54,000 / (1.1 x 1.00 x 1,005) = 38.0 OK
Discharge air temperature (°F) = 70 + 38.0 = 108.0 OK

Entering Air Temperature

Normally, an entering air temperature value is not used for equipment selection. It may be an issue when the thermostat set-point is unusually low, and/or the net winter design condition value for the return duct load, and/or outdoor air load is unusually large. For this example, the Appendix 2 calculation procedure returns a 67.9°F value for entering air temperature, is demonstrated here:

Outdoor air temperature = 34°F
Temperature at return grille = 70°F
Figure A5-1 ACF = 1.00
Return duct load = 1,155 Btuh
Design value for blower Cfm for heating = 1,005
Outdoor air = 75 Cfm; Sensible eff = 0.55
Return Cfm = 1,005 - 75 = 930
Return duct temperature drop (°F) = TD
TD (°F) = 1,155 / (1.1 x 1.00 x 1,005) = 0.95
Return duct exit temperature (°F) = 70 - 0.95 = 69.05
Recovery exit temperature (°F) = RET
RET (°F) = 34 + 0.55 x (69.05 - 34) = 53.28
Mixed air temperature (°F) = MAT
MAT (°F) = (930 x 69.05 + 75 x 53.28) / 1,005 = 67.87
Entering air temperature (°F) = MAT = 67.87

7-10 Dry Summer Cold Winter Example

The over-size limit from Table N2-4 applies to furnaces. When the furnace is equipped with a cooling coil, the over-size limit from Table N2-1 applies to cooling-only equipment. See Section 8 when dual fuel heating is provided by a furnace and a heat pump.

Heating Load and Operating Conditions

Furnace size is based on the *Manual J* heating load for Boise, ID, as summarized below. Return duct loads and engineered ventilation details are relevant because they affect entering dry-bulb temperature, which affects leaving air temperature. The 0.88 altitude adjustment factor for 2,838 feet applies to *Manual J* calculations and to psychrometric calculations for entering air temperature. Equipment performance is adjusted for altitude when it exceeds 2,500 Feet (see Appendix 5).

Altitude = 2,838 Feet; Figure A5-1 ACF = 0.88
Outdoor design temperature = 9°F
Indoor conditions: 70°F db; no humidification
Sensible heating load = 58,349 Btuh
Winter humidification load on furnace = None
Sensible return duct load (Section A2-3) = 2,420 Btuh
Outdoor air = 75 Cfm; Sensible eff. for heating = 0.55
Preferred furnace OSL = 1.40

Candidate XYZ Performance for Heating

Furnace performance data is searched for something close to 58,000 Btuh of output heating capacity for full burner capacity. Figure 7-5 shows actual heating performance data for a F80 size product that has one firing rate and three blower motor/wheel options. The 1.03 over-size factor complies with the 1.40 limit, and the temperature rise (TR) values for the models are acceptable, so all three products are tentatively acceptable for heating.

OEM's altitude adjustment for burner = 2% per 1,000 Ft
Input Btuh factor = 0.02 x (2,838 / 1,000) = 0.057
Input Btuh at altitude = 80,000 x (1.0- 0.057) = 75,440
Steady-state efficiency = 64,000 / 80,000 = 0.80
Output Btuh = 0.80 x 75,440 = 60,352
OSF = 60,352 / 58,349 = 1,034
TR (°F) = Output Btuh / (1.1 x ACF x Cfm)
Blower power must be adequate for the duct system.

Candidate XYZ Performance for Cooling

The Section 5 example for cooling-only equipment shows that the 036 size is appropriate for the Boise location. The example also shows that the design air flow rate for the 036 unit is 1,200 Cfm. So, when the furnace blower is used for heating and cooling, it must be able to deliver 1,200 Cfm (or a little more, or less) when the equipment operates in the cooling mode. Figure 7-5 shows that the F80-OP2 furnace is the choice for heating and cooling, because the OP1 model does not have enough blower power, and the OP3 model has too much blower power.

Manual D Compatibility

The F80-OP2 blower, operating at high-speed, can deliver 1,189 Cfm against 0.70 IWC of airflow resistance. Therefore, the air-side performance of this model should be adequate for cooling and heating. However, the ideal solution would be to use a furnace that provides something close to 1,200 Cfm at a medium PSC blower speed. Or a furnace that has an ECM blower that can maintain something close to 1,200 Cfm over a 0.50 to 0.80 IWC pressure range.

- The *Manual D* Friction Rate Worksheet is used to confirm adequate blower performance. A ballpark version of this calculation is provided by Figure 7-5. This shows 0.26 IWC may be available for the fittings and straight runs in the critical circulation path (this should be adequate).

- The *Manual D* version of this calculation requires OEM pressure drop values for air-side components that are not factored into the OEM's blower data, plus a duct plan that shows duct system geometry, fitting identification numbers, straight run lengths; plus fitting equivalent length values from *Manual D*, Appendix 3.

Furnace Performance Data — OEM xyz			
Model	F80-OP1	F80-OP2	F80-OP3
Input Btuh	80,000	80,000	80,000
Output Btuh	64,000	64,000	64,000
Rise (°F)	50–80	30-60	25-55
AFUE	80%	80%	80%
Blower Watts	150	250	560
Wheel Size	9 x 7	10 x 7	11 x 10
Mid Cfm 0.50 IWC	681 - 809	1,008 - 1,147	1,674 - 1,933
Max Cfm 0.50 IWC	956	1,296	2,163
Max Cfm 0.70 IWC	803	1,189	2,026
Min Cfm 0.70 IWC	428	808	1,404

1) One-stage burner, PSC blower motor has 4 speed settings
2) Blower data is for heat exchanger only, no filter, no AC coil.
3) Sea level performance.
4) Rise = Air temperature rise through heat exchanger.
5) Maximum discharge air temperature = 140°F.

Candidate Suitability			
Mid Cfm - Heating	809	1,147	1,674
Mid Cfm Rise (°F)	77.1 ok	54.4 ok	37.7 ok
Cool Cfm @ 0.70"	NA	1,189	1,404
Cool Cfm Rise (°F)		52.4 ok	44.4 ok
Available ESP for 1,404 Cfm (min blower speed)			0.70 IWC

F80-OP2 static pressure for 1,189 Cfm = 0.70 IWC. Deduct standard filter = 0.10; wet cooling coil = 0.25; supply grille, return grille and hand damper = 0.09. Net pressure for fittings and straight runs for critical circulation path = 0.70 - 0.44 = 0.26 IWC.

Figure 7-5

Discharge Air Temperature

As explained for the Fayetteville example, the default discharge air temperature value equals the thermostat set-point value plus the temperature rise for a given burner output value, and the corresponding blower Cfm value. The default discharge air temperature for the F80-OP2 furnace is 122.4°F, as demonstrated here:

Figure A5-1 ACF = 0.88
Thermostat set-point = 70°F
Temperature rise (°F) = TR
F80 burner output = 60,367 Btuh
Design value for blower Cfm = 1,189
TR (°F) = 63,367 / (1.1 x 0.88 x 1,189) = 52.4 OK
Discharge air temperature (°F) = 70 + 52.4 = 122.4 OK

Section 7

Entering Air Temperature

Normally, an entering air temperature value is not used for equipment selection. It may be an issue when the thermostat set-point is unusually low, and/or the net winter design condition value for the return duct load, and/or outdoor air load is unusually large. For this example, the Appendix 2 calculation procedure returns a 66.2°F value for entering air temperature, is demonstrated here:

Outdoor air temperature = 9°F
Temperature at return grille = 70°F
Figure A5-1 ACF = 0.88
Return duct load = 2,420 Btuh
Design value for blower Cfm for heating = 1,189
Outdoor air = 75 Cfm; Sensible eff = 0.55
Return Cfm = 1,189 − 75 = 1,114
Return duct temperature drop (°F) = TD
TD (°F) = 2,420 / (1.1 x 1.00 x 1,189) = 2.1
Return duct exit temperature (°F) = 70 − 2.1 = 67.9
Recovery exit temperature (°F) = RET
RET (°F) = 9 + 0.55 x (67.9 − 9) = 41.4
Mixed air temperature (°F) = MAT
MAT (°F) = (1,114 x 67.9 + 75 x 41.4) / 1,189 = 66.2
Entering air temperature (°F) = MAT = 66.2

7-11 Oil or Propane Furnace

Oil and propane furnaces have an input Btuh rating, an output Btuh rating, a steady-state efficiency, an AFUE rating, low and high temperature rise limits, and a high-limit for discharge air temperature. The Table N2-4 size limit factors apply to all types of fossil fuel furnaces. Furnace blower size options, and blower motor options, are similar to natural gas equipment options. Therefore, procedures demonstrated by the preceding examples for natural gas equipment apply to oil and propane equipment.

7-12 Electric Furnace

Electric furnaces have an input KW value that determines output Btuh (1 KW produces 3,413 Btuh). There is a high-limit for discharge air temperature. The steady-state efficiency is 1.00 (ignoring cabinet loss). The concept of an AFUE rating is not an electric furnace issue. The over-size factor concept applies to all types of furnaces. Table N2-3 provides size limit values for electric furnaces. Furnace blower size options, and blower motor options, are similar to natural gas equipment options. Therefore, procedures demonstrated by the examples for natural gas equipment apply to electric coil equipment, except Table N2-3 provides the over-size limit, and there is only one temperature rise limit.

Section 8
Dual Fuel Heating Procedures and Examples

The possibility of significant heating cost savings provides motivation to investigate the performance of a hybrid heating system. This system normally consists of a natural gas furnace and an air-air heat pump, but the application principles and design procedures also apply to oil and propane furnaces, and to water-air heat pumps.

8-1 Economic Question

For a year-round comfort system, is it better to use a furnace equipped with a cooling evaporator coil, or a furnace equipped with an indoor heat pump coil? Either system provides adequate comfort when properly designed and installed; so for a homeowner, this depends on annual energy cost, and on the installed cost of a cooling coil furnace vs. the installed cost of a heat pump coil furnace.

8-2 Heat Pump Outputs and Energy Inputs

For heat pump heating, momentary compressor heating capacity (CHC in Btuh units) per input KW depends on heat source temperature (outdoor air temperature, or entering water temperature). Since the furnace provides the blower for the indoor heat pump coil, blower power is roughly the same for furnace heating and compressor heating, so blower power is not a KW input for heat pump COP. Since a dual fuel heat pump has no electric heating coil, the momentary input KW is the sum of the compressor KW_C and the outdoor fan KW_{OF}. Figure 8-1 summarizes this concept, per OEM data, for an air-air heat pump.

Heat pump output (Btuh) = CHC
Heat pump input KW = KW_C + KW_{OF}

8-3 Furnace Outputs and Energy inputs

For a furnace, the heat (Btu) contained in a unit of fuel (CuFt or gallon) is a constant value. For equivalent heat output, the furnace fuel flow rate (CuFt per hour, or gallons per hour) equals the compressor heating capacity (CHC) divided by the heat content of a unit of fuel (HCF), adjusted for the steady-state furnace efficiency (SS_{eff}). Blower power is the same for furnace heating, and for compressor heating (when blower wheel speed is constant).

SS_{eff} = Output Btuh / Input Btuh
Burner output Btuh = CHC
Fuel flow rate = CHC / (HCF x SS_{eff})

The heat content of fossil fuel (HCF) varies somewhat, depending on the source. The default values for *Manual S* procedures are provided here:

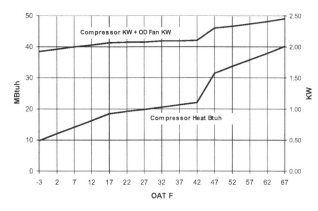

Figure 8-1

Natural gas Btu per CuFt = 1,000
Therm = 100 CuFt = 100,000 Btu
Propane Btu per Gallon = 91,500
Fuel oil Btu per Gallon = 138,000

8-4 Economic Balance Point

The economic balance point temperature is the heat source temperature that causes equal cost for compressor heat vs. fossil fuel heat. Figure 8-2 (next page) shows how OEM compressor heating data is used to estimate the economic balance point for a gas furnace.

- It is more economical to use compressor heat above the economic balance point.

- It is more economical to use furnace heat below the economic balance point.

- A relatively high economic balance point favors a furnace with a cooling-only coil.

- A relatively low economic balance point favors a hybrid system.

- The economic balance point may be higher, about equal to, or lower than the thermal balance point (Figure 8-3, next page).

- The compressor cannot operate continuously below the thermal balance point, but it may operate when the furnace is off.

- OEM controls determine how the heat pump operates when the heat source temperature is below the thermal balance point temperature, and above the economic balance point.

Section 8

| Air-Air Heat Pump plus Natural Gas Furnace ||||||||
| Fuel Cost Comparison for $ 0.10 / KWH Power and $ 0.90 per Therm Gas ||||||||
OAT (°F)	CHC (MBtuh)	Input KW	Heating COP	CuFt / Hr Input	Electric Cost / HR	Gas Cost / Hr	Cost Ratio Gas / Elect
–3	9.83	1.92	1.50	10.92	0.192	0.098	0.51
2	12.00	1.96	1.79	13.33	0.196	0.120	0.61
7	14.20	2.00	2.08	15.78	0.200	0.142	0.71
12	16.30	2.03	2.35	18.11	0.203	0.163	0.80
17	18.50	2.07	2.62	20.56	0.207	0.185	0.89
22	19.20	2.08	2.70	21.33	0.208	0.192	0.92
27	19.90	2.08	2.80	22.11	0.208	0.199	0.96
32	20.60	2.09	2.89	22.89	0.209	0.206	0.99
37	21.30	2.09	2.99	23.67	0.209	0.213	1.02
42	22.00	2.10	3.07	24.44	0.210	0.220	1.05
47	31.50	2.30	4.01	35.00	0.230	0.315	1.37
52	33.70	2.33	4.24	37.44	0.233	0.337	1.45
57	35.80	2.37	4.43	39.78	0.237	0.358	1.51
62	38.00	2.41	4.62	42.22	0.241	0.380	1.58
67	40.20	2.45	4.81	44.67	0.245	0.402	1.64

1) Compressor heating capacity (CHC) and KW values for the compressor and outdoor fan provided by OEM performance data.
2) Heating COP = CHC / (3.413 x Input KW).
3) CuFt / Hr = CHC Btuh / (1,000 Btuh per CuFt x 0.90 Efficiency).
4) Electric cost per hour = $ 0.10 x Input KW; Gas cost per hour = $ 0.009 per CuFt x CuFt per hour input.
5) Cost ratio = Gas cost / Electric cost.
6) Fuel cost are equal when the outdoor air temperature is about 33°F, so the economic balance point is about 33°F.

Figure 8-2

8-5 Break-Even COP

Figure 8-2 shows economic equivalence for compressor heat and furnace heat when it is about 33°F outdoors. The corresponding COP value for the heat pump is about 2.9, so 2.9 is the break-even COP (BECOP).

The break-even COP value depends on the cost of electricity ($/KWH), the unit cost of the fossil fuel (dollars per 1,000 CuFt for natural gas, or dollars per Gallon for propane or oil), and the steady-state efficiency (SS_{eff}) of the furnace. These equations return BECOP values for natural gas heat, oil heat, and propane heat.

Gas BECOP = 293 x SS_{eff} x ($/KWH / $/1,000 CuFT)
Oil BECOP = 41 x SS_{eff} x ($/KWH / $ / Gallon)
Propane BECOP = 27 x SS_{eff} x ($/KWH / $/Gallon)

Break-even COP is an indicator of the economic benefit of a dual fuel system. A relatively high BECOP value translates to a relatively high economic balance point, and vice versa. Therefore, a relatively high BECOP value favors a furnace with a cooling-only coil; and a relatively low BECOP value favors a furnace with a heat pump coil.

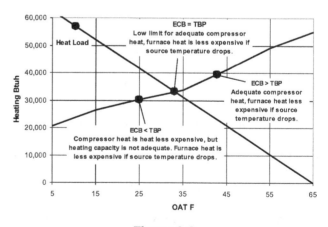

Figure 8-3

Figure 8-4 (next page) shows how the BECOP value varies with the price of natural gas, for ten cent, fifteen cent and twenty cent electricity. However, BECOP thinking is ballpark thinking. A calculation similar to a Figure 8-2 determines the economic balance point.

8-6 Water-Air Heat Pump

Water-air heat pumps tend to have a higher heating COP than air-air heat pumps of the same nominal size, and there is no defrost penalty. An inspection of OEM performance data shows that heating COP for 30°F water is in the 3.0 range, and that this increases to the 3.6 range for 50°F water, then up to the 4.8 range for 90°F water.

- Momentary heating COP depends on momentary entering water temperature, which may range from less than 30°F to more than 90°F, depending on the type of water system, and the day of year.
- For Figure 8-4, the shaded cells suggest a possible economic benefit from an air-air heat pump.
- The heating COP for once-through water may be in the 3.6 range. Figure 8-4 shows that a 3.6 COP significantly increases the number of shaded cells for possible economic benefit.
- The heating COP for earth-loop water may be in the 4.8 rage at the start of the heating season, and in the 3.0 range at the end of the heating season. The average COP will be somewhere in the 3.5 to 4.0 range. Figure 8-4 shows a significant increase the number of shaded cells for possible economic benefit.
- A calculation similar to a Figure 8-2 determines the economic balance point. Water pump KW is part of the input KW for this calculation.

8-7 Return on Investment

It may be true that a hybrid system saves energy and reduces heating cost. However, this has no meaning unless the savings are quantified by a proper energy and op-cost calculation. Then, the capital cost of the hybrid system can be compared to the capital cost of an ordinary system, and the deferential can be compared to the annual savings in energy cost.

- A comprehensive hourly or bin-hour calculation determines annual heating cost savings (see Appendix 6).
- For acceptable pay-back criteria, *Manual S* defers to homeowner judgment

8-8 Furnace Sizing

The furnace sizing rules provided by Table N2-4 apply to dual fuel systems. Per the *Manual D* Friction Rate Worksheet, the furnace blower must have adequate power to move the design Cfm through the critical circulation path. The air flow resistance for this path includes the resistance produced by the air-side components that are external to the OEM's blower data, plus path fitting resistance, and straight run resistance.

Natural Gas BECOP Scenarios			
$ 0.10 / KWH	Steady-State Efficiency		
$ / 1,000 CuFt	0.80	0.85	0.90
6.00	3.91	4.15	4.40
8.00	2.93	3.11	3.30
10.00	2.34	2.49	2.64
12.00	1.95	2.08	2.20
14.00	1.67	1.78	1.88
16.00	1.47	1.56	1.65
18.00	1.30	1.38	1.47
20.00	1.17	1.25	1.32
$ 0.15 / KWH	Steady-State Efficiency		
$ / 1,000 CuFt	0.80	0.85	0.90
6.00	5.86	6.23	6.59
8.00	4.40	4.67	4.94
10.00	3.52	3.74	3.96
12.00	2.93	3.11	3.30
14.00	2.51	2.67	2.83
16.00	2.20	2.33	2.47
18.00	1.95	2.08	2.20
20.00	1.76	1.87	1.98
$ 0.20 / KWH	Steady-State Efficiency		
$ / 1,000 CuFt	0.80	0.85	0.90
6.00	7.81	8.30	8.79
8.00	5.86	6.23	6.59
10.00	4.69	4.98	5.27
12.00	3.91	4.15	4.40
14.00	3.35	3.56	3.77
16.00	2.93	3.11	3.30
18.00	2.60	2.77	2.93
20.00	2.34	2.49	2.64

1) Shaded cells indicate a possible economic benefit based on a 2.50 or less BECOP value for air-air equipment. However, a BECOP value, by itself, is not conclusive, and does not claim to be conclusive.
2) A calculation similar to a Figure 8-2 determines the economic balance point, and a comprehensive hourly or bin-hour calculation determines annual heating cost savings.

Figure 8-4

8-9 Heat Pump Sizing

The heat pump sizing rules provided by Table N2-2 apply to dual fuel systems. The heat pump size limit for total cooling capacity may be for Condition A equipment,

Section 8

or Condition B equipment, depending on the *Manual J* sensible heat ratio, and the HDD/CDD ratio for the application.

8-10 Retrofit Application

An indoor refrigerant coil may be added to an existing heating-only furnace, or an existing cooling-only coil may be replaced by a heat pump coil. For this scenario, the existing blower must have enough power for the new design Cfm value, for the new set of air-side components in the critical circulation path, and for the existing fittings and straight runs in the critical circulation path. The sidebar on this page provides related procedures.

8-11 Economic Balance Points – Fayetteville

Since Fayetteville, AR, is lower than 2,500 Feet, there is no adjustment to the OEM's cooling and heating capacity data. Section 5-10 shows that the Fayetteville location requires a Condition A heat pump, and that 042 size equipment has a 0.99 over-size factor for total cooling capacity. Figure 6-3 shows that the default thermal balance point is about 37°F.

The economic balance point calculation for this example is similar to Figure 8-2, but the CHC values and input KW values are for a 042 heat pump size. Figure 8-5 shows that five-cent electricity may justify a dual fuel system, that ten-cent electricity may justify a dual-fuel system for ten dollar gas; and that fifteen cent electricity disqualifies the dual fuel concept.

Economic Balance Points — Fayetteville Example Condition A heat Pump – 042 Size Furnace Efficiency = 0.90			
$ / 1,000 CuFt	$ / KWH		
	0.05	0.10	0.15
6.00	5°F	47°F	> 70°F
8.00	– 2°F	42°F	59°F
10.00	Way below 0°F	12°F	45°F

1) Per Section 5-10, a Condition A heat pump in the 042 size has a 0.99 factor for excess cooling capacity.
2) Per Section 6-4, the thermal balance point is about 37°F.

Figure 8-5

8-12 Economic Balance Points – Brunswick

Since Brunswick, GA, is at sea level, there is no adjustment to the OEM's cooling and heating capacity data. Section 5-11 shows that the Brunswick location requires a Condition A heat pump, and that 042 size equipment has a 1.06 over-size factor for total cooling capacity. Figure 6-4 shows that the default thermal balance point is about 41°F.

Validating Retrofit Airflow

The size of the refrigeration cycle equipment is determined by applying the Section N2 sizing rules to an accurate *Manual J* load calculation. This requires a brand new load calculation for existing conditions.

The design Cfm for refrigeration cycle equipment is determined when the equipment is selected and sized by *Manual S* procedures.

Available Pressure Validation by Calculation

The *Manual D* Friction Rate Worksheet determines when blower power is adequate (the design friction rate value must be somewhere in the wedge shown by the graph at the bottom of the worksheet).

When the Friction Rate Worksheet shows that maximum blower power is significantly deficient, use more efficient fittings, install a blower that has more power, exchange the furnace for one that has a more blower power, or abandon the project.

Available Pressure Validation by Field Test

The alternative to calculations is to see when there is a blower speed setting that is compatible with the new design Cfm value. Simulate refrigerant coil pressure drop by blocking off a portion of the filter area.

- Filter pressure drop with an engineered restriction equals coil pressure drop (from OEM data) plus filter pressure drop when system airflow is at the design Cfm value.

- Start with maximum blower power and all balancing dampers open. Adjust the restriction size for the required pressure drop, and see how the measured Cfm compares with the design Cfm.

- When the measured Cfm is significantly deficient at maximum blower power, use more efficient fittings, install a blower that has more power, exchange the furnace for one that has a more blower power, or abandon the project.

- When measured Cfm is excessive, repeat the experiment with less blower power. When the choice is between excessive Cfm and deficient Cfm, use more blower power, and adjust hand dampers for the design Cfm.

Local Airflow Rates

Adequate blower pressure for the critical circulation path does not guarantee that all duct airway sizes are correct. *Manual J* room loads and *Manual D* procedures provide room Cfm values and airway sizes for all duct runs.

The economic balance point calculation for this example is similar to Figure 8-2, but the CHC values and Input KW values are for a 042 heat pump size. Figure 8-6 shows that five-cent electricity may justify a dual fuel system, that ten-cent electricity may justify a dual-fuel system for ten dollar gas; and that fifteen-cent electricity disqualifies the dual fuel concept.

Economic Balance Points — Brunswick Example Condition A heat Pump - 042 Size Furnace Efficiency = 0.90			
$ / 1,000 CuFt	$ / KWH		
	0.05	0.10	0.15
6.00	5°F	47°F	> 70°F
8.00	− 2°F	42°F	59°F
10.00	Way below 0°F	12°F	45°F

1) Per Section 5-11, a Condition A heat pump in the 042 size has a 1.06 factor for excess cooling capacity.
2) Per Section 6-6, the thermal balance point is about 41°F.

Figure 8-6

8-13 Economic Balance Points – Boise

Since Boise is at 2,838 Ft, a 0.95 adjustment factor is applied to the OEM's cooling and heating capacity data. Section 5-12 shows that the Boise location qualifies for a Condition B heat pump, and that 048 size equipment has 10,591 Btuh of excess total cooling capacity. Figure 6-6 shows that the default thermal balance point is about 33°F.

The economic balance point calculation for this example is similar to Figure 8-2, but the CHC values and Input KW values are for a 048 heat pump size. Figure 8-7 shows that five-cent electricity may justify a dual fuel system, that ten-cent electricity may justify a dual-fuel system for nine dollar, or more, gas; and that fifteen-cent electricity disqualifies the dual fuel concept.

- When an airway size is too small, shorten the effective length of the path (use more efficient fittings), or increase the airway size of the duct run (when this requires new fittings, use efficient fittings.).
- Hand dampers are required to balance local airflow rates. Adjust existing dampers, based on *Manual D* Cfm values, or install and adjust new dampers.

Economic Balance Points — Boise Example Condition B heat Pump - 048 Size Furnace Efficiency = 0.90			
$ / 1,000 CuFt	$ / KWH		
	0.05	0.10	0.15
6.00	5°F	47°F	> 70°F
8.00	− 2°F	42°F	59°F
10.00	Way below 0°F	12°F	45°F

1) Per Section 5-12, a Condition B heat pump in the 048 size has 10,591 Btuh of excess cooling capacity.
2) Per Section 6-6, the thermal balance point is about 33°F.

Figure 8-7

Section 8

This section is not part of the this standard. It is merely informative and does not contain requirements necessary for conformance to the standard. It has not been processed according to the ANSI requirements for a standard, and may contain material that has not been subject to public review or a consensus process. Unresolved objectors on informative material are not offered the right to appeal at ACCA or ANSI.

Section 9

Central Ducted Water-Air Heat Pump Examples

One selection/sizing procedure applies to all types of cooling-only equipment and to heat pumps. This section shows how water-air heat pump equipment is sized for cooling. After make, model and size have been determined, the OEM's expanded performance data for heating is used to evaluate heating performance. Appendix 19 provides supporting detail for the example problems in this section.

9-1 Redundant Instructions

The commentary and the related sidebar exhibits provided by Sections 5-1 through 5-9 (for air-air cooling examples), and Sections 6-1 through 6-3 (for air-air heat pump heating examples) apply to water-air equipment. Therefore, these procedures are used for the examples in this section. However, there is one significant difference, which is that water-air equipment performance depends on entering water temperature instead of outdoor air temperature. Section 9-2 deals with this issue.

9-2 Entering Water Temperature

Figure A1-26 shows that the cooling and heating capacity of a water-air heat pump depends on the temperature of the water that enters the equipment package. When ground water is pumped from a source and discarded, entering water temperature is fairly constant through the year. When the water circulates through a closed piping-loop system that is buried in the ground, entering water temperature will change on a monthly basis, reaching a maximum value in late fall, and a minimum value in early spring.

- Local well drillers can provide a value for ground water temperature.
- Pipe loops may be vertical or horizontal.
- Entering water temperature depends on soil properties, pipe loop geometry, the length of pipe, etc.
- The person (and software) responsible for designing a buried, or submerged, piping loop provides maximum and minimum values for entering water temperature. These calculations are based on heating and cooling load calculations provided by the practitioner. See Appendix 9.
- The size of the maximum-minimum temperature excursion is inversely related to piping loop cost. This is unfavorably non-linear (an additional increment of temperature benefit requires more than one increment of additional cost).

Ballpark Values for Entering Water Temperature

Prior to producing a proper water-loop design, maximum (WTH) and minimum (WTL) water temperature values may be estimated by the following equations. Equation use requires values for the historical hottest and coldest outdoor air temperatures experienced by the local climate. These extreme temperatures seldom occur, but when they do, they can be 10°F to 20°F hotter or colder than the *Manual J* design temperature (refer to national weather service data, or just web-search for... *Extreme Temperatures USA*).

WTH = Extreme summer temperature - 10°F
WTL = Extreme winter temperature + 40°F

Akron, OH, Example:
Manual J 1% db value = 85°F
Extreme summer db = 104°F
WTH = 104 – 10 = 94°F
Manual J 99% db value = 5°F
Extreme winter db = –25°F
WTL = –25 + 40 = 15°F
Antifreeze is required when HTL is below freezing.
Antifreeze affects loop heat transfer rate.

Use of OEM Performance Data

When a GWHP (open, pump and dump) system is designed, a single water temperature determines heating and cooling performance. For a closed piping loop, heating performance is evaluated for the minimum water temperature value (WTL), and cooling performance is evaluated for the maximum water temperature value (WTH).

- OEM performance data may have to be adjusted for antifreeze in the piping loop (ask the OEM).
- Heating capacity increases with increasing water temperature.
- Total, sensible, and latent cooling capacity decrease with increasing water temperature.
- Heating and cooling capacity increase somewhat with increasing water flow rate (Gpm though the equipment).
- Pumping power increases with water flow rate.
- For best heat transfer, the design Gpm value should cause turbulent flow in loop piping runs (responsibility lies with the person and software that produces the pipe loop design).

Section 9

Equipment Size Limits

For cooling, the design value for entering water temperature (WTH) is normally lower for once-through systems, vs. buried, closed-loop systems (roughly 40°F to 60°F, vs. 85°F to 110°F). Since latent capacity increases as entering water temperature drops, the limit for excess total cooling capacity for open-piping systems is somewhat larger than for closed-loop systems (see Tables N2-1 and N2-2).

9-3 Balanced Climate Humid Summer Example

The over-size limits from Table N2-1 apply to cooling-only equipment. These limits apply to all cooling-only equipment, regardless of the local degree day ratio and the application's JSHR value.

The over-size limits from Table N2-2 apply to heat pump equipment. Fayetteville, AR, has 4,166 heating degree days and 4,267 cooling degree days (NOAA data), so it's degree day ratio value is 0.98, which means that the over-size limit is for a Condition A heat pump. In addition, the *Manual J* sensible heat ratio for this example is much less than 0.95, so there are two reasons why this is a Condition A heat pump (either reason is sufficient).

Inspection of Tables N2-1 and N2-2 show that the size limit for total cooling capacity is the same for cooling-only equipment, and for Condition A heat pumps. Therefore, the following solutions apply to both types of equipment.

Cooling Loads and Operating Conditions

Equipment size is based on the *Manual J* cooling loads for the Figure A19-3 floor plan located in Fayetteville, AR. Return duct loads and engineered ventilation details are important because they affect entering wet-bulb and entering dry-bulb temperatures. The 0.96 altitude adjustment factor for 1,251 feet applies to *Manual J* calculations and to psychrometric calculations for entering air temperature (the ACF adjustment is made for procedure consistency, even when the effect is small). Altitude also affects equipment performance, but this effect may be ignored when the altitude is 2,500 Feet or less (this industry-wide default is superseded by OEM guidance). Local ground water temperature is about 62°F. The extreme summer air temperature is 115°F, and the extreme winter air temperature is –15°F (web page values for Ft. Smith).

Sensible cooling load = 33,954 Btuh
Latent cooling load = 5,586 Btuh
Total cooling load = 39,540 Btuh
***Manual J** tons = 39,540 / 12,000 = 3.29*
Floor area = 3,300 SqFt
*SqFt floor area per **Manual J** ton = 3,300 / 3.29 = 1,002*
Altitude = 1,251 Feet; Figure A5-1 ACF = 0.96
Outdoor conditions cooling: 93°F db / 75°F wb
Indoor conditions cooling: 75°F db and 50% RH
Sensible return duct load (Section A2-3) = 1,630 Btuh
Latent return duct load (Section A2-3) = 640 Btuh
Outdoor air = 75 Cfm; Sensible Eff. for cooling = 0.50
JSHR = 33,954 / 39,540 = 0.86
HDD / CDD = 3,935 / 4,368 = 0.90
Ground water temperature = 62°F
Extreme summer temperature = 115°F
WTH = 115 –10 = 105°F
For a single-speed cooling-only, or Condition A heat pump
OSL for open-pipe ground water = 0.90 to 1.25
OSL for buried closed-loop water = 0.90 to 1.15

Data Search

Expanded performance data is searched for something close to 39,000 Btuh of total cooling capacity, for a preliminary value for the entering wet-bulb temperature. To get started, use the wet-bulb temperature for the indoor air.

Condition of the indoor air = 75°F db and 50% RH
Indoor wb temperature at 1,251 feet = 62.35°F
Ballpark wb temperature value for search = 62°F to 63°F

Note: The actual entering wet-bulb temperature depends on the return duct load and the outdoor air load, but these adjustments require a blower Cfm value, which is not known until a candidate unit is selected.

Candidate Single-Speed Equipment

The entering water temperature is 62°F for an open-pipe system, and 105°F for a buried-loop system. Figure 9-1 (next page) shows actual cooling performance data for a single-speed heat pump in the 042 size, 048 size, and 060 size for water with 15% methanol (values for no antifreeze will be somewhat different). This data was extracted from many pages of data for this product. Since 1,350 Cfm, 1,550 Cfm and 2,000 CFM are mid-range values, they are used to find a total cooling capacity values for the 042, 048, and 060 sizes.

Open-Pipe System (GWHP) Candidate

For 62°F water; 75°F db / 63°F wb entering air, the 042 size operating at 5 Gpm has 41,240 Btuh of total cooling capacity, and the 048 size operating at 9 Gpm has 48,100 Btuh of total cooling capacity. The over-size factor for the 042 unit is 1.04, and 1.22 for the 048 unit. Both of these values are within the 0.90 to 1.25 limit for an open-pipe system, so both sizes are tentatively acceptable for 62°F water.

042 OSF for 62°F = 41,240 / 39,540 = 1.04
048 OSF for 62°F = 48,100 / 39,540 = 1.22

Buried Closed-Loop System (GLHP) Candidate

For 105°F entering water; 75°F db / 63°F wb entering air, the 042 size operating at 5 Gpm has 31,750 Btuh of total cooling capacity, the 048 size operating at 9 Gpm has 37,000 Btuh of total cooling capacity, and the 060 size operating at 8 Gpm has 47,950 Btuh of total capacity. The over-size factor for the 042 unit is 0.80, 0.94 for the 048 unit, and 1.21 for the 060 unit. The 0.80 value is less than the 0.90 minimum for total cooling capacity, so the 042 unit is too small for 105°F water. The 0.94 value for the 048 unit is within the 0.90 to 1.15 limit for a closed-loop system, so the 048 unit is tentatively acceptable for 105°F water. The 1.21 value exceeds the 1.15 maximum for a closed-loop system, so the 060 unit is too large for this application.

042 OSF for 105°F = 31,750 / 39,540 = 0.80
048 OSF for 105°F = 37,000 / 39,540 = 0.94
060 OSF for 105°F = 47,950 / 39,540 = 1.21

Entering Dry-Bulb and Wet-Bulb Values

For cooling, return duct loads and outdoor air loads increase the entering dry-bulb and wet-bulb temperatures. Per Section A2-3 procedures, the sensible return duct load is 1,630 Btuh, the latent return duct load is 640 Btuh. The altitude is 1,251 feet, the altitude adjustment is 0.96, the outdoor air is at 93°F dry-bulb / 75°F wet-bulb, and the sensible recovery effectiveness for cooling is 0.50.

When Sections A2-4 and A2-7 procedures are applied to the return duct loads and outdoor air loads for 1,350 blower Cfm (042 size), the condition of the entering air for cooling is 76.6°F db and 63.5°F wb. For 1,550 blower Cfm (048 size), the condition of the entering air for cooling is 76.4°F db and 63.4°F wb.

Equipment size = 042
Blower Cfm = 1,350; Return Cfm = 1,275; OA Cfm = 75
Cooling dry-bulb °F at return grille = 75.0
Cooling wet-bulb °F at return grille = 62.347
Cooling dry-bulb °F out of return duct = 76.143
Cooling wet-bulb °F out of return duct = 62.884
Cooling entering (mixed air) dry-bulb °F = 76.604 (76.6)
Cooling entering (mixed air) wet-bulb °F = 63.481 (63.5)

Equipment size = 048
Blower Cfm = 1,550; Return Cfm = 1,475; OA Cfm = 75
Cooling dry-bulb °F at return grille = 75.0
Cooling wet-bulb °F at return grille = 62.347
Cooling dry-bulb °F out of return duct = 75.996
Cooling wet-bulb °F out of return duct = 62.815
Cooling entering (mixed air) dry-bulb °F = 76.400 (76.4)
Cooling entering (mixed air) wet-bulb °F = 63.399 (63.4)

Interpolated Cooling Capacity Values

Total cooling capacity may be interpolated from the OEM's performance data (Figure 9-1) because total capacity only depends on entering wet-bulb temperature. However, this OEM's data format is not sufficient for sensible capacity interpolation, because sensible capacity depends on entering wet-bulb temperature, and entering dry-bulb temperature.

Water-Source Heat Pump Cooling — 042 Size
Blower Operating at 1,350 Cfm; 15% Methanol by Volume

EWT (°F)	Gpm	EAc db/wb (°F)	TC 1,000 Btuh	SC 1,000 Btuh	LC 1,000 Btuh	EAh db (°F)	HC 1,000 Btuh
25	5.0	75/63	~	~	~	60	~
		80/67	~	~	~	70	~
62		75/63	41.24	31.16	10.08	60	~
		80/67	44.80	31.56	13.24	70	~
105		75/63	31.75	25.75	6.00	~	~
		80/67	31.50	26.85	7.65	~	~

Water-Source Heat Pump Cooling — 048 Size
Blower Operating at 1,550 Cfm; 15% Methanol by Volume

EWT (°F)	Gpm	EAc db/wb (°F)	TC 1,000 Btuh	SC 1,000 Btuh	LC 1,000 Btuh	EAh db (°F)	HC 1,000 Btuh
25	9.0	75/63	~	~	~	60	~
		80/67	~	~	~	70	~
62		75/63	48.10	33.40	14.70	60	~
		80/67	52.26	34.80	17.46	70	~
105		75/63	37.00	30.50	6.50	~	~
		80/67	40.20	31.80	8.40	~	~

Water-Source Heat Pump Cooling — 060 Size
Blower Operating at 2,000 Cfm; 15% Methanol by Volume

EWT (°F)	Gpm	EAc db/wb (°F)	TC 1,000 Btuh	SC 1,000 Btuh	LC 1,000 Btuh	EA_h db (°F)	HC 1,000 Btuh
25	8.0	75/63	~	~	~	60	~
		80/67	~	~	~	70	~
62		75/63	60.80	42.78	17.02	60	~
		80/67	66.06	45.58	20.48	70	~
105		75/63	47.95	39.25	8.70	~	~
		80/67	52.10	40.90	11.20	~	~

EWT = Entering water temperature, Gpm = gallons per minute.
EAc = Entering air for cooling (db = dry-bulb, wb = wet-bulb).
TC = Total cooling capacity, SC = Sensible cooling capacity.
LC = Latent cooling capacity.
EA_h = Entering air dry-bulb for heating.
HC = Heating capacity. Capacities adjusted for blower heat.
25°F values extrapolated from 30-40°F data with OEM approval.
62°F and 105°F values interpolated from 60–70°F; 100–110°F data.

Figure 9-1

042 Performance

For the 042 size, the design value for blower Cfm is 1,350 Cfm. The design values for entering water temperature is 62°F or 105°F. The design values for entering wet-bulb and entering dry-bulb are 63.5°F and 76.6°F.

For 62°F water
Total Btuh @ 63.5°F wb = 41,685
Sensible and latent Btuh closer to the 75°F/63°F values
Sensible Btuh @ 75°F/63°F = 31,160
Latent Btuh @ 75°F/63°F = 10,080

For 105°F water
Total Btuh @ 63.5°F wb = 32,094
Sensible and latent Btuh closer to the 75°F/63°F values
Sensible Btuh @ 75°F/63°F = 25,750
Latent Btuh @ 75°F/63°F = 6,000

048 Performance

For the 048 size, the design value for blower Cfm is 1,550 Cfm. The design values for entering water temperature are 62°F and 105°F. The design values for entering wet-bulb and entering dry-bulb are 63.4°F and 76.4°F.

For 62°F water
Total Btuh @ 63.5°F wb = 48,516
Sensible and latent Btuh closer to the 75°F/63°F values
Sensible Btuh @ 75°F/63°F = 33,400
Latent Btuh @ 75°F/63°F = 14,700

For 105°F water
Total Btuh @ 63.5°F wb = 37,320
Sensible and latent Btuh closer to the 75°F/63°F values
Sensible Btuh @ 75°F/63°F = 30,500
Latent Btuh @ 75°F/63°F = 6,500

Job Site Performance

The total cooling load is 39,540 Btuh, the sensible load is 33,954 Btuh, and the latent load is 5,586 Btuh. Interpolated capacity values are provided above. Figure 9-2 compares cooling performance for the 042 size vs. the 048 size for 62°F water, and for 105°F water.

Open-Pipe System

For 62°F water, the 042 size and the 048 size are compatible with the size limit (0.90 to 1.25) for total cooling capacity. Both units exceed the preferred (non-mandatory) limit for excess latent capacity (the XSLC value should be 1.5 or less), but this tends to be the case when entering water temperature is relatively cool. Both units have adequate sensible capacity (the sensible capacity ratio must be 0.90 or greater).

- The 042 size is the best match for cooling.
- The 048 size provides more compressor heating capacity for heating, and is acceptable for cooling per Table N2-2 rules.

Buried Closed-Loop System

The 048 size is the only choice for 105°F water. The over-size factor is compatible with the size limit (0.90 to 1.15) for total cooling capacity. There is some excess latent capacity, but the LCR value is significantly less than 1.5; and the SCR value is slightly more than the 0.90 limit.

Cooling Performance Summary Fayetteville, AR							
62°F Water – Open-Pipe System 042 @ 1,350 Cfm; 048 @ 1,550 Cfm							
Size	TC	OSF	LC	LCR	XSLC	ASC	SCR
042	41,685	1.05	10,800	1.93	5,214	33,767	0.99
048	48,516	1.23	14,700	2.63	9,114	37,957	1.12
105°F Water - Closed Buried-Loop System 042 @ 1,350 Cfm; 048 @ 1,550 Cfm							
Size	TC	OSF	LC	LCR	XSLC	ASC	SCR
042	32,094	0.81	The OSF is less than the 0.90 limit.				
048	37,320	0.94	6,500	1.16	914	30,957	0.91
060	47,950	1.21	The OSF exceeds the 1.15 limit.				
Capacity (Btuh): TC = Total; LC = Latent; SC = Sensible. OSF = Total capacity over-size factor = Total capacity / Total load. LCR = Latent capacity ratio = OEM data latent capacity / Latent Load. XSLC = Excess latent capacity (Btuh). = OEM data latent capacity – Latent Load. ASC = Adjusted sensible capacity. = OEM data sensible capacity +1/2 excess latent capacity. SCR = Sensible capacity ratio. = Adjusted sensible capacity / Sensible load. Cooling loads (Btuh): Total = 39,540; Sensible = 33,954; Latent = 5,586.							

Figure 9-2

- Entering water temperature values for most of the cooling season will be significantly cooler than 105°F, which is the default value for the end of the cooling season. Therefore, the OSF and SCR values will be larger than the Figure 9-1 values for most of the cooling season.

- For any given project, the worst-case value for entering water temperature may be significantly cooler than the 105°F default used for this example. This depends on the details of the water system design, per Section 9-2.

Square Feet per Ton Values

There is 3,300 SqFt or floor area, and the total cooling load is 39,540 Btuh, so there is 1,002 SqFt per *Manual J* ton. Figure 9-3 (next page) provides square feet per ton values for open-pipe equipment in the 042 and 048 sizes, and for closed-loop, earth-coupled equipment in the 048 size.

- Total cooling capacity is very sensitive to entering water temperature, somewhat sensitive to water flow Gpm, and significantly sensitive to the entering air wet-bulb temperature.

- Square feet per ton values depend on total cooling capacity, so they are equally sensitive to the variables that affect total cooling capacity.
- The AHRI rating value for total cooling capacity (and the corresponding SqFt/Ton value) usually does not correlate with application circumstances (possible, but statistically uncommon).

Heating Loads and Operating Conditions

A Condition A heat pump is compatible with the *Manual J* cooling loads and the attributes of Fayetteville, AR, weather. For cooling, the 042 and 048 sizes are acceptable for an open-pipe system, and the 048 size is acceptable for a buried, closed-loop system.

The extreme winter temperature is –15°F. The *Manual J* heating load and corresponding equipment operating conditions are summarized below. Figure 9-4 (next page) shows the heating performance data for 042 equipment and 048 equipment.

Sensible heating load = 56,236 Btuh
Altitude = 1,251 Feet; Figure A5-1 ACF = 0.96
Outdoor air temperature = 13°F db
Indoor conditions: 70°F db, no humidification
Sensible return duct load (Section A2-3) = 2,272 Btuh
Outdoor air = 75 Cfm; Sensible Eff. for heating = 0.55
Ground water temperature = 62°F
Extreme winter temperature = -15°F
WTL = -15 + 40 = 25°F

Entering Dry-Bulb Temperature

Return duct loads and outdoor air loads decrease the entering dry-bulb temperature. Per Section A2-3 procedures, the sensible return duct load is 2,272 Btuh. The altitude is 1,251 feet, the altitude adjustment is 0.96, the outdoor temperature is 13°F, and the sensible recovery effectiveness for heating is 0.55.

Entering dry-bulb for the 042 Size

When Sections A2-4 and A2-7 procedures are applied to the return duct load and outdoor air load (using altitude psychrometrics), the dry-bulb temperature of the entering air is 67.0°F for 1,350 blower Cfm.

Blower Cfm = 1,350; return Cfm = 1,275; OA Cfm = 75
Dry-bulb °F at return grille = 70.0
Dry-bulb °F out of return duct = 68.406
Entering (mixed air) dry-bulb °F = 67.021 (67.0)

Entering dry-bulb for the 048 Size

When Sections A2-4 and A2-7 procedures are applied to the return duct load and outdoor air load (using altitude psychrometrics), the dry-bulb temperature of the entering air is 67.4°F for 1,550 blower Cfm.

Square Feet per Ton Values Fayetteville, AR					
Manual J SqFt per Ton = 1,002					
Open system	EWT °F	Gpm	EDB °F / EWB °F	TC Btuh	SqFt per Ton
042 Applied	62	5	76.6 / 63.5	41,685	951
042 Rated	59	11	80.6 / 66.2	48,700	813
048 Applied	62	9	76.4 / 63.4	48,516	817
048 Rated	59	12	80.6 / 66.2	54,600	725
Closed system	EWT °F	Gpm	EDB °F / EWB °F	TC Btuh	SqFt per Ton
048 Applied	105	9	76.4 / 63.4	37,320	1,061
048 Rated	77	12	80.6 / 66.2	47,100	841

1) Applied relates to actual project circumstances. Rated relates to AHRI rating data.
2) For open-pipe systems, entering water temperature depends on ground water temperature, which depends on local conditions, and the Gpm is a practitioner decision.
3) For buried closed-loop systems, entering water temperature and Gpm depend on decisions made by the person (and software) responsible for the piping loop design.
4) Appendix 2 procedures, applied to *Manual J* data, return values for entering dry-bulb and wet-bulb temperatures.
5) Cooling capacity values extracted from OEM data.
6) 3,300 SqFt of floor area for this example.

Figure 9-3

Blower Cfm = 1,550; return Cfm = 1,475; OA Cfm = 75
Dry-bulb °F at return grille = 70.0
Dry-bulb °F out of return duct = 68.612
Entering (mixed air) dry-bulb °F = 67.401 (67.4)

Interpolated Heating Capacity Values

For the 042 size, the design value for blower Cfm is 1,350 Cfm and the design value for entering air temperature is 67.0°F. For the 048 size, the design value for blower Cfm is 1,550 Cfm and the design value for entering air temperature is 67.4°F. Applied heating capacity values for 67.0°F and 67.4°F entering air are interpolated from OEM performance data values (per Figure 9-4, on the next page).

Heating capacity for 62°F once-through water
042 size for 67.0°F air = 41,500 Btuh
048 size for 67.4°F air = 54,000 Btuh

Heating capacity for 25°F closed-loop water
048 size for 67.4°F air = 31,300 Btuh

Caveats for the Buried Closed-Loop Heating

Entering water temperature values for most of the heating season will be significantly warmer than 25°F, which is the default value for the end of the heating season. For

Section 9

any given project, the worst-case value for entering water temperature may be significantly warmer than the 25°F value used for this example. This depends on the details of the water system design, per Section 9-2.

Supplemental Heat

Figure 9-5 shows the balance point diagram for this application. The supplemental heat requirement depends on equipment size and entering water temperature.

Supplemental KW for 62°F once-through water
042 size = 4.32 KW (use 5 KW)
048 size = 0.66 KW (use none, or smallest KW available)

Supplemental KW for 25°F closed-loop water
048 size = 7.31 KW (use 7.5 KW)

Default Thermal Balance Point

Figure 9-5 shows that the default thermal balance points are about 15°F, 26°F, and 36°F, depending on equipment size and entering water temperature.

- Supplemental heat must be locked out when the outdoor air temperature is above the thermal balance point.
- Supplemental heating capacity may be activated by a simple outdoor air temperature sensor control that has manually adjusted set-points, or microprocessor control that evaluates the momentary need for electric coil heat.

Emergency Heat

The default value for emergency heat is 85% of the heating load. This is 47,801 Btuh, which is close to 14 KW.

0.85 x 56,236 = 47,801 Btuh
47,801 / 3,413 = 14.1 KW

Auxiliary Heat

Because of standard sizes offered by this OEM, the total amount of electric coil heat is 15 KW. For the 048 size and 25°F water, this is preferably split into 7.5 KW for supplemental heat, with an additional 7.5 KW available by emergency switch. For the 042 size and 62°F water, this is preferably split into 5 KW steps for supplemental heat, with and additional 10 KW available by emergency switch. For the 048 size and 62°F water, this may be split into 0 KW, 2.5 KW or 5 KW for supplemental heat, with balance available by emergency switch.

Sizing Decision for an Open-Pipe System

The 042 and 048 sizes are compatible with the equipment sizing rules when 62°F water flows through an open-pipe system. Total cooling capacity falls within the minimum and maximum limits, sensible cooling capacity satisfies the minimum requirement for the sensible cooling capacity

Water-Air Heat Pump Heating — 042 Size Blower Operating at 1,350 Cfm; 15% Methanol by Volume							
EWT (°F)	Gpm	EAc db/wb (°F)	TC 1,000 Btuh	SC 1,000 Btuh	LC 1,000 Btuh	EA_h db (°F)	HC 1,000 Btuh
25	5.0	75/63	~	~	~	60	23.9
		80/67	~	~	~	70	23.1
62		75/63	~	~	~	60	42.6
		80/67	~	~	~	70	41.1

Water-Air Heat Pump Heating — 048 Size Blower Operating at 1,550 Cfm; 15% Methanol by Volume							
EWT (°F)	Gpm	EAc db/wb (°F)	TC 1,000 Btuh	SC 1,000 Btuh	LC 1,000 Btuh	EA_h db (°F)	HC 1,000 Btuh
25	9.0	75/63	~	~	~	60	32.2
		80/67	~	~	~	70	31.0
62		75/63	~	~	~	60	55.5
		80/67	~	~	~	70	53.5

EWT = Entering water temperature, Gpm = gallons per minute.
EAc = Entering air for cooling (db = dry-bulb, wb = wet-bulb).
TC = Total cooling capacity, SC = Sensible cooling capacity.
LC = Latent cooling capacity, EA_h = Entering air db for heating.
HC = Reverse cycle heating capacity.
25°F values extrapolated from 30–40°F data with OEM approval.
62°F values interpolated from 60–70°F data.

Figure 9-4

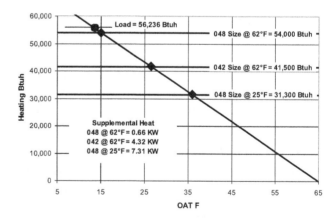

Figure 9-5

ratio, and latent cooling capacity satisfies the recommended (non-mandatory) limit for the latent cooling capacity ratio (see Table N2-2 and Figure 9-2).

- Figure 9-2 shows that the 042 size is the preferred choice for cooling because the OSF, SCR and LCR values are closer to 1.00, than for the 048 size.
- Figure 9-5 shows that the 048 size may be the preferred choice for heating because the thermal balance point is 15°F, vs. 26°F for the 042 size. However,

Figure A19-3 shows that there are not many bin-hours for outdoor air temperatures that are less than 25°F, so the 042 size is the preferred choice for this location.

Sizing Decision for a Buried Closed-Loop System

For a buried, closed-loop system, the 048 size is the only size (042, vs. 048, vs. 060) that is compatible with the equipment sizing rules. Total cooling capacity falls within the minimum and maximum limits, sensible cooling capacity satisfies the minimum requirement for the sensible cooling capacity ratio, and latent cooling capacity satisfies the recommended (non-mandatory) limit for the latent cooling capacity ratio (see Table N2-2 and Figure 9-2).

For heating, the design value for the thermal balance point is about 36°F for 25°F water. However, the 25°F water temperature is the worst-case temperature for the end of the heating season. The water temperature will be significantly warmer than 25°F, and the thermal balance point will be significantly lower than 36°F for most of the heating season.

- This example problem is about equipment sizing for a given set of entering water temperatures. Worst-case water temperatures were used for this purpose. A water system may be designed for a maximum water temperature that is less than 105°F, and a minimum water temperature that is more than 25°F. See Appendix 9.

- Different entering water temperature values have no affect on the equipment sizing procedure, but they do affect the design values for cooling and heating capacity; which may, or may not, affect the size of the installed equipment when cooling capacity values are compared to Table N2-2 limits.

9-4 Hot-Humid Climate Example

The over-size limits from Table N2-1 apply to cooling-only equipment. These limits apply to all cooling-only equipment, regardless of the local degree day ratio and the application's JSHR value.

The over-size limits from Table N2-2 apply to heat pump equipment. Brunswick, GA, has 1,545 heating degree days and 6,765 cooling degree days (NOAA data), so it's degree day ratio value is 0.23, which means that the over-size limit is for a Condition A heat pump. In addition, the *Manual J* sensible heat ratio for this example is much less than 0.95, so there are two reasons why this is a Condition A heat pump (either reason is sufficient).

Inspection of Tables N2-1 and N2-2 show that the size limit for total cooling capacity is the same for cooling-only equipment, and for Condition A heat pumps. Therefore, the following solutions apply to both types of equipment.

Cooling Loads and Operating Conditions

Equipment size is based on the *Manual J* cooling loads for the Figure 19-2 floor plan located in Brunswick, GA. Return duct loads and engineered ventilation details are important because they affect entering wet-bulb and entering dry-bulb temperatures. Since Brunswick is 20 feet above sea level, there is no altitude adjustment (ACF = 1.0) for *Manual J* calculations or for the psychrometric calculations for entering air temperature, and there is no altitude adjustment for equipment performance. Local ground water temperature is about 70°F. The extreme summer air temperature is 105°F, and the extreme winter air temperature is 7°F (web page values for Jacksonville, Florida).

Sensible cooling load = 29,413 Btuh
Latent cooling load = 8,801 Btuh
Total cooling load = 38,214 Btuh
***Manual J** tons = 38,214 / 12,000 = 3.18*
Floor area = 3,300 SqFt
*SqFt floor area per **Manual J** ton = 3,300 / 3.18 = 1,038*
Altitude = 20 Feet; Figure A5-1 ACF = 1.00
Outdoor conditions: 91°F db / 79°F wb
Indoor conditions: 75°F db and 50% RH
Sensible return duct load (Worksheet G) = 1,461 Btuh
Latent return duct load (Worksheet G) = 948 Btuh
Outdoor air = 75 Cfm; Sensible Eff. for cooling = 0.50
JSHR = 29,413 / 38,214 = 0.77
HDD / CDD = 1,523 / 6,676 = 0.23
Ground water temperature = 70°F
Extreme summer temperature = 105°F
WTH = 105 -10 = 95°F
For a single-speed cooling-only, or Condition A heat pump
OSL for open-pipe ground water = 0.90 to 1.25
OSL for buried closed piping loop = 0.90 to 1.15

Data Search

Expanded performance data is searched for something close to 38,000 Btuh of total cooling capacity, for a preliminary value for the entering wet-bulb temperature. To get started, use the wet-bulb temperature for the indoor air.

Condition of the indoor air = 75°F db and 50% RH
Indoor wb temperature at 20 feet = 62.54°F
Ballpark wb temperature value for search = 62°F to 63°F

Note: The actual entering wet-bulb temperature depends on the return duct load and the outdoor air load, but these adjustments require a blower Cfm value, which is not known until a candidate unit is selected.

Candidate Single-Speed Equipment

The entering water temperature is 70°F for an open-pipe system, and 95°F for a buried-loop system. Figure 9-6 shows actual cooling performance data for a single-speed heat pump in the 042 size and 048 size for water with 15% methanol (values for no antifreeze will be somewhat

Section 9

different). This data was extracted from many pages of data for this product. Since 1,350 Cfm and 1,550 Cfm are mid-range values, they are used to find a total cooling capacity values for the 042 and 048 sizes.

Open-Pipe System Candidate

For 70°F water; 75°F db/ 63°F wb entering air, the 042 size operating at 5 Gpm has 39,400 Btuh of total cooling capacity, and the 048 size operating at 9 Gpm and 1,550 Cfm has 46,500 Btuh of total cooling capacity. The over-size factor for the 042 unit is 1.03, and 1.22 for the 048 unit. Both of these values are within the 0.90 to 1.25 limit for an open-pipe system, so both sizes are tentatively acceptable for 70°F water.

042 OSF for 62°F = 39,400 / 38,214 = 1.03
048 OSF for 62°F = 46,500 / 38,214 = 1.22

Buried Closed-Loop System Candidate

For 95°F entering water; 75°F db/ 63°F wb entering air, the 042 size operating at 5 Gpm has 34,450 Btuh of total cooling capacity, and the 048 size operating at 9 Gpm and 1,550 Cfm has 39,750 Btuh of total cooling capacity. The over-size factor for the 042 unit is 0.90, and 0.94 for the 048 unit. The 0.90 value for the 042 unit just meets the 0.90 minimum for total cooling capacity. The 1.04 value for the 048 unit is within the 0.90 to 1.15 limit for a closed-loop system, so both sizes are tentatively acceptable for 95°F water.

042 OSF for 105°F = 34,450 / 38,214 = 0.90
048 OSF for 105°F = 39,750 / 38,214 = 1.04

Entering Dry-Bulb and Wet-Bulb Values

For cooling, return duct loads and outdoor air loads increase the entering dry-bulb and wet-bulb temperatures. Per Section A2-3 procedures, the sensible return duct load is 1,461 Btuh, the latent return duct load is 948 Btuh. The altitude is 20 feet, the altitude adjustment is 1.00, the outdoor air is at 91°F dry-bulb / 79°F wet-bulb, and the sensible recovery effectiveness for cooling is 0.50.

When Sections A2-4 and A2-7 procedures are applied to the return duct loads and outdoor air loads for 1,350 blower Cfm (042 size), the condition of the entering air for cooling is 76.4°F db and 64.0°F wb. For 1,550 blower Cfm (048 size), the condition of the entering air for cooling is 76.2°F db and 63.8°F wb.

Equipment size = 042
Blower Cfm = 1,350; Return Cfm = 1,275; OA Cfm = 75
Cooling dry-bulb °F at return grille = 75.0
Cooling wet-bulb °F at return grille = 62.543
Cooling dry-bulb °F out of return duct = 75.984
Cooling wet-bulb °F out of return duct = 63.105
Cooling entering (mixed air) dry-bulb °F = 76.395 (76.4)
Cooling entering (mixed air) wet-bulb °F = 63.990 (64.0)

Water-Air Heat Pump Cooling — 042 Size
Blower Operating at 1,350 Cfm; 15% Methanol by Volume

EWT (°F)	Gpm	EAc db/wb (°F)	TC 1,000 Btuh	SC 1,000 Btuh	LC 1,000 Btuh	EAh db (°F)	HC 1,000 Btuh
47	5.0	75/63	~	~	~	60	~
		80/67	~	~	~	70	~
70	5.0	75/63	39.40	29.80	9.60	60	~
		80/67	42.80	31.00	11.80	70	~
95	5.0	75/63	34.45	26.05	8.40	~	~
		80/67	37.45	27.15	10.30	~	~

Water-Air Heat Pump Cooling — 048A Size
Blower Operating at 1,550 Cfm; 15% Methanol by Volume

EWT (°F)	Gpm	EAc db/wb (°F)	TC 1,000 Btuh	SC 1,000 Btuh	LC 1,000 Btuh	EAh db (°F)	HC 1,000 Btuh
47	9.0	75/63	~	~	~	60	~
		80/67	~	~	~	70	~
70	9.0	75/63	46.50	33.00	13.50	60	~
		80/67	50.50	34.40	16.10	70	~
95	9.0	75/63	39.75	30.50	6.55	~	~
		80/67	40.20	31.80	8.40	~	~

EWT = Entering water temperature; Gpm = gallons per minute.
EAc = Entering air for cooling (db = dry-bulb, wb = wet-bulb).
TC = Total cooling capacity, SC = Sensible cooling capacity.
LC = Latent cooling capacity. EA_h = Entering air db for heating.
HC = Heating capacity.
Capacities adjusted for blower heat.
47°F values interpolated from 40-50°F data.
70°F values copied from the OEM's data table.
95°F values interpolated from 90-100°F data.

Blower Cfm Adjustment Factors

Load Item	Percent of Nominal Blower Cfm for Capacity Data						
	85%	90%	95%	100%	105%	110%	115%
TC	0.972	0.982	0.993	1.000	1.007	1.010	1.013
SC	0.926	0.948	0.974	1.000	1.027	1.055	1.066
HC	0.967	0.978	0.990	1.00	1.009	1.017	1.024

Water-Air Heat Pump Cooling — 048B Size
Blower Operating at 1,395 Cfm; 15% Methanol by Volume

EWT (°F)	Gpm	EAc db/wb (°F)	TC 1,000 Btuh	SC 1,000 Btuh	LC 1,000 Btuh	EAh db (°F)	HC 1,000 Btuh
47	9.0	75/63	~	~	~	60	~
		80/67	~	~	~	70	~
70	9.0	75/63	45.66	31.28	14.38	60	~
		80/67	49.59	32.61	12.61	70	~
95	9.0	75/63	39.03	29.67	9.36	~	~
		80/67	42.42	30.90	11.52	~	~

Figure 9-6

Equipment size = 048
Blower Cfm = 1,550; Return Cfm = 1,475; OA Cfm = 75
Cooling dry-bulb °F at return grille = 75.0
Cooling wet-bulb °F at return grille = 62.543
Cooling dry-bulb °F out of return duct = 75.857
Cooling wet-bulb °F out of return duct = 63.033
Cooling entering (mixed air) dry-bulb °F = 76.219 (76.2)
Cooling entering (mixed air) wet-bulb °F = 63.808 (63.8)

Interpolated Cooling Capacity Values

Total cooling capacity may be interpolated from this OEM's performance data (Figure 9-6) because total capacity only depends on entering wet-bulb temperature. However, this OEM's data format is not sufficient for sensible capacity interpolation, because sensible capacity depends on entering wet-bulb temperature, and entering dry-bulb temperature.

O42 Performance

For the 042 size, the design value for blower Cfm is 1,350 Cfm. The design values for entering water temperature is 70°F or 95°F. The design values for entering wet-bulb and entering dry-bulb are 64.0°F and 76.4°F.

For 70°F water
Total Btuh @ 64.0°F wb = 40,250
Sensible and latent Btuh closer to the 75°F/63°F values
Sensible Btuh @ 75°F/63°F = 29,800
Latent Btuh @ 75°F/63°F = 9,600

For 95°F water
Total Btuh @ 63.5°F wb = 35,200
Sensible and latent Btuh closer to the 75°F/63°F values
Sensible Btuh @ 75°F/63°F = 26,050
Latent Btuh @ 75°F/63°F = 8,400

O48A Performance

For 048A performance, the design value for blower Cfm is 1,550 Cfm. The design values for entering water temperature are 70°F and 95°F. The design values for entering wet-bulb and entering dry-bulb are 63.8°F and 76.2°F.

048A for 70°F water
Total Btuh @ 63.8°F wb = 47,300
Sensible and latent Btuh closer to the 75°F/63°F values
Sensible Btuh @ 75°F/63°F = 33,000
Latent Btuh @ 75°F/63°F = 13,500

048A for 95°F water
Total Btuh @ 63.8°F wb = 40,440
Sensible and latent Btuh closer to the 75°F/63°F values
Sensible Btuh @ 75°F/63°F = 31,300
Latent Btuh @ 75°F/63°F = 8,450

O48B Performance

For 048B performance, the design value for blower Cfm is 1,395 Cfm. The design value for entering water temperature is 95°F. The design values for entering wet-bulb and entering dry-bulb are 63.3°F and 76.3°F.

048B for 95°F water
Total Btuh @ 63.3°F wb = 39,284
Sensible and latent Btuh closer to the 75°F/63°F values
Sensible Btuh @ 75°F/63°F = 29,670
Latent Btuh @ 75°F/63°F = 9,360

Job Site Performance

The total cooling load is 38,212 Btuh, the sensible load is 29,413 Btuh, and the latent load is 8,801 Btuh. Interpolated capacity values are provided above. Figure 9-7 (previous page) compares cooling performance for the 042 size vs. the 048 size for 70°F water, and for 95°F water.

Open-Pipe System

For 70°F water, the 042 and 048A sizes are compatible with the size limit (0.90 to 1.25) for total cooling capacity. Both units are compatible with the preferred (non-mandatory) limit for excessive latent capacity (the LCR value should be 1.5 or less). Both units have adequate sensible capacity (the SCR value must be 0.90 or greater).

- The 042 size is the best match for cooling.
- The 048 size complies with the size limits for cooling and has excessive compressor heating capacity (cooling is the primary concern for Brunswick).

Cooling Performance Summary Brunswick, GA						
70°F Water - Open-Pipe System 042 @1,350 Cfm; 048A @ 1,550 Cfm						
Size	TC	OSF	LC	LCR	XSLC	ASC	SCR
042	40,250	1.05	9,600	1.09	799	30,200	1.03
048A	47,300	1.24	13,500	1.53	4,699	35,350	1.20
95°F Water - Closed Buried-Loop System 042 @1,350 Cfm; 048A@1,550 Cfm; 048B @1,395 Cfm						
Size	TC	OSF	LC	LCR	XSLC	ASC	SCR
042	35,200	0.92	8,400	0.95	- 401	26,050	0.89
048A	40,440	1.06	8,450	0.96	-351	31,300	1.06
048B	39,284	1.03	9,360	1.06	559	29,670	1.02

Capacity (Btuh): TC = Total; LC = Latent; SC = Sensible.
OSF = Total capacity over-size factor = Total capacity / Total load.
LCR = Latent capacity ratio.
  = OEM data latent capacity / Latent Load.
XSLC = Excess latent capacity (Btuh).
  = OEM data latent capacity - Latent Load.
ASC = Adjusted sensible capacity.
  = OEM data sensible capacity + ½ excess latent capacity.
SCR = Sensible capacity ratio.
  = Adjusted sensible capacity / Sensible load.
Cooling loads (Btuh):
Total = 39,540; Sensible = 33,954; Latent = 5,586.

Figure 9-7

Section 9

Buried Closed-Loop System

For 95°F water, Figure 9-7 shows that the 042 size is sightly deficient in latent and sensible cooling capacity. These deficiencies may be rectified by designing the water-loop for a cooler entering water temperature (85°F should do it), but this goes beyond the scope of this example.

Figure 9-7 also shows that the 048B size operating at 1,395 blower Cfm is the perfect size for 95°F water. The 1.03 over-size factor complies with the size limit (0.90 to 1.15) for total cooling capacity. Latent capacity exceeds latent load by 559 Btuh, and the 1.06 LCR value is significantly less than 1.5. The 1.02 SCR value means that the adjusted sensible capacity is about 2% more than the sensible load.

- Entering water temperature values for most of the cooling season will be significantly cooler than 95°F, which is the default value for the end of the cooling season. Therefore, momentary cooling capacity values will be larger than the Figure 9-6 values for most of the cooling season.

- For any given project, the worst-case value for entering water temperature may be significantly cooler than the 95°F default used for this example. This depends on the details of the water system design, per Section 9-2.

Square Feet per Ton Values

There is 3,300 SqFt or floor area, and the total cooling load is 38,214 Btuh, so there is 1,038 SqFt per *Manual J* ton. Figure 9-8 provides square feet per ton values for open-pipe equipment in the 042 and 048A sizes, and for closed-loop, earth-coupled equipment in the 048B size.

- Total cooling capacity is very sensitive to entering water temperature, somewhat sensitive to water flow Gpm, and significantly sensitive to the entering air wet-bulb temperature.

- Square feet per ton values depend on total cooling capacity, so they are equally sensitive to the variables that affect total cooling capacity.

- The AHRI rating value for total cooling capacity (and the corresponding SqFt/Ton value) usually does not correlate with application circumstances (possible, but statistically uncommon).

Heating Loads and Operating Conditions

A Condition A heat pump is compatible with the *Manual J* cooling loads and the attributes of Brunswick, GA, weather. For cooling, the 042 and 048A sizes are acceptable for an open-pipe system, and the 048B size is acceptable for a buried, closed-loop system.

The extreme winter temperature is 7°F. The *Manual J* heating load and corresponding equipment operating conditions are summarized below. Figure 9-9 (next page)

Square Feet per Ton Values Brunswick, GA					
Manual J SqFt per Ton = 1,038					
Open system	EWT °F	Gpm	EDB °F / EWB °F	TC Btuh	SqFt per Ton
042 Applied	70	5	76.4 / 64.0	40,250	985
042 Rated	59	11	80.6 / 66.2	48,700	815
048A Applied	70	9	76.2 / 63.8	47,300	838
048 Rated	59	12	80.6 / 66.2	54,600	725
Closed system	EWT °F	Gpm	EDB °F / EWB °F	TC Btuh	SqFt per Ton
048B Applied	95	9	76.3 / 63.3	39,284	1,008
048 Rated	77	12	80.6 / 66.2	47,100	841

1) Applied relates to actual project circumstances. Rated relates to AHRI rating data.
2) For open-pipe systems, entering water temperature depends on ground water temperature, which depends on local conditions, and the Gpm is a practitioner decision.
3) For buried closed-loop systems, entering water temperature and Gpm depend on decisions made by the person (and software) responsible for the piping loop design.
4) Appendix 2 procedures, applied to *Manual J* data, return values for entering dry-bulb and wet-bulb temperatures.
5) Cooling capacity values extracted from OEM data.
6) 3,300 SqFt of floor area for this example.

Figure 9-8

shows the heating performance data for 042 equipment and 048 equipment.

Sensible heating load = 34,880 Btuh
Altitude = 20 Feet; Figure A5-1 ACF = 1.00
Outdoor air temperature = 34°F db
Indoor conditions: 70°F db, no humidification
Sensible return duct load (Section A2-3) = 1,155 Btuh
Outdoor air = 75 Cfm; Sensible Eff. for heating = 0.55
Ground water temperature = 70°F
Extreme winter temperature = 7°F
WTL = 7 + 40 = 47°F

Entering Dry-Bulb Temperature

Return duct loads and outdoor air loads decrease the entering dry-bulb temperature. Per Section A2-3 procedures, the sensible return duct load is 1,155 Btuh. The altitude is 20 feet, the altitude adjustment is 1.00, the outdoor temperature is 34°F, and the sensible recovery effectiveness for heating is 0.55.

Entering dry-bulb for the 042 Size

When Sections A2-4 and A2-7 procedures are applied to the return duct load and outdoor air load (using altitude psychrometrics), the dry-bulb temperature of the entering air is 68.3°F for 1,350 blower Cfm.

Blower Cfm = 1,350; return Cfm = 1,275; OA Cfm = 75
Dry-bulb °F at return grille = 70.0
Dry-bulb °F out of return duct = 69.222
Entering (mixed air) dry-bulb °F = 68.341 (68.3)

Entering dry-bulb for the 048B Size

When Sections A2-4 and A2-7 procedures are applied to the return duct load and outdoor air load (using altitude psychrometrics), the dry-bulb temperature of the entering air is 68.4°F for 1,395 blower Cfm.

048B
Blower Cfm = 1,395; return Cfm = 1,320; OA Cfm = 75
Dry-bulb °F at return grille = 70.0
Dry-bulb °F out of return duct = 69.247
048B entering (mixed air) dry-bulb °F = 68.394 (68.4)

Interpolated Heating Capacity Values

The 042 size is the best match for 70°F (open-system) water. The 048B size is the best match for 47°F (buried, closed-loop) water. The 042 size operates at 1,350 blower Cfm, and the design value for entering air temperature is 68.3°F. The 048B size operates at 1,395 blower Cfm, and the design value for entering air temperature is 68.4°F. Applied heating capacity values for 68.3°F and 68.4°F entering air are interpolated from OEM performance data values (per Figure 9-9).

Heating capacity for 70°F once-through water
042 size for 68.3°F air = 45,600 Btuh

Heating capacity for 47°F closed-loop water
048B size for 68.4°F air = 43,000 Btuh

Caveats for Buried Closed-Loop Heating

Entering water temperature values for most of the heating season will be significantly warmer than 47°F, which is the default value for the end of the heating season. For any given project, the worst-case value for entering water temperature may be significantly warmer than the 47°F value used for this example. This depends on the details of the water system design, per Section 9-2.

Supplemental Heat

Figure 9-10 shows the balance point diagram for this application. The supplemental heat requirement depends on equipment size and entering water temperature. The cooling load dominates the heating load for this location, so there is no supplemental heating load for either type of water system.

Supplemental KW for 70°F once-through water
042 size = 0.00 KW (heating capacity exceeds load)

Supplemental KW for 47°F closed-loop water
048B size = 0.00 KW (heating capacity exceeds load)

Water-Source Heat Pump Heating — 042 Size Blower Operating at 1,350 Cfm; 15% Methanol by Volume							
EWT (°F)	Gpm	EAc db/wb (°F)	TC 1,000 Btuh	SC 1,000 Btuh	LC 1,000 Btuh	EA$_h$ db (°F)	HC 1,000 Btuh
47	5.0	75/63	~	~	~	60	34.6
		80/67	~	~	~	70	33.4
70		75/63	~	~	~	60	46.8
		80/67	~	~	~	70	45.3

Water-Source Heat Pump Heating — 048A Size Blower Operating at 1,550 Cfm; 15% Methanol by Volume							
EWT (°F)	Gpm	EAc db/wb (°F)	TC 1,000 Btuh	SC 1,000 Btuh	LC 1,000 Btuh	EA$_h$ db (°F)	HC 1,000 Btuh
47	9.0	75/63	~	~	~	60	45.4
		80/67	~	~	~	70	43.7
70		75/63	~	~	~	60	60.9
		80/67	~	~	~	70	58.9

Water-Source Heat Pump Heating — 048B Size Blower Operating at 1,395 Cfm; 15% Methanol by Volume							
EWT (°F)	Gpm	EAc db/wb (°F)	TC 1,000 Btuh	SC 1,000 Btuh	LC 1,000 Btuh	EAh db (°F)	HC 1,000 Btuh
47	9.0	75/63	~	~	~	60	44.4
		80/67	~	~	~	70	42.7
70		75/63	~	~	~	60	59.6
		80/67	~	~	~	70	57.6

EWT = Entering water temperature, Gpm = gallons per minute.
EAc = Entering air for cooling (db = dry-bulb, wb = wet-bulb).
TC = Total cooling capacity, SC = Sensible cooling capacity.
LC = Latent cooling capacity, EA$_h$ = Entering air db for heating.
HC = Reverse cycle heating capacity.
25°F values extrapolated from 30-40°F data.
62°F values interpolated from 60-70°F data.

Figure 9-9

Default Thermal Balance Point

Figure 9-10 shows that the default thermal balance point for the 042 size with 47°F water is about 24°F. It also shows that the default thermal balance point for the 048B size with 47°F water is about 26°F. Both balance points are lower than the winter design temperature (34°F).

- In general, supplemental heat must be locked out when the outdoor air temperature is above the thermal balance point. However, it is not needed for this particular set of circumstances.

- When supplemental heat is needed, it may be activated by a simple outdoor air temperature sensor control that has manually adjusted set-points, or microprocessor control that evaluates the momentary need for electric coil heat.

Section 9

Emergency Heat

The default value for emergency heat is 85% of the heating load. This is 29,648 Btuh, or about 8.7 KW.

0.85 x 34,880 = 29,648 Btuh
29,648 / 3,413 = 8.69 KW

Auxiliary Heat

Because of standard sizes offered by this OEM, the total amount of electric coil heat is 10 KW. This may be activated in one-stage, or split into two 5 KW stages, per the action of the emergency heat controls.

Sizing Decision for an Open-Pipe System

The 042 and 048 sizes are compatible with the equipment sizing rules when 70°F water flows through an open-pipe system. Total cooling capacity falls within the minimum and maximum limits, sensible cooling capacity satisfies the minimum requirement for the sensible cooling capacity ratio, and latent cooling capacity satisfies the recommended (non-mandatory) limit for the latent cooling capacity ratio (see Table N2-2 and Figure 9-2).

- Figure 9-7 shows that the 042 size is the preferred choice for cooling because the OSF, SCR and LCR values are closer to 1.00, than for the 048 size.

- The 048 size pushes the upper limit for cooling and has about 59,000 Btuh of heating capacity, which is decidedly excessive when compared to the 35,000 Btuh heating load.

- Brunswick, GA, has many hours of warm/hot summer weather with a lot of outdoor humidity, and mild winters, so the 042 size is the preferred choice for this location.

Sizing Decision for a Buried-Loop System

For a buried, closed-loop system, the 048B size is the only size (042 vs. 048A vs. 048B) that is compatible with the equipment sizing rules. Total cooling capacity falls within the minimum and maximum limits, sensible cooling capacity satisfies the minimum requirement for the sensible cooling capacity ratio, and latent cooling capacity satisfies the recommended (non-mandatory) limit for the latent cooling capacity ratio (see Table N2-2 and Figure 9-7).

For heating, the design value for the thermal balance point is significantly lower than the winter design temperature for outdoor air. However, the 47°F water temperature is the worst-case temperature for the end of the heating season. The water temperature will be significantly warmer than 47°F, and the thermal balance point will be significantly lower than 26°F for most of the heating season.

- This example problem is about equipment sizing for a given set of entering water temperatures. Worst-case water temperatures were used for this purpose.

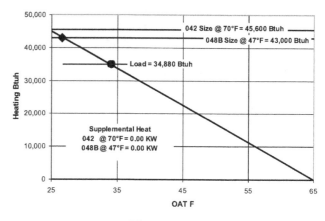

Figure 9-10

A water system may be designed for a maximum water temperature that is less than 95°F, and a minimum water temperature that is more than 47°F. See Appendix 9.

- Different entering water temperature values have no affect on the equipment sizing procedure, but they do affect the design values for cooling and heating capacity; which may, or may not, affect the size of the installed equipment when cooling capacity values are compared to Table N2-2 limits.

9-5 Dry Summer Cold Winter Example

The over-size limits from Table N2-1 apply to cooling-only equipment. These limits apply to all cooling-only equipment, regardless of the local degree day ratio and the application's JSHR value.

The over-size limit from Table N2-2 applies to heat pump equipment. Boise, ID, has 5,727 heating degree days and 2,856 cooling degree days (NOAA data), so it's degree day ratio value is 2.01, which means that the over-size limit is for a Condition B heat pump. Per *Manual J*, Table 1A; the elevation is 2,838 feet, and the grains difference value for 45% RH indoors is -21 Grains, so the cooling coil will be dry. A JSHR value of 0.95, or more, is the second, and necessary, reason why this is a Condition B heat pump.

Table N2-2 procedures for a Condition B heat pump supersede Table N2-1 procedures for cooling-only equipment. Therefore, the solutions for cooling-only equipment and heat pump equipment are different. Water-air equipment is typically heat pump equipment, so the scope of this example is limited to heat pump equipment.

Cooling Loads and Operating Conditions

Equipment size is based on the *Manual J* cooling loads for the Figure 19-2 floor plan located in Boise, ID. The return duct load and engineered ventilation details are important because they affect entering dry-bulb temperature. The 0.88 altitude adjustment factor for 2,838 feet applies to *Manual J* calculations and to psychrometric calculations for entering air temperature. Altitude also affects equipment performance, per the air mass-flow adjustment factor from Table A5-3. Local ground water temperature is about 52°F. The extreme summer air temperature is 111°F, and the extreme winter air temperature is −28°F (web page values).

Sensible cooling load = 30,145 Btuh
Latent cooling load = Negative (dry-coil)
Total cooling load = 30,145 Btuh
***Manual J** tons = 30,145 / 12,000 = 2.51*
Floor area = 3,300 SqFt
*SqFt floor area per **Manual J** ton = 3,300 / 2.51 = 1,315*
Altitude = 2,838 Feet; Figure A5-1 ACF = 0.88
Outdoor conditions: 94°F db / 63°F wb
Indoor conditions: 75°F db and less than 45% RH
Sensible return duct load (Worksheet G) = 1,346 Btuh
Latent return duct load (Worksheet G) = NA; dry-coil
Outdoor air = 75 Cfm; Sensible Eff. for cooling = 0.50
JSHR = 30,145 / 30,145 = 1.00
HDD / CDD = 5,658 / 3,036 = 1.86
Ground water temperature = 52°F
Extreme summer temperature = 111°F
WTH = 111 -10 = 101°F
OSL for a Condition B heat pump = +15,000 Btuh TC

Data Search

Expanded performance data is searched for something close to 42,000 Btuh total cooling capacity (30,000 Btuh cooling load plus 12,000 Btuh of excess cooling capacity), for a preliminary value for the entering wet-bulb temperature. Since there is no latent load the cooling coil will be dry, so use a dry-coil value for entering wet-bulb temperature (typically 59°F or less).

Candidate Single-Speed Equipment

The entering water temperature is 52°F for an open-pipe system, and 101°F for a buried-loop system. Figure 9-11 (previous page) shows actual cooling performance data for a single-speed heat pump in the 042 size, 048 size, and 060 size for water with 15% methanol (values for no antifreeze will be somewhat different). This data was extracted from many pages of data for this product. Since 1,350 Cfm, 1,550 Cfm and 2,000 Cfm are mid-range values, they are used to find preliminary total cooling capacity values for the 042, 048, and 060 sizes.

Note that this OEM does not provide total cooling capacity values for a dry cooling coil. Therefore, total cooling capacity values for 75°F dry-bulb and 63°F wet-bulb are used to select equipment.

Water-Air Heat Pump Cooling — 042 Size
Blower Operating at 1,350 Cfm; 15% Methanol by Volume

EWT (°F)	Gpm	EAc db/wb (°F)	TC 1,000 Btuh	SC 1,000 Btuh	LC 1,000 Btuh	EAh db (°F)	HC 1,000 Btuh
12	5.0	75/63	~	~	~	60	17.5
		80/67	~	~	~	70	16.9
52		75/63	43.54	31.06	12.48	60	37.2
		80/67	47.38	32.34	15.04	70	35.8
101		75/63	32.83	25.87	6.96	~	~
		80/67	35.70	26.97	8.73	~	~

Water-Air Heat Pump Cooling — 048 Size
Blower Operating at 1,550 Cfm; 15% Methanol by Volume

EWT (°F)	Gpm	EAc db/wb (°F)	TC 1,000 Btuh	SC 1,000 Btuh	LC 1,000 Btuh	EAh db (°F)	HC 1,000 Btuh
12	9.0	75/63	~	~	~	60	24.4
		80/67	~	~	~	70	23.5
52		75/63	50.10	33.98	16.12	60	48.6
		80/67	54.38	35.38	19.00	70	46.7
101		75/63	38.12	30.82	7.30	~	~
		80/67	41.40	32.12	9.28	~	~

Water-Air Heat Pump Cooling — 060 Size
Blower Operating at 2,000 Cfm; 15% Methanol by Volume

EWT (°F)	Gpm	EAc db/wb (°F)	TC 1,000 Btuh	SC 1,000 Btuh	LC 1,000 Btuh	EAh db (°F)	HC 1,000 Btuh
12	8.0	75/63	~	~	~	60	25.9
		80/67	~	~	~	70	25.0
52		75/63	63.30	45.30	18.00	60	58.4
		80/67	68.76	47.18	21.58	70	56.2
101		75/63	48.79	39.69	9.10	~	~
		80/67	52.98	41.38	11.60	~	~

EWT = Entering water temperature, Gpm = gallons per minute.
EAc = Entering air for cooling (db = dry-bulb, wb = wet-bulb).
TC = Total cooling capacity, SC = Sensible cooling capacity.
LC = Latent cooling capacity. EA_h = Entering air db for heating.
HC = Heating capacity. Capacities adjusted for blower heat.
12°F values extrapolated from 30–40°F data.
52°F and 101°F values interpolated from 60-70°F; 100–110°F data.

Figure 9-11

- Total cooling capacity for a dry-coil will be somewhat less than the 75°F/63°F values, but the allowance for excess cooling capacity is 15,000 Btuh or less, and latent capacity is not an issue, so 75°F/63°F values for total capacity may be used to size equipment for a dry-coil scenario.

- It may be that upon request, the OEM can provide dry-coil data. When so, use the dry-coil data for equipment selection and sizing.

Section 9

- Other OEMs may publish dry-coil data for their products. When so, consider the use of those products.

Open-Pipe System Candidate

At sea level, for 52°F water; 75°F db / 63°F wb entering air, the 042 size operating at 5 Gpm and 1,350 Cfm has 43,540 Btuh of total cooling capacity; and the 048 size operating at 9 Gpm and 1,550 Cfm has 50,100 Btuh of total cooling capacity. The excess cooling capacity for the 042 unit is 13,395 Btuh, and the excess cooling capacity for the 048 unit is 19,955 Btuh. The 042 size is within the 15,000 Btuh limit. The 048 size is too large for 52°F water.

042 excess capacity = 43,540 - 30,145 = 13,395 Btuh
048 excess capacity = 50,100 - 30,145 = 19,955 Btuh
Excess capacity limit = 15,000 Btuh

Buried Closed-Loop System Candidate

At sea level, for 101°F entering water and 75°F db / 63°F wb entering air, the 042 size operating at 5 Gpm and 1,350 Cfm has 32,830 Btuh of total cooling capacity; the 048 size operating at 9 Gpm and 1,550 Cfm has 38,120 Btuh of total cooling capacity; and the 060 size operating at 8 Gpm and 2,000 Cfm has 48,790 Btuh of total cooling capacity. The 048 size is too large for 101°F water. The 042 and 048 sizes are within the 15,000 Btuh limit. The 048 size is used because it has more heating capacity than the 042 unit.

042 excess capacity = 32,830 - 30,145 = 2,685 Btuh
048 excess capacity = 38,120 - 30,145 = 7,975 Btuh
060 excess capacity = 48,790 - 30,145 = 18,645 Btuh
Excess capacity limit = 15,000 Btuh

Entering Dry-Bulb and Wet-Bulb Values

Return duct and outdoor air loads increase the entering dry-bulb temperature (wet-bulb temperature is not an issue for a dry climate). Per Section A2-3 procedures, the sensible return duct load is 1,346 Btuh. The altitude is 2,838 feet, the altitude adjustment is 0.88, the outdoor air is at 94°F dry-bulb and 63°F wet-bulb, and the sensible recovery effectiveness for cooling is 0.50

When Sections A2-4 and A2-7 procedures are applied to the return duct loads and outdoor air loads for 1,350 blower Cfm (042 size), the temperature of the entering air for cooling is 76.4°F db. For 1,550 blower Cfm (048 size), the temperature of the entering air for cooling is 76.2°F db.

Equipment size = 042
Blower Cfm = 1,350; Return Cfm = 1,275; OA Cfm = 75
Cooling dry-bulb °F at return grille = 75.0
Cooling dry-bulb °F out of return duct = 76.030
Cooling entering (mixed air) dry-bulb °F = 76.529 (76.5)

Equipment size = 048
Blower Cfm = 1,550; Return Cfm = 1,475; OA Cfm = 75
Cooling dry-bulb °F at return grille = 75.0
Cooling dry-bulb °F out of return duct = 75.897
Cooling entering (mixed air) dry-bulb °F = 76.355 (76.3)

Interpolated Cooling Capacity Values

Total cooling capacity may be interpolated from this OEM's performance data (Figure 9-11) because total capacity only depends on entering wet-bulb temperature. As note above, this OEM does not provide total cooling capacity values for a dry cooling coil. Therefore, total cooling capacity values for 75°F dry-bulb and 63°F wet-bulb are used to select equipment.

042 Performance

For the 042 size, the design value for blower Cfm is 1,350. The design values for entering water temperature is 52°F or 101°F. Figure 9-11 provides capacity values for sea level air density.

For 52°F water
Approximate total Btuh @ 63.0°F wb = 43,540
Approximate sensible Btuh = 43,540

For 101°F water
Approximate total Btuh @ 63.0°F wb = 32,830
Approximate sensible Btuh = 32,830

048 Performance

For the 042 size, the design value for blower Cfm is 1,550. The design values for entering water temperature is 52°F or 101°F. Figure 9-12 provides capacity values for sea level air density.

For 52°F water
Approximate total Btuh @ 63.0°F wb = 50,100
Approximate sensible Btuh = 50,100

For 101°F water
Approximate total Btuh @ 63.0°F wb = 38,120
Approximate sensible Btuh = 38,120

Check Capacity at Altitude

OEM data is for sea level. For equivalent altitude performance, the air mass-flow through the evaporator coil must be equal to the sea level mass-flow. Per Figure A5-1, the altitude correction factor for 3,000 Feet is 0.89, so the effectiveness of a blower Cfm value at altitude is equivalent to 89% of the same value at sea level. Since the coil is dry, the sensible capacity equals total capacity.

042 Cooling capacity at altitude
Sea level Cfm = Design Cfm = Altitude Cfm = 1,350
Mass-flow Cfm at altitude = 0.89 x 1,350 = 1,202
Cfm adjustment factor for OEM's sea level data = 89%
OEM data provides capacity factors for 90% Cfm

OEM's total capacity factor for 90% Cfm = 0.982
OEM sea level data adjusted fro 90% Cfm
For 52°F water = 0.982 x 43,540 = 42,756 Btuh
For 101°F water = 0.982 x 32,830 = 32,239 Btuh

048 Performance at altitude
Sea level Cfm = 1,550
Mass-flow Cfm at altitude = 0.89 x 1,550 = 1,380
Cfm adjustment factor for OEM's sea level data = 89%
OEM data provides capacity factors for 90% Cfm
OEM's total capacity factor for 90% Cfm = 0.982
OEM sea level data adjusted for 90% Cfm
For 52°F water = 0.982 x 50,100 = 49,198 Btuh
For 101°F water = 0.982 x 38,120 = 37,434 Btuh

Note 1: The OEM's minimum Cfm is 85% of the Cfm used for the expanded performance data (0.85 factor). Figure A5-1 shows that the ACF for 5,000 feet is 0.84, so the method demonstrated above may be used to 5,000 feet for this make and model.

Note 2: An 85% limit for sea level Cfm is equivalent to a 85% air mass-flow limit for any altitude. Discuss equipment application and performance with the OEM when the Table A5-1 ACF factor is less than the OEM's percentage (as a decimal factor) for minimum sea level blower Cfm.

Note 3: For this make and model, the OEM's total capacity adjustment factor for 85% sea level blower Cfm is 0.972, so the altitude effect on total cooling capacity is not a significant equipment sizing issue. However, refrigeration cycle performance at significantly reduced air mass-flow may be an equipment duty issue that must be discussed with the OEM.

Job Site Performance

The total cooling load is 30,145 Btuh, the sensible load is 30,145 Btuh, and the latent load is 0 Btuh. Interpolated capacity values are provided above. Figure 9-12 compares cooling performance for the 042 size vs. the 048 size for 52°F water, and for 101°F water.

Open-Pipe System

For 52°F water, the 042 size is compatible with the 15,000 Btuh limit for excess cooling capacity. The 048 size fails this test.

- The 1.42 SCR value for the 042 size means that equipment runtime per hour for cooling will be less than desirable. Short runtimes reduce air distribution effectiveness.
- Less air distribution effectiveness (which is not quantified by a standard procedure) is the cost of improved heating efficiency (which may be estimated by a defensible procedure).

Buried Closed-Loop System

The 048 size operating at 1,550 blower Cfm is the preferred choice for 101°F water. There is about a half-ton of extra compressor capacity for improved heating efficiency.

Cooling Performance Summary Boise, ID						
52°F Water - Open-Pipe System 042 @1,350 Cfm; 048 @ 1,550 Cfm						
Size	TC	XSTC	LC	LCR	XSLC	ASC	SCR
042	42,756	12,611	0	NA	NA	42,756	1.42
048	49,198	19,053	0	NA	NA	49,198	1.63
101°F Water - Closed Buried-Loop System 042 @1,350 Cfm; 048@1,550 Cfm						
Size	TC	XSTC	LC	LCR	XSLC	ASC	SCR
042	32,239	2,094	0	NA	NA	32,239	1.07
048	37,434	7,289	0	NA	NA	37,434	1.24
060	47,912	17,767	0	NA	NA	47,912	1.59

Capacity (Btuh): TC = Total; LC = Latent; SC = Sensible.
Capacity adjusted for altitude. NA = Not applicable.
XSTC = Excess total capacity = Total capacity - Total load.
LCR = Latent capacity ratio.
  = OEM data latent capacity / Latent Load.
XSLC = Excess latent capacity (Btuh).
  = OEM data latent capacity - Latent Load.
ASC = Adjusted sensible capacity.
  = OEM data sensible capacity + ½ excess latent capacity.
SCR = Sensible capacity ratio.
  = Adjusted sensible capacity / Sensible load.
Cooling loads (Btuh):
Total = 30,145; Sensible = 30,145; Latent = 0.

Figure 9-12

- The 1.24 SCR value for the 048 size is somewhat compatible with air distribution effectiveness for cooling (when heating efficiency is not an issue, the upper limit for cooling capacity is 1.15).
- An XSTC value of 7,289 Btuh is less than half of the 15,000 Btuh allowed, but the XSTC value for the next larger size (060 unit) operating at it's nominal (2,000) blower Cfm value, exceeds the 15,000 Btuh limit for excess cooling capacity.
- Less air distribution effectiveness due to excess compressor capacity (which is not quantified by a standard procedure) is the cost of improved heating efficiency (which may be estimated by a defensible procedure).
- This OEM has a 25°F low-limit for entering water temperature. When the water-loop design has to use more pipe to satisfy this requirement, the improvement for entering water temperature for heating reduces the entering water temperature for cooling.
- A lower entering water temperature for cooling increases cooling capacity, and this will cause some increase in the Figure 9-12 XSTC values.
- Considering all circumstances, the 048 size is the appropriate choice for this application.

Square Feet per Ton Values

There is 3,300 SqFt or floor area, and the total cooling load is 30,145 Btuh, so there is 1,315 SqFt per *Manual J* ton. Figure 9-13 provides square feet per ton values for open-pipe equipment in the 042 size, and for buried closed-loop equipment in the 048 size.

- Total cooling capacity is very sensitive to entering water temperature, somewhat sensitive to water flow Gpm, and significantly sensitive to the entering air wet-bulb temperature.
- Square feet per ton values depend on total cooling capacity, so they are equally sensitive to the variables that affect total cooling capacity.
- The AHRI rating value for total cooling capacity (and the corresponding SqFt/Ton value) usually does not correlate with application circumstances (possible, but statistically uncommon).

Heating Loads and Operating Conditions

A Condition B heat pump is compatible with the *Manual J* cooling loads and the attributes of Boise, ID, weather. For cooling, the 042 size is acceptable for an open-pipe system, and the 048 size is the preferred choice for a buried, closed-loop system.

The extreme winter temperature is -28°F. The *Manual J* heating load and the corresponding equipment operating conditions are summarized here:

Sensible heating load = 58,349 Btuh
Altitude = 2,838 Feet; Figure A5-1 ACF = 0.88
Outdoor air temperature = 9°F db
Indoor conditions: 70°F db, no humidification
Sensible return duct load (Section A2-3) = 2,420 Btuh
Outdoor air = 75 Cfm; Sensible Eff. for heating = 0.55
Ground water temperature = 52°F
Extreme winter temperature = –28°F
WTL = -28 + 40 = 12°F

Heating Performance

Figure 9-14 shows the OEM's heating performance data for 042 equipment and 048 equipment. The entering water temperature for an open-pipe system is 52°F.

The heating data stops at 30°F for entering water temperature, but this OEM allows extrapolation down to 25°F. However, the default entering water temperature (WTL) for a buried, closed-loop system is 12°F, so the piping loop must be designed for an entering water temperature that is compatible with the 25°F limit. Therefore, the piping loop is designed for 30°F water (see Appendix 9).

- Enhancing the performance of the piping loop for heating also improves cooling performance. Therefore, the entering water temperature for cooling will be less than the 101°F WTH default for Boise, ID.
- When the design value for entering water temperature is reduced, cooling capacity will be more than the 37,434 Btuh value from Figure 9-12. Therefore, excess cooling capacity will be more than the 7,289 Btuh value from Figure 9-12, but the adjusted excess capacity will still be significantly less than the 15,000 Btuh limit.
- At some point, the heating-cooling design values for entering water temperature become an economic issue. Appendix 9 provides additional commentary.

Entering Dry-Bulb Temperature

Return duct loads and outdoor air loads decrease the entering dry-bulb temperature. Per Section A2-3 procedures, the sensible return duct load is 2,420 Btuh. The altitude is 2,838 feet, the altitude adjustment is 0.88, the outdoor temperature is 9°F, and the sensible recovery effectiveness for heating is 0.55.

Entering dry-bulb for the 042 Size

When Sections A2-4 and A2-7 procedures are applied to the return duct load and outdoor air load (using altitude psychrometrics), the dry-bulb temperature of the entering air is 66.7°F for 1,350 blower Cfm.

Square Feet per Ton Values Boise, ID					
Manual J SqFt per Ton = 1,314					
Open system	EWT °F	Gpm	EDB °F / EWB °F	TC Btuh	SqFt per Ton
042 Applied	52	5	75.0 / 63.0	42,756	927
042 Rated	59	11	80.6 / 66.2	48,700	813
Closed system	EWT °F	Gpm	EDB °F / EWB °F	TC Btuh	SqFt per Ton
048 Applied	101	9	75.0 / 63.0	37,434	1,058
048 Rated	77	12	80.6 / 66.2	47,100	840

1) Applied relates to actual project circumstances. Rated relates to AHRI rating data.
2) For open-pipe systems, entering water temperature depends on ground water temperature, which depends on local conditions, and the Gpm is a practitioner decision.
3) For buried closed-loop systems, entering water temperature and Gpm depend on decisions made by the person (and software) responsible for the piping loop design.
4) Appendix 2 procedures, applied to *Manual J* data, return values for entering dry-bulb and wet-bulb temperatures.
5) Cooling capacity values extracted from OEM data.
6) 3,300 SqFt of floor area for this example.
7) Entering air at 75/63°F used for applied because OEM data had no dry-coil values.

Figure 9-13

Blower Cfm = 1,350; return Cfm = 1,275; OA Cfm = 75
Dry-bulb °F at return grille = 70.0
Return duct load = 2,420 Btuh
Dry-bulb °F out of return duct = 68.148
Entering (mixed air) dry-bulb °F = 66.669 (66.7)

Entering dry-bulb for the 048 Size

When Section A2-4 and A2-7 procedures are applied to the return duct load and outdoor air load (using altitude psychrometrics), the dry-bulb temperature of the entering air is 67.1°F for 1,550 blower Cfm.

Blower Cfm = 1,550; return Cfm = 1,475; OA Cfm = 75
Dry-bulb °F at return grille = 70.0
Return duct load = 2,420 Btuh
Dry-bulb °F out of return duct = 68.387
Entering (mixed air) dry-bulb °F = 67.094 (67.1)

Interpolated Heating Capacity Values

For the 042 size, the design value for blower Cfm is 1,350 Cfm, and the design value for entering air temperature is 66.7°F. For the 048 size, the design value for blower Cfm is 1,550 Cfm, and the design value for entering air temperature is 67.1°F. Heating capacity values for 66.7°F and 67.1°F entering air are interpolated from OEM performance data values (per Figure 9-14). The OEM's 0.978 heating capacity factor for reduced air mass-flow is applied to interpolated values.

Heating capacity for 52°F once-through water
042 size for 66.7°F air = 35,464 Btuh

Heating capacity for 30°F closed-loop water
048 size for 67.1°F air = 33,523 Btuh

Caveats for Buried Closed-Loop Heating

Entering water temperature values for most of the heating season will be significantly warmer than 30°F, which is the temperature at the end of the heating season. For any given project, the value for entering water temperature may be significantly different than the 30°F value used for this example. This depends on the details of the water system design, per Section 9-2.

Supplemental Heat

Figure 9-15 shows the balance point diagram for this application. The supplemental heat requirement depends on equipment size and entering water temperature.

Supplemental KW for 52°F once-through water
042 size = 6.71 KW

Supplemental KW for 30°F closed-loop water
048 size = 7.27 KW

Water-Air Heat Pump Heating — 042 Size
Blower Operating at 1,350 Cfm; 15% Methanol by Volume

EWT (°F)	Gpm	EAc db/wb (°F)	TC 1,000 Btuh	SC 1,000 Btuh	LC 1,000 Btuh	EA$_h$ db (°F)	HC 1,000 Btuh
30	5.0	75/63	~	~	~	60	26.3
		80/67	~	~	~	70	25.4
52		75/63	~	~	~	60	37.2
		80/67	~	~	~	70	35.8

Water-Air Heat Pump Heating — 048 Size
Blower Operating at 1,550 Cfm; 15% Methanol by Volume

EWT (°F)	Gpm	EAc db/wb (°F)	TC 1,000 Btuh	SC 1,000 Btuh	LC 1,000 Btuh	EA$_h$ db (°F)	HC 1,000 Btuh
30	9.0	75/63	~	~	~	60	35.2
		80/67	~	~	~	70	33.9
52		75/63	~	~	~	60	48.6
		80/67	~	~	~	70	46.7

EWT = Entering water temperature, Gpm = gallons per minute.
EAc = Entering air for cooling (db = dry-bulb, wb = wet-bulb).
TC = Total cooling capacity, SC = Sensible cooling capacity.
LC = Latent cooling capacity, EA$_h$ = Entering air db for heating.
HC = Reverse cycle heating capacity.
52°F values interpolated from 50-60°F data.

Figure 9-14

Default Thermal Balance Point

Figure 9-15 shows that the default thermal balance point for the 042 size with 52°F (once-though) water is about 32°F. The default thermal balance point for the 048 size with 30°F (loop) water is about 33°F.

- Supplemental heat must be locked out when the outdoor air temperature is above the thermal balance point.
- Supplemental heating capacity may be activated by a simple outdoor air temperature sensor control that has manually adjusted set-points, or microprocessor control that evaluates the momentary need for electric coil heat.

Emergency Heat

The default value for emergency heat is 85% of the heating load. This is 29,648 Btuh, or about 8.7 KW.

0.85 x 58,349 = 49,597 Btuh
49,597 / 3,413 = 14.53 KW

Auxiliary Heat

Because of standard sizes offered by this OEM, the total amount of electric coil heat is 15 KW. For the 042 size with 52°F water, this is preferably split into 7.5 KW for supplemental heat, with an additional 7.5 KW available by emergency switch. For the 048 size with 30°F water, this is preferably split into 7.5 KW for supplemental heat, with an additional 7.5 KW available by emergency switch.

Sizing Decision for an Open-Pipe System

For an open-pipe system (52°F water), the 042 size is the only size (042 vs. 048) that is compatible with the equipment sizing rules. Total cooling capacity falls within the minimum and maximum limits (see Table N2-2 and Figure 9-12). Sensible cooling capacity equals total cooling capacity, and zero latent cooling capacity is compatible with a dry-coil application.

Sizing Decision for a Buried-Loop System

For a buried, closed-loop system (30°F water), the 048 size is the only size (042 vs. 048 vs. 060) that is compatible with the equipment sizing rules. Total cooling capacity falls within the minimum and maximum limits (see Table N2-2 and Figure 9-12). Sensible cooling capacity equals total cooling capacity, and zero latent cooling capacity is compatible with a dry-coil application.

For heating, the design thermal balance point value is about 33°F. However, the 30°F water temperature is the worst-case temperature for the end of the heating season. The water temperature will be significantly warmer than 30°F, and the thermal balance point will be significantly lower than 33°F for most of the heating season.

- This example problem is about equipment sizing for a given set of entering water temperatures. A 30°F temperature for heating is used for this purpose (the corresponding water temperature for cooling will be less than the 101°F default).

- A water system may be designed for a minimum water temperature that is more than 30°F.

- Different entering water temperature values have no affect on the equipment sizing procedure, but they do affect the design values for cooling and heating capacity; which may, or may not, affect the size of the installed equipment when cooling capacity values are compared to Table N2-2 limits.

9-6 Multi-Speed Performance

Expanded cooling performance data for two-speed equipment is similar to the single-speed examples in the section, except there will be two sets of data, one for reduced (stage 1) speed, and one for full (stage 2) speed.

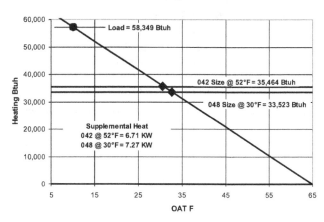

Figure 9-15

The data for full compressor speed, and the associated range of blower speeds, are used to select and size equipment. Therefore, the equipment section and sizing procedure for multi-speed equipment is identical to the procedure used for single-speed equipment. For heat pumps, cooling and heating capacity for full compressor speed is used to size the equipment, and to draw the thermal balance point diagram.

9-7 Variable-Speed Performance

Expanded cooling and heating performance data for variable-speed equipment is similar to the single-speed examples in the section, except there may be two or more sets of data. The possibilities are, minimum compressor speed, an intermediate compressor speed, the compressor speed used for the AHRI rating test, and enhanced compressor speed. The maximum and minimum compressor speeds are determined by the OEM's design and controls.

It may be that maximum compressor speed is the speed used for advertising the AHRI values for total cooling capacity and heating capacity (full capacity), or the maximum speed may be higher than the speed used for the AHRI rating tests (enhanced speed). For cooling, expanded performance data for full capacity (compressor operating at the AHRI rating speed), is used to select and size equipment. For heating, expanded heating performance data for the maximum, continuously available, compressor speed is used to draw the thermal balance point diagram.

This section is not part of the this standard. It is merely informative and does not contain requirements necessary for conformance to the standard. It has not been processed according to the ANSI requirements for a standard, and may contain material that has not been subject to public review or a consensus process. Unresolved objectors on informative material are not offered the right to appeal at ACCA or ANSI.

Section 10
Hydronic Heating Equipment Examples

One selection/sizing procedure applies to residential water boilers that serve convective devices (gravity convectors, fan coils, ventilating fan coils, and duct coils).

- For selecting and sizing terminal devices, and for pipe system design, refer to hydronic industry guidance, OEM guidance, and related codes and standards.
- This section does not apply to radiant hot water heating systems. Refer to radiant heating industry guidance, OEM guidance, and related codes and standards.

10-1 Hot Water Heating System Design

Refer to OEM guidance and performance data for selecting, sizing, and controlling convective (gravity or forced air) terminal units. Refer to OEM venting guidance. Refer to OEM guidance for selecting and sizing hydronic specialties (pump, expansion tank, valves, etc.), and for water piping instructions and piping details. Refer to OEM guidance for fuel piping requirements and details, for electrical requirements and details, and for control requirements and details. When the installation is above 2,000 to 2,500 feet, refer to OEM guidance pertaining to altitude.

10-2 Space Heating Load

The space heating load for boiler, or hot water heater selection/sizing, is the block heating load for the rooms and spaces served by the equipment. This load is for the winter design temperature for outdoor air (per *Manual J* Table 1A or 1B, or code value), and the winter design temperature for indoor air (70°F per *Manual J*, or code value). The block heating load is not adjusted for internal gain, or for heat gain due to solar radiation. The block heating load includes:

- Space heat provided by gravity convection terminals (typically baseboard coils).
- Space heat provided by fan coil terminals (no outdoor air capability).
- Space heat provided by unit ventilators (fan coil terminal with outdoor air capability).
- Duct or equipment cabinet coils that provide space heat (include duct load and outdoor air load, where applicable).
- Heat loss for water pipe in an unheated space.
- *Manual J* (full version, Eighth-Edition) procedures provide the necessary values.

10-3 Maximum Space Heating Capacity

Over-sized heating equipment causes equipment cycling (or throttling) on a winter design day, and reduces runtime for all part-load hours. This provides no efficiency or economic advantage. This may, or may not, effect occupant comfort (depending on the water temperature vs. time behavior at the terminal devices). Table N2-5 provides maximum heating capacity limits for boilers, and duct or cabinet water coils, based on aggressive use of *Manual J* procedures.

10-4 Minimum Space Heating Capacity

Output heating capacity must be equal to, or greater than, the block heating load. For staged or modulating equipment, output heating capacity is for full capacity.

10-5 Water Temperature Limits

Investigate and observe the OEM's limits for low entering water temperature, high leaving water temperature, and water temperature rise. Temperatures that are out of range may cause condensation on equipment parts, may damage equipment parts, or may be produce a serious safety hazard. Conform to local code and OEM guidance.

10-6 Equipment Selection Examples

The equipment selection examples in this section are for the heating loads produced by a surrogate dwelling built in a cold winter location, and a mild winter location. The intent is to demonstrate the sizing procedure for primary hydronic heating equipment. Therefore, the solution for an example problem is not a general solution for the housing stock in a given location or region, as explained here:

- The outdoor design condition for heating does not depend on dwelling's attributes and the HVAC system's attributes. So this value is common to the housing stock in a given location.
- The heating load depends on dwelling's features and attributes, and may depend on a duct load and/or an engineered ventilation load, and there may be a piping load. So these values are not common to the housing stock in a given location.
- Therefore, practitioners must apply *Manual J* and *Manual S* procedures to the actual dwelling in the actual location when selecting and sizing equipment, and should consider the full range of products offered by OEMs.

10-7 Attributes of the Example Dwelling

The dwelling used for the cooling-only and heat pump examples is used for these hydronic heating examples. Envelope efficiency is good, but not exceptional. Glass area is modest. Attic ducts are insulated and sealed, but the workmanship is average. The dwelling has no engineered ventilation. Basic information is summarized here, Appendix 19 provides more detail.

- Slab on grade, one story, 3,300 SqFt (Figure A19-2 shows the floor plan).
- Two pane, clear glass, wood frame, tight fenestration. Fenestration area is 10.9 percent of the floor area. No AED excursion.
- Commonly used ceiling, wall and floor R-values.
- Average structural tightness.
- Hot water piping in heated space, or in locations that approximate a heated space.

10-8 Cold Winter Example

The over-size limit from Table N2-5 applies to boilers. A boiler typically provides hot water heat when the location has a harsh winter design temperature and a significant amount of cold weather hours. The dwelling may have a ducted cooling-only system, or a ductless cooling-only system that is subject to Table N2-1 sizing limits (see the Section 5 example for Boise, ID).

- Hot water heat is commonly provided by gravity baseboard fixtures. These may be zoned.
- When the dwelling has a duct system for cooling, hot water heat may be provided by a hot water coil at the air handler.
- A duct system makes it easier to comply with a code/standard/regulation, or design preference that requires a significant amount of outdoor air for engineered ventilation (something like 50 to 100 Cfm, for example).
- A duct system makes it easier to comply with a code/standard/regulation, or design preference that requires heat recovery for engineered ventilation.

Heating Load and Operating Conditions

Boiler size is based on the **Manual J** heating load for Boise, ID, weather; as summarized below. Duct loads and engineered ventilation loads apply when heat is provided by one hot water coil at the air handler for the cooling system. The 0.88 altitude adjustment factor for 2,838 feet applies to *Manual J* calculations and to psychrometric calculations for entering air temperature. Equipment performance is adjusted for altitude per OEM guidance, or when it exceeds 2,500 Feet (see Appendix 5).

Water Boiler Performance					
Product	Model	AFUE	TD Ratio	Input Btuh	Output Btuh
ABC DV; MB	55	0.96	5:1	55,000	51,000
	85			85,000	79,000
XYZ DV; MB	50	0.96	5:1	50,000	45,000
	80			80,000	72,000

1) DV = Direct vent; MB = Modulating burner; TD = Turn down.
2) Input = Maximum burner input Btuh.
3) Output = Heating capacity Btuh (not Net IBR).

Figure 10-1

Altitude = 2,838 Feet; Figure A5-1 ACF = 0.88
Outdoor design temperature = 9°F
Indoor conditions: 70°F db; no humidification
Sensible heating load = 58,349 Btuh
Winter humidification load = None
Sensible return duct load (Section A2-3) = 2,420 Btuh
Outdoor air = 75 Cfm; Sensible eff. for heating = 0.55
Boiler OSL = 1.40
Hot water coil OSL = 1.25 to 1.50

Boiler Performance

Boiler performance data is searched for something close to 58,000 Btuh of output heating capacity for full-burner capacity (or electric element capacity). Figure 10-1 shows actual heating performance data for a condensing direct vent product that has a modulating burner with a 5:1 turn down ratio. The 1.16 over-size factor for the XYZ, Model 80 product complies with the 1.40 limit for full heating output capacity.

OEM's altitude adjustment for burner = 2% per 1,000 Ft
Input Btuh factor = 0.02 x (2,838 / 1,000) = 0.057
Input Btuh at altitude = 80,000 x (1.0–0.057) = 75,440
Steady-state efficiency = 72,000 / 80,000 = 0.90
Output Btuh = 0.90 x 75,440 = 67,896
OSF = 67,896 / 58,349 = 1.16

Hot Water Coil Performance

When a central hot water coil is used, the sea level heating capacity of the coil depends on entering water temperature and Gpm, entering air temperature and Cfm, coil face area, number of tubing rows, number of circuits, and fins per inch. For hot water from a boiler, the following defaults may be used to estimate coil performance. Final values depend on operating temperatures and details. Work with the heating coil OEM for coil selection.

Entering water temperature = 180°F
Entering air temperature = 70°F
Entering water - Entering air = 110°F
Water temperature drop (WTD) = 20°F to 30°F

Section 5-12 shows that the cooling-only system for the Boise dwelling operates at 1,200 Cfm. So 1,200 Cfm is used to select a hot water coil (this is not mandatory, it may be that some other Cfm value is used for heating). The attic duct load and the engineered ventilation load causes a 66°F entering air temperature.

Blower Cfm = 1,200, Outdoor air Cfm = 75, Sen. Eff =0.55
Air temperature at return grill = 70°F, OAT = 9°F
Air temperature out of the return duct = 67.917°F
Entering air temperature = 66.260°F (66°F)

Figure 10-2 shows OEM performance data for a two row, multi-circuit coil with a specific face area value. The data provides sea level heating capacity values (Btuh) for combinations of Cfm and Gpm values, based on a 125°F water-air temperature difference. Sea level capacity values are adjusted for altitude by using a look-up Cfm that equates sea level mass-flow to altitude mass-flow.

Design Cfm for altitude = 1,200 Cfm
Altitude adjustment factor = 0.88
Look-up Cfm = 0.88 x 1,200 = 1,056 Cfm

The OEM's sea level data is for 1,000 Cfm and 1,400 Cfm. The 1,000 Cfm value is close enough to 1,056 Cfm for this application (interpolation is required when the there is a significant difference). For 1,000 Cfm, 5 Gpm, and a 125°F water-air temperature difference, the OEM's data shows 66,100 Btuh of heating capacity.

OEM Sea level data
Default water-air temperature difference = 125°F
Lookup values = 1,000 Cfm and 5 Gpm
Lookup heating capacity = 66,100 Btuh

The OEM's sea level data is for a 125°F water-air temperature difference. The design value for entering water temperature is 180°F, and the entering air temperature is 66°F, so the interpolated adjustment factor for a 114°F temperature difference is 0.91, and the adjusted heating capacity is 60,283 Btuh.

Capacity for 1,000 Cfm and 125°F TD = 66,100 Btuh
Adjustment for 114°F water-air TD = 0.91
Capacity for 114°F TD = 0.91 x 66,100 = 60,283 Btuh

The heating capacity at altitude is 60,283 Btuh and the heating load is 58,349 Btuh, so the over-size factor for the heating coil is 1.03.

Altitude capacity for 114°F TD = 60,283 Btuh
Heating load = 58,349 Btuh
Coil OSF for sea level data = 60,283 / 58,349 = 1.03

Hot Water Coil Performance - Boise					
Coil Attributes	GPM	Head Loss (Ft)	MBtuh at 1,000 Cfm	MBtuh at 1,400 Cfm	
Two Row Multi-Circuit Size 16	3.0	0.50	59.2	68.5	
	5.0	1.26	66.1	78.4	
	7.0	2.25	69.6	83.6	
	9.0	3.46	71.7	86.8	
Air-Side Pressure Drop (IWC)			0.07	0.13	

1) Data based on 180°F entering water and 55°F entering air.
2) Multiply listed capacity by a temperature difference (TD) factor when the water-air temperature difference is not 125°F.

TD °F	60	70	80	90	110	125	140
Factor	0.48	0.56	0.64	0.72	0.80	1.00	1.20

Figure 10-2

A set of equations relates coil water-side performance to air-side performance. These are provided here, with demonstrated use. Note that the actual (1,200 Cfm) blower Cfm is used for these calculations.

Water Btuh Loss = 500 x Gpm x WTD
Air Btuh Gain = 1.1 x ACF x Cfm x ATR
LWT (°F) = EWT - WTD
LAT (°F) = EAT + ATR

Where:
WTD = Water temperature drop (°F)
ACF = Altitude correction factor
ATR = Air temperature Rise (°F)
LWT = Leaving water temperature (°F)
LAT = Leaving air temperature (°F)

WTD = 63,283 / (500 x 5) = 24.1°F
LWT = 180 - 24.1 = 155.9 F
ATR = 63,283 / (1.1 x 0.88 x 1,200) = 51.9°F
LAT = 66 + 51.9 = 117.9°F

Manual D Compatibility

When a hot water coil is installed in the duct system, the blower for duct system cooling must have adequate power to compensate for the pressure drop produced by a hot water heating coil. The *Manual D* Friction Rate Worksheet determines when blower power is compatible with the pressure dissipating items (the components, fittings and straight runs in the critical circulation path of the duct system).

Manual D calculations are not adjusted for altitude (see Section A5-13), so the air-side pressure drop for the hot water coil is based on the OEM's sea level data with no adjustment for altitude. Per Figure 10-2, the pressure drop for 1,000 Cfm is 0.07 IWC. Since the pressure drop increases with the square of the Cfm ratio, the pressure drop for 1,200 Cfm is 0.10 IWC, as demonstrated here:

Reference point = 1,000 Cfm and 0.07 IWC
Application Cfm = 1,200
Pressure drop for 1,200 Cfm = 0.07 x (1,200 / 1,000)^2
Pressure drop for 1,200 Cfm = 0.10 IWC

10-9 Mild Winter Humid Climate Example

Since summer cooling and dehumidification are the primary concern, and because the heating load is relatively small, a potable water heater may be used for space heating. The dwelling may have a ducted, or ductless, cooling-only system that is subject to Table N2-1 sizing limits (see the Section 5 example for Brunswick, GA).

- When the dwelling has a duct system for cooling, hot water heat may be provided by a hot water coil at the air handler.

- A duct system makes it easier to comply with a code/standard/regulation, or design preference that requires a significant amount of outdoor air for engineered ventilation (something like 50 to 100 cfm, for example).

- A duct system makes it easier to comply with a code/standard/regulation, or design preference that requires heat recovery for engineered ventilation.

Heating Load and Operating Conditions

The heating capacity of the closed hot water circuit for space heat is based on the *Manual J* heating load for Brunswick, GA, weather; as summarized below. Duct loads and engineered ventilation loads apply when heat is provided by one hot water coil at the air handler for the cooling system. Brunswick is close to sea level, so there is no altitude adjustment factor for *Manual J* calculations and psychrometric calculations. OEM equipment performance data is for sea level conditions.

Altitude = 20 Feet; Figure A5-1 ACF = 1.00
Outdoor design temperature = 34°F
Indoor conditions: 70°F db; no humidification
Sensible heating load = 34,880 Btuh
Winter humidification load = None
Sensible return duct load (Section A2-3) = 1,155 Btuh
Outdoor air = 75 Cfm; Sensible eff. for heating = 0.55
Water heater OSL per OEM guidance.
Hot water coil OSL = 1.25 to 1.50

Water Heater Performance

The full output capacity for the space heating circuit must be equal to, or greater than, the *Manual J* heating load, which is about 35,000 Btuh for this example. The total heating load on the water heater equals the space heating load plus the water heating load (see Section N2-10). For equipment sizing, output capacity is compared to the total heating load.

Standard Vent Tank Water Heater with Side Taps					
Tank Size (Gallons)	Input Btuh	Output Btuh	Steady State Effi'cy	Energy Factor	Recover GPH 90 (RGPH)
40 or 50	40,000	30,400	0.76	0.62	41
40 or 50	50,000	38,000	0.76	0.59	51
50 or 65	65,000	50,050	0.77	0.58	67
74	75,100	60,080	0.80	na	81

1) Tank size for space heat only should be 40 Gallons or more, discuss this with the OEM.
2) Output Btuh must be equal to or larger than the **Manual J** heating load, plus additional heat for potable water.
3) The steady-state efficiency (SS_{eff}) for various tank and tank-less products may be somewhat lower or higher, or significantly higher than the values for this product.
4) The energy factor only relates to potable water heating use.
5) Refer to local codes/standards/regulations for efficiency requirements for space heating use.
6) Recover GPH 90 (RGPH) is the gallons per hour that can have a 90°F temperature rise.
7) Some OEM data does not provide output Btuh values. This equation provides approximate values (ask the OEM for the official values). **Output Btuh = (500 / 60) x RGPH x 90**.
8) Some OEM data does not provide steady-state efficiency values. This equation provides approximate values (ask the OEM for the official values). SS_{eff} = **Output Btuh / Input Btuh**.

Figure 10-3

Figure 10-3 shows actual heating performance data for a standard vent, tank water heater, that has side taps for a closed-water circuit. The 50,000 input Btuh model has 9% excess capacity (1.09 factor) for space heat, but may be too small for space heat plus potable water heat. The 65,000 input Btuh model has 43% excess capacity (1.43 factor) for space heat, so it may be adequate for space heat plus potable water heat.

Space heat ratio for 50K input = 38,000 / 34,880 = 1.09
Space heat ratio for 65K input = 50,050 / 34,880 = 1.43

Hot Water Coil Performance

The sea level heating capacity of a central hot water coil depends on entering water temperature and Gpm, entering air temperature and Cfm, coil face area, number of tubing rows, number of circuits, and fins per inch. For hot water from a water heater, the following defaults may be used to estimate coil performance. Final values depend on operating temperatures and details. Work with the heating coil OEM for coil selection.

Entering water temperature = 140°F
Entering air temperature = 70°F
Entering water - Entering air = 70°F
Water temperature drop 10°F to 15°F.

Section 5-11 shows that the cooling-only system for the Brunswick dwelling operates at 1,400 Cfm. So 1,400 Cfm is used to select a hot water coil (this is not mandatory, it may be that some other Cfm value is used for heating). The attic duct load and the engineered ventilation load causes a 68°F entering air temperature.

Blower Cfm = 1,400, Outdoor air Cfm = 75, Sen. Eff =0.55
Air temperature at return grill = 70°F, OAT = 34°F
Air temperature out of the return duct = 69.25°F
Entering air temperature = 68.40°F (68°F)

Figure 10-4 shows OEM performance data for a two row, multi-circuit coil with a specific face area value. The data provides sea level heating capacity values (Btuh) for combinations of Cfm and Gpm values, based on a 125°F water-air temperature difference. Sea level capacity values apply to Brunswick, GA.

The OEM's data is for 1,000 Cfm and 1,400 Cfm. The 1,400 Cfm value applies to this example. For 1,400 Cfm, 3 Gpm, and a 125°F water-air temperature difference, the OEM's data shows 68,500 Btuh of heating capacity.

OEM Sea level data
Default water-air temperature difference = 125°F
Lookup values = 1,400 Cfm and 3 Gpm
Lookup heating capacity = 68,500 Btuh

The OEM's sea level data is for a 125°F water-air temperature difference. The design value for entering water temperature is 140°F, and the entering air temperature is 68°F, so the interpolated adjustment factor for a 72°F temperature difference is 0.58, and the adjusted heating capacity is 39,456 Btuh.

Capacity for 1,400 Cfm and 125°F TD = 68,500 Btuh
Adjustment for 72°F water-air TD = 0.58
Capacity for 72°F TD = 0.58 x 68,500 = 39,456 Btuh

The hot water coil heating capacity is 39,456 Btuh and the heating load is 34,880 Btuh, so the over-size factor for the coil is 1.13.

Altitude capacity for 72°F TD = 39,456 Btuh
Heating load = 34,880 Btuh
Coil OSF for sea level data = 39,456 / 34,880 = 1.13

A set of equations relates coil water-side performance to air-side performance. These are provided here, with demonstrated use:

Water Btuh Loss = 500 x Gpm x WTD
Air Btuh Gain = 1.1 x ACF x Cfm x ATR
LWT (°F) = EWT - WTD
LAT (°F) = EAT + ATR

Hot Water Coil Performance — Brunswick				
Coil Attributes	GPM	Head Loss (Ft)	MBtuh at 1,000 Cfm	MBtuh at 1,400 Cfm
Two Row Multi-Circuit Size 16	3.0	0.50	59.2	68.5
	5.0	1.26	66.1	78.4
	7.0	2.25	69.6	83.6
	9.0	3.46	71.7	86.8
Air-Side Pressure Drop (IWC)			0.07	0.13

1) Data based on 180°F entering water and 55°F entering air.
2) Multiply listed capacity by a temperature difference (TD) factor when the water-air temperature difference is not 125°F.

TD °F	60	70	80	90	110	125	140
Factor	0.48	0.56	0.64	0.72	0.80	1.00	1.20

Figure 10-4

Where:
WTD = Water temperature drop (°F)
ACF = Altitude correction factor
ATR = Air temperature Rise (°F)
LWT = Leaving water temperature (°F)
LAT = Leaving air temperature (°F)

WTD = 39,456 / (500 x 3) = 26.3°F
LWT = 140 - 26.3 = 113.7°F
ATR = 39,456 / (1.1 x 1.00 x 1,400) = 25.6°F
LAT = 68 + 25.6 = 93.6°F

Manual D Compatibility

The blower for the duct system for cooling must have adequate power to compensate for the pressure drop produced by a hot water heating coil. The *Manual D* Friction Rate Worksheet determines when blower power is compatible with the pressure dissipating items (the components, fittings and straight runs in the critical circulation path of the duct system). Per Figure 10-4, the coil pressure drop for 1,400 Cfm is 0.13 IWC.

10-10 Hydronic Air Handler

When cooling is provided by a duct system, a hydronic air handler may provide blower power for cooling and heating, a hot water coil, and a filter. The hot water supply may be provided by a water heater or boiler. Figure 10-5 (next page) shows an OEM package that consists of a tank-less water heater, and a hydronic air handler.

- A cooling coil module that is external to the air handler allows use of OEM expanded performance data for an OEM matched evaporator, condensing unit combination (per *Manual S* requirements), and there is an AHRI rating for certified equipment supplied by one OEM.

Section 10

- The blower must be able to provide the Cfm needed for cooling. This would be the Cfm used to select and size the cooling equipment.
- There must be an adequate blower table for the air handler.
- Blower table notes may, or may not, state what air-side components produce a pressure drop that must be subtracted from the pressure values in the blower table. It may be that one or more of these components are not accounted for—filter, hot water coil, cooling coil. Discuss this with the OEM.
- Components that are external to the blower table must be accounted for on the *Manual D* Friction Rate Worksheet.

Heating Capacity Data

Figure 10-6 (next page) provides an example of the heating capacity data for an OEM product. This is just a sample of a much larger matrix that summarizes the performance for four air handler sizes served by five tank-less water heater sizes. The full table shows a wide range of heating capacities in relatively small steps.

Blower Data

Figure 10-7 (next page) shows part of a PSC motor blower table for four air handler sizes (the actual table shows Cfm values for 0.10 IWC through 1.0 IWC). The footnote informs the reader that the filter is an external static pressure item, but says nothing about the hot water coil and cooling coil. The most likely scenario is that the hot water coil was in place for the blower test, and that a cooling coil is an external static pressure item, but this must be verified by the OEM. This product also is available with an ECM blower motor, and the OEM provides the blower table for this option.

Water Heat Source

The water heating equipment may be a water heater or boiler. This equipment may, or may not, be provided by the hydronic air handler vendor. A water heater may be a tank type, or a tank-less type, but either type must be appropriate for closed-circuit heating (Section N2-10 summarizes code issues).

Pump and Hydronic Accessories

The pump and hydronic accessories may, or may not, be provided by the hydronic air handler vendor. Refer to vendor product literature for availability and guidance.

Cooling Equipment

The evaporator coil condensing unit combination may, or may not, be provided by the hydronic air handler vendor. It does not make any difference who provides the cooling equipment, but the hydronic air handler blower must be

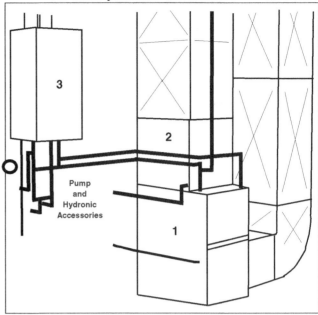

Hydronic Air Handler

Hydronic Air Handler - Item 1
A hydronic air handler provides the blower, hot water coil, and filter. Comprehensive blower data (per Section A1-10) is required for the *Manual D* Friction Rate Worksheet. The blower must have the power to move the design Cfm (largest value when cooling Cfm is compared to heating Cfm) through the water coil, the cooling coil, the filter, all the components, duct fittings, and straight duct runs in the critical circulation path. When the blower data has not been adjusted for the airflow resistance produced by the heating coil and/or filter, then pressure drop data for the coil and/or filter is required for duct sizing calculations.

The hot water-coil load is based on the *Manual J* heating load for the space served by the equipment. Heating capacity depends on coil size and the details of coil construction, heating Cfm, entering air temperature, entering water temperature and Gpm. Air temperature rise and water temperature drop must be in an acceptable range. Comprehensive performance data is required to validate water coil performance.

Cooling Coil Module - Item 2
An external cooling coil allows use of a rated condensing unit - evaporator coil combination that is supported by comprehensive performance data (per Section A1-9 requirements).

A generic cooling coil in the air handler must not be used unless the hydronic air handler OEM can provide cooling system rating data that conforms to industry standards, and expanded performance data that conforms to *Manual S* requirements.

Pressure drop data for the cooling coil (wet or dry, where applicable) is required for duct sizing calculations.

Water Heater - Item 3
The water heater may be the tank type or the tank-less type. The water heater may be provided by the air handler OEM, or by a third party vendor. The water heater provides space heat and potable water heat.

The water heater must be listed for space heating use (refer to Section N2-10, and OEM guidance). Some tank heaters have dedicated side taps for closed-loop heat, some have conversion fittings, some may not have the desired/necessary hardware.

Tank size and maximum output heating capacity (in Btuh units) must be suitable for the intended duty. Refer to OEM sizing guidance.

Figure 10-5

Heating Capacity (Btuh) for Tank-less Heater Model 84					
AH Size	Heating Cfm	Entering Water Temperature (F)			
		120	130	140	150	160
4	1,235	25,700	30,900	33,900	39,600	44,800
6	1,622	40,000	47,800	52,100	60,300	68,100
8	1,586	45,800	53,300	56,900	66,900	76,000
10	1,620	43,200	51,800	56,900	65,100	75,400

1) 150°F water recommended for system design.
2) High-limit for entering water temperature = 160°F.
3) 72°F air entering heating coil.
4) Heating capacity values for 53, 64, 56, 74 and 95 water heater sizes typically vary by 10% or less, a few by 15% or less.
5) The lowest capacity value in the full data set is 26,400 Btuh and the largest capacity value is 89,700 Btuh.

Figure 10-6

PSC Blower Performance					
AH and Blower Size	Motor Speed	External Static Pressure (IWC)				
		0.30	0.40	0.50	0.60	0.70
Size 4 11 x 7 Wheel ½ HP	Low	749	719	686	655	621
	M-Lo	1,002	977	922	896	865
	M-Hi	1,160	1,100	1,073	1047	1,008
	High	1,301	1,266	1,235	1,202	1,156
Size 6 11 x 7 Wheel ¾ HP	Low	886	876	855	841	817
	M-Lo	1,179	1,137	1,131	11,02	1,072
	M-Hi	1,306	1,307	1,277	1,246	1,210
	High	1,747	1,681	1,622	1,560	1,500
Size 8 11 x 10 Wheel ¾ HP	Low	1,300	1,240	1,236	1,210	1,177
	M-Lo	1,471	1,463	1,418	1,385	1,359
	M-Hi	1,671	1,611	1,586	1,553	1,513
	High	1,948	1,929	1,871	1,806	1,751
Size 10 11 x 10 Wheel ¾ HP	Low	1,308	1,279	1,257	1,231	1,205
	M-Lo	14,99	14,87	1,415	1,418	1,394
	M-Hi	1,693	1,663	1,620	1,586	1,569
	High	1,974	1,982	1,973	1,944	1,917

Units tested without filter in place.

Figure 10-7

compatible with the Cfm and external static pressure requirements for the cooling equipment.

Potable Water Heat

When hot water equipment provides space heat and potable water heat, *Manual J* provides the load value for space heat, and OEM guidance provides the value for the potable water load. For dual use, conform to code and OEM guidance for equipment selection and sizing.

10-11 Engineered Ventilation

The fresh air (outdoor air) requirement for a dwelling depends on local code. It may be that the potential for natural ventilation through operable windows is an adequate solution. It may be that a significant amount of mechanical outdoor air Cfm (perhaps as much as 0.35 air changes per hour) is required on an intermittent or continuous basis. When engineered ventilation is required, it may be that heat recovery is required.

- Providing engineered ventilation (when required, or desired) is a routine matter when the dwelling has a duct system (a ducted cooling system with hot water baseboard heat, for example). The sidebar on the next page reviews fundamental issues for this scenario.

- When there is no duct system (no cooling, or ductless cooling), engineered openings and an exhaust fan may satisfy the ventilation requirement. However, forcing infiltration into heated spaces may cause discomfort, and this method is not compatible with a recovery mandate.

- When there is no duct system for cooling, and depending on the applicable code, standard, or government program, a dedicated ventilation system that distributes outdoor air to more than one room or space may be required. Heat recovery is typically required for this scenario. Introducing cool air or relatively cold air into a heated room or space may cause a comfort problem. The sidebar on the next page relates to these issues.

10-12 Freeze Protection

Hot water coils (and the associated piping) that process outdoor air, or a mixture of outdoor and return air, must not freeze. Investigate leaving water temperatures for all possible operating conditions. Provide appropriate operating and safety controls.

- The outdoor air damper may be open, modulated, closed, or stuck in some open position. (Also true for return dampers, exhaust dampers, and relief dampers).
- Closed dampers have some leakage.
- The ambient temperature surrounding the equipment may be an issue.
- The blower may be operating at it's design Cfm, a staged Cfm, a modulated Cfm, or it may be inoperative (shut off, or failed).

Cooling Duct System Provides Ventilation

When the dwelling has a duct system for cooling-only, a modest amount of raw outdoor air (something like 5% to 10% of the blower Cfm) may be mixed with a much larger amount of return air, or the outdoor air may be processed by a heat recovery device before mixing with return air.

- The cooling system blower will operate intermittently, or continuously, depending on the code requirement. All conditioned spaces served by the duct system receive fresh air.

- The temperature of the supply air will be colder than the air in the conditioned space.

    For 70°F return air and 5% outdoor air, the supply air temperature at the air handler varies from 65.5°F when it is –20°F outdoors, to 69°F when it is 50°F outdoors.

    For 70°F return air and 10% outdoor air, the supply air temperature at the air handler varies from 61°F when it is –20°F outdoors, to 68°F when it is 50°F outdoors.

    Supply air temperatures will be modestly warmer when outdoor air flows through heat recovery equipment.

    When 65°F to 69°F supply air causes discomfort, a heating coil in the air handler corrects the problem. For 1,000 Cfm, it takes about 4,500 Btuh to 5,500 Btuh (depending on altitude) to increase supply air temperature by 5°F.

- Duct runs in a cold space (typically an attic) must be tightly sealed and properly insulated (duct system condensation caused by thermosyphoning must not occur when the blower is not operating).

- Entering air temperature depends on outdoor air temperature and outdoor air Cfm, and on return air temperature (adjusted for a duct load, when applicable) and return air Cfm.
- Water-coil Gpm may be for full-flow, reduced flow, or no-flow.
- Leaving water temperature depends on the coil's design, on entering water temperature and Gpm, and on entering air temperature and Cfm.
- OEM data that deals with the relevant variables determines coil performance.
- Pipe running through an unconditioned space that will, or possible could, experience freezing conditions must have freeze protection.

Informative Material Pertaining to Ductless Air-Air Equipment

Section 11 – Ductless Single-Split Equipment

Section 12 – Ductless Multi-Split Systems

Section 13 – Single-Package Equipment

Section 11

Ductless Single-Split Equipment

Ductless single-split equipment has an outdoor compressor unit and one indoor fan coil unit. The fan coil unit has it's own programmable thermostat, and controls that interface with the outdoor unit's controls. One piece of equipment is used for a defined comfort zone.

- Equipment capacity must be compatible with the zone load (the zone includes all spaces served by the fan coil unit).
- Equipment capacity may be fixed or variable. When capacity is staged or modulated, there is a maximum capacity value, a rated capacity value, and a minimum capacity value.
- The fan coil unit may have a multiple-speed blower and an electronic expansion valve, or some other type of expansion valve.
- A fan coil unit may be free blow (supply grille, no ducting), or ducted (supply grille, and a return grille, at the end of duct runs).
- A wall, flush-ceiling, recessed-ceiling, or low-wall (floor) fan coil has an internal supply air diffuser, which may have variable throw and spread, may automatically vector the throw in a repetitive pattern, or vector the throw toward portions of the space that are too warm, or too cool.
- External static pressure is an important issue for ducted fan coil units. The available static pressure must be compatible with the pressure required for it's duct system.
- A simple multi-run duct system that has supply grilles, a return grille (with no filter), a hand damper, and a few aerodynamic fittings, may require 0.20 IWC of external pressure, or more.

11-1 Applications

Single-split equipment is used for new construction, and for retrofit and replacement work. This may be cooling-only equipment, or heat pump equipment.

- Cooling may be added to an existing living space that only has heating.
- An independent source of heat is required when cooling-only equipment is used for new construction (radiant-floor or baseboard heat may be hot water heat or electric resistance heat, for example).
- Heat pump equipment may be used for new construction, for a new addition, or it may replace an existing year-round comfort system.
- When heat pump equipment does not have integrated supplemental heat, an independent source of supplemental heat is required when it's maximum heating capacity at the winter design condition is less than the *Manual J* heating load.
- One piece of equipment per zone allows simultaneous heating and cooling for a set of zones.
- The total cooling capacity of the equipment must be compatible with the rooms and spaces served.

  The smallest equipment in a product line may have 6,000 to 9,000 Btuh of total AHRI cooling capacity. Most room loads are much smaller than this (i.e., zoning by room requires a large room load).

  The aggregate cooling load for a group of compatible rooms (zone load) must be compatible with the cooling capacity of the equipment.

- The equipment must have enough latent capacity for the climate. (This is a summer design day issue, see Section 11-6).
- Engineered ventilation (outdoor air with recovery, or without recovery) may be mandated by code, or desired for good practice reasons, but the indoor units for a given product line may not have an outdoor air feature.

  Some indoor units provide outdoor air with no recovery, but this may be a commercial product.

  An independent ventilation system is required when the indoor unit cannot provide the desired ventilation rate, and recovery effectiveness.

- In general, the air distribution pattern of the indoor unit must be compatible with the geometry of the rooms and spaces served.

  For free blow (no duct) equipment, the zone should have an open, relatively compact, floor plan (there is a limit to the effective throw of the supply grille, even when it has an enhanced throw-vector feature).

  A ducted fan coil unit should be used when the zone has partitioned spaces, or for a group of open rooms that have a sprawling floor plan.

11-2 Design Goals

The design goal is to match the heating-cooling capacity of the equipment with the zone heating-cooling loads. This requires *Manual J* loads for a zoned dwelling, and OEM performance data for heating and cooling.

- A zone may be one room or space, or a combination of rooms and spaces.
- The rooms and spaces in a zone must have compatible load patterns and use schedules (see *Manual Zr*, Section 3 and Section 4).
- The total cooling capacity of the equipment must be compatible with the zone's design day cooling load, and must have adequate heating capacity for the design day heating load (or supplemented by other means).
- For cooling, the indoor humidity should be 55% RH or less on a design day, and should not exceed 60% RH for part-load conditions.
- A ductless fan coil unit may serve a zone that is not divided by partition walls (the supply air grille should be able to affect the air motion in the collective space that it serves).
- A ducted fan coil unit provides a way to match equipment capacity with zone load when a zone has two or more partitioned rooms and/or spaces, a large floor area, or a sprawling floor plan.

11-3 Outdoor Equipment

Outdoor units (Figure 11-1) may be cooling-only equipment, or may be reverse-cycle equipment that provides heating and cooling. Various makes and models are available in a range of sizes for single-phase power.

- Nominal size is based on total cooling capacity for the AHRI rating-test condition. Sizes typically range from about 8,000 Btuh to about 24,000 Btuh, but may be as large as 48,000 Btuh.
- Nominal size may be stated in KW units. Since 1 KW is 3,413 Btuh, KW values are easily converted to Btuh values. For example, 4.0 KW is about 13,650 Btuh.

11-4 Indoor Equipment

The primary issues for indoor units (Figure 11-2) are sensible and latent cooling capacity at the *Manual J* summer design condition, heating capacity at the *Manual J* winter design temperature, compatibility with outdoor air requirements (per code, or preference), and air distribution (correspondence between the zone's floor plan and the available air pattern). Available external static pressure is very important for ducted units.

- Most products do not have integrated supplemental (electric resistance) heat.
- Some products have enhanced heat pump heating when it is cold outdoors (Figure 11-3, next page).
- Most fan coil units do not have an outdoor air feature (may be available as a commercial product).

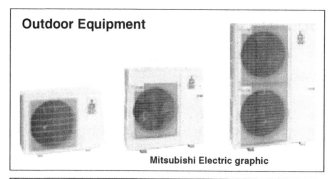

Outdoor Equipment

Mitsubishi Electric graphic

Features and Options	
Item	Consideration
Heating-cooling mode	Heating or cooling with automatic change-over.
Compressor capacity control	Variable, staged, fixed.
Compressor motor speed	Type of control, as applicable.
Requires crankcase heater	Yes or no; or conditional yes.
Low ambient cooling	Minimum approved outdoor air temperature (may require wind baffle, low ambient pressure control, crankcase heater, etc.).
Enhanced refrigerant cycle heat for cold weather	47°F heating capacity held relatively constant to 15°F (or so) outdoors; then drops 75% to 85% for below zero outdoors.
Hard start, and/ fast warm-up	Avoid nuisance, and comfort.
Heat pump defrost control	Document method.
Motor protection	Voltage; amperage; temperature.
Refrigerant safety controls	Pressure; temperature.
Water for space humidification	Condensate.
SEER; HSPF; Noise Ratings	Equipment is generally quiet.

Figure 11-1

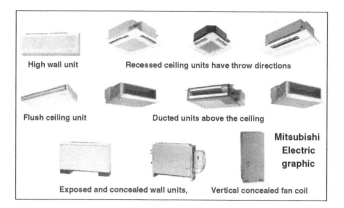

High wall unit — Recessed ceiling units have throw directions
Flush ceiling unit — Ducted units above the ceiling
Exposed and concealed wall units, — Vertical concealed fan coil

Mitsubishi Electric graphic

Figure 11-2

- The available static pressure for ducted fan coils may be relatively low (about 0.10 IWC, possibly 0.20 IWC).

- Filter options may be an issue for some applications.
- Figure 11-4 lists common features and options.

11-5 Performance Data and Data Use

The OEM provides a map (or equivalent) of the system's approved operating range. An example of this information is provided by Figure 11-5 (next page). Make sure that the OEM's operating range is compatible with the winter and summer design temperatures for the dwelling's comfort system.

OEMs publish AHRI rating data, which include total cooling capacity values for a special set of conditions, and heating capacity values for a special set of conditions.

- For heating, the outdoor dry-bulb is 47°F and 17°F, and the indoor entering dry-bulb is 70°F.
- For cooling, the outdoor dry-bulb is 95°F, the indoor entering dry-bulb is 80°F, and the indoor entering wet-bulb is 67°F.
- For cooling and heating, the compressor operates at it's rated capacity (rating speed) with the indoor unit operating at maximum blower Cfm.
- Heating capacity data may not be adjusted for the defrost cycle effect.

A piece of OEM literature may, or may not, show the rated capacity for 17°F heating. This is important information (most locations have a design temperature that is much colder than 47°F), so find it in the OEM's technical or installation literature, or ask for it.

OEM's publish a capacity range for equipment that has variable compressor capacity. These values are for the AHRI rating conditions for cooling and heating (as noted above). For example:

Rated cooling capacity = 9,000 Btuh
Cooling capacity range = 3,800 to 12,200 Btuh
Rated heating capacity (47°F) = 10,900 Btuh
Heating capacity range (47°F) = 4,500 to 14,100 Btuh

Rated heating capacity (17°F) = 6,600 Btuh
A 17°F capacity range value not relevant (the heating load normally requires full capacity).

Rated cooling capacity and rated heating capacity values do not represent actual full-load performance when the equipment is installed in a given dwelling, at a specific location, except by coincidence.

- The design value for summer outdoor dry-bulb may not be 95°F.
- The design values for summer entering dry-bulb and wet-bulb may not be 80°F and 67°F.

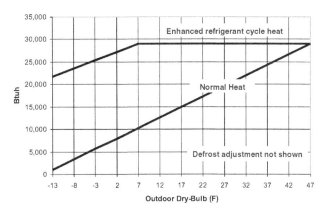

Figure 11-3

Indoor Equipment — Features and Options	
Item	Consideration
Outdoor air feature	Engineered ventilation.
Cooling condensate disposal	Evaporation, pan, drain, pump.
Heating-cooling mode	Heating or cooling with automatic change-over.
Control refrigerant flow	Type of expansion valve affects capacity control; reverse cycle required for heat pumps.
Dehumidification cycle	Enhanced moisture removal for a limited time (comfort issue).
Low ambient cooling	Compatible with outdoor unit.
Enhanced refrigerant cycle heat for cold weather	Compatible with outdoor unit.
Electric resistance coil [1]	Supplemental heat.
Blower speeds [2]	Minimum / maximum Cfm; need a blower table or graph for a ducted unit.
Air pattern control [3]	Manual or automatic vanes.
Filter options	Particle, mold-mildew, odors.
Motor protection	Voltage; amperage; temperature.
Refrigerant safety controls	Temperature; frost and ice.
Operating controls	Run schedules; set-point schedules; blower schedules; wired control, remote control.
Warm start-up	Heating season comfort.
Space humidification [4]	Source of water supply.
SEER; HSPF; Noise Ratings	Equipment is generally quiet.

1) Some form of supplemental heat is required when compressor heat is inadequate during cold weather.
2) External static pressure is extremely important for ducted units.
3) One-way, two-way, 3-D, vectored by infrared sensor.
4) Outdoor unit condensate may be used for humidification.

Figure 11-4

Section 11

- The design value for winter outdoor dry-bulb may not be 47°F or 17°F.
- The design value for winter entering dry-bulb may not be 70°F.
- Defrost cycles may reduce effective heating capacity between 17°F and 47°F.
- For variable-speed equipment, the compressor motor speed for a rating test may be less than the maximum motor speed (for enhanced capacity).
- Equipment rating tests are conducted with a specific length of refrigerant pipe and a specific change in piping elevation (usually zero). Correction factors reduce equipment capacity for longer piping lengths, and larger elevation changes.

An OEM may publish expanded performance data for heating and cooling. This determines equipment performance when it serves an actual dwelling, at a specific location. This information correlates sensible and latent cooling capacity with sets of summer operating conditions, and heating capacity with sets of winter operating conditions. This is a fundamental equipment sizing issue, so Section 11-6 covers it in detail.

Discharge air should mix supply air with room air and produce adequate air motion in the occupied space. An OEM may provide air pattern data for free blow equipment (see Section 11-7).

A ducted indoor unit must be compatible with the duct system it serves. An OEM may provide a blower table or graph (see Section 11-9).

Compressor capacity and refrigerant management are an inherent attribute of multi-split equipment. The OEM's design determines the operation of the outdoor and indoor equipment (described in OEM literature).

11-6 Expanded Performance Data

For ¾ tons of rated cooling, total capacity can vary by about ½ ton (roughly) as the outdoor air condition and entering air condition change. In addition, the coil sensible heat ratio for common entering wet-bulb temperatures (59°F to 67°F) can vary from 0.7 (or less), to 1.0 (i.e., latent capacity can range from less than seventy percent of total capacity to zero). Expanded performance data summarizes these tendencies for a given piece of equipment.

For air-air heat pumps, heating capacity can decrease by a factor of 3.0 to 4.0 as the outdoor temperature drops from 70°F to 0°F, or less.

Expanded performance summarizes this behavior, so it is used to evaluate the heating capacity for a piece of equipment that has the appropriate cooling capacity.

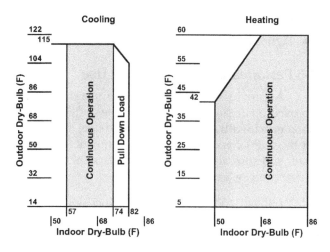

Figure 11-5

Conditional Cooling Capacity

For a given amount of compressor capacity (for a stage or speed), the conditional cooling capacity (sensible, latent and total) of a single-split system is sensitive to outdoor dry-bulb temperature, the dry-bulb temperature of the air entering the indoor coil, the wet-bulb temperature of the air entering the indoor coil, and the Cfm value at the indoor coil. Figure 11-6 (next page) provides an example of conditional cooling capacity data.

- Note that the total capacity varies from 7,080 Btuh (for a dry climate at 104°F) to 10,700 Btuh (for a wet climate at 68°F). Also note that the rated capacity is 8,500 Total Btuh (for 95°F db and 67°F WB).

  Figure 11-5 shows that the high outdoor air temperature limit for cooling is 115°F, but the cooling capacity data (Figure 11-6) stops at 104°F. Question the OEM about such discrepancies.

- Note that the sensible capacity varies from 4,790 Btuh (for a hot, dry climate) to 5,680 Btuh (for a cool, wet climate).

- Latent capacity equals total capacity minus sensible capacity. This calculation shows that latent capacity varies from 2,290 Btuh (for a hot-dry climate) to about 4,240 Btuh (for a cool-wet climate).

  Note that this particular piece of equipment, by design, has significant latent capacity over it's operating range. This example may not apply to some other piece of equipment. Always refer to the performance data for the equipment used.

- Climate humidity, building envelope infiltration, the use of engineered ventilation (and the type of recovery equipment), return duct leakage from an unconditioned space, and internal moisture loads are the primary factors that determine the *Manual J* sensible heat ratio (JSHR). Climate design temperature and solar azimuth angles have a smaller effect (the JSHR value depends on the latent load and sensible load).

- For indoor humidity control, the coil sensible heat ratio (CSHR) must be equal to (or less than) the JSHR when the equipment operates at the summer design condition. This will produce acceptable indoor humidity values as outdoor air temperature decreases.

Conditional Heating Capacity

For a given amount of compressor capacity (stage or speed), the conditional heating capacity of a single-split system is very sensitive to outdoor dry-bulb temperature; and somewhat sensitive to the dry-bulb temperature of the air entering the indoor coil, and to the Cfm value at the indoor coil, as demonstrated by Figure 11-7.

- Note that for 70°F indoors, the heating capacity varies from 5,800 Btuh (14°F outdoors), to 11,050 Btuh (50°F outdoors). Also note that the rated heating capacity is about 10,500 Btuh for 47°F outdoors.

Figure 11-5 shows that the low outdoor air temperature limit for heating is 5°F, but the heating capacity data (Figure 11-7) stops at 14°F. Question the OEM about such discrepancies.

- In this case, the OEM has not adjusted heating capacity for defrost when the outdoor temperature is in the 17°F to 47°F range.
- Note that heating capacity is not very sensitive to indoor temperature (70°F values may be used for common design work).

11-7 Air Distribution

For supply air, the primary concern is mixing supply air with room air, and air motion in the occupied space. In this regard, the principles for selecting and sizing ducted supply air diffusers, grilles and registers, equally apply to fan-coil grilles and diffusers.

- A fan coil unit only affects the air motion in it's local open space; it does not affect the air motion in other partitioned spaces that are in the same zone (and may not closely control the temperature in other partitioned spaces).
- Throw, spread, and drop (for ceiling or high-wall units), should be compatible with the geometry of the open space served by the fan coil unit.
- Air distribution should be relatively quiet. For non-ducted equipment, this depends on the OEM's design. For ducted equipment, this depends on the practitioner's design for duct runs, grilles and registers.

Cooling Performance for a Small System							
Entering		Outdoor Dry-Bulb (°F)					
EWB °F	EDB °F	68		77		86	
		TC	SHC	TC	SHC	TC	SHC
57.2	68.0	8.67	5.68	8.27	5.46	7.88	5.24
60.8	71.6	9.13	5.87	8.73	5.65	8.33	5.43
64.4	77.0	9.52	6.02	9.13	5.81	8.73	5.59
67.0	80.0	9.72	6.10	9.32	5.89	8.92	5.67
71.6	86.0	10.31	6.33	9.91	6.12	9.51	5.91
75.2	89.6	10.70	6.46	10.30	6.27	9.91	6.06
Entering		Outdoor Dry-Bulb (°F)					
EWB °F	EDB °F	89		95		104	
		TC	SHC	TC	SHC	TC	SHC
57.2	68.0	7.72	5.14	7.48	5.01	7.08	4.79
60.8	71.6	8.18	5.34	7.94	5.21	7.54	4.99
64.4	77.0	8.57	5.52	8.33	5.38	7.93	5.16
67.0	80.0	8.77	5.58	8.50	5.44	8.13	5.24
71.6	86.0	9.35	5.82	9.12	5.69	8.72	5.48
75.2	89.6	9.75	5.97	9.51	5.85	9.11	5.64

TC = Total cooling MBtu; SC = Sensible cooling MBtuh.
Capacities have a deduction for indoor fan motor heat.
Refrigerant piping length = 25 Ft; Elevation change = 0 Ft.

Figure 11-6

Heating Performance for a Small System					
Entering Dry-Bulb (°F)	Outdoor Dry-Bulb (°F)				
	14	23	32	43	50
	Heat Output (MBtuh)				
60.8	6.20	7.51	8.83	10.40	11.45
64.4	6.04	7.35	8.67	10.24	11.29
68.0	5.88	7.19	8.51	10.08	11.13
70.0	5.80	7.11	8.43	10.00	11.05
71.6	5.72	7.03	8.34	9.92	10.97
75.2	5.56	6.87	8.18	9.76	10.81

Capacities include fan motor heat for high fan speed.
Heating capacity not adjusted for defrost cycle.
Refrigerant piping length = 25 Ft; Elevation change = 0 Ft.

Figure 11-7

Section 11

The amount of OEM-published information pertaining to throw, spread and drop varies considerably. At one extreme, there may be no information, at the other extreme, the guidance may be comprehensive, as demonstrated by Figure 11-8.

OEM's tend to be very sensitive to noise issues, so ductless, split-coil equipment tends to be quiet. In this regard, the human ear is sensitive to sound pressure, but perception also depends on the frequency of the sound, so a noise criteria (NC) curve summarizes ear perception across eight octave bands.

- Figure 11-9 (next page) provides an example of comprehensive information, but this may, or may not, appear in OEM literature.
- A single decibel value does not summarize noise (eight values are required for a NC chart).

11-8 Blower Data

A ducted fan coil unit is used when the geometry of the space served by a fan coil is not compatible (too large, or too irregular) with it's free blow air pattern. Or, a ducted fan coil is used when it serves two or more partitioned spaces that are in the same zone.

The fan coil unit is sized to neutralize the loads for the space or spaces served, this determines maximum blower Cfm. Blowers usually operate at more than one speed, so maximum Cfm occurs at maximum blower speed.

The OEM's blower data (table or chart) correlates available static pressure with blower Cfm (Figure 11-10, next page, for example). The available static pressure for maximum blower Cfm must be compatible with the duct system served.

- A circulation path will have a supply grille, a return grille, and may have a hand damper for balancing. These components will require 0.04 to 0.09 IWC of static pressure (0.09 is the *Manual D* default).
- Efficient boot fittings at the supply grille and return grille will require an additional 0.03 to 0.06 IWC of static pressure.
- Efficient elbows and/or takeoffs may require an additional 0.03 to 0.06 IWC of static pressure.
- Straight duct may dissipate about 0.01 IWC of pressure per 10 foot section.
- A simple 10 foot duct system (one supply, two boots, no elbow or tees), may require 0.08 to 0.16 IWC of static pressure.
- A distribution system that serves two or more rooms may require 0.15 to 0.25 IWC of static pressure.

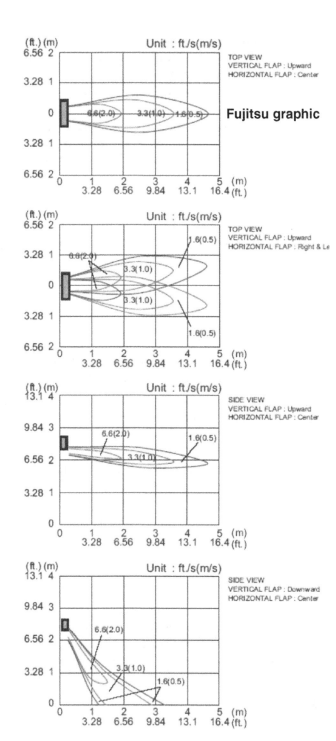

Figure 11-8

11-9 Duct System Design

The cooling and heating loads for most rooms and spaces are much smaller than the cooling-heating capacity of the smallest fan coil unit. Some, or all, of these spaces may be partitioned. This is reconciled by combining the spaces into a zone, and using a ducted fan coil unit to distribute supply air to the spaces.

- *Manual J* procedures determine room heating and cooling loads, then *Manual D* procedures convert these loads to supply air Cfm values.
- *Manual D* procedures convert supply air Cfm values to duct airway sizes (subject to air velocity limits for duct-generated noise).
- Make sure that the blower data is for a filter in place, and do not add accessory pressure drop devices that are incompatible with blower power.
- Efficient duct fittings are absolutely essential. Use items that have the shortest equivalent length in Appendix 3, *Manual D*.

11-10 Equipment Selection and Sizing

Size single-split equipment for cooling, then (where applicable) check the heating capacity of the system. Relevant procedures are summarized here:

Size for Cooling

Expanded cooling performance data is used to size the equipment (Figure 11-6, for example). The goal is to match total, sensible and latent capacity to the zone cooling load values from *Manual J* calculations.

- The equipment serves one zone. The zone consists of one or more rooms/spaces that have compatible loads, as far as time-of-day, and month-of-year are concerned.
- For heat pumps, the equipment operates in the cooling mode, or heating mode, depending on the nature of the load.
- The equipment is sized for full cooling capacity when operating at summer design conditions.
- Per Table N2-2 and Table N2-1, total cooling capacity (sensible plus latent) may range from 90% of the block load (0.90 factor) to 120% of the block load (1.20 factor), for cooling-only equipment, and for a Condition A heat pump.
- For a Condition B heat pump, total cooling capacity may be as much as 15,000 Btuh more than the block cooling load.
- Latent capacity must be equal to, or greater, than the latent load, and the sensible capacity must not be less than 90% of the sensible block load.

Evaluate Heating Capacity

The design heating load for the system occurs at the winter design condition, and the value for the block heating load is determined by *Manual J* procedures. Performance data for the AHRI rating test is limited to heating capacity at 17°F and 47°F (or just 47°F); so the expanded performance data (Figure 11-7, for example) must be used to evaluate heating capacity for the winter design condition.

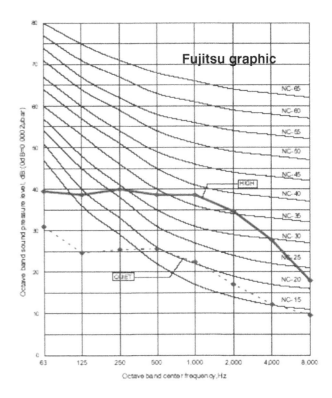

Figure 11-9

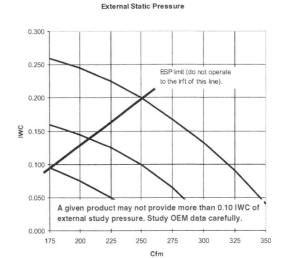

Figure 11-10

- Heat pump equipment is sized for cooling, per Table N2-2 rules.
- Expanded performance data for heating is used to draw the thermal balance point diagram. Use the performance data for maximum compressor heating capacity.

Some products can operate at an enhanced compressor speed during cold weather (see Figure 11-3). This must be available on a continuous basis, for an unlimited amount of time.

When the heating capacity data does not have a defrost knee, ask the OEM for data that does have a defrost knee.

- Use Table N2-3 rules and Section 6 procedures to size supplemental electric coil heat, and emergency electric coil heat.

- When the indoor fan-coil unit does not have supplemental electric coil heat, another source of heat is required to satisfy the ancillary heating needs (electric baseboard heat, for example).

- When an indoor fan coil unit has electric coil heat, the combined heating capacity of the refrigerant coil (when compressor heat is available for the winter design condition), and the electric resistance coil, must satisfy the supplemental heat requirement, and the electric coil heat must satisfy the emergency heat requirement.

- When the indoor fan coil unit has electric coil heat, the full electric resistance coil capacity must be equal to, or greater than, the **Manual J** heating load for the zone served when compressor heat is not available at the winter design condition.

The heat pump is fully functional, but operation is prohibited by a low outdoor air temperature control, so electric coil heat is the only source of heat.

Section 12

Ductless Multi-Split Systems

Multi-split systems have an outdoor compressor unit and two or more indoor fan coil units. Each fan coil unit has it's own proprietary wired or wireless remote controller. The outdoor unit operates when one or more indoor units call for heat or cooling. To optimize system operation, the indoor units communicate with the outdoor unit, and the outdoor unit communicates with the indoor units.

Indoor fan coil units provide comfort zones. Compressor capacity distribution may be by refrigerant piping only, or by a combination of refrigerant piping and air ducts.

- Indoor unit (fan coil) capacity should be compatible with the zone load (the zone includes all spaces served by the fan coil unit).
- Outdoor unit capacity must be compatible with the fan coil units served (OEM guidance authorizes combinations and configurations).
- System capacity (outdoor units and fan coil units) may be fixed or variable. When capacity is staged or modulated, there is a rated capacity, a maximum capacity, and a minimum capacity.
- Fan coil units may have multiple-speed blowers, and electronic expansion valves.
- Fan coil units may be free blow (supply grille, no ducting), or ducted (supply grilles, and a return grille at the end of duct runs).
- A wall, flush-ceiling, recessed-ceiling, or low-wall (floor) fan coil has an internal supply air diffuser; which may have variable throw and spread, or may automatically vector the throw in a repetitive pattern, or vector the throw toward portions of the space that are too warm, or too cool.
- External static pressure is an important issue for ducted fan coil units. The available static pressure must be compatible with the pressure required for the duct system.
- A simple multi-run duct system that has supply grille, a return grille (with no filter), a hand damper, and a few aerodynamic fittings, may require 0.20 IWC of external pressure, or more.

12-1 Applications

Multi-split equipment is used for new construction, and for retrofit and replacement work. This may be a cooling-only system, or a heat pump system. Smaller, single-phase equipment is used for most homes. Larger, three-phase equipment may be used for a very large home (when the site has access to three-phase power).

- Multi-split cooling may be added to an existing dwelling, or living space that only has heating.
- An independent source of heat is required when cooling-only equipment is used for new construction (radiant-floor or baseboard heat may be hot water heat or electric resistance heat, for example).
- A multi-split heat pump may be used for new construction, for a new addition; or it may replace an existing year-round comfort system.
- When multi-split equipment does not have integrated supplemental heat, an independent source of supplemental heat is required when the maximum compressor heating capacity at the winter design condition is less the *Manual J* heating load.
- Some dwellings require simultaneous heating and cooling. This requires separate systems, or a multi-split heat pump system that has variable refrigerant flow (VRF) and heat recovery (VRF may require three-phase power).
- The total cooling capacity of an indoor unit should be compatible with the rooms and spaces served.

  The smallest indoor unit in a product line may have 6,000 to 9,000 Btuh of total AHRI cooling capacity. Most room loads are much smaller than this (i.e., zoning by room requires a large room load).

  The aggregate cooling load for a group of compatible rooms (zone load) should be compatible with the cooling capacity of an indoor unit.

- The equipment must have adequate latent capacity for a summer design day (see Section 12-6).
- Engineered ventilation (outdoor air with recovery, or without recovery) may be mandated by code, or desired for good practice reasons, but the indoor units for a given product line may not have an outdoor air feature.

  Some indoor units provide outdoor air with no recovery, but this may be a commercial product.

  An independent ventilation system is required when a multi-split system cannot provide the desired ventilation rate, and recovery effectiveness.

- In general, the air distribution pattern of an indoor unit must be compatible with the geometry of the rooms and spaces served.

For free blow (no duct) equipment, the zone should have an open, relatively compact floor plan (there is a limit to the effective throw of the supply grille, even when it has an enhanced throw-vector feature).

A ducted fan coil unit should be used when the zone has partitioned spaces, or for a group of open rooms that have a complex floor plan.

12-2 Design Goals

The design goal is to match the heating-cooling capacity of the indoor fan coils with the corresponding zone loads, and to match the capacity range of the outdoor unit with the indoor units that it serves. This requires *Manual J* loads for a zoned dwelling, and OEM performance data for heating and cooling.

- A zone may be one room or space, or a combination of rooms and spaces.

- The rooms and spaces in a zone must have compatible load patterns and use schedules (see *Manual Zr*, Section 3 and Section 4).

- The total cooling capacity of the indoor unit must be compatible with the zone's design day cooling load; and must have adequate heating capacity (where applicable) for the design day heating load (or supplemented by other means).

- For cooling, the indoor humidity should be 55% RH or less on a design day, and should not exceed 60% RH at part-load conditions.

- A ductless fan coil unit may serve a zone that is not divided by partition walls (the supply air grille must be able to affect the air motion in the collective space that it serves).

- A ducted fan coil unit provides a way to match fan coil capacity with a zone load when the zone has two or more partitioned rooms and/or spaces, or when the zone has a large or sprawling floor plan.

- A given set of fan coil units must be compatible with the outdoor unit (as specified by the OEM's design guidance).

12-3 Outdoor Equipment

Outdoor units (Figure 12-1) may be cooling-only equipment, or may be reverse-cycle equipment that provides heating and cooling. Various makes and models are available in a range of sizes.

Nominal Size for Outdoor Units

Nominal system size is based on total cooling capacity for the AHRI rating-test condition, with a specific set of indoor units operating at their rated capacity. Residential system sizes typically range from about 12,000 Btuh to about 48,000 Btuh, but may be as large as 65,000 Btuh.

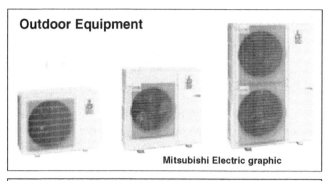

Outdoor Equipment

Mitsubishi Electric graphic

Features and Options for Smaller Systems	
Item	Consideration
Power, phase and voltage	Match available service.
Variable refrigerant flow [1]	May require three-phase power.
Number of refrigerant pipes [2]	Two-pipe or three-pipe.
Heating-cooling mode [3]	Heating or cooling with automatic change-over; or simultaneous heating and cooling.
Maximum number of indoor units (4 to 5 tons total)	Two to eight.
Compressor	Type, and number in cabinet.
Compressor capacity control	Variable, staged, fixed.
Compressor motor speed	Type of control, as applicable.
Requires crankcase heater	Yes or no; or conditional yes.
Low ambient cooling	Minimum approved outdoor air temperature (may require wind baffle, low ambient pressure control, crankcase heater, etc.).
Enhanced refrigerant cycle heat for cold weather	47 °F heating capacity held relatively constant to 15 °F (or so) outdoors; then 75% to 85% for below zero outdoors.
Hard start, and fast warm-up	Avoid nuisance, and comfort.
Heat pump defrost control	Investigate the method used.
Motor protection	Voltage; amperage; temperature.
Refrigerant safety controls	Pressure; temperature.
Water for space humidification	Condensate.
SEER; HSPF; Noise Ratings	Equipment is generally quiet.

1) At least one OEM has single-phase equipment.
2) At least one OEM has two-pipe systems.
3) Simultaneous H-C requires VRF and heat recovery.

Figure 12-1

Commercial sizes range from about 18,000 Btuh to about 360,000 Btuh.

- Nominal size may be stated in KW units. For example, a multi-split product may have five size classes that range from 4.0 KW to 10.0 KW.

- Since 1 KW is 3,413 Btuh, KW values are easily converted to Btuh values. For example, 4.0 KW is about 13,650 Btuh.

Power Supply

Residential equipment uses single-phase power. Commercial equipment generally uses three-phase power, but smaller sizes may use single-phase power.

- Most single family and low-rise, multi-family structures have single-phase power, so three-phase equipment is not an option for the majority of residential systems.
- The entire range of residential and commercial equipment is an option when a very large home has three-phase power, or access to three-phase power.

The power supply issue is important because a desirable feature may not be available with single-phase equipment. Where applicable, this issue should be discussed with the OEM, or the OEM's representative.

- Single-phase equipment is generally limited to two to eight indoor units.
- Three-phase, VRF equipment may have more than eight indoor units that are served by a two-pipe, or three-pipe refrigerant system (commercial systems 65,000 Btuh or larger).
- Single-phase equipment may not provide simultaneous heating and cooling (but may have automatic heat-cool changeover).
- Three-phase, VRF equipment may provide simultaneous heating and cooling.

12-4 Indoor Equipment

The primary design issues for indoor units (Figure 12-2) are sensible and latent cooling capacity at the *Manual J* summer design temperature, heating capacity at the *Manual J* winter design temperature, compatibility with outdoor air requirements (per code, or preference), and air distribution (correspondence between the zone's floor plan and the available air pattern). Available external static pressure is very important for ducted units.

- Residential fan coil sizes (for rated cooling capacity) typically range from 5,000 Btuh to 24,000 Btuh, and may be as large as 42,000 Btuh.
- Most products do not have integrated supplemental (electric resistance coil) heat, but some do. Study OEM literature carefully, or ask the OEM.
- Some products have enhanced heat pump heating when it is cold outdoors (see Figure 12-3).

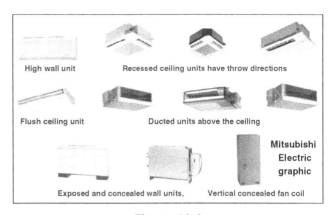

Figure 12-2

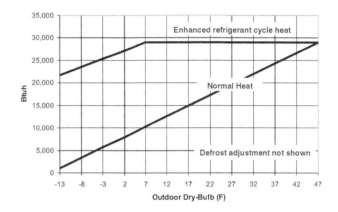

Figure 12-3

- Most fan coil units do not have an outdoor air feature (may be available as a commercial product).
- For single-phase equipment, the available static pressure for ducted fan coils may be relatively low (about 0.10 IWC, possibly 0.20 IWC).
- Ducted fan coils for three-phase equipment may provide 0.20 to 0.30 IWC of pressure.
- Filter options may be an issue for some applications.
- Figure 12-4 (next page) lists common features and options.

12-5 Performance Data and Design Procedures

The OEM provides a map (or equivalent) of the system's approved operating range. An example of this information is provided by Figure 12-5 (page 141). Make sure that the OEM's operating range is compatible with the winter and summer design temperatures for the dwelling's comfort system.

The OEM authorizes combinations of indoor units for a given outdoor unit. An example of this information is provided by Figure 12-6 (next page). Note that the total nominal capacity of the indoor units may exceed the nominal capacity of the outdoor unit. When so, the actual capacity will be limited to the outdoor unit capacity (the OEM's refrigerant system design and controls deal with this issue).

OEMs publish AHRI rating data, which include total cooling capacity values for a specific (standard) set of conditions, and heating capacity values for a specific (standard) set of conditions.

- For heating, the outdoor dry-bulb is 47°F and 17°F, and the indoor entering dry-bulb is 70°F.
- For cooling, the outdoor dry-bulb is 95°F, the indoor entering dry-bulb is 80°F, and the indoor entering wet-bulb is 67°F.
- For cooling and heating, the compressor operates at it's rated capacity (rating speed) with all indoor units operating at their rated capacities.

For variable-speed equipment, maximum capacity can be greater than rated (full) capacity. This depends on the outdoor-indoor speeds for the rating test vs. maximum compressor speed.

Use of an enhanced speed feature increases capacity for any operating condition. For example, Figure 12-3 shows that programmed speed increases maintain rated (47°F) heating capacity as the outdoor air temperature drops.

- Heating capacity data may not be adjusted for the defrost cycle effect.

A piece of OEM literature may, or may not, show the rated capacity for 17°F heating. This is important information (most locations have a design temperature that is much colder than 47°F), so find it in the OEM's technical or installation literature, or ask for it.

OEM's publish a capacity range for equipment that has variable compressor capacity. These values are for the AHRI rating conditions for cooling and heating (as noted above). For example:

Rated cooling capacity = 20,000 Btuh
Cooling capacity range = 7,800 to 20,000 Btuh
Rated heating capacity (47°F) = 22,000 Btuh
Heating capacity range (47°F) = 8,500 to 22,000 Btuh

Rated heating capacity (17°F) = 14,500 Btuh
Rated capacity values for 17°F may not be published.
Reduced capacity values for 17°F may not be relevant to cold weather operation.

Rated cooling capacity and rated heating capacity values do not represent actual full-load performance when the

Indoor Equipment — Features and Options	
Item	Consideration
Power supply	Match available service.
Indoor unit styes	Match application needs (below).
Outdoor air feature	Engineered ventilation.
Cooling condensate disposal	Evaporation, pan, drain, pump.
Refrigerant piping	Not VRF; or has VRF.
Heating-cooling mode [1]	Heating or cooling with automatic change-over; or simultaneous heating and cooling.
Control refrigerant flow	Type of expansion valve affects capacity control; reverse cycle required for heat pumps.
Dehumidification cycle	Enhanced moisture removal for a limited time (comfort issue).
Low ambient cooling	Compatible with outdoor unit.
Enhanced refrigerant cycle heat for cold weather	Compatible with outdoor unit.
Electric resistance coil [2]	Supplemental heat.
Blower speeds [3]	Minimum / maximum Cfm; need a blower table or graph for a ducted unit.
Air pattern control [4]	Manual or automatic vanes.
Filter options	Particle, mold-mildew, odors.
Motor protection	Voltage; amperage; temperature.
Refrigerant safety controls	Temperature; frost and ice.
Operating controls	Run schedules; set-point schedules; blower schedules; wired control, remote control.
Warm start-up	Heating season comfort.
Space humidification [5]	Source of water supply.
Noise ratings	Indoor blowers are generally quiet at rated speed, and more quiet at reduced speed.

1) Simultaneous H-C requires VRF and heat recovery.
2) Some form of supplemental heat is required when compressor heat is inadequate during cold weather.
3) External static pressure is extremely important for ducted units.
4) One-way, two-way, 3-D, vectored by infrared sensor.
5) Outdoor unit condensate may be used for humidification.

Figure 12-4

equipment is installed in a given dwelling, at a specific location, except by coincidence.

- The design value for summer outdoor dry-bulb may not be 95°F.
- The design values for summer entering dry-bulb and wet-bulb may not be 80°F and 67°F.
- The design value for winter outdoor dry-bulb may not be 47°F or 17°F.

- The design value for winter entering dry-bulb may not be 70°F.
- Defrost cycles may reduce effective heating capacity between 17°F and 47°F.
- For variable-speed equipment, the compressor motor speed for a rating test may be less than the maximum motor speed (for enhanced capacity).
- Equipment rating tests are conducted with a specific length of refrigerant pipe and a specific change in piping elevation (usually zero). Correction factors reduce equipment capacity for longer piping lengths, and larger elevation changes.

An OEM may publish expanded performance data for cooling and heating. This determines equipment performance when it serves an actual dwelling, at a specific location. This information correlates total, sensible, and latent cooling capacity with sets of summer operating conditions, and heating capacity with sets of winter operating conditions. This is a fundamental equipment sizing issue, so Sections 12-6 and 12-7 cover it in detail.

Discharge air should mix supply air with room air, and produce adequate air motion in the occupied space. An OEM may provide air pattern data for free blow equipment (see Section 12-8).

A ducted indoor unit must be compatible with the duct system it serves. An OEM may provide a blower table or graph (see Section 12-9).

Compressor capacity and refrigerant management are an inherent attribute of multi-split VRF equipment. The OEM's design determines the operation of the outdoor and indoor units (described in OEM literature).

12-6 Expanded Performance Data for Cooling

For 2-1/2 tons of rated cooling, total capacity can vary by almost two tons as the outdoor air condition and entering air condition change. In addition, the coil sensible heat ratio for common entering wet-bulb temperatures (59°F to 67°F) can vary from about 0.5 to 1.0 (i.e., latent capacity can range from fifty percent of total capacity to zero). Expanded performance data quantifies these tendencies for a given equipment set.

Conditional Cooling Capacity for the System

For a given amount of compressor capacity (for a stage or speed), the conditional cooling capacity (sensible, latent and total) of a multi-split system is sensitive to outdoor dry-bulb temperature, the dry-bulb temperature of the air entering the indoor coils, the wet-bulb temperature of the air entering the indoor coils, and the Cfm values at the indoor coils. Figure 12-7 (next page) provides an example of conditional cooling capacity data.

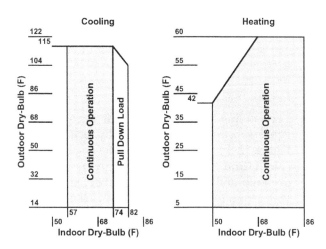

Figure 12-5

Authorized Configurations			
Outdoor Unit Capacity (Btuh)	24,000	30,000	36,000
Indoor Unit Capacities (1,000 Btuh)	9 + 9	9 + 9	9 + 9 + 9
	9 + 12	9 + 12	9 + 9 + 12
	9 + 15	9 + 15	9 + 9 + 15
	12 + 12	9 + 18	9 + 9 + 18
		9 + 24	9 + 9 + 24
		12 + 12	9 + 12 + 12
		12 + 15	9 + 12 + 15
		12 + 18	9 + 12 + 18
		15 + 15	9 + 15 + 18
		15 + 18	12 + 12 + 12
		18 + 18	12 + 12 + 15
		9 + 9 + 9	12 + 12 + 18
		9 + 9 + 12	12 + 15 + 18
		9 + 9 + 15	9 + 9 + 9 + 9
		9 + 9 + 18	9 + 9 + 9 + 12
			9 + 9 + 9 + 15
			9 + 9 + 12 + 12

Figure 12-6

- Note that the total capacity varies from 16,690 Btuh (for a hot-dry climate) to 36,040 Btuh (for a cool-wet climate). Also note that the rated capacity is 30,600 Total Btuh (95°F db and 67°F WB).
- Note that the sensible capacity varies from 5,240 Btuh (for a hot, wet-coil climate) to 32,490 Btuh (for a cool, dry-coil climate).

- Latent capacity equals total capacity minus sensible capacity. This calculation shows that latent capacity varies from 0 Btuh (for a hot-dry climate) to about 15,000 Btuh (for a cool, wet-coil climate), to 25,320 Btuh when the entering air is extremely humid.

- The cooling coil's sensible heat ratio (CSHR) equals sensible capacity divided by total capacity. Figure 12-8 (next page) shows the results of this calculation. Note that for normal entering dry-bulb and wet-bulb values, the CSHR value varies from 1.00 to about 0.50, and can be as low as 0.29 when the entering air is extremely humid.

- Climate humidity, building envelope infiltration, the use of engineered ventilation (and the type of recovery equipment), return duct leakage from an unconditioned space, and internal moisture loads are the primary factors that determine the *Manual J* sensible heat ratio (JSHR). Climate design temperature and solar azimuth angles have a smaller effect (the JSHR value depends on the latent load and sensible load).

- For indoor humidity control, the coil sensible heat ratio (CSHR) must be equal to (or less than) the JSHR when the equipment operates at the summer design condition. This will produce acceptable indoor humidity values as outdoor air temperature decreases.

Conditional Cooling Capacity for Indoor Units

Data for indoor unit cooling capacity would be similar to Figure 12-7. That is, total capacity and sensible capacity depend on outdoor dry-bulb temperature, entering wet-bulb and dry-bulb temperature at the fan coil, and fan-coil Cfm. However, indoor unit capacity also depends on the size of the outdoor unit, the number of indoor units, and the sizes of the indoor units.

Mapping all possible permeations of outdoor units and indoor units for the entire range of operating conditions is impractical, as far as publishing table sets is concerned. Therefore, OEM data for indoor units may be limited to a table that shows AHRI cooling capacity for a particular outdoor unit serving a specific set of indoor units.

For example, an outdoor unit that has 19,100 Btuh of rated (AHRI) cooling capacity may serve three indoor units that have 7,500 Btuh of rated cooling capacity, or three indoor units that have 11,900 Btuh of rated (AHRI) cooling capacity. Note that the aggregate rated capacity of the indoor units may be marginally more, or significantly more, than the rated capacity of the outdoor unit.

Outdoor Unit = 19,100 Btuh
Indoor units = 3 x 7,500 = 22,500 Btuh
Indoor units = 3 x 11,500 = 35,700 Btuh

Outdoor Unit: 31-MBH (30,600 Btuh rated total cooling capacity) Indoor Units: Four 9-MBH (9,000 Btuh nominal rated cooling capacity)							
System Cooling Capacity (Btuh)							
Entering Air Condition (°F)		TC-SC Split	Outdoor Dry-Bulb (°F)				
WB	DB		65	75	85	95	105	115
		TC	31,170	30,000	28,730	28,010	22,960	16,690
	72		25,580	24,900	24,440	23,980	21,700	16,690
	76		29,470	29,010	28,320	28,010	22,960	16,690
59	80	SC	31,170	30,000	28,730	28,010	22,960	16,690
	84		31,170	30,000	28,730	28,010	22,960	16,690
	88		31,170	30,000	28,730	28,010	22,960	16,690
WB	DB	TC	32,490	31,280	29,960	29,310	23,400	16,970
	72		21,010	20,550	19,870	19,640	17,120	14,610
	76		24,900	24,440	23,980	23,520	21,240	16,970
63	80	SC	29,010	28,550	28,100	27,640	23,400	16,970
	84		32,490	31,280	29,960	29,310	23,400	16,970
	88		32,490	31,280	29,960	29,310	23,400	16,970
WB	DB	TC	33,790	32,540	31,170	30,600	23,770	17,200
	72		16,440	15,980	15,290	15,070	12,550	10,270
	76		20,320	19,870	19,410	19,180	16,670	14,150
67	80	SC	24,440	23,980	23,520	23,300	20,780	17,200
	84		28,550	28,100	27,410	27,180	23,770	17,200
	88		32,440	31,980	31,170	30,600	23,770	17,200
WB	DB	TC	35,020	33,730	32,320	31,860	24,020	17,350
	72		11,410	10,950	10,490	10,490	7,750	5,690
	76		15,520	15,070	14,610	14,380	11,640	9,580
71	80	SC	19,640	19,180	18,720	18,500	15,980	13,690
	84		23,520	23,070	22,610	22,610	19,870	17,350
	88		27,640	27,180	26,720	26,500	23,750	17,350
WB	DB	TC	36,040	34,730	33,270	32,940	24,130	17,390
	76		10,720	10,270	9,810	9,810	7,070	5,240
	80		14,840	14,610	14,150	13,920	11,180	9,350
75	84	SC	18,950	18,500	18,040	17,810	15,290	13,240
	88		22,840	22,380	21,920	21,920	19,180	17,350

1) Total Cfm for indoor units = 1,177; specific values for refrigerant pipe length and rise.
2) Outdoor and indoor units operating at a declared motor speed.

Figure 12-7

The preceding values are rated component values, not system performance values. In other words, the capacity of the outdoor unit may be less than 19,100 Btuh, and the capacity of an indoor unit may be less than 7,500 Btuh, or less than 11,500 Btuh. This depends on the number and size of the indoor units that operate simultaneously.

For example, a 19,100 Btuh outdoor unit may serve three indoor units; and three, two, or one unit may operate, so there are three system capacity scenarios. When the compressor has capacity control, there are minimum and a maximum system capacities; and minimum and a maximum indoor unit capacities.

> One 7,500 Btuh indoor unit:
> System capacity = 4,700 to 8,800 Btuh
> One indoor unit = 4,700 to 8,800 Btuh
>
> Two 7,500 Btuh indoor units (15,000 Btuh):
> System capacity = 6,800 to 17,400 Btuh
> One indoor unit = 3,400 to 8,700 Btuh
>
> Three 7,500 Btuh indoor units: (22,500 Btuh):
> System capacity = 8,600 to 19,100 Btuh
> One indoor unit = 2,867 to 6,367 Btuh

The preceding exhibit shows that system capacity nearly doubled for two units, but only increased by a factor of 2.17 for three units. This is because the rated capacity of the outdoor unit, and this three-unit set is 19,100 Btuh (a larger outdoor unit would increase system capacity).

Note that the capacity range of one unit varies as other units operate or shut-down. For example, the minimum cooling capacity for one operating unit is 4,700 Btuh, but this drops to 3,400 Btuh (6,800 x 7,500 / 15,000) when two units operate, and to 2,867 Btuh (8,600 x 7,500 / 22,500) when three units operate. The corresponding values for maximum cooling capacity are 8,800 Btuh, 8,700 Btuh and 6,367 Btuh.

Also note that the capacity range concept deals with variable compressor capacity (steps in outdoor unit size, or equipment that has capacity control). When the outdoor unit only has one capacity at AHRI conditions, there are unique values for indoor coil capacity.

Figure 12-7 shows substantial variation in system capacity as operating conditions change. This behavior also applies to indoor units, so AHRI total cooling capacity values do not apply to a specific dwelling in a given location, except by coincidence. So the question is, what are the approximate on-site capacities for the indoor units?

Figure 12-9 provides adjustment factors for actual operating conditions (this is a *Manual Zr* procedure — not from OEM guidance). For example, the adjusted cooling capacities for AHRI conditions, and for a dry-warm climate (outdoor db = 100°F, entering wb = 59°F), are compared here (adjustment factor = 0.83).

> AHRI capacities from OEM literature
> One 7,500 Btuh unit = 4,700 to 8,800 Btuh
> Two 7,500 Btuh units = 6,800 to 17,400 Btuh
> Three 7,500 Btuh units = 8,600 to 19,100 Btuh

Coil Sensible Heat Ratio for Figure 12-7							
Entering Temp (°F)		Outdoor Dry-Bulb (°F)					
Wet-Bulb	Dry-Bulb	65	75	85	95	105	115
59	72	0.82	0.83	0.85	0.86	0.95	1.00
	76	0.95	0.97	0.99	1.00	1.00	1.00
	80	1.00	1.00	1.00	1.00	1.00	1.00
	84	1.00	1.00	1.00	1.00	1.00	1.00
	88	1.00	1.00	1.00	1.00	1.00	1.00
63	72	0.65	0.66	0.66	0.67	0.73	0.86
	76	0.77	0.78	0.80	0.80	0.91	1.00
	80	0.89	0.91	0.94	0.94	1.00	1.00
	84	1.00	1.00	1.00	1.00	1.00	1.00
	88	1.00	1.00	1.00	1.00	1.00	1.00
67	72	0.49	0.49	0.49	0.49	0.53	0.60
	76	0.60	0.61	0.62	0.63	0.70	0.82
	80	0.72	0.74	0.75	0.76	0.87	1.00
	84	0.84	0.86	0.88	0.89	1.00	1.00
	88	0.96	0.98	1.00	1.00	1.00	1.00
71	72	0.33	0.32	0.32	0.33	0.32	0.33
	76	0.44	0.45	0.45	0.45	0.48	0.55
	80	0.56	0.57	0.58	0.58	0.67	0.79
	84	0.67	0.68	0.70	0.71	0.83	1.00
	88	0.79	0.81	0.83	0.83	0.99	1.00
75	76	0.30	0.30	0.29	0.30	0.29	0.30
	80	0.41	0.42	0.43	0.42	0.46	0.54
	84	0.53	0.53	0.54	0.54	0.63	0.76
	88	0.63	0.64	0.66	0.67	0.79	1.00

Figure 12-8

Capacity Adjustment for System Cooling							
Ewb (°F)	Outdoor Dry-Bulb (°F)						
	85	90	95	100	105	110	115
59	0.94	0.93	0.92	0.83	0.75	0.65	0.55
63	0.98	0.97	0.96	0.86	0.76	0.66	0.55
67	1.02	1.01	1.00	0.89	0.78	0.67	0.56

1) Conditional capacity / AHRI rated capacity (95°F/ 80°F/ 67°F).
2) Entering dry-bulb = 75°F.
3) For entering wet-bulb, use 59°F for dry-coil cooling; use 63°F for wet-coil cooling with JSHR 0.80 or higher; use 67°F for wet coil cooling with JSHR less than 0.80.
4) Approximate adjustment factors based on total capacity values from Figure 12-7.

Figure 12-9

Section 12

Capacities when installed in a dry-warm climate
One 6,225 Btuh unit = 3,901 to 7,304 Btuh
Two 6,225 Btuh units = 5,644 to 14,442 Btuh
Three 6,225 Btuh units = 7,138 to 15,853 Btuh

An OEM may publish a moisture removal value for the indoor units. This may be in pints per hour, which is approximately 1,050 Btuh of latent capacity per pint of condensation. However, this is the latent capacity for air entering the indoor coil at 67°F wet-bulb and 80°F dry-bulb. The latent capacity will be a less when air enters the indoor coil at 63°F wet-bulb (50% RH) and 75°F dry-bulb, and could be considerably less, or more, for other entering conditions (see Figure 12-8).

- Nominal moisture removal values for indoor units may not represent the latent capacity for a given size outdoor unit, and a given set of indoor units, operating at a given outdoor air temperature, and a given entering air condition.

- The humidity ratio (moisture level) for space air tends to equalize across the dwelling's rooms and spaces, so moisture removal calculations are made for the block load space.

- The *Manual J* block load for the space served by the outdoor equipment determines the sensible heat ratio for the block load space (JSHR).

- The OEM's expanded performance data (Figure 12-7) determines the coil sensible heat ratio (CSHR) for the equipment that cools the block load space.

- The desired indoor humidity will be maintained, or will be lower than design, when the CSHR value is equal to, or less than, the JSHR value.

- For indoor units, the design goal is to match sensible and latent cooling capacity with the zone loads from *Manual J* procedures. Then, the capacity of the outdoor unit must be compatible with the set of indoor units.

12-7 Expanded Performance Data for Heating

For air-air heat pumps, heating capacity can decrease by a factor of 3.0 to 4.0 as the outdoor temperature drops from 70°F to 0°F, or less. Expanded performance summarizes this behavior, so it is used to evaluate the heating capacity for a piece of equipment that has the appropriate cooling capacity.

Conditional Heating Capacity for the System

For a given amount of compressor capacity (stage or speed), the conditional heating capacity of a multi-split system is very sensitive to outdoor dry-bulb temperature; and somewhat sensitive to the dry-bulb temperature of the air entering the indoor coils, and to the Cfm values at the indoor coils, as demonstrated by Figure 12-10.

Outdoor Unit: 31-MBH (30,600 Btuh rated total cooling capacity)					
Indoor Units: Four 9-MBH (9,000 Btuh nominal rated cooling capacity)					
Refrigerant Cycle Heating Capacity (Btuh)					
Outdoor Dry-Bulb (°F)	Indoor Dry-bulb (°F)				
	60	65	70	75	80
0	18,270	18,260	18,230	18,200	18,150
3	18,860	18,850	18,820	18,790	18,740
8	20,260	20,250	20,230	20,200	20,150
13	21,720	21,710	21,680	21,650	21,600
18	23,310	23,300	23,280	23,240	23,190
23	24,970	24,960	24,940	24,910	24,850
28	26,690	26,690	26,660	26,630	26,570
33	28,460	28,450	28,430	28,400	28,340
38	30,190	30,190	30,170	30,140	30,080
43	32,020	32,020	32,000	31,960	31,900
48	33,850	33,850	33,840	33,800	33,740
53	35,680	35,680	35,670	35,630	35,570
58	37,420	37,430	37,420	37,380	37,320
63	39,190	39,200	39,190	39,160	39,100
65	39,870	39,880	39,880	39,850	39,790

Not adjusted for defrost (18°F to 48°F).
Total Cfm for indoor units = 1,130; specific values for refrigerant pipe length and rise.
Compressor operating at a declared motor speed.

Figure 12-10

- Note that the heating capacity varies from 18,150 Btuh (0°F outdoors, 80°F indoors), to 39,870 Btuh (65°F outdoor, 60°F indoors). Also note that the rated heating capacity is about 33,840 Btuh (for 47°F outdoors and 70°F indoors).

- In this case, the OEM has not adjusted heating capacity for defrost when the outdoor temperature is in the 17°F to 47°F range.

- Note that heating capacity is not very sensitive to indoor temperature (70°F values may be used for common design work).

- The table stops at 0°F outdoors. This implies a lower limit for the equipment's operating range. This is verified by the OEM's operating range map (see Figure 12-5), or ask the OEM for guidance.

Conditional Heating Capacity for Indoor Units

Data for indoor unit heating capacity would be similar to Figure 12-10. That is, heating capacity depends on outdoor dry-bulb temperature, the entering dry-bulb temperature at the fan coil, and fan-coil Cfm. However, indoor unit capacity also depends on the size of the outdoor unit, the number of indoor units, and the sizes of the indoor units.

Mapping all possible permeations of outdoor units and indoor units for the entire range of operating conditions is a significant task, and performance summaries require many paper and/or electronic pages. Therefore, OEM data for indoor units tend to be limited to a table that shows AHRI heating capacity for a particular outdoor unit serving a specific set of indoor units. (Practitioners would be able to design with more precision when comprehensive data was generated and published.)

For example, an outdoor unit that has 19,100 Btuh of nominal (AHRI) cooling capacity, and 24,800 Btuh of nominal heating capacity at 47°F may serve three indoor units that each have 8,500 Btuh of nominal (AHRI) heating capacity, or three indoor units that each have 14,300 Btuh of nominal (AHRI) heating capacity. Note that the aggregate nominal capacity of the indoor units may be marginally more, or significantly more, than the nominal capacity of the outdoor unit.

Outdoor dry-bulb temperature = 47°F
Outdoor Unit = 24,800 Nominal Btuh
Indoor units = 3 x 8,500 = 25,500 Nominal Btuh
Indoor units = 3 x 14,300 = 42,900 Nominal Btuh

The preceding values are maximum component values, not system performance values. In other words, the capacity of the outdoor unit may be less than 24,800 Btuh, and the capacity of the indoor units may be less than 8,500 Btuh, or less than 14,300 Btuh. This depends on the number and size of the indoor units that operate simultaneously.

For example, a 24,800 Btuh outdoor unit may serve three indoor units; and three, two, or one unit may operate at the same time, so there are three capacity scenarios. When the compressor has capacity control, there is a minimum system capacity, and a maximum system capacity; and a minimum indoor unit capacity, and a maximum indoor unit capacity.

One 8,500 Btuh indoor unit at 47°F
System capacity = 6,100 to 14,600 Btuh
One indoor unit = 6,100 to 14,600 Btuh

Two 8,500 Btuh indoor units at 47°F (17,000 Btuh)
System capacity = 6,800 to 21,800 Btuh
One indoor unit = 3,400 to 10,900 Btuh

Three 8,500 Btuh indoor units: at 47°F (25,500 Btuh)
System capacity = 9,200 to 24,800 Btuh
One indoor unit = 3,067 to 8,267 Btuh

The preceding exhibit shows that maximum heating capacity increases by a factor of 1.49 for two units, but this factor is only 1.70 for three units. This is because the rated heating capacity of the outdoor unit, and this three unit set is 24,800 Btuh (a larger outdoor unit would increase indoor unit capacity).

Note that the capacity range of one unit varies as other units operate or shut-down. For example, the minimum heating capacity for one operating unit is 6,100 Btuh, but this drops to 3,400 Btuh (6,800 x 8,500 / 17,000) when two units operate, and to 3,067 Btuh (9,200 x 8.500 / 25,500) when three units operate. The corresponding values for maximum cooling capacity are 14,600 Btuh, 10,900 Btuh and 8.267 Btuh.

As previously noted for cooling, the capacity range concept deals with variable compressor capacity (steps in outdoor unit size, or equipment that has capacity control). When the outdoor unit only has one capacity at AHRI rating conditions, there are unique values for indoor coil capacity.

Figure 12-10 shows substantial variation in system capacity as outdoor dry-bulb temperature changes. This behavior also applies to each indoor unit, so the rating values for AHRI heating capacity do not apply to a specific dwelling in a given location, except by coincidence. So, the question is; what are the approximate on-site capacities for the indoor units?

Figure 12-11 provides adjustment factors for actual outdoor air temperatures (this is a *Manual Zr* procedure — not from OEM guidance). For example, the adjusted heating capacities for 47°F outdoors and 0°F outdoors (70°F indoors), are compared here (adjustment factor = 0.54).

AHRI 47°F capacities from OEM literature
One 8,500 Btuh unit = 6,100 to 14,600 Btuh
Two 8,500 Btuh units = 6,800 to 21,800 Btuh
Three 8,500 Btuh units = 9,200 to 24,800 Btuh

Capacity Adjustment for Indoor Unit Heating							
Outdoor Dry-Bulb (°F)							
0	3	8	13	18	23	28	33
0.54	0.56	0.60	0.64	0.69	0.74	0.79	0.84
Outdoor Dry-Bulb (°F)							
38	43	48	53	58	63	65	
0.89	0.95	1.00	1.05	1.11	1.16	1.18	

1) Conditional capacity / AHRI Rated Capacity.
2) Entering air dry-bulb = 70°F.
3) Approximate adjustment factors based on heating capacity values from Figure 12-10.

Figure 12-11

Section 12

Capacities when the outdoor temperature is 0°F
One 4,590 Btuh unit = 3,294 to 7,884 Btuh
Two 4,590 Btuh units = 3,672 to 11,772 Btuh
Three 4,590 Btuh units = 4,968 to 13,392 Btuh

For indoor units, the design procedure compares maximum heating capacity with the zone load from *Manual J* procedures. Since system components are sized for cooling, the indoor units may, or may not, have adequate heating capacity.

- For wet-coil cooling, continuous compressor operation (at full capacity, or near full capacity) on a summer design day is preferred for moisture removal, so over sizing for the heating load is not recommended.

- Moisture removal is not an issue for a dry climate that does not have a rainy season, so there is considerable leeway for excess cooling capacity (the system may have 15,000 Btuh of excess total cooling capacity, per Table N2-2).

- Some form of supplemental heat is required when compressor heat is deficient at the winter design condition (or use a different type of system).

12-8 Air Distribution

For supply air, the primary concern is mixing supply air with room air, and air motion in the occupied space. In this regard, the principles for selecting and sizing ducted supply air diffusers, grilles and registers, equally apply to fan-coil grilles and diffusers.

- A fan coil unit only affects the air motion in it's local open space; it does not affect the air motion in other partitioned spaces that are in the same zone (and may not closely control the temperature in other partitioned spaces).

- Throw, spread, and drop (for ceiling or high-wall units), should be compatible with the geometry of the open space served by the fan coil unit.

- Air distribution should be relatively quiet. For non-ducted equipment, this depends on the OEM's design. For ducted equipment, this depends on the practitioner's design (for duct runs, grilles and registers).

The amount of OEM-published information pertaining to throw, spread and drop varies considerably. At one extreme, there may be no information, at the other extreme, the guidance may be comprehensive, as demonstrated by Figure 12-12.

OEM's tend to be very sensitive to noise issues, so multi-split equipment tends to be quiet. In this regard, the human ear is sensitive to sound pressure, but perception also depends on the frequency of the sound, so a noise criteria

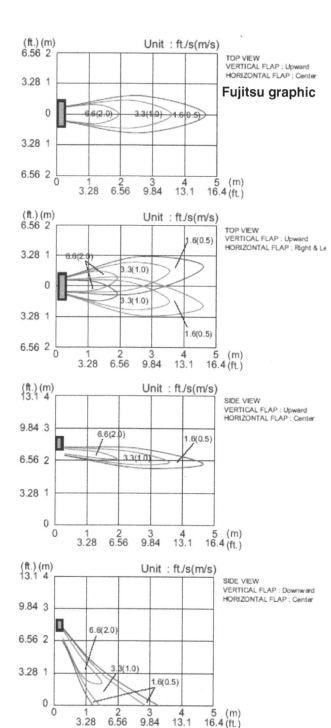

Figure 12-12

(NC) curve summarizes ear perception across eight octave bands.

- Figure 12-13 provides an example of comprehensive information, but this may, or may not, appear in OEM literature.

- A single decibel value does not summarize noise (eight values are required for a NC chart).

12-9 Blower Data

A ducted fan coil unit is used when the geometry of the fan coil's local space is not compatible (too large, or too irregular) with it's free blow air pattern. Or, a ducted fan coil is used when it serves two or more partitioned spaces that are in the same zone.

The fan coil unit is sized to neutralize the loads for the space or spaces served. This determines maximum blower Cfm. Blowers usually operate at more than one speed, so maximum Cfm occurs at maximum blower speed.

The OEM's blower data (table or chart) correlates available static pressure with blower Cfm (Figure 12-14, for example). The available static pressure for maximum blower Cfm must be compatible with the duct system served.

- A circulation path will have a supply grille, and a return grille, and may have a hand damper for balancing. These components will require 0.04 to 0.09 IWC of static pressure.
- Efficient boot fittings at the supply grille and return grille will require an additional 0.03 to 0.06 IWC of static pressure.
- Efficient elbows and/or takeoffs may require an additional 0.03 to 0.06 IWC of static pressure.
- Straight duct may dissipate about 0.01 IWC of pressure per 10 foot section.
- A simple 10 foot duct system (one supply, two boots, no elbow or tees), may require 0.08 to 0.16 IWC of static pressure.
- A distribution system that serves two or more rooms, may require 0.15 to 0.25 IWC of static pressure.

12-10 Duct System Design

The cooling and heating loads for most rooms and spaces are much smaller than the cooling-heating capacity of the smallest fan coil unit; some, or all, of these spaces may be partitioned. This is reconciled by combining the spaces into a zone, and using a ducted fan coil unit to distribute supply air to the spaces.

- *Manual J* procedures determine room heating and cooling loads, then *Manual D* procedures convert these loads to supply air Cfm values.
- *Manual D* procedures convert supply air Cfm values to duct airway sizes (subject to air velocity limits for duct-generated noise).
- Make sure that the blower data is for a filter in place, and do not add accessory pressure drop devices that are incompatible with blower power.

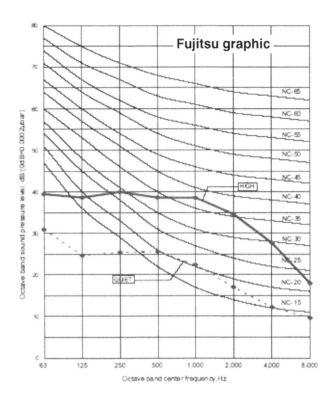

Figure 12-13

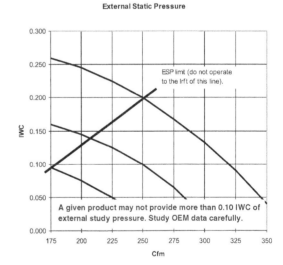

Figure 12-14

- Efficient duct fittings are absolutely essential (use items that have the shortest equivalent length in Appendix 3, *Manual D*).

12-11 Equipment Selection and Sizing

Size the outdoor unit for cooling, size the indoor units for cooling, then verify that the outdoor unit is compatible with the set of indoor units. Then check the heating performance of the indoor units.

Relevant procedures are summarized below. See ACCA *Manual Zr* for zoning procedures and example problems.

Size Outdoor Equipment for Cooling

Expanded cooling performance data is used to size the outdoor unit (see the sidebar to the right). The goal is to match sensible and latent capacity to the block cooling load values from *Manual J* calculations.

- The outdoor unit serves two or more zones. Each zone consists of one or more rooms/spaces that have compatible loads, as far as time-of-day, and month-of-year are concerned.
- The zones may, or may not, have compatible load patterns through the day (zone control deals with this issue).
- For heat pumps, cycling between heating or cooling, or simultaneous heating and cooling, may be required when zone load patterns are not compatible through the year.
- Outdoor equipment is sized for maximum (or near maximum) cooling capacity when operating at summer design conditions.
- Total cooling capacity (sensible plus latent) may range from 90% of the block load (0.90 factor) to 120% of the block load (1.20 factor), for cooling-only equipment, and for a Condition A heat pump.
- For a Condition B heat pump, total cooling capacity may be as much as 15,000 Btuh more than the block cooling load.
- Latent capacity must be equal to, or greater, than the latent load, and the sensible capacity must not be less than 90% of the sensible block load.
- The outdoor unit must be compatible with the set of indoor units. The candidate is confirmed, or not, after the indoor units are selected and sized.

Size Indoor Equipment for Cooling

Indoor units are sized for the peak zone cooling load (sensible plus latent) obtained from *Manual J* procedures. Cooling performance data for indoor units may be (and usually is) limited to total capacity (sensible plus latent) at AHRI conditions; so the expanded data for the outdoor unit is used to estimate indoor unit performance for the actual summer design condition.

- Fan coil units are sized for full compressor capacity (AHRI rating speed), when operating at summer design conditions.

> **Adequate Performance Data**
>
> Equipment capacity varies over a wide range as the operating condition deviates from the AHRI test condition (see Sections 12-6 and 12-7). Therefore, equipment selection requires expanded performance data (for cooling, and heat pump heating) when the actual operating conditions are different than the AHRI test condition. In this regard, *Manual Zr* procedures are identical to *Manual S* procedures, which requires the use of expanded performance data.

- Cooling capacity data for the indoor units must be for the candidate outdoor unit.
- Expanded performance data for the outdoor unit may be used to produce conditional performance data for the indoor units (see Figure 12-9).
- Indoor units are initially selected for one fan coil operating (maximum cooling capacity).
- The total capacity (sensible plus latent) of a fan coil unit may range from 90% of the peak zone load (0.90 factor) to 120% of the peak zone load (1.20 factor).

Verify Outdoor Unit Compatibility

The sum of the indoor units cooling capacity values may be larger than the capacity of the outdoor unit. This is caused by time-of-day diversity for zone cooling loads. However, the actual operating capacity is determined by the outdoor unit capacity.

An OEM compatibility table verifies component capacity (see Figure 12-6). When the outdoor unit is too small, or too large, for the indoor units, select the next available size, and repeat the indoor unit calculations for new outdoor unit (to see when indoor unit capacities are in the 1.00 to 1.25 range).

Evaluate Indoor Unit Heating Capacity

The design heating load for an indoor unit occurs at the winter design condition, and the value for the zone heating load is determined by *Manual J* procedures. Heating performance data for indoor units may be (and usually is) limited to heating capacity at AHRI conditions (17°F and 47°F; or just 47°F); so the expanded data for the outdoor unit is used to estimate indoor unit performance for the winter design condition.

- Heat pump equipment is sized for cooling, per Table N2-2 rules.
- Expanded performance data for heating is used to draw the thermal balance point diagram. Use the performance data for maximum compressor heating capacity.

Some products can operate at an enhanced compressor speed during cold weather (see Figure 11-3). This must be available on a continuous basis, for an unlimited amount of time.

When the heating capacity data does not have a defrost knee, ask the OEM for data that does have a defrost knee.

- Heating capacity data for the indoor units must be for the candidate outdoor unit.
- Expanded performance data for the outdoor unit may be used to produce conditional performance data for indoor units (see Figure 12-11).
- Fan coil performance is evaluated for all fan coils operating (minimum heating capacity per unit).
- Use Table N2-3 rules and Section 6 procedures to size zone supplemental electric coil heat, and emergency electric coil heat.
- When the indoor fan-coil unit does not have supplemental electric coil heat, another source of heat is required to satisfy the zone's ancillary heating need (electric baseboard heat, for example).
- When a indoor fan coil unit has electric coil heat, the combined heating capacity of the refrigerant coil (when compressor heat is available for the winter design condition), and the electric resistance coil, must satisfy the zone's supplemental heat requirement, and the electric coil heat must satisfy the zone's emergency heat requirement.
- When the indoor fan coil unit has electric coil heat, the full electric resistance coil capacity must be equal to, or greater than, the *Manual J* heating load for the zone served when compressor heat is not available at the winter design condition.

The heat pump is fully functional, but operation is prohibited by a low outdoor air temperature control, so electric coil heat is the only source of heat.

Section 12

Section 13

Single-Package Equipment

Packaged terminal air conditioners (PTAC), packaged terminal heat pumps (PTHP), and their thru-the-wall, or window equivalents, have all their components in one cabinet, except for the space thermostat, which may be in the cabinet, or at a remote location. One piece of equipment is used for each comfort zone.

- The unit's cooling capacity should be compatible with the zone load (a zone includes all spaces served by a piece of equipment).
- Cooling-cycle equipment may have electric resistance heat in the cabinet.
- For heat pumps, refrigerant cycle heating must be supplemented by another source of heat for most USA locations.

  This is determined by drawing a balance point diagram.

  This may be an electric resistance, or hot water, or steam coil in the cabinet, or external equipment.

- Compressors are single-stage, single-speed (for Year 2014).
- Indoor blowers may have multiple-speeds. Outdoor blowers may have multiple-speeds.
- PTAC and PTHP equipment may be free blow (integral supply grille), or ducted (supply grille at the end of a duct).

PTAC or PTHP

Vertical PTAC or PTHP

13-1 Applications

Unitary equipment is used for new construction and for retrofit and replacement work. This may be cooling-only equipment, or cooling and heating equipment.

- Cooling equipment packages may be added to an existing dwelling, or living space, that does not have cooling.
- An independent source of heat is required when cooling-only equipment is used for new construction (integral electric heating coil, radiant-floor, or baseboard heat may have hot water or electric resistance circuits).
- Heat pump equipment may be used for new construction, for a new addition, or, it may replace an existing year-round comfort system.
- A source of supplemental heat is required when a heat pump does not have enough compressor heat for the winter design condition. In this regard, it may be that the low-limit temperature for compressor heat is significantly warmer than the winter design temperature for outdoor air (a 25°F to 40°F low-limit is common).
- Heat pump equipment normally has electric resistance heat. There may be two or more KW options. A large heating coil may be staged.
- For all applications, the combined heating capacity (refrigerant cycle heat plus electric resistance heat) at the winter design condition must be equal to, or greater than, the *Manual J* heating load for the space served. An additional source of heat is required when this is not true (a piece of electric baseboard heat, for example).
- One piece of equipment per zone allows simultaneous heating and cooling for a set of zones.
- In general, the total cooling capacity of a piece of equipment should be appropriate for the zone it

serves. In this regard, the smallest unit in a product line may have 5,000 to 9,000 Btuh of total AHRI cooling capacity. Most room loads are much smaller than this (i.e., zoning by room requires a large room load).

- The equipment must have enough latent capacity for the climate. In this regard, some types of equipment have an enhanced moisture removal feature.

- Engineered ventilation (outdoor air with recovery, or without recovery) may be mandated by code, or desired for good practice reasons, but a given product may not provide the desired performance.

  When the equipment provides outdoor air, the Cfm value should be compatible with the code requirement.

  The code may require heat recovery.

  An independent ventilation system is required when the equipment cannot provide the appropriate ventilation rate, and recovery effectiveness.

- For free blow (no duct) equipment, the zone should have an open, relatively compact, floor plan (there is a limit to the effective throw of the supply grille). Integral supply grilles may have fixed vanes, or adjustable vanes (for optimizing throw and spread).

- There is not much external static pressure for ducted air, so the total fitting pressure drop of a duct run must be very small, and the straight duct length must be short (see OEM guidance).

- The equipment is in the occupied space, so quiet operation is important.

13-2 Design Goals

The design goal is to match the cooling-heating capacity of a piece of equipment with the zone cooling-heating loads. This requires **Manual J** loads for a zoned dwelling and OEM performance data for heating and cooling.

- A zone may be one room or space, or a combination of rooms and spaces.

- The rooms and spaces in a zone must have compatible load patterns and use schedules (see **Manual Zr**, Section 3 and Section 4).

- The total cooling capacity of the equipment should be compatible with the zone's design condition cooling load; and must have adequate heating capacity for the design condition heating load (or supplemented by other means).

- For cooling, indoor humidity should be 55% RH or less for the summer design condition, and should not exceed 60% RH for part-load conditions.

Single-Package Features and Options	
Item	Consideration
Power supply	Single-phase.
Summer humidity control	Enhanced moisture removal. [1]
Low ambient cooling limit	See OEM guidance.
Electric heating coils	2 to 6 KW range, capacity may be staged. [2]
Low ambient heating limit	Auto switch to electric coil heat only when it is 25°F to 45°F outdoors. [2]
High ambient heating limit	Lock out electric coil heat when it is more than 45°F outdoors. [2]
Emergency heat or cold space	Activate electric coil and blower if compressor heat is deficient.
Heat Pump defrost	Reverse cycle with active electric coil heat, or other. [2]
Hot water or steam coil	Available for some products.
Outdoor air Cfm	Vent provides outdoor air Cfm, may be staged, no reclaim. [2]
Blower speed or Cfm	Outdoor fan and indoor fan, fans may be staged. [2]
Air distribution	Manually adjustable vanes, option for short duct to an adjacent room. [2]
Filter options	See OEM literature.
Noise Rating	See OEM literature.
Operating controls	Fan on-off or speed; high-low capacity, run schedules; set-point schedules; remote control. [2]
Condensate for cooling mode	Evaporate on outdoor coil, and/or drain. [2]
Condensate for heating mode	Evaporate on indoor coil, condensate pump; or drip. [2]
Start-up amperage	Random start for multiple units, hard start kit. [2]
Start-up issues	Anti short cycle relay, warm start for heating comfort. [2]
Motor protection	Volts; amps; temperature. [2]
Refrigerant safety controls	Pressure; temperature. [2]
SEER; HSPF; Noise Rating	Noise may be an issue.

1) Some products use a refrigerant heat pipe loop for more moisture removal and reheat.
2) See OEM guidance for actual values or details.
3) External static pressure is extremely important for ducted units.

Figure 13-1

- A ductless unit may serve a zone that is not divided by a partition wall (the supply air grille should be able to affect the air motion in the collective space that it serves).

- A ducted unit may serve two adjacent rooms in the same zone, providing the duct airflow resistance is relatively small.

13-3 Equipment Attributes

Single-package equipment may be cooling-only equipment, or may be reverse-cycle equipment that provides heating and cooling. Various styles, makes and models are available in a range of sizes.

Nominal Size and Power

Nominal size is based on total cooling capacity for the AHRI rating-test condition, or a testing standard published by the Association of Home Appliance Manufacturers (AHAM). Sizes range from about 5,000 Btuh to about 36,000 Btuh total cooling capacity. Single-phase power is adequate for all types of equipment.

Features and Options

The primary issues are summer humidity control for all types of equipment and cold weather heating performance for heat pump equipment. Air distribution and noise are important comfort issues. Operating and safety controls provide convenience and protect the equipment. Figure 13-1 (previous page) lists common features and options.

13-4 PTAC and PTHP Rating Data

OEMs publish AHRI rating data for PTAC and PTHP equipment. This consists of total cooling capacity values for a special set of conditions, and heating capacity values for a special set of conditions.

- For cooling, the outdoor dry-bulb is 95°F, the indoor entering dry-bulb is 80°F, and the indoor entering wet-bulb is 67°F.
- For PTHP heating, the outdoor dry-bulb is 47°F and the indoor entering dry-bulb is 70°F.
- A heating value for 17°F outdoors may, or may not, be available. This depends on the low-limit temperature for compressor operation (see Figure 13-3, next page).
- For cooling and heating, the compressor operates at full capacity at maximum blower Cfm.
- Heating capacity is not to be adjusted for defrost; with no credit for supplemental heat.

The low outdoor air temperature limit for compressor heating is important information because most locations have a design temperature that is much colder than 47°F. Find the low-limit for compressor heating, and the available electric heating coil KW values in the OEM's technical or service literature, or ask for it.

Rated cooling capacity and rated heating capacity values do not represent actual full-load performance when the equipment is installed in a given dwelling, at a specific location, except by coincidence.

- The design value for summer outdoor dry-bulb may not be 95°F.
- The design values for summer entering dry-bulb and wet-bulb may not be 80°F and 67°F.
- The design value for winter outdoor dry-bulb may not be 47°F or 17°F.
- The design value for winter entering dry-bulb may not be 70°F.
- Defrost cycles may reduce effective heating capacity between 47°F and 17°F.

An OEM may publish expanded performance data for heating and cooling. This determines equipment performance when it serves an actual dwelling, at a specific location. This information correlates total, sensible, and latent cooling capacity with sets of summer operating conditions, and heating capacity with sets of winter operating conditions. This is a fundamental equipment sizing issue, so Sections 13-6 and 13-7 cover it in detail.

13-5 Home Appliance Rating Data

Window units and thru-the-wall equipment are classified as home appliances. The AHAM rating data for this type of equipment is summarized here:

- For cooling, the outdoor dry-bulb is 95°F, the indoor entering dry-bulb is 80°F, and the indoor entering wet-bulb is 67°F.
- For heat pump heating, the outdoor dry-bulb is 47°F, and the indoor entering dry-bulb is 70°F.

OEM literature may not say that heat pump heating capacity is for 47°F outdoors, and may not provide heating capacity values for colder temperatures. This is important information because most locations have a design temperature that is much colder than 47°F. Determine the low-limit value for compressor heating, and the available electric heating coil KW values in the OEM's technical or service literature, or ask for it.

There is no expanded performance data for heating and cooling for appliances. However, the affect of the outdoor air dry-bulb temperature and the entering air condition is similar to other types of residential equipment.

- Total capacity, sensible capacity, and latent capacity vary with outdoor dry-bulb temperature, and entering dry-bulb and wet-bulb. Heating capacity depends on outdoor dry-bulb temperature and entering dry-bulb temperature.

- A heating capacity graph provides a useful model of heating performance. Draw a capacity line through the 47°F point, and the low-limit temperature point (when a second point is available).

13-6 Expanded Performance Data for Cooling

The conditional cooling capacity (sensible, latent and total) of PTAC and PTHP equipment is sensitive to outdoor dry-bulb temperature, the dry-bulb temperature of the air entering the indoor coil, the wet-bulb temperature of the air entering the indoor coil, and the Cfm value at the indoor coil. Figure 13-2 provides an abbreviated example of such data.

- Outdoor air temperature values may go to 115°F.
- Entering air wet-bulb values may range from 57°F to 73°F.
- Entering air dry-bulb values may range from 70°F to 85°F.
- Capacity values may, or may not, be adjusted for blower heat.
- Some OEM data shows total capacity values and sensible heat ratio values.
- The cooling coil sensible heat ratio (CSHR) equals sensible capacity divided by total capacity.
- Climate humidity, building envelope infiltration, the use of engineered ventilation, and internal moisture loads are the primary factors that determine the *Manual J* sensible heat ratio (JSHR). Climate design temperature and solar azimuth angles have a smaller effect (the JSHR value depends on the latent load and sensible load).
- For indoor humidity control, the CSHR should be equal to (or less than) the JSHR when the equipment operates at the summer design condition. This will produce acceptable indoor humidity values as outdoor air temperature decreases.

13-7 Expanded Performance Data for Heating

Heating capacity is very sensitive to outdoor dry-bulb temperature, and somewhat sensitive to the dry-bulb temperature of the air entering the indoor coil, and the Cfm value at the indoor coil. Figure 13-3 provides an abbreviated example of such data.

- Outdoor air temperature values may be colder than 32°F (depends on the OEM's low-limit value).
- The entire heating load must be carried by electric coil heat when the outdoor temperature is below the low-limit for compressor heat.
- Entering air dry-bulb values may range from 60°F to 80°F.

Model 07 — 7,000 Btuh Nominal Cooling Capacity							
Cooling Capacity (Btuh)							
Entering Air Condition (°F)		Outdoor Dry-Bulb (°F)					
		85		95		105	
WB	DB	TC	SC	TC	SC	TC	SC
61	75	6,680	5,695	6,380	5,545	6,030	5,665
	80	6,930	6,930	6,665	6,665	6,270	6,270
	85	7,205	7,205	7,030	7,030	6745	6,745
67	75	7,440	4,005	7,155	4,140	6,680	4,150
	80	7,345	5,385	7,000	5,250	6,680	5,295
	85	7,390	6,570	7,105	6,445	6,690	6,270

1) TC = Total cooling capacity; SC = Sensible cooling capacity; maximum blower Cfm.
2) Capacity values adjusted for blower heat.

Figure 13-2

| Model 07 — Heating Performance (Btuh) |||||||
| EDB (°F) | Outdoor Temperature (°F) ||||||
	32	37	42	47	52	57	62
70	4,300	4,900	5,500	6,200	6,900	7,800	8,200

1) Capacity values include blower heat.
2) Capacity values not adjusted for defrost cycle.
3) Compressor stops (electric coil heat active) when the indoor refrigerant coil is 25°F or colder. This occurs when the outdoor temperature is about 35°F.

Figure 13-3

- Capacity values may, or may not, be adjusted for blower heat.
- Capacity values may, or may not, be adjusted for defrost.

13-8 Air Distribution and Noise

For supply air, the primary concern is mixing supply air with room air, and air motion in the occupied space. In this regard, the principles for selecting and sizing ducted supply air diffusers, grilles and registers, apply to packaged equipment grilles.

- A unit only affects the air motion in it's local open space; it does not affect the air motion in other partitioned spaces that are in the same zone (and may not closely control the temperature in other partitioned spaces).
- Throw, spread, and drop should be compatible with the geometry of the space served by the unit (the OEM may not publish grille performance data).

- Air distribution should be relatively quiet. When provided, sound data should be based on the ear's response to sound pressure across eight octave bands (a noise criteria chart, or rating).
- Sound data should include a test for full compressor capacity, with fans operating at full-speed.

13-9 Equipment Size

Expanded cooling performance data is used to size cooling-only equipment and heat pump equipment. The goal is to match total, sensible, and latent capacity to the zone cooling load values from *Manual J* calculations.

- The *Manual J* peak load procedure provides values for the sensible, latent, and total cooling loads.
- The equipment is sized for full cooling capacity (compressor operates at the AHRI or AHAM rating speed) for the summer design conditions used for the cooling load calculation.
- The Table N2-1 sizing rules for total, latent, and sensible cooling capacity apply to PTAC and PTHP equipment.
- The Section N2-14 sizing rules for total, latent, and sensible cooling capacity apply to AHAM appliances.

13-10 Heating Performance

Heat pump equipment is sized for cooling, then compressor heating capacity and the supplemental heat requirement are investigated. The goal is to provide adequate heating capacity for the winter design condition.

- The design heating load occurs at the winter design temperature for outdoor air, and the value for this load is determined by *Manual J* procedures.
- The combined heating capacity of the refrigerant coil and the electric resistance coil (or hot water, or steam) must be equal to, or greater than, the *Manual J* load for the zone served.
- The OEM's heating performance data and the *Manual J* heating load are used to draw a balance point diagram for heating.
- Various amounts of supplemental electric-coil heat (or some other source of integrated, or external heat) are required below the thermal balance point.
- The maximum amount of supplemental heat is read from the balance point diagram at the winter design temperature.

The OEM's heating data for compressor heat may be limited to heating capacity at AHRI test conditions, or the OEM may provide conditional data (heating Btuh vs.

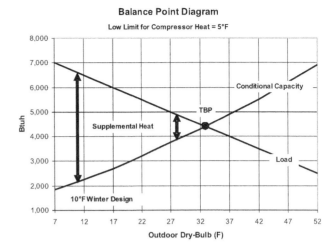

Figure 13-4

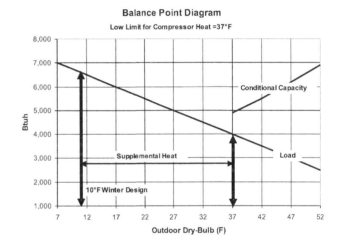

Figure 13-5

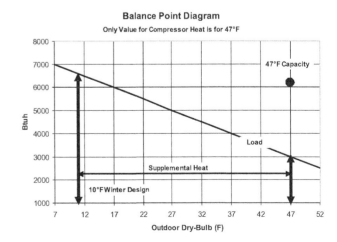

Figure 13-6

outdoor air temperature). The balance point diagram is based on available data. For example:

- Figure 13-4 (previous page) shows that the balance point diagram for a piece of single-package equipment is similar to a balance point diagram for a central heat pump, when the package provides compressor heat when it is very cold outdoors.

*Note that the maximum amount of supplemental heat is less than the **Manual J** heating load when the low-limit temperature for compressor heat is colder than the **Manual J** design temperature.*

*Or, the maximum amount of supplemental heat equals the **Manual J** heating load when the low-limit temperature for compressor heat is warmer than the **Manual J** design temperature.*

- Figure 13-5 (previous page) shows the balance point diagram for a piece of single-package equipment that stops the compressor when it is moderately cold outdoors. For this example, the cutoff temperature is warmer than the thermal balance point temperature, so compressor heat is used above the low-limit temperature, and supplemental heat is used below the low-limit temperature.

*Note that the maximum amount of supplemental heat is equal to the **Manual J** heating load.*

- Figure 13-6 (previous page) shows the balance point diagram for a piece of single-package equipment that has no heating performance data, except for the 47°F heating value. For this scenario, assume the maximum amount of supplemental heat is equal to the **Manual J** heating load

Supplemental heat is used when compressor heat is not available.

Supplemental heat is used when compressor heat is available, but compressor heating capacity is inadequate.

Informative Material Pertaining to Implementation

Appendix 1 – Basic Concepts for Air System Equipment

Appendix 2 – Entering Air Calculations

Appendix 3 – Searching OEM Data for Candidate Equipment

Appendix 4 – Requirements for Expanded Performance Data

Appendix 5 – Altitude Effects

Appendix 1
Basic Concepts for Air System Equipment

An accurate load calculation determines equipment operating conditions and provides values for the sensible and latent cooling loads, the heating load, and the winter humidification load (where applicable), or the summer humidification load for a dry climate (when desired). The sensible and latent cooling loads determine the total cooling load, which is a sizing value for the cooling equipment selection, and the *Manual J* sensible heat ratio. The design value for cooling Cfm is determined when expanded cooling performance data is used to select and size equipment. Heating performance data is used to select heating-only equipment, or to evaluate heat pump performance for the heating mode. AHRI rating data is not adequate for equipment selection and sizing.

A1-1 Load Calculations

A load analysis must be performed before equipment is selected and sized. Use the latest version of the ANSI/ACCA *Manual J* — Residential Load Calculation (MJ8), and Form J1 to calculate design values for the heating load, sensible cooling load, and latent cooling load. Conform to *Manual J*, Section 2 accuracy protocol.

A1-2 Operating Conditions for Cooling Equipment

Cooling equipment may be an air conditioner, or a heat pump operating in the cooling mode. For either case, equipment capacities (total Btuh, sensible Btuh and latent Btuh) depend on the condition of the air or water that enters the condenser, and the condition of the air that enters the evaporator.

Condition at the Condenser

For air-cooled equipment (Figure A1-1), cooling performance depends on the temperature of the air entering the condenser (outdoor coil). This temperature may be equal to, or warmer than, the outdoor air temperature.

- When the outdoor coil is not affected by the sun or a confined space, the design value for the ambient dry-bulb temperature is the *Manual J* 1% dry-bulb temperature from Table 1A or Table 1B.
- When the outdoor coil is near a sunlit roof or wall, or in a confined space, the ambient air temperature may be 5°F to 20°F warmer than the *Manual J* value.

Air-Cooled Equipment

Use the local design temperature when selecting air-cooled equipment (the 1% dry-bulb value from *Manual J*, Table 1).

- Adjust for the temperature near a hot roof or wall.
- The outdoor coil should not be installed in a confined space (the outdoor fan must have access to new air).

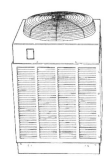

Figure A1-1

Water-Cooled Equipment

Use the water-loop temperature for late summer, or the ground water temperature when selecting water-cooled equipment.

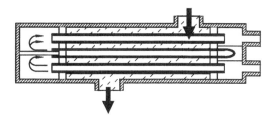

Figure A1-2

For water-cooled equipment (Figure A1-2), cooling performance depends on the temperature of the water entering the condenser.

- For a once-though system, the design value for entering water temperature (EWT) is equal to the ground water temperature.
- For an earth-loop system, the design value for the entering water temperature is warmer than the ground water temperature (loop temperature peaks during late summer, or early fall).
- For an earth-loop system, the design value for the entering water temperature may be as warm, or warmer than the summer design temperature for outdoor air.

Cooling performance also depends on the fluid flow rate through the condenser. This value may be set by the original equipment manufacturer (OEM), or may be selected by the practitioner.

Appendx 1

- The OEM's design determines the Cfm through an air-cooled condenser.
- The practitioner's design determines the Gpm through a water-cooled condenser. However, this is a secondary issue (cooling capacity is somewhat sensitive to Gpm).

Condition at the Indoor Coil

Cooling performance also depends on the dry-bulb (DB) and wet-bulb (WB) temperatures of the air that enters the indoor coil. These temperatures depend on the condition of the air leaving the conditioned space at return grilles (the indoor air), the conduction and leakage loads for the return duct, and the use of engineered ventilation (see Figure A1-3).

No Return Duct Load and No Engineered Ventilation

When there is no return duct load (the duct is in the conditioned space, or an unconditioned space that is similar to a conditioned space), and no engineered ventilation (raw or processed outdoor air is not mixed with return air), the dry-bulb and wet-bulb temperatures for entering air are equal to the dry-bulb and wet-bulb temperatures of the indoor air (see Figure A1-4).

- The default condition for indoor air depends on the *Manual J* design values for dry-bulb temperature (75°F) and relative humidity (RH). Use 45% RH for a dry climate, or use 50% or 55% RH for a humid climate.

    Dry and humid climates are defined in the glossary.

    50% RH is preferred for a humid climate, providing the equipment has enough latent capacity for this value.

    55% RH is acceptable when the equipment does not have enough latent capacity for 50% RH.

    The Manual J DB and RH defaults are superseded by values specified by code or utility regulation.

- When the location is at 2,500 feet of elevation or less, there may be a latent load on the indoor coil. When this is the case, Figure A1-5 converts a relative humidity value and a dry-bulb temperature to an entering wet-bulb (EWB) temperature.
- When the location is at or above 2,500 feet, there is normally no latent load for the summer design condition.

    At elevation, Manual J Table 1A or 1B typically shows zero or negative grains difference values for 45% RH.

    A few locations in a few states are exceptions when the elevation is 2,500 to 3,200 feet (see Hawaii, Kansas, Montana, Nebraska, Texas, and West Virginia).

- There is no latent infiltration load for *Manual J* Table 1 locations that have grains difference values that are zero or negative.

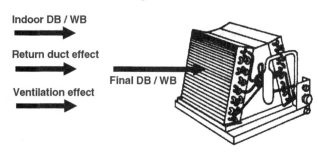

Entering Air Condition

Figure A1-3

For no return duct load and no ventilation, the condition of the entering air is the same as the condition of the indoor air.

Entering DB default = 75°F.
Entering WB depends on the local climate (see Figure A1-5).

Figure A1-4

Entering Wet-Bulb Temperature (EWB) 2,500 Feet or Less No Return Duct Load, No Engineered Ventilation					
Indoor RH%	Indoor DB (°F)	EWB (°F)		
		0 Ft	2,500 Ft	Round To
55	75	63.95	63.60	64
50		62.55	62.15	63 or 62
45		61.11	60.65	61
40		59.63	59.10	60 or 59
35		58.10	57.51	58

1) The coil may be dry when the RH is 45%, or less (this is determined by inspecting the equipment performance data).
2) Use altitude sensitive metrics for other RH-DB pairs.

Figure A1-5

- When there is no latent infiltration load, the indoor coil is typically dry when operating at the summer design condition.

    Internal latent load, by itself, is normally a minor issue (MJ8 sensible heat ratio 0.95 to 1.00).

    When the cooling coil is dry, the entering wet-bulb temperature is typically 59°F or less.

- A dry-climate may have no latent load for the Table 1 design condition (which is defined by a 1% dry-bulb temperature and a coincident wet-bulb temperature), but may have a latent load during the rainy season.

The outdoor design condition for rainy season humidity control is determined by 1% wet-bulb temperature and a coincident dry-bulb temperature (see the American Society of Heating, Refrigeration and Air-Conditioning Engineers weather data).

*For example, the grains difference value for the rainy season in Tucson, AZ; is similar to the **Manual J** summer design value for Milwaukee, WI.*

*For ordinary comfort cooling, **Manual J** and **Manual S** do not investigate rainy season issues. However, this is important when continuous humidly control is critical for spaces that have a swimming pool and/or spa (see ACCA **Manual SPS**).*

Return Duct Effect

A return duct in an unconditioned space may have a sensible cooling load (Btuh), and/or a latent cooling load (Btuh). A sensible load increases the dry-bulb and wet-bulb temperatures of the entering air. A latent load increases the wet-bulb temperature of the entering air. Figure A1-6 summarizes the issue. A negative latent load decreases the wet-bulb temperature of the entering air (which is a moot point when there is no latent load for the air that passes through the return grille).

- *Manual J* Table 7 provides sensible and latent duct load values for the entire duct system (supply-side and return-side). The return-side loads are some fraction of the duct system loads.

- Appendix Sections A2-3 and A2-4 provide procedures for determining the return duct loads, and the associated DB/WB temperature gains.

- A sensible return duct load can occur for any Table 1 location, regardless of altitude, because the ambient dry-bulb temperature can be significantly warmer than the temperature of the indoor air.

- When the return duct has a sensible cooling load, it may increase the dry-bulb temperature of the return air (i.e., the entering air) by about 1/2°F to more than 5°F (see Figure A1-7, next page).

- When the return duct has some sensible and latent load combination, it may increase the wet-bulb temperature of the return air (i.e., the entering air) by 1/2°F to more than 3°F (see Figure A1-7).

- There is no latent return duct load for Table 1 locations that have grains difference values that are zero or negative.

For a dry climate, *Manual J* advises a design based on 45% RH in the conditioned space. However, this goal is not possible when the corresponding latent load is negative.

- Indoor humidity will be lower than 45% RH when the internal moisture gains cannot balance the moisture losses for infiltration and ventilation, (assuming no summer humidification).

- When the entering air humidity is less than 45% RH on a summer design day, the indoor coil will be dry, providing the indoor coil is not colder than it needs to be for a dry climate. Use 500, or more, blower Cfm per nominal AHRI ton of total capacity (or maximum allowed by the OEM).

- When the indoor coil is dry, sensible capacity equals total capacity (for the threshold entering wet-bulb value, and for all lower values).

For a return duct load with no ventilation, the condition of the entering air is not the same as the condition of the indoor air.

Entering dry-bulb increases when there is a sensible duct load.

Entering wet-bulb increases when there is a sensible and/or latent duct load.

Figure A1-6

In general, there is no latent return load when the location's elevation is 2,500 feet, or higher.

There are a few 2,500 to 3,200 foot locations that have positive grains difference values (see Hawaii, Kansas, Montana, Nebraska, Texas and West Virginia).

- When outdoor air is not mixed with return air, the DB and WB temperature of the air entering the indoor coil are equal to the temperature of the air at the return grille plus the temperature rise for the return duct.

- When outdoor air is mixed with return air, the DB/WB temperature of the mixture that enters the indoor coil depends on mixed air psychrometrics, as explained below.

Engineered Ventilation with no Heat Recovery

Mechanical introduction of outdoor air with no heat recovery will produce a sensible cooling load (Btuh), and may produce a latent cooling load (Btuh). A sensible load

Appendx 1

Dry-Bulb Rise (°F) Vs. Sensible Return Duct Load				
Sensible Load (Btuh)	Return Duct Cfm			
	1,000	1,500	2,000	2,500
	Sea Level			
1,000	0.91	0.61	0.45	0.36
2,000	1.82	1.21	0.91	0.73
3,000	2.73	1.82	1.36	1.09
4,000	3.64	2.42	1.82	1.45
5,000	4.55	3.03	2.27	1.82
6,000	5.45	3.64	2.73	2.18
	2,500 Feet			
1,000	0.83	0.55	0.41	0.33
2,000	1.65	1.10	0.83	0.66
3,000	2.48	1.65	1.24	0.99
4,000	3.31	2.21	1.65	1.32
5,000	4.14	2.76	2.07	1.65
6,000	4.96	3.31	2.48	1.99
	5,000 Feet			
1,000	0.76	0.51	0.38	0.31
2,000	1.53	1.02	0.76	0.61
3,000	2.29	1.53	1.15	0.92
4,000	3.05	2.04	1.53	1.22
5,000	3.82	2.55	1.91	1.53
6,000	4.58	3.05	2.29	1.83

Wet-Bulb Rise (°F) Vs. Sensible & Latent R-Duct Load				
Sensible and Latent Load (Btuh)	Return Duct Cfm			
	1,000	1,500	2,000	2,500
	Sea Level			
1,000 / 1,000	0.63	0.42	0.31	0.25
2,000 / 2,000	1.25	0.83	0.57	0.50
3,000 / 3,000	1.86	1.25	0.94	0.75
4,000 / 4,000	2.47	1.66	1.25	1.00
5,000 / 5,000	3.07	2.06	1.56	1.25
6,000 / 6,000	3.65	2.47	1.86	1.49
	2,500 feet			
1,000 / 1,000	0.54	0.36	0.27	0.22
2,000 / 2,000	1.08	0.72	0.54	0.43
3,000 / 3,000	1.61	1.08	0.81	0.65
4,000 / 4,000	2.13	1.41	1.08	0.86
5,000 / 5,000	2.65	1.79	1.35	1.08
6,000 / 6,000	3.17	2.13	1.61	1.29

1) For interpolating wet-bulb scenarios, half of the rise is caused by the sensible load, and half is caused by the latent load.
2) Appendix 2 provides procedures for determining return duct loads and the associated DB/WB temperature gains.
3) The DB/WB temperatures leaving the return duct are equal to the temperature at the return grille plus the return duct rise.

Figure A1-7

Mixing outdoor air with air that exits the return duct affects the condition of the air entering the indoor coil.

Entering dry-bulb increases when there is a sensible ventilation load.

Entering wet-bulb increases when there is a sensible and/or latent ventilation load.

Figure A1-8

Mixed Air DB (°F) for any Elevation with no Recovery 10% Outdoor Air for Cooling			
Return Duct Air DB (°F)	Outdoor DB (°F)		
	85	95	105
75	76.0	77.0	78.0
77	77.8	78.8	79.8
79	79.6	80.6	81.6
81	81.4	82.4	83.4
Mixed Air WB for 0 – 2,500 Ft with no Recovery 10% Outdoor Air			
Return Duct Air DB 75 to 81 (°F)	Outdoor Air Dry-Bulb (°F)		
	85, 95, 105	95, 105	95
Return Duct Air WB (°F)	Outdoor Air WB (°F)		
	70	75	80
	Mixed Air WB (°F)		
59	60.2	60.8	61.5
61	62.0	62.5	63.2
63	64.6	64.3	65.0
65	65.5	66.1	66.7
67	67.3	67.8	68.4

1) The maximum WB error for simplifying parametric dependancies is ± 0.05 °F.
2) In general, the indoor coil will be dry when the location's elevation is 2,500 feet, or higher.
3) There are a few 2,500 to 3,200 foot locations that have positive grains difference values (see Hawaii, Kansas, Montana, Nebraska, Texas and West Virginia; *Manual J* Table 1).
4) Appendix 2 provides procedures for calculating the entering air condition for any set of circumstances.

Figure A1-9

increases the dry-bulb and wet-bulb temperature of the entering air. A latent load increases the wet-bulb temperature of the entering air. A negative latent load decreases the wet-bulb temperature of the entering air (which is a moot point when there is no latent load for the air that passes through the return duct). Figure A1-8 summarizes the issue.

- A sensible ventilation load occurs for any location, regardless of altitude when the 1% dry-bulb temperature for outdoor air is greater than 75°F (assuming the thermostat is set for 75°F, or less).

- There is a latent ventilation load for *Manual J* Table 1 locations that have grains difference values that are greater than zero.

- There is no latent ventilation load for Table 1 locations that have grains difference values that are zero or negative.

In general, there is no latent ventilation load when the location's elevation is 2,500 feet, or higher.

There are a few 2,500 to 3,200 foot locations that have positive grains difference values (see Hawaii, Kansas, Montana, Nebraska, Texas and West Virginia).

- Figure A1-9 (previous page) provides entering DB values and approximate entering WB values for 10% outdoor air, for relevant combinations of outdoor air DB/WB values applied to relevant combinations of return air DB/WB values.

Note that 10% outdoor air may add 0.4°F to 3.0°F to the entering air DB temperature, and 0.3°F to 2.5°F to the entering air WB temperature.

Ten percent outdoor air is generally compatible with the 0.35 air change per hour (ACH) value that appears (or has appeared) in some standards and codes.

- Sections A2-5 and A2-6 discuss the 0.35 ACH issue, and provide procedures for determining entering DB/WB temperatures when any amount of raw outdoor air is mixed with return air.

Engineered Ventilation with Heat Recovery

Mechanical introduction of outdoor air with heat recovery will produce a sensible cooling load (Btuh), and may produce a latent cooling load (Btuh). A sensible load increases the dry-bulb and wet-bulb temperatures of the entering air, but the effect is smaller with sensible heat recovery. A latent load increases the wet-bulb temperature of the entering air, but the effect is smaller with latent heat recovery. A negative latent load decreases the wet-bulb temperature of the entering air (which is a moot point when there is no latent load for the air that passes through the return duct).

- A sensible ventilation load will occur for any *Manual J* Table 1 location, regardless of altitude, when the outdoor 1% dry-bulb temperature is greater than 75°F (when the thermostat is at 75°F, or less).

- There is a latent ventilation load for Table 1 locations that have grains difference values that are greater than zero.

Mixed Air DB for any Elevation with Heat Recovery 10% Outdoor Air and 0.60 Effectiveness for Cooling			
Return Duct Air DB (°F)	Outdoor DB (°F)		
	85	95	105
75	75.4	75.8	76.2
77	77.3	77.7	78.1
79	79.2	79.6	80.0
81	81.2	81.6	82.0

Mixed Air WB for 0 - 2,500 Ft with Heat Recovery 10% Outdoor Air and 0.60 Effectiveness for Cooling			
Return Duct Air DB 75 to 81 (°F)	Outdoor Air Dry-Bulb (°F)		
	85, 95, 105	95, 105	95
Return Duct Air WB (°F)	Outdoor Air WB (°F)		
	70	75	80
	Mixed Air WB (°F)		
59	59.5	59.7	60.1
61	61.4	61.6	61.9
63	63.3	63.5	63.8
65	65.2	65.4	65.7
67	67.1	67.3	67.6

1) The maximum WB error for simplifying parametric dependancies is ± 0.2 °F.
2) Figure A1-9 provides entering wet-bulb values when the heat recovery equipment is limited to sensible recovery.
3) In general, the indoor coil will be dry when the location's elevation is 2,500 feet, or higher.
4) There are a few 2,500 to 3,200 foot locations that have positive grains difference values (see Hawaii, Kansas, Montana, Nebraska, Texas and West Virginia; *Manual J* Table 1).
5) Appendix 2 provides procedures for calculating the entering air condition for any set of circumstances.

Figure A1-10

- There is no latent ventilation load for Table 1 locations that have grains difference values that are zero or negative.

In general, there is no latent ventilation load when the location's elevation is 2,500 feet, or higher.

There are a few 2,500 to 3,200 foot locations that have positive grains difference values (see Hawaii, Kansas, Montana, Nebraska, Texas and West Virginia).

- Figure A1-10 provides entering DB/WB values for 10% outdoor air with 0.60 recovery effectiveness, for relevant combinations of outdoor air DB/WB values applied to relevant combinations of return air DB/WB values.

Note that 10% outdoor air with 0.60 effectiveness may add 0.2°F to 1.2°F to the entering air DB temperature, and 0.1°F to 1.1°F to the entering air WB temperature.

The 0.60 effectiveness value applies to sensible recovery and to latent recovery. Figure A1-9 provides entering wet-bulb values when the heat recovery equipment is limited to sensible recovery.

Ten percent outdoor air is generally compatible with the 0.35 air change per hour (ACH) value that appears (or has appeared) in standards and codes.

A particular piece of heat recovery equipment may have a different effectiveness rating.

- Section A2-7 provides procedures for determining entering DB/WB temperatures when any amount of outdoor air is mixed with return air. There are procedures for no heat recovery, and for recovery effectiveness values specified by the practitioner.

A1-3 Operating Conditions for Heat Pump Heating

Heat pump equipment may be air-air or water-air. For either case, heating capacity (Btuh) primarily depends on the temperature of the fluid that enters the evaporator, but also is effected by the temperature of the air that enters the indoor coil.

Condition at the Evaporator

For air-air equipment (Figure A1-11), heating performance depends on the air temperature at the outdoor coil. By default, this temperature is the 99% dry-bulb temperature from *Manual J* Table 1.

For water-air equipment (Figure A1-12), heating performance depends on the temperature of the water entering the water to refrigerant heat exchanger. This temperature depends on the water supply source.

- For a once-though system, the entering water temperature (EWT) is equal to the ground water temperature.
- For an earth-loop system, the design value for the entering water temperature may be significantly colder than the ground water temperature (loop water temperature is at it's lowest value during late winter, or early spring).
- For an earth-loop system, the design value for the entering water temperature may be less than 32°F (antifreeze must be added to the loop water).

Heating performance also depends on the fluid flow rate through the evaporator. This value may be set by the original equipment manufacturer (OEM), or may be selected by the practitioner.

- For air-air equipment, the OEM's design determines the Cfm through the outdoor coil.

Air-Air Heat Pump Heating Capacity

Use the local winter design temperature to evaluate heating performance (the 99% dry-bulb value from *Manual J*, Table 1).

The outdoor coil should not be installed in a confined space (the outdoor fan must have access to new air).

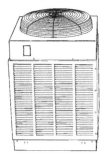

Figure A1-11

Water-Air Equipment

Use the ground water temperature for once-through equipment, or the water-loop temperature for late winter, to evaluate heating performance.

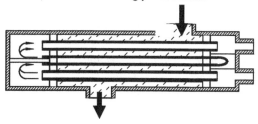

Figure A1-12

- For water-air equipment, the practitioner's design determines the Gpm through the water to refrigerant heat exchanger. However, this is a secondary issue (heating capacity is somewhat sensitive to Gpm).

Condition at the Indoor Coil

Heating performance also depends on the dry-bulb temperature of the air that enters the indoor coil. This temperature depends on the condition of the air leaving the conditioned space (indoor air), the conduction and leakage loads for the return duct, and the use of engineered ventilation (mixing outdoor air with return air).

- Entering air temperature affects compressor heat output, the thermal balance point diagram, and the amount of supplemental electric coil heat.
- Figure A1-13 (next page) shows that the size of the entering air temperature effect depends on the make and model of the heat pump equipment.
- An entering air temperature below 50°F to 60°F (depending on the product) may result in incomplete defrost cycles, and increased use of supplement heat.

Appendx 1

Heating Capacity Vs. Entering Air Temperature				
Air-Air Heat Pump from OEM A				
OAdb (°F)	EAdb (°F)			
	60 [3]	70	75	80
2	+ 1.2%	Reference Capacity	–0.7%	–1.3%
7	+ 0.9%		–0.9%	–1.8%
12	+ 1.6%		–0.8%	–1.6%
17	+ 0.7%		–0.7%	–1.3%
22	+ 1.3%		–0.6%	–1.3%
27	+ 1.2%		–0.6%	–1.2%
32	+ 1.7%		–0.6%	–1.1%
37	+ 1.6%		–0.5%	–1.0%
42	+ 1.5%		–0.5%	–1.5%
47	+ 1.1%		–0.8%	–1.1%
52	+ 1.4%		–0.4%	–1.1%
57	+ 1.3%		–0.7%	–1.3%
62	+ 1.2%		–0.6%	–1.2%
67	+ 1.2%		–0.9%	–1.5%

Air-Air Heat Pump from OEM B			
OAdb (°F)	EAdb (°F)		
	65	70	75
–3	+ 6.1%	Reference Capacity	–6.4%
7	+ 4.4%		–4.7%
17	+ 2.8%		–3.8%
27	+ 2.1%		–2.1%
37	+ 2.0%		–2.0%
47	+ 2.0%		–1.9%
57	+ 1.9%		–1.9%
67	+ 1.8%		/1.8%

Air-Air Heat Pump from OEM C			
OAdb (°F)	EAdb (°F)		
	55 [3]	70	80
–10	+11.2%	Reference Capacity	–17.9%
0	+ 9.3%		–14.8%
10	+ 7.6%		–12.3%
20	+ 6.3%		–10.1%
30	+ 5.3%		–8.3%
40	+ 4.4%		–6.9%
50	+ 3.6%		–5.7%
60	+ 3.0%		–4.7%

1) OAdb = Outdoor air dry-bulb, EAdb = Entering air dry-bulb.
2) Baseline heating capacity is for 70°F EAdb; a cooler EAdb increases capacity, a warmer EAdb decreases capacity.
3) Values below 60°F may degrade defrost cycle performance.

Figure A1-13

Dry-Bulb Drop (°F) Vs. Sensible Return Duct Load				
Heating Load Btuh	Return Duct Cfm			
	1,000	1,500	2,000	2,500
Sea Level				
1,000	0.91	0.61	0.45	0.36
2,000	1.82	1.21	0.91	0.73
3,000	2.73	1.82	1.36	1.09
4,000	3.64	2.42	1.82	1.45
5,000	4.55	3.03	2.27	1.82
6,000	5.45	3.64	2.73	2.18
2,500 Feet				
1,000	0.83	0.55	0.41	0.33
2,000	1.65	1.10	0.83	0.66
3,000	2.48	1.65	1.24	0.99
4,000	3.31	2.21	1.65	1.32
5,000	4.14	2.76	2.07	1.65
6,000	4.96	3.31	2.48	1.99
5,000 Feet				
1,000	0.76	0.51	0.38	0.31
2,000	1.53	1.02	0.76	0.61
3,000	2.29	1.53	1.15	0.92
4,000	3.05	2.04	1.53	1.22
5,000	3.82	2.55	1.91	1.53
6,000	4.58	3.05	2.29	1.83

1) Appendix 2 provides procedures for determining return duct loads and the associated dry-bulb temperature drop.
2) The dry-bulb temperature at the exit of the return duct is equal to the temperature at the return grille minus the return duct temperature change.
3) The temperature drop values in this table show two decimal places, rounding to one place is adequate for actual practice.

Figure A1-14

Mixed Air DB for any Elevation with no Recovery 10% Outdoor Air for Heating							
Return DB (°F)	Outdoor DB (°F)						
	-20	-10	0	10	20	30	40
60	52.0	53.0	54.0	55.0	56.0	57.0	58.0
65	56.5	57.5	58.5	59.5	60.5	61.5	62.5
70	61.0	62.0	63.0	64.0	65.0	66.0	67.0
75	65.5	66.5	67.5	68.5	69.5	70.5	71.5

Appendix 2 provides procedures for calculating the entering air condition for any set of circumstances.

Figure A1-15

No Return Duct Load and No Engineered Ventilation

When there is no return duct load (the duct is in the conditioned space, or an unconditioned space that is similar to a conditioned space), and no engineered ventilation (raw or processed outdoor air is not mixed with return air), the

Appendx 1

dry-bulb temperature for entering air is equal to the dry-bulb temperature of the indoor air.

- The default condition for indoor air equals the *Manual J* design value for dry-bulb temperature for heating (70°F).
- The *Manual J* dry-bulb default is superseded by the value specified by code or utility regulation.

Return Duct Effect

A return duct in an unconditioned space will have a sensible heating load (Btuh). This load reduces the dry-bulb temperature of the entering air.

- *Manual J* duct load tables provide a value for the sensible heating load for the entire duct system (supply-side and return-side). The return-side load is some fraction of the system load.
- Sections A2-3 and A2-4 provide procedures for determining the return duct load, and the associated dry-bulb temperature drop.
- A return duct heating load can occur for any Table 1 location, because the ambient dry-bulb temperature can be significantly colder than the temperature of the indoor air.
- When the return duct has a sensible heating load, it may decrease the dry-bulb temperature of the return air (i.e., the entering air) by about 1/2°F to more than 5°F (see Figure A1-14, previous page).

Engineered Ventilation with no Heat Recovery

For engineered ventilation, using raw outdoor air with no heat recovery produces a sensible heating load (Btuh). This load decreases the entering air temperature.

- Figure A1-15 (previous page) provides entering dry-bulb values for 10% outdoor air, for the relevant range of outdoor air dry-bulb values, and a relevant range of return air dry-bulb values.

  Note that 10% outdoor may cause the entering air to be 2°F to 9.5°F cooler than the return air.

  Ten percent outdoor air is generally compatible with the 0.35 air change per hour (ACH) value that appears (or has appeared) in standards and codes.

- Sections A2-5 and A2-6 discuss the 0.35 ACH issue, and provide procedures for determining the entering DB temperature when any amount of raw outdoor air is mixed with return air.

Engineered Ventilation with Heat Recovery

Mechanical introduction of outdoor air with heat recovery will produce a sensible heating load (Btuh). A sensible load decreases the dry-bulb temperature of the entering air, but the effect is smaller with sensible heat recovery.

Winter Humidification Loads

Duct leakage to/from an unconditioned space produces a winter humidification load. *Manual J* Version 2.00 or later evaluates the latent load for duct leakage.

- Leakage on either side of an exposed duct system may cause a condensation problem (for summer or winter).
- An inadequate overall R-value at any point along an exposed duct system may cause a condensation problem (for summer or winter).

Mixing outdoor air with return air produces a winter humidification load. *Manual J* 8th Edition Version 2.00 or later evaluates the latent load for winter ventilation.

Infiltration produces a winter humidification load. *Manual J* Version 2.00 or later evaluates the latent load for winter infiltration.

Moisture migration produces a winter humidification load. *Manual J* Version 2.00 or later evaluates the latent load for moisture migration.

Mixed Air DB for any Elevation with Recovery
10% Outdoor Air and 0.60 Effectiveness for Heating

Return DB (°F)	Outdoor DB (°F)						
	-20	-10	0	10	20	30	40
60	56.8	57.2	57.6	58.0	58.4	58.8	59.2
65	61.6	62.0	62.4	62.8	63.2	63.6	64.0
70	66.4	66.8	67.2	67.6	68.0	68.4	68.8
75	71.2	71.6	72.0	72.4	72.8	73.2	73.6

Appendix 2 provides procedures for calculating the entering air condition for any set of circumstances.

Figure A1-16

- A sensible ventilation load will occur for any *Manual J* Table 1 location, regardless of altitude, when the outdoor 1% dry-bulb temperature is less than 70°F (thermostat is at 70°F, or less).
- Figure A1-16 provides entering DB/WB values for 10% outdoor air with 0.60 recovery effectiveness, for relevant outdoor air DB values applied to relevant return air DB values.

  Note that 10% outdoor air with 0.60 recovery effectiveness may reduce the entering air temperature by 0.8°F to 3.8°F (compared to the return air temperature).

  Ten percent outdoor air is generally compatible with the 0.35 air change per hour (ACH) value that appears (or has appeared) in standards and codes.

A particular piece of heat recovery equipment may have a different effectiveness rating.

- Section A2-7 provides procedures for determining entering DB temperature when any amount of outdoor air is mixed with return air. There are procedures for no heat recovery, and for a recovery effectiveness value specified by the practitioner.

A1-4 Operating Conditions for Forced Air Furnaces

Furnace output capacity (Btuh) is not significantly effected by the outdoor temperature, or entering dry-bulb temperature. However, furnace heat exchangers have air temperature rise limits, and there is a high-limit temperature for discharge air (see Section 3). In addition, an entering air temperature less than 55°F may cause rust damage for air-side components not made of stainless steel.

A1-5 Design Values for Supply Air Cfm

Supply air that has a higher dry-bulb value than room/space air compensates for a sensible room/space heat loss. Supply air that has a lower dry-bulb value than room/space air compensates for a sensible room/space heat gain. For steady-state conditions, the amount of supply air for a given heat loss or heat gain value is uniquely determined by these psychrometric equations:

Cooling Cfm = SCL / (1.1 x ACF x CTD)
Heating Cfm = SHL / (1.1 x ACF x HTD)

Where:
SCL = Sensible cooling load (MJ8 summer Btuh)
SHL = Sensible heating load (MJ8 winter Btuh)
ACF = Altitude correction factor (see Figure A5-1)
HTD (°F) = Supply air DB - Room/Space DB
CTD (°F) = Room/Space DB - Supply air DB

Note that these equations are the only possible solution to the heat balance problem.

- A thermostat's set-point can only be maintained when the rate of sensible heat (Btuh) entering a room/space equals the rate of sensible heat (Btuh) leaving a room/space.

- The number of air turnovers (air changes) for a room/space depends on the psychrometric Cfm that provides a heat balance (per the previous equations), and the volume (CuFt) of the room/space.

In other words, procedures that recommend an arbitrary air change value for determining supply air Cfm ignores the principle of conservation of energy, and can only be correct by fortunate coincidence (pure luck).

The desire to mandate an air change value is due to the legitimate need for adequate air movement in the occupied zone (see the air distribution effectiveness sidebar on this page).

- Since the sensible heating load or sensible cooling load is what it is, per **Manual J** procedures, the only option for adjusting supply air Cfm is to manipulate the CTD value or HTD value.

- Smaller CTD and HTD values increase the supply air Cfm, and vice versa. However, there are important issues that limit the use of this concept.

OEM's have limits for the maximum and minimum temperature of the air leaving a heat exchanger, heating coil, or cooling coil.

For cooling and heat pump equipment, indoor coil Cfm, Btuh capacity, and CTD or HTD are interdependent. Therefore, equipment is selected for the appropriate capacity at a given blower Cfm, and the CTD and HTD are what they are for the associated Cfm value.

For humid climate cooling, colder supply air is required for adequate indoor humidity control (a larger CTD value translates to a lower supply Cfm value).

Air Distribution Effectiveness

The amount of supply Cfm for a room/space heat balance decreases as construction efficiency increases. This means that supply air registers, grilles and diffusers, must be pushed to their performance limits, as far as throw is concerned.

- In general, supply air hardware must be as small a size as possible, without causing objectionable noise.

- For a given type/style outlet, some makes/models have stronger throws than others. Search for products that have the longer throws for a given size and Cfm value, with an acceptable amount of noise.

- Supply air hardware manufacturer's need to invest in research that results in products that provide more ventilation effectiveness for a relatively small supply Cfm value.

- Practitioners should investigate the performance of the supply air nozzles that are commonly used with high air velocity systems.

- Primary heating-cooling equipment OEM's need to offer equipment that has a relatively large supply Cfm for the amount of heating-cooling capacity. By-pass air (around a coil or heat exchanger) provides solution to this problem, but requires more blower power.

A1-6 Sensible Heat Ratio

There is a sensible heat ratio for the *Manual J* cooling loads (JSHR), and there is a sensible heat ratio for a cooling coil (CSHR). These equations provide sensible heat ratio values for *Manual J* output, and for values extracted from expanded equipment performance data.

$JSHR = SL / (SL + LL) = SL / TL$
$CSHR = SC / (SC + LC) = SC / TC$

Where:
Loads and capacities are in Btuh units.
SL = Sensible load; SC = Sensible capacity
LL = Latent load; LC = Latent capacity
TL = Total load; TC = Total capacity

Akron, OH Outdoor Condition = 90°FDB / 26 Grains Difference; Indoor Condition = 75°F DB/ 50% RH					
Configuration	Manual J Output	Infiltration Load		
		Tight	Average	Loose
All ducts in conditioned space, no mechanical ventilation	Sensible Btuh	20,877	21,681	22,486
	Latent Btuh	2,242	3,105	3,967
	JSHR	0.90	0.87	0.85
Attic ducts @ 135°F ambient, 10% duct gain for conduction, no duct leakage, no mechanical ventilation	Sensible Btuh	22,964	23,850	24,735
	Latent Btuh	2,242	3,105	3,967
	JSHR	0.91	0.88	0.86
All ducts in conditioned space, mechanical ventilation at 100 Cfm	Sensible Btuh	22,527	23,331	24,136
	Latent Btuh	4,010	4,873	5,736
	JSHR	0.85	0.83	0.81
Attic ducts @ 135°F ambient, 10% duct gain for conduction (return-side contributes 5%), 100 Cfm supply-side leakage, 100 Cfm return-side leakage	Sensible Btuh	31,214	32,100	32,985
	Latent Btuh	5,778	6,641	7,503
	JSHR	0.84	0.83	0.81
Open crawlspace ducts, 10% duct gain for conduction (return-side contributes 5%),100 Cfm supply-side leakage,100 Cfm return-side leakage, no mechanical ventilation	Sensible BTUH	26,624	27,150	28,035
	Latent BTUH	5,778	6,641	7,503
	JSHR	0.82	0.80	0.79

Charleston, SC Outdoor Condition = 91°F DB / 60 Grains Difference; Indoor Condition = 75°F DB/ 50% RH					
Configuration	Manual J Output	Infiltration Load		
		Tight	Average	Loose
All ducts in conditioned space, no mechanical ventilation	Sensible Btuh	20,093	21,789	22,647
	Latent Btuh	3,370	5,360	7,350
	JSHR	0.86	0.80	0.75
Attic ducts @ 135°F ambient, 10% duct gain for conduction, no duct leakage, no mechanical ventilation	Sensible Btuh	23,023	23,968	24,912
	Latent Btuh	3,370	5,360	7,350
	JSHR	0.87	0.82	0.77
All ducts in conditioned space, mechanical ventilation at 100 Cfm	Sensible Btuh	22,690	23,544	24,407
	Latent Btuh	7,450	9,440	11,430
	JSHR	0.75	0.71	0.68
Attic ducts @ 135°F ambient, 10% duct gain for conduction (return-side contributes 5%), 100 Cfm supply-side leakage, 100 Cfm return-side leakage	Sensible Btuh	31,273	32,218	33,162
	Latent Btuh	6,906	8,896	10,886
	JSHR	0.82	0.78	0.75
Open crawlspace ducts, 10% duct gain for conduction (return-side contributes 5%),100 Cfm supply-side leakage,100 Cfm return-side leakage, no mechanical ventilation	Sensible BTUH	26,323	27,268	28,212
	Latent BTUH	6,906	8,896	10,886
	JSHR	0.79	0.75	0.72

Figure A1-17

For perfect indoor humidity control when the equipment operates continuously at *Manual J* design conditions (or the local code/utility conditions that supersede *Manual J* procedures), the CSHR value should be identical to the JSHR value. This value may range from 1.0 for no latent load, to 0.75 or less for a relatively large latent load (compared to the total load).

- Climate has a significant affect on latent load (see the grains difference values in *Manual J*, Table 1). For a given location, this is what it is.
- The design value for indoor relative humidity has some affect on the latent load (see the Grains difference values in *Manual J*, Table 1). Designing for a higher indoor humidity (55% RH instead of 50% RH) reduces the *Manual J* latent load (but diminishes part-load humidity control).

When there is a latent load, indoor humidity drifts up when the compressor cycles. This is not a problem when it stays below 60% RH (per industry comfort studies).

Designing for 50% RH (vs. 55% RH) leaves more room to drift when the equipment cycles at part-load.

The maximum design value for Manual J calculations is 55% RH (for dwellings that push the limit of the equipment's ability to control latent load).

- Infiltration loads, outdoor air loads for engineered ventilation, and duct leakage loads can have a significant affect on the latent load.
- Designs and construction that reduce the latent load increase the JSHR value (this is very desirable for humidity control and energy use).
- Designs and construction that reduce the sensible load decrease the JSHR value (this is very undesirable for humidity control, but is desirable for energy use).

Figure A1-17 (previous page) shows how design and construction affect the *Manual J* sensible heat ratio for an Akron, OH, dwelling (significant summer humidity), and for the same dwelling in Charleston, SC, (oppressive summer humidity). Note that the Akron SHR values range from 0.79 to 0.91, and the Charleston values range from 0.68 to 0.87.

- Sensible heat ratios of 0.80 or higher are no problem for cooling equipment, so a 50% RH design value is compatible with all Akron scenarios.
- The Charleston example has many scenarios that have sensible heat ratios that are somewhat, or significantly, less than 0.80. This may be a problem for the cooling equipment.

Take measures to reduce the latent load.

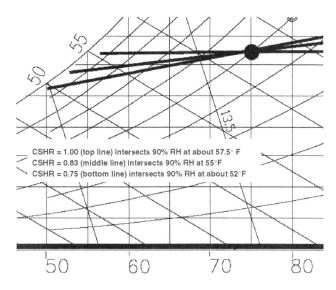

CSHR = 1.00 (top line) intersects 90% RH at about 57.5° F
CSHR = 0.83 (middle line) intersects 90% RH at 55°F
CSHR = 0.75 (bottom line) intersects 90% RH at about 52°F

Figure A1-18

Theoretical Cooling Equipment Designs
For 24,900 Btuh sensible load, 0.83 SHR, 75°F room

Unit	LA (°F)	Cfm	LA (RH)	LA (Gr)	Δ Gr	Lat Cap
A	55	1,132	90.0%	57.85	6.80	5,234
B	60	1,509	77.5%	59.66	4.99	5,121
C	65	2,264	66.7%	61.36	3.29	5,064

1) LA = Leaving air; Gr = Grains; Lat Cap = Latent capacity
2) Unit A is the only practical solution considering duct sizes, equipment cost and energy use, but A, B and C are psychrometrically correct solutions.

Figure A1-19

Coil sensible heat ratios depend on the OEM's design. Search for makes and models that are compatible with the Manual J sensible heat ratio.

It may be that a whole-house dehumidifier or a ventilation dehumidifier is required for summer humidity control.

Design for 55% RH instead of 50% RH (as the last resort).

A1-7 Cooling Cfm Determined by Design

Sensible heat ratio lines can be drawn on a psychrometric chart, as demonstrated by Figure A1-18 (ACCA *Manual P* provides related instructions). When the cooling equipment is perfect for the design condition cooling load, it's coil sensible heat ratio line will be identical to the *Manual J* sensible heat ratio line.

- This simply means that the sensible to total ratio for the equipment matches the sensible to total ratio for the loads.

Appendix 1

- This overlap, or a close approximation, is a must when the equipment is to maintain the desired indoor relative humidity for the summer design condition.

Demonstration of Principle

All points on a sensible heat ratio line have the same sensible to total ratio, so any point is a suitable leaving air condition for the sensible and latent loads. For example, the following set of loads is compatible with a 0.83 sensible heat ratio value (middle line on Figure A1-18).

Sensible load = 24,900 Btuh
Latent load = 5,100 Btuh
Total load = 30,000 Btuh = 2.5 Tons
CSHR = JSHR = 0.83

So, an OEM could design the equipment for a 55°F leaving dry-bulb temperature (LAT), or for 60°F, or 65°F (or any point on the 0.83 line). Compatibility with the *Manual J* loads for a sea level home is demonstrated by Figure A1-19 (previous page). The procedure that provides the Figure A1-19 values is summarized here, for Unit A:

Space design condition = 75°F, 50% RH, 64.65 Grains.
Supply air condition = 55°F, 90% RH, 57.85 Grains.
CTD = 75 − 55 = 20°F
Supply air Cfm = 24,900 / (1.1 x 1.0 x 20) = 1,132
Grains difference (DGr) = 64.65 − 57.85 = 6.80
Latent Btuh = 0.68 x ACF x Cfm x DGr
Latent Btuh = 0.68 x 1.0 x 1,132 x 6.80 = 5,234

Notes:
a) Latent Btuh = 0.68 x ACF x Cfm x ΔGr is the psychrometric equation for latent load or latent capacity.

b) 5,234 Btuh of latent capacity is not exactly equal to the 5,100 Btuh latent load because the hand cannot draw a perfect SHR line, and because the eye cannot perfectly resolve the information on the psychrometric chart.

c) There is a big difference in Cfm/Ton values
Cfm/Ton for Unit A = 1,132 / 2.5 = 453
Cfm/Ton for Unit B = 1,509 / 2.5 = 604
Cfm/Ton for Unit C = 2,264 / 2.5 = 906

At this point, a thoughtful observer may ask... *Why are Cfm per ton values for actual equipment so low? When OEM's would design for higher Cfm/Ton values, the air distribution effectiveness problem would go away.*

As is normally the case in life, multiple conflicting issues must be resolved by tradeoffs. Such as achieving a SEER goal, coil size and cost issues, blower size and blower power issues, meeting a production cost goal, avoiding condensate blow off (and probably many more, if we could question equipment designers).

Cooling Equipment Designs Based on Climate For 30,000 Btuh total load, 75°F room, 90% RH off coil					
Unit	SHR	S-Load	LAT	CTD	Cfm	Cfm/Ton
D	1.00	30,000	57.5	17.5	1,558	623
E	0.83	24,900	55.0	20.0	1,132	453
F	0.75	22,500	52.5	22.5	909	364

The Cfm/Ton values are psychrometrically correct. OEMs also consider how Cfm/Ton affects condensate blow off and the SEER/HSPF ratings.

Figure A1-20

Prerequisites for Equipment Selection For sensible and latent cooling, and sensible heating	
From *Manual J*	Calculate or Look-Up
Design Loads (Btuh) Sensible cooling Latent cooling Sensible heating Form J1, bottom line	**Entering Air Temperatures (°F)** Dry-bulb for cooling Wet-bulb for cooling Dry-bulb for heating This manual, Sections A1-2, A1-3
For Air-Air Equipment Summer 1% dry-bulb (°F) Winter 99% dry-bulb (°F) From Table 1A or Table 1B, or code/utility values	**For Water-Air Equipment** Entering water temperature (°F) End of cooling season End of heating season Ground water temperature, or values from piping loop design
Indoor Conditions Cooling dry-bulb (°F) Cooling relative humidity (%RH) Heating dry-bulb (°F) *Manual J* defaults, or code/utility values	**Candidate Search Methods** Total *Manual J* cooling load Ballpark Cfm See, Appendix 3

Figure A1-21

It turns out that the optimum design, considering all issues, results in a leaving air humidity in the 85% RH to 95% RH range. So for this discussion, Unit A performance (90% RH) is similar to what we get from OEM equipment.

Application of Principle

One thing that OEMs can do, is to match equipment components (compressor, evaporator, condenser, and refrigerant metering device) to the climate. In this regard, Figure A1-18 shows that the 1.00 SHR line (dry-coil climate) intersects the 90% RH line at about 57.5°F, and the 0.83 SHR line (significant humidity climate) intersects the 90% RH line at about 55°F, and the 0.75 SHR line (oppressive humidity climate) intersects the 90% RH line at about 52.5°F. So there could be three types of indoor units for one outdoor unit, as demonstrated by Figure A1-20.

Practitioners benefit when an OEM provides expanded performance for one outdoor unit working with different indoor unit configurations. This way, equipment sensible and latent capacities can be closely matched to the sensible and latent loads produced by the local climate.

- Some may ask... What does 400 Cfm per ton (or whatever value that is popular) have to do with equipment sizing.
- The answer... Absolutely nothing, except by coincidence.

A1-8 Prerequisites for Equipment Selection

Manual J calculations provide design day operating conditions and equipment load values for a particular dwelling. OEM expanded performance data correlates equipment performance (sensible and latent cooling capacity, and/or heating capacity) with operating conditions. Figure A1-21 (previous page) summarizes the information that is required for equipment selection and sizing.

A1-9 Expanded Performance Data

After equipment selection data has been collected, OEM expanded performance data for cooling is used to select a cooling-only unit, or heat pump. This data is presented as a series of tables that are organized according to equipment size (normally from smaller sizes to larger sizes).

- Cooling-only equipment and heat pump equipment is sized for the sensible and latent cooling loads.

However, the limit for excess cooling capacity depends on the type of equipment, the JSHR value, and the type of climate (see Section N2).

- Carefully search the data sheets for the product that provides the desired performance.

Must have adequate latent capacity, adequate sensible capacity; and excess total capacity must not exceed high-low limits.

- Start with the data sheet that has a total capacity or ballpark Cfm value that is close to the total load or desired ballpark Cfm value (see Appendix 3).
- It may be that more than one model size can satisfy the performance requirements without being unacceptably over-sized or under-sized.

Air-Air Cooling or Air-Air Heat Pump Cooling

An example of expanded cooling performance data for equipment that has one indoor refrigerant coil is provided by Figure A1-22. Notice that this exhibit accounts for all the variables that affect the performance of air-air equipment (blower Cfm, outdoor air temperature, entering air dry-bulb and entering air wet-bulb).

- A data sheet must provide information on total capacity, sensible capacity and latent capacity. For the format that this OEM uses, sensible capacity equals total capacity multiplied by the sensible heat ratio, and latent capacity equals total capacity minus sensible capacity.

Expanded Performance Data for Cooling with an Air-Cooled Condenser

EWB °F	Cfm	Outdoor DB 85°F				Outdoor DB 90°F				Outdoor DB 95°F				Outdoor DB 100°F			
		TC Btuh	CSHR			TC Btuh	CSHR			TC Btuh	CSHR			TC Btuh	CSHR		
			EDB °F				EDB °F				EDB °F				EDB °F		
			75	80	85		75	80	85		75	80	85		75	80	85
59	1,000	27,205	0.94	1.00	1.00	26,080	0.97	1.00	1.00	24,955	0.99	1.00	1.00	23,830	1.00	1.00	1.00
	1,125	27,621	0.98	1.00	1.00	26,496	1.00	1.00	1.00	25,371	1.00	1.00	1.00	24,246	1.00	1.00	1.00
	1,250	28,038	1.00	1.00	1.00	26,913	1.00	1.00	1.00	25,788	1.00	1.00	1.00	24,663	1.00	1.00	1.00
63	1,000	29,205	0.75	0.88	1.00	28,080	0.78	0.91	1.00	26,955	0.80	0.93	1.00	25,830	0.83	0.96	1.00
	1,125	29,621	0.79	0.92	1.00	28,496	0.82	0.95	1.00	27,371	0.84	0.97	1.00	26,246	0.87	1.00	1.00
	1,250	30,038	0.83	0.96	1.00	28,913	0.86	0.99	1.00	27,788	0.88	1.00	1.00	26,663	0.91	1.00	1.00
67	1,000	31,205	0.56	0.69	0.82	30,080	0.59	0.72	0.85	28,955	0.61	0.74	0.87	27,830	0.64	0.77	0.90
	1,125	31,621	0.60	0.73	0.86	30,496	0.63	0.76	0.89	29,371	0.65	0.78	0.91	28,246	0.68	0.81	0.94
	1,250	32,038	0.64	0.77	0.90	30,913	0.67	0.80	0.93	29,788	0.69	0.82	0.95	28,663	0.72	0.85	0.98

EWB = Entering wet-bulb temperature; EDB = Entering dry-bulb temperature; DB = Dry-bulb temperature.
Cfm = Blower Cfm setting; TC = Total cooling capacity (sensible plus latent); CSHR = Coil sensible heat ratio = Sensible Btuh / Total Btuh
Capacity values have been adjusted for blower heat (default value = 500 blower motor Watts).

Figure A1-22

Appendx 1

- A data sheet will show available blower speeds, or blower speed settings (low-, medium-, and high-speed for this PSC blower product).
- A data sheet must show a full range of outdoor air temperatures (105°F, 110°F and 115°F not shown to make Figure A1-22 more readable).
- A data sheet must show a range of entering wet-bulb temperatures.

  The lowest value should be compatible with dry-coil cooling (EWB 59°F or lower).

  The highest value should be compatible with a large moisture removal load (EWB 67°F, or higher).
- A data sheet must show a range of entering dry-bulb temperatures (70°F to 85°F, for example).
- A data sheet should show a power input (KW) value for each total capacity value (not relevant to capacity searches, not shown to make Figure A1-22 more readable).
- A data sheet note should state whether or not the cooling capacity values have been adjusted for blower heat (blower heat is a *Manual J* load when the data has not been adjusted for blower heat).

Air-Air Heat Pump Heating

An example of expanded heating performance data for equipment that has one indoor refrigerant coil is provided by Figure A1-23. Notice that this exhibit accounts for all the variables that affect the heat output of air-air equipment (blower Cfm, outdoor air temperature, and entering air dry-bulb).

- A data sheet must provide heating Btuh values for heat pump (compressor) heating.
- A data sheet will show available blower speeds, or blower speed settings (low-, medium-, and high-speed for this PSC blower product).
- A data sheet must show a full range of outdoor air temperatures for heating (values typically from 70°F or so, to 0°F, to -15°F, depending on the low-limit for the equipment.
- A data sheet should show a range of entering dry-bulb temperatures (typically 60°F or 65°F to 75°F or 80°F).
- A data sheet should show a power input (KW) value for each heating capacity value (not relevant to heating capacity issues, not shown to make Figure A1-23 more readable).
- A data sheet note should state whether or not the heating capacity values are discounted for reverse cycle operation during the defrost cycle. (One OEM refers to this as the integrated heating capacity.)

Air-Air Heat Pump Heating Capacity (MBtuh) Operating at 1,200 Cfm				
Outdoor Dry-Bulb (°F)	Entering Air Temperature (°F)			
	60	70	75	80
–3	10.1	9.8	9.7	9.6
2	12.3	12.0	11.8	11.7
7	14.6	14.2	14.0	13.7
12	16.8	16.3	16.1	15.8
17	19.1	18.5	18.2	17.9
22	19.8	19.2	18.9	18.6
27	20.5	19.9	19.6	19.3
32	21.2	20.6	20.3	20.0
37	21.9	21.3	21.0	20.6
42	22.6	22.0	21.6	21.3
47	32.5	31.5	31.0	30.5
52	34.7	33.7	33.1	32.6
57	36.9	35.8	35.3	34.7
62	39.2	38.0	37.4	36.8
67	41.4	40.2	39.5	38.9
72	43.7	42.3	41.7	41.0
Blower Cfm		1,050	1,200	1,350
Capacity adjustment		0.97	1.00	1.03

1) Heating values in the 17°F to 47°F range discounted for defrost cycles.
2) Heating values not adjusted (increased) for blower heat.

Figure A1-23

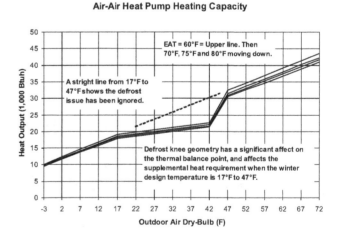

Figure A1-24

- A data sheet note should state whether or not the heat output values include blower heat.

  Values that do not include blower heat are conservative.

  Values that do include blower heat are based on a default value for blower watts (actual power when installed may be different).

- A graph similar to Figure A1-24 (previous page) shows an alternative way to summarize heating performance (some OEM's use a table, some use a graph).

This format is convenient because the practitioner only needs to draw the load-line for the dwelling to obtain a balance point diagram.

The jog in the heating capacity line represents the defrost effect. A straight line means that the OEM has not adjusted the performance data for defrost cycles.

Defrost Issues

A defrost adjustment for heating capacity applies (as far as data presentations are concerned) when the outdoor air temperature is 17°F to 47°F. This is known as the defrost knee.

- The size and shape (geometry) of the performance data defrost knee may be based on a default frosting condition specified by an AHRI standard, as shown by Figure A1-25.

- The size and shape of the defrost knee for an actual heat pump system installed in a given location may be similar to the OEM's knee, less severe (for a cold-dry winter), or more severe (for a lot of humid and wet winter hours when the outdoor temperature is 30°F to 40°F).

- Heating data that has a defrost knee should be used for the default thermal balance point diagram.

- When the geometry of the actual defrost knee is significantly different than indicated by OEM data, the actual balance point diagram will be different than the default balance point diagram.

The supplemental heat load is evaluated at the winter design temperature. Since defrost reduces net heating capacity, the supplemental heat load (electric heating coil KW) may be significantly effected when the winter design temperature is between 17°F and 47°F.

Defrost may occur when the outdoor temperature is less than 17°F, but OEM defrost knees do not show this relatively minor effect.

- In general, the defrost knee for the AHRI defrost condition is adequate for estimating the supplemental heat requirement (standard electric coil sizes, internal heat gain, and solar heat provide an adequate margin of safety).

Water-Air Equipment

Figure A1-26 (next page) provides an example of cooling data and compressor heat output for a water-air heat pump. Note that this data is conceptually identical to air-air data (Figures A1-22 and A1-23), except performance

Defrost Time is Conditional

Between 17°F and 47°F, defrost time is very sensitive to the wetness of the local climate, and the type of defrost control (time or demand). The figure below shows that the AHRI test chamber adjustment (HSPF test point) is about right when the outdoor air is relatively dry. It also shows that the defrost adjustment can be larger than the AHRI adjustment when the outdoor air is moderately cold and wet (Akron, Ohio, for example).

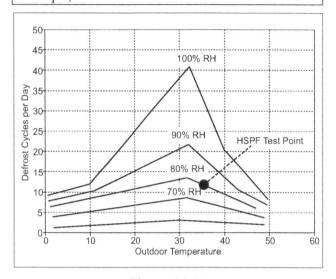

Figure A1-25

depends on entering water temperature (outdoor air temperature is not relevant), and there are no defrost issues for compressor heating.

- A data sheet must provide information on total capacity, sensible capacity and latent capacity. This OEM lists all three values. Coil sensible heat ratios may be computed when needed.

- A data sheet will show available blower speeds, or blower speed settings (multiple-speed settings for this PSC blower product).

- A data sheet must show a full range of entering water temperatures (40°F, 60°F, 80F and 100°F not shown to make Figure A1-26 more readable).

For water-loop systems, loop water temperature can range from below freezing to more than 110°F, depending on the climate, and the details of the piping loop design (see Appendix 9).

- A data sheet may show two or more water Gpm values (a third Gpm value was omitted to make Figure A1-26 more readable).

Gpm has a minor affect on cooling and heating capacity, but it is an important variable for water-loop design.

Pumping power and pumping cost increase as Gpm increases.

Water-side pressure drop values for each Gpm were omitted to make Figure A1-26 more readable (not relevant to capacity searches).

- A data sheet must show a range of entering wet-bulb temperatures.

The lowest value should be compatible with dry-coil cooling (59°F or lower). Not true for Figure A1-26, so when needed, a system designer would have to ask the OEM for the missing data.

The highest value should be compatible with a large moisture removal load (67°F, or higher).

- A data sheet must show a range of entering dry-bulb temperatures (70°F to 85°F, for example).

- A data sheet should show a power input (KW) value for each total capacity value (not relevant to capacity searches, not shown to make Figure A1-26 more readable).

- A data sheet note should state whether or not the cooling capacity values have been adjusted for blower heat (blower heat is a *Manual J* load when the data has not been adjusted for blower heat).

Ductless Equipment

Ductless equipment may be a one-to-one split cooling-only system, or heat pump system; a multi-split cooling-only system, or heat pump system; a packaged terminal air conditioner (PTAC), or packaged terminal heat pump (PTHP); or consumer equipment (a AHAM window or wall cooling unit, or heat pump). As far as basic heating-cooling performance is concerned, there is no difference between ductless equipment and central ducted equipment.

- Cooling equipment has sensible, latent, and total cooling capacity, and a coil sensible heat ratio.

- For air-air equipment, cooling capacity values depend on outdoor air temperature, indoor blower Cfm, entering wet-bulb temperature, and entering dry-bulb temperature.

- For heating, compressor heat output depends on outdoor air temperature, indoor blower Cfm, and entering dry-bulb temperature.

Ductless Multi-Split Equipment—Outdoor Unit

For ductless multi-split equipment, the sensible, latent and total cooling capacity, and the coil sensible heat ratio, and compressor heating capacity of the outdoor unit (where applicable), depend on the variables mentioned above. Since there are two or more indoor units, performance also depends on the system configuration.

Expanded Performance Data for a Water-Air HP
Blower Operating at 1,550 Cfm; 15% Methanol by Volume

EWT (°F)	Gpm	EAc db/wb (°F)	TC 1,000 Btuh	SC 1,000 Btuh	LC 1,000 Btuh	EAh db (°F)	HC 1,000 Btuh
30	6.0	75/63	~	~	~	60	33.8
		80/67	~	~	~	70	32.5
		85/71	~	~	~	80	31.3
	9.0	75/63	~	~	~	60	35.2
		80/67	~	~	~	70	33.9
		85/71	~	~	~	80	32.6
50	6.0	75/63	50.0	34.4	15.6	60	45.0
		80/67	54.3	35.8	18.5	70	43.4
		85/71	58.7	37.3	21.4	80	41.8
	9.0	75/63	50.5	34.1	16.4	60	47.2
		80/67	54.8	35.5	19.3	70	45.4
		85/71	59.2	36.9	22.3	80	43.7
70	6.0	75/63	45.8	33.4	12.4	60	57.6
		80/67	49.8	34.8	15.0	70	55.7
		85/71	53.8	36.1	17.7	80	53.8
	9.0	75/63	46.5	33.0	13.5	60	60.9
		80/67	50.5	34.4	16.1	70	58.9
		85/71	54.6	35.7	18.9	80	56.8
90	6.0	75/63	40.4	31.4	9.0	60	70.7
		80/67	43.9	32.7	11.2	70	68.7
		85/71	47.5	34.0	13.5	80	66.8
	9.0	75/63	41.1	31.7	9.4	60	75.4
		80/67	44.7	33.0	11.7	70	73.3
		85/71	48.3	34.3	14.0	80	71.2
110	6.0	75/63	35.6	29.2	6.4	60	~
		80/67	38.6	30.4	8.2	70	~
		85/71	41.7	31.6	10.1	80	~
	9.0	75/63	35.6	30.1	5.5	60	~
		80/67	38.7	31.4	7.3	70	~
		85/71	41.8	32.6	9.2	80	~

EWT = Entering water temperature, Gpm = gallons per minute.
EAc = Entering air for cooling (db = dry-bulb, wb = wet-bulb)
TC = Total cooling capacity, SC = Sensible cooling capacity
LC = Latent cooling capacity, EAh = Entering air db for heating
HC = Reverse cycle heating capacity

Blower Cfm Adjustment

Cfm	85%	90%	95%	100%	105%	110%	115%
TC	0.972	0.982	0.993	1.000	1.007	1.010	1.013
SC	0.926	0.948	0.974	1.000	1.027	1.055	1.066
HC	0.967	0.978	0.990	1.000	1.990	1.017	1.024

Figure A1-26

Appendx 1

Example of Authorized Multi Split Configurations			
Indoor Units Total Capacity at 95°F, 80°F, 67°F	Outdoor Unit Capacity (Btuh)		
	24,000	30,000	36,000
9,000 Btuh 12,000 Btuh 15,000 Btuh 18,000 Btuh 24,000 Btuh	9 + 9	9 + 9	9 + 9 + 9
	9 + 12	9 + 12	9 + 9 + 12
	9 + 15	9 + 15	9 + 9 + 15
	12 + 12	9 + 18	9 + 9 + 18
		9 + 24	9 + 9 + 24
		12 + 12	9 + 12 + 12
		12 + 15	9 + 12 + 15
		12 + 18	9 + 12 + 18
		15 + 15	9 + 15 + 18
		15 + 18	12 + 12 + 12
		18 + 18	12 + 12 + 15
		9 + 9 + 9	12 + 12 + 18
		9 + 9 + 12	12 + 15 + 18
		9 + 9 + 15	9 + 9 + 9 + 9
		9 + 9 + 18	9 + 9 + 9 + 12
			9 + 9 + 9 + 15
			9 + 9 + 12 + 12

1) System motors operating at rating speed.
2) Expanded performance data determines applied performance.

Figure A1-27

Multi-Split Cooling Data
Outdoor Unit: 30-MBH (30,600 Btuh rated total cooling capacity)
Indoor Units: Three 9-MBH (9,000 Btuh nominal rated cooling capacity)

System Cooling Capacity (Btuh)								
Entering Air (°F)		T/S Split	Outdoor Dry-Bulb (°F)				
			65	75	85	95	105	115
WB	DB	TC	31,170	30,000	28,730	28,010	22,960	16,690
59	72	SC	25,580	24,900	24,440	23,980	21,700	16,690
	76		29,470	29,010	28,320	28,010	22,960	16,690
	80		31,170	30,000	28,730	28,010	22,960	16,690
	84		31,170	30,000	28,730	28,010	22,960	16,690
	88		31,170	30,000	28,730	28,010	22,960	16,690
WB	DB	TC	32,490	31,280	29,960	29,310	23,400	16,970
63	72	SC	21,010	20,550	19,870	19,640	17,120	14,610
	76		24,900	24,440	23,980	23,520	21,240	16,970
	80		29,010	28,550	28,100	27,640	23,400	16,970
	84		32,490	31,280	29,960	29,310	23,400	16,970
	88		32,490	31,280	29,960	29,310	23,400	16,970
WB	DB	TC	33,790	32,540	31,170	30,600	23,770	17,200
67	72	SC	16,440	15,980	15,290	15,070	12,550	10,270
	76		20,320	19,870	19,410	19,180	16,670	14,150
	80		24,440	23,980	23,520	23,300	20,780	17,200
	84		28,550	28,100	27,410	27,180	23,770	17,200
	88		32,440	31,980	31,170	30,600	23,770	17,200
WB	DB	TC	35,020	33,730	32,320	31,860	24,020	17,350
71	72	SC	11,410	10,950	10,490	10,490	7,750	5,690
	76		15,520	15,070	14,610	14,380	11,640	9,580
	80		19,640	19,180	18,720	18,500	15,980	13,690
	84		23,520	23,070	22,610	22,610	19,870	17,350
	88		27,640	27,180	26,720	26,500	23,750	17,350

1) Total Cfm for indoor units = 1,177; specific values for refrigerant pipe length and rise.
2) Outdoor and indoor units operating at a declared motor speed.

Figure A1-28

- One outdoor unit serves a set of indoor units. OEM's provide tables that show authorized configurations (see Figure A1-27).
- The sensitivities of expanded cooling performance data for a given configuration must be similar to Figure A1-28.
- The sensitivities of expanded performance data for compressor heating must be similar to Figure A1-29 (next page).
- When heat pump equipment has an over-speed feature, expanded performance data for enhanced compressor speed may be used to construct a balance point diagram for heating as demonstrated by Figure A1-30 (next page).

Ductless Multi-Split Equipment - Indoor Unit

Data for indoor unit cooling capacity will be similar to Figure A1-28. That is, total capacity and sensible capacity depend on outdoor dry-bulb temperature, entering wet-bulb and dry-bulb temperature at the fan coil, and fan-coil Cfm. Data for indoor unit heating capacity would be similar to Figure A1-29. That is, heating capacity depends on outdoor dry-bulb temperature, the entering dry-bulb temperature at the fan coil, and fan-coil Cfm.

However, indoor unit capacity also depends on the size of the outdoor unit, the number of indoor units, the sizes of the indoor units, and the number of indoor units that are active at a given time, and on how each indoor unit is controlled (for refrigerant flow and blower speed). Mapping all possible permeations of outdoor units and indoor units for the entire range of operating conditions is a significant task. Therefore, OEM performance data for

Appendx 1

Multi-Split Heating Data				
Outdoor Unit: 31-MBH (30,600 Btuh rated total cooling capacity)				
Indoor Units: Three 9-MBH (9,000 Btuh nominal rated cooling capacity)				
Refrigerant Cycle Heating Capacity (Btuh)				
Outdoor Dry-Bulb (°F)	Indoor Dry-Bulb (°F)			
	60	65	70	75	80
0	18,270	18,260	18,230	18,200	18,150
3	18,860	18,850	18,820	18,790	18,740
8	20,260	20,250	20,230	20,200	20,150
13	21,720	21,710	21,680	21,650	21,600
18	23,310	23,300	23,280	23,240	23,190
23	24,970	24,960	24,940	24,910	24,850
28	26,690	26,690	26,660	26,630	26,570
33	28,460	28,450	28,430	28,400	28,340
38	30,190	30,190	30,170	30,140	30,080
43	32,020	32,020	32,000	31,960	31,900
48	33,850	33,850	33,840	33,800	33,740
53	35,680	35,680	35,670	35,630	35,570
58	37,420	37,430	37,420	37,380	37,320
63	39,190	39,200	39,190	39,160	39,100
65	39,870	39,880	39,880	39,850	39,790

1) Not adjusted for defrost (18°F to 48°F).
2) Total Cfm for indoor units = 1,130; specific values for refrigerant pipe length and rise.
3) Compressor operating at a rating motor speed.

Figure A1-29

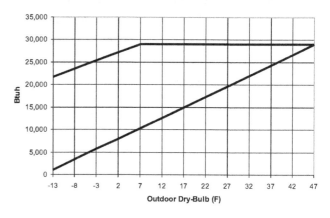

Figure A1-30

Air Delivery (Cfm) for a Five Speed Blower Blower Wheel Driven by a PSC Motor						
Unit Size	Blower Speed	External Static Pressure (IWC)				
		0.20	0.40	0.60	0.80	1.00
024	Low	721	611	-	-	-
	Low-Med	769	694	610	-	-
	Medium	882	812	736	651	-
	Med-High	971	916	851	775	681
	High	-	-	957	887	788
030	Low	828	759	-	-	-
	Low-Med	991	934	868	783	-
	Medium	1,091	1,041	983	910	785
	Med-High	1,189	1,144	1,091	1,027	912
	High	-	1,235	1,186	1,125	1,007
036	Low	1,025	906	-	-	-
	Low-Med	1,214	1,125	1,034	942	-
	Medium	1,370	1,276	1,179	1,078	971
	Med-High	-	1,416	1,314	1,206	1,083
	High	-	-	1,441	1,326	1,182

Tested with a dry cooling coil. Subtract pressure drops for a wet cooling coil, an electric heater, and a standard air filter.

Component Pressure Drop (IWC)				
Cfm	600	800	1,000	1,200	1,400
Wet cooling coil	0.01	0.02	0.02	0.04	0.03
Electric Coil	0.03	0.03	0.04	0.06	0.08
Standard Filter	0.03	0.05	0.08	0.12	0.16

For a speciality filter, substitute the pressure drop from the OEM's performance data.

Figure A1-31

indoor units may be limited to AHRI rated cooling capacity and AHRI rated heating capacity where applicable).

- The indoor units may all be in one zone, or shared by two or more zones.
- For single-zone applications, the expanded performance data for the complete system (Figures A1-28 and A1-29) is adequate.
- For zoned systems, the primary issue is that the total cooling capacity of the indoor unit is compatible with the total cooling load for the zone.
- For zoned systems, actual expanded performance data for an indoor unit, or an approximation of this data is useful. Section 11 and Section 12 provide procedures for ductless, split-coil equipment.

A1-10 Blower Performance Data

Blower performance data is a mandatory requirement for *Manual D* duct sizing calculations. OEM performance data for a given product normally includes a table or graph that summarizes blower performance.

- For the Figure A1-31 (previous page) exhibit, blower Cfm values and the corresponding external static pressure values are tabulated for five blower speeds (blowers with PSC motors typically have two to five speed settings).

Air Delivery (Cfm) for a Variable-Speed Blower
Blower Wheel Driven by a ECM Motor

Function	Cfm Set Point	ESP (IWC) Range	External Static Pressure (IWC)									
			0.10	0.20	0.30	0.40	0.50	0.60	0.70	0.80	0.90	1.00
Low Heat	735	0.0 – 0.5		735			725			~		
High Heat	1,180	0.0 – 1.0	1,160	1,165	1,175	1,180						1,175
Cooling Set-point Options	525	0.0 – 0.5		525			510			~		
	700	0.0 – 0.5		700		695	685			~		
	875	0.0 – 1.0	875					865	855	845		840
	1,050	0.0 – 1.0	1,050								1,045	1,035
	1,225	0.0 – 1.0	1,205	1,215	1,225							1,210
Maximum	1,400	0.0 – 1.0	1,395	1,400						1,385	1,360	1,310

There may be no footnotes concerning air-side components in place when blower was tested. When this is the case, the practitioner must scrutinize OEM literature for guidance on this matter (exactly what was in place when the blower was tested, and find pressure drop information for components that were not in place during the test). It may be necessary to call the OEM and ask for the information. Make no assumptions.

Figure A1-32

- For the Figure A1-32 exhibit, blower Cfm values and the corresponding external static pressure values are tabulated for eight Cfm set-points (blowers with ECM motors typically have multiple Cfm settings).
- Practitioners must pay close attention to blower table footnotes, as explained here:

Figure A1-31 shows that the heat pump's blower was tested with just a dry cooling coil in the indoor equipment cabinet, so when the duct system is designed (per Manual D procedures), the pressure drops for an electric heating coil and filter must be subtracted from the external statice pressure read from the blower table.

Figure A1-32 shows an example of a blower table that has no footnotes. Such presentation occurrences may be due to a lack of due diligence on the part of the OEM, or a conscious effort to make blower performance look better than it is. When such situations are encountered, practitioners must asked the OEM for the missing footnote information (it may, or may not, be in some other part of the OEM's engineering literature).

- For a PSC blower operating at a given speed, external static pressure decreases when undocumented components are installed in the blower cabinet.
- For an ECM blower operating at a Cfm set-point, blower speed increases when undocumented components are installed in the blower cabinet.

Blower speed controls try to hold the desired Cfm set-point.

The desired duct system Cfm will be maintained when the total resistance to airflow (cabinet components plus the pressure drop for the critical external circulation path) is less than the maximum blower pressure (for Figure A1-32, this is 0.5 IWC for low heat, and 1.0 IWC for all other options).

There may be undesirable consequences when the blower is driven to it's maximum pressure limit (less than the desired supply air Cfm, and/or an equipment problem).

A1-11 Component Pressure Drop Data

Air-side components are commonly installed in the equipment cabinet, or in plenums and duct runs. Components that were not in place when the blower was tested reduce the amount of pressure that is available to force air through duct fittings and straight duct runs. The *Manual D* Friction Rate Worksheet takes this into consideration, and provides a friction rate for airway sizing.

- OEM pressure drop data for cabinet components that were not in place when the blower was tested is required for *Manual D* calculations (the bottom of Figure A1-31 shows example pressure drops).
- OEM or vendor pressure drop data for components installed in duct runs (coil, filter, grille, diffuser, control damper, hand damper, etc.) is required for *Manual D* calculations.
- The sidebar on the next page summarizes the *Manual D* procedure for determining the duct slide rule friction rate value for airway sizing.

Appendx 1

A1-12 Performance Data Formats

OEMs publish expanded performance data for cooling and heating performance, blower data, and pressure drop data for air-side components in different formats. It may be that an OEM computer model, or an OEM authorized software product, accepts input pertaining to the operating conditions for a summer design day and a winter design day (where applicable), and returns cooling performance values and heating performance values (where applicable). Practitioners must study and properly apply the engineering guidance for the products they use.

Cooling Data Issues

A cooling data sheet may show total capacity values and coil sensible heat ratio values, or may show total capacity and sensible capacity values. Both formats provide total, sensible, and latent capacity values, and a sensible heat ratio value.

- Some tables have capacity data for two or more blower Cfm values. Some tables have capacity data for one mid-range Cfm value, and capacity adjustment factors for other Cfm values.

- The maximum and minimum values for outdoor air temperature (OAT) or entering water temperature (EWT), and the increment between the listed temperatures values vary from table to table. The values on a particular data sheet may not be adequate, or convenient, for some applications.

  Some locations have a summer design temperature that is less than 90°F, and possibly less than 85°F. Some locations have a summer design temperature that is more than 110°F, and possibly more than 115°F. Entering water temperature may range from less than 30°F to more than 100°F. Ten degree temperature jumps for OAT or EWT make interpolation more of an issue than five degree jumps.

- OEM tables show different ranges of entering wet-bulb (EWB) values. The values on a particular sheet may not be adequate for some applications.

  An EWB bulb value for a coil sensible heat ratio of 1.00 is needed for dry-coil applications. An EWB value for a relatively low coil sensible heat ratio (0.75 or lower) is needed for applications that have a relatively large latent load.

- OEM tables show different ranges of entering dry-bulb (EDB) values. The values on a particular data sheet may not be adequate for some scenarios.

  The entering dry-bulb temperature may be less than 70°F, or more than 80°F.

Manual D Friction Rate for Airway Sizing

Blower power must be adequate for the air flow resistance produced by all air-side components that are external to the OEM's blower data, and the air flow resistance produced by the duct fittings, and the straight duct runs in the duct system.

A circulation path is the supply air path from the blower to a room/space, plus the return path from the room/space, back to the blower. The critical circulation path is the path that has the largest pressure drop for the path's air flow rate (path Cfm).

- The various circulation paths are parallel paths. When the blower has enough power for the path that has the most air flow resistance (largest pressure drop), it has more than enough power for all other paths.

- Closing balancing dampers in the lower resistance paths makes blower power compatible with all circulation paths.

A filter, cooling coil, or electric heating coil are examples of components that may be installed in, or on, a furnace or air-handler cabinet. An item becomes an external component when it was not in place for the blower test (i.e., not relevant to the blower data).

A supply grille, a return grille, a balancing damper, a zone damper, and a duct coil are examples of external pressure dissipating components that may be installed in a circulation path.

Blower external static pressure (ESP) is the pressure that moves the air though all pressure dissipating items that are not relevant to the blower data.

Available static pressure (ASP) is the pressure that moves the air though the fittings and straight runs in the critical circulation path.

Available pressure equals external pressure minus the pressure dissipated by critical-path components that are not relevant to the blower data.

The available static pressure, and the total effective length (TEL) of the critical circulation path (fitting equivalent lengths plus straight run lengths), determine the friction rate value (pressure drop per 100 feet of duct) for duct air way sizing.

The *Manual D* Friction Rate Worksheet evaluates the preceding issues and determines when blower performance is compatible with the TEL of the critical circulation path. When blower performance is acceptable, the Friction Rate Worksheet provides a friction rate value for sizing every duct run in the duct system. Then the friction sizes are checked for air velocity, and a size is increased when the velocity is too high.

One OEM's tables are for 80°F entering dry-bulb, supplemented by sensible capacity adjustment factors for other dry-bulb temperatures. Serious errors occur when a practitioner fails to notice this when using the data. (The adjustment may range from about 2,000 Btuh to more than 5,000 Btuh, depending on circumstances.)

- Some OEM's provide expanded performance data for an indoor unit nominal capacity that is equally matched to the outdoor unit nominal capacity, and for larger and smaller indoor unit nominal capacities. Others only provide data for an equal match. When the outdoor and indoor nominal sizes are not compatible with the type of climate, the performance data may show a large amount of unneeded latent capacity. The sidebar starting on the right side of the previous page discusses this issue.

Heating Data Issues

Data sheets for refrigeration-cycle heat show compressor heating capacity values. These presentations may, or may not, account for the defrost knee.

- Some tables have capacity data for two or more blower Cfm values. Some tables have capacity data for one mid-range Cfm value, and capacity adjustment factors for other Cfm values.
- OEM tables show different ranges of entering dry-bulb (EDB) values. The values on a particular sheet may not be adequate for some applications.

    The entering dry-bulb temperature may be less than 65°F, or more than 75°F.

- Data that does not have an appropriate defrost knee may cause a significant error for the thermal balance point estimate, and will underestimate the supplemental heat requirement when the winter design temperature is in the 17°F to 47°F range.
- Some OEM's show heating performance as a heating capacity vs. outdoor air temperature table, or as a graph. A graph is the more convenient format because one can readily see the shape of the defrost knee, and because a thermal balance point diagram is easily produced by drawing a straight, heating load vs. OAT line on the graph.

Capacity Control Issues

Compressor and/or blower motor speed may be staged or modulated, a heating burner may be staged or modulated. It is appropriate, and necessary, that OEM expanded performance data shows how output capacity varies with staging controls, or modulating controls.

There is only one data set for equipment that operates at one compressor speed, so there is no question about which data set to use for equipment sizing. Since multi-speed and variable-speed equipment may have two or more sets of performance data, the data set that must be used for equipment sizing is specified here:

Single Compressor Speed Equipment

For single-speed equipment, there is one compressor speed and a corresponding data set. There fore, expanded cooling performance data for the only possible compressor speed must be used for equipment sizing.

Variable Blower Speed with No Capacity Control

For the equipment sizing procedures in this standard, equipment that operates at one compressor speed is single-speed equipment, regardless of the technology used to control indoor blower speed, and outdoor fan speed for air-air equipment.

- Compressor speed staging or modulation has a dramatic effect on system performance, as far as compressor run time at part-load is concerned.
- Blower/fan speed modulation may have a useful effect on compressor run time at part-load, but this is not equivalent to the benefit offered by compressor speed control.

Two Compressor Speed Equipment

For two or more distinct compressor speeds, there may be performance data for each compressor speed (typically low, or stage-one speed; and high, or stage-two speed). The expanded cooling performance data for high-speed (full compressor capacity) shall be used for equipment sizing.

Variable Compressor Speed Equipment

At this time (Year 2014), data presentation for variable compressor speed equipment (that typically uses inverter technology), varies with the product. There could be data exhibits for maximum capacity, an intermediate capacity, and minimum capacity. A given OEM may provide all three sets, a maximum-minimum set, or just the data for maximum capacity; or no data at all (just the AHRI rating values).

Per the Section N1-1 definition, full capacity is the capacity for the compressor speed used for the AHRI rating test for cooling and for heat pump heating. It may be that maximum capacity is the same as full capacity, or it may be that maximum capacity is for a compressor speed that exceeds the value used for a AHRI rating test (i.e., for the maximum compressor speed allowed by the OEM's design).

For this document, enhanced speed refers to compressor speeds that exceed the speed used for the AHRI rating test for heating or cooling. Enhanced speed may, or may not, be available on a continuous basis (i.e., enhanced speed may have a time limit triggered by a monitored refrigeration-side, electric power, or motor heat variable).

Appendx 1

The expanded cooling performance data for the compressor speed used for the AHRI rating test that produces the advertised value for AHRI total cooling capacity must be used for equipment sizing. The actual compressor speed value used for the rating test is of interest, but this information is not required for equipment sizing.

- The AHRI rating test is common to all products.
- Product SEER is based on the AHRI rating test.
- This eliminates questions pertaining to what maximum or full capacity terminology actually means.
- This eliminates questions pertaining to enhanced speed availability, and endurance.
- This eliminates questions about actual compressor speed values.

Blower Data Issues

Blower data may be presented as a table or graph. Either way, obvious and comprehensive footnotes are required so the practitioner knows what air-side components were in place when the blower was tested.

- *Manual D* Third Edition, Section 2 shows that the system operating point can only occur at the intersection of the blower curve and duct curve.
- The graphical format is more convenient for investigating the effect of a blower speed change because a blower table, by itself, cannot be used to evaluate the system Cfm consequence of a blower speed change.
- Superimposing a duct system resistance curve on an OEMs blower performance graph, shows the system balance point, the system Cfm, and the system pressure drop.

Air-Side Component Data Issues

Pressure drop vs. Cfm data for air-side components may be presented as a table or graph. A graph is more convenient because it eliminates any need for interpolation. This information is required for duct system design.

A1-13 Standard Formats

Appendix 4 provides *Manual S* suggestions for standard data presentation formats for cooling and heating equipment. Standard formats are desirable because one training experience would apply to any product.

A1-14 Alternative to Published Data

For cooling-only equipment, and for heat pumps, the equipment sizing goal is to show that equipment latent and sensible capacities are compatible with *Manual J* cooling loads when the equipment operates at summer

AHRI Rating Data — Test Chamber Performance		
Air-Air Equipment	Cooling	Total cooling capacity (Btuh) for 95°F outdoor air, 80°F entering air dry-bulb, and 67°F entering air wet-bulb, and a SEER value.
	Heating	Heating capacity (Btuh) for 47°F outdoor air, 70°F entering air dry-bulb temperature, and a HSPF value.

Equipment selection and in-situ performance issues:
1) No blower Cfm value for duct design.
2) No sensible and latent capacity values for comparison with sensible and latent loads.
3) Sensible, latent, and total capacity depend on outdoor dry-bulb, entering wet-bulb, entering dry-bulb, and blower Cfm, actual installed values can be (and usually are) different than the test chamber values.
4) A heating value for 47°F outdoor air temperature may be useful for some southern Florida locations and most of Hawaii, but has no relevance to the rest of the USA.
5) A heating Btuh vs. outdoor dry-bulb graph (with defrost knee) is required for a balance point diagram.
6) SEER and HSPF are based on test chamber scenarios that may be quite different than the operating conditions for a specific dwelling in a given location.
7) Genesis (DOE, Federal Register) documents show that HSPF depends on the climate zone. The HSPF for AHRI listing is for weather that is similar to Pittsburgh, PA. The HSPF value can be significantly lower or higher for other climate zones.
8) The HSPF calculation is based on a heating load for Pittsburgh type weather. The value used is much lower than what would be normal for this climate zone. This affects the thermal balance point, and minimizes the amount of supplemental heat for cold weather, and maximizes the published HSPF value.

Water-Air Equipment	Cooling	Total cooling capacity (Btuh) for 85°F entering water and 95°F exiting water, 80°F entering air dry-bulb, and 67°F entering air wet-bulb, and an EER value.
	Heating	Heating capacity (Btuh) for 70°F entering water, and 70°F entering air temperature, and a COP value.

Equipment selection and in-situ performance issues:
1) No blower Cfm value for duct design.
2) No sensible and latent capacity values for comparison with sensible and latent loads.
3) Sensible, latent, and total capacity depend on entering water temperature, entering wet-bulb, entering dry-bulb, and blower Cfm, actual installed values can be (and usually are) different than the test chamber values.
4) Cooling values for 85°F entering water do not generally apply to once-through systems, and only apply to loop systems for a few days, twice a year. Heating values for 70°F entering water do not generally apply to once-through systems, and only apply to loop systems for a few days, twice a year.
5) A heating Btuh vs. outdoor dry-bulb graph (for the coldest EWT for the heating season) is required for a balance point diagram.
6) For once-through piping, EER depends on the local ground water temperature. For loop piping, EER depends on the seasonal average water temperature for cooling.
7) For once-through piping, COP depends on the local ground water temperature. For loop piping, EER depends on the seasonal average water temperature for heating.

Figure A1-33

design conditions. The OEM verification path may be used when published expanded performance data is not commonly available to an OEM-authorized audience, when available data is incomplete for intended equipment use, or when an authorized party needs help with, and/or confirmation of, available data use (see Section N3).

A1-15 AHRI-Certification Data

The rating information that appears in the Air Conditioning, Heating and Refrigeration Institute (AHRI) **Certified Products Directory**, or on OEM data sheets, applies to test chamber performance, per operating conditions specified by an AHRI testing standards. The rating information for air-air equipment and water-air equipment is summarized by Figure A1-33 (previous page).

Figure A1-33 also explains why rating data must not be used to select and size cooling equipment and heat pumps. This mandate is defended here:

- Equipment performance depends on blower Cfm.

    *Note that the Cfm that is appropriate for the **Manual J** loads is the Cfm for **Manual D** duct airway sizing.*

- The design values for indoor temperature and indoor humidity are maintained when latent cooling capacity matches the latent cooling load, and sensible cooling capacity matches the sensible cooling load.

    Total capacity may be used to size equipment when there is no latent load (because sensible capacity equals total capacity).

    Latent and sensible capacity values must be used when there is a latent load.

- **Manual J**, Table 1A and Table 1B show that outdoor dry-bulb and wet-bulb temperatures for cooling can be significantly different than the AHRI rating condition. They also show that outdoor dry-bulb temperature for heating is not even close to 47°F for most locations.

    The local summer dry-bulb temperature affects air-air condenser performance, and may affect the entering air dry-bulb and wet-bulb temperatures when there is a return duct load, and/or an engineered ventilation load.

    The local summer wet-bulb temperature may affect the entering air wet-bulb temperature when there is a return duct load and/or an engineered ventilation load.

    *When there is no return duct load, and/or ventilation load, the entering air dry-bulb for cooling is likely to be less than 80°F, and the entering air wet-bulb is likely to be less than 67°F (the **Manual J** default is 75°F/63°F for a wet-coil, or 75°F DB, and 59°F WB or less for a dry-coil.*

    *The winter design dry-bulb temperature determines the worst-case scenario for heat pump heating (maximum **Manual J** load, minimum compressor heat), and may affect the entering dry-bulb temperature (when there is a return duct load, and/or an engineered ventilation load).*

- For water-air equipment, the entering water temperature value may be relatively constant for the whole year, or may have a large swing during the year. This depends on the type of water system.

    For once-though systems, ground water temperature varies significantly, depending on location.

    For buried pipe-loop systems, entering water temperature may vary from below freezing to more than 100°F during the year (depending on location and piping loop design).

- Expanded performance data published by OEMs show large variations in equipment performance as operating conditions change.

    For cooling, see Figure A1-22 (air-air equipment) and Figure A1-26 (water-air equipment).

    For heating, see Figure A1-23 (air-air equipment) and Figure A1-26 (water-air equipment).

- A thermal balance point diagram is produced by plotting compressor heat output vs. outdoor air temperature and the heating load-line on the same graph.

    The default heating load-line runs from the winter design condition to zero load at 65°F.

    The thermal balance point diagram determines the design value for supplemental heat.

    The thermal balance point value is a parameter of interest for system designers, and people that produce codes, regulations and standards.

    The thermal balance point value has significant affect on seasonal efficiency.

    A thermal balance point diagram is required for air-air equipment, and for water-air equipment.

- A thermal balance point with a defrost knee is required for air-air equipment.

    It takes more than one point to draw a heating capacity vs. outdoor temperature line.

    It takes more than two points (17°F and 47°F) to draw a heating capacity line with a defrost knee.

- For water-air equipment, one performance point may be used to draw a horizontal capacity line on a thermal balance point graph.

    The default heating load-line runs from the winter design condition to zero load at 65°F.

The heating capacity line is for the coldest entering water temperature for the heating season.

Defrost is not an issue.

- Momentary equipment efficiency (EER and COP) depends on the momentary loads (including defrost, where applicable) and the corresponding operating conditions, the momentary heat/cool output and corresponding power draw, and a cycling penalty; and other details, such as the type of defrost control. Integrating momentary performance over seasonal time produces a seasonal efficiency value (in EER/COP terms, or SEER/HSPF terms).

- Seasonal efficiency (SEER/HSPF) for a given dwelling in a particular location, with a given piece of equipment, will normally be different than indicated by the advertised rating values.

The actual climate may be significantly different than the climate model for the efficiency rating calculation.

The actual heating-cooling loads may be significantly different than the defaults used for the rating test, and efficiency rating calculation.

The seasonal effect of the actual operating variables may be significantly different than the models used for the rating test, and efficiency rating calculation.

The actual cycling degradation coefficient and defrost penalty may be significantly different than the models used for the rating test, and efficiency rating calculation.

A1-16 Degree Day Data

Per Table N2-2, the limit for excess cooling capacity for heat pump equipment depends on the ratio of heating degree days to the base 65°F (HDD-65) to the cooling degree days to the base 50°F (CDD-50). A significant increase in excess total cooling capacity is allowed when this ratio is 2.0, or more, providing that the sensible heat ratio for the total and sensible cooling loads for the summer design condition is 0.95, or greater. The Condition B sizing rule for heat pump equipment applies when the answer to both questions is yes.

Degree day information is provided by the sources listed below. This data is not homogenized. For a given location, there will be differences in the degree day ratio, depending on the source of the data. This is not an issue for locations that are decidedly cold, or decidedly warm, but it is an issue for locations that are at the tipping point for the 2.0 DD-ratio test.

Figure A1-34 provides an example of the degree day values and degree day ratios, for the Boise, ID, area. Note that the results of the degree day ratio test are exactly opposite, depending on the data source. Also note that the NOAA data has degree day values for three nearby locations, vs. one location for the ASHRAE data. All of these locations are close to each other, and the consensus per the Figure A1-34 ratios, is that the Boise area qualifies for the Condition B sizing rule.

Degree Day Data Comparison For Bosie, ID, and Vicinity				
ASHRAE Note 1	Boise Air Port	Caldwell	Lucky Peak Dam	7N Station
HDD-65	5,658	5,698	~	~
CDD-50	3,036	2,624	~	~
DD Ratio	1.86	2.13	~	~
NOAA Note 2	Boise Air Port	Caldwell	Lucky Peak Dam	7N Station
HDD-65	5,727	5,606	5,730	6,325
CDD-50	2,856	3,119	2,840	2,527
DD Ratio	2.01	1.80	2.02	2.50

1) CD-ROM in back of the in the 2009 ASHRAE Handbook of Fundamentals.
2) NOAA: Annual Degree Days to Selected Bases, 1971-2000; Climatography of the United States No. 81; Supplement No. 2

Figure A1-34

ASHRAE Weather Data

Climatic design information (including degree day data) for 5,564 locations, as provided by a CD-ROM in back of the in the 2009 ASHRAE Handbook of Fundamentals (or the latest version of this data base). To access this data, load Chapter 14 from the ASHRAE CD, and click on the following link in the first paragraph of Chapter 14.

The complete data tables for all 5,564 stations are contained on the CD-ROM that accompanies this book.

Or use the computer's operating system to open CD files. Right-click on the CD, and use Explore command to open the Program Files Folder. Double left-click (DLC) on this folder, DLC on the ASHRAE folder, DLC on the 2009 ASHRAE Handbook folder, DLC on the Stations folder, DLC on the StaList_P.pdf file; then find the state of interest, then DLC on the town of interest.

NOAA Degree Day Data

Heating and cooling degree day values for various base temperatures are provided by the following NOAA document. This may be down loaded from the NOAA web site at no cost.

Annual Degree Days to Selected Bases, 1971-2000;

Climatography of the United States No. 81; Supplement No. 2; National Climate Data Center, Asheville N.C.

http://cdo.ncdc.noaa.gov/climatenormals/clim81_supp/CLIM81_Sup_02.pdf.

This appendix is not part of the this standard. It is merely informative and does not contain requirements necessary for conformance to the standard. It has not been processed according to the ANSI requirements for a standard, and may contain material that has not been subject to public review or a consensus process. Unresolved objectors on informative material are not offered the right to appeal at ACCA or ANSI.

Appendix 2

Entering Air Calculations

Appendix 1, Figures A1-5, A1-7, A1-9 and A1-10 provide a quick way to estimate entering dry-bulb and wet-bulb temperatures for a limited set of circumstances. This appendix provides procedures that produce a solution for a particular set of circumstances.

A2-1 Summary of Procedure

For cooling, the dry-bulb and wet-bulb temperatures of the air that enters the indoor coil depends on the condition of the air at the return grille, the sensible and latent return duct loads (where applicable), and the sensible and latent outdoor air loads (where applicable). This also applies to the entering air dry-bulb temperature for heat pump heating. Proceed as follows:

Adjust for altitude for locations above sea level (use altitude sensitive psychrometric software).

1) Determine the dry-bulb and wet-bulb temperatures at the return grille (see Section A2-2).

Note: When there are no return duct loads and no engineered ventilation loads (outdoor air is not mixed with return air), these are the dry-bulb and wet-bulb values for entering air (steps 2 and 3 do not apply).

2) When there is a return duct load, determine the dry-bulb and wet-bulb temperatures at the exit of the return duct.

a) Determine the sensible and latent loads for the return-side of the duct system (see Section A2-3).

b) Convert return duct loads to a dry-bulb temperature rise and a wet-bulb temperature rise (see Section A2-4).

c) Add the return duct rise to the temperature at the return grille to find the dry-bulb and wet-bulb temperatures at the exit of the main return trunk.

Note: When there are no engineered ventilation loads (outdoor air is not mixed with return air), these are the DB and WB values for entering air (step 3 does not apply).

3) Determine the dry-bulb and wet-bulb temperatures of the outdoor air, return air, mixture.

- See Section A2-6 for no heat recovery.
- See Section A2-7 with heat recovery.

A2-2 Dry-Bulb and Wet-Bulb at the Return Grille

The dry-bulb and wet-bulb temperatures at the return grille depend on the design values for indoor air dry-bulb and relative humidity. Then, altitude sensitive psychrometric software provides a wet-bulb temperature value, and a humidity ratio (Grains/Lb) value.

- The indoor dry-bulb temperature and relative humidity values are the same as the load calculation values for the summer design conditions.
- When the **Ma***nual J* calculation shows no latent load for 45% RH indoors, the indoor coil will be dry for the summer design condition (assuming correct equipment selection and size for the climate), and the indoor humidity will be less than 45% RH.
- When there is no latent load on the indoor coil, the entering wet-bulb temperature defaults to the value that produces a coil sensible heat ratio of 1.00 (no latent capacity) when expanded performance data is used to select cooling equipment.

A2-3 Return Duct Loads

Manual J (unabridged Eighth Edition, versions 2.00 and later) duct tables provide performance values for the entire duct system that is described in the table's heading. When these values are processed by *Manual J* Worksheet G, it returns a heat loss factor, a sensible gain factor, and a latent cooling load value for the entire duct system, based on the duct surface areas listed in a duct table. Worksheet G also provides duct performance factors for the actual duct surface areas (from the drawing board, or field measured).

Worksheet G is modified to accommodate the purposes of the procedures in this manual. This revised version of Worksheet G will appear in future versions of *Manual J*. Appendix 21 provides a blank copy of Worksheet G.

Figure A2-1 (next page) shows Worksheet G calculations for a radial duct system in a vented attic under a dark shingle roof (*Manual J* Table 7B-R; 2,500 SqFt floor area; 0°F winter, 95°F and 40 Δgrains summer. The duct has R-4 insulation and has not been sealed (0.35 Cfm/SqFt supply-side leakage, and 0.70 Cfm/SqFt return-side leakage).The installed supply duct surface area is 350 SqFt, and the installed return duct surface area is 115 SqFt (as measured, or estimated by the practitioner).

The left side of Figure A2-1 shows Worksheet G calculations for the entire duct system. Note that the default supply and return areas from *Manual J* Table 7B-R are 312 SqFt and 95 SqFt. In this case the duct loads are adjusted for the actual installed surface areas (350 SqFt of supply duct, and 115 SqFt of return duct).

Appendx 2

- The heat loss factor for the entire duct system is 0.469.
- The sensible gain factor for the entire duct system is 0.643.
- The latent cooling load value for the entire duct system is 2,871 Btuh.
- These duct load factors and latent load value are large because duct efficiency is poor (R4 is mediocre, and 0.35/0.70 leakage is unacceptable).

The right side of Figure A2-1 shows Worksheet G calculations for the return-side of the duct system. Note that the supply-side surface areas have been set to zero.

- The heat loss factor for the return-side of the duct system is 0.160.

  Multiply the heating load for the space served by the duct system by the return-side heat loss factor to obtain a heating load for the return duct. For example, when the space heating load is 52,000 Btuh (per line 14 on the J1 form), the heating load for the return-side of the duct system is 0.160 x 52,000 = 8,320 Btuh.

- The sensible gain factor for the return-side of the duct system is 0.219.

  Multiply the sensible cooling load for the space served by the duct system by the return-side heat gain factor to obtain a cooling load for the return duct. For example, when the sensible space load is 25,000 Btuh (per line 14 on the J1 form), the sensible cooling load for the return-side of the duct system is 0.219 × 25,000 = 5,475 Btuh.

- The latent cooling load value for the return-side of the duct system is 2,190 Btuh.

- When the efficiency of this duct system is improved to R8 with 0.12/0.24 leakage, the sensible and latent return duct loads are dramatically reduced:

  8,320 heating Btuh drops to 2,635 Btuh

  5,475 sensible cooling Btuh drops to 1,620 Btuh

  2,190 latent cooling Btuh drops to 751 Btuh

A2-4 Dry-Bulb and Wet-Bulb at the Exit of the Return Duct

The sensible heat equation (below) converts a sensible return duct load (sensible Btuh) to a dry-bulb gain, or dry-bulb loss (± DT). Then for cooling and heating, the dry-bulb temperature of the air that exits the return duct equals the indoor dry-bulb temperature plus the return duct gain.

Indoor DB = Given
$\Delta T\ (°F) = \pm$ **Sensible Btuh / (1.1 x ACF x R_{Cfm})**
Exiting DB = Indoor DB $\pm \Delta T$

Worksheet G - Return Duct Loads

Duct Table Number	Case Number	Look-Up Floor Area (SqFt)	SAT (°F) Heating	99% (°F) Dry-Bulb	1% (°F) Dry-Bulb	Table 1 ΔGrains
7B-R	1	2,500	100	0	95	40

Step 1) Enter base-case load factors and latent heat value from Table 7 (eyeball interpolation is acceptable)

		Supply and Return Ducts			Return-Side Only	
	Base-case factors from duct table			Copy the base-case supply and return duct values		
1	Heat loss factor =	0.170		Heat loss factor =	0.170
2	Sensible gain factor =	0.220		Sensible gain factor =	0.220
3	Latent gain (Btuh) =	601		Latent gain (Btuh) =	601

Step 2) R-Value Correction (WIF) — Copy the WIF supply and return duct values

4	R-Value	For heat loss =	1.370		Heat loss =	1.370
5	4	For sensible gain =	1.330		Sensible gain =	1.330
6		Adjusted heat loss factor =	0.233	< Line 1 factor x line 4 adjustment	Adj loss fact =	0.233
7		Adjusted sensible gain factor =	0.293	< Line 2 factor x line 5 adjustment	Adj sens fact =	0.293

Step 3) Leakage Rate Correction (LCF) — Copy the LCF supply and return duct values

8	Cfm / SqFt	For heat loss =	1.750		Heat loss =	1.750
9	0.35	< SSL Sensible gain =	1.910		Sensible gain =	1.910
10	0.70	< RSL Latent gain =	4.020		Latent gain =	4.020
11		Adjusted heat loss factor =	0.408	< Line 6 factor x line 8 adjustment	Adj loss fact =	0.408
12		Adjusted sensible gain factor =	0.559	< Line 7 factor x line 9 adjustment	Adj sens fact =	0.559
13		Adjusted latent gain (ALG) =	2,416	< Line 3 value x line 10 adjustment	ALG =	2,416

Step 4) Surface Area Adjustment (duct surface area units = SqFt, and Kr = 1 - Ks)

14	Installed supply area =	350	DSF for MJ8 Sect 23-18 shortcut	Installed supply area = Zero	0.00
15	Default (Table 7) supply area =	312		Default supply area = Zero	0.00
16	Rs = Installed area / default area =	1.122		Rs = Zero	0.00
17	Installed return area =	115		Copy the installed return area =	115
18	Default (Table 7) return area (DFR) =	95		Copy the default return area (DFR) =	95
19	Rr = Installed area / default area =	1.211		Copy the Rr value =	1.211
20	Ks = 0.676 Kr =	0.324		Copy Ks = 0.676 Copy Kr =	0.324
21	SAA (heating and sensible cooling) =	1.151	< Ks x Rs + Kr x Rr >		0.392
22	RSL (default return-side latent gain) =	1,809	< 0.68 x DFR x RSL x ΔGrains >		1,809
23	LGA (latent gain adjustment) =	1.188	< Rr x RSL / ALG + Rs x (ALG - RSL) / ALG >		0.906
24	Effective heat loss factor (EHLF) =	0.469	< Line 11 Factor x Line 21 SAA value >		0.160
25	Effective sensible gain factor (ESGF) =	0.643	< Line 12 Factor x Line 21 SAA value >		0.219
26	Effective latent gain Btuh (ELG) =	2,871	< Line 13 gain x Line 22 LGA adjustment >		2,190

Figure A2-1

Default Outdoor Air Fraction

Floor Area SqFt	Outdoor Air Cfm [1]	Blower Cfm [2]		OA Fraction [3]	
		Low	Medium	Low Cfm	Med Cfm
1,000	47	400	500	0.12	0.09
2,000	93	800	1,000	0.12	0.09
3,000	140	1,200	1,500	0.12	0.09
4,000	187	1,600	2,000	0.12	0.09
5,000	233	2,000	2,500	0.12	0.09
6,000	280	2,400	3,000	0.12	0.09

1) 0.35 ACH outdoor air for an 8 Ft ceiling height.
2) 1,000 SqFt/ Ton of total cooling capacity; 400 to 500 Cfm/Ton.
3) Outdoor air fraction = Outdoor Air Cfm/ Blower Cfm.

Figure A2-2

Where:
ACF is an altitude correction factor (see Figure A5-1)
R_{Cfm} = Return air Cfm = Blower Cfm—Outdoor Air Cfm
Return air Cfm may be equal to the blower Cfm, or somewhat larger or smaller. For the purpose of this calculation, R_{Cfm} defaults to blower Cfm minus outdoor air Cfm.

For cooling, altitude sensitive psychrometrics provides an indoor humidity ratio value (grains of moisture per pound of air), based on the indoor dry-bulb and relative humidity values. Then, the latent heat equation (below), converts a latent return duct load (latent Btuh) to a grains of moisture gain (DGR). Then, the exiting grains value equals the indoor grains value plus the latent moisture gain.

Indoor Grains = Psychrometric value
ΔGR *= Latent Load Btuh / 1.1 x ACF x* R_{Cfm}
Exiting Grains = Indoor Grains + ΔGR

For cooling, altitude sensitive psychrometrics converts an exiting dry-bulb temperature and grains value to a exiting wet-bulb temperature, and converts an indoor dry-bulb temperature and relative humidity value to an entering wet-bulb temperature. The wet-bulb rise (ΔWB) equals the difference between the two wet-bulb values.

Exiting WB = Psychrometric value
Indoor WB = Given psychrometric state point
ΔWB *= Exiting WB - Indoor WB*

A2-5 Outdoor Air Fraction

The outdoor air fraction (OAF) for a specific installation depends on the blower Cfm and the outdoor air Cfm used by the practitioner.

OAF = Outdoor Cfm / Blower Cfm

For *Manual J* Table 8, the default value for outdoor air is 0.35 air changes per hour (ACH). This translates to about 10% percent outdoor air for efficient construction that has adequate exposure diversity (i.e., the aggregate fenestration load does not have a significant peak during some hour of the day). Figure A2-2 (previous page) summarizes this concept.

- Blower Cfm is determined when the equipment is selected and sized.
- Outdoor air Cfm depends on the local code/utility requirement. When the local code does not address the issue, good practice is defined by model codes and indoor air quality standards.

A2-6 Entering Dry-Bulb and Wet-Bulb Temperatures for Raw Air Ventilation

Entering air may be a mixture of return air and raw outdoor air. For cooling, altitude sensitive psychrometrics provides dry-bulb and wet-bulb temperatures for mixed air. For heating, an equation provides a dry-bulb value.

- The mixed air calculation for cooling depends on the outdoor air fraction, the dry-bulb and wet-bulb temperatures of the outdoor air, and the dry-bulb and wet-bulb temperatures of the air at the exit of the return duct.
- The outdoor air fraction for cooling and heating is determined by the practitioner (subject to codes, regulations, and good practice procedures).

Mixed Air DB/WB for 10% OA with no Heat Recovery				
Outdoor Air at 95°F DB and 75°F WB				
RA DB 75°F	MA DB °F		MA WB °F	
RA WB °F	Sea Level	2,500 Ft	Sea Level	2,500 Ft
59	77.0	77.0	60.800	60.809
61			62.547	62.553
63			64.302	Note 3
65			66.066	
67			67.836	
RA DB 77°F	MA DB °F		MA WB °F	
RA WB	Sea Level	2,500 Ft	Sea Level	2,500 Ft
59	78.8	78.8	60.806	60.814
61			62.552	62.559
63			64.307	Note 3
65			66.069	
67			67.839	
RA DB 79°F	MA DB °F		MA WB °F	
RA WB	Sea Level	2,500 Ft	Sea Level	2,500 Ft
59	80.6	80.6	60.812	60.820
61			62.557	62.563
63			64.311	Note 3
65			66.072	
67			67.842	
RA DB 81°F	MA DB °F		MA WB °F	
RA WB	Sea Level	2,500 Ft	Sea Level	2,500 Ft
59	82.4	82.4	60.818	60.826
61			62.562	62.568
63			64.314	Note 3
65			66.076	
67			67.844	

1) OA = Outdoor air, RA = Return air; MA = Mixed air.
2) Raw outdoor air mixed with air leaving the return duct.
3) RA WB will be 61°F or less at 2,500 feet or higher (space humidity will be 45% RH or less with no summer humidification).

Figure A2-3

- The cooling load calculation determines elevation, and the dry-bulb and wet-bulb temperatures of the outdoor air (per *Manual J*, Tables 1A or 1B).
- The cooling load calculation determines the sensible and latent return duct loads, which determine the condition of the air leaving the return duct (see Sections A2-2, A2-3 and A2-4).
- For cooling, Figure A2-3 (previous page) shows mixed air conditions (psychrometric output) for 95°F DB and 75°F WB outdoors, and a variety of return air conditions at sea level, and at 2,500 feet.
- For heating, this equation determines the mixed air dry-bulb temperature (MAT), where RA_{db} and

OA_{db} are return air and outdoor air temperatures, and OAF is the outdoor air fraction.

$$MAT\ (°F) = RA_{db} \times (1 - OAF) + OA_{db} \times OAF$$

A2-7 Entering Dry-Bulb and Wet-Bulb Temperatures for Heat Recovery Ventilation

Entering air may be a mixture of return air and processed outdoor air. For this scenario, heat recovery equations and altitude sensitive psychrometrics provide dry-bulb and wet-bulb temperatures for mixed air.

- For cooling, the mixed air condition depends on the outdoor air fraction, the dry-bulb and wet-bulb temperatures of the outdoor air, the dry-bulb and wet-bulb temperatures of the air exiting the return duct, and the sensible and latent effectiveness of the heat recovery equipment.

- For heating, the mixed air temperature depends on the outdoor air fraction, the dry-bulb temperature of the outdoor air, the dry-bulb temperature of the air at the exit of the return duct, and the sensible effectiveness of the heat recovery equipment.

- The outdoor air fraction is determined by the practitioner (subject to codes, regulations and good judgement).

- The outdoor design conditions for a cooling load calculation determines local elevation, and the dry-bulb and wet-bulb temperatures of the outdoor air (per *Manual J*, Tables 1A or 1B).

- The load calculation determines the sensible and latent return duct loads for cooling, and the sensible load for heating, which determines the condition of the air leaving the return duct (see Sections A2-2, A2-3 and A2-4).

- The sensible and latent effectiveness rating of the heat recovery equipment is determined by the practitioner (inspect OEM data).

Condition of Processed Air for Cooling

The heat recovery effectiveness (E) for cooling determines the condition of the ventilation air that leaves the heat recovery equipment (discharge air). These equations provide state point values for discharge air (DA).

$$DA_{db} = OA_{db} - E_{sen} \times (OA_{db} - RA_{db})$$
$$DA_{gr} = OA_{gr} - E_{lat} \times (OA_{gr} - RA_{gr})$$

Where:
DA_{db} = Discharge air dry-bulb temperature
OA_{db} = Outdoor air dry-bulb temperature
RA_{db} = Return air dry-bulb temperature
DA_{gr} = Discharge air grains
OA_{gr} = Outdoor air grains
RA_{gr} = Return air grains

Figures A2-3 and A2-4 show mixed air conditions for sea level and 2,500 feet. Note that the mixed dry-bulb temperature is not sensitive to altitude, and that the mixed wet-bulb temperature is relatively insensitive to altitude (even when the altitude exceeds 2,500 feet).

- Altitude does affect the return air wet-bulb temperature because return duct leakage produces a negative latent load at 2,500 feet or higher.

  *At elevation, **Manual J** Table 1 typically shows zero or negative grains difference values for 45% RH.*

  A few locations in a few states are exceptions when the elevation is 2,500 to 3,200 feet (see Hawaii, Kansas, Montana, Nebraska, Texas and West Virginia).

- When the indoor coil is dry at altitude, the relative humidity of the return air will be less than 45% RH, and it's wet-bulb temperature will be less than 61°F, and may be less than 59°F.

- When the indoor coil is dry, the entering wet-bulb temperature defaults to a value that is compatible with a dry-coil.

  The expanded performance data published by OEMs correlates coil sensible heat ratio (sensible capacity / total capacity) with entering wet-bulb values.

  The coil is dry when the coil sensible heat ratio is 1.00.

  Some versions of OEM data stop at 63°F WB. This may not be low enough for a dry climate (coil sensible heat ratios tend to be less than 1.00 for 63°F WB).

  When expanded data is not adequate for a dry climate, ask the OEM for dry-coil performance data.

E_{sen} = Sensible recovery effectiveness
E_{lat} = Latent recovery effectiveness (zero for no recovery)

Condition of Processed Air for Heating

The heat recovery effectiveness (E) for heating determines the temperature of the ventilation air that leaves the heat recovery equipment (discharge air). This equation provides a dry-bulb value discharge air (DA).

$$DA_{db} = OA_{db} + E_{sen} \times (RA_{db} - OA_{db})$$

Where:
DA_{db} = Discharge air dry-bulb temperature
OA_{db} = Outdoor air dry-bulb temperature
RA_{db} = Return air dry-bulb temperature
E_{sen} = Sensible recover psychrometric effectiveness

Condition of Mixed Air

The condition of the air at the exit of the return duct, and the condition of the air leaving the recovery equipment are inputs to the psychrometric calculation for mixed air. These values, and the outdoor air fraction, determine the condition of the air that enters the indoor coil.

- For cooling, Figure A2-4 shows mixed air conditions for 95°F DB and 75°F WB, and for a variety of return air conditions at sea level, and at 2,500 feet. The effectiveness value for sensible heat recovery is 0.60, and 0.60 for latent heat recovery.

- For heating, this equation determines the mixed air dry-bulb temperature (MAT), where RA_{db} and DA_{db} are return air and outdoor air temperatures, and OAF is the outdoor air fraction.

MAT (°F) = RA_{db} x (1 − OAF) + DA_{db} x OAF

A2-8 Comprehensive Example

An example that deals with all the issues that affect the condition of the entering air is provided below. All psychrometric calculations are altitude sensitive. The calculations are simplified when there are no return duct loads, or no outdoor air loads. The calculations are as simple as they can possibly be when there are no return duct loads, and no outdoor air loads.

Cooling Calculations

At sea level, the outdoor air is at 95°F DB, 75°F WB, and 98.53 grains. The return grille air is at 75°F DB and 50% RH. The return duct loads are 2,500 sensible Btuh and 1,500 latent Btuh. The blower operates at 1,200 Cfm. The outdoor air fraction is 0.10. The sensible and latent effectiveness ratings for heat recovery are 0.60 and 0.55.

Dry-bulb and Wet-Bulb at the Return Grille

At sea level, the psychrometric chart shows that 75°F DB and 50% RH is equivalent to 75°F DB and 62.547°F WB and that the humidity ratio is 64.65 Grains. When there are no return duct loads, and no outdoor air loads, the condition of the entering air is 75°F DB and 62.5°F WB.

Entering DB (°F) = 75.0
Entering WB (°F) = 62.5

Dry-bulb and Wet-Bulb Leaving the Return Duct

The psychrometric equations for air convert duct loads to a change in dry-bulb temperature and a change in humidity ratio. Since the sensible and latent loads are positive, the dry-bulb and grains values at the exit of the return duct are larger than the values at the return grille. When there are no outdoor air loads, the condition of the entering air is about 76.9°F DB and 63.7°F WB.

Return Air Cfm = 1,200 − (0.10 x 1,200) = 1,080
Dry-bulb rise (°F) = 2,500 / (1.1 x 1.0 x 1,080) = 2.104
Exit dry-bulb (F) = 75.00 + 2.104 = 77.104

Grains rise (°F) = 1,500 / (0.68 x 1.0 x 1,080) = 2.042
Exit grains = 64.65 + 2.042 = 66.692
Exit wet-bulb is read from a psychrometric chart
Exit wet-bulb (°F) for 77.104 DB / 66.692grains = 63.705

Mixed Air DB/WB for 10% OA with 0.60 Recovery					
Outdoor Air at 95°F DB and 75°°F WB					
RA DB 75°F	MA DB °F		MA WB °F	
RA WB °F	Sea Level	2,500 Ft	Sea Level	2,500 Ft
59	75.8	75.8	59.745	59.749
61			61.638	61.642
63			63.536	Note 3
65			65.438	Note 3
67			67.343	
RA DB 77°F	MA DB °F		MA WB °F	
RA WB	Sea Level	2,500 Ft	Sea Level	2,500 Ft
59	77.7	77.7	59.747	59.751
61			61.640	61.643
63			63.537	Note 3
65			65.438	Note 3
67			67.343	
RA DB 79°F	MA DB °F		MA WB °F	
RA WB	Sea Level	2,500 Ft	Sea Level	2,500 Ft
59	79.6	79.6	59.747	59.752
61			61.641	61.644
63			63.538	Note 3
65			65.439	Note 3
67			67.345	
RA DB 81°F	MA DB °F		MA WB °F	
RA WB	Sea Level	2,500 Ft	Sea Level	2,500 Ft
59	81.6	81.6	59.749	59.753
61			61.643	61.645
63			63.539	Note 3
65			65.344	Note 3
67			67.345	

1) RA = Return air; MA = Mixed air.
2) Raw outdoor air mixed with air leaving the return duct.
3) RA WB will be 61°F or less at 2,500 feet or higher (space humidity will be 45% RH or less with no summer humidification).

Figure A2-4

Entering DB (°F) = 77.1
Entering WB (°F) = 63.7

Mixed Air Dry-bulb and Wet-Bulb — No Recovery

When there is no heat recovery, 120 Cfm of outdoor air at 95°F DB and 75°F WB is mixed with 1,080 Cfm of return air at 77.104°F DB and 62.677°F WB. The mixed air condition from the psychrometric chart is 78.845°F DB and 64.924°F WB, which is the entering air condition.

Entering DB (°F) = 78.8
Entering WB (°F) = 64.9

Appendix 2

Entering Air Worksheet for Cooling

Outdoor Air (OA) and Altitude Correction Factor

Dry-Bulb (°F)	Wet-Bulb (°F)	A-Psych Grains	ACF Figure A5-1
95.00	73.00	98.534	1.00

Outdoor air values from MJ8, Table 1; or per code/utility value.
A-Psych grains from altitude sensitive psychrometrics.

Indoor Air at Return Grille

Dry-Bulb (°F)	RH (%)	A-Psych Wet-Bulb	A-Psych Grains
75.00	50.00	62.547	64.650

Indoor air per MJ8 default, or per code/utility value.
A-Psych values from altitude sensitive psychrometrics.

System Air Flow Values

Blower Cfm	OA Cfm	RA Cfm	OAF
1,200	120	1,080	0.10

Blower Cfm from OEM's expanded performance data.
OA Cfm per practitioner's design (observe code/utility guidance).
RAcfm = Bcfm - OAcfm
Outdoor air fraction = OAF = OAcfm / Bcfm

Return Duct Loads, Dry-Bulb Rise, and Grains Rise

Sensible Btuh	Latent Btuh	Dry-Bulb Rise (°F)	Grains Rise
2,500	1,500	2.104	2.042

Return duct loads from MJ8 Worksheet G (see Section A2-3).
Dry-Bulb rise = Sensible Btuh / (1.1 x ACF x RAcfm)
Grains rise = Latent Btuh / (0.68 x ACF x RAcfm)

Air Leaving Return Duct

Return DB RAdb (°F)	Return Grains RAgr	A-Psych WB (°F)	Return WB RAwb (°F)
77.104	66.692	63.705	63.705

RAdb = Indoor air DB + Return duct rise
RAgr = Indoor air A-Psych grains + Return duct rise
RAwb from altitude sensitive psychrometrics

Recovery Performance and Discharge Air (DA)

Sensible Effectiveness Seff	Latent Effectiveness Leff	Discharge Air Dry-Bulb DAdb (°F)	Discharge Air Grains DAgr
0.60	0.55	84.263	81.021

Effectiveness ratings from OEM performance data.
DAdb (°F) = OAdb - Seff x (OAdb - RAgr)
DAgr = OAgr - Leff x (OAgr - RAgr)

Air Entering the Equipment (read from A-Psych)

OAF	Entering DB EAdb (°F)	Entering WB EAwb (°F)	Entering Grains EAgr
0.10	77.813	63.325	63.762

Raw or processed outdoor air mixed with return duct air.
Use altitude sensitive psychrometrics for the outdoor air fraction.
Use the dry-bulb and wet-bulb values for air leaving return duct.
Use the dry-bulb and grains values for discharge air.

Figure A2-5

Entering Air Worksheet for Heating

Outdoor Air (OA) and Altitude Correction Factor

Dry-Bulb (°F)	Wet-Bulb (°F)	A-Psych Grains	ACF Figure A5-1
95.00	73.00	98.534	1.00

Outdoor air values from MJ8, Table 1; or per code/utility value.
A-Psych grains from altitude sensitive psychrometrics.

Indoor Air at Return Grille

Dry-Bulb (°F)	RH (%)	A-Psych Wet-Bulb	A-Psych Grains
75.00	50.00	62.547	64.650

Indoor air per MJ8 default, or per code/utility value.
A-Psych values from altitude sensitive psychrometrics.

System Air Flow Values

Blower Cfm	OA Cfm	RA Cfm	OAF
1,200	120	1,080	0.10

Blower Cfm from OEM's expanded performance data.
OA Cfm per practitioner's design (observe code/utility guidance).
RAcfm = Bcfm - OAcfm
Outdoor air fraction = OAF = OAcfm / Bcfm

Return Duct Loads, Dry-Bulb Rise, and Grains Rise

Sensible Btuh	Latent Btuh	Dry-Bulb Rise (°F)	Grains Rise
2,500	1,500	2.104	2.042

Return duct loads from MJ8 Worksheet G (see Section A2-3).
Dry-Bulb rise = Sensible Btuh / (1.1 x ACF x RAcfm)
Grains rise = Latent Btuh / (0.68 x ACF x RAcfm)

Air Leaving Return Duct

Return DB RAdb (°F)	Return Grains RAgr	A-Psych WB (°F)	Return WB RAwb (°F)
77.104	66.692	62.677	62.677

RAdb = Indoor air DB + Return duct rise
RAgr = Indoor air A-Psych grains + Return duct rise
RAwb from altitude sensitive psychrometrics

Recovery Performance and Discharge Air (DA)

Sensible Effectiveness Seff	Latent Effectiveness Leff	Discharge Air Dry-Bulb DAdb (°F)	Discharge Air Grains DAgr
0.60	0.55	84.263	81.021

Effectiveness ratings from OEM performance data.
DAdb (°F) = OAdb - Seff x (OAdb - RAgr)
DAgr = OAgr - Leff x (OAgr - RAgr)

Air Entering the Equipment (read from A-Psych)

OAF	Entering DB EAdb (°F)	Entering WB EAwb (°F)	Entering Grains EAgr
0.10	77.813	63.325	63.762

Raw or processed outdoor air mixed with return duct air.
Use altitude sensitive psychrometrics for the outdoor air fraction.
Use the dry-bulb and wet-bulb values for air leaving return duct.
Use the dry-bulb and grains values for discharge air.

Figure A2-6

Mixed Air Dry-bulb and Wet-Bulb — With Recovery

With heat recovery, 120 Cfm of discharge air at 84.263°F DB and 81.021 grains is mixed with 1,080 Cfm of return air at 77.104°F DB and 66.692 grains. The mixed air condition from the psychrometric chart is 77.813°F DB and 63.325°F WB, which is the entering air condition.

DA_{db} (°F) = 95.00 – 0.60 x (95.00 – 77.104) = 84.263
DA_{grains} = 98.534 – 0.55 x (98.534 – 66.692) = 81.021

Entering DB (°F) = 77.8
Entering WB (°F) = 63.3

Heating Calculations

At sea level, the outdoor air is at 5°F DB. The air entering the return grille air is at 70°F DB. The return duct load is minus 4,500 sensible Btuh. The blower operates at 1,200 Cfm. The outdoor air fraction is 0.10. The sensible effectiveness rating for winter heat recovery is 0.65 (latent recovery is not common for ordinary comfort heating, but is relevant to swimming pool and spa applications).

Dry-bulb at the Return Grille

The working value for the dry-bulb temperature at the return grille is equal to the design value for indoor dry-bulb temperature. When there are no return duct loads, and no outdoor air loads, the condition of the entering air is 70°F DB.

Dry-bulb Leaving the Return Duct

The psychrometric equations for air convert the sensible duct load to a change in dry-bulb temperature. Since the duct load is negative, the dry-bulb value at the exit of the return duct is less than the value at the return grille. When there is no outdoor air load, the condition of the entering air is about 66.2°F DB.

Return Air Cfm = 1,200 – (0.10 x 1,200) = 1,080
Dry-bulb rise (°F) = – 4,500 / (1.1 x 1.0 x 1,080) = - 3.788
Exit dry-bulb (°F) = 70.00 - 3.788 = 66.212

Mixed Air Dry-bulb — No Recovery

When there is no heat recovery, 120 Cfm of outdoor air at 5°F DB is mixed with 1,080 Cfm of return air at 66.212°F DB. The mixed air dry-bulb from the psychrometric chart is 59.377°F DB, so the entering dry-bulb temperature is about 59.4°F.

Mixed Air Dry-bulb — With Recovery

With heat recovery, 120 Cfm of discharge air at 44.788°F DB is mixed with 1,080 Cfm of return air at 66.212°F DB. The mixed air condition from the psychrometric chart is 63.988°F DB, so the entering dry-bulb temperature is about 64.0°F.

DA_{db} (°F) = 5.00 + 0.65 x (5.00 - 66.212) = 47.788

A2-9 Entering Air Worksheet for Cooling

Figure A2-5 (previous page) shows the entering air worksheet for the cooling part of the Section A2-8 example. Use may require sensible and latent load values for a return duct (see Figure A2-1), and may required an outdoor air Cfm value for engineered ventilation, and may require a sensible effectiveness value, or sensible and latent values, for heat recovery equipment.

A2-10 Entering Air Worksheet for Heating

Figure A2-6 (previous page) shows the entering air worksheet for the heating part of the Section A2-8 example. Use may require the sensible load value for a return duct (see Figure A2-1), and may required an outdoor air Cfm value for engineered ventilation, and may require a sensible effectiveness value for heat recovery equipment.

A2-11 Entering Air Worksheet Psychrometrics

The psychrometric equations that relate a sensible or latent load to Cfm, and to the change in dry-bulb temperature (ΔT), or humidity ratio(ΔGrains), have sensitivity to altitude. This is implemented by using an altitude correction factor (ACF value) from Figure A5-1.

Sensible Btuh = 1.1 x ACF x Cfm x ΔT
Latent Btuh = 0.68 x ACF x Cfm x ΔGrains

Altitude affects the psychrometric relationship between dry-bulb temperature, wet-bulb temperature, relative humidity, and humidity ratio. This is implemented by using an altitude sensitive software (which is commonly available as an accessory to *Manual J* load calculation software).

Appendx 2

This appendix is not part of the this standard. It is merely informative and does not contain requirements necessary for conformance to the standard. It has not been processed according to the ANSI requirements for a standard, and may contain material that has not been subject to public review or a consensus process. Unresolved objectors on informative material are not offered the right to appeal at ACCA or ANSI.

Appendix 3
Searching OEM Data for Candidate Equipment

Expanded equipment performance data sheets published by OEMs start with the smallest unit (which has the smallest capacity and blower Cfm), and progress through larger sizes (total capacity and Cfm values increase according). There are usually many data sheets (or data sets), but only a few apply to a given set of *Manual J* loads.

When a search for suitable equipment begins, the data set entry point may be based on a total cooling capacity value, or a ballpark Cfm value.

- Students and practitioners tend to be more comfortable with the total capacity method.
- The ballpark Cfm method works best when an OEM provides data for different indoor unit sizes matched to the same outdoor unit. For example, nominal indoor capacity may be 2-1/2, 3, or 3-1/2 tons for a nominal 3-ton outdoor unit (as demonstrated by Figure A1-20 (copied to this page).
- Either method provides an entry point for equipment performance evaluation, and either method will find equipment that is appropriate for the *Manual J* loads.
- Practitioners may exercise their preference.
- Section 2 provides step by step procedures for selecting and sizing refrigeration cycle equipment. See also, Sections 5, 11, 12 and 13.

A3-1 Total Capacity Method

OEM data sheets normally start with the sheet for the unit that has the smallest total capacity, and progress through larger and larger values. So, the search for appropriate equipment may be based on total cooling capacity.

- There may be many total capacity values on a data sheet. Use the total capacity value that correlates with the *Manual J* outdoor air temperature (or entering water temperature), and the expected entering wet-bulb temperature (see Section A1-2).
- Use the total capacity value that correlates with the medium or mid-range blower speed.
- The search may terminate when the first data sheet shows that equipment performance is compatible with the *Manual J* loads (per Section 2-1 procedures), and has acceptable excess capacity; or the practitioner may decide to search for a closer match (a smaller unit may have adequate latent and sensible capacity, with less excess capacity).

Cooling Equipment Designs Based on Climate For 30,000 Btuh total load, 75°F room, 90% RH off coil							
Unit	SHR	S-Load	LAT	CTD	Cfm	Cfm/Ton
D	1.00	30,000	57.5	17.5	1,558	623
E	0.83	24,900	55.0	20.0	1,132	453
F	0.75	22,500	52.5	22.5	909	364
The Cfm/Ton values are psychrometrically correct. OEMs also consider how Cfm/Ton affects condensate blow off and the SEER/HSPF ratings.							

Copy of Figure A1-20

- The search continues (check the data for the next larger or smaller unit) when the first data sheet shows that equipment performance is not compatible with the *Manual J* loads, or does not comply with Table N2-1 or Table N2-2 sizing rules.
- When a search continues, one or two iterations usually find a suitable size.
- The practitioner may use a blower speed other than medium-speed at any point in the search (but this leaves less room for adjusting blower Cfm after the equipment has been installed).
- The final design Cfm value for *Manual D* duct sizing calculations equals the Cfm from the data sheet that proves equipment performance is compatible with the *Manual J* loads, and the Table N2-1 or Table N2-2 sizing rules.

A3-2 Ballpark Cfm Method

A ballpark value for cooling Cfm may be used to find an equipment data sheet that proves the equipment is the correct size, or it may show that the equipment is not quite compatible with the *Manual J* loads.

- Section A3-3 provides step by step instructions for producing a ballpark Cfm value.
- Use a medium or mid-range blower speed for the search (blower Cfm at medium-speed should be similar to ballpark Cfm).
- The search may terminate when the data sheet for the ballpark Cfm shows that equipment performance is compatible with the *Manual J* loads (per Section 2-1 procedures), and has acceptable excess capacity; or the practitioner my decide to search

for a closer match (a smaller unit may have adequate latent and sensible capacity with less excess total capacity).

- The search continues when the first data sheet shows that equipment performance is not compatible with the *Manual J* loads, or does not comply with Table N2-1 or Table N2-2 sizing rules. Check the data for the next larger or smaller unit.

- As a search continues, one or two iterations usually find a suitable model.

- The practitioner may use a blower speed other than medium-speed at any point in the search (but this leaves less room for adjusting blower Cfm after the equipment has been installed).

- The ballpark Cfm value is not the final design Cfm value (except by coincidence).

- The final design Cfm value for *Manual D* duct sizing calculations equals the Cfm from the data sheet that proves equipment performance is compatible with the *Manual J* loads, and the excess capacity limit (i.e., the blower Cfm for the unit that will actually be installed).

A3-3 Ballpark Cfm Calculation

An approximate blower Cfm for cooling is obtained by using *Manual J* loads to estimate the appropriate dry-bulb temperature drop for the cooling coil. Then the psychrometric equation for sensible heat provides the Cfm value. Procedure steps are provided here:

Step 1

Use the design-day loads (from the bottom of the J1 Form) to calculate the *Manual J* sensible heat ratio (JSHR).

Total Load = Sensible Load + Latent Load

$$JSHR = \frac{Manual\ J\ Sensible\ Load}{Manual\ J\ Total\ Load}$$

For example, if the sensible load is 30,000 Btuh and the latent load is 5,000 Btuh, so the total load is 35,000 Btuh, and the sensible heat ratio is 0.86. This means that 86 percent of the cooling load is a sensible load and that 14 percent of the cooling load is a latent load.

SHR = 30,000 / (30,000 + 5,000) = 0.86

Step 2

Determine the compatible discharge air temperature for cooling. This temperature will depend on the relative size of the sensible and latent loads, as indicated by the sensible heat ratio.

- The default for indoor air temperature is 75°F.

Default TD Values for Ballpark Cooling Cfm			
JSHR	LAT (°F db)	IAT (°F db)	TD (°F db)
Below 0.80	53	75	22
0.80 to 0.85	55	75	20
Above 0.85	57	75	18

1) LAT = Dry-bulb temperature for air off the cooling coil.
   IAT = Default indoor air temperature for cooling.
   TD = IAT - LAT.
2) The TD value is applied to the sensible block load on the cooling coil for the summer design day, per this equation:
   Cfm = Sensible Btuh / (1.1 x ACF x TD)
3) When there is a duct system, the dry-bulb temperature of the air leaving supply air outlets may be warmer than the LAT value. However, the air leaving the cooling coil has adequate sensible capacity because the duct system load is embedded in the block cooling load value (per *Manual J* procedure).
   - The *Manual J* duct load is for the entire duct system.
   - Because duct run shapes and airway sizes vary (and perhaps exposures, insulation values, and leakage rates), the sensible and latent duct loads per foot of trunk run or branch run are not the same as the average values for the entire duct system.
   - Runs with smaller loads have cooler supply air than runs with larger loads, so the temperature differences across a set of supply air outlets can be significant.
   - After the system is installed, hand dampers are adjusted to compensate for variations in supply air temperature.

Figure A3-1

- For 75°F in the conditioned space, a 55°F leaving air temperature (LAT) is roughly compatible with a normal latent load.

- When the sensible heat ratio is relatively low, the latent load is relatively large compared to the sensible load, so indoor humidity is controlled by a colder cooling coil (LAT 52°F to 53°F).

- When the sensible heat ratio is relatively high, the latent load is relatively small compared to the sensible load, so indoor humidity is controlled by a warmer cooling coil (LAT 57°F to 58°F).

- Figure A3-1 provides default temperature difference (TD) values for ballpark Cfm calculations, and explains duct load effects.

Step 3

After the appropriate TD value is determined, the sensible heat equation provides the ballpark Cfm value.

Cfm = Sensible load / (1.1 x ACF x TD)

For example, if the sensible load for a sea level home is 32,000 Btuh, and the TD value is 22°F (humid climate), the ballpark Cfm is 1,322 Cfm. Or, if the sensible load is 32,000 Btuh, and the TD value is 18°F (low outdoor humidity, no latent load), the ballpark Cfm is 1,616 Cfm.

This appendix is not part of the this standard. It is merely informative and does not contain requirements necessary for conformance to the standard. It has not been processed according to the ANSI requirements for a standard, and may contain material that has not been subject to public review or a consensus process. Unresolved objectors on informative material are not offered the right to appeal at ACCA or ANSI.

Appendix 4
Requirements for Expanded Performance Data

This appendix applies to residential, vapor compression cycle equipment that is tested and rated according to AHRI protocol. It applies to single-package and split systems. It applies to air-air equipment and to water-air equipment. It applies to equipment that has one indoor coil, and to multi-split equipment. It applies to equipment that has a single-speed compressor, a multi-speed compressor, or a variable-speed compressor.

The intent of this Appendix is to define minimum requirements for presenting expanded performance data for equipment selection and sizing (see Section A1-9). Therefore, reporting requirements are limited to steady-state performance (i.e., continuous compressor operation) for a comprehensive set of operating conditions.

Additional information required for energy use and operation cost modeling is beyond the scope of this Appendix. See the current versions of ANSI/AHRI testing standards for the noted types of equipment. Await publication of ASHRAE Standard 205P — Standard Representation of Performance Simulation Data for HVAC&R and Other Facility Equipment.

A4-1 Cooling Capacity Values

Cooling equipment has a total capacity value, a sensible capacity value, and latent capacity value. These values depend on the operating conditions (see Sections A4-3, A4-4, A4-7 and A4-9). However, the latent capacity value will be zero when the entering air wet-bulb and dry-bulb temperatures cause a dry evaporator coil.

Per *Manual S* procedures, all three values are used for equipment selection and sizing. The common methods for presenting this information provides a total capacity value and a sensible capacity value; or a total capacity value and a coil sensible heat ratio value. The missing capacity value or values are calculated per these equations.

Total Capacity = Sensible Capacity + Latent Capacity
Sensible Capacity = CSHR x Total Capacity

Where:
Capacity values are in Btuh units
CSHR = Coil Sensible Heat Ratio

A4-2 Compressor Heating Capacity Values

Compressor heating capacity is just sensible heat. The magnitude of the heating capacity value depends on the operating conditions (see Sections A4-5, A4-6, A4-8 and A4-9). Per *Manual S* procedures, one value is associated with the winter design condition, and a set of values for a range of outdoor air temperatures is used to draw a balance point diagram.

A4-3 Temperature Range for Air-Air Cooling

Air-air cooling performance data must be compatible with the outdoor summer design conditions, and the possible entering air wet-bulb and dry-bulb temperatures, for the dwelling and it's location. Suitable ranges and requirements are summarized here:

- Outdoor dry-bulb temperatures 70°F to 115°F, preferably in 5°F increments for look-up tables.
- Entering air wet-bulb temperatures 57°F to 72°F, preferably in 3°F increments for look-up tables.
- Entering air dry-bulb temperatures 65°F to 85°F, preferably in 5°F increments for look-up tables.
- Software models can process user-specified input values (incremental scenarios do not apply).
- High- and low-limits for outdoor air temperature, and the condition of the entering air, for standard OEM controls.
- High and low-limits for outdoor air temperature, and the condition of the entering air, for optional OEM controls/accessories, where applicable.

A4-4 Temperature Range for Water-Air Cooling

Water-air cooling performance data must be compatible with possible entering water temperatures, and the possible entering air wet-bulb and dry-bulb temperatures, for the dwelling and it's location. The water flow rate (Gpm) affects performance. Suitable ranges and requirements are summarized here:

- Entering water temperatures from 40°F (or the OEM's low-limit for cooling) to 105°F (or the OEM's high-limit for cooling), preferably in 10°F increments for look-up tables.
- The range of water flow rates and the Gpm values are specified by the OEM.
- Entering air wet-bulb temperatures 57°F to 72°F, preferably in 3°F increments for look-up tables.
- Entering air dry-bulb temperatures 65°F to 85°F, preferably in 5°F increments for look-up tables.
- Software models can process user-specified input values (incremental scenarios do not apply).

- High- and low-limits for entering water temperature, and the condition of the entering air, for standard OEM controls.
- High- and low-limits for entering water temperature, and the condition of the entering air, for optional OEM controls/accessories, where applicable.

A4-5 Temperature Range for Air-Air Heating

Air-air heat pump heating performance data must be compatible with a range of outdoor temperatures, and the possible entering air dry-bulb temperature, for the dwelling and it's location. Suitable ranges and requirements are summarized here:

- Outdoor dry-bulb temperatures −15°F to 70°F, preferably in 5°F increments for hard copy data.
- Entering air dry-bulb temperatures 60°F to 80°F, preferably in 5°F increments for look-up tables.
- Heating capacity values for outdoor air temperatures in the 17°F to 47°F range must be adjusted for defrost cycle effects.

  Document the frosting condition (air temperature and relative humidity at the outdoor coil).

  Identify the type of defrost control, and document applicable settings.

- Software models can provide a heating capacity vs. outdoor air temperature graph for a user-specified entering air temperature (incremental scenarios do not apply).
- High- and low-limits for outdoor air temperature, and entering air temperature, for standard OEM controls.
- High- and low-limits for outdoor air temperature, and entering air temperature, for optional OEM controls/accessories, where applicable.

A4-6 Temperature Range for Water-Air Heating

Water-air heating performance data must be compatible with possible entering water temperatures, and the possible entering air dry-bulb temperature, for the dwelling and it's location. The water flow rate (Gpm) affects performance. Suitable ranges and requirements are summarized here:

- Entering water temperatures from 20°F (or the OEM's low-limit for heating) to 80°F (or the OEM's high-limit for heating), preferably in 10°F increments for look-up tables.
- The range of water flow rates and the Gpm values are specified by the OEM.
- Entering air dry-bulb temperatures 60°F to 80°F, preferably in 5°F increments for look-up tables.

- Software models can provide a heating capacity vs. outdoor air temperature graph for user-specified values for entering water temperature and entering air temperature (incremental scenarios do not apply).
- High- and low-limits for entering water temperature, and entering air temperature, for standard OEM controls.
- High- and low-limits for entering water temperature, and entering air temperature, for optional OEM controls/accessories, where applicable.

A4-7 Compressor Speed for Expanded Cooling Data

Provide expanded cooling performance data for the compressor speed used for the AHRI rating test. For air-air equipment this is the speed used for the 95°F/80°F/67°F test for total cooling capacity. For water-air equipment this is the speed used for the 85°F entering water, 95°F leaving water, 80°F/67°F entering air test for total cooling capacity.

- Expanded cooling data for the AHRI rating speed is used for the *Manual S* equipment sizing method.
- For multi-speed equipment and variable-speed equipment, a performance map, or maps, for continuous compressor operation at a lower speed, or speeds, may provide suitable documentation for the *Manual S* performance sizing method.

A4-8 Compressor Speed for Expanded Heating Data

Provide expanded compressor heating data for the compressor speed used for the AHRI rating test, and additional data for enhanced compressor speed (where applicable). For air-air equipment this is the speed used for the 47°F outdoor air, 70°F entering air test for heating capacity. For water-air equipment this is the speed used for the 70°F entering water, 70°F entering air test for heating capacity.

- When the product's compressor does not operate at enhanced speed, expanded heating data for the AHRI rating speed is used for the *Manual S* thermal balance point diagram, and for sizing supplemental heat.
- For variable-speed equipment, expanded heating data for continuous, unrestricted, compressor operation at enhanced speed is used for the *Manual S* thermal balance point diagram, and for sizing supplemental heat.

A4-9 Indoor Blower Speed for Expanded Data

The default indoor blower speed, or speeds, for two or more indoor units, is the speed, or speeds, used for the AHRI rating test. Or, there may be a blower Cfm setting, or settings, for two or more indoor units, for the AHRI rating test. Either way, there is a blower Cfm value for one indoor unit, or values for two or more indoor units, for the AHRI rating test. The blower Cfm value, or values, used for the AHRI rating test should be included in the AHRI rating test report.

Expanded performance data for a range of indoor blower Cfm values is common and desirable. Any blower Cfm value listed by expanded performance data for cooling, or compressor heating, may be used for *Manual S* equipment sizing, and balance point diagram construction.

A4-10 Interpolation

Interpolation of the capacity values in look-up tables is required when one or more of the design condition values do match the choices offered by the table. Interpolation is not an issue when a software model process user-specified input values and returns algorhythmic capacity values.

A4-11 Additional Reporting Requirements

Expanded performance data and AHRI certification test data is also used for energy and op-cost calculations. Such efforts use the performance data for continuous equipment operation (steady-state performance), as described above; plus additional data sets for equipment cycling or throttling during part-load conditions. ASHRAE Standard 205P — Standard Representation of Performance Simulation Data for HVAC&R and Other Facility Equipment — addresses this issue (in the development stage as of the second half of 2012). The possible and desirable goals and objectives for this effort are summarized here:

- Centralize Data Location (authorized people will be able to investigate the performance any OEM product by accessing an industry-wide data base).
- Standardized Data File Format (one learning experience allows a person to use data provided by any OEM, and this standardizes software input routines).
- Explicitly Define Performance Metrics (uniform reporting requirements pertaining to operating conditions and the related capacity values, power requirements, and cycling penalties).
- Standardized Definition of Operating Conditions (an enhanced version of the requirements in this appendix).
- Provide Validation Rules (certification of published data, as far as accuracy limits are concerned).
- Provide Data Consistent with Simulation Inputs (standardized data formats must be compatible with software program needs).
- Establish Industry Consensus (OEM's agree to uses one presentation format, and to post their data in a central data base for use by authorized persons).

Appendx 4

This appendix is not part of the this standard. It is merely informative and does not contain requirements necessary for conformance to the standard. It has not been processed according to the ANSI requirements for a standard, and may contain material that has not been subject to public review or a consensus process. Unresolved objectors on informative material are not offered the right to appeal at ACCA or ANSI.

Appendix 5

Altitude Effects

Expanded equipment performance data published by equipment manufacturers must be used to select and size heating equipment, air conditioning equipment, and heat pumps. However, published performance data applies to sea-level air density. This Appendix provides procedures for estimating equipment capacity at altitude.

A5-1 Psychrometric Calculations

Altitude affects the psychrometric state point of air. Use psychrometric software that adjusts for altitude to determine the properties of outdoor air, indoor air, and the air at any point in the air distribution.

For a set of dry-bulb and wet-bulb values, as altitude increases:
- Grains of moisture increases
- Relative humidity increases
- Dew-point increases
- Specific volume increases

For a set of dry-bulb and relative humidity values, as altitude increases:
- Wet-bulb decreases (slightly)
- Grains of moisture increases
- Dew-point does not change
- Specific volume increases

For mixing two streams of air:
- Use psychrometric software that adjusts for altitude when moisture (wet-bulb, relative humidity, humidity ratio) is involved.
- Altitude sensitive software may be used for mixed air dry-bulb (DB) calculations, or a heat balance equation may be used, regardless of altitude.

Mixed Cfm = Cfm_M = Cfm_1 + Cfm_2
Mixed DB = (Cfm_1 x DB_1 + Cfm_2 x DB_2) / Cfm_M

Altitude affects the psychrometric equation for sensible heating and cooling processes (the calculation for a sensible Btuh load, or a sensible Btuh capacity). Figure A5-1 provides altitude correction factor (ACF) values.

Sensible Btuh = 1.1 x ACF x Cfm x ΔT (°F)

Altitude affects the psychrometric equation for latent heating and cooling processes (the calculation for a latent Btuh load, or a latent Btuh capacity). Figure A5-1 provides altitude correction factor (ACF) values.

Latent Btuh = 0.68 x ACF x Cfm x ΔGrains at altitude

Altitude Correction Factors For Psychrometric Equations	
Feet	ACF
0	1.00
1,000	0.97
2,000	0.93
3,000	0.89
4,000	0.87
5,000	0.84
6,000	0.80
7,000	0.77
8,000	0.75
9,000	0.72
10,000	0.69
11,000	0.66
12,000	0.63

Calculations for air-to-air heat exchangers, desiccant wheels heat industrial process equipment, and special heating and cooling applications may require adjustment factors that include the effect of air temperature.

Figure A5-1

A5-2 Altitude Affects Equipment Performance

Altitude reduces air density, which affects the performance of indoor and outdoor fin-tube refrigerant coils, furnace heat exchangers, electric heating coils, gas burners, air-to-air heat exchangers, equipment blowers, air-side components, and duct runs.

- Refrigerant coils, air-to-air heat exchangers, and furnace heat exchangers are affected because surface-to-air heat transfer depends on air mass-flow (pounds of air per minute), which depends on volume flow (cubic feet or air per minute) and air density (pounds of air per cubic foot).

  Mass-flow also depends on entering air temperature. This is ignored for most HVAC equipment, because entering air temperature falls into a narrow band of temperatures.

- Heat-rejection refrigerant coils are affected because altitude air mass-flow affects condensing temperature and head pressure.

- The relationships between gauge pressures and condenser or evaporator temperatures depend on altitude (refrigerant-side performance is not affected when absolute pressures at altitude are equal to absolute pressures at sea level).

- Expansion valves, capillary tubes and orifices selected for air mass-flow and refrigerant-side pressure drop at sea level may be too large for reduced air mass-flow at altitude (metering pressure drop and refrigerant flow increase, with possible refrigerant slugging at part-load).

- For a given Cfm value and input KW, the temperature rise across an electric heating coil increases with altitude, because heat input is constant and mass-flow decreases.

- Gas burner heating capacity is reduced when a fuel orifice sized for a sea level air mass-flow and oxygen content is not compatible with the air mass-flow and oxygen content at altitude.

- For a given output Btuh value and blower Cfm value, the temperature rise across a furnace heat exchanger increases with altitude, because heat input is constant and mass-flow decreases.

- Hot water coil heat transfer depends on air mass-flow. For a given coil Cfm value, heating capacity decreases with altitude because air mass-flow decreases with altitude.

- When blower wheel Rpm is constant, blower Cfm is not affected by altitude, but mass-flow and external pressure decrease with altitude, and input horsepower decreases with decreasing mass-flow.

- The aerodynamic resistance of duct airways decreases with altitude because velocity pressure and duct friction depend on air density.

- For a given air volume flow (supply Cfm), supply grille, register and air diffuser performance is affected by altitude, because pressure drop and discharge momentum depend on air density.

- Altitude also affects air balancing instruments, air balancing procedures, and air balancing calculations, but this is not a topic for this manual.

A5-3 Air-Air Cooling Equipment

Figure A5-2 provides an example of expanded performance data for air-air cooling equipment (cooling-only, or heat pump). Such performance summaries are for sea level operation. Performance at altitude is obtained by applying Figure A5-3 factors (next page) to sea level data.

For example, load and psychrometric calculations for a Denver, CO, dwelling (90°F summer design temperature) show that the state-point of the entering air is less than 59°F wet-bulb (for a dry cooling coil), and about 75°F dry-bulb. Figure A5-2 provides cooling performance values for 90°F outdoor dry-bulb, 59°F entering wet-bulb, 1,125 Cfm, and 75°F entering dry-bulb. The 59°F wet-bulb data shows a dry-coil, so the data is compatible with a dry cooling coil. Sea level data (Figure A5-2) provides these values:

Total capacity (Btuh) = 26,496
CSHR = 1.00
Sensible capacity (Btuh) = 1.00 x 26,496 = 26,496
Latent capacity (Btuh) = 0

Expanded Performance Data for Cooling with an Air-Cooled Condenser															
EWB °F	Cfm	Outdoor DB 85°F			Outdoor DB 90°F			Outdoor DB 95°F			Outdoor DB 100°F				
		TC Btuh	CSHR		TC Btuh	CSHR		TC Btuh	CSHR		TC Btuh	CSHR			
			EDB °F				EDB °F				EDB °F				EDB °F	
			75	80	85		75	80	85		75	80	85		75	80	85
59	1,000	27,205	0.94	1.00	1.00	26,080	0.97	1.00	1.00	24,955	0.99	1.00	1.00	23,830	1.00	1.00	1.00
	1,125	27,621	0.98	1.00	1.00	26,496	1.00	1.00	1.00	25,371	1.00	1.00	1.00	24,246	1.00	1.00	1.00
	1,250	28,038	1.00	1.00	1.00	26,913	1.00	1.00	1.00	25,788	1.00	1.00	1.00	24,663	1.00	1.00	1.00
63	1,000	29,205	0.75	0.88	1.00	28,080	0.78	0.91	1.00	26,955	0.80	0.93	1.00	25,830	0.83	0.96	1.00
	1,125	29,621	0.79	0.92	1.00	28,496	0.82	0.95	1.00	27,371	0.84	0.97	1.00	26,246	0.87	1.00	1.00
	1,250	30,038	0.83	0.96	1.00	28,913	0.86	0.99	1.00	27,788	0.88	1.00	1.00	26,663	0.91	1.00	1.00
67	1,000	31,205	0.56	0.69	0.82	30,080	0.59	0.72	0.85	28,955	0.61	0.74	0.87	27,830	0.64	0.77	0.90
	1,125	31,621	0.60	0.73	0.86	30,496	0.63	0.76	0.89	29,371	0.65	0.78	0.91	28,246	0.68	0.81	0.94
	1,250	32,038	0.64	0.77	0.90	30,913	0.67	0.80	0.93	29,788	0.69	0.82	0.95	28,663	0.72	0.85	0.98

EWB = Entering wet-bulb temperature; EDB = Entering dry-bulb temperature; DB = Dry-bulb temperature.
Cfm = Blower Cfm setting; TC = Total cooling capacity (sensible plus latent); CSHR = Coil sensible heat ratio = Sensible Btuh / Total Btuh
Capacity values have been adjusted for blower heat (default value = 500 blower motor Watts).

Figure A5-2

Figure A5-3 factors are used to adjust performance for Denver, CO, (about 5,000 feet). Since the cooling coil is dry, the equipment will have this altitude performance for 1,125 Cfm:

Total capacity (Btuh) = 0.92 x 26,496 = 24,376
Sensible capacity (Btuh) = 24,376
Latent capacity (Btuh) = 0

When the adjusted equipment capacity value is compatible with the cooling load and the equipment size limits, the air distribution system is designed for 1,125 Cfm. When this capacity value is deficient, capacity is evaluated at a higher Cfm (for Figure A5-2 data, the limit is 1,250 Cfm); or investigate the altitude adjusted performance of next larger unit. In any case, the Cfm used to determine cooling capacity at altitude is the design Cfm for psychrometric calculations, and for the air distribution system.

For comfort conditioning, cooling coils tend to be dry when the altitude is 2,500 Feet or higher (because of dry infiltration, dry outdoor air for ventilation, and relatively low latent internal gain).

*A few locations in a few states are exceptions when the elevation is 2,500 to 3,200 feet (see **Manual J**, Table 1 data for Hawaii, Kansas, Montana, Nebraska, Texas and West Virginia).*

When an application has a wet-coil, use the wet-coil factors provided by Figure A5-3.

A5-4 Water-Air Cooling Equipment

The water-side of water-air cooling equipment is not affected by altitude. Sea level cooling capacity is maintained when the air mass-flow rate through the indoor refrigerant coil at altitude equals the air mass-flow rate at sea level. This applies to cooling-only equipment and to heat pumps.

- Obtain values for blower Cfm, total capacity, sensible capacity, latent capacity and sensible heat ratio from manufacturer's expanded performance data for sea level operation. (This data is similar to Figure A5-2, but entering water temperature replaces outdoor air temperature.)
- Use an ACF value (Figure A5-1) to find the blower Cfm that will produce an equivalent mass-flow rate at altitude (sea level performance is maintained, and sea level capacity data applies at altitude).
- The OEM's performance data determines the maximum blower Cfm value.
- When the altitude Cfm exceeds the OEM's limit, investigate the performance of larger equipment.

Altitude Adjustment Factors
Cooling Evaporator with Air-Cooled Condenser

Altitude (Feet)	Total Capacity		Sensible Capacity	
	Wet-Coil	Dry-Coil	Wet-Coil	Dry-Coil
Sea Level	1.00	1.00	1.00	1.00
1,000	0.99	0.98	0.97	0.98
2,000	0.98	0.97	0.94	0.97
3,000	0.98	0.95	0.91	0.95
4,000	0.97	0.94	0.88	0.94
5,000	0.96	0.92	0.85	0.92
6,000	0.95	0.90	0.82	0.90
7,000	0.94	0.89	0.80	0.89
8,000	0.94	0.87	0.77	0.87
9,000	0.93	0.86	0.74	0.86
10,000	0.92	0.84	0.71	0.84
11,000	0.91	0.82	0.68	0.82
12,000	0.90	0.81	0.65	0.81

1) Interpolation and extrapolation of values published by the Carrier Corp (***Engineering Guide for Altitude Effects***, 1967).
2) Use wet-coil values for sensible heat ratios (SHR) less than 0.95.

Figure A5-3

For example, the ACF value for 5,000 Feet is 0.84, so 1,600 Cfm at sea level is about 1,900 Cfm at altitude. Design the air distribution system for 1,900 Cfm.

Blower Cfm at altitude = 1,600 / 0.84 = 1,905 Cfm
Capacity at altitude = Sea level capacity

A5-5 Hot Water Coil or Chilled Water Coil

Sea level heating capacity or cooling capacity is maintained at altitude when the air mass-flow rate through the water coil at altitude equals the air mass-flow rate at sea level. Use the Section A5-4 procedure.

A5-6 Electric Heating Coil

The output heating capacity of an electric resistance heating coil is not affected by altitude, but the temperature rise (TR) across the coil depends on air mass-flow through the coil. When Cfm is held constant, the temperature rise at altitude is larger than at sea level. When temperature rise is held constant, the air mass-flow rate must increase at altitude.

Temperature rise (TR) is evaluated by applying an altitude correction to the psychrometric equation for sensible heat. Figure A5-1 provides altitude correction factor (ACF) values.

TR °F = (Kilowatts x 3.413) / (1.1 x ACF x Cfm)

For example, suppose 1,500 Cfm flows through a 10 KW coil in Denver, CO, (approximately 5,000 Feet).

Sea level TR = (10.0 x 3,413) / (1.1 x 1.00 x 1,500) = 20.7 °F
Denver TR = (10.0 x 3,413) / (1.1 x 0.84 x 1,500) = 24.6 °F
Denver Cfm for 20.7 °F rise = 1,500 x 24.6 / 20.7 = 1,786

A5-7 Gas Burner

The input heating capacity of a gas burner depends on the mass-flow of the gas-air mixture that flows to the burner, which depends on the pressure drop across the metering orifice, the density of the combustion air, and the oxygen content of the combustion air. This is affected by altitude. Refer to OEM guidance on this matter.

- OEM specifications have derating tables or charts (for input capacity) for burner assemblies at altitude. This guidance may call for a replacement burner orifice or burner kit for altitudes above 2,000 Feet. These kits reduce gas flow to match the reduced oxygen content of the air. Such kits are based on National Fuel Gas Code ANSI Z223.1, which calls for a reduction of input capacity for each 1,000 Feet above sea level.

- Many OEMs use the derating from the National Fuel Gas Code (2% to 4 % less input capacity per 1,000 Feet of elevation, depending on furnace efficiency). To determine output capacity, adjust input capacity and multiply the adjusted input capacity by the sea level steady-state efficiency (not the AFUE) of the furnace.

For example, a sea level furnace that has 100,000 Btuh of input capacity and a 86% steady-state efficiency is installed in Denver, CO, (5,000 Feet). The OEM's derating factor is 0.04 per 1,000 Feet of elevation.

Input adjustment factor = 0.04 x (5,000 / 1,000) = 0.20
Input Btuh at altitude = 100,000 x (1.00- 0.20) = 80,000
Output Btuh = 0.86 x 80,000 = 68,800

The temperature rise across the furnace heat exchanger is affected by altitude. This behavior is evaluated by applying an air density adjustment to the psychrometric equation for sensible heat (as demonstrated for an electric heating coil).

For example, evaluate Denver, CO, performance when 1,600 Cfm flows through a furnace that has 80,000 input Btuh and 86% SS efficiency at sea level.

Sea level output Btuh = 80,000 x 0.86 = 68,800
Sea level TR = (68,800) / (1.1 x 1.00 x 1,600) = 39.1 °F
Denver adjustment factor = 0.04 x (5,000 / 1,000) = 0.20
Denver input Btuh = 80,000 x (1.00 - 0.20) = 64,000
Denver output Btuh = 0.86 x 64,000 = 55,040
ACF for Denver = 0.84
Denver TR = (55,040) / (1.1 x 0.84 x 1,600) = 37.2 °F

A5-8 Oil Burner

The input heating capacity of an oil burner depends on the mass-flow of oil that is pumped to the burner. This is not affected by altitude, but the amount of oxygen in a cubic foot of combustion air is reduced at altitude. Refer to OEM guidance on this matter.

- The fuel rate and input capacity of an oil furnace are reduced at altitude when the volume flow rate (Cfm) of combustion air equals the sea level flow rate.

- For natural draft furnaces, sea level input capacity is maintained at altitude by increasing the chimney height (to maintain the sea level mass-flow rate for combustion air).

- For forced draft furnaces, sea level input capacity is maintained at altitude by increasing the combustion air Cfm (to maintain the sea level mass-flow rate for combustion air).

- The temperature rise calculation for gas furnaces applies to oil furnaces. Determine output Btuh and apply an air density adjustment to the psychrometric equation for sensible heat (as demonstrated by Section A5-7.)

A5-9 Hot-Gas Coil

When the pressure and temperature for the refrigerant-side of a hot-gas coil is the same at altitude as for sea level, heating capacity depends on air mass-flow rate. When Cfm is held constant, the temperature rise at altitude is larger than at sea level. When temperature rise is held constant, the air mass-flow rate must increase at altitude.

Temperature rise (TR) is evaluated by applying an altitude correction to the psychrometric equation for sensible heat. Figure A5-1 provides the approximate altitude correction factor (ACF).

TR (°F) = Btuh Capacity / (1.1 x ACF x Cfm)

For example, suppose 1,500 Cfm flows through a 24,000 Btuh coil in Denver, CO (approximately 5,000 Feet).

Sea level TR = 24,000 / (1.1 x 1.00 x 1,500) = 14.5 °F
Denver TR = 24,000 / (1.1 x 0.84 x 1,500) = 17.3 °F
Denver Cfm for 14.5 °F rise = 1,500 x 17.3 / 14.5 = 1,790

A5-10 Heat Pump Heating

Air-air heat pump manufacturers publish heating capacity tables for refrigerant cycle heating at sea level. Figure A5-4 shows that heating capacity is very sensitive to outdoor temperature, and marginally sensitive to indoor temperature (*integrated capacity* means that the data has a default adjustment for defrost cycles).

For a heat pump at altitude, the dry-coil adjustment factors for a cooling evaporator served by an air-cooled condenser may be used for heat pump heating (Figure A5-3). This is an approximate adjustment, but approximate data is adequate for the intended purpose.

- The actual defrost cycle effect at altitude may be less than the default effect embedded in the OEM's performance data.
- Integrated heating capacities are used to draw a thermal balance point diagram for heat pump heating.
- Because air-air (and water-air) heat pumps are sized for cooling, the balance point diagram for heating need not be perfect.
- An approximate balance point value is sufficient for selecting the set-point of a control that deactivates supplemental electric resistance heat when outdoor temperature is above the thermal balance point.
- Thermal balance point diagrams are used to size electric resistance heaters for supplemental heat. The defrost knee has little effect when the winter design temperature for outdoor air is 20°F or less. In any case, because of standard sizes, the installed KW for supplemental heat is usually more than adequate.
- When an electric resistance heating coil is sized for 100 percent back-up heat, the installed heating capacity of electric coil is normally excessive for normal operation.

A5-11 Blower Performance

When blower speed (Rpm) is constant, blower Cfm is not affected by altitude. However, for a given Rpm, air mass-flow is reduced at altitude, and reduced mass-flow translates to less fan pressure, less airflow horsepower and less motor horsepower.

A5-12 Duct System Performance

When duct system airflow rates (Cfm values) are the same at altitude as for sea level, system resistance to airflow (external static pressure) is less than at sea level. And, because a given Cfm value has less mass-flow at altitude, the heating or cooling capacity for a supply air Cfm value is less than sea level capacity for the same Cfm.

Integrated Heating Capacity (MBtuh)				
Outdoor DB (F)	Entering Dry-Bulb (°F)			
	60	70	75	80
–5	78.1	75.8	74.9	74.0
0	86.8	84.4	83.4	82.5
5	96.0	93.6	92.4	91.4
10	106.4	103.8	102.0	100.9
15	119.9	117.1	115.0	114.0
20	131.0	120.6	120.0	119.5
25	142.5	139.4	137.9	136.4
30	154.5	151.2	149.6	148.0
35	167.2	163.6	161.7	160.0
40	180.8	176.9	174.8	172.9
45	194.0	189.8	187.5	185.3
50	213.9	209.0	206.6	204.3
55	243.4	237.4	234.5	231.7
60	262.1	255.5	252.3	249.1
70	278.3	271.2	267.7	264.1
75	295.6	286.3	284.3	280.5

Figure A5-4

A5-13 Duct System Design

Duct sizing procedures are not affected by altitude. Use sea level blower data, sea level friction charts, and sea level pressure drop data for air-side components and duct fittings to size duct runs.

- The duct system is designed for the blower Cfm value that was used to select equipment. (This Cfm tends to be larger than the value that would be used for a sea level application because heating and cooling capacity depends on mass-flow.)
- The fraction of blower Cfm flowing through a supply outlet or return grille is the same at altitude as for sea level.

A5-14 Effect on Duct System Operating Point

Flow-pressure relationships for the blower and the duct system are summarized by two curves on a pressure vs. volume flow rate graph (Figure A5-5, for example). The intersection of these two curves is the only possible operating point for the blower (for a particular blower Rpm, and a particular set of damper positions).

- Duct system design procedures use sea level blower data, so blower performance is plotted as curve B1.
- Duct system design procedures use sea level values for component pressure drops and fitting pressure drops, so duct system performance is plotted as curve S1.
- When duct sizing procedures are correctly applied, the operating point Cfm equals the design value for blower Cfm (as determined by the equipment selection procedure).
- The system operating point is affected by altitude because blower pressure and system flow resistance are reduced by altitude.
- Blower pressure is proportional to air density, so all points on the blower curve are multiplied by an altitude factor from Figure A5-5. This produces curve B2, which represents blower performance at altitude.
- System resistance is proportional to air density, so all points on the system curve are multiplied by an altitude factor from Figure A5-5. This produces curve S2, which represents system performance at altitude.
- At altitude, the operating point Cfm is equal to the sea level operating point Cfm, and the operating pressure is reduced (therefore, blower power is reduced).

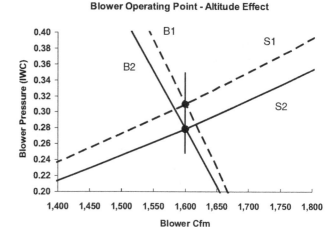

Figure A5-5

A5-15 Air-to-Air Heat Exchangers and Desiccant Wheels

The performance of air-to-air heat exchangers and desiccant wheels (and the hot-gas coil or gas burner for a desiccant wheel) depends on altitude and entering air temperatures. Refer to published engineering guidance provided by the product manufacturer, or use performance data provided by the product manufacturer's engineering department or technical representative.

Related Information

Appendix 6 – Energy and Op-Cost Calculations

Appendix 7 – Moisture and Condensation Issues

Appendix 8 – Condensation Calculations

Appendix 9 – Water-Loop Issues for Water-Air Heat Pumps

Appendix 10 – Multi-Split Piping

Appendix 11 – Furnace Cycling Efficiency

Appendix 12 – Matching Evaporators and Condensing Units

Appendix 13 – Performance Models for Cooling-Only and Heat Pump Equipment

Appendix 14 – Air-Air Heat Pump Supply Air Temperature

Appendix 15 – Whole-House Dehumidifier Performance

This appendix is not part of the this standard. It is merely informative and does not contain requirements necessary for conformance to the standard. It has not been processed according to the ANSI requirements for a standard, and may contain material that has not been subject to public review or a consensus process. Unresolved objectors on informative material are not offered the right to appeal at ACCA or ANSI.

Appendix 6

Energy and Op-Cost Calculations

The first portion of this section provides the rationale for requiring that HDD-65 divided by CDD-50 must be less than 2.0 to qualify a heat pump for 15,000 Btuh of excess cooling capacity. The balance of the section summarizes the requirements of a credible and defensible energy and op-cost calculation.

A6-1 Heat Pump Heating—Reducing Use of Electric Coil Heat

When indoor humidity control is not an issue (*Manual J* sensible heat ratio ranges from 0.95 to 1.00), the limit for excess total cooling capacity is greatly increased (+15,000 Btuh), providing this allowance results in a significant reduction in annual energy use. The issues that affect annual energy use are summarized here:

- The base case is for no set-back or set-up schedule, with supplemental heat locked out when the outdoor air temperature is above the thermal balance point temperature, and using equipment that has demand defrost.
- Compressor heat is more desirable than electric coil heat because compressor COP is significantly more than 1.0 (even when it is very cold outdoors), and because electric coil heat has a COP of 1.0.
- For heating, when the outdoor air temperature is below the thermal balance point, the compressor operates continuously with no cycling penalty.
- For heating, when the outdoor air temperature is above the thermal balance point, the compressor cycling penalty in KWH units increases with the amount of excess cooling capacity.
- For cooling, the compressor cycling penalty in KWH units increases with the amount of excess cooling capacity.
- The size of the cycling penalty depends on the cycling degradation coefficient (Cd) for the equipment. This is a secondary effect.
- The size of the cycling penalty also depends on how the cooling energy efficiency ratio (EER, not SEER) changes with steps in equipment size. This effect varies from negligible to significant, depending on equipment performance data.
- Blower and fan Cfm and power tend to increase with steps in equipment size. Larger equipment tends to use more annual blower and fan power.

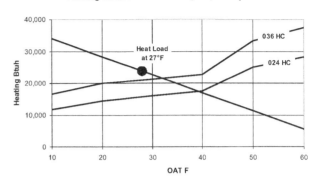

Seattle City Office Bin-Hours					
Outdoor Air Temperature (°F)					
Below 25	26 to 35	36 to 45	46 to 55	56 to 65	66 to 75
43	271	1,945	2,988	2,332	890

1) 1,750 SqFt dwelling, Seattle, WA., sea-level, 99% outdoor dry-bulb is 27°F, and 70°F indoors; 1% outdoor dry-bulb is 82°F, with 13 Grains moisture difference for 75°F and 45%RH indoors; bin data from AFM-88-8.
2) Double pane, metal break windows and skylights. Total fenestration area is 242 SqFt, distributed on four exposures.
3) Dark shingle roof over vented attic with R-30 ceiling insulation; wall U-value is 0.097; slab floor with R5 edge and under edge.
4) Winter infiltration at 0.26 ACH, summer infiltration at 0.14 ACH.
5) Attic duct system, R6 insulation; supply leakage 0.12 Cfm/sqFt duct area; return leakage 0.24 Cfm/SqFt duct area.
6) No engineered ventilation.
7) Manual J heating load is 24,348 Btuh; the sensible cooling load is 23,425 Btuh, and the latent cooling load is 1,206 Btuh.
8) The Manual J sensible heat ratio is 0.951.
9) Heat pump capacity curves from actual OEM data for a nominal 24,000 total cooling Btuh system, and for a nominal 36,000 total cooling Btuh system.

Tacoma McChord AFB Bin-Hours					
Outdoor Air Temperature (°F)					
Below 25	26 to 35	36 to 45	46 to 55	56 to 65	66 to 75
65	399	3,033	4,892	3,889	1,744

Figure A6-1

- Annual energy use equals compressor KWH for the heating season, plus electric coil heat for the heating season, plus compressor KWH for the cooling season, plus indoor blower and outdoor fan power for the year.

Appendx 6

Bin-Hour Calculation Summary for Figure A6-1 Circumstances (Seattle, WA)										
Nominal Size	AHRI Tons 95/80/67 (°F)	OEM's 95/80/67°F EER Values	Thermal Balance Point (°F)	Cooling KWH	Compressor Heating KWH	Electric Coil KWH	Total Heating KWH	Annual Heat-Cool KWH	Annual KWH Saved	Annual Saving Percent
Annual energy use for equipment that has a 0.25 cycling degradation coefficient										
024	2.08	11.88	39	1,271	8,816	707	9,523	10,794	~	~
036	2.92	11.39	32	1,321	9,379	211	9,591	10,912	-118	-1.09%
Annual energy use for equipment that has a 0.15 cycling degradation coefficient										
024	2.08	11.88	39	1,222	8,504	707	9,211	10,433	~	~
036	2.92	11.39	32	1,245	8,913	211	9,125	10,370	63	0.61%

1) Cooling capacity adjusted for blower heat, per OEM data.
2) Annual KWH includes blower KWH and outdoor fan KWH. Note 3 shows KW values from the OEM's expanded data.
3) For the 024 size, blower KW = 0.26, and outdoor fan KW = 0.25; for the 036 size, blower KW = 0.28, and outdoor fan KW = 0.25
4) For the 024 size the supplemental electric coil load is 2.59 KW; 5.0 KW used for the bin calculation. For the 036 size the supplemental electric coil load is 1.01 KW; 2.5 KW used for the bin calculation.
5) OEM EER values for the AHRI rating condition include compressor power, and OEM defaults for indoor blower and outdoor fan power. The OEM did not provide Cd values, so the EER values are not necessarily for the Cd values used for this example. Because EER values are not used for the bin calculation, they do not affect the size of the KWH values.
6) No electric coil heat when the outdoor air temperature is above the thermal balance point temperature. Electric coil is one-stage.

Figure A6-2

A6-2 Intuitive Indicator

A thermal balance point diagram for the dwelling and the candidate equipment shows when electric coil heat is needed. When there are a large number of bin-hours below the thermal balance point temperature, excess compressor capacity for cooling will result in a significant KWH savings for the heating season. On the other hand, a small number of bin-hours below the thermal balance point will not produce a significant KWH savings for the heating season.

Excessive compressor capacity increases energy use for heating above the thermal balance point, and for all cooling hours, due to unnecessary equipment cycling. Therefore, larger equipment for locations that have a large number of bin-hours above the thermal balance point may not produce significant annual energy savings, and for some cases, energy annual use may increase somewhat.

- The best circumstances for energy savings occur when a location has a large number of bin-hours below the thermal balance point, and relatively small number of cooling bin-hours.
- The worst circumstances for energy savings occur when a location has a small number of bin-hours below the thermal balance point, and relatively large number of cooling bin-hours.
- Some locations have a large number of bin-hours below the thermal balance point, and a large number of cooling bin-hours. This tends to reduce the benefit of excess compressor capacity for heating efficiency.

Seattle Example

Figure A6-1 (previous page) summarizes the situation for a location that has relatively mild weather year-round. The 024 system has a 0.96 over-size factor, and the thermal balance point for compressor heating is about 39°F. Figure A6-1 also shows that an additional ton of cooling capacity lowers the thermal balance point to about 32°F, and reduces the need for electric coil heat. Also note that there are only 314 bin-hours below 35°F.

An intuitive conclusion about the benefit of using an extra ton of cooling capacity requires some experience. A 7°F reduction in the thermal balance point looks impressive, but the small number of cold weather bin-hours is the primary issue.

Figure A6-2 shows the results of a bin energy calculation for the Figure A6-1 situation. Note that for this particular product, the OEM's EER value decreases from 11.88 to 11.39 for a one-ton increase in equipment size.

EER vs. size behavior is peculiar to this product, the effect may be significantly different for some other product. The ideal scenario is that EER increases with size, or at least stays relatively constant with size.

For a 0.25 cycling degradation coefficient (the default value when the OEM does not provide a value), annual energy use increases by about 1%; and for a 0.15 cycling degradation coefficient, annual energy use decreases by about 1%. Larger equipment reduces electric coil energy use by about 495 KWH, but for a 0.25 Cd, this benefit is less than the penalty for compressor cycling (total KWH increases), and for a 0.15 Cd the compressor cycling penalty reduces the 495 KWH benefit by 87% (total savings is 63 KWH).

Therefore, for a relatively common dwelling, an extra ton of cooling capacity for a specific OEM product does not provide a significant reduction in energy use for a benign climate. A bin-hour calculation for a dwelling that has different attributes, and/or equipment EER vs. size behavior may produce a somewhat different result, possibly a few more percentage points of positive or negative energy savings, depending on circumstances.

Tacoma, WA is close to Seattle. Figure A6-1 shows that Tacoma has more cold weather bin-hours than Seattle, so the Tacoma energy savings for excess compressor capacity will be somewhat larger than the Seattle values, everything else being equal.

Spokane Example

Figure A6-3 summarizes the situation for a location that has a relatively cold winter, and moderate summer weather. The 030 system has an 1.00 over-size factor, and the thermal balance point for compressor heating is about 35°F. Figure A6-3 also shows that an additional ton of cooling capacity lowers the thermal balance point to about 27°F, and reduces the need for electric coil heat. Also note that there are 2,215 bin-hours below 35°F.

For this example, an 8°F reduction in the thermal balance point looks impressive, but 2,215 bin-hours below 35°F outdoors is the primary issue.

Figure A6-4 (next page) shows the results of a bin energy calculation for the Figure A6-3 situation. Note that for this particular product, the OEM's EER value decreases from 12.45 to 11.37 for a one-ton increase in equipment size.

EER vs. size behavior is peculiar to this product, the effect may be significantly different for some other product. The ideal scenario is that EER increases with size, or at least stays relatively constant with size.

For a 0.25 cycling degradation coefficient (the default value when the OEM does not provide a value), annual energy use decreases by about 3.5%; and for a 0.15 cycling degradation coefficient, annual energy use decreases by about 4.8%. Electric coil energy use is reduced by 2,923 KWH, but 80% to 73% of this savings, depending on the Cd value, is offset by increased energy use do to equipment cycling (the net savings is 585 KWH for a 0.25 Cd, and 797 KWH for a 0.15 Cd).

Therefore, for a relatively common dwelling, an extra ton of cooling capacity for a specific OEM product does provide a significant reduction in energy use for a cold winter climate. A bin-hour calculation for a dwelling that has

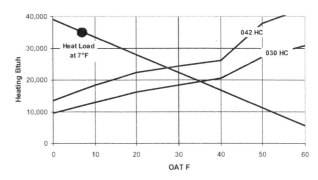

Spokane Bin-Hours					
Outdoor Air Temperature (°F)					
Below 25	26 to 35	36 to 45	46 to 55	56 to 65	66 to 75
591	1,624	1,986	1,569	1,323	942

1) 1,750 SqFt dwelling, Spokane, WA.; 2,366 Feet, 99% outdoor dry-bulb is 7°F, and 70°F indoors; 1% outdoor dry-bulb is 89°F, with -23 Grains moisture difference for 75°F and 45%RH indoors; bin data from AFM-88-8.
2) Double pane, metal break windows and skylights. Total fenestration area is 242 SqFt, distributed on four exposures.
3) Dark shingle roof over vented attic with R-30 ceiling insulation; wall U-value is 0.097; slab floor with R5 edge and under edge.
4) Winter infiltration at 0.26 ACH, summer infiltration at 0.14 ACH.
5) Attic duct system, R6 insulation; supply leakage 0.12 Cfm/sqFt duct area; return leakage 0.24 Cfm/SqFt duct area.
6) No engineered ventilation.
7) Manual J heating load is 35,239 Btuh; the sensible cooling load is 25,901 Btuh, and the latent cooling load is zero.
8) The *Manual J* sensible heat ratio is 1.00.
9) Heat pump capacity curves from actual OEM data for a nominal 29,400 total cooling Btuh system, and for a nominal 40,500 total cooling Btuh system.

Boise, ID, Bin-Hours					
Outdoor Air Temperature (°F)					
Below 25	26 to 35	36 to 45	46 to 55	56 to 65	66 to 75
524	1,336	1,782	1,535	1,293	1,019

Figure A6-3

different attributes, and/or equipment EER vs. size behavior may produce a somewhat different result, possibly a few more percentage points of more, or less, energy savings, depending on the scenario.

Figure A6-3 also show bin-hours for Boise, ID. For Boise, the winter is a little milder than for Spokane, and the summer is somewhat warmer. Therefore, everything else being equal, the energy savings for one-ton of excess cooling capacity for Boise, ID, will be somewhat less than the Spokane, WA, savings. In general, the energy savings for excess cooling capacity decrease as bin-hours shift from colder bins to warmer bins.

Bin-Hour Calculation Summary for Figure A6-3 Circumstances (Spokane, WA)										
Nominal Size	AHRI Tons 95/80/67°F	OEM's 95/80/67°F EER Values	Thermal Balance Point (F)	Cooling KWH	Compressor Heating KWH	Electric Coil KWH	Total Heating KWH	Annual Heat-Cool KWH	Annual KWH Saved	Annual Saving Percent
Annual energy use for equipment that has a 0.25 cycling degradation coefficient										
030	2.45	12.45	35	1,923	10,654	4,421	15,075	16,998	~	~
042	3.38	11.37	27	2,335	12,581	1,498	14,078	16,413	585	3.44%
Annual energy use for equipment that has a 0.15 cycling degradation coefficient										
030	2.45	12.45	35	1,845	10,412	4,421	14,833	16,678	~	~
042	3.38	11.37	27	2,197	12,186	1,498	13,684	15,881	797	4.78%

1) Cooling capacity adjusted for blower heat, per OEM data. The altitude adjustment factor for total cooling and heating capacity is 0.97.
2) Annual KWH includes blower KWH and outdoor fan KWH. Note 3 shows KW values from the OEM's expanded data.
3) For the 030 size, blower KW = 0.26, and outdoor fan KW = 0.255; for the 042 size, blower KW = 0.49, and outdoor fan KW = 0.25.
4) For the 030 size the supplemental electric coil load is 6.92 KW; 7.5 KW used for the bin calculation. For the 042 size the supplemental electric coil load is 5.50 KW; 7.5 KW used for the bin calculation.
5) OEM EER values for the AHRI rating condition include compressor power, and OEM defaults for indoor blower and outdoor fan power. The OEM did not provide Cd values, so the EER values are not necessarily for the Cd values used for this example. Because EER values are not used for the bin calculation, they do not affect the size of the KWH values.
6) No electric coil heat when the outdoor air temperature is above the thermal balance point temperature. Electric coil is one stage.

Figure A6-4

A6-3 Simplified Indicator

Heating degree days and cooling degree days are related to bin-hour data, so for simplification and convenience, heating degree days to the base 65°F (HDD-65), and cooling degree days to the base 50°F (CDD-50) are used to anticipate the consequences of a bin-hour calculation. Per Table N2-2 procedures, 15,000 Btuh of excess cooling capacity for reduced annual energy use is allowed when the HDD-65 to CDD-50 ratio is equal to, or greater than 2.0, providing that latent cooling capacity is not an issue.

- Degree day information is readily available for thousands of locations (see Section N1-5). Bin-hour data and hourly weather summaries are not as prolific as degree day data. Processing historical hourly summaries for a particular weather station is possible, but not practical for commercial purposes.
- A degree day ratio calculation is a simple task. A bin-hour calculation, or hourly simulation, is considerably more than what most practitioners are able and willing to do, unless software provides credible solutions that require minimal practitioner skill and input.
- Figure A6-5 shows degree day ratios for a few dry summer locations that may, or may not, benefit from excess compressor capacity for cooling.

A6-4 Alternative to the Degree Day Ratio Method

Spot checks for locations that may benefit from more compressor heating capacity show that the HDD-65 to CDD-50 ratio method is compatible with conclusions that

Sampling of NOAA Degree Day Ratios for Dry Locations			
Location	HDD-65	CDD-50	HDD/CDD
Seattle, WA.	4,615	2,159	2.14
Tacoma, WA.	4,650	2,123	2.19
Spokane, WA.	6,820	2,060	3.31
Boise, ID	5,727	2,856	2.01
Billings, MT.	7,006	2,496	2.81
Bozman, MT.	7,729	1,780	4.34
Tucson, AZ.	1,888	6,616	0.29
Las Vegas, NV.	2,239	6,677	0.33
Reno, NV.	5,600	2,513	2.23
Denver, CO.	2,128	3,724	2.24
San Francisco, CA.	3,653	2,036	1.79
Albuquerque, NM.	4,281	4,013	1.07
Santa Fe, NM.	6,073	2,399	2.53

Figure A6-5

are based on bin-hour calculations. However, authoritative organizations, software houses, and practitioners have the option to use a credible bin-hour calculation, or hourly simulation to justify more compressor capacity for reduced annual energy use (see Section A20-6).

- The annual energy use consequences of excess compressor capacity depend on local weather patterns; the dwelling's floor plan, fenestration plan, and construction details; duct loads and engineered ventilation loads; equipment performance maps for heating and cooling, equipment EER vs. steps in compressor size; and equipment cycling degradation coefficient.

- The criteria for justifying excess compressor capacity may be the peak KW demand on a winter peaking utility, vs. it's annual KWH load.

- Excess compressor capacity for cooling affects installation cost and operating cost. This raises a return on investment question that may, or may not, be affected by a utility rebate or incentive program, or a tax policy.

A6-5 Basic Bin-Hour Calculation

A simplified bin-hour calculation for a dwelling is based on a 65°F outdoor air temperature for heating-cooling change-over (no heat or cooling required at 65°F). The line for heating load vs. outdoor dry-bulb temperature runs from the Manual J heating load value to zero Btuh for 65°F outdoors; and the line for cooling load vs. outdoor dry-bulb temperature runs from the **Manual J** cooling load value to zero Btuh for 65°F outdoors. OEM data provides lines for heating and cooling capacity vs. outdoor air temperature (or entering water temperature). Bin-hours are assigned to steps in outdoor air temperature.

The Figure A6-6 graphs and the Figure A6-7 (next page) procedure (next page) show how the preceding instructions are implemented. Note that a default solar load plus internal gain effect is embedded in the way the load-lines are drawn on the graph. (For heating, no solar/internal load for the winter design temperature, with a default solar/internal load for 65°F outdoors; for cooling, full solar/internal load for the summer design temperature, with a default solar/internal load for 65°F outdoors.)

The indoor thermostat (70°F default for heating, 75°F default for cooling) responds to sensible capacity vs. sensible load. When there is no latent load, total capacity equals sensible capacity, so equipment runtime is based on total capacity vs. total load. This provides a significant simplification of the calculation procedure, and is appropriate for a Condition B heat pump.

Note that the bin-hour values are for 24 hours per day, because this simplified method does not make separate calculations for sunshine hours and night time hours, and does not use an internal load vs. time of day schedule. Also note that the OEM's defrost knee provides a default adjustment for the effect of defrost cycles.

This simplified procedure deals with the basic issues that affect annual energy use for a Condition B heat pump, and returns a reasonable approximation of the annual

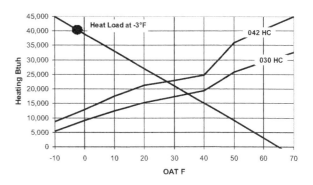

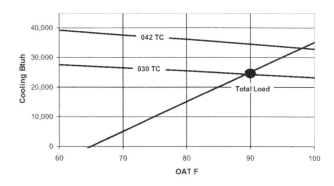

Denver, Co; Bin-Hours											
–10 F	0 F	10 F	20 F	30 F	40 F	50 F	60 F	70 F	80 F	90 F	100 F
22	76	221	637	1,259	1,476	1,468	1,570	1,112	675	245	7

1) 1,750 SqFt dwelling, Denver, CO, 5,283 Feet, 99% outdoor dry-bulb is –3°F, and 70°F indoors; 1% outdoor dry-bulb is 90°F, with -33 Grains moisture difference for 75°F and 45%RH indoors; bin data from AFM-88-8.
2) Double pane, metal break windows and skylights. Total fenestration area is 242 SqFt, distributed on four exposures.
3) Dark shingle roof over vented attic with R-30 ceiling insulation; wall U-value is 0.097; slab floor with R5 edge and under edge.
4) Winter infiltration at 0.26 ACH, summer infiltration at 0.14 ACH.
5) Attic duct system, R6 insulation; supply leakage 0.12 Cfm/sqFt duct area; return leakage 0.24 Cfm/SqFt duct area.
6) No engineered ventilation.
7) **Manual J** heating load is 40,848 Btuh; the sensible cooling load is 25,152 Btuh, and the latent cooling load is zero.
8) The **Manual J** sensible heat ratio is 1.00.
9) Heat pump capacity curves from actual OEM data for a nominal 29,400 total cooling Btuh system, and for a nominal 40,500 total cooling Btuh system.

Figure A6-6

energy load. A similar procedure appears in Section 19 of the 2009 ASHRAE Handbook of Fundamentals.

Figure A6-8 shows bin calculation results for Figure A6-6 circumstances. Note that for this particular product, the OEM's EER value decreases from 12.45 to 11.37 for a one-ton increase in equipment size. Alternative products may behave differently, as far as EER vs. equipment size is concerned.

Appendx 6

Bin Heating Energy Calculation for Figure A6-6 Circumstances for the 030 Size; Cd = 0.25 (Denver, CO)

Note 1	Note 2	Note 3	Note 4	Note 5	Note 6	Note 7	Note 8	Note 9	Note 10	Note 11	Note 12
Bin-Hour Temp° F	Bin-Hours 10°F Range	MJ8 Heat Load (HL) Btuh	Compressor Heat (CHC) OEM Btuh	Load Factor (LF)	Input KW Compressor and Fans	part-load Factor (PLF) Cd = 0.25	Compressor Blower and Fan KWH	Electric Coil Btuh Capacity ECC Btuh	Electric Coil Btuh Load ECL	Electric Coil Run Factor ECF	Electric Coil KWH	Total Package KWH
−10	22	45,053	5,299	1.00	0.20	1.00	4	34,130	39,754	1.00	220	224
0	76	39,046	8,987	1.00	2.00	1.00	152	34,130	30,059	0.88	669	821
10	221	33,039	12,365	1.00	2.05	1.00	453	34,130	20,674	0.61	1,339	1,791
20	637	27,032	15,327	1.00	2.09	1.00	1,329	34,130	11,705	0.34	2,185	3,513
30	1,259	21,025	17,351	1.00	2.11	1.00	2,651	34,130	3,674	0.11	1,355	4,007
40	1,476	15,018	19,430	0.77	2.13	0.94	2,579	34,130	0	0.00	0	2,579
50	1,468	9,011	25,834	0.35	2.25	0.84	1,375	34,130	0	0.00	0	1,375
60	1,570	3,004	29,238	0.10	2.30	0.78	478	34,130	0	0.00	0	478
70	0	-3,004	32,605	~	2.35	0.73	0	34,130	0	0.00	0	0
						Total compressor, blower, fan KWH =	9,020	Electric coil KWH and Total Package KWH =			5,768	14,788

1) Ten degree bin temperature steps used to simplify the example. AFM-88-8 bin data has bin-hours for five degree steps. Values for two five degree steps are summed to obtain value for a ten degree step. Five degree steps preferred for actual design work.
2) Two points define a straight line. The **Manual J** heating load provides one point, and the no heating load at 65°F outdoors provides the second point. The general equation for a straight line is Btuh Load = Line slope x Outdoor air temperature + Intercept. Regression analysis provides values for the slope and intercept. Or, draw it up on a piece of graph paper.
3) OEM expanded heating data that has a default defrost knee provides heating capacity values vs. outdoor air temperature.
4) LF = HL / CHC; Maximum value = 1.00; Minimum value = 0.
5) OEM expanded heating data provides KW values for the compressor, blower, and outdoor fan vs. outdoor air temperature.
6) PLF = 1 − Cd x (1.0 - LF).
7) Package KWH = (Bin-Hours x LF x Input KW) / PLF.
8) Amount of electric coil heat activated by the second stage of the indoor thermostat. One stage of heat shown for this example. When electric coil heat is staged, correlate eclectic coil heat capacity with the temperature bins. (1 KW = 3,413 Btuh).
9) ECL = HL - CHC; Minimum value = 0.
10) ECF = ECL / ECC; Maximum = 1.0; Minimum = 0.
11) Electric coil KWH = Bin-Hours x (ECC / 3,413) x ECF.
12) Total package KWH = Total compressor, blower, fan KWH + Electric coil KWH.

Bin Cooling Energy Calculation for Figure A6-6 Circumstances for the 030 Size; Cd = 0.25 (Denver, CO)

Note 1	Note 2	Note 3	Note4	Note 5	Note 6	Note 7
Bin-Hour Temp° F	Bin-Hours 10°F Range	MJ8 Cool Load Btuh (TL)	Total Cool Capacity Btuh (TC)	Load Factor (LF)	Input KW Compressor and Fans	part-load Factor (PLF) Cd = 0.25	Total Package KWH
100	7	35,213	23,276	1.00	2.550	1.00	18
90	245	25,152	24,380	1.00	2.320	1.00	568
80	675	15,091	25,484	0.59	2.090	0.90	930
70	1,112	5,030	26,588	0.19	1.860	0.80	491
60	0	-5,030	27,692	-0.18	1.630	0.70	0
						Total Package KWH =	2,007

1) See Note 1 for heating.
2) See Note 2, for heating. In this case, the **Manual J** cooling load provides one point, and the no cooling load at 65°F outdoors provides the second point.
3) OEM expanded cooling data provides total capacity values vs. outdoor air temperature.
4) LF = TL / TC; Maximum value = 1.00; Minimum value = 0.
5) OEM expanded cooling data provides KW values for the compressor, blower, and outdoor fan vs. outdoor air temperature.
6) PLF = 1 − Cd x (1.0 - LF).
7) Package KWH = (Bin-Hours x LF x Input KW) / PLF.

Total Cooling Load: Equipment runtime may be based on the total cooling load when the latent cooling load is zero or insignificant. The bin calculation procedure for cooling is much more complicated when the coil sensible heat ratio depends on momentary operating conditions.

Water-Air Heat Pumps: For water-air equipment, entering water temperature, and the associated values for compressor heating/cooling capacity, and package input KW must be correlated with the bin-hour temperatures. For GWHP (open, pump and dump) systems, one Btuh value and one KW value applies to all temperature bins. For buried-loop systems, entering water temperature and the associated Btuh and KW values depend on month of year. For loop systems bin calculations are performed for each month, then results are summed. A less accurate solution assigns a cold water temperature to the cold temperature bins, a mid-range water temperature to the middle temperature bins, and a warm water temperature to the warm temperature bins.

Figure A6-7

Bin-Hour Calculation Summary for Figures A6-6 and A6-7 Circumstances (Denver, CO)										
Nominal Size	AHRI Tons 95/80/67°F	OEM's 95/80/67°F EER Values	Thermal Balance Point (F)	Cooling KWH	Compressor Heating KWH	Electric Coil KWH	Total Heating KWH	Annual Heat-Cool KWH	Annual KWH Saved	Annual Saving Percent
Annual energy use for equipment that has a 0.25 cycling degradation coefficient										
030	2.45	12.45	35	2,007	9,020	5,768	14,788	16,795	~	~
042	3.38	11.37	27	2,418	10,821	2,889	13,710	16,128	667	3.97%
Annual energy use for equipment that has a 0.15 cycling degradation coefficient										
030	2.45	12.45	35	1,922	8,811	5,768	14,579	16,501	~	~
042	3.38	11.37	27	2,270	10,502	2,889	13,391	15,661	839	5.09%

1) Cooling capacity adjusted for blower heat, per OEM data. The altitude adjustment factor for total cooling and heating capacity is 0.92.
2) Annual KWH includes blower KWH and outdoor fan KWH. Note 3 shows KW values from the OEM's expanded data.
3) For the 030 size, blower KW = 0.26, and outdoor fan KW = 0.255; for the 042 size, blower KW = 0.49, and outdoor fan KW = 0.25.
4) For the 030 size the supplemental electric coil load is 9.7 KW; 10.0 KW used for the bin calculation. For the 042 size the supplemental electric coil load is 8.7 KW; 10.0 KW used for the bin calculation.
5) OEM EER values for the AHRI rating condition include compressor power, and OEM defaults for indoor blower and outdoor fan power. The OEM did not provide Cd values, so the EER values are not necessarily for the Cd values used for this example. Because EER values are not used for the bin calculation, they do not affect the size of the KWH values.
6) No electric coil heat when the outdoor air temperature is above the thermal balance point temperature. Electric coil is one-stage.

Figure A6-8

A6-6 Advanced Methods

Practitioners, stake holders and software houses have the option to use a more sophisticated energy calculation procedure. Such procedures apply to cooling-only equipment, Condition A heat pumps, Condition B heat pumps, and to fossil fuel heating equipment.

A Simultaneous Solution is Required

Outdoor solar and outdoor air conditions continuously interact with building construction details to produce momentary sensible and latent envelope loads, and may affect momentary duct loads. Outdoor solar conditions depend on hour of year, latitude, altitude, momentary cloud cover, and momentary atmospheric haze. Outdoor air conditions affect momentary engineered ventilation loads, where applicable.

Drape and blind positions affect momentary fenestration loads. Momentary fenestration loads also depend on the interior thermal mass that is heated by solar radiation passing through fenestration, and fenestration shading devices. Momentary structural panel loads depend on the beam radiation impinging on roof and wall areas, the thermal mass of these panels, and the absorptivity and emissivity of their surfaces.

Occupants produce a variety of momentary sensible and latent cooling loads. Momentary internal loads also depend on the interior thermal mass that is affected by temperature difference radiation. The consequences of occupant behavior is superimposed on the loads produced by outdoor circumstances. An indoor blower produces a momentary fan heat load.

For the simplest case, one indoor thermostat reacts to the sum of the momentary sensible loads and cycles single-speed equipment on and off. Zoning adds significant complexity to energy modeling, as does set-up and set-back, with or without zoning. Multi-speed and variable-speed equipment adds significant complexity. OEM control strategies for enhanced indoor humidity control add complexity.

For cooling, momentary equipment sensible and latent capacity attempts to balance with momentary sensible and latent loads, depending on outdoor air conditions or entering water temperature, and entering air wet-bulb and dry-bulb temperatures. This determines momentary values for coil sensible heat ratio, equipment runtime per hour, and indoor relative humidity. Modeling this process is significantly complicated by the pull-down transient for indoor coil temperature after equipment start-up, and a possible failure to bring the indoor humidity to the desired level before the equipment cycles off on dry-bulb temperature. The system's cycling degradation coefficient for the cooling mode affects seasonal energy use.

For heat pump heating, the momentary thermal balance point depends on the momentary solar and internal loads, and on how the momentary outdoor air condition affects the defrost cycle. The first stage of the thermostat activates the compressor. Above the momentary thermal balance point, compressor runtime depends on momentary heating capacity vs. the momentary heating load, or the compressor operates continuously below the thermal balance point. Above the thermal balance point, the cycling degradation coefficient for compressor heating affects seasonal energy use.

For heat pump heating, supplemental electric coil heat should be locked out above the momentary thermal balance point (or for an appropriate value for outdoor air temperature). Below the momentary thermal balance point, the electric coil runtime depends on the demand for electric coil heat vs. momentary compressor heat.

Heat pump heating energy depends on the type of defrost control, and depends on a timer setting for timed defrost. Demand defrost is common, but the shape of the defrost knee for compressor heat depends on the local frosting potential (outdoor air dry-bulb and coincident wet-bulb temperatures) for the location's outdoor air temperature bins.

The amount of electric coil heat energized during defrost affects seasonal energy use, because the space is heated at a COP of 1.0 when the electric coil heat added during a defrost cycle exceeds the reheat heat load for the defrost cycle. Space heating during defrost reduces the amount of heat that must be provided by the compressor after a defrost cycle. Crankcase heat uses energy.

Fossil fuel heating is relatively simple. runtime depends on heating capacity vs. the heating load. Momentary efficiency depends on momentary runtime. Staged or modulation burners add calculation complexity.

Blower power and water pump power may be relatively constant through the season. The calculations are more complicated when the motor speed setting changes or modulates during the season. Continuous blower operation significantly increases seasonal energy use. Heat recover equipment for engineered ventilation, and/or use of supplemental dehumidification equipment adds significant complexity to the calculations.

The local electric utility may have one rate for the whole year, with no demand changes. There may be different rates for heating and cooling. There may be a demand charge. The rate plan may be linked to an incentive program. Electric, natural gas, propane and oil prices are momentary. Momentary utility or tax rebates affect installed cost, but the benefit may, or may not, go to the homeowner (in the past, some programs routed the incentive to the installer).

Conclusion

This incomplete list of energy use, energy cost, and project pay-back issues is more than enough to show that simplified procedures based on rating SEER, HSPF, AFUE, degree days, or average heating and cooling hours are inadequate. Even a comprehensive investigation for a particular dwelling in a particular location is inadequate for drawing general conclusions, because of large differences in most of the variables that affect the calculations.

A 12 month load calculation procedure, or at least a four season version, has adequate sensitivity to load producing circumstances, and a proper set of expanded performance data has sensitivity to equipment capacity and power/fuel use circumstances. Energy rates and rate schedules are what they are for a particular location. Software that performs a proper hourly simulation for a typical meteorological year, of a sophisticated bin-hour calculation, provides defensible, case specific, values for energy use and operating cost.

A6-7 Weather Data for Energy Modeling

For bin-hour modeling, AFM 88-29, Engineering Weather Data was published in 1978. This has been improved and updated, and is available on a CD, per the following address. The web-page provides a link to a PDF summary (at no charge) of the capabilities, features, formats, and sensitivities of the data sets on the CD.

http://ols.nndc.noaa.gov/plolstore/plsql/olstore. prodspecific? prodnum=C00515-CDR-A0001.

This link provides a summary of what is in the current version of AFM 88-29.

UFC-3-400-02, Design: Engineering Weather Data, Unified Facilities Criteria, is dated February, 2003.

http://www.wbdg.org/ccb/DOD/UFC/ufc_3_400_02.pdf

An ASHRAE CD has bin-hour data and degree hour data for simplified energy calculations. Visit their web-site for an inventory of available products.

Typical mean year data is used for hourly simulations. The National Renewable Energy Laboratory's (NREL) TMY3 data set (Wilcox and Marion 2008) contains data for 1,020 U.S. locations. TMY3, along with the 1991-2005 National Solar Radiation Data Base (NSRDB) (NREL 2007), contains hourly solar radiation [global, beam (direct), and diffuse} and meteorological data for 1,454 stations, and is available at:

http://ols.nndc.noaa.gov/plolstore/plsql/olstore. prodspecific?prodnum=C00668-TAP-A0001.

The Climate Atlas of the United States; as provided by the National Climatic Data Center (NCDC/NOAA) has useful data for energy modeling. This CD-ROM replaces a popular paper Atlas last published in 1968, and supersedes version 1.0 of the Climate Atlas of the Contiguous United States published on CD in 2000. The new CD Atlas contains 2023 color maps of climatic elements such as temperature, precipitation, cloud cover, snow, wind, pressure, etc., that define the USA climate, see:

http://www.ncdc.noaa.gov/oa/about/cdrom/climatls2/ atlashelp.html

These weather data sources, and additional sources are listed in Chapter 14 of the 2009 ASHRAE Book of Fundamentals. See page 14.1, page 14-15 and page 14.16.

Section N1-5 of this manual provides two sources for heating degree day values and cooling degree day values for various base temperatures. These are used to comply with Table N2-2 sizing procedures. Degree day models, and heating-hour and cooling-hour models, do not have adequate capability and sensitivity for energy modeling.

A6-8 Proximity Issues for Weather Data Use

Weather data for a nearby location may be used when bin-hour data or typical mean year data is not available for the location of interest. However, the location of interest must be climatologically compatible with the weather data location.

- Nearby refers to the vector distance (miles or kilometers) between two latitude/longitude points.
- Locations may be climatologically similar for a 50 mile distance to more than a hundred mile distance, when they are at about the same elevation; and not near the ocean, an unusually large lake, or in a river basin.
- Locations are not climatologically similar when there is a significant difference in elevation (500 feet may be significant, 1,000 feet is significant).
- Locations that have similar elevations are not similar when one is near a large body of water, or in a river basin, and the other is remote (perhaps 20 miles, or less) from significant aquatic influence.

Appendx 6

Appendix 7

Moisture and Condensation Issues

For cold climate heating, condensation problems may occur when indoor humidity exceeds 20% to 35% RH. For humid climates, mold, mildew and condensation problems may occur during summer cooling. Use of appropriate system design procedures and equipment sizing rules prevent such occurrences.

A7-1 Design Values for Indoor Humidity

The optimum range for space humidity is 40% RH to 60% RH for health and comfort (see Figure A7-1). For wet-coil operation, cooling systems are designed for 50% RH. For very humid locations, cooling systems may be designed for 55% RH. For dry-coil climates, cooling systems are designed for 45% RH (see Figure A7-2).

A7-2 Moisture Issues for Winter

For cold weather, with an adequate vapor retarder, there will be no surface condensation problems when the dew-point of the space air is lower than the dry-bulb temperature of the coldest surface that is in contact with space air (including exposed duct surfaces).

Comfort Zone Condensation (Winter)

When the comfort system has winter humidification, the task is usually performed by central humidifier that adds moisture to the air flowing through a primary supply duct. Surface condensation problems are avoided by using an appropriate set-point for the humidistat (see Figure A7-2), an effective vapor retarding membrane, adequate insulation, and adequate fenestration performance (provide appropriate R-values and workmanship for all construction details).

For zone damper systems, the effect of engineered humidification depends on where the moisture goes as zone dampers close, and on zone isolation, the location of the humidistat, and the sophistication of the control system. Condensation is possible when a comfort zone, dump zone, or non-zoned space is over humidified. See *Manual Zr*, Appendix 2 for more information on this subject.

Condensation Calculations for Winter

Make sure the dew-point temperature of space air is less than the dry-bulb temperature of any structural surface that contacts space air. Also make sure that the dew-point temperature of ducted air is less than the dry-bulb temperature of any duct surfaces that contact ducted air (supply air, return air and bypass air can have different dew-points). See Appendix 8 for related procedures.

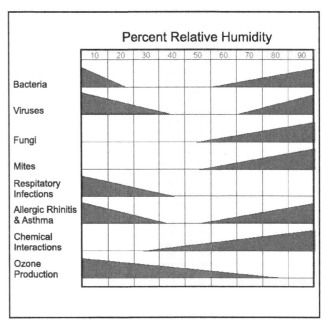

Figure A7-1

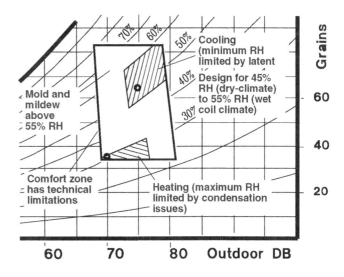

Figure A7-2

A7-3 Moisture Issues for Summer

Summer humidity may cause condensation on the outside surfaces of windows, glass doors and skylights, and/or condensation within structural panels. This depends on the dew-point temperature of the outdoor air and the dry-bulb temperature of the surfaces that contact outdoor air.

- On a very humid summer day, the peak humidity ratio (grains of moisture per pound of air) for outdoor air can be significantly higher that the humidity ratio that is used for cooling load calculations (compare weather data for the 1% dew-point condition and the 1% dry-bulb condition).
- For warm, humid climates, a vapor retarding membrane is installed near the outdoor surface (this prevents moisture migration to a cool hidden surface).
- Condensation on the outdoor surface of a window can occur for any location that has significant summer humidity (an Ohio window that has a relatively high U-value, for example).
- Condensation may occur for a normal space temperature (75°F), so the probability of condensation increases as space temperature drops (a cold dump zone, for example).

Duct Condensation (Summer)

Condensation occurs when the dry-bulb temperature of a duct surface is less than the dew-point temperature of the air that is in contact with the surface. This applies to the exterior surface of vapor retarding membrane (wrap) that covers duct insulation, and to the duct material when there is no vapor retarding wrap (moisture may migrate through duct insulation).

- Duct runs in unconditioned spaces are vulnerable to condensation during humid weather.
- Duct condensation may occur for normal operating temperatures (55°F to 75°F), so the probability of condensation increases as duct air temperature drops (cold air through a bypass duct, or cold return air from a dump zone, for example).

Condensation Calculations for Summer

The dry-bulb temperature of any structural surface that contacts outdoor air must be warmer than the dew-point temperature of the outdoor air. Also make sure the dry-bulb temperature of any duct surface that contacts outdoor air is warmer than the dew-point temperature of the outdoor air. See Appendix 8 for related procedures.

Conditions for Mold and Mildew

Biological spores are ubiquitous. Mold and Mildew blooms are activated by a source of moisture, which can be humid air, or surface condensation.

- Figure A7-1 shows that blooms may occur when space humidity exceeds 60% RH.
- Some climates are more susceptible to mold and mildew than others because infiltration and engineered ventilation increase the latent load when the outdoor air dew-point is greater than the indoor air dew-point.
- For 75°F dry-bulb and 50% RH, the dew-point of indoor air is 55°F, for 75°F and 60% RH the dew-point of indoor air is close to 60°F.
- For humid climates, duct insulation may not prevent summer condensation on duct walls and/or insulating materials. An external facing or wrap (vapor retarding membrane) is required when the average outdoor air dew-point for cooling (July/August) exceeds 60°F.
- Figure A8-5 provides outdoor air dew-point information for USA cities.
- During cold weather, there may be condensation in attic ducts when the ducts are not used for heating (baseboard heat, for example).

Minimize or Neutralize Moisture Gains

Humidity control is improved when moisture gains are minimal. The practitioner should provide observations, advice and counsel pertaining to envelope gains and internal gains. The practitioner is solely responsible for mechanical system gains.

- Minimize structural infiltration (building seams and joints must be sealed, windows and doors must be tight, an air barrier must be properly installed with no flaws or damage).
- Prevent infiltration through duct runs (seal all seams and joints in exposed duct runs; seal all seams and joints in an exposed air handler).
- Infiltration is increased by negative space pressure (direct vented furnaces and water heaters do not affect infiltration).
- Engineered ventilation may produce a sizable latent load. Routing outdoor air through cooling equipment moderates latent load to some extent (moisture removal depends on runtime). For very humid climates, a ventilation dehumidifier reduces indoor humidity.
- Vents, chimneys and exhaust fans increase infiltration. Routing make-up air through cooling equipment moderates latent load to some extent (moisture removal depends on runtime).

- Occupants, showers, baths, cooking, a dishwasher, an unvented clothes dryer and maintenance routines are significant sources of moisture. Plants and fish tanks add moisture to space air.
- Moisture must not migrate through structural panels (a vapor retarding membrane must be properly installed with no flaws or damage).
- Foundations must not leak, the dirt below a crawlspace must be covered by an effective vapor retarding membrane.
- Moisture from a hot tub must not flow from the tub space to other rooms (by air-coupled diffusion, by duct-coupled diffusion, by migration through building materials, or by forced airflow through duct runs).
- For wet-coil cooling, continuous indoor blower operation adds moisture to supply air when the compressor is off.

Maximize Humidity Control by Design

Approved design and installation procedures maximize humidity control. This is important for wet-coil climates.

- Cooling equipment must not be over-sized (aggressive and competent use of *Manual J* and *Manual S* procedures are required).
- For *Manual J* design conditions, the cooling coil sensible heat ratio must be equal to or less than the *Manual J* sensible heat ratio.
- For cooling, continuous indoor blower operation may cause space humidity to drift out of the desired range (evaporation from a wet-coil and drip pan increase indoor air humidity and dew-point temperature).
- Overcooling a space (dump zone for a zone damper system, basement, closet, internal room, or typical living space) drives space air temperature down and relative humidity up, and may cause mold and mildew, or possible visible or concealed condensation.
- Condensation may be caused when a jet of cold supply air blows on a surface (primary air from a supply air outlet, or a supply duct leak).
- The refrigerant charge must be correct (the apparatus dew-point must not be too warm, airflow must not be diminished by frost or ice).
- The cooling coil must be clean (condensation is blown off the coil when the free area of the coil is reduced by an accumulation of dirt).
- Provide an effective drip pan and condensate drain (no leaks or blockage, trap height must be adequate for the negative pressure caused by a blocked filter, or for a clean filter that has a high pressure drop).
- Zone dampers should not close when zone humidity is excessive (a single-zone system that short cycles has the same problem).
- A whole-house dehumidifier provides indoor humidity control.
- A common dehumidifier appliance reduces indoor humidity, and increases the *Manual J* sensible heat ratio (provide a dedicated drain).

Appendx 7

This appendix is not part of the this standard. It is merely informative and does not contain requirements necessary for conformance to the standard. It has not been processed according to the ANSI requirements for a standard, and may contain material that has not been subject to public review or a consensus process. Unresolved objectors on informative material are not offered the right to appeal at ACCA or ANSI.

Appendix 8

Condensation Calculations

Airborne and migrating moisture can cause visible condensation, concealed condensation and freezing condensation. Airborne moisture and/or condensation may cause mold and mildew, cosmetic damage to interior materials and surfaces, or serious damage to structural materials and surfaces. Condensation must not occur during any month-of-year, or hour of day.

A8-1 Condensation on Surfaces

Structural condensation can form on interior surfaces, concealed surfaces and exterior surfaces. Condensation can form on the inside or the outside of duct runs and/or equipment cabinets. Condensation occurs when a surface temperature is colder than the dew-point temperature of the air that contacts the surface.

- During winter, condensation is caused by a building surface temperature, or duct surface temperature, that is colder than the dew-point temperature of the indoor air, or the ducted air.

- During summer, condensation is caused by a building surface temperature, or duct surface temperature, that is colder than the dew-point temperature of the outdoor air, or the air in a duct-run space.

- Condensation calculations must show that air temperature and humidity are compatible with system components, construction techniques and construction materials.

A8-2 Dew-Point Temperature

The dew-point temperature for air depends on dry-bulb temperature and relative humidity. Dew-point temperature does not depend on altitude. Dew-point temperature may be read from a sea-level psychrometric chart, or determined by psychrometric software.

- The *Manual J* design value for space dry-bulb temperature is 70°F for winter, and 75°F for summer. However, the summer dry-bulb value for a dump zone can be significantly colder than 75°F.

- For cooling, the value for ducted supply air may range from 53°F (humid climate) to 58°F (dry climate). However, supply air may be significantly colder than 53°F when supply air flows through a bypass air duct, or dump zone.

- A space that has 20% RH or higher during cold weather may be vulnerable to visible and/or concealed condensation (see Figure A7-2). Condensation also can occur inside of a duct that is surrounded by cold air.

- A 45% RH to 60% RH value for space humidity applies to summer air conditioning applications that have a latent load (the space humidity for dry climate cooling may be less than 45 % RH). For 60% RH, condensation will not occur when structural surfaces are warmer than 60°F (approximately).

- For summer, the dew-point temperature for outdoor air depends on the weather. The dew-point temperature for the 1% dew-point condition may be significantly higher than the dew-point temperature for the 1% dry-bulb condition.

- For summer, structural and/or duct condensation may form on surfaces that contact humid outdoor air, or humid ambient air in an unconditioned space. Summer condensation calculations should be based on the 1% dew-point condition.

A8-3 Condensation Models

Condensation occurs when the dry-bulb temperature of a surface is less than the dew-point temperature of the air that is in contact with the surface. The procedure for using this simplified model is provided below.

Condensation can also occur when water vapor migrates through building materials. In this case, condensation occurs when the partial pressure of the water vapor is greater than the saturation pressure of the water vapor (see the 2005 ASHRAE Handbook of Fundamentals, page 23.10). This depends on local dry-bulb temperature because saturated vapor pressure varies with dry-bulb temperature. (Software is used for sophisticated calculations. See Section A8-12 and Section A8-15.)

A8-4 Minimum Surface Temperature

Building surfaces, cold duct surfaces, and cold pipe surfaces may be protected by a suitable vapor retarding membrane. The dry-bulb temperature at the membrane surface should be about 5 °F warmer than the dew-point temperature of the contacting air.

A8-5 Minimum R-Value

The temperature at a vapor membrane surface depends on outdoor air dry-bulb temperature, indoor air dry-bulb temperature and the R-values of the materials in the heat transmission path, including the air film coefficients. Therefore, dry-bulb temperature and relative humidity determine dew-point temperature, dew-point temperature determines minimum membrane temperature, and minimum membrane temperature determines overall R-value. Calculations are made for visible and concealed condensation.

A8-6 Condensation on Interior Surfaces

Condensation on interior surfaces will not occur when the dew-point temperature of the indoor air is lower than the temperature of the coldest indoor surface. The following equation shows that surface temperature (T_s) depends on the overall R-value (R_t) of the structural panel (with the indoor and outdoor air film resistance), the indoor temperature (T_i) and the outdoor temperature (T_o).

$T_s = T_i - (T_i - T_o) \times (k / R_t)$

Where k equals the indoor air film coefficient for still air:
k = 0.68 for vertical surface (horizontal heat flow)
k = 0.95 for horizontal panel or skylight (heat flow down)
k = 0.76 for 45 degree panel or skylight (heat flow down)
k = 0.62 for exposed floor (heat flow up)
k = 0.95 for cold pipes and ducts (heat flow down)

When the thermal envelope complies with energy codes, windows, skylights and glass doors will have a lower R-value than walls, ceilings and exposed floors. R-values for windows, skylights, doors and frames exposed to outdoor temperatures may need to be higher than required by a local energy code.

For example, a double pane, clear glass window (k = 0.68) can have a 1.59 R-value (0.63 U-value), so the temperature at the inside surface is 40.1°F when the indoor air temperature is 70°F and the outdoor design temperature is 0°F. Therefore, condensation will occur when the dew-point of the indoor air exceeds 40.1°F.

Window R-value including air films = 1.59
Ts = 70 - (70 - 0) x (0.68 / 1.59) = 40.1°F

Overall R-values (with air film resistance) are commonly assigned to ceilings, walls and floors, but window manufacturer's normally publish U-Values Btuh/(SqFt·°F). In this case, the R-value is the reciprocal of the U-value.

Acceptable window performance is determined for the desired design condition when the surface condensation equation is solved for R_t ((SqFt•°F)/Btuh). This version of the equation is provided here:

$R_t = k \times (T_i - T_o) / (T_i - T_s)$

For example, when the design value for indoor dry-bulb is 70°F, the window R-value for 30% relative humidity is 1.72 (U = 0.58), as demonstrated here:

Outdoor dry-bulb = 0°F
Indoor air = 70°F
Indoor air relative humidity = 30%
Indoor air dew-point = 37.3 F
Safety factor = 5 °F
Minimum surface temperature = 42.3°F
k = 0.68
R_t = 1.72 (includes air films)
U-value = 0.58

Note that the minimum R-value requirement (R_t) applies to any point on the interior surface of a window, skylight or glass door assembly. This means that the local R-value at any point on a glass-frame assembly must equal or exceed the minimum requirement.

- The National Fenestration Rating Council (NFRC) U-value represents the average performance of the entire assembly. The U-value at a particular point on the surface can be larger or smaller.
- The NFRC U-value rating is for a default frame size, the U-value for some other frame size may be somewhat different.
- The 5°F cushion for dew-point temperature compensates for small differences in performance at various points on the fenestration assembly.

The overall R-value equation for interior surface temperature also applies to opaque panels. In this case, the vapor membrane surface could be a low perm paint or a covering on the inside surface of a ceiling, wall or floor.

A8-7 Condensation on Exterior Glass

Surface condensation will form when the temperature of the outside surface of a window light or it's framing is colder than the dew-point temperature of the outdoor air. This equation estimates the temperature at the outside surface of window glass (T_g).

$T_g = T_i + (R_g - 0.25) / R_g \times (T_o - T_i)$

Where:
T_i = Indoor air temperature (°F)
T_o = Outdoor air temperature (°F)
R_g = Total R through glass, including air films
0.25 = Default R-Value for the outside air film

Figure A8-1 (next page) shows that the common dew-point temperature for a humid climate ranges from 71°F (80°F outdoors) to 73°F (90°F outdoors). However, the dew-point temperature can be significantly higher than these values. For example, the ASHRAE 1% dew-point value for Miami, FL, is about 77°F with a mean coincident dry-bulb of 83°F (equivalent to 82% RH).

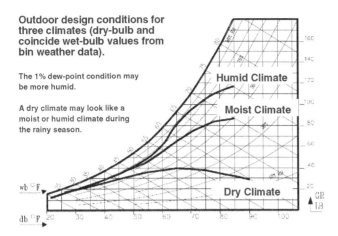

Outdoor design conditions for three climates (dry-bulb and coincide wet-bulb values from bin weather data).

The 1% dew-point condition may be more humid.

A dry climate may look like a moist or humid climate during the rainy season.

Figure A8-1

Therefore, when indoor temperature is a little cool (a supply air dump zone at 60°F to 70°F, for example), surface condensation may occur when the outdoor humidity is high. This is demonstrated by Figure A8-2 for glass U-values that range from 1.0 to 0.25 and indoor temperatures that range from 60°F to 70°F (T_g values that are below a 77°F dew-point temperature are in shaded boxes).

A8-8 Winter Condensation in Structural Panels

Concealed condensation occurs whenever the temperature of a surface or membrane within a wall, ceiling, or floor is below the dew-point temperature of the indoor air that contacts the surface. The following equation evaluates the temperature distribution across a structural panel. This equation shows that the temperature at a concealed surface (T_s) depends on the R-value for the path from the vapor membrane to the outdoor air (R_o), the total R-value across the panel (R_t), the outdoor temperature (T_o), and the indoor temperature (T_i).

$$T_s = T_o + (R_o / R_t) \times (T_i - T_o)$$

Figure A8-3 (next page) shows two constructions that have the same overall R-value. However, the condensation potential for insulation and retarder at the indoor side of the block is significantly lower than the condensation potential for insulation and retarder at the outdoor side of the block.

- The R-value for the interior finish and the exterior finish is 0.50.
- The R-value for the block is 2.0.
- The R-value of the insulation is 10.0.
- The R-values for the indoor and outdoor air films are 0.68 and 0.17.
- The indoor and outdoor temperatures are 70°F and -5°F. Indoor humidity is 30% RH.

Temperature (°F) at Outside Surface of Glass

Glass R	Total R	T_o	T_i	T_g
0.07	R = 1.0 U = 1.0	75	60	71.3
			65	72.5
			70	73.8
		80	60	75.0
			65	76.3
			70	77.5
1.07	R = 2.0 U = 0.50	75	60	73.1
			65	73.9
			70	74.4
		80	60	77.5
			65	78.1
			70	78.8
2.07	R = 3.0 U = 0.33	75	60	73.8
			65	74.2
			70	74.6
		80	60	78.3
			65	78.8
			70	79.2
3.07	R = 4.0 U = 0.25	75	60	74.1
			65	74.4
			70	74.7
		80	60	78.8
			65	79.1
			70	79.4

1) Glass R = R-value from outside surface to inside surface.
2) Total R = Glass R plus inside (0.68) and outside (0.25) air films.
3) Glass U = 1 / Total R.

Figure A8-2

Insulation and Vapor Membrane near Inside Surface

The dew-point temperature of indoor air at 70°F and 30% RH is 37.3°F. When the insulation and membrane are inside of the block, the temperature at the vapor membrane is warmer than the dew-point temperature of the indoor air (R-values provided by Figure A8-3).

$$T_s = -5 + (12.67 / 13.85) \times (70 - (-5)) = 63.6°F$$

Insulation and Vapor Membrane near Outside Surface

When the insulation and membrane are outside of the block, this calculation shows that the design is obviously inadequate for air that has a 37.3°F dew-point. Moist air migrating to the vapor membrane will condense and freeze.

Appendx 8

$T_s = -5 + (0.67 / 13.85) \times (70 - (-5)) = -1.4\ °F$

Even when a structural panel has a robust overall R-value, concealed condensation will occur when there is no vapor retarding surface or membrane; or when the surface or membrane is on the wrong side of the structural panel; or when the surface or membrane is improperly installed, cut or damaged; or when there is a thermal bridge that has a low R-value.

A8-9 Summer Condensation in Structural Panels

Concealed condensation will form when the temperature of a surface within a structural panel is lower than the dew-point temperature of outdoor air that contacts the surface. This equation estimates the temperature at the vapor retarding wrap (T_s).

$T_s = T_i + (0.68 + R_x) / R_t \times (T_o - T_i)$

Where:
T_i = Indoor air temperature (°F)
T_o = Outdoor air temperature (°F)
R_x = Total R for materials inside of wrap (no air film)
Default R_x for wrap behind wall board = 0.45
Default R_x for wrap behind siding = 0.45 + $R_{insulation}$
R_t = Total R-value for wall, including air films
0.68 = Default for the inside air film

As previously noted, the 1% dew-point temperature for Miami is about 77°F. When outdoor moisture migrates to the vapor retarding warp, surface condensation may occur when the outdoor humidity is high. This is demonstrated by Figure A8-4 (next page) for wall insulation that ranges from R-11 to R-19 and indoor temperatures that range from 60°F to 70°F.

Note that the transmission path through a stud has a smaller R-value than the path through the insulation. For a wrap behind wallboard, the wrap temperature at the stud will be warmer than the wrap temperature at the insulation. For a wrap behind the siding, the wrap temperature at the stud will be colder than the wrap temperature at the insulation.

A8-10 Condensation Inside of Duct Runs

Condensation on interior duct surfaces will not occur when the dew-point temperature of the ducted air is lower than the temperature of the airway surface. This equation shows that airway surface temperature (T_s) depends on duct air temperature (T_i) and ambient temperature (T_o), the overall R-value (R_t) of the duct package (duct material, insulation and air film resistance), and the resistance of the inside air film (R_i).

$T_s = T_i - (T_i - T_o) \times (R_i / R_t)$

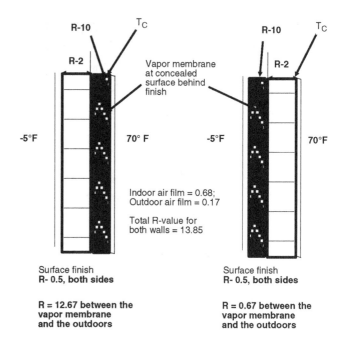

Figure A8-3

Where R_i equals the air film coefficient for airway air:
R_i is about 0.25 for typical air velocities
R_i is about 0.68 for no air velocity (blower off)

For example, a dwelling has engineered humidification (media humidifier in duct), and the dew-point of space air is 37.3°F for 70°F dry-bulb and 30% RH. When the blower is off, this air may migrate through an attic duct system.

When the blower is off, the total R-value of a sealed metal duct that has no insulation is about 1.36 (metal is negligible and both air films are about 0.68). When the ambient temperature is 0°F and the duct air temperature is 70°F, the temperature for the duct airway surface is about 35°F, so condensation is possible.

Dew-point for duct air = 37.3°F
$T_s = 70 - (70 - 0) \times (0.68 / 1.36) = 35.0°F$

For example, when the blower operates, 1,400 Cfm of 105°F air moves through the duct system. The *Manual J* humidification load is 4,760 Btuh, so the humidifier must add 4.5 pounds of water per continuous hour of operation. But the furnace only operates for 42 minutes per hour because it is over-sized, so the humidifier adds 6.5 pounds of water per hour when the furnace operates. This means that return air enters the furnace at 70°F and 32.5 Grains and leaves the furnace at 105°F and 39.6 Grains, so the dew-point of the supply air is about 42.3°F.

When the blower runs, the total R-value of a sealed metal duct that has no insulation is about 0.93 (metal is negligible, the inside air film is 0.25 and the outside air film is 0.68). When the ambient temperature is 0°F and the duct air temperature is 105°F, the temperature for the duct airway surface is about 76.8°F, so supply duct condensation will not occur. A similar calculation shows that return duct condensation will not occur.

Dew-point for supply air (105°F, 12% RH) = 42.3 °F
$T_S = 105 - (105 - 0) \times (0.25 / 0.93) = 76.8°F$
Dew-point for return air (70°F, 30% RH) = 37.3 °F
$T_S = 70 - (70 - 0) \times (0.25 / 0.93) = 51.2°F$

Duct systems installed outside of the conditioned space should be insulated (R4 is common, R6 or R8 may be a code/utility requirement). This makes the duct airway surface much warmer than the dew-point of ducted air (for the 30% RH scenario). However, condensation may occur at places where the duct leaks.

A8-11 Condensation Outside of Duct Runs

For humid climates, duct insulation may not prevent condensation on exposed duct walls and/or insulating materials. An external facing or wrap (vapor retarding membrane) is required when the average outdoor air dew-point for cooling (July/August) exceeds 60°F. Figure A8-5 (next page) provides outdoor air dew-point information for USA cities.

Condensation occurs when the dry-bulb temperature of a duct surface is less than the dew-point temperature of the air that is in contact with the surface. This applies to the exterior surface of vapor retarding membrane (wrap) that covers duct insulation and to the duct material when there is no vapor retarding wrap (moisture may migrate through duct insulation). These equations estimate the temperature at the outside surface of a duct wrap (T_w) and at the inside surface of the duct insulation (T_d).

$T_w = T_o - (0.95 / R_t) \times (T_o - T_i)$
$T_d = T_o - ((0.95 + R_{ins}) / R_t) \times (T_o - T_i)$

Where:
T_o = Ambient temperature surrounding the duct (°F)
T_i = Air temperature inside the duct (°F)
0.95 = Default for the outside air film
0.17 = Default for the inside air film
R_{ins} = Insulation R-value (no credit for air films)
Pure series path conduction (use worst-case for R_{ins})
Defaults for R_{ins} = 2.0; 4.0; 6.0; 8.0
R-value for metal wall or membrane wall is negligible
$R_t = R_{ins} + 0.95 + 0.17$

Temperature (°F) at Vapor Membrane					
Wrap Behind Wall Board					
T_o	T_i	T_s		
		R11	R13	R19
75	60	61.3	61.1	60.8
	65	65.8	65.7	65.5
	70	70.4	70.4	70.3
80	60	61.7	61.5	61.1
	65	66.3	66.1	65.8
	70	70.8	70.7	70.5
85	60	62.1	61.8	61.3
	65	66.7	66.5	66.1
	70	71.3	71.1	70.8
Wrap Behind Siding					
T_o	T_i	T_s		
		R11	R13	R19
75	60	73.6	73.8	74.1
	65	74.1	74.2	74.4
	70	74.5	74.6	74.7
80	60	78.1	78.4	78.8
	65	78.6	78.8	79.1
	70	79.1	79.2	79.4
85	60	82.7	83.0	83.5
	65	83.1	83.4	83.8
	70	83.6	83.8	84.1

1) Wall board R-value = 0.45; siding R-value = 1.0.
2) The shaded boxes show that the wrap temperature may be lower than the Miami dew-point temperature.
3) Approved moisture migration calculations are more complex (see the ASHRAE Handbook of Fundamentals, or use building science software (WUFI-ORNL or H.A.M).

Figure A8-4

Condensation on Duct Wrap

When the duct is protected by a comprehensive vapor retarding membrane, determine the duct wrap temperature (T_w) and compare it with the dew-point temperature of the surrounding air. This applies to a rigid metal or wire helix duct with exterior insulation protected by a wrap, to duct board that has a protective wrap, and to completely sealed metal duct that has duct liner.

For example, Figure A8-1 shows that for a humid climate, outdoor air (and vented attic air) may be near 90% RH when the outdoor dry-bulb temperature is 65°F, so the ambient dew-point temperature is about 62°F.

Appendix 8

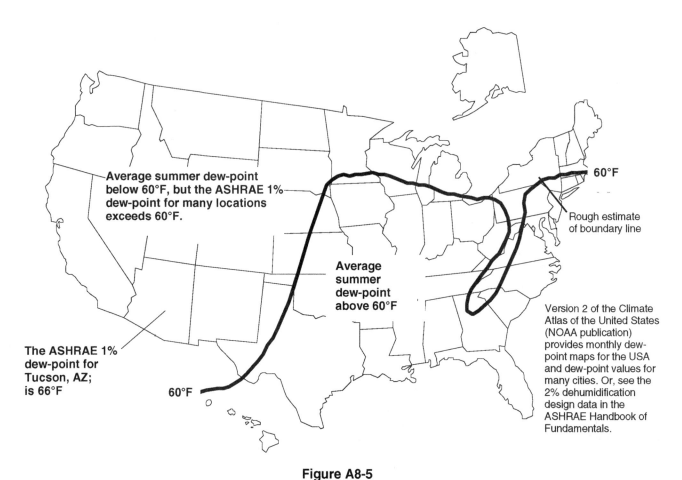

Figure A8-5

Figure A8-6 shows that with R4 insulation, the wrap temperature (T_w) is a little warmer (62.2°F to 63.1°F) than the dew-point temperature (62°F) when the ducted air (T_i) is 50°F to 55°F; and that it is a little colder (61.3°F) than the dew-point temperature (62°F) when the ducted air is 45°F. Therefore, wrap condensation is possible for a worst-case scenario:

- Cool attic air at 90% RH or higher.
- Insulation R-value is R4 or less.
- Ducted air is unusually cold (45°F)

However, the attic temperature is normally warmer than outdoor temperature. When the attic is only five degrees warmer, Figure A8-6 shows that the wrap temperature is 65.4°F or higher for a 70°F attic. In addition, duct insulation should be R6, or preferably R8, and the equipment may shut-down on a safety before duct air temperature drops to 45°F.

Condensation on Duct Insulation

When the duct is not protected by a comprehensive vapor retarding wrap, investigate the temperature at the inside surface of the duct insulation (T_d). This applies to externally insulated ducts that have no wrap or a defective

\multicolumn{6}{c}{Wrap Temperature (T_w) and Duct Surface Temperature (T_d) for R4 Insulation}
R_{ins}	R_t	T_o	T_i	T_w	T_d
4	5.12	65	55	63.1	55.3
			50	62.2	50.5
			45	61.3	45.7
		70	55	67.2	55.5
			50	66.3	50.7
			45	65.4	45.8
		100	55	91.7	56.5
			50	90.7	51.7
			45	89.8	46.8
		130	55	116.1	57.5
			50	115.2	52.7
			45	114.2	47.8

T_o = Attic temperature; T_i = Temperature of duct air.
T_w = Temperature of external vapor retarding membrane.
T_d = Temperature at the inside surface of the insulation.

Figure A8-6

wrap (seam leaks, cuts, penetrations), to duct board that has a defective wrap, and to an unsealed metal duct that has duct liner. (The assumption is that moisture will migrate through the insulation and condense in the insulation or on the surface covered by the insulation.)

For example, Figure A8-1 shows that when the outdoor dry-bulb temperature is 65°F or higher, dew-point temperature ranges from 55°F to 60°F for a moist climate and from 62°F to 67°F for a humid climate; and Figure A8-7 shows that the temperature at the inside surface of the insulation is predominately less than 55°F and occasionally close to 55°F. Therefore, condensation is possible within the insulation, or on the surface that is covered by the insulation. These circumstances apply:

- Moist or humid climate
- Ineffective vapor wrap
- Outdoor dry-bulb temperature 65°F or higher
- Ducted air 45°F to 60°F

Figure A8-7 shows that increasing insulation R-value has little effect on the temperature at the inside surface of the insulation. The integrity of the wrap determines when condensation is possible.

A8-12 Condensation Software

The preceding sections provide simplified (ballpark) tools for predicting condensation. However, there are various types of climates and each climate has an outdoor air condition for each month and hour of the year. There are many options for the condition of space air, ducted air and ambient air. There are many types of fenestration and structural panels, and various types of duct construction. Therefore, subtle technical issues may not be modeled by a simple R-value procedure.

Comprehensive condensation calculations are performed by the WUFI and H.A.M software (see Section A8-15). Go to these sources for related information:

- See the Oak Ridge National Laboratories (ORNL's) Buildings Technology Center web site.
- Search the web for *Heat, Air and Moisture Building Science Toolbox*.

A8-13 Consequences of Humidity

For health and comfort, 50% RH to 60% RH is best. Even when there is no significant condensation, mold, mildew, bacteria, fungi and viruses tend to grow or thrive when relative humidity exceeds 60% RH (see Figure A7-1). High humidity also causes rot, corrosion and rust.

Wrap Temperature (T_w) and Duct Surface Temperature (T_d) for R6 and R8 Insulation					
R_{ins}	R_t	T_o	T_i	T_w	T_d
6	7.12	65	55	63.7	55.2
			50	63.0	50.4
			45	62.3	45.5
		70	55	68.0	55.4
			50	67.3	50.5
			45	66.7	45.6
		100	55	94.0	56.1
			50	93.3	51.2
			45	92.7	46.3
		130	55	120.0	56.8
			50	119.3	51.9
			45	118.7	47.0
8	9.12	65	55	64.0	55.2
			50	63.4	50.3
			45	62.9	45.4
		70	55	68.4	55.3
			50	67.9	50.4
			45	67.4	45.5
		100	55	95.3	55.8
			50	94.8	50.9
			45	94.3	46.0
		130	55	122.2	56.4
			50	121.7	51.5
			45	121.1	46.6

Figure A8-7

A8-14 Consequences of Condensation

Indoor humidity in the 50% RH to 60% RH range will cause condensation when the thermal performance of the building is deficient. Related problems are listed here:

- Window or skylight glass covered with haze, frames may be stained; or may rot, or corrode.
- Stain or corrosion on interior finishes and metal.
- Wet ceiling tiles and ceiling insulation.
- Stains on exterior finish or masonry.
- Mold and mildew on carpets and furniture, on the visible and concealed surfaces of the building, on mechanical system components.

- Wet wall or ceiling insulation loses most of it's effectiveness.
- Electrical wiring problems.
- A ceiling assembly may sag or collapse when soaked with moisture.
- When structural connections and fasteners rust or corrode, framing may fail when exposed to normal wind, snow and rain loads.
- Exterior masonry cracks, splits or breaks off due to freezing condensation.
- Air leakage paths carry moisture to cold surfaces, where it freezes and causes icicles or a ice dam.

A8-15 Building Science Software

The WUFI and H.A.M computer programs evaluate the thermal and hygrothermal performance of building materials and structural panels. Proper use of these programs may require relevant experience and training.

WUFI

The menu-driven PC program WUFI-ORNL/IBP developed by Fraunhofer Institute of Bauphysics and Oak Ridge National Laboratory and validated using data derived from outdoor and laboratory tests, allows realistic calculation of the transient hygrothermal behavior of multi-layer building components exposed to natural climate conditions.

WUFI-ORNL/IBP can be used for assessing:

- The drying time of masonry with trapped construction moisture.
- The danger of interstitial condensation.
- The influence of driving rain on exterior building components.
- The effect of repair and retrofit measures.
- The hygrothermal performance of roof and wall assemblies under unanticipated use, or in different climate zones.

Proper application of WUFI requires experience in the field of hygrothermics and some basic knowledge in the use of numerical calculation methods.

H.A.M.

The Heat, Air and Moisture Building Science Toolbox is a computer program that applies building science principles to the design of any cladding and exterior wall system. This program will determine thermal properties and temperature gradients, locate winter and summer dew-point temperatures, analyze potential winter and summer wall condensation, determine air leakage rates through openings, determine the effect of height and temperature on stack effect and fan pressurization on the building envelope.

The Building Science Toolbox was developed specifically for architects, engineers, technologists and technicians designing building envelope systems. It contains five building science tools, which are:

- The "R" Value Analysis Tool
- The Condensation Analysis Tool
- The Air Leakage Analysis Tool
- The Building Pressure Analysis Tool
- The Psychrometric Tool

Appendix 9
Water-Loop Issues for Water-Air Heat Pumps

Even though water-air heat pumps are notably efficient, they are not as common as air-air heat pumps. The primary reason for the disparity is the need for an adequate supply of water.

A9-1 Once-Through Water

Most residential properties do not have access to a pond, lake or river, and most do not have a well. When a dwelling has a well, it is typically the source of potable water. When an existing well, or new well has adequate capacity for heat pump equipment, it's use and design may depend on local codes and regulations.

Water disposal is an issue. A second well may be required to return discharge water to the aquifer, or this practice may be forbidden, depending on local codes and regulations. Dumping water on the property may, or may not, be physically possible; and when possible, this may be subject to local codes and regulations. Dumping water off the property most likely will not be tolerated by a neighbor, and/or local authority.

Water quality may be an issue. Mineral deposits will foul the water-side of heat transfer surfaces, degrade performance, and possibly cause a mechanical problem. Water treatment and maintenance solutions may, or may not, be acceptable, depending on the effort and cost.

A9-2 Earth-Loop Water

A buried piping loop may provide a solution to some, or all, water problems. For heating, the water that circulates through the loop extracts heat from the ground and delivers captured heat to the heat pump. For cooling, the heat pump heats loop water, then the circulating water transfers this heat to the ground.

For a buried-loop system, the aquifer is protected, and water disposal is not an issue. However, the quality of the water in the buried pipe runs may be an issue. Follow water-air equipment manufacturer guidance pertaining to water treatment and filtration.

Note that, horizontal loop systems require adequate acreage, and a considerable amount of excavation and back-filling. Vertical loop systems do not require very much acreage, but they do require a lot of drilling. For cold climate use, earth-coupled systems require freeze protection, which is provided by some type of water and antifreeze solution. Significant materials and installation cost are associated with a closed piping loop.

The annual energy efficiency of a GLHP (buried, closed-loop) system is less than a GWHP (open, pump and dump) system. This is because equipment heating-cooling capacity and efficiency depend on entering water temperature.

- As far as refrigeration cycle equipment is concerned, excellent year-round performance is provided by once-through ground water in the 40°F to 55°F temperature range.

- As far as refrigeration cycle equipment is concerned, heating capacity is reduced when loop water temperature is lower than ground water temperature, and cooling capacity is reduced when loop water temperature is warmer than ground water temperature (see Figure A1-26).

- Water pumping energy is an issue. For once-through systems, momentary pump watts and annual pump KWH tend to be significantly more than for earth-loop water systems. Therefore, a higher well-pump power draw will offset some of the efficiency provided by a steady 40°F to 55°F water temperature.

- A proper energy and op-cost calculation, or utility bill study for local circumstances, will show how heat pump system types compare, as far as annual energy use, and annual operating cost are concerned.

- In general, both types of water-air heat pump systems are more efficient than an air-air heat pump system.

A9-3 Buried Water-Loop Design

Once it has been decided that an earth-coupled, water-loop heat pump is the system of choice, the closed piping loop must be designed, and the heat pump equipment must be selected and sized. In this regard, three interrelated questions arise:

- What is the entering water temperature for heating, and for cooling?
- What is the geometry of the loop system?
- What is the total length of the buried pipe?

The answer to these questions depends on the heating and cooling loads, the climate, the month of the year, the type of soil, the moisture in the soil; the type, depth and geometry of the buried piping, the length of the buried piping, the Gpm water flow rate in the piping, the

Appendx 9

water-loop pressure drop, the water velocity in the piping, the pipe diameter, the physical properties of the pipe, and the properties of the fluid (water-antifreeze solution) in the loop. Clearly, these are fairly difficult questions to answer.

Once the loop is designed, and the entering water temperatures for heating and cooling are known, the remaining design work is routine. For equipment selection and sizing, and for air-side design, there is no procedural difference between a water-air heat pump system and an air-air heat pump system.

- Tables N2-1 and N2-2 provide sizing limits for water-air equipment.
- Section 2 provides step-by-step instructions.
- Section 9 provides example equipment selection-sizing problems.
- OEM blower data and *Manual D* procedures determine duct airway sizes.

A9-4 Piping Geometry

Figure A9-1 shows an example of a vertical loop system and a horizontal loop system. There are many possible variations of these themes, and numerous decision making issues.

- There may be one loop, or multiple loops.
- Multiple loops may be in series or parallel.
- Vertical loop depth, cross-sectional pipe pattern, and pipe-to-pipe clearances are issues.
- Horizontal loop stacking pattern, buried depths, and pipe-to-pipe clearances are issues.
- Decisions depend on available acreage, local soil conditions, the amount of pipe required for the size of the equipment, the pump power requirement, materials cost, and installation cost.

A9-5 Length of Buried Pipe

The length of buried pipe is estimated by using the latest version of the following equations. These equations may be solved by hand with the aid of many charts and tables, but this exercise in trial and error mathematics exceeds the scope of this appendix. Fortunately, dedicated software is normally used for this work. Section A9-12 identifies the source for loop design and installation procedures, and related software.

$$L_h = \frac{HC \times ((COP - 1 / COP) \times (R_p + R_s \times F_h)}{(GTL - WTL)}$$

$$L_c = \frac{TC \times ((EER + 3.142) / COP) \times (R_p + R_s \times F_c)}{(WTH - GTH)}$$

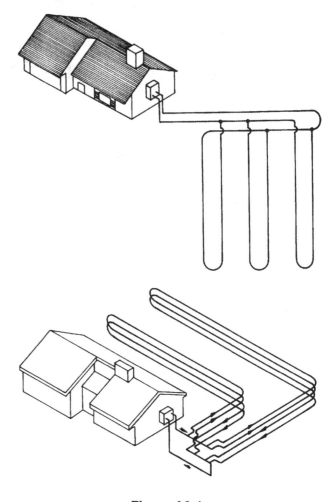

Figure A9-1

Where::
L_h = Pipe length for heating (Ft)
L_c = Pipe length for cooling (Ft)
HC = Design heating capacity value (Btuh)
TC = Design value for total cooling capacity (Btuh)
COP = Heat pump COP for HC value
EER = Heat pump EER for TC value
R_p = Thermal resistance of pipe (Hr-Ft-°F/Btu)
R_s = Thermal resistance of soil (Hr-Ft-°F/Btu)
F_h = Compressor heating run fraction (%)
F_c = Compressor cooling run fraction (%)
EWT = Entering water temperature
WTL = Minimum EWT for year (°F)
WTH = Maximum EWT for year (°F)
GTL = Coldest ground temperature for year (°F)
GTH = warmest ground temperature for year (°F)

- The pipe length for heating (Lh) and for cooling (Lc) will normally be different values. The largest value determines pipe length.
- The amount of buried pipe depends on the size of the equipment (the HC and TC values). Therefore, equipment over sizing, translates to more buried pipe than needed, and higher installation cost.

- The amount of buried pipe depends on the WTL and WTH water temperature values. Note that colder temperatures for heating and warmer temperature for cooling translate to less pipe length.

- However, compressor heating capacity decreases as the entering water temperature (WTL) gets colder, and compressor cooling capacity decreases as the entering water temperature (WTH) gets warmer. So there is a trade-off between equipment size and the amount of pipe in the ground.

- Antifreeze in pipe loop water affects the performance of the heat pump equipment and the performance of the piping system.

- Heat pump performance data must be compatible with the properties of the fluid flowing through the equipment.

- Pipe loop pressure drop, pumping power, and buried pipe diameter depend on the properties of the fluid flowing through the pipe.

- Pipe loop pressure drop, pumping power, and buried pipe diameter also depend on the geometry of the pipe runs, the use of series or parallel loops, and the length of the pipe runs.

- When pipe runs are the wrong size, and/or, when the water pump is not correctly selected and sized, a water-air heat pump system may use more momentary power (Watts), and more annual energy (KWH) than needed, with the consequence of significantly reduced system efficiency.

- OEM's have reported cases where pump failure was caused by incorrect water system design.

- Water-air equipment manufacturer, and pump manufacturer guidance, must be used to select and size water pumps.

A9-6 Summary of Design Issues

System design, as far as primary components are concerned, requires a proper load calculation; use of expanded performance data (for the fluid that will be in the piping loop) for equipment selection and sizing; and pipe length calculations for heating and cooling. Then water pipe runs must be sized, and loop pressure drops must be determined (including the pressure drop through the equipment). Then a pump product must be selected and sized. Then, blower data and air-side component pressure drop data that is compatible with *Manual D* procedures must be used to size duct airways. OEM performance data and *Manual T* procedures are used to select and size supply air outlet and return grille hardware.

A9-7 Other Issues

There are guidelines and procedures for drilling and grouting, trenching and back filling. There are piping methods and materials requirements. There are guidelines and procedures for water-side flushing, for mixing an anti-freeze solution, and for pipe system charging and air purging. There are guidelines for piping details (fittings, valves and accessories). The system designer must select and integrate appropriate HVAC equipment operating and safety controls, and water system operating and safety controls.

A9-8 Energy Calculations

When energy use and operating cost benefits are mathematically evaluated, the estimates must be is generated by a bin-hour calculation or hourly simulation that is compatible with Appendix 6 procedures. This requirement is identical, in principle, to procedures provided by the source cited in Section A9-12.

Energy calculations for GLHP (buried, closed-loop) systems are more complex than for GWHP (open, pump and dump) systems. This is because the temperature of loop water, and therefore, equipment capacity and efficiency, depend on momentary conditions, such as the time of year, and HVAC equipment operating time. For once-though systems the entering water temperature is essentially constant year-round, providing that the source water is not significantly affected by solar beam radiation.

A9-9 Comprehensive Instructions and Software

A collection of design and installation manuals, and design software, may be purchased from the International Ground Water Heat Pump Association, Oklahoma State University. Also inquire about training courses provided by the association, and by water-air equipment OEMs.

Appendx 9

This appendix is not part of the this standard. It is merely informative and does not contain requirements necessary for conformance to the standard. It has not been processed according to the ANSI requirements for a standard, and may contain material that has not been subject to public review or a consensus process. Unresolved objectors on informative material are not offered the right to appeal at ACCA or ANSI.

Appendix 10

Ductless Multi-Split Piping

Multi-split OEMs have various refrigerant distribution methods. The primary difference is the number of pipes.

There are two-pipe systems and three-pipe systems. For heat pump systems, two refrigerant pipes may provide heating or cooling, or simultaneous heating and cooling. Three refrigerant pipes are used to provide simultaneous heating and cooling.

- Simultaneous heating and cooling may improve zone temperature control.
- Simultaneous heating and cooling system may recover energy.

A10-1 Pipe Names

Traditional refrigerant pipe names can be confusing because expansion valves may be at the indoor units, at the outdoor unit, or at an indoor refrigerant distribution block. For the purpose of this discussion, there is a heating refrigerant pipe, a cooling refrigerant pipe, a supply refrigerant pipe, and a return refrigerant pipe.

A10-2 Basic Two-Pipe System

A basic two-pipe system operates in the heating mode or cooling mode. The outdoor unit may provide heating refrigerant to all indoor units, or cooling refrigerant to all indoor units. Figure A10-1 demonstrates the concept.

- Each indoor unit may have it's own supply pipe and a return pipe (for separate compressors or a distribution block in the outdoor unit).
- Indoor units may be served by a supply header and a return header.
- Indoor units may be served by supply branches and return branches from a distribution block.
- For both designs, the entire system operates in the heating mode or cooling mode.

A10-3 Two-Pipe Recovery System

This design features a refrigerant management block (RMB). The outdoor unit processes refrigerant returned by the RMB, and feeds processed refrigerant to the RMB, per RMB need. The RMB provides heating refrigerant or cooling refrigerant to an indoor unit. Each indoor unit returns refrigerant to the RMB. Figure A10-2 demonstrates the concept.

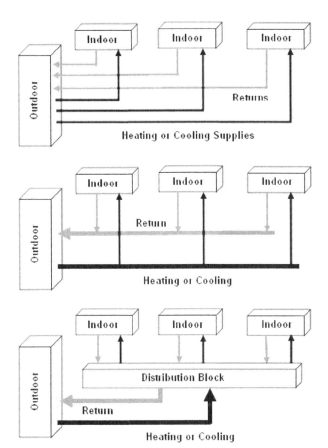

Figure A10-1

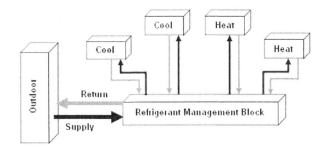

Figure A10-2

- The entire system may operate in the heating mode or cooling mode.
- The system may provide simultaneous heating and cooling for a set of indoor units.

A10-4 Three-Pipe Recovery System

For a three-pipe design, the outdoor unit provides heating refrigerant and cooling refrigerant to a set of mode valves, and refrigerant is returned from the mode valves. Each mode valve feeds refrigerant to indoor units and accepts refrigerant from it's indoor units. Figure A10-3 demonstrates the concept.

- All indoor units served by a particular mode valve provide heating-only, or cooling-only.
- A set of mode valves may provide heating and cooling within the overall system.

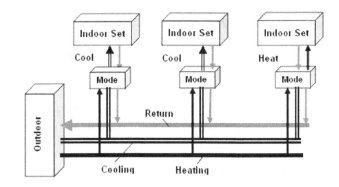

Figure A10-3

Appendix 11

Furnace or Water Boiler Cycling Efficiency

The cycling efficiency of a fossil fuel furnace or boiler depends on the percentage of the time per hour (run fraction) that the furnace burner operates. At full-load, the furnace operates continuously, so the cycling efficiency is equal to the steady-state efficiency. At part-load conditions, the cycling efficiency is less than the steady-state efficiency.

A11-1 Part-Load Efficiency Curves

Figure A11-1 provides curves that correlate the cycling efficiency ratio (CER) with the heating load ratio (HLR). (The heating load ratio equals the heating load divided by the output capacity of the furnace.) These curves are based on research that was published by the Department of Energy and the National Bureau of Standards.

A11-2 Part-Load Efficiency Equations

The part-load efficiency curves provided by Figure A11-1 are produced by the following equations. In the third equation, the C_i constant has different values, which depend on the AFUE rating of the furnace. Figure A11-2 correlates C_i values with furnace AFUE values.

AFUE Vs. C Value	
AFUE	Conditional C Value (C_i)
Above 0.75	22.0
0.70 to 0.75	15.0
0.65 to 0.70	12.0
Below 0.65	10.5

Figure A11-2

CER = Cycling Efficiency / Steady-State Efficiency
HLR = Heating Load / Output Capacity
$CER = 1 - [(1 / e^{HLR})]^{C_i}$

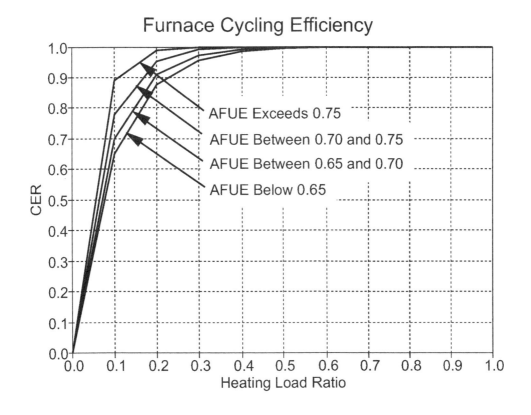

Figure A11-1

A11-3 Energy Use and Furnace Over Sizing

The cycling efficiency curves (Figure A11-1) explain why furnace and boiler operating costs are not as sensitive to over sizing as one may expect. Notice that the cycling efficiency ratio is essentially equal to the steady-state efficiency ratio when the heating load exceeds 25 percent of the output heating capacity. Also notice that a small reduction in the cycling efficiency ratio is associated with heating loads that are between 15 and 25 percent of the output heating capacity. As far as the annual heating-cycle energy requirement is concerned, the effect of the efficiency reduction in this range of load ratios is buffered by the small number of bin-load hours for this range of load ratios. Below 15 percent output capacity, the cycling penalty is severe, but the net effect on the annual energy requirement for heating is negligible because there are only a few bin-hours associated with this range of load ratios.

Appendix 12
Matching Evaporators and Condensing Units

The evaporator coil must be matched to the condensing unit to obtain the desired cooling performance. This is not a concern when cooling is provided by packaged equipment because the components are matched by the equipment manufacturer (with adequate expanded performance data). However, practitioners who mix and match evaporator coils and condensing units must select components that will provide the desired performance.

A12-1 Evaporator Performance

Evaporator capacity decreases as the suction temperature increases. This occurs because evaporator capacity depends on the temperature difference between the air that flows through the coil and the refrigerant that is evaporating in the coil. Also note that as the suction temperature increases, the surface temperature of the coil increases, causing the latent capacity of the coil to decrease.

A12-2 Condensing Unit Performance

The capacity of the condensing unit increases when the suction temperature increases. This occurs because the increase in gas density for a higher suction pressure translates into an increase in the amount of gas that is circulated by the compressor.

A12-3 Refrigerant-Side Operating Point

The condensing unit and the evaporator will always balance out at a specific operating point. This operating point may be determined by plotting condensing unit performance and evaporator coil performance on a suction temperature versus total cooling capacity graph. An example of this procedure is provided by Figure A12-1. Notice that the components balance out at a specific tonnage, and at a specific suction temperature. It is important to remember that the latent capacity of the coil is closely related to the suction temperature. When the balance point results in a suction temperature that is too high, the coil will not be able to properly control the humidity of the air that flows through the evaporator coil.

A12-4 Optimum Refrigerant-Side Balance Point

Figure A12-2 shows that more tonnage is extracted from a condensing unit when it serves a larger evaporator coil. Unfortunately, the tonnage increase is accompanied by

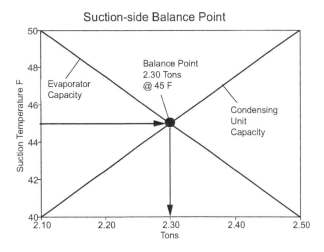

Figure A12-1

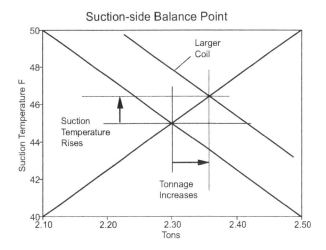

Figure A12-2

an increase in suction temperature, and a corresponding decrease in latent capacity. This means that the indoor humidity may be unacceptably high when the evaporator capacity is too large for the condensing unit capacity. Indoor humidity control requires suction temperatures that cause discharge evaporator air to have a dry-bulb temperature (apparatus dew-point) that is compatible with the latent load.

This appendix is not part of the this standard. It is merely informative and does not contain requirements necessary for conformance to the standard. It has not been processed according to the ANSI requirements for a standard, and may contain material that has not been subject to public review or a consensus process. Unresolved objectors on informative material are not offered the right to appeal at ACCA or ANSI.

Appendix 13

Performance Models for Cooling-Only and Heat Pump Equipment

The manufacturer's expanded performance data for a particular make, model and size may be approximated by a set of linear equations. Converting a data table to a set of equations has certain uses and advantages. Accuracy, as it relates to the OEM's data set may be good, but not perfect (see Figures A13-6 and A13-11, and Section A13-16).

A13-1 Performance Model Use

An equation set correlates sea level equipment performance with operating conditions. When the equation set is evaluated by a computerized spreadsheet, operating conditions are entered into input cells and performance values are returned in output cells. Figure A13-1 provides an example. A partial list of uses is provided here:

- The model provides automated interpolation.

- Figure A13-2 (next page) shows how a limited matrix of operating scenarios is converted to a more comprehensive matrix of scenarios.

- The model provides extrapolation. Figure A13-7 (ahead four pages) also shows how performance data for 59°F entering wet-bulb is estimated when OEM data ignores the possibility of dry-climate use. Also note that values for 70°F, 75°F and 80°F entering dry-bulb are generated, vs. the 75°F, 80°F and 85°F values for the OEM's data.

- The model may be used for final equipment selection and sizing when the accuracy of the calculation engine is acceptable (i.e., model output values favorably compare with the values shown by official OEM performance data).

- An accurate model may be used by a code official to verify final equipment selection and sizing.

- A sophisticated bin-hour energy calculation, or an hourly energy calculation, requires a reasonably accurate equipment performance model.

- A model that has 1% to 10% error (typically 5% or less) over a comprehensive range of operating conditions may be used for preliminary design work.

- Expanded performance data for old equipment may not be available. The model provides a ballpark summary of equipment performance.

- Models produced by the procedures in this section are more than adequate for class room, or on-line training, and the associated home work. Or they may b e used to demonstrate equipment behavior in a seminar environment.

- A model may be used (and has been used) to evaluate the temperature ramp consequences of bypass air for a zone damper system. (Entering air conditions and equipment performance continuously change with every time-step iteration of the situation.)

Spreadsheet Engine for Expanded Performance Data Air-Air Equipment			
Input for Sea Level Conditions			
Blower Cfm	Outdoor Air Dry-Bulb (°F)	Entering Air Wet-Bulb (°F)	Entering Air Dry-Bulb (°F)
1,215	95	63	75
Equation Set Output for Sea Level Conditions			
Total Cooling Capacity Btuh	Coil Sensible Heat Ratio CSHR	Sensible Capacity Btuh	Latent Capacity Btuh
34,400	0.83	28,552	5,848
Altitude Adjustment for dry-coil Cooling			
Altitude (Feet)		EWB Default	57°F

1) OEM data is for sea level conditions. For locations above 2,500 Feet, altitude adjustments are applied to sea level data. See Appendix 5, Section 2-5, and Section 5-12.
2) Dry-coil cooling is typical for elevations above 2,500 Feet. A few locations are exceptions when the elevation is 2,500 to 3,200 feet (see MJ8 Table 1 Grains Difference data for Hawaii, Kansas, Montana, Nebraska, Texas and West Virginia).
3) The elevation adjustment for air-air dry-coil operation may be provided by Figure A5-3, or OEM guidance.
4) Output error depends on the accuracy of the model's equations.
5) When OEM equations are used, the spreadsheet solution should be identical to the OEM's published performance data.
6) When surrogate equations are produced by the procedures in this appendix, the error typically ranges from 0% to 5% for most scenarios, but may be as high as 10% for some scenarios.
7) The scenario accuracy of surrogate equations may be improved when the practitioner fine tunes the equations for local operating conditions. For example, if 93°F/64°F/75°F is the typical design condition for practitioner projects, accuracy for 105°F/57°F/75°F is not an issue, and vice versa.
8) An engine for water-air equipment will have additional input for entering water temperature. Water-side performance is not affected by altitude, so water-air equipment has it's own altitude adjustment procedure (see Section A5-4 and Section 9-5).

Figure A13-1

A13-2 Altitude Effects — General Solution

For altitude applications, Appendix 2 procedures provide entering wet-bulb and dry-bulb values for extracting capacity values from sea level data. Then an Appendix 5 adjustment, or an OEM guidance adjustment, is applied to sea level capacity values.

- An altitude version of the Figure A13-1 spreadsheet engine must integrate a sea level data model, altitude psychrometrics, an entering air condition model, and an altitude adjustment model.

- An altitude version of the Figure A13-1 spreadsheet engine would require an input value for altitude, *Manual J* Table 1 values for outdoor air dry-bulb and wet-bulb, values for indoor air dry-bulb and relative humidity, a sensible return duct load, a latent return duct load, and outdoor air Cfm value, and a return air Cfm value (outdoor air Cfm plus return air Cfm equals blower Cfm).

A13-3 Air-Air Cooling Model

OEM expanded data for a particular make, model and size may be reduced to an equation set that is sensitive to momentary operating conditions. The cooling performance of air-air equipment depends on four variables.

- Outdoor dry-bulb temperature (OAT)
- Entering dry-bulb temperature (EDB)
- Entering wet-bulb temperature (EWB)
- Cfm flowing through the refrigerant coil (Cfm)

These variables are processed by a set of linear equations that summarize the information provided by OEM performance data. These equations are presented below in general form. The first equation yields values for the total capacity (TC), the second equation provides values for the coil sensible-to-total capacity ratio (CSHR), and the third equation provides input power values (Watts).

TC = K + M1 x Cfm + M2 x EWB + M3 x OAT
CSHR = Q + N1 x Cfm + N2 x EWB + N3 x EDB + N4 x OAT
Watts = V + O1 x Cfm + O2 x EWB + O3 x OAT

When a matrix of comprehensive performance data is available, the slopes (M_i, N_i and O_i) and intercepts (K, Q, and V) of the preceding equations may by evaluated by performing a crude regression analysis on the data.

- For a given make and model, one set of equations is required for each step in size.

- The procedure prefers OEM data that has adequate set of sensitivities (Figure A13-2, for example).

- OEM data that uses a few dry-bulb, wet-bulb pairs (see Figure A13-3, next page) is deficient for equipment selection and sizing work, and makes equation set modeling more difficult, and less accurate.

- OEM data for water-air equipment commonly uses a few dry-bulb, wet-bulb pairs, so Section A13-9 deals with the issue.

- Section A13-14 discusses modeling issues in more detail.

OEM Sea Level Data as Published						SEER = 13.0					Total 95°F / 80°F / 67°F Rating Btuh = 35,000							
		Outdoor Dry-Bulb 85°F				Outdoor Dry-Bulb 95°F					Outdoor Dry-Bulb 105°F					Outdoor Dry-Bulb 115°F			
EWB °F	Blower cfm	TC Btuh	Comp KW	CSHR vs. EDB			TC Btuh	Comp KW	CSHR vs. EDB			TC Btuh	Comp KW	CSHR vs. EDB			TC Btuh	Comp KW	CSHR vs. EDB		
				75°F	80°F	85°F			75°F	80°F	85°F			75°F	80°F	85°F			75°F	80°F	85°F
62	1,050	34.1	2.6	0.789	0.935	1.000	32.1	3.0	0.798	0.956	1.000	29.1	3.3	0.787	0.962	1.000	26.2	3.7	0.775	0.966	1.000
	1,200	35.1	2.7	0.821	0.989	1.000	32.9	3.1	0.830	1.000	1.000	29.8	3.4	0.815	1.000	1.000	26.7	3.8	0.798	1.000	1.000
	1,350	35.5	2.8	0.806	0.992	1.000	33.3	3.1	0.805	1.000	1.000	30.2	3.5	0.785	1.000	1.000	27.0	3.9	0.763	1.000	1.000
67	1,050	37.0	2.7	0.578	0.714	0.851	34.5	3.1	0.577	0.725	0.870	31.7	3.4	0.587	0.748	0.905	28.9	3.8	0.599	0.775	0.945
	1,200	38.1	2.8	0.601	0.753	0.906	35.4	3.2	0.599	0.763	0.927	32.5	3.5	0.606	0.785	0.960	29.5	3.8	0.617	0.814	1.000
	1,350	38.5	2.9	0.616	0.790	0.953	35.8	3.2	0.620	0.804	0.964	32.8	3.6	0.622	0.826	0.982	29.9	3.9	0.625	0.849	1.000
72	1,050	40.7	2.8	0.356	0.482	0.607	38.0	3.1	0.368	0.503	0.634	35.1	3.5	0.368	0.513	0.655	32.3	3.9	0.365	0.520	0.678
	1,200	41.9	2.9	0.370	0.508	0.647	39.0	3.2	0.379	0.528	0.679	35.9	3.6	0.376	0.538	0.702	32.9	4.0	0.371	0.550	0.726
	1,350	42.3	3.0	0.376	0.532	0.690	39.4	3.3	0.388	0.558	0.726	36.4	3.7	0.382	0.563	0.747	33.3	4.1	0.375	0.574	0.772

Figure A13-2

A13-4 Modeling an Exhibit of Air-Air Data

Figure A13-4 (next page) summarizes a possible solution for slope and intercept values for Figure A13-2 data. Procedure detail is provided here:

M1 Value
M1 Per Figure A13-2
OAT = 95°F, EWB = 62°F, EDB = 75°F
TC for 1,050 Cfm = 32,100 Btuh
TC for 1,350 Cfm = 33,300 Btuh
M1 = (33,300 − 32,100) / (1,350 − 1,050) = 4.00

M2 Value
M2 Per Figure A13-2
OAT = 95°F, 1,200 Cfm, EDB = 75°F
TC for 62°F EWB = 32,900 Btuh
TC for 67°F EWB = 35,400 Btuh
M2 = (35,400 − 32,900) / (67 − 62) = 500.0

M3 Value
M3 Per Figure A13-2
1,200 Cfm, EWB = 62°F, EDB = 75°F
TC for 95°F OAT = 32,900 Btuh
TC for 105°F OAT = 29,800 Btuh
M3 = (29,800 − 32,900) / (105 − 95) = −310.0

K value
OAT = 95°F, Cfm = 1,200, EWB = 62°F, EDB = 75°F
TC = 32,900 Btuh
K = 32,900 − (4.00 x 1,200 + 500 x 62 − 310 x 95) = 26,550

N1 Value
N1 Per Figure A13-2
OAT = 95°F, EWB = 62°F, EDB = 75°F
CSHR for 1,050 Cfm = 0.798
CSHR for 1,350 Cfm = 0.805
N1 = (0.805 − 0.798) / (1,350 − 1,050) = 0.0002

N2 Value
N2 Per Figure A13-2
OAT = 95°F, 1,200 Cfm, EDB = 75°F
CSHR for 62°F EWB = 0.830
CSHR for 67°F EWB = 0.599
M2 = (0.599 − 0.830) / (67 − 62) = −0.0462

N3 Value
N3 Per Figure A13-2
1,200 Cfm, EWB = 62°F, EDB = 75°F
CSHR for 95°F OAT = 0.830
CSHR for 105°F OAT = 0.815
N3 = (0.815 − 0.830) / (105 − 95) = −0.0015

N4 Value
N4 Per Figure A13-2
OAT = 95°F, 1,200 Cfm, EWB = 67°F
CSHR for 75°F EDB = 0.
CSHR for 80°F EDB = 0.
N4 = (0.763 − 0.599) / (80 − 75) = 0.0328

Deficient Format for Air-Air Cooling Data
1,350 Nominal Blower Cfm

Cfm	OAT °F	EDB °F	EWB °F	TC MBtuh	SC MBtuh	KW	SEER
1,350	80	75	63	37.5	27.0	2.930	12.8
		80	67	40.8	28.2	2.978	13.7
	90	75	63	35.0	26.0	3.153	11.1
		80	67	38.0	27.0	3.220	11.8
	100	75	63	32.6	24.9	3.432	9.5
		80	67	35.5	25.9	3.480	10.2

A dry-bulb, wet-bulb pair format does not summarize sensible capacity sensitivity to dry-bulb temperature (see Figure A13-2).

Figure A13-3

Slopes and Intercepts for Figure A13-2 Data

M Slopes (TC)	N Slopes (CSHR)	O Slopes (Watts)
M1 (Cfm) = 4.00	N1 (Cfm) = 0.0002	O1 (Cfm) = 0.3333
M2 (EWB) = 500.0	N2 (EWB) = −0.0462	O2 (EWB) = 20.0
M3 (OAT) = −310.0	N3 (OAT) = −0.0015	O3 (OAT) = 30.0
~	N4 (EDB) = 0.0328	~
K intercept = 26,550	Q intercept = 1.3489	V intercept = −1,390

Figure A13-4

Q value
OAT = 95°F, Cfm = 1,200, EWB = 62°F, EDB = 75°F
CSHR = 0.830
Q = 0.830 − (0.0002 x 1,200 − 0.0462 x 62 − 0.0015 x 95 + 0.0328 x 75) = 1.3489

O1 Value
M1 Per Figure A13-2
OAT = 95°F, EWB = 62°F, EDB = 75°F
Watts for 1,050 Cfm = 3,000
Watts for 1,350 Cfm = 3,100
O1 = (3,100 − 3,000) / (1,350 −1,050) = 0.3333

O2 Value
M2 Per Figure A13-2
OAT = 95°F, 1,200 Cfm, EDB = 75°F
Watts for 62°F EWB = 3,100
Watts for 67°F EWB = 3,200
O2 = (3,200 − 3,100) / (67 − 62) = 20.0

O3 Value
M3 Per Figure A13-2
1,200 Cfm, EWB = 62°F, EDB = 75°F
Watts for 95°F OAT = 3,100
Watts for 105°F OAT = 3,400
O3 = (3,400 − 3,100) / (105 − 95) = 30.0

Appendx 13

		Equation Set Version of Figure A13-2 Data																		
		Outdoor Dry-Bulb 85°F					Outdoor Dry-Bulb 95°F					Outdoor Dry-Bulb 105°F					Outdoor Dry-Bulb 115°F			
EWB °F	Blower cfm	TC Btuh	Comp KW	CSHR vs. EDB			TC Btuh	Comp KW	CSHR vs. EDB			TC Btuh	Comp KW	CSHR vs. EDB			TC Btuh	Comp KW	CSHR vs. EDB		
				75°F	80°F	85°F			75°F	80°F	85°F			75°F	80°F	85°F			75°F	80°F	85°F
62	1,050	35,400	2,750	0.842	1.000	1.000	32,300	3,050	0.827	0.991	1.000	29,200	3,350	0.812	0.976	1.000	26,100	3,650	0.797	0.961	1.000
	1,200	36,000	2,800	0.845	1.000	1.000	32,900	3,100	0.830	0.994	1.000	29,800	3,400	0.815	0.979	1.000	26,700	3,700	0.800	0.964	1.000
	1,350	36,600	2,850	0.849	1.000	1.000	33,500	3,150	0.834	0.998	1.000	30,400	3,450	0.819	0.983	1.000	27,300	3,750	0.804	0.968	1.000
67	1,050	37,900	2,850	0.611	0.775	0.939	34,800	3,150	0.596	0.760	0.924	31,700	3,450	0.581	0.745	0.909	28,600	3,750	0.566	0.730	0.894
	1,200	38,500	2,900	0.614	0.778	0.942	35,400	3,200	0.599	0.763	0.927	32,300	3,500	0.584	0.748	0.912	29,200	3,800	0.569	0.733	0.897
	1,350	39,100	2,950	0.618	0.782	0.946	36,000	3,250	0.603	0.767	0.931	32,900	3,550	0.588	0.752	0.916	29,800	3,850	0.573	0.737	0.901
72	1,050	40,400	2,950	0.380	0.543	0.708	37,300	3,250	0.365	0.528	0.692	34,200	3,550	0.350	0.514	0.678	31,100	3,850	0.335	0.498	0.663
	1,200	41,000	3,000	0.383	0.547	0.711	37,900	3,300	0.368	0.532	0.696	34,800	3,600	0.353	0.517	0.681	31,700	3,900	0.338	0.502	0.666
	1,350	41,600	3,050	0.387	0.551	0.715	38,500	3,350	0.372	0.535	0.700	35,400	3,650	0.357	0.521	0.685	32,300	3,950	0.342	0.506	0.670

Figure A13-5

		Error = (Model Value - Published Value) / Published Value																		
		Outdoor Dry-Bulb 85°F					Outdoor Dry-Bulb 95°F					Outdoor Dry-Bulb 105°F					Outdoor Dry-Bulb 115°F			
EWB °F	Blower cfm	TC Btuh	Comp KW	CSHR vs. EDB			TC Btuh	Comp KW	CSHR vs. EDB			TC Btuh	Comp KW	CSHR vs. EDB			TC Btuh	Comp KW	CSHR vs. EDB		
				75°F	80°F	85°F			75°F	80°F	85°F			75°F	80°F	85°F			75°F	80°F	85°F
62	1,050	3.8%	5.8%	6.7%	6.9%	0.0%	0.6%	1.7%	3.6%	3.6%	0.0%	0.3%	1.5%	3.1%	1.4%	0.0%	-0.4%	-1.4%	2.8%	-0.5%	0.0%
	1,200	2.6%	3.7%	3.0%	1.2%	0.0%	0.0%	0.0%	0.0%	-1.2%	0.0%	0.0%	0.0%	-0.1%	-3.4%	0.0%	0.0%	-2.6%	0.3%	-5.4%	0.0%
	1,350	3.1%	1.8%	5.3%	0.9%	0.0%	0.6%	1.6%	3.6%	-0.5%	0.0%	0.7%	-1.4%	4.3%	-2.1%	0.0%	1.1%	-3.8%	5.3%	-4.3%	0.0%
67	1,050	2.4%	5.6%	5.6%	8.5%	10.2%	0.9%	1.6%	3.2%	4.8%	6.2%	0.0%	1.5%	-1.1%	-0.4%	0.3%	-1.0%	-1.3%	-5.5%	-5.9%	-5.4%
	1,200	1.0%	3.6%	2.2%	3.3%	4.0%	0.0%	0.0%	0.0%	0.0%	0.0%	-0.6%	0.0%	-3.7%	-4.7%	-5.0%	-1.0%	0.0%	-7.8%	-9.9%	-10.3%
	1,350	1.6%	1.7%	0.3%	-1.0%	-0.8%	0.6%	1.6%	-2.8%	-4.7%	-3.4%	0.3%	-1.4%	-5.5%	-9.0%	-6.7%	-0.3%	-1.3%	-8.5%	-13.3%	-9.9%
72	1,050	-0.7%	5.4%	6.5%	12.9%	16.6%	-1.8%	4.8%	-1.1%	5.1%	9.2%	-2.6%	1.4%	-4.9%	0.1%	3.4%	-3.7%	-1.3%	-8.4%	-4.2%	-2.3%
	1,200	-2.1%	3.4%	3.5%	7.6%	9.9%	-2.8%	3.1%	-3.0%	0.7%	2.4%	-3.1%	0.0%	-6.1%	-3.8%	-3.0%	-3.6%	-2.5%	-8.9%	-8.8%	-8.3%
	1,350	-1.7%	1.7%	2.8%	3.5%	3.5%	-2.3%	1.5%	-4.3%	-4.1%	-3.6%	-2.7%	-1.4%	-6.6%	-7.6%	-8.4%	-3.0%	-3.7%	-9.0%	-11.9%	-13.3%

Figure A13-6

V value

OAT = 95°F, Cfm = 1,200, EWB = 62°F, EDB = 75°F
Watts = 3,100
V = 3,100 − (0.3333 x 1,200 + 20.0 x 62 − 30.0 x 95)
 = −1,390

Figure A13-5 shows how the equation set interprets equipment performance, and Figure A13-6 compares model output with published data (Figure A13-2) values. Model output shows good compatibility with OEM data, especially for the 95°F to 105°F outdoor air range, and the and 62°F to 67°F entering wet-bulb range that were used to generate slope and intercept values. See Section A13-15 for commentary on modeling issues.

A13-5 Data Presentation Adjustment

The OEM's format for the cooling data has 10°F jumps in outdoor air temperature. The OEM's format has no data for an entering dry-bulb that is cooler than 75°F, and data for an 85°F entering dry-bulb value is unless for normal circumstances. Note that there is no data for an entering wet-bulb temperature of 59°F, or less. In addition, data for a 72°F entering wet-bulb temperature is of no use for residential applications that have a normal latent load.

Manual J sensible heat ratios typically are 0.70 or more. Anything less than 0.65 is unusual, and may indicate an error in the load calculation; and/or an unusual latent load, or loads, for infiltration, outdoor, and duct leakage.

Figure A13-7 shows how the equation set is used to cast performance data in a more useful format. However, the resulting values are subject to OEM approval.

- OEM's usually allow interpolation, so 5°F jumps in outdoor air temperature should not be a problem.
- OEM's usually do not allow extrapolation, unless it is approved by the OEM. This caveat applies to performance values for 59°F entering wet-bulb temperature.

A13-6 Air-Air Heating Model

The steady-state heating performance data of an air-air heat pump may be represented as a piecewise, linear function of outdoor air temperature (see Figure A13-8, next page). The need for a set of capacity lines is due to the defrost effect when the outdoor dry-bulb temperature ranges from 17°F, to 35°F, to 47°F. Compressor heating capacity is modeled by the following procedure, which returns a heating capacity value (Btuh), and the compressor power value (Watts).

Heating Btuh = A_i + M_i x OAT
Watts = B_i + N_i x OAT

In this case, there are three sets of intercepts (A_i and B_i) and slopes (M_i and N_i). One set models performance when the outdoor temperature is below 17°F and above 47°F (no defrost effect). The second set models performance when the outdoor temperature is between 17°F and 35°F. And the third set models performance when the outdoor temperature is between 35°F and 47°F.

		\multicolumn{5}{c}{Model Output for a more Useful Collection of Condition Sets}												
		Outdoor Dry-Bulb 80°F					Outdoor Dry-Bulb 90°F					Outdoor Dry-Bulb 100°F					Outdoor Dry-Bulb 110°F				
EWB °F	Blower cfm	TC Btuh	Comp KW	CSHR vs. EDB			TC Btuh	Comp KW	CSHR vs. EDB			TC Btuh	Comp KW	CSHR vs. EDB			TC Btuh	Comp KW	CSHR vs. EDB		
				70°F	75°F	80°F			70°F	75°F	80°F			70°F	75°F	80°F			70°F	75°F	80°F
59	1,050	35,450	2,540	0.82	0.99	1.00	32,350	2,840	0.81	0.97	1.00	29,250	3,140	0.79	0.96	1.00	26,150	3,440	0.78	0.94	1.00
59	1,200	36,050	2,590	0.83	0.99	1.00	32,950	2,890	0.81	0.98	1.00	29,850	3,190	0.80	0.96	1.00	26,750	3,490	0.78	0.95	1.00
59	1,350	36,650	2,640	0.83	0.99	1.00	33,550	2,940	0.82	0.98	1.00	30,450	3,240	0.80	0.96	1.00	27,350	3,540	0.79	0.95	1.00
62	1,050	36,950	2,600	0.69	0.85	1.00	33,850	2,900	0.67	0.83	1.00	30,750	3,200	0.66	0.82	0.98	27,650	3,500	0.64	0.80	0.97
62	1,200	37,550	2,650	0.69	0.85	1.00	34,450	2,950	0.67	0.84	1.00	31,350	3,250	0.66	0.82	0.99	28,250	3,550	0.64	0.81	0.97
62	1,350	38,150	2,700	0.69	0.86	1.00	35,050	3,000	0.68	0.84	1.00	31,950	3,300	0.66	0.83	0.99	28,850	3,600	0.65	0.81	0.98
67	1,050	39,450	2,700	0.45	0.62	0.78	36,350	3,000	0.44	0.60	0.77	33,250	3,300	0.42	0.59	0.75	30,150	3,600	0.41	0.57	0.74
67	1,200	40,050	2,750	0.46	0.62	0.79	36,950	3,050	0.44	0.61	0.77	33,850	3,350	0.43	0.59	0.76	30,750	3,650	0.41	0.58	0.74
67	1,350	40,650	2,800	0.46	0.63	0.79	37,550	3,100	0.45	0.61	0.77	34,450	3,400	0.43	0.60	0.76	31,350	3,700	0.42	0.58	0.74
EWB °F	Blower cfm	Outdoor Dry-Bulb 85°F					Outdoor Dry-Bulb 95°F					Outdoor Dry-Bulb 105°F					Outdoor Dry-Bulb 115°F				
		TC Btuh	Comp KW	CSHR vs. EDB			TC Btuh	Comp KW	CSHR vs. EDB			TC Btuh	Comp KW	CSHR vs. EDB			TC Btuh	Comp KW	CSHR vs. EDB		
				70°F	75°F	80°F			70°F	75°F	80°F			70°F	75°F	80°F			70°F	75°F	80°F
59	1,050	35,450	2,540	0.82	0.99	1.00	32,350	2,840	0.81	0.97	1.00	29,250	3,140	0.79	0.96	1.00	26,150	3,440	0.78	0.94	1.00
59	1,200	36,050	2,590	0.83	0.99	1.00	32,950	2,890	0.81	0.98	1.00	29,850	3,190	0.80	0.96	1.00	26,750	3,490	0.78	0.95	1.00
59	1,350	36,650	2,640	0.83	0.99	1.00	33,550	2,940	0.82	0.98	1.00	30,450	3,240	0.80	0.96	1.00	27,350	3,540	0.79	0.95	1.00
62	1,050	36,950	2,600	0.69	0.85	1.00	33,850	2,900	0.67	0.83	1.00	30,750	3,200	0.66	0.82	0.98	27,650	3,500	0.64	0.80	0.97
62	1,200	37,550	2,650	0.69	0.85	1.00	34,450	2,950	0.67	0.84	1.00	31,350	3,250	0.66	0.82	0.99	28,250	3,550	0.64	0.81	0.97
62	1,350	38,150	2,700	0.69	0.86	1.00	35,050	3,000	0.68	0.84	1.00	31,950	3,300	0.66	0.83	0.99	28,850	3,600	0.65	0.81	0.98
67	1,050	39,450	2,700	0.45	0.62	0.78	36,350	3,000	0.44	0.60	0.77	33,250	3,300	0.42	0.59	0.75	30,150	3,600	0.41	0.57	0.74
67	1,200	40,050	2,750	0.46	0.62	0.79	36,950	3,050	0.44	0.61	0.77	33,850	3,350	0.43	0.59	0.76	30,750	3,650	0.41	0.58	0.74
67	1,350	40,650	2,800	0.46	0.63	0.79	37,550	3,100	0.45	0.61	0.77	34,450	3,400	0.43	0.60	0.76	31,350	3,700	0.42	0.58	0.74

TC = K + M1 x Cfm + M2 x EWB + M3 x OAT
CSHR = Q + N1 x Cfm + N2 x EWB + N3 x OAT + N4 x EDB
Watts = V + O1 x Cfm + O2 x EWB + O3 x OAT

TC = 26,550 + 4.0 x Cfm + 500 x EWB − 310 x OAT
CSHR = 1.3489 + 0.0002 x Cfm − 0.0462 x EWB + 0.0015 x OAT + 0.0328 x EDB
Watts = −1,390 + 0.3333 x Cfm + 20.0 x EWB + 30.0 x OAT

Figure A13-7

The following formulas evaluate the slopes and intercepts for each temperature range. To use these formulas, the AHRI high (47°F) Btuh capacity value and low (17°F) Btuh capacity value are required. The corresponding (47°F and 17°F) values for compressor watts are required. A Btuh capacity value for 35°F, and a watt value for 35°F are required.

Set 1 - Below 17°F or above 47°F
M1 = (Btuh @ 47°F – Btuh @ 17°F) / 30
A1 = Btuh @ 17°F – (M1 x 17)
N1 = (Watts @ 47– Watts @ 17°F) / 30
B1 = Watts @ 17°F – (N1 x 17)

Set 2 - Between 17° and 35°F
M 2= (Btuh @ 35°F – Btuh @ 17°F) / 18
A2 = Btuh @ 35°F – (M2 x 35)
N2 = (Watts @ 35°F – Watts @ 17°F) / 18
B2 = Watts @ 35°F – (N2 x 35)

Set 3 - Between 35°F and 47°F
M3 = (Btuh @ 47°F – Btuh @ 35°F) / 12
A3 = Btuh @ 35°F – (M3 x 35)
N3 = (Watts @ 47°F – Watts @ 35°F) / 12
B3 = Watts @ 35°F – (N3 x 35)

Note: The defrost knee is the default knee embedded in the OEM data. The actual defrost knee for a particular location may be similar, somewhat different, or considerably different. **Manual S** *procedures use the default defrost knee for a default balance point diagram, which provides an approximate outdoor air temperature for locking out supplemental heat. Energy and op-cost models should use the defrost knee for the local frosting potential, and the type of installed defrost control. See the sidebar on this page, and see Figure A1-25.*

A13-7 Water-Air Cooling Model

OEM expanded data for a particular make, model and size may be reduced to an equation set that is sensitive to momentary operating conditions. The cooling performance of water-air equipment depends on these variables:

- Water temperature entering the condenser (EWT)
- Entering air dry-bulb temperature (EDB)
- Entering air wet-bulb temperature (EWB)
- Cfm flowing through the indoor coil (Cfm)
- Gpm of water flowing through the condenser

When the water flow rate effect is small, as demonstrated by Figure A13-9 (next page), Gpm may be dropped from the equation set. When Gpm sensitivity is desired, it may be modeled as a simple multiplier that is applied to a capacity value, or electrical power value for a nominal Gpm.

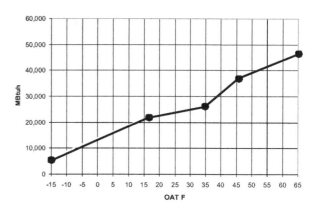

Figure A13-8

Defrost Control Comments

When the equipment has a simple defrost cycle timer, the annual number of defrost cycles will not vary with outdoor air conditions because the defrost cycle is initiated by time lapse. However, for a given winter temperature bin, the duration of a defrost cycle will vary from climate to climate because ice buildup depends on the amount of moisture in the outdoor air.

Demand defrost improves the situation because defrost cycle initiation depends on need. Therefore, a dry winter climate provokes fewer defrost cycles than a wet winter climate. However, for a given winter temperature bin, the duration of a defrost cycle will vary from climate to climate because ice buildup depends on the amount of moisture in the outdoor air.

This leaves four variables that may be combined into a set of linear equations that summarize the information provided by OEM expanded cooling performance data. These equations are presented below in general form. For this set, the first equation yields a value for the total capacity (TC), the second equation provides values for the coil sensible-to-total capacity ratio (CSHR), and the third equation provides input power values (Watts).

TC = K + M1 x Cfm + M2 x EWB + M3 x EWT
CSHR = Q + N1 x Cfm + N2 x EWB + N3 x EWT + N4 x EDB
Watts = V + O1 x Cfm + O2 x EWB + O3 x EWT

When adequate cooling performance data is available, the slopes (M_i, N_i and O_i) and intercepts (K, Q, and V) of the preceding equations are evaluated by performing a crude regression analysis on OEM data.

- For a given make and model, one set of equations is required for each step in size (i.e., six sets of equations are required for a product that has six nominal ton sizes).
- The procedure applies to any set of OEM data that has an adequate set of sensitivities.

A13-8 Deficient Format for Cooling Data

Figure A13-10 (next page) shows a popular format for presenting water-air heat pump data (also used by some OEM's for air-air equipment). The use of entering dry-bulb and wet-bulb pairs is unfortunate because it is not possible to interpolate sensible cooling performance for dry-bulb temperature, and it is not possible to evaluate the dry-bulb temperature effect on sensible heat ratio (the N4 slope in the CSHR equation).

The second issue relates to the OEM's choice of entering wet-bulb values (63°F, 67°F and 71°F, for the Figure A13-9 example). Data for an entering wet-bulb temperature of 59°F, or less, is required for dry-climate applications. The 71°F wet-bulb value is typically of no interest.

Since an equation set has sensitivity to entering dry-bulb and wet-bulb temperature, the organization and limits of OEM data may be unofficially recast to a format that compensates for these deficiencies.

A13-9 Modeling an Exhibit of Water-Air Data

Figure A13-10 provides an exhibit of expanded performance data for water-air equipment. Figure A13-11 (next page) shows a solution for the slope and intercept values for the Figure A13-10 data. Procedure detail is provided here:

M1 Value

The Figure A13-10 blower adjustment factors correlate total capacity change with blower Cfm change, so the M1 slope value is determined by the following equation. The equation is applied to six cases (85%, 90%, 95%, 105%, 110% and 115%), and the resulting slope values are averaged. The average M1 value for 36,000 Btuh of total cooling capacity and 1,200 Cfm is 4.17. A 36,000 Btuh value is near the middle of the product size range, so the 4.17 value is used for all sizes for this make and model.

Other Cfm = 1,200 x Percent adjustment
Other TC Btuh = 36,000 x Blower Cfm factor for TC

$$M1 = \frac{(TC\ Btuh\ nominal\ Cfm - TC\ Btuh\ other\ Cfm)}{(Nominal\ Cfm - Other\ Cfm)}$$

M2 Value

M2-A Per Figure A13 –10; EWT = 50°F
TC for 63°F EWB = 43,900 Btuh
TC for 67°F EWB = 47,800 Btuh
M2–A = (47,800 – 43,900) / (67 – 63) = 975
M2–B Value Per Figure A13-10; EWT = 100°F
TC for 63°F EWB = 32,600 Btuh
TC for 67°F EWB = 35,500 Btuh
M2–B = (32,600 – 35,500) / (67 – 63) = 725
M2 = (975 + 725) / 2 = 850

Gpm Effect for Nominal 8 Gpm
Adjustment Factors for 5 Gpm and 11 Gpm
Nominal Blower Cfm = 1,350

EWT °F	Gpm	Ewb/Edb °F	TC Btuh	SC Btuh	KW
50	5	75 / 63	0.98	0.98	1.08
		80 / 67	0.98	0.98	1.08
		85 / 71	0.98	0.98	1.08
	11	75 / 63	1.01	1.01	0.97
		80 / 67	1.01	1.01	0.97
		85 / 71	1.01	1.01	0.97
80	5	75 / 63	0.98	0.99	1.05
		80 / 67	0.98	0.99	1.03
		85 / 71	0.98	0.99	1.05
	11	75 / 63	1.03	1.03	0.98
		80 / 67	1.03	1.02	0.97
		85 / 71	1.03	1.03	0.98
110	5	75 / 63	0.99	0.99	1.00
		80 / 67	0.99	0.99	1.00
		85 / 71	0.99	0.99	1.00
	11	75 / 63	1.02	1.03	0.96
		80 / 67	1.02	1.03	0.96
		85 / 71	1.02	1.03	0.96

1) EWT = Entering water temperature; Gpm = Gallons per Minute
TC = Total cooling capacity; SC = Sensible cooling capacity;
KW = Compressor input plus a default blower input, no pump.
2) Factor = Data value for 5 Gpm or 11 Gpm divided by data value for 8 Gpm.
3) Use averages for modeling purposes. For example: total capacity is about 2.0% less for 5 Gpm, and about 2.0 more for 11 Gpm.
4) Based on data published by a prominent water-air heat pump manufacturer.

Figure A13-9

M3 Value

M3-A Per Figure A13–10; EWB = 63°F
TC for 50°F EWT = 43,900 Btuh
TC for 100°F EWT = 32,600 Btuh
M3-A = (32,600 – 43,900) / (100 – 50) = –226
M3-B Value Per Figure A13–10; EWB = 67°F
TC for 50°F EWT = 47,800 Btuh
TC for 100°F EWT = 35,500 Btuh
M3-B = (35,500 – 47,800) / (100 – 50) = –246
M3 = –(226 + 246) / 2 = –236

K value

TC for 50°F EWT and 63°F EWB = 43,900 Btuh
K = 43,900 – (4.17 x 1,350 + 850 x 63 – 236 x 50) = –3,480

Appendx 13

N1 Value
The procedure for producing the 0.0002 N1 value is the same as the procedure for producing the M1 value. In this case the procedure is applied to the sensible heat ratio, per these defaults and equations.

Nominal total capacity (TC) = 36,000 Btuh
Nominal sensible capacity for 75°F / 63°F = 24,950 Btuh
Nominal CSHR = 24,950 / 36,000 = 0.693
Other CSHR = Other SC / Other TC
Other TC Btuh = 36,000 x Blower Cfm factor for TC
Other SC Btuh = 24,950 x Blower Cfm factor for SC
Other Cfm = 1,200 x Percent adjustment

$$N1 = \frac{(CSHR\ nominal\ Cfm - CSHR\ other\ Cfm)}{(Nominal\ Cfm - Other\ Cfm)}$$

N2 Value (CSHR = SC / TC)
N2–A Per Figure A13-10; EWT = 50°F
CSHR for 63°F EWB = 0.0683
CSHR for 67°F EWB = 0.642
N2–A = (0.642 – 0.683) / (67 - 63) = –0.01028
M2–B Value Per Figure A13-10; EWT = 100°F
CSHR for 63°F EWB = 0.764
CSHR for 67°F EWB = 0.730
M2–B = (0.730 – 0.764) / (67 – 63) = –0.00856
M2 = –(0.01028 + 0.00856) / 2 = –0.00942

N3 Value (CSHR = SC / TC)
N3-A Per Figure A13-10; EWB = 63°F
CSHR for 50°F EWT = 0.683
CSHR for 100°F EWT = 0.764
N3–A = (0.764 – 0.683) / (100 – 50) = 0.00161
N3–B Value Per Figure A13-10; EWB = 67°F
CSHR for 50°F EWT = 0.642
CSHR for 100°F EWT = 0.730
N3–B = (0.730 – 0.642) / (100 - 50) = 0.00175
N3 = (0.00161 + 0.00175) / 2 = 0.00168

N4 Value
For N4, a 0.0010 value is carried forward from **Manual S**, First edition, Table A3-2, because the Figure A13-10 format does not have segregated dry-bulb sensitivity.

Q Value
CSHR for 50°F EWT and 63°F EWB = 0.683
Q = 0.683 – (0.0002 x 1,350 – 0.00942 x 63 +
    0.00168 x 50 + 0.001 x 75) = 0.84778

O1 Value
The procedure for producing the 0.347 O1 value is the same as the procedure for producing the M1 value. In this case the procedure is applied to power input (KW), per these defaults and equations.

Nominal input power for 36,000 Brtuh unit = 2.4 KW
Other Cfm = 1,200 x Percent adjustment
Other TC Btuh = 36,000 x Blower Cfm factor for TC

Water-Air Heat Pump Cooling Data 1,350 Nominal Cfm, 85°F/71°F DB/WB Data Ignored							
Gpm	EWT °F	EDB °F	EWB °F	TC MBtuh	SC MBtuh	KW	EER
8	50	75	63	43.9	30.0	2.275	19.3
		80	67	47.0	31.3	2.320	20.6
	60	75	63	42.0	29.1	2.485	16.9
		80	67	45.6	30.3	2.533	18.0
	70	75	63	40.0	28.1	2.685	14.9
		80	67	43.5	29.3	2.736	15.9
	80	75	63	37.5	27.0	2.930	12.8
		80	67	40.8	28.2	2.978	13.7
	90	75	63	35.0	26.0	3.153	11.1
		80	67	38.0	27.0	3.220	11.8
	100	75	63	32.6	24.9	3.432	9.5
		80	67	35.5	25.9	3.480	10.2
	110	75	63	30.3	23.8	3.695	8.2
		80	67	32.9	24.8	3.739	8.8

1) Similar data is provided by the OEM for 5 Gpm and 11 Gpm.
2) Capacity values are 1% to 2% less for 5 Gpm, and 1% to 2% more for 11 Gpm.
3) A dry-bulb, wet-bulb pair format does not summarize sensible capacity sensitivity to dry-bulb temperature.

Blower Cfm Adjustment Factors						
Load Item	Percent of Nominal Blower Cfm for Capacity Data					
	85%	90%	95%	100%	105%	110%	115%
TC	0.972	0.982	0.993	1.000	1.007	1.010	1.013
SC	0.926	0.948	0.974	1.000	1.027	1.055	1.066
HC	0.967	0.978	0.990	1.00	1.009	1.017	1.024
KW	0.977	0.984	0.993	1.00	1.011	1.018	1.028

Figure A13-10

Slopes and Intercepts for Figure A13-10 Data		
M Slopes (TC)	N Slopes (CSHR)	O Slopes (Watts)
M1 (Cfm) = 4.17	N1 (Cfm) = 0.0002	O1 (Cfm) = 0.347
M2 (EWB) = 850	N2 (EWB) = -0.00942	O2 (EWB) = 41.294
M3 (EWT) = -236	N3 (EWT) = 0.00168	O3 (EWT) = 20.812
~	N4 (EDB) = 0.0010	~
K = –3,480	Q = 0.84778	V = 1,836

1) M1, N1, O1 slopes are based on the Cfm adjustment factors.
2) The remaining values are based on Figure A13-10 body data.

Figure A13-11

$$O1 \text{ for KW} = \frac{KW \text{ nominal Cfm} - KW \text{ other Cfm}}{(\text{Nominal Cfm} - \text{Other Cfm})}$$

O1 for Watts = 1,000 x O1 for KW

O2 Value

O2–A Per Figure A13-10; EWT = 50°F
Watts for 63°F EWB = 2,275
Watts for 67°F EWB = 2,556
O2–A = (2,556 – 2,275) / (67 – 63) = 70.385
O2–B Value Per Figure A13–10; EWT = 100°F
Watts for 63°F EWB = 3,432
Watts for 67°F EWB = 3,480
O2–B = (3,480 – 3,432) / (67 – 63) = 12.203
O2 = (70.385 + 12.203) / 2 = 41.294

O3 Value

O3–A Per Figure A13–10; EWB = 63°F
Watts for 50°F EWT = 2,275
Watts for 100°F EWT = 3,432
O3–A = (3,432 – 2,275) / (100 – 50) = 23.139
O3–B Value Per Figure A13–10; EWB = 67°F
Watts for 50°F EWT = 2,556
Watts for 100°F EWT = 3,480
O3–B = (3,480 – 2,256) / (100 – 50) = 18.485
O3 = (23.139 + 18.485) / 2 = 20.812

V value

Watts for 50°F EWT and 63°F EWB = 2,275
V = 2,275 – (0.347 x 1,350 + 41.294 x 63 +
    20.812 x 50) = –1,836

Equation Set for Figure A13-10 Data

TC = –3,480 + 4.17 x Cfm + 850 x EWB – 236 x EWT
CSHR = 0.84778 + 0.0002 x Cfm - 0.00942 x EWB +
    0.00168 x EDB + 0.001 x EWT
Watts = –1,836 + 0.347 x Cfm + 41.294 x EWB +
    20.812 x EWT

A13-10 Error Check

To check on model error, output from the preceding equation set is compared to Figure A13-10 data for a few data points. Figure A13-12 shows that the equation set is a reasonable simulation of the OEM's expanded data.

- The Section A13-9 equations are based on two entering water temperatures (slope values for 50°F and 100°F are averaged). This is compatible with an earth-loop system because entering water temperature varies from relatively cold to relatively warm during the cooling season.

- Entering water temperature is constant, or approximately constant, for a once-through system. For this scenario, an equation set developed for one entering water temperature, is best for modeling accuracy.

Equation Set Error					
Output and Error for 8 Gpm; 1,350 Cfm; 75°F DB and 63°F WB					
EWT °F	TC Bruh	SC Btuh	CSHR	EER	Watts
50	43,900	30,000	0.683	19.3	2,275
100	32,100	24,629	0.767	9.7	3,315
Error	TC	SC	CSHR	EER	Watts
50	0.00%	0.00%	0.00%	0.00%	0.00%
100	1.53%	1.09%	-0.45%	-1.92%	3.39%
Output and Error for 8 Gpm; 1,350 Cfm; 80°F DB and 67°F WB					
EWT °F	TC Btuh	SC Btuh	CSHR	EER	Watts
50	47,300	30,778	0.651	19.4	2,440
100	35,500	26,078	0.735	10.2	3,480
Error	TC	SC	CSHR	EER	Watts
50	1.05%	-0.25%	-1.31%	-3.67%	4.55%
100	0.00%	-0.69%	-0.69%	0.00%	0.00%

Figure A13-12

A13-11 Water-Air Equation Set Use

Equation sets are approximations of OEM data. When the ability to show due diligence is required (professional design/sizing, or energy modeling projects), use OEM published data when it applies to the operating conditions of interest, or ask the OEM for data when an operating condition, or conditions, is not addressed by the OEM's published data. Otherwise:

- Section A13-1 explains that electronic spreadsheet input may be processed by an embedded equation set for a given make/model and size. The output cells provide conditional performance values. Figure A13-1, Footnote 8, advices that spreadsheet input for water-air equipment includes a value for entering water temperature.

- An equation set for a given make/model and size may be used to produce an expanded data table that has sensitivity to conditional circumstances that are ignored by the OEM's published data. The next section provides an example of this use.

A13-12 Water-Air Cooling Example

An equation set for a given make/model and size may be used to produce an expanded performance data table that is more relevant than the OEM's table. For example, the Section A13-9 equation set (repeated below) produces the Figure A13-13 data table.

Appendx 13

Data Table Provided by Equation Set									
Mid Gpm	EWT °F	Blower Cfm	EWB °F	Watts	TC Btuh	SC Btuh vs. EDB			EER
						70°F	75°F	80°F	
8	70	1,148	59	2,455	34,936	24,772	24,947	25,122	14.23
		1,350		2,526	35,780	26,820	26,999	27,178	14.17
		1,553		2,596	36,624	28,937	29,120	29,303	14.11
		1,148	63	2,621	38,336	25,739	25,931	25,673	14.63
		1,350		2,691	39,180	27,893	28,089	27,825	14.56
		1,553		2,761	40,024	30,115	30,315	30,045	14.50
		1,148	67	2,786	41,736	26,450	26,659	26,657	14.98
		1,350		2,856	42,580	28,710	28,923	28,921	14.91
		1,553		2,926	43,424	31,038	31,255	31,253	14.84
OEM's Data Values for 1,350 Cfm, or Adjusted for Other Cfm Values per OEM Factors									
8	70	1,148	63	2,623	38,880	26,021			
		1,350		2,685	40,000	28,100			14.9
		1,553		2,760	40,520	29,955			
		1,148	67	2,673	42,282			27,132	
		1,350		2,736	43,500			29,300	15.9
		1,553		2,812	44,066			31,234	
(Equation Set Value - OEM Value) / OEM Value									
8	70	1,148	63	-0.09%	-1.40%	-0.34%			
		1,350		0.23%	-2.05%	-0.04%			-1.82%
		1,553		0.05%	-1.22%	1.20%			
		1,148	67	4.22%	-1.29%			-1.75%	
		1,350		4.39%	-2.11%			-1.29%	-5.78%
		1,553		4.05%	-1.45%			0.06%	

1) Sea level data. See Appendix 5 for altitude adjustment procedure.
2) Figure A13-9 provides adjustment factors for 5 Gpm or 11 Gpm,

Figure A13-13

TC = -3,480 + 4.17 x Cfm + 850 x EWB - 236 x EWT
CSHR = 0.84778 + 0.0002 x Cfm - 0.00942 x EWB + 0.00168 x EDB + 0.001 x EWT
Watts = -1,836 + 0.347 x Cfm + 41.294 x EWB + 20.812 x EWT

- Compare the Figure A13-13 format with the Figure A13-10 format. Note that Figure A13-13 provides values for 59°F wet-bulb, and sensitivity to entering dry-bulb temperature.
- To save space, Figure A13-13 data is for a 70°F entering water temperature. A similar matrix may be produced for any entering water temperature.
- Figure A13-13 also shows values from the OEM's data table for 70°F water (see Figure A13-10).
- Figure A13-13 compares equation set values with OEM data values. The comparison shows a 1% to 2% error for total and sensible capacity, a small to 5% error for watts, and a 2% to 6% error for EER.

A13-13 Water-Air Heating Model

Since water-air equipment does not have a defrost cycle, the heating capacity and power are modeled by linear equations that are a function of entering water temperature (EWT). These equations are provided here:

Heating Btuh = A + M x EWT
Watts = B + N x EWT

In this case, one set of intercepts (A and B) and slopes (M and N) is adequate. The following formulas can be used to generate values for A, B, M and N:.

M = (Btuh @ 70°F − Btuh @ 50°F) / 20
A = Btuh @ 50°F − (M x 50)
N = (Watts @ 70°F − Watts @ 50°F) / 20
B = Watts @ 50°F − (N x 50)

A13-14 OEM Data Format Issues

Some OEMs show a total capacity value and a sensible heat ratio value, some show a total capacity value and a sensible capacity value. The procedure for evaluating equation constants is the same for both cases, just use a spread sheet to convert total capacity values and the corresponding sensible capacity values to sensible heat ratio values.

Some OEMs show total capacity and sensible capacity, but the sensible capacity value is for 80°F entering dry-bulb. For this format, the OEM provides an adjustment procedure for other entering dry-bulb values. This means the adjustment procedure must be used to recast the data into a usable format. The easiest way to do this is to use a spreadsheet to convert the OEM's data format to a format that is compatible with the modeling procedures provided by this appendix:

It has already been noted that some OEM data uses dry-bulb, wet-bulb pairs (see Figures A13-3 and A13-10). Section A13-9 procedures apply for this type of data (outdoor air dry-bulb temperature replaces entering water temperature for air-air equipment).

Some OEM's present table data for one nominal Cfm value, and use adjustment factors for other Cfm values (Figure A13-10, for example). Section A13-9 procedures apply for this type of data (outdoor air dry-bulb temperature replaces entering water temperature for air-air equipment).

For two compressor speeds, build a model for each speed. For variable compressor speed, build a model for maximum speed and for minimum speed.

A13-15 Modeling Issues and Caveats

Figure A13-6 shows that model error is smaller when operating condition values are similar to the values used to calculate model slopes and intercepts. For example, a model based on mid-range Cfm values, 95°F and 105°F outdoors, 63°F and 67°F entering wet-bulb, and 75°F and 80°F entering dry-bulb may have better accuracy for these conditions, than for hot dry climate conditions (say 110°F, 57°F EWB and 75°F EDB).

- Base the modeling on a set of operating conditions that apply to the dwelling's location.
- Use a spreadsheet to check model error (Figures A13-2, A13-5 and A13-6, for example).
- For advanced study, use a spreadsheet to see if a slope is constant through the whole data range. For example, hold Cfm, entering wet-bulb and entering dry-bulb constant, and plot total cooling capacity (or CSHR, or Watts) vs. outdoor air temperature. When the result is a perfect straight line, the slope applies to any outdoor design temperature. When the plot has two or more lines with different slopes, the modeling should be adjusted to the local climate. Then perform similar investigations for variable entering wet-bulb, variable entering dry-bulb, and variable Cfm.

An equation set for a given make/model and size, may, or may not, apply to other makes/models of the same size. To see if one equation set applies to more than one product, produce an equation set for a default product, and a separate equation set for some other make/model/size and see if the M, N, O slopes are the same or, about the same, for both models.

When the slopes are similar, the K, Q and V intercepts depend on the product. For example, a two ton unit and a four ton unit that are the same make and model may have similar slopes, but must have different K and V intercepts for total capacity and Watts sensitivity. The Q intercept may, or may not, apply to both products, check and see.

The background work for producing this section found that one set of slopes for a particular make/model/size did not apply to the same make/model in a different size. This however, does not prove that one set of slopes for all sizes for a given make/model is impossible, but this must be investigated on a case-by-case basis.

A13-16 Accuracy of OEM Data

Models attempt to duplicate OEM data whether it is correct, or not. However, OEM data should show the tendencies that are summarized by Figure A13-14. When this is not the case, compare the questionable data with data for similar makes/models of the same size.

The background work for producing this section found OEM data that has positive and negative total capacity slopes that depend on the range of outdoor air temperature (positive for 85°F to 95°F vs. negative for 95°F to 105°F, for example). Then a data set from a different OEM showed no watt-value sensitivity to blower Cfm, or entering wet-bulb temperature.

Appendx 13

Data from other OEMs for similar products showed slope behavior that is consistent with Figure A13-13 tendencies. So, the questionable data was discarded, and replaced with data that is consistent with expected tendencies.

Discussing data accuracy with an OEM is not a simple matter. To resolve data issues, one must talk to the person that produces the data. Then this person must look into the matter, and confirm data accuracy, or clarify data use, or provide corrected data.

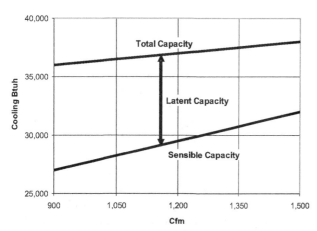

Total capacity and sensible capacity increase as Cfm increases. Latent capacity decreases because the rate of sensible capacity increase is greater than the rate total capacity increase. Input power (KW or Watts) increases as Cfm increases.

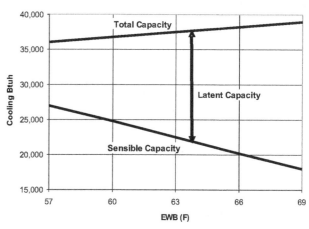

Total capacity increases and sensible capacity decreases as entering wet-bulb increases. Latent capacity increases because the capacity lines diverge as entering wet-bulb increases. Input power (KW or Watts) increases as entering wet-bulb increases.

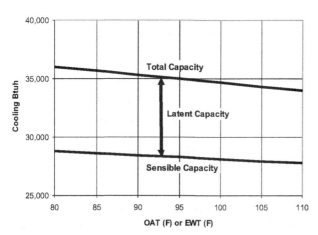

Total capacity and sensible capacity decrease as outdoor air temperature, or entering water temperature increase. Latent capacity decreases because the rate of sensible capacity decrease is less than the rate total capacity decrease. Input power (KW or Watts) increases as condensing temperature increases.

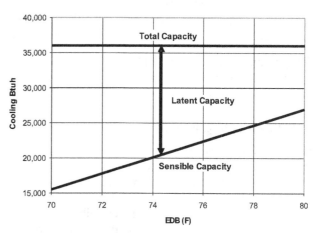

Total capacity is constant and sensible capacity increases as entering dry-bulb increases. Latent capacity decreases because the capacity lines converge as entering dry-bulb increases. Input power (KW or Watts) is constant as entering dry-bulb increases.

Figure A13-14

Appendix 14

Air-Air Heat Pump Supply Air Temperature

During heating, the temperature of the supply air delivered by an air-to-air heat pump gets noticeably cooler as the outdoor temperature declines. This means that there may be many operating hours associated with supply air temperatures that are 85°F or cooler. In fact, when the weather is extremely raw, the temperature of the supply air may fall below 80°F. However, when the supplemental heat is energized, the supply air temperature may range from 90°F to 120°F or more, depending on the outdoor temperature and on how much supplemental heat is activated. So, when it is cold outside, the supply air temperature can be expected to fluctuate by 20°F to 30°F, or more.

Of course, the warmer supply air temperatures that occur when the supplemental heat is energized may be desirable; however, this operating condition may only last for a few minutes out of each hour. Therefore, it is important to understand that an excessive amount of supplemental heating capacity produces short periods of operation with warm supply temperatures, and long periods of operation with cool supply temperatures.

A14-1 Balance-point Diagram

Figure A14-1 shows the balance-point diagram for a cold climate dwelling. The heating load for this home is about 42,000 Btuh at an outdoor design temperature of 0°F. Notice that the balance point is equal to 30°F (BP1) when the heat pump is the only source of heat. When 5 KW of supplemental heat is added to the system, the balance point is about 11°F (BP2). When 10 KW of supplemental heat is added to the system, the balance point is about –6°F (BP3). And, when 15 KW of supplemental heat is added to the system, the balance point is off the chart, somewhere below -10°F. (In this example, 10 KW is an appropriate amount of supplemental heat because BP3 is just a little below the 0°F design temperature.)

A14-2 Supply Air Temperatures

Figure A14-2 (next page) shows what the supply air temperature (SAT) is when the heat pump is the only source of heat, and when 5, 10 and 15 KW of supplemental heat is energized. These supply air temperatures were estimated by using the sensible heat equation (below) to evaluate the temperature rise across the indoor air handler.

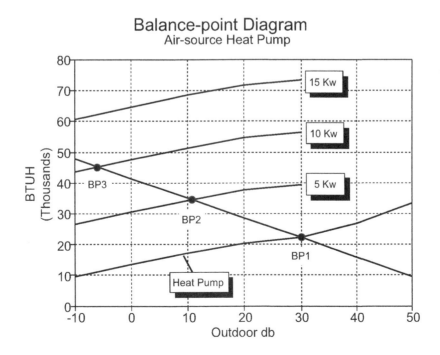

Figure A14-1

Appendx 14

$$\text{Rise (°F)} = \frac{\text{(Heat Pump Btuh + Supplemental Btuh)}}{1.1 \times \text{ACF} \times \text{Blower Cfm}}$$

SAT (°F) = 70 + Rise

Figure A14-2 shows that when no supplemental heat is energized, the supply air temperature ranges from a low of 80°F, when the outdoor temperature is 0°F, to a high of 87°F, when the outdoor temperature is equal to the 30°F balance point. With 5 KW of supplemental heat active, the diagram shows that the supply air temperature will range from 93°F to 100°F. When 10 KW is active, the supply air temperature ranges between 106 F and 113 F; and, when 15 KW is active, the supply air temperature ranges between 119°F and 126°F.

A14-3 Supplemental KW Run Fraction

As indicated by Figure A14-2, a larger amount of supplemental heating capacity will result in a warmer supply temperature. However, this condition only occurs for a few minutes an hour. This means that there will be many minutes per hour when the heat-pump-only supply temperature, which is relatively cool. This behavior is quantified by the following equation, which evaluates the number of minutes per hour for active supplemental heat:

$$\text{Min/Hr} = \frac{60 \times \text{(Heating Load - Heat Pump Capacity)}}{3,413 \times \text{Supplemental KW}}$$

Figures A14-3 and A14-4 (next page) show the supply air temperatures and the corresponding run fractions for air-to-air heat pump packages that have 10 KW and 15 KW of supplemental heat. Notice how the 10 KW system causes the supply temperature to be warmer for more minutes per hour.

For example, at the 0°F outdoor temperature, the supply temperature of the 10 KW system is above 100°F for 49 minutes per hour compared to 33 minutes per hour for the 15 KW system. It follows that the 10 KW system will have a supply temperature that is below 85°F for 11 minutes per hour compared to 27 minutes per hour for the 15 KW system. A similar analysis at other outdoor temperatures shows that the 10 KW system will always provide more minutes per hour of 100°F plus supply air temperature than the 15 KW system.

A14-4 Two Stages Improve Performance

When the outdoor temperature is above 10°F, Figures A14-3 and A14-4 indicate that both the 10 KW system and the 15 KW system spend most of the hour operating at the lower, heat-pump-only supply air temperature. Therefore, during moderate weather, the 10 KW system is not that much better than the 15 KW system. For example, for a 20°F outdoor temperature, the supply temperature of the 10 KW system is above 100°F for 14 minutes per hour compared to 10 minutes per hour for the 15 KW system.

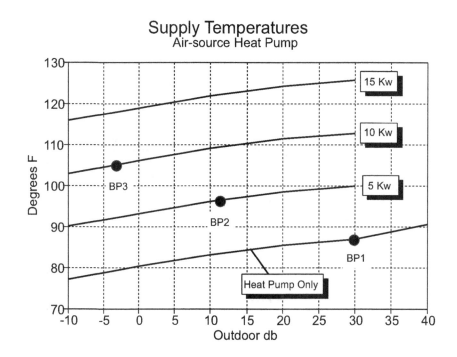

Figure A14-2

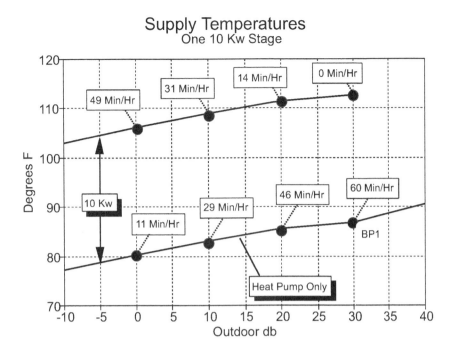

Figure A14-3

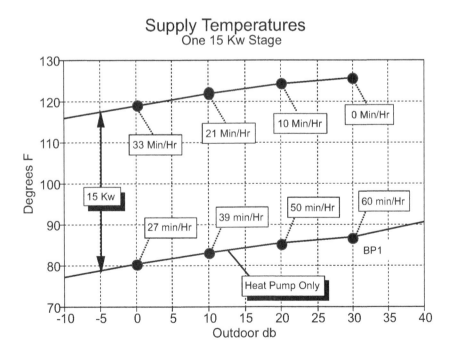

Figure A14-4

The performance of the 10 KW system may be improved by using two 5 KW coils instead of one 10 KW coil. Two outdoor thermostats are required for this design. When the outdoor temperature drops below 30°F, the first outdoor thermostat energize 5 KW of supplemental heat, and when the outdoor temperature drops below 11°F degrees, the second outdoor thermostat energizes an additional 5 KW of supplemental heat.

The benefit of a staged system is demonstrated by Figure A14-5, which shows that when the outdoor temperature is above 11°F, one 5 KW stage of supplemental heat produces a warmer supply air temperatures for more minutes per hour. For example, at 12°F, the supply temperature of the staged system is above 95°F for about 60 minutes per hour, compared to 31 minutes per hour for the 10 KW system. At 20°F, the supply temperature of the staged system is above 98°F for about 29 minutes per hour, compared to 14 minutes per hour for the 10 KW system.

A14-5 Sizing Supplemental Heat

Keeping supplemental KW to a minimum reduces the minutes-per-hour for relatively cool supply air temperatures. The maximum amount of electric resistance heat controlled by the second stage of the room thermostat should not be much larger than the supplemental heat requirement read from a thermal balance point diagram. (The supplemental heat requirement is equal to the difference between the winter design heating load and compressor heat output when the equipment operates at the winter design temperature.) This means that when an additional increment of electrical resistance heat is required to satisfy a 100 percent (or less) emergency heat requirement, the additional heat should be controlled by a manual switch.

A14-6 Staging Supplemental Heat

Staging the supplemental heat will increase the number of minutes per hour that the system operates with a relatively warm supply temperature. As indicated above, two 5 KW stages provide warmer supply temperatures when the outdoor air temperature is between the first balance point and the second balance point (10°F and 30°F in this case.) This range of outdoor temperatures is very important because most of the winter heating hours occur at intermediate outdoor air temperatures.

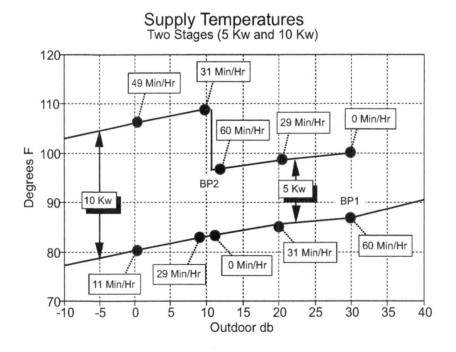

Figure A14-5

This appendix is not part of the this standard. It is merely informative and does not contain requirements necessary for conformance to the standard. It has not been processed according to the ANSI requirements for a standard, and may contain material that has not been subject to public review or a consensus process. Unresolved objectors on informative material are not offered the right to appeal at ACCA or ANSI.

Appendix 15

Whole-House Dehumidifier Performance

The latent load for sizing primary cooling equipment is calculated for the summer design condition. Section A15-1 shows that large latent loads may occur during spring, midsummer, and fall. Sections A15-2 and A15-3 provide the basis for the Figure N2-1 dehumidifier performance adjustment curves (see Section N2-12).

Monthly Moisture Removal Loads for Brunswick, GA Example Dwelling Maintained at 75°F and 55% RH Indoors												
Outdoor DB °F	88-29 Bin-Hours	88-29 MCWB °F	Outdoor Air Grains	Bin Delta Grains	Latent Load Factor	Pints per Day	Outdoor DB °F	88-29 Bin-Hours	88-29 MCWB °F	Outdoor Air Grains	Bin Delta Grains	Latent Load Factor	Pints per Day
May							June					
95 / 99	1	73	83.4	12.2	0.20	37	95 / 99	3	80	127.6	56.4	0.91	171
90 / 94	14	73	91.5	20.3	0.33	62	90 / 94	23	78	122.4	51.2	0.83	155
85 / 89	44	73	99.6	28.4	0.46	86	85 / 89	86	76	117.8	46.6	0.75	141
80 / 84	101	71	96.3	25.1	0.40	76	80 / 84	147	75	119.7	48.5	0.78	147
75 / 79	141	70	98.9	27.7	0.45	84	75 / 79	203	73	115.9	44.7	0.72	135
70 / 74	203	68	96.4	25.2	0.41	76	70 / 74	195	70	107.1	35.9	0.58	109
July							August					
95 / 99	5	78	114.2	43.0	0.69	130	95 / 99	2	80	127.6	56.4	0.91	171
90 / 94	50	79	129.0	57.8	0.93	175	90 / 94	44	79	129.0	57.8	0.93	175
85 / 89	134	78	130.6	59.4	0.96	180	85 / 89	124	78	130.6	59.4	0.96	180
80 / 84	158	76	126.0	54.8	0.88	166	80 / 84	148	76	126.0	54.8	0.88	166
75 / 79	230	74	121.9	50.7	0.82	154	75 / 79	250	74	121.9	50.7	0.82	154
70 / 74	162	71	112.6	41.4	0.67	125	70 / 74	160	72	117.7	46.5	0.75	141
65 / 69	7	66	94.2	23.0	0.37	70	65 / 69	14	67	98.8	27.6	0.45	84
September							October					
95 / 99	~	~	~	~	~	~	95 / 99	~	~	~	~	~	~
90 / 94	11	77	115.9	44.7	0.72	135	90 / 94	9	77	115.9	44.7	0.72	135
85 / 89	72	77	124.1	52.9	0.85	160	85 / 89	60	74	105.5	34.3	0.55	104
80 / 84	127	75	119.7	48.5	0.78	147	80 / 84	105	72	102.0	30.8	0.50	93
75 / 79	211	73	115.9	44.7	0.72	135	75 / 79	160	70	98.9	27.7	0.45	84
70 / 74	199	70	107.1	35.9	0.58	109	70 / 74	166	68	96.3	25.1	0.40	76
65 / 69	72	66	94.2	23.0	0.37	70	65 / 69	115	64	84.4	13.2	0.21	40

1) Bin-hours and Mean Coincident Wet-bulb (MCWB) values from Engineering Weather Data AFM 88-29.
2) Altitude psychrometrics (Brunswick is near sea level), provides humidity ratio (grains) values. 75°Fdb / 55% RH = 71.2 Grains.
3) Bin delta grains = Bin grains value - Indoor grains for 75°F / 55% RH. **Manual J** Table 1A grains difference for 75°F / 55% RH = 62.
4) Latent load factor = Bin delta grains / 62 (this is a simplification of a complex relationship, but it serves the purpose).
5) For the summer design condition (91°F / 79°F) and 75°F / 55% RH indoors, the latent load for the dwelling is 8,250 Btuh = 188 pints/day.
6) Bin pints per day = (24 x 8,250 x Latent load factor) / 1,054 [24 = Hours / Day; 1,054 = Default phase change latent heat for 1 Lb water].
7) For 75°F / 55% RH entering air, the latent capacity of a 210 pint / day product is about 76% of it's rated capacity = 0.76 x 210 = 160 pint / day.
8) Shaded cells show outdoor conditions that challenge dehumidifier capacity. Hours of occurrence is a significant issue.

Figure A15-1

Appendx 15

A15-1 Latent Load Vs. Month of Year

The dehumidifier helps the primary cooling equipment when the primary equipment compressor cycles, or operates at reduced capacity. There will be times when the dehumidifier is the primary source of humidity control, and occasions when the dehumidifier is the only significant source of humidity control, as demonstrated by Figure A15-1 (previous page).

- Brunswick, GA, has a very humid climate. The summer design condition for outdoor air is 91°F dry-bulb and 79°F wet-bulb.
- For the summer design condition outdoors, and for 75°F and 55% RH indoors, the moisture load for the Figure A15-1 dwelling is 188 pints/day.
- Per the Section N2 sizing rule, minimum dehumidifier capacity is 85% of the design load, or 160 Pints per day.
- The default capacity adjustment factor for a whole-house dehumidifier is 0.76 (per Figure N2-2), so the required dehumidifier capacity rating is about 160 / 0.76, or 210 pints/day.
- The shaded Figure A15-1 cells show when the moisture load is close to, or exceeds, 160 pints/day. In some cases this is only for a few hours per month, in other cases for many hours per month.
- The primary equipment operates less as the bin dry-bulb temperature decreases, and substantially less when there is no solar load, so the dehumidifier must carry more of the moisture load, or most of the moisture load, for theses circumstances.
- Figure A15-1 shows that there are a substantial number of hours when the outdoor temperature is in the upper 70's to low 80's, and the moisture load is 145 pints/day, or more. The majority of these hours will be night time hours, or cloudy day hours.
- The moisture load for 60% RH indoors is about 165 pints per day. The default capacity adjustment factor for 75°F db, 60% RH entering air is 0.90, so dehumidifier capacity for 75°F db, 60% RH is 90% of 210 pints /day, or 189 pints per day.
- Therefore, for benign sensible load conditions, humidity excursions will be in the 55% to 60% RH range, and will not exceed 60% RH.

A15-2 Expanded Capacity Data

Whole-house dehumidifier performance data is limited to a single steady-state pints per day capacity value, and a pints per KWH efficiency value for 75°F, 60% RH entering air. Research performed by Jon Winkler, Ph.D., Dane Christensen, Ph.D., and Jeff Tomerlin; National Renewable

Dehumidifier Manufacturer's Specifications				
Brand Name	Model #	Capacity [1] Pints / Day	Energy [1] Factor L / KWH	Air Flow Rate Cfm
A	See the NREL report	150	3.7	415
B		70	2.32	160
C [3]		70	2.37	170
D		65	1.8	195 / 175 / 155
E		45	1.5	103 / 91 / 81
F		35	1.4	N/A
G		25	1.2	N/A

1) Performance at the rated inlet condition of 80°F, 60% relative humidity (RH).
2) Flow rate specified at 0 inches water gauge (IWG).
3) Unit was not tested under all operating conditions due to nearly identical performance with Product B.
4) Make and model numbers are listed in the NREL report.

Figure A15-2

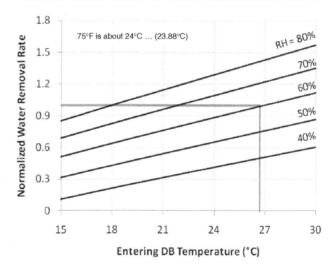

Generic Water Removal Rate Performance Curve

Figure A15-3

Energy Laboratory (NREL) provides default performance data for other operating conditions. The actual report is at:

http://www.nrel.gov/docs/fy12osti/52791.pdf.

Figure A15-2 summarizes the range of products tested. Figure A15-3 shows expanded capacity (moisture removal) data, and Figure A15-4 (next page) shows expanded efficiency data.

The expanded data models (generic performance curves) are output from a regression analysis of laboratory test output values for Figure A15-2 equipment. The actual report makes this comment, pertaining to using default models for products produced by different OEMs (Appendix D is in the NREL report):

"Despite subtle differences in the individual performance curves (see Appendix D), a single set of performance curves can accurately predict the performance of all the dehumidifiers tested."

A15-3 Dehumidifier Performance Equations

The NREL report cited above also provides the equation that was used to produce Figures A15-3 and A15-4. This equation is provided below. Figure A15-5 provides values for the a, b, c, d, e and f constants, r2 is a correlation index (not used in the equation).

Performance Variable = a + b x T + c x T^2 + d x RH + e x RH^2 + f x T x RH

Where:
The performance variable may be moisture removal capacity (pints / day), or the energy factor (liters / KWH).
T is the degrees centigrade (°C) dry-bulb temperature.
RH is the relative humidity value.

To investigate performance for degrees Fahrenheit (°F), convert the Fahrenheit temperature to a centigrade temperature, and use the centigrade value for the equation.

°C = 5 / 9 x (°F – 32)

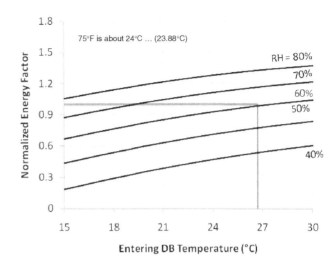

Generic Energy Factor Performance Curve

Figure A15-4

Constants for Dehumidifier Performance Equation		
Equation Constant	Pints / Day	Liters / KWH
a	-1.1625	-1.9022
b	0.022715	0.063467
c	-0.00011321	-0.00062284
d	0.021111	0.03954
e	-6.9303E-05	-0.00012564
f	0.00037884	-0.00017672
r2	0.977	0.969

Figure A15-5

Appendx 15

Ancillary Pages

Appendix 16 – Glossary

Appendix 17 – Symbols, Acronyms and Abbreviations

Appendix 18 – Summary of Equations

Appendix 19 – Supporting Detail for Equipment Sizing Examples

Appendix 20 – Rationale for Equipment Sizing Limits

Appendix 21 – Related Resources

Appendix 22 – Blank Forms

Index

This appendix is not part of the this standard. It is merely informative and does not contain requirements necessary for conformance to the standard. It has not been processed according to the ANSI requirements for a standard, and may contain material that has not been subject to public review or a consensus process. Unresolved objectors on informative material are not offered the right to appeal at ACCA or ANSI.

Appendix 16

Glossary

A

Adequate exposure diversity (AED)

No significant spike in the total (block) fenestration cooling load during a summer design day.

AED excursion

The total fenestration cooling load exceeds the AED limit (spikes) for some hour of a summer design day.

AHAM appliance

OEM air conditioning and heat pump products that are certified by the Association of Home Appliance Manufacturers.

AHJ

Authority Having Jurisdiction: As it pertains to local code requirements.

AHRI-Certified equipment

OEM air conditioning and heat pump products tested and rated by the Air-Conditioning, Heating, and Refrigeration Institute.

AHRI defrost condition

See Figure A1-25.

AHRI rating speed

See Section N1-1 definitions.

AHRI rating test for cooling

See Section N1-1 definitions.

AHRI rating test for heating

See Section N1-1 definitions.

AHRI Ton

The advertised value for rated total cooling capacity, per the AHRI rating test for cooling, in Btuh units, divided by 12,000 (Btuh per ton).

Air-air

For cooling-only equipment and heat pumps, the heat source is outdoor air and the heat sink is indoor air, or vice versa.

Air changes per hour

For infiltration and engineered ventilation, the number of indoor space-air volumes replaced by outdoor air during one hour of time.

Air-coupled space

Rooms and spaces that are not isolated by partition wall and/or interior doors.

Air distribution

Supply air enters conditioned space through a free blow grille at the equipment, or through supply air outlets fed by duct runs, plus an adequate return air path.

Air distribution effectiveness

Supply air must be adequately mixed with space air, must induce adequate air movement in the space used by occupants, and must not cause drafts or stagnate air in the space used by occupants. The ability of supply air grilles, registers, or diffusers to adequately mix a given amount of supply air with room air.

Air loading factor (ALF)

The supply air Cfm to a space divided by the floor area of the space. (Grilles, registers and diffusers are designed for low, medium, or high air loading.)

Air-side

For water-air and air-air equipment, all components, devices, and piping associated with the supply/return air circuit.

Air turnover

For ventilation effectiveness, the number of indoor space-air volumes replaced by supply air for one hour of time.

Air zoning

An air distribution system that is equipped with a set of supply air dampers and associated controls, that provides zone temperature control.

Airway

The inside dimensions of a duct run, fitting or plenum.

Applied capacity

See Section N1-1 definitions.

Ancillary dehumidification

See Section N2-12

Attributes

Attributes define the issues that affect actual performance, and the performance predicted by a mathematical model. For example, a cooling load calculation is affected by a set of fenestration attributes (directions, rough opening areas, U-values,

SHGC values, internal shade adjustments, and external shade adjustments). An attribute may be a constant (a U-value, for example), or a variable (an over hang adjustment, for example). For defined or limited circumstances, an attribute may be a defensible default. An attribute may be independent constant or variable. Two or more attributes may be inter-dependant variables. An attribute can have a large, moderate, or small affect on performance. The sensitivity and accuracy of a robust model depends on the accuracy and interlacing of it's attribute models.

Auxiliary heat

For heat pump heating, electric coil heat used for supplemental heat and/or emergency heat.

Available static pressure

For *Manual D*, the blower pressure that is available to move air through the duct fittings and duct runs in the critical circulation path.

B

Balance point

In general, the load and the available capacity, are identical (there is a balance point for compressor cooling Btuh and heating Btuh, for furnace heating Btuh, for electric coil heating Btuh, for blower Cfm, and for pump Gpm, etc.).

Balance point diagram

A graph of a load and the related equipment capacity (typically, the heating/cooling load vs. heat pump compressor heating/cooling capacity; or blower/pump capacity vs. duct/pipe system resistance).

Beam radiation

Direct radiant heat from the sun to some surface on the earth, with no interference from clouds, haze, trees, or man-made shade.

Bin hours

The average number of observed hours (over 20 years, or so) that outdoor dry-bulb temperature falls in a given range (typically five degree bands ranging from the location's coldest temperature to the location's warmest temperature). Each bin-hour total may be split into three values for three eight-hour groups. The bin-hour data usually includes values for average coincident wet bulb temperature.

Bin model

Circumstantial equipment loads, and circumstantial equipment capacities, are associated with bin-hours that are parsed for time of day.

Bin temperature or temperature bin

The range of normal outdoor air temperatures (winter low to summer high) for a location are divided into 5°F or 10°F bins (from the coldest temperature to the warmest temperature).

Block load

The total heating or cooling load for the entire space served by a piece of heating or cooling equipment. This always includes the building envelope loads and all applicable system load, internal loads only apply to cooling.

Block Load Space

For a block load calculation, one room or space, a group of rooms and spaces, or the entire dwelling.

Blower balance point

The Cfm and pressure produced by the blower equals the Cfm and airflow resistance produced by the air distribution system.

Bonus room

Any room or space that is completely or effectively isolated from the rooms and spaces for the primary floor plan. Typically a room over a garage, an attic room, or a basement room. (i.e., a buffer space is converted to a living space).

Break-even COP

Operating circumstances cause heat pump compressor heating cost to be identical to fossil fuel heating cost.

Buffer zone air

Air in an enclosed unconditioned space.

Buried earth loop

See earth loop.

Bypass air

Air that leaves the primary equipment and short circuits back to the equipment through a dedicated duct run (bypass duct). The condition of the bypass air is essentially the same as the supply air. Bypass air is mixed with normal return air, and possibly outdoor air, before it enters the equipment. This process causes a temperature ramp at the equipment; which means that the discharge air temperature increases over time for heating, or decreases over time for cooling, but settles at a final value. Should the final values exceed the equipment's limit temperature for discharge air, the equipment's limit control will stop the equipment (assuming appropriate controls).

C

Candidate

A piece of cooling or heating equipment that has the desired set of performance attributes, that may, or may not, be compatible with size limit rules.

Capabilities

HVAC system or HVAC equipment functions (zoning, heating, cooling, humidification, dehumidification, filter air, provide outdoor air, heat recovery, etc.). Mathematical model functions (determine or evaluate sensible and latent heating and cooling loads, blower operating point, supply air Cfm, duct airway size, supply air outlet throw and drop, bypass air temperature ramp, for example). See also, attributes and sensitivities.

Capacity control

Sensor input to control logic adjusts some aspect, or aspects, of equipment performance to provide some amount of correlation between the momentary equipment output and the momentary equipment load. This may involve on-off cycling, a few distinct capacity steps, or an infinite number of capacity steps (variable capacity).

Central system or equipment

A piece of HVAC equipment and it's distribution system. The primary equipment is usually external to the rooms and spaces served, but may be in one of the rooms or spaces. Most dwellings have one central system. A zoned dwelling may have two or more central systems.

Change-Over

A given set of load conditions usually produces a net heating load or a net cooling load on the HVAC equipment. The size of this load varies as load conditions vary. At some point there is no load condition (the change-over point). Then more movement along this trajectory produces an increasingly larger heating load or cooling load. The heating-cooling change-over point is quantified by an outdoor air temperature value, but this varies with circumstances (the change-over temperature depends on the size of the solar gain, the internal load, and the effective thermal mass of the conditioned space). For a thermal balance point diagram, the default change-over temperature for outdoor is 65°F.

Coil sensible heat ratio

A cooling coil has total capacity, sensible capacity and latent capacity. The magnitude of these Btuh values depend on the momentary heat sink temperature (for air or water), and the momentary condition of the air entering the indoor coil (dry-bulb and wet-bulb temperature). The conditional coil sensible heat ratio equals the momentary sensible capacity divided by the momentary total capacity. This value can range from less than 0.50 (large latent load) to 1.0 (no latent load) as operating conditions change. Summer design condition circumstances apply to equipment selection.

Coincident dry-bulb temperature

Outdoor dry-bulb and wet-bulb temperatures do not move in unison, therefore, an average wet-bulb value is associated with a particular dry-bulb value.

Coincident wet-bulb temperature

Outdoor wet-bulb and dry-bulb temperatures do not move in unison, therefore, an average dry-bulb value is associated with a particular wet-bulb value.

Cooling load

A cooling load (Btuh for inch-pound units) may be a sensible load, a latent load, or a total (sensible plus latent) load.

Comfort space or comfort zone

The interior portion of a conditioned space that is two feet from any wall, and about 6½ feet high (where we are most likely to find people).

Comprehensive (conditional) performance data

See Expanded performance data.

Condition A or Condition B

See Section N2-5, and Table N2-2 And Section 1-9.

Critical circulation path

The path of maximum airflow resistance from the blower, to the conditioned space, and back to the blower. There is one path per supply outlet, one of these paths produces more airflow resistance than the other paths. For air zoning, a bypass duct or dump zone produces an additional path. All circulation path are parallel paths.

Cyclic

Observed or measured behavior repeats after an increment of time, then repeats for the next time-step, and so on. For example, outdoor air temperature and solar loads cycle in 24 hour periods, and by the year.

Cycling degradation coefficient

Inefficiency caused by starting and stopping equipment (similar to driving an automobile in stop and go traffic).

D

Default balance point diagram

A thermal balance point diagram that uses defaults for circumstantial solar loads, internal loads, and heat pump heating capacity.

Default defrost knee

For air-air heat pumps, the circumstantial compressor heating capacity in the 17°F to 47°F outdoor air temperature range has a default adjustment for the effect of the defrost cycle.

Default heating load-line

The graph of the heating load vs. outdoor air temperature uses default values for solar load and internal load for each outdoor air temperature value.

Defrost knee

Air-air heat pumps operate in the cooling mode to melt frost/ice on ten outdoor coil; compressor heating capacity is reduced when the outdoor air temperature is in the 17°F to 47°F range.

Demand charge

The electrical bill increases when the KW load exceeds some threshold value (or some schedule of values).

Design Day

A convenient misnomer for summer and winter design conditions, and the corresponding design loads for summer cooling and winter heating.

Dedicated return air path

An engineered return air path from room air to the entrance of a return duct. There may be a return grille for each room or space that has supply air; or there may be a transfer grille or transfer duct from a space that has supply air to a space that has a return grille (which must be sized for the total amount of supply air Cfm that flows to it). The total pressure drop for a transfer path (from room air to the entrance of a remote return duct opening) should be 0.06 IWC, or less (space pressure affects supply air Cfm and the operation of interior doors).

Diffuser

An supply air outlet that has engineered performance, as far as it's air pattern is concerned (i.e., vanes, blades, or cones are designed to provide specific throws and spreads over a certain range of supply air Cfm). The diffuser design determines when it is compatible with low, medium, or relatively high air loading. See also, air loading factor.

Direct evaporative cooling

Moisture is evaporated to supply air, then routed to the conditioned space. This lowers the supply air dry-bulb temperature (provides sensible cooling capacity), and rises the supply air humidity ratio (adds moisture to the conditioned space).

Direct saturation efficiency

See Section 4-4.

Discharge air

The airflow out of primary cooling or heating equipment, leaving a cooling or heating device, or leaving a supply air outlet.

Distribution loads

Duct system loads, piping system loads, blower heat, water pump heat.

Diversity or diversity factor

For cooling or heating, the loads for a set of spaces do not peak simultaneously, and/or are not simultaneously active, so the sum of the set of the peak loads for these spaces is greater than the largest possible momentary aggregate load.

Drop

The vertical distance between the supply air outlet and the bottom of the primary air pattern at the end of the horizontal throw. An air distribution effectiveness issue.

Dry climate

The indoor evaporator (cooling coil) is typically dry during the cooling season (ignoring a short rainy season).

Dry coil or dry cooling coil

The moisture in the air passing through a cooling coil does not condenses on coil surfaces (coil surfaces are warmer than the dew-point of the air).

Dual fuel

For heat pump heating, an air-air heat pump or water-air heat pump, plus a fossil fuel furnace.

Ductless multi-split

An air conditioner or heat pump that has an outdoor unit, two or more indoor units, and a set of refrigerant lines. Most types of indoor units have integral supply air grilles; however, some indoor units are designed to serve a local (modest) duct system (essentially, a small air handler). Most indoor units do not have an outdoor air feature, but some do. Indoor units use various types of filters.

Ductless split-coil

An air conditioner or heat pump that has an outdoor unit, one indoor unit, and a set of refrigerant lines. Most types of indoor units have integral supply air grilles; however, some indoor units are designed to serve a local (modest) duct system (essentially, a small air handler). Most indoor units do not have an outdoor air feature, but some do. Indoor units use various types of filters.

Dump zone

A zone damper system may route excess air through a conditioned room or space that is of no, or minor, importance to occupant comfort (a utility space, for example).

Earth coupled heat pump

Refrigeration cycle equipment that uses buried pipe-loop water, for a heat source and a heat sink.

Earth loop

A buried pipe-loop (horizontal or vertical) filled with freeze-protected water provides a heat source and a heat sink for water-air equipment.

Economic balance point

For heat pump heating, the outdoor air temperature that produces equality for refrigerant cycle heating cost (compressor heat) and fossil fuel heating cost.

Energy

For the purposes of this manual, input or savings (typically per month, per season, or per year) in KWH units or Btu units.

Energy factor

Energy factor (for whole-house and ventilation dehumidifiers, the rated moisture removal efficiency (Pints/KWH, for example). For water heaters, the ratio of output energy to input energy for a rating test.

Engineered humidification

Selection, size and placement of a winter humidification device, based on a calculated load.

Engineered value

A performance goal set by a standard or code, and/or proper application of the laws of physics.

Engineered ventilation

Outdoor air that is purposely introduced to the occupied space by the action of a mechanical device. This may be as simple as a small, dampered duct from the outdoors to the return side of an air handler, or as complex as an air-to-air heat exchanger that provides enthalpy recovery.

Enhanced compressor speed

See Section N1-1 definitions.

Envelope load

The heating or cooling load for the structure, ignoring loads produced by the comfort system.

Excess Air

For zone damper systems, the difference between the momentary need for supply air Cfm, and the momentary value for blower Cfm.

Excess latent capacity

See Section N1-1 definitions.

Expanded performance data

For cooling, total capacity, sensible capacity, latent capacity, and power draw (KW) conditionally depend on the blower Cfm, heat sink temperature (for air or water), and the condition of the air entering the indoor coil (dry-bulb and wet-bulb temperature). For heat pump heating, refrigerant cycle heating capacity and power draw (KW), conditionally depend on the blower Cfm, heat source temperature (for air or water), and the temperature of the air entering the indoor coil. These relationships are summarized by published data tables or software equivalents. This information is required for selecting and sizing refrigeration-cycle equipment. See the Section N1-1 definitions and see Section A1-9. See also, *performance map*.

External static pressure

The blower pressure that is available to move air through air-side components not accounted for by the blower data, through duct fittings, and through duct runs.

Face velocity

The average velocity of supply air across the face of an outlet (roughly the supply Cfm divided by the inside frame area).

Fan

Fans have propeller type blades, blowers have a vaned wheel and a scroll housing. The two terms are often used as equivalents (for example, fan coil is common jargon for an air handler cabinet that has a blower).

Fan coil unit

A cabinet equipped with a blower and one or more coils for heating and/or cooling. The cabinet may accommodate an air filter. The cabinet may have integral supply and return grilles, or it may have inlet and outlet collars for attaching duct runs. When it has outdoor air capability, it may be called a unit ventilator.

Fan stall

Blower airflow becomes unstable, erratic, or negligible when the airflow over the blades is not compatible with the blade design (system resistance to airflow exceeds a limit value for a given blower wheel speed).

Fenestration

Engineered openings in structural panels (windows, doors and skylights). For *Manual J*, subassemblies that have glass (windows, glass doors, and skylights).

Fixed default or fixed value

For equations and mathematical models, reducing input for a variable to a selected numerical constant. This is done to simplify the calculation, and is justified when the practice does not make a significant difference in equation or model output.

Free blow

Air discharged through a supply air outlet that has no upstream zone damper. Supply air discharged from a grille that is part of the equipment (indoor unit of a ductless-split system, for example).

Free blow space

A room or space served by indoor equipment that has an integral supply air grill. A room or space that receives supply air though a duct run that has no zone damper.

Frosting potential

For air-air heat pumps, the amount of moisture in the outdoor air when the outdoor coil temperature is colder than dew point of the outdoor air.

Full capacity

See Section N1-1 definitions.

Full compressor speed

See Section N1-1 definitions.

G

Grains difference

The humidity ratio difference for two psychrometric statepoints in grains of water per pound of dry air units.

Grille

A supply air outlet that has a frame and a set of louvers (horizontal, vertical or both). The louvers may be fixed (no air pattern adjustment) or adjustable (affects throw and spread). Grilles are compatible with lower air loading values.

Gross output

For boiler performance, no output capacity (Btuh) deduction for piping and pick-up loads.

Ground water heat pump

Refrigeration cycle equipment that uses once-through ground water, or buried pipe-loop water, for a heat source and a heat sink.

H

Head

For ductless multi-split equipment, one indoor unit.

Heating Load

For equipment sizing, the heating load for the winter design condition.

Heat recovery

For this manual, sensible and/or latent heat recovered from exhaust air; or the total amount of heat transferred from one flow of refrigerant to another flow of refrigerant.

Heat recovery effectiveness

For heating, the amount of heat that is reclaimed from exhaust air and added to outdoor air used for ventilation, or the direction of heat flow is reversed for cooling. Some equipment recovers sensible heat only, some equipment recovers sensible heat and latent heat. The net effect is to moderate the condition of the entering outdoor air.

Heat sink

Typically, air, water, or soil that absorbs heat rejected by refrigeration cycle equipment.

Heat source

Typically, air, water, or soil that transfers heat to refrigeration cycle equipment.

High-Limit

The maximum value allowed by the OEM.

Hourly simulation

Circumstantial loads and circumstantial equipment capacities are associated with each hour of the year. Calculations are normally based on a typical mean year for the location of interest.

Humid climate

The indoor evaporator (cooling coil) is typically wet during the cooling season.

Humidity ratio

The amount of moisture in a pound of air at a given psychrometric condition. Grains of moisture per pound of dry air units are used for this manual, but pounds of moisture per pound of dry air is commonly used. One pound of water is 7,000 grains of water.

Hydronic heat

Hot water heat provided by gravity convectors; fan coil units, air-handlers, unit ventilators; or by radiant heating coils.

I

Indoor air
The air in a conditioned space.

Indoor air condition
The state point (typically summarized by dry-bulb temperature and relative humidity values) of the indoor air.

Integrated heating capacity
For air-air heat pumps, compressor heating capacity is adjusted for the OEM's default defrost knee.

Isolated room or space
Any comfort room or space that has natural convection air-coupling to adjacent spaces by virtue of a partition opening that is no larger than a normal interior door. (Air mixing tends to reduce room-to-room temperature difference. There can be no significant mixing for a closed door; and the mixing for an open door, or for no door, may be deficient.)

L

Large glass area
The total glass area for a room or space is greater than 15% of it's floor area. (This value is only a threshold default for a possible temperature control problem. Load calculations, AED curves, and excursion values are required to see when a fenestration load is a zoning issue. See MJ8, Section 4.)

Latent capacity or load
The moisture removal ability of refrigeration cycle equipment, or the moisture gain for a dwelling and it's comfort system.

load-line
A line on a graph that correlates a heating load or cooling load (Y-axis) with outdoor air temperature (X-axis). The heating load-line on a thermal balance point diagram, for example.

Load patterns
Local cooling and heating loads depend on time of day, and day of year. To investigate this behavior, the heating or cooling load for a room, a space, a zone, a dwelling, etc., is plotted for each hour-of day, for each month of year (twelve graphs with twenty-four data points per graph). The loads for these plots are obtained from load calculations for hourly-monthly, outdoor conditions and sun angles, and for hourly-monthly internal load values.

Load sensible heat ratio
See, *Manual J* sensible heat ratio. (There is a load sensible heat ratio for each momentary operating condition. The value for summer design conditions is used for equipment selection and sizing.)

Low-Limit
The minimum value allowed by the OEM.

M

Manual J sensible heat ratio
For cooling, the sensible load to total load ratio for a given set of operating circumstances. Summer design condition circumstances apply to equipment selection and sizing.

Mass flow
For inch-pound units, pounds per hour, pounds per minute, pounds per second, etc.

Maximum capacity
The maximum capacity of refrigeration cycle equipment (cooling units and heat pumps) operating at a fixed compressor speed occurs when the heat sink/source temperature, and the entering air condition, are most favorable (see comprehensive performance data). When refrigeration cycle equipment has staged or modulated compressor performance, the maximum output capacity occurs at maximum compressor speed, when the sink/source temperature, and the entering air condition, are the most favorable. The AHRI rating condition is not the most favorable operation condition, so maximum capacity may be greater than rated capacity. In some cases, the maximum capacity of variable compressor speed equipment, operating at the AHRI rating condition, is greater than it's AHRI rated capacity (because maximum compressor speed was not used for the AHRI rating test). Furnace burners that are staged, or modulated, have a maximum output Btuh capacity. Blowers that operate at staged, or modulated, wheel-speeds have a maximum air power capacity (which depends on a set of Cfm and external static pressure values).

Minimum Capacity
The minimum capacity of refrigeration cycle equipment (cooling units and heat pumps) operating at a fixed compressor speed occurs when the heat sink/source temperature, and the entering air condition, are least favorable (see comprehensive performance data). When refrigeration cycle equipment has staged or modulated compressor performance, the minimum output capacity occurs for minimum compressor speed, when the sink/source temperature, and entering air condition, are least favorable. Minimum equipment capacity is always less (normally much less) than the equipment's AHRI rated capacity. Furnace burners that are staged, or modulated, have a minimum output Btuh capacity. Blowers that operate at staged, or modulated, wheel-speeds have a minimum wheel-speed (to avoid aerodynamic stall), and a minimum air power capacity (which depends on a set of Cfm and external static pressure values).

Multi-speed equipment

Cooling and heat pump equipment that operates at two or more distinct compressor speeds.

Multi-Split

A ductless split-coil cooling system or heat pump that has two or more indoor coils.

Multi-Zone

A single comfort system that simultaneously controls the air temperature in two or more zones.

N

Net output

For boiler performance, output capacity (Btuh) has a default adjustment (deduction) for piping and pick-up loads.

Noise

A negative human reaction to the sound pressure or sound power values for eight octave bands (Figure 11-9, for example). The net affect may be summarized by a single value descriptor; a noise criteria (NC) value.

Nominal AHRI ton

The AHRI rating value for total cooling capacity divided by 12,000.

Nominal cooling tons

Total cooling capacity at the AHRI rating condition (95°F/80°F/67°F) divided by 12,000.

O

Occupied zone or occupied space

A virtual room that is 6½ feet high, with vertical boundaries that are two feet inside the physical walls of the surrounding physical room.

OEM

For this manual, the source for the primary heating-cooling equipment (air conditioner, heat pump, furnace, etc.). See also, zone damper equipment vendor.

OEM package

An OEM may provide single-zone equipment that has no zoning features, or an equipment package that has zoning capability. An OEM package that provides zoning may be a mandatory one-source package (the OEM provides everything), or it may be that zone damper vendor devices can be substituted for the OEM's devices (as specified by the OEM).

OEM verification path

See Section N3.

Once-through

Ground water enters a water-air heat pump, flows through the equipment, and is discarded.

Operating cost (op-cost)

The total amount of money paid for electrical and fossil fuel HVAC energy over a period of time (usually a season, or a year). These charges are normally less than utility bills indicates because HVAC energy is only part of the total amount of energy delivered to the dwelling.

Outdoor air fraction

Outdoor air Cfm divided by blower Cfm.

Outlet

Hardware designed for mixing ducted supply air with room air (grille, register, diffuser).

Over-size factor

See Section N1-1 definitions.

Over-size limit

See Section N1-1 definitions.

Owner

The party that has the authority to commission HVAC work This may be the current or future occupant, a land lord, or a builder that intends to use the structure, or sell the structure.

P

Packaged terminal air conditioner (PTAC)

All the refrigerant cycle components and controls for cooling are housed in one decorative cabinet that has integral supply and return air grilles, and some type of air filter. There may be an outdoor air feature. There may be a way to attach a minimal duct run to a remote supply air grille. There may be an electric resistance heat option.

Packaged terminal heat pump (PTHP)

All the refrigerant cycle components and controls for reverse cycle operation (for heating and cooling) are housed in one decorative cabinet that has integral supply and return air grilles, and some type of air filter. There may be an outdoor air feature. There may be a way to attach a minimal duct run to a remote supply air grille. There may be an electric resistance heat option.

Part-load

The momentary heating-cooling load for a room, space, zone, or dwelling is normally less, or much less, than the *Manual J* load. This applies to the heating load, the sensible cooling load, the latent cooling load, or the total cooling load.

Peak block load

The *Manual J* value for the total cooling load for all the rooms and spaces served by a piece of central equipment. The sensible and latent components of this value are used for equipment sizing. The standard *Manual J* procedure provides this value for single zone systems and multi-zone systems.

Peak zone load

For air-zoning with central equipment, the *Manual J* value for the peak sensible cooling load for a zone. For zoning with multi-split equipment or unitary equipment, the peak total (sensible plus latent) load. The zone may be one room, or a set of rooms and spaces. The optional *Manual J* procedure provides peak load values for zone system design (not applicable to single zone systems that serve a set of rooms and spaces).

Performance map

Cooling or heating capacity performance (output) as a function of circumstantial operating conditions (input). See expanded performance data.

Pick-up load

See recovery load.

Practitioner

The authority that is responsible for system design and system installation. This may be one person or a team. When it is a team, the leader-coordinator of the project is responsible for the actions of the group. When the system designer is not the system installer, the designer is responsible for it's work and the installer is responsible for it's work, which means that the owner, or the owners representative, is the leader-coordinator of the project, and the authority that is responsible for system design and system installation.

Pull-down

See recovery load.

R

Rated capacity

The cooling equipment's total capacity when operating at the AHRI rating condition for the heat sink air or fluid, the rating condition for the air entering the indoor coil, and the minimum requirement for blower performance. Heat pump heating capacity when operating at the AHRI rating conditions for the heat sink air or fluid, the rating condition for the air entering the indoor coil, and the minimum requirement for blower performance and defrost action. For variable compressor speed equipment, the rating test speed may not be the maximum speed.

Rating test speed

See Section N1-1 definitions.

Recovery effectiveness

See heat recovery effectiveness.

Recovery load

The momentary load (Btuh value) for bringing the temperature of interior space materials and space air back to the occupied set-point temperature after a set-back or set-up period.

Refrigerant side

All components, piping, and devices associated with the refrigeration circuit of a piece of cooling-only equipment, or heat pump equipment.

Register

A supply air outlet that has a frame and a set of fixed or adjustable louvers (horizontal, vertical or both), and an adjustable damper for flow control. Registers are compatible with lower air loading values.

Remote space

A room or space that is not adequately air-coupled to the room or space that has the thermostat.

Return

The entrance to an effective return air path. (Return path resistance must be compatible with return Cfm, and the portion of blower pressure that is available for return air.)

Reserve heat

The portion of installed heat pump electric coil heat not needed for supplemental heat, but is available for emergency heat (operated by a manual switch).

Room

A living space, or ancillary space, that is defined by some combination of partition walls and exposed walls.

Room load

The heating or cooling load for a partitioned space that is isolated from adjacent spaces (an interior door provided connectivity).

Run fraction or runtime fraction

The decimal value for operating time per hour (may vary from 0.00 to 1.00). For example, when the momentary load is half the momentary capacity, the run fraction is 0.50.

S

Sensible heat ratio

For cooling, the momentary, circumstantial, sensible load or sensible capacity; divided the momentary, circumstantial, total load, or total capacity.

Sensible capacity or load

The ability of equipment to change the dry-bulb temperature of the air in the conditioned space. Envelope loads and system loads tend to increase or decrease the dry-bulb temperature in the conditioned space.

Sensitivity

The behavior of a physical system depends on a set of constants, and a set of space-time variables. When conditional behavior is to be accurately summarized by a mathematical model, the equation set must accommodate inputs for all relevant constants, and have defensible models for all relevant variables. The degree to which this is accurately accomplished determines the sensitivity of the model. For example, the solar heat gain coefficient (SHGC) for a piece of fenestration may be modeled as constant, but a load calculation procedure that only uses a SHGC value for clear glass would not apply to dwellings that have improved glass. For example, the published AHRI value for total cooling capacity ignores the conditional behavior of cooling equipment.

Set-back or set-up

A thermostat's set-point is automatically or manually reduced or increased for a period of time. This may be occasional (occupants on vacation), or scheduled by day of week. The goal is to save energy, but the net affect depends on a complex set of interrelated issues. In general, longer set-up or set-back periods (say eight hours or more) are more productive than shorter periods (four hours or less).

Simultaneous heating-cooling

The comfort system can continuously heat one or more zones, while cooling one or more zones. The need for this capability may depend on glass direction, glass area, and/or internal loads.

Single-split

A ductless split-coil cooling system or heat pump that has one indoor coil.

Single-speed equipment

Cooling and heat pump equipment that operates at two or more distinct compressor speeds.

Single Zone

A comfort system that has one point of temperature control for all rooms and spaces served by it's central equipment. This thermostat cycles the equipment, or adjusts it's output capacity to it's satisfaction, with no regard to the temperature in the rooms and spaces that are remote to the thermostat.

Sizing value

The sizing value is the *Manual J* total cooling load for the summer design condition, for the space served by cooling-only equipment, or heat pump equipment.

Solar gain and solar load

Solar gain is the radiant heat the enters the conditioned space, or impinges on exterior surfaces. Solar load is combined with the effect of solar gain and the thermal mass affected by the solar gain.

Southern glass

Glass that faces southeast, south, or southwest.

Space

One or more rooms with partition walls; one or more open floor plan areas; or any combination thereof.

Space load

The heating or cooling load for one room or space, a set of rooms and spaces (a zone), or all the rooms and spaces in a dwelling.

Spread

For a floor outlet blowing up a wall, or wall air outlet blowing across the room, the width of the primary air pattern at the end of the throw.

Staged

Equipment capacity increases in steps, as defined by the OEM's design (compressor capacity, blower capacity, burner capacity, electric heating coil capacity, for example).

Stake holder

Anyone that manufacturers, purchases, provides, designs, installs, tests or investigates performance, regulates (or has standing to comment on codes and standards), or teaches residential HVAC design, installation and maintenance principles.

Standard sizes

OEM's tend to design cooling-only equipment and heat pump equipment for the same steps in increasing capacity. For a product line, the smallest size may range from one-half of a cooling ton to 2 cooling tons. For a product line, the largest size may range from one cooling ton to 5 cooling tons. Size steps tend to be in half-ton, or one-ton increments. The cooling ton values are for the AHRI rating conditions for air-air, or water-air equipment.

Start-up load

Depending on circumstances, a start-up recovery load may be substantially larger than the recovery load for a set-back or set-up period.

Steady-State

Observed or measured behavior does not change with time.

Summer design condition

The outdoor air conditions used for a cooling load calculation (MJ8, Table 1A and Table 1B is the ANSI standard, unless local code says otherwise).

Supplemental heat

For heat pump heating, electric coil heat that makes up for the monetary difference between the heating load and the available compressor heat.

Supply air outlet

A grille, register or diffuser.

Survey

A survey may be based on a set of plans, and/or a field inspection. It should provide comprehensive documentation of all issues and conditions that affect design procedures and installation decisions. For new construction, produce a summary of construction details (for load calculations), and available space (for placing equipment and routing distribution). For modifying or replacing an existing comfort system, produce a summary of construction details (for load calculations), a summary of the attributes of the existing equipment (obtain OEM performance data when possible), a summary of the attributes of the existing distribution system (airflow measurements may be useful), and notes pertaining to available space (for placing new or additional equipment and/or routing distribution). All surveys include an interview with the owner, or owner's representative (document attitudes and preferences).

System loads

Duct loads, piping loads, outdoor air mixed with return air, blower heat, pump heat, any form of reheat, winter or summer humidification loads.

T

Terminal velocity

The OEM's default velocity for measuring throw (supply air outlet discharge air slows down as it moves away from the outlet).

Temperature bin or bin temperature

The range of normal outdoor air temperatures (winter low to summer high) for a location are divided into 5°F or 10°F bins (from the coldest temperature to the warmest temperature).

Temperature swing

The variation in space air temperature over time (in the comfort zone). When a space has a thermostat, the deviation from the thermostat's set-point tends to be cyclic (a few cycles per hour), and moderate in amplitude (the thermostat's differential). When a space does not have a thermostat, the deviation from the remote thermostat's set-point can be noticeable (say 2°F), or substantial (more than 5°F).

Thermal balance point

For heat pump heating, the outdoor temperature that produces equality for the heating load and compressor heating capacity. Note that there is a default balance point (no credit for solar gain and internal loads), and a conditional (dynamic) balance point (which depends on momentary values for solar gain, internal gain, and the momentary heat transfer to or from the effective thermal mass of the conditioned space). The default balance point is commonly used to lock out supplemental electric coil heat. A comprehensive model of dynamic balance point is required for energy and op-cost calculations. See also; change-over.

Thermal mass

The ability of an object (floor, desk, or wall, for example) to store heat (Btu) depends on the specific heats (Btuh / (Lb·°F)) of the materials in the object, and the weights (lb) of these materials.

Thermostat differential

The thermostat-sensed temperature change (drop or rise) that causes a thermostat to change it's instructions to the equipment. For example, heating equipment stops at a break temperature, and restarts at a somewhat lower temperature (0.5 to 2.0 °F). For automatic heating-cooling change-over, heating may stop at a break temperature, and the thermostat-sensed temperature may have to rise by a significant amount to activate cooling (5 °F, for example).

Third party

Equipment and devices provided by someone other than the OEM, or owner.

Throw

The distance that it takes for the primary flow from a supply air outlet to slow from the face velocity at the outlet (typically 600 Fpm to 800 fpm, when the outlet is sized correctly) to a relatively slow value (typically 50 Fpm to 100 Fpm, as designated by the OEM's performance data for the product).

Ton

For total cooling capacity, 12,000 Btuh per hour.

Total load

The sum of all envelope loads and system loads for the space served by the cooling or heating equipment.

Total capacity or load

For equipment sizing, the sum of the sensible cooling load and the latent cooling load for the summer design condition.

Total effective length

For *Manual D*, the duct fitting equivalent lengths plus straight run lengths for the critical circulation path.

Total heating load

The sum of the circumstantial building envelope loads and HVAC system loads.

Transient

Observed or measured behavior changes with time.

Variable-speed equipment

Cooling and heat pump equipment that operates at any speed that ranges from a minimum value to a maximum value, per the OEM's design and limits.

Ventilation dehumidifier

See Section N1-1 definitions and see Section N2-12.

Volume flow

Typically, Cfm or Gpm for inch-pound units.

Water-air

For cooling-only equipment and heat pumps, the heat source is some form of ground water and the heat sink is indoor air, or vice versa.

Water-side

For water-air equipment, all components, devices, and piping associated with the water circuit.

Water-source heat pump

Refrigeration cycle equipment that uses once-through ground water, or buried pipe-loop water, for a heat source and a heat sink.

Wet coil or wet cooling coil

Moisture in the air passing through a cooling coil condenses on coil surfaces, the condensation is collected and routed to a drain.

Whole-house dehumidifier

See Section N1-1 definitions and see Section N2-12.

Winter design condition

The outdoor air conditions used for a heating load calculation (MJ8, Table 1A and Table 1B is the ANSI standard, unless local code says otherwise).

Zone

A room or space, or a set of rooms and spaces, that has it's own point of temperature sensing and control. (The associated comfort system/equipment/devices must be capable of satisfying the instructions issued by local control.)

Zone damper

An automated open-close damper, multi-position damper, or modulating damper in a supply air duct, typically controlled by a zone thermostat.

Zone damper system

An engineered package of heating-cooling equipment and it's operating and safety controls, ductwork, supply air outlets and returns, zone thermostats and dampers, local zoning controls, and a central zone-control panel. There may be a bypass air duct and a bypass damper. The zoning controls and bypass controls (where applicable) must be compatible with the actions of the heating-cooling equipment controls.

Zone equipment vendor (ZEV)

A source of air zoning devices and controls. Such equipment may be added to heating-cooling equipment supplied by others, or a heating-cooling equipment manufacturer may provide all of the system components.

Zone load

The heating or cooling load for one room or space that has it's own thermostat, or for a set of rooms and spaces that have their own thermostat.

Appendix 17

Symbols, Acronyms and Abbreviations

1% db	One percent dry-bulb. (Outdoor dry-bulb temperature will be more than the 1% value for 1% of the hours per year.)
1% wb	One percent wet-bulb. (Outdoor wet-bulb temperature will be more than the 1% value for 1% of the hours per year.)
99% db	Ninety-nine percent dry-bulb. (Outdoor dry-bulb temperature will be more than the 99% value for 99% of the hours per year.)
°C	Degrees Centigrade.
°F	Degrees Fahrenheit.
Δ	Delta (difference or change).

A

A	A is an intercept value for a straight line (see Appendix 13). B; K; Q and V serve the same purpose.
ACCA	Air Conditioning Contractors of America.
ACF	Altitude correction factor.
AED	Adequate exposure diversity (pertains to the *Manual J* cooling load calculation for fenestration).
AFUE	For fossil fuel furnaces, the annual fuel utilization efficiency (per AHRI test and calculation criteria).
AHAM	Association of Home Appliance Manufacturers.
AHC	Adjusted heating capacity (see Section N2-15).
AHJ	Authority Having Jurisdiction (AHJ)
AHRI	Air Conditioning, Heating and Refrigeration Institute.
AHRI Ton	AHRI rating test cooling capacity divided by 12,000 Btuh.
AHRI 47 or AHRI 17	Air-air heat pump heating capacity test for 17°F or 47°F outdoors.
ANSI	American National Standard Institute.
ASHRAE	American Society of Heating Refrigeration and Air Conditioning Engineers.
ASC	Adjusted sensible capacity (OEM data sensible capacity +1/2 excess latent capacity).
ASP	Available static pressure.
ATD	Air temperature difference (see Section N2-15).
ATR	Air temperature rise.

B

B	B is an intercept value for a straight line (see Appendix 13). A; K; Q and V serve the same purpose.
BECOP	Break even COP (for dual fuel heating systems).
BKW	Blower KW.
Btu	British thermal Unit
Btuh	British thermal units per hour

C

CD or CD-ROM	Compact disk.
Cd	Cycling degradation coefficient.
CDD; CDD-50	Cooling degree day. Cooling degree day to the base 50°F.
CER	Furnace or boiler cycling efficiency ratio (see Appendix 11).
CHC	For heat pumps, compressor heating capacity.
COP	Coefficient of performance.
Cfm	Cubic feet per minute.
Cfm/Ton	Blower Cfm per Ton of total cooling capacity
CKW	Compressor KW.
CSHR	Coil sensible heat ratio (sensible capacity divided by total capacity).
CTD	Cooling temperature difference.
CuFt	Cubic foot.

D

DA	Discharge air (outdoor air leaving air-air heat recovery equipment).
DAdb or DAgr	Discharge air dry-bulb temperature, or discharge air grains.
DB or db	Dry-bulb temperature.
DD	Degree day.
DDR	Degree day ratio (HDD-65 / CDD-50, for example).
DSE	Direct saturation efficiency (determines the condition of the air leaving an evaporative cooling unit, see Section 4-4).

E

E, or E_{sen}, or E_{lat}	Heat recovery effectiveness, or sensible effectiveness, or latent effectiveness.
EA	Entering air.
EAC	Entering air condition (the psychrometric state point for the relevant altitude).
EAT; eat	Entering air temperature.
EBP	Economic balance point.
ECC	Electric coil heating capacity for a bin-hour calculation (see Figure A6-7).
ECF	Electric coil run factor load for a bin-hour calculation (see Figure A6-7).
ECL	Electric coil load for a bin-hour calculation (see Figure A6-7).
ECM	Electronically commutated motor.
EDB	Entering dry-bulb temperature.
EER	A circumstantial energy efficiency ratio for cooling equipment (typically a rating condition value).
EEV	Electronic expansion valve.
EF	Energy factor (dehumidifier efficiency pints/KWH or liters/KWH; or water heater efficiency (output-input ratio).
ERV	Energy recovery ventilator.
ESP	External static pressure.
EWB	Entering wet-bulb temperature.
EWT	Entering water temperature.

F

Fc; Fh	For Appendix 9, Fc = compressor run fraction for cooling; Fh = compressor run fraction for heating.
Fs	Full compressor speed.
Ft	Foot

G

GLHP	Ground loop heat pump (water in buried closed pipe loop).
Gpm	Gallons per minute.
Grains	Absolute humidity (grains of moisture per pound of dry air).
GTH; GTL	For water-air equipment, the highest and lowest ground temperature for the year.
GWHP	Ground water heat pump (ground water from well, pond, lake, river, etc., flows though equipment and is discarded).

H

HC or HC47	Heating capacity, or air-air heat pump heating capacity for 47°F outdoors.
HCF	Heat content of fossil fuel (Btuh per CuFt, Btuh per gallon).
HDD; HDD-65	Heating degree day; Heating degree day to the base 65°F.
HL	Heating load.
HLR	Furnace or boiler heating load ratio (see Appendix 11).
HLT	High-limit temperature for air or water heating equipment.
HP; hp	Heat pump.
HSPF	For air-air heat pumps, the heating season performance factor (per AHRI test and calculation criteria).
HTD	Heating temperature difference.
HVAC	Heating ventilation and air conditioning.

I

IAT	Indoor air temperature.
IWC	Inches water column (pressure).

J

JSHR	Sensible heat ratio for *Manual J* cooling loads (sensible load divided by total load).

K

K	Capital K is an intercept value for a straight line (see Appendix 13). A; B; Q and V serve the same purpose.
k	Small k is an air-film coefficient value (see Section A8-6).
KW	Kilowatts (3,413 Btuh).
KWH	Kilowatts per hour.

L

LA	Leaving air.
LAT	Leaving air temperature.
LC	Latent cooling capacity.
Lc	For water-air heat pumps, required buried pipe length for cooling.
LCR	Latent capacity ratio (OEM data latent capacity / Latent Load).
LF	Load factor for compressor cycling rate (see Figure A6-7).
Lh	For water-air heat pumps, required buried pipe length for heating.
LL	Latent load (for summer dehumidification; for winter humidification; possibly for summer humidification).
LWT	Leaving water temperature.

M

M	Slope of a straight line; with subscript I indicates an item in a set of slopes (see Appendix 13). N and O serve the same purpose.
MA	Mixed air.
MAT; mat	Mixed air temperature (typically outdoor air mixed with return air).
MBH or MBtuh	1,000 Btuh
MCDB	Mean coincident dry-bulb temperature.
MCWB	Mean coincident wet-bulb temperature.
MJ8	The full (unabridged) version of the latest edition of *Manual J*.
MRA	Moisture removal adjustment (for whole-house and ventilation dehumidifier performance).

N

N	Slope of a straight line; with subscript I indicates an item in a set of slopes (see Appendix 13). M and O serve the same purpose.
NA; na	Not applicable.
NC	Noise criteria (OEM performance data quantifies supply air outlet noise).
NOAA	National Oceanic and Atmospheric Administration.

O

O	Slope of a straight line; with subscript I indicates an item in a set of slopes (see Appendix 13). M and N serve the same purpose.
OA	Outdoor air.
OAdb; OAgr	Outdoor air dry-bulb, or outdoor air grains.
OAF	Outdoor air fraction.
OAT	Outdoor air temperature.
OEM	Original Equipment Manufacturer.
OSF	Over-size factor.
OSL	Over-size limit.

P

PKW	Pump KW.
PLF	part-load factor for compressor cycling (see Figure A6-7).
PSC	Permanent split capacitor.
PTAC	Packaged terminal air conditioner.
PTHP	Packaged terminal heat pump.

Q

Q Q is an intercept value for a straight line (see Appendix 13). A; B; K and V serve the same purpose.

R

R-, or R before a number
 R = R-value, or a specific R-value (R11, for example).

RA, or RAdb, or RAgr
 Return air, or return air dry-bulb, or return air grains.

Rcfm Return Cfm.

RET Recovery exit temperature (for air leaving air-air recovery equipment).

Rg; Ri; Rins; Rt; Rx
 See Appendix 8; Rg = R-value of a pane of glass; Ri = air film coefficient at inside surface of a duct airway; Rins = R-value of a piece of duct insulation; Rt = total effective R-value for a structural panel; Rx = R-value to some point in a structural panel.

RH; rh Relative humidity.

RKW Electric resistance coil KW.

RMB For ductless multi-split equipment piping, refrigerant management block (see Appendix 10, Section A10-3).

Rpm Revolutions per minute.

Rp; Rs See Appendix 9, Rp = T-value for a pipe wall; Rs= = Soil R-value.

RS Compressor speed used for 95/80/67 rating test.

RTF Runtime fraction (operating minutes per hour / 60).

S

SA Supply air.

SAT Supply air temperature.

SC Sensible cooling capacity, or sensible heating capacity.

SCL Sensible cooling load.

SCR Sensible capacity ratio (adjusted sensible capacity / sensible load).

SEER For air-air cooling equipment, the seasonal energy efficiency ratio (per AHRI test and calculation criteria).

SHC Supplemental heat capacity Btuh.

SHL Sensible heating load.

SHR Sensible heat ratio (sensible load divided by total load, sensible capacity divided by total capacity).

SL Sensible cooling load, or sensible heating load.

SqFt Square feet.

SSeff Steady state efficiency.

T

T; Td; Tg; To; Ti; Ts; Tw
 T = Temperature; Td = duct material surface temperature; Tg = temperature at a glass surface; To = outdoor air temperature, Ti = inside air temperature; Ts = surface temperature; Tw = temperature at surface of a duct wrap.

TBP Thermal balance point.

TC Total (sensible plus latent) cooling capacity.

TD or ΔT Temperature difference.

TEL Total effective length of a duct run, or ducted air circulation path.

TKW Total package power input KW.

TL Total cooling load, or total heating load.

Ton For total cooling capacity, 12,000 Btuh per hour.

TR Air or water temperature rise.

TRmax Maximum air or water temperature rise.

TRmin Minimum air or water temperature rise.

TXV Thermostatic expansion valve.

U

U- U-value = 1 / R-value.

V

V	V is an intercept value for a straight line (see Appendix 13). A; B; K and Q serve the same purpose.
VDH	Ventilation dehumidifier.
VKW	Vent fan KW
VFR	Variable refrigerant flow

W

WB; wb	Wet-bulb temperature
WHD	Whole-house dehumidifier.
WPD	Water pressure drop.
WTD	Water temperature drop (for hot water heating terminal device).
WTH or WTL	For water-air equipment, the highest and lowest entering water temperature for the year.
WTR	Water temperature rise (through a boiler or water heater).

X

XHC	Excess heating capacity (see Section N2-15).
XSLC	Excess latent capacity (OEM data latent capacity - Latent Load).

Z

ZEV	Zoning equipment vendor.

Appendx 17

Appendix 18

Summary of Equations

The conversion factors and equations used in this document are summarized here. The equations appear in alphabetical order, based on the descriptions of equation use.

Conversion Factors

1 KW = 1,000 Watts.
3,413 Btuh = 1 KW.
Pints per day = 24 × (Latent Btuh load / 1,054).
1 pound of water = 1 Pint.
2.113 Pints = 1 Liter.

Air-Side Pressure Drop for a Duct System Component

The pressure drop across air-side component (coil or filter, for example) increases with the square of the Cfm ratio.

$$IWC_2 = IWC_1 \times (Cfm_2 / Cfm_1)^2$$

Where:
IWC_2 is the pressure drop for the desired Cfm (Cfm_2).
IWC_1 is the known pressure drop for Cfm_1.

Air Temperature Rise or Drop Through Equipment

The psychrometric equation for sensible heat determines the air temperature rise across a furnace heat exchanger, electric heating coil, or indoor refrigerant coil that provides space heat; or the temperature drop for an indoor refrigerant coil that provides sensible cooling.

Rise (°F) = Output heating capacity Btuh / (1.1 × ACF × Blower Cfm)

Drop (°F) = Sensible cooling capacity Btuh / (1.1 × ACF × Blower Cfm)

Where:
ACF = Altitude correction factor (see Figure A5-1).
Blower Cfm = The chosen air flow rate for heating or cooling, which may be the Cfm that was used to select cooling equipment; or for furnace heating, a value that is compatible with the temperature rise limits. Note that the blower must provide adequate external static pressure for air distribution when delivering the desired Cfm.

Buried Water-Loop Design Equations

See Appendix 9.

Cooling Tons

There is a ton value for the *Manual J* total cooling load, a ton value for the conditional total cooling equipment capacity, and a ton value for the AHRI rating value for total cooling capacity. These values may be similar, or quite different, depending on excess cooling capacity, and equipment operating circumstances.

Manual J Tons = Manual J total cooling Btuh / 12,000

Conditional Equipment Tons = Conditional total cooling Btuh / 12,000

AHRI Rating Tons = AHRI total cooling Btuh / 12,000

Degree Day Ratio (DDR) for Allowing a Condition B Heat Pump

A heat pump may have up to 15,000 Btuh excess total cooling capacity when the DDR value is 2.0 or more, and the *Manual J* sensible heat ratio (JSHR) for the cooling load calculation is 0.95, or greater.

DDR = HDD65 / CDD50

Where:
Heating degree days (HDD) is to base 65 °F.
Cooling degree days (CDD) is to base 50 °F.

Design Values for Entering Water Temperature for a Water-Loop Heat Pump

Extreme summer and winter temperatures for outdoor air determine default values for entering water temperature for cooling and heating. Extreme temperature may be 10°F to 20°F hotter or colder than the *Manual J* design temperature (refer to national weather service data, or just web-search for… Extreme Temperatures USA).

WTH = Extreme summer outdoor air temperature – 10°F

WTL = Extreme winter outdoor air temperature + 40°F

Antifreeze is required when HTL is below freezing. Antifreeze affects loop heat transfer rate.

Direct Saturation Efficiency for Evaporative Cooling Equipment

This equation determines the direct saturation efficiency (DSE) of the equipment.

DSE (%) = 100 × (DB_{in} - DB_{out}) / (DB_{in} - WB_{in})

Where:
DB_{in} = Air dry-bulb entering equipment.
DB_{out} = Air dry-bulb out of equipment.
WB_{in} = Air wet-bulb entering equipment.

Economic Balance Point for Dual Fuel Systems

The following equations return BECOP values for natural gas heat, oil heat, and propane heat. The economic balance point is the outdoor air temperature, or entering water temperature, that produces the break-even COP value for an air-air, or water-air, heat pump.

Gas BECOP = 293 x SS_{eff} x ($/KWH / $/1,000 CuFt)
Oil BECOP = 41 x SS_{eff} x ($/KWH / $ / Gallon)
Propane BECOP = 27 x SS_{eff} x ($/KWH / $/Gallon)

Where:
SS_{eff} = Steady state efficiency.

Equipment Runtime Fraction (RTF) for Energy and Operation Cost Calculations

For a sensible heat control, and given operating condition, the runtime fraction is roughly equal to the momentary sensible load divided by the momentary sensible capacity; however, start-up transients cause s to be somewhat longer than indicated by a steady-state model. Actual runtime and energy use also depend on the equipment's cycling degradation coefficient.

RTF = Operating minutes per hour / 60
Approximate RTF = Sensible load / Sensible capacity

High-Limit for Discharge Air Temperature

Indoor refrigerant coils that provide space heat and electric heating coils have a high-limit for leaving air temperature. The maximum leaving air temperature value is specified by the OEM. Use these equations to see when coil Cfm is compatible with coil heating capacity.

HPl_{at} = HP_{eat} + HC / (1.1 x ACF x Cfm)
EAT_{coil} = LAT_{hp}
LAT_{coil} = EAT_{coil} + (3,413 x KW) / (1.1 x ACF x Cfm)

Where:
HP_{lat} = Air temperature leaving the refrigerant coil (°F).
HP_{eat} = Air temperature entering the refrigerant coil (°F).
HC = Maximum compressor heating capacity (Btuh).
ACF = Altitude correction factor (see Figure A5-1).
Cfm = The air flow rate through the equipment.
EAT_{coil} is the air temperature into the electric coil (°F).
LAT_{coil} is the air temperature off the electric coil (°F).
KW is the capacity of the electric heating coil.

a) The electric coil is locked out when the outdoor air temperature is warmer than the thermal balance point.
b) For air-air equipment, use the heating capacity for a 65°F outdoor air temperature for the refrigerant coil, and use the heating capacity for the thermal balance point temperature for the electric coil.
c) For water-air equipment, use the heating capacity for the warmest entering water temperature for the heating season for both coils.

Outdoor Air Fraction for Engineered Ventilation

The outdoor air fraction (OAF) for a specific installation depends on the blower Cfm and the outdoor air Cfm used by the practitioner.

OAF = Outdoor Cfm / Blower Cfm

Over-Size Factor (OSF) for Equipment Sizing

The over-size factor equals the equipment's total cooling capacity, or maximum heating capacity (electric heating coils), or full heating capacity (fossil fuel furnaces), when operating at the summer or winter design conditions used for the load calculation, divided by the sizing value.

OSF for cooling = Total cooling capacity / Sizing Value

OSF for electric coil heat = Maximum heating capacity / Sizing Value

OSF for fossil fuel furnace heat = Full heating capacity / Sizing Value

Psychrometric Equation for Air Processed by an Air-Air Heat Exchanger

The heat recovery effectiveness (E) for cooling determines the condition (dry-bulb temperature and humidity ratio grains) of the ventilation air that leaves the heat recovery equipment (discharge air). The following equations provide state point values for discharge air (DA). Note that grains values for a given db/rh, or db/wb, state point depend on altitude.

DA_{db} = OA_{db} - E_{sen} x (OA_{db} - RA_{db})
DA_{gr} = OA_{gr} - E_{lat} x (OA_{gr} - RA_{gr})

Where:
DA_{db} = Discharge air dry-bulb temperature.
OA_{db} = Outdoor air dry-bulb temperature.
RA_{db} = Return air dry-bulb temperature.
DA_{gr} = Discharge air grains.
OA_{gr} = Outdoor air grains.
RA_{gr} = Return air grains.
E_{sen} = Sensible recovery effectiveness.
E_{lat} = Latent recovery effectiveness (zero for no recovery).

Condition of Processed Air for Heating

The heat recovery effectiveness (E) for heating determines the temperature of the ventilation air that leaves the heat recovery equipment (discharge air). This equation provides a dry-bulb value discharge air (DA).

DA_{db} = OA_{db} + E_{sen} x (RA_{db} - OA_{db})

Where:
DA_{db} = Discharge air dry-bulb temperature.
OA_{db} = Outdoor air dry-bulb temperature.
RA_{db} = Return air dry-bulb temperature.
E_{sen} = Sensible recover psychrometric effectiveness.

Psychrometric Equation for Mixed Air Temperature

Dry-bulb temperature calculations for mixing outdoor air with return air do not depend on altitude. This equation determines the mixed air dry-bulb temperature (MAT) for heating, or for sensible cooling.

MAT (°F) = RA_{db} x (1 - OAF) + OA_{db} x OAF

Where:
RA_{db} and OA_{db} are the return air and outdoor air dry-bulb temperatures.
OAF is the outdoor air fraction.

Psychometric Equation for Sensible Cooling and Sensible Heating Cfm

For sensible cooling or heating, blower Cfm, and supply air Cfm to a room or space, depend on the sensible cooling or heating load, and the difference (absolute value) between the upstream air temperature and the downstream air temperature.

Cfm = Sensible Btuh Load / (1.1 x ACF x TD)

Where:
Sensible Btuh Load = The load on the equipment, or the room/space load.
ACF = Altitude correction factor (see Figure A5-1).
TD (or Δ) = Dry-bulb temperature difference (absolute value).
TD for blower Cfm = Difference for equipment leaving air and entering air.
TD for a supply air outlet = Difference for supply air and room/space air.

Psychometric Equation for Sensible Cooling by Direct Evaporative Equipment

The design Cfm for the evaporative cooling equipment depends on the summer design value for the sensible cooling load, the summer design values for the outdoor air dry-bulb and wet-bulb temperatures, the direct saturation efficiency for evaporative cooling equipment, and the difference between the dry-bulb temperature in the room/space and the dry-bulb temperature of the air leaving the evaporative cooling equipment.

Cfm = Sensible Btuh Load / (1.1 x ACF x TD)

Where:
Sensible Btuh Load = The load for the room/space load.
ACF = Altitude correction factor (see Figure A5-1).
TD (or ΔT) = Dry-bulb temperature difference (absolute value).
TD for a blower Cfm = Difference for supply air and room/space air.
The direct saturation efficiency equation provides the supply air temperature value.

Psychrometric Equation for a Latent Duct Load

For cooling, altitude sensitive psychrometrics provides an indoor humidity ratio value (grains of moisture per pound of air), based on the indoor dry-bulb and relative humidity values. Then, the latent psychrometric equation for air converts a latent return duct load (latent Btuh), and a return Cfm value (R_{cfm}) to a grains of moisture gain (DGR). Then, the exiting grains value equals the indoor grains value plus the latent moisture gain.

Indoor Grains = Psychrometric value
DGR = Latent Load Btuh / 1.1 x ACF x R_{Cfm}
Exiting Grains = Indoor Grains + DGR

For cooling, altitude sensitive psychrometrics converts an exiting dry-bulb temperature and grains value to a exiting wet-bulb temperature, and converts an indoor dry-bulb temperature and relative humidity value to an entering wet-bulb temperature. The wet-bulb rise (DWB) equals the difference between the two wet-bulb values.

Exiting WB (°F) = Psychrometric value
Indoor WB (°F) = Given psychrometric state point
DWB (°F) = Exiting WB - Indoor WB

Psychrometric Equation for a Sensible Duct Load

The sensible psychrometric equation for air converts a sensible return duct load (sensible Btuh) to a dry-bulb gain, or dry-bulb loss (± TD or ΔT). Then, for cooling and heating, the dry-bulb temperature of the air that exits the return duct equals the indoor dry-bulb temperature plus the return duct gain.

Indoor DB (°F) = Given
TD (°F) = ± Sensible Load Btuh / (1.1 x ACF x R_{Cfm})
Exiting DB (°F) = Indoor DB ± TD

Where:
ACF is an altitude correction factor (see Figure A5-1).
R_{Cfm} = Return air Cfm = Blower Cfm - Outdoor Air Cfm. Return air Cfm may be equal to the blower Cfm, or somewhat larger or smaller. For the purpose of this calculation, RCfm defaults to blower Cfm minus outdoor air Cfm.

Sensible Heat Ratio for Cooling

The following equations provide a sensible heat ratio value for a cooling load calculation (JSHR), or for cooling equipment performance (CSHR).

JSHR = Sensible load Btuh / Total load Btuh
JSHR = Sensible load / (Sensible load + Latent load)

CSHR = Sensible capacity / Total capacity
CSHR = Sensible capacity / (Sensible capacity + Latent capacity)

Surface Condensation Calculations

See Appendix 8.

Appendx 18

Water Temperature Drop and Air Temperature Rise for Hot Water Coils

A set of equations relates coil water-side performance to air-side performance. These are provided here:

Water Btuh Loss = 500 x Gpm x WTD
Air Btuh Gain = 1.1 x ACF x Cfm x ATR
LWT (°F) = EWT - WTD
LAT (°F) = EAT + ATR

Where:
WTD = Water temperature drop (°F).
ACF = Altitude correction factor.
ATR = Air temperature Rise (°F).
LWT = Leaving water temperature (°F).
LAT = Leaving air temperature (°F).

Water Temperature Rise through Equipment

For boilers and water heating equipment, the water temperature rise through the equipment is determined by this equation:

Water Rise (°F) = Output Btuh / (500 x Water Gpm)

Where:
Output Btuh = Heat added to entering water.
Water Gpm = Water flow rate through the equipment.

This appendix is not part of the this standard. It is merely informative and does not contain requirements necessary for conformance to the standard. It has not been processed according to the ANSI requirements for a standard, and may contain material that has not been subject to public review or a consensus process. Unresolved objectors on informative material are not offered the right to appeal at ACCA or ANSI.

Appendix 19
Supporting Detail for Equipment Sizing Examples

Equipment selection and sizing procedures are based on *Manual J* heating and cooling loads. This Appendix provides supporting detail for the example equipment sizing problems in Sections 5, 6, 7, 8, 9, and 10.

A19-1 Dwelling Performance and Attributes

The performance of one floor plan with one set of construction details is investigated for various climate types. Figure A19-1 summarizes *Manual J* output for this study. The primary attributes of the dwelling are summarized below. Survey details are summarized by Figure A19-2 (next page).

- Slab on grade, one story, 3,300 SqFt.
- Two pane, clear glass, wood frame, tight fenestration. Fenestration area is 10.9 percent of the floor area. No AED excursion.
- Commonly used ceiling, wall and floor R-values; average structural tightness.
- Attic ducts: R6, default sealed, 0.12/0.24 (Cfm/SqFt) in vented attic under a white shingle roof (16C).
- Engineered ventilation: 75 Cfm OA and 75 Cfm exhaust though a sensible heat exchanger. Heat recovery effectiveness: 0.55 heating, 0.50 cooling.

A19-2 Balanced Climate with Summer Humidity

Fayetteville, AR, has a climate that produces robust heating and sensible cooling loads, and a significant latent cooling load. This scenario is compatible with a furnace plus electric cooling equipment, or heat pump equipment. Heating load hours and cooling load hours are similar.

	How Location Effects *Manual J* Loads							
MJ8 output for indoor dry-bulb values: Heating = 70°F Cooling = 75°F	Used for Sections 5, 6, 7, 9, and 10			For comparison only, values not used for example problems.				
	Fayetteville Balanced Humid	Brunswick Mild Hot Humid	Boise Cold Hot Dry	Seattle Moderate Some Humid	Tacoma Moderate Almost Dry	Spokane Cold Warm Dry	Aims Cold Hot Humid	Tucson Mild Very Hot Dry
Elevation (Ft) / Latitude°	1,251 / 36	20 / 31	2,838 / 43	14 / 47	429 / 47	2,366 / 47	955 / 42	2,641 / 32
Winter 99% db °F	13	34	9	27	24	7	-6	24
Summer1% db/wb °F	93 / 75	91 / 79	94 / 63	82 /	82 /	89 /	90 /	102 /
Indoor RH for cooling	50%	50%	45%	45%	45%	45%	50%	45%
ΔGrains : Daily Range	40 : M	66 : M	-21 : H	13 : M	6 : M	-23 : M	38 ; M	-24 : H
Heating Btuh	56,236	34,880	58,349	41,298	44,739	60,643	76,136	43,922
Sensible cooling Btuh	33,954	29,413	30,145	23,721	23,701	27,592	28,793	34,677
Latent cooling Btuh	5,586	8,801	Negative [3]	2,352	1,590	Negative [3]	5,252	Negative [3]
MJ8 SHR[1]	0.86	0.77	1.00	0.91	0.94	1.00	0.85	1.00
Ballpark Cfm	1,786	1,215	1,730	1,198	1,221	1,531	1,349	1,925
SFper MJ8 ton [2]	1,002	1,036	1,314	1,519	1,566	1,435	1,163	1,142
EDB / EWB cooling (°F)	76.2 / 63.2	76.6 / 64.1	76.2 / Dry	76.0 / 61.6	76.0 / 61.4	76.0 / Dry	76.2 / 63.3	76.3 / Dry
EDB heating (°F)	68.9	69.0	68.8	68.8	68.7	68.6	68.0	69.2
NOAA HDD for 65°F base	4,166	1,145	5,227	4,165	4,650	6,820	6,791	1,578
NOAA CDD for 50°F base	4,267	6,765	2,856	2,159	2,123	2,081	3,070	7,077
NOAA HDD / CDD	0.98	0.23	2.01	1.93	2.19	3.28	2.21	0.22

1) Sensible load / (Sensible load + Latent load).
2) 12,000 x Floor area / (Sensible load + Latent load).
3) No latent load, space RH will be less than 45%.

Figure A19-1

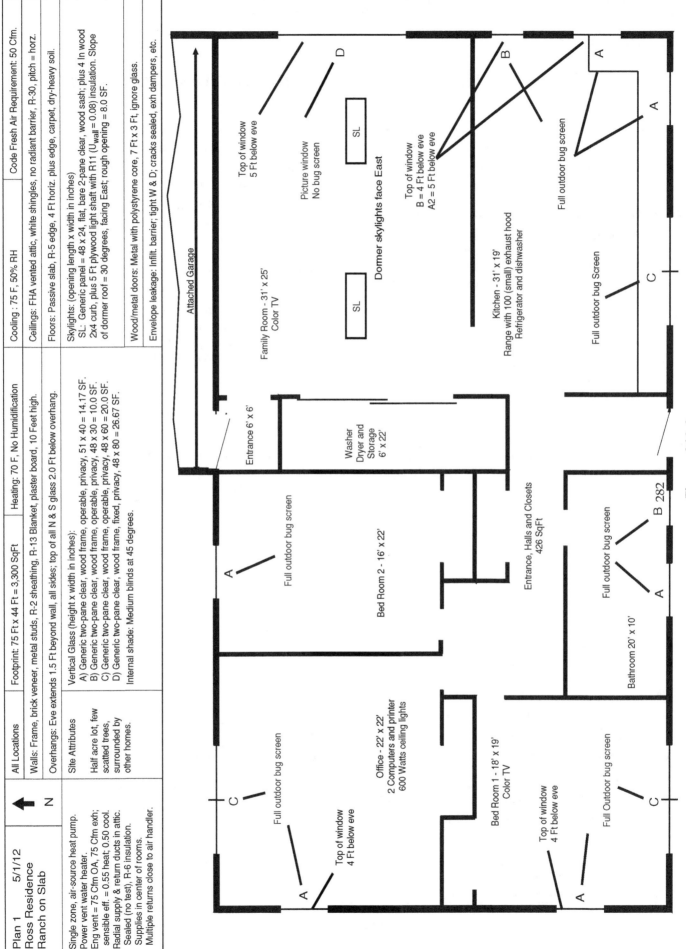

Figure A19-2

A19-3 Warm and Very Humid Climate

Brunswick, GA, has oppressive summer humidly and mild winter temperatures. This scenario favors a heat pump, or a cooling-only system with some form of ancillary heat. Summer dehumidification is a primary concern. Cooling load hours are dominate.

A19-4 Cold Winter Hot Dry Summer Climate

Boise, ID, and Spokane, WA, have a climate that produces robust heating and sensible cooling loads. The climate is very dry, so there is no latent cooling load. This scenario is compatible with a furnace plus electric cooling equipment, or heat pump equipment. Heating load hours are dominate.

A19-5 Moderate Climate with Some Humidity

Seattle, WA, and Tacoma, WA, have a climate that produces moderate heating and sensible cooling loads. Both climates have modest latent cooling loads (Tacoma is somewhat colder and dryer than Seattle). This scenario favors a heat pump, or a cooling-only system with some form of ancillary heat. Heating load hours are dominate.

A19-6 Cold Winter Hot Humid Summer

Ames, IW, has a climate that produces robust heating and sensible cooling loads, and a significant latent cooling load. This scenario is compatible with a furnace plus electric cooling equipment, or heat pump equipment. Heating load hours are dominate.

A19-7 Hot Dry Climate

Tucson, AZ; has a climate that produces a moderate heating load and a robust sensible cooling load. The climate is very dry, so there is no latent cooling load. Cooling load hours are dominate.

A19-8 Bin Weather Data

Bin weather data summarizes the attributes of the local climate, as far as dry-bulb temperature and coincident wet-bulb temperature are concerned. Bar graphs of the bin dry-bulb temperature data for the Figure A19-1 cities are provided below. Figure A19-3 (next page) shows the bin data in a table format.

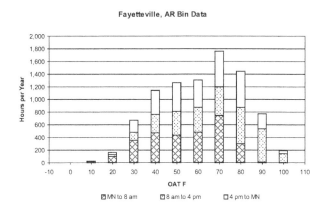

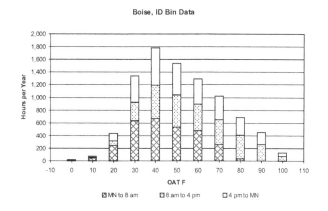

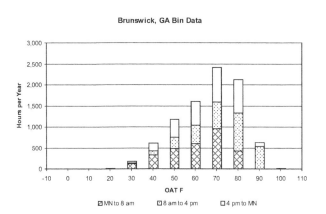

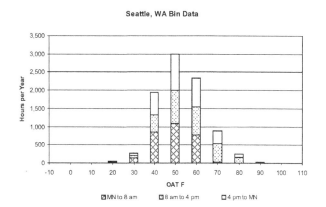

Appendx 19

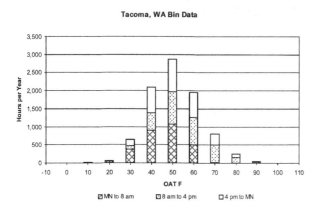
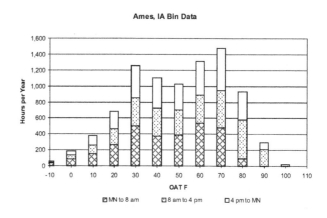
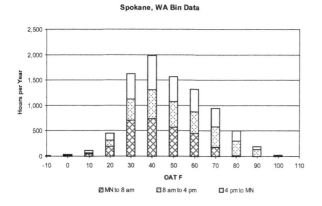
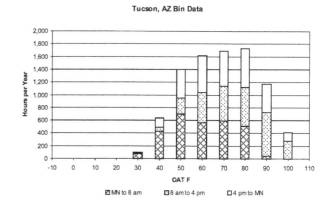

Bin Data for Appendix 19 Cities												
Bin Temp	-10	0	10	20	30	40	50	60	70	80	90	100
Fayetteville, AR												
MN - 8 AM		2	18	100	359	470	437	479	743	298	12	
8 AM-4 PM			5	29	123	293	373	397	457	579	521	143
4 PM - MN			6	38	195	379	450	432	566	567	241	44
Totals	0	2	29	167	677	1,142	1,260	1,308	1,766	1,444	774	187
Coinc-WB	-8	-1	9	19	28	36	45	54	64	70	74	76
Brunswick, GA (Glynco nAS)												
MN - 8 AM				11	123	322	476	600	960	421		
8 AM-4 PM				1	18	99	284	445	624	904	535	9
4 PM - MN				2	35	197	419	556	822	793	92	2
Totals	0	0	0	14	176	618	1,179	1,601	2,406	2,118	627	11
Coinc-WB				18	28	38	47	57	66	73	78	78
Boise, ID (Mt. Home AFB)												
MN - 8 AM	2	10	43	243	634	672	530	476	266	37		
8 AM-4 PM		2	15	76	293	521	511	420	383	370	265	69
4 PM - MN		5	15	113	409	589	494	397	370	283	192	54
Totals	2	17	73	432	1,336	1,782	1,535	1,293	1,019	690	457	123
Coinc-WB	-13	-2	9	19	27	35	42	48	53	57	61	64

Figure A19-3 (continued next page)

Appendx 19

Bin Data for Appendix 19 Cities													
Bin Temp	-10	0	10	20	30	40	50	60	70	80	90	100
Seattle CO, WA												
MN - 8 AM			1	20	143	857	1,084	775	36			
8 AM-4 PM			1	9	57	469	925	773	503	157	22	1
4 PM - MN			1	11	71	619	979	784	351	93	10	
Totals	0	0	3	40	271	1,945	2,988	2,332	890	250	32	1
Coinc-WB	3	5	7	18	28	38	47	55	61	65	69	71
Tacoma, WA (McChord AFB)												
MN - 8 AM		1	6	40	377	902	1,070	504	23			
8 AM-4 PM			1	7	92	486	896	760	481	165	28	
4 PM - MN			2	13	182	706	905	696	305	95	16	
Totals		1	9	60	651	2,094	2,871	1,960	809	260	44	0
Coinc-WB	-10	3	10	19	29	38	46	54	59	63	67	69
Spokane, WA (Fairchild AFB)												
MN - 8 AM	4	14	47	196	705	736	568	452	180	12		
8 AM-4 PM	2	8	25	113	411	574	507	427	408	296	129	13
4 PM - MN	3	9	35	135	508	676	494	444	354	191	65	4
Totals	9	31	107	444	1,624	1,986	1,569	1,323	942	499	194	17
Coinc-WB	0	1	8	18	28	36	43	50	54	58	62	64
Ames, IA (Des Moines, IW)												
MN - 8 AM	36	87	153	269	502	370	390	538	482	93	1	0
8 AM-4 PM	8	47	105	196	352	356	311	351	468	489	209	18
4 PM - MN	12	53	122	220	405	381	325	424	531	353	82	4
Totals	56	187	380	685	1,259	1,107	1,026	1,313	1,481	935	292	22
Coinc-WB	-10	0	9	18	28	36	45	54	63	69	73	76
Tucson, AZ (Davis, Mt.)												
MN - 8 AM				4	81	432	698	565	588	508	42	
8 AM-4 PM					5	60	253	473	550	614	683	279
4 PM - MN					16	146	447	573	544	610	446	136
Totals	0	0	0	4	102	638	1,398	1,611	1,682	1,732	1,171	415
Coin-WB				17	27	34	41	47	54	61	64	67

Figure A19-3 (continued from previous page)

Appendx 19

Appendix 20

Rationale for Section N2 Sizing Limits

Minimum and maximum equipment sizing limits prescribed by Section N2 determine occupant comfort because they affect indoor temperature and humidity control. Sizing limits also effect annual energy use (Btu/Yr and/or KWH/Yr) for the HVAC system, the peak KW load on the local electrical utility grid, and installation cost. These issues tend to conflict with each other. For example, improving seasonal comfort may add to energy use and/or installation cost, or improving annual energy efficiency may diminish comfort and/or increase installation cost, or minimizing installation cost may reduce comfort and/or increase annual energy use.

Stated differently, the design of a complex system requires a significant amount of give-and-take among competing goals. This appendix explains the rationale for the Section N2 size limits.

A20-1 Prescriptive vs. Performance Procedure

Industry standards tend to provide two options for dealing with complex design problems. In this regard, practitioners may apply prescriptive guidance (per Section N2), or do performance modeling.

- Prescriptive guidance must be conservative because a simplified solution must be compatible with a wide range of issues that affect momentary heating and cooling loads and their interaction with momentary equipment performance, as applicable to local weather patterns. The simplified solution also must consider large differences in local energy costs, installation costs, and maintenance costs. This limits design options, but it is compatible with the skill-set of a typical practitioner, it is implemented with minimal time and cost, and it is easily checked by a code authority.

- Performance modeling maximizes system design options because it deals with a specific set of circumstances. However, most practitioners are not positioned to undertake such evaluations, the market place will not absorb the cost of such efforts, and most code officials do not have the skill-set, or time, to check the calculations.

- The intent of the prescriptive guidance provided by Sections N1, N2 and N3 of this manual is to effect rules based on sound physics and engineering that work for locations across the country, and keep practitioners from getting into unforeseen difficulties.

A20-2 Dry-Bulb Temperature Control

The simplest technology (single-speed compressor, PSC blower, orifice or cap-tube metering, on-off control) is perfectly adequate for dry-bulb temperature control for the space that has the thermostat, providing all aspects of the capacity distribution system, refrigerant system, and wiring/control system are correct. The temperature swing at the thermostat depends on the thermostat's differential, which will be 1°F, or less.

Dry-bulb temperature control becomes an issue when the occupant manually switches the HVAC system on and off, or when the thermostat set-point is manipulated to reduce seasonal energy consumption, or when the thermostat set-point is manipulated to improve indoor humidity control for cooling, or when multiple thermostats control zoning devices.

Dry-Bulb Temperature Control for Heating

Dry-bulb temperature control is not an issue when the heating equipment has adequate sensible capacity for the winter design condition. The minimum sizing factor for heating capacity is 1.0, regardless of the source of heat (fossil fuel or electric furnace or boiler, or some combination of compressor heat and electric coil heat).

Dry-Bulb Temperature Control for Cooling

Dry-bulb temperature control is not an issue when cooling equipment has adequate sensible capacity for the summer design condition. In other words, if sensible capacity is sufficient for the summer design condition, it is excessive for all part load conditions, but the comfort space thermostat resolves the issue.

However, indoor relative humidity has a powerful effect on occupant health and comfort, so the sizing rules favor humidity control. Therefore, the minimum sizing factor for sensible cooling capacity is 0.90, as explained here:

- The minimum size factor for total cooling capacity is 0.90 for all types of compressor speed control. This allows some equipment under sizing vs. jumping to a larger nominal size, or may be used for improved indoor humidity control, by design.

- The minimum size factor for latent cooling capacity is 1.0 because indoor humidity control is critical for occupant comfort.

- Total cooling capacity equals sensible capacity plus latent capacity, so it is mathematically possible for the sensible capacity factor to be less than

0.90 when the total capacity factor is less than 1.0. Therefore, the minimum value for the sensible capacity factor is set at 0.90.

- The sidebar on this page explains why occupants may never experience the effect of the 0.90 size factor for sensible capacity.

A20-3 Indoor Humidity Control for Cooling

Conventional residential comfort systems do not control indoor humidity because dry-bulb temperature control has no sensitivity to the momentary value for indoor humidity. If the system is designed and installed properly, indoor relative humidity will be in a preferred range when the compressor is fully loaded (i.e., for steady-state circumstances that occur for a few hours per season). Indoor humidity tends to drift up as the load on the compressor is reduced (i.e., for transient circumstances that occur for thousands of hours per season).

- Poor indoor humidity control causes discomfort which may result in a lower thermostat set-point with increased energy use. High indoor humidity may cause mold and mildew.

- For heat pumps, indoor humidity control takes precedence over electric heating coil use.

- Indoor humidity control is not an issue for a climate that has no latent cooling load, so for this case, the upper limit for excess total cooling capacity depends on the type of equipment.

- For cooling-only equipment installed in any type climate (very dry to very humid), there is no justification for excess cooling capacity.

Air distribution effectiveness improves with blower runtime, use of continuous blower significantly increases energy use.

Larger equipment tends to use more energy. This may be a minor issue, or a significant issue, depending on the Btuh output per KW input values for a smaller size vs. a larger size (the Cd effect is a minor issue).

Larger equipment cost more to install, and requires large duct airways.

- For heat pumps installed in climate that has dry summer weather and bin-hour data that causes seasonal energy use for heating to be significantly more than seasonal energy for cooling, the upper limit for total cooling capacity is substantially increased (see Section A20-4).

Low and High-Limit for Latent Cooling Capacity

Because indoor humidity control is so important for cooling, the low-limit factor for latent capacity is 1.0. This means that the latent cooling capacity of the equipment, when subject to the operating circumstances (indoor

---

> **Dry-Bulb Temperature Excursions**
>
> For no excess cooling capacity, small indoor air temperature excursions (say one to three degrees) may occur, by design, for statistically infrequent incidents of unusually hot or cold weather. However:
>
> - The mathematical models embedded in a load calculation procedure are based on conservative assumption and defaults, which is standard engineering practice for producing a simplified methodology.
>
> - For no practitioner error, or safety factor use, the actual cooling load for the summer design condition is somewhat less than the calculated value, so dry-bulb temperature excursions for the summer design condition may not occur.
>
> - For acceptable, but less than perfect use of a load calculation procedure, a temperature excursion is even less likely to occur because the practitioner adds a factor of safety to the output of the load calculation (the accuracy of a tool depends on the skill of a conscientious user).
>
> - Properly sized equipment may have some excess capacity.
>
> - A few degrees of occasional, short-term, temperature excursion is not a health and safety issue.
>
> - Complaints about inadequate cooling or inadequate heating are typically caused by design errors or methods-and-materials errors in the distribution system, the refrigerant system, and the control system; or zoning may be required.
>
> - Indoor air temperature excursions in one or more rooms and/or spaces indicate a need for zoning, providing all the design and installation aspects of a single-zone system are correct.
>
> - Supplemental cooling, or appropriate zoning is required for entertaining a relatively large number of people.

---

temperature and RH, outdoor temperature, heat sink temperature, blower Cfm, entering wet-bulb temperature and entering dry-bulb temperature) used for the load calculation and equipment selection, is equal to, or greater than, the latent load for the summer design condition.

When an OEM's expanded performance data is used to select and size equipment, the latent capacity for the summer design condition may be greater than the latent load. This means that the latent capacity of the equipment for summer design circumstances exceeds what is required for the indoor humidity value that was used for the load calculation. If a new load calculation is made for an indoor humidity value that is compatible with equipment performance (determined by trial and error) latent capacity will equal latent load, as explained by the sidebar on this page.

Some excess latent capacity is not a problem; it just means that the indoor humidity for a summer design day will be somewhat less than the value used for the load calculation, which is a good thing. However, a lower indoor RH value reduces the entering air wet-bulb temperature, which reduces latent capacity and increases sensible capacity.

The fraction of excess latent capacity used to reduce indoor RH is about half of the excess. The other half appears as an increase in sensible capacity, as caused by a lower entering wet-bulb temperature. The fraction value for a particular dwelling, with particular equipment, in a particular location may be somewhat more or less than 0.50, but the industry is not positioned to make such calculations a matter of routine design procedure.

It may be that the sensible capacity adjustment for excess latent capacity is used to satisfy the sensible capacity requirement (to match a 0.90 limit, or to achieve something close to the a 1.0 factor). This does not diminish seasonal humidity control.

It may be that the sensible capacity adjustment for excess latent capacity is not needed to satisfy the sensible capacity requirement (a 0.90 to 1.0 factor). This is undesirable for part-load humidity control (causes smaller compressor runtime fractions). Therefore, the suggested (not mandatory) upper limit for excess latent capacity is a 1.5 factor (1.5 more than the latent cooling load).

High-Limit for Total Cooling Capacity

OEM expanded performance data summarizes steady state performance (the compressor operates continuously because the imposed testing load matches the available capacity). When the equipment is installed in a dwelling, continuous compressor operation will generally not occur unless the equipment is purposely undersized (see the sidebar on the preceding page). Therefore, expanded performance data does not model installed performance (the summer design condition is a special case that estimates the maximum amount of capacity that will be needed during the entire cooling season).

Equipment that has One Compressor Speed

Applied equipment performance is transient in nature, as demonstrated by the Figure 1-7 curves. Such curves determine effective total, sensible and latent capacity after equipment has been installed in a dwelling (i.e., when the compressor cycles).

Excess or Deficient Latent Capacity Depends on the Indoor Relative Humidity Value used for the Cooling Load Calculation

For a particular piece of equipment installed in a particular dwelling in a particular location, cooling performance is what it is, the attributes of the structure and it's comfort system are what they are, and the climate is what it is. So, the only variable that affects the latent cooling load is the design value for indoor air relative humidity, and the most convenient variable that affects latent cooling capacity is the design value for blower Cfm.

The ability to adjust blower Cfm so that latent capacity matches latent load is limited by the minimum and maximum values allowed by the OEM's performance data. The latent capacities for this range of blower Cfm values may not be compatible with the latent load for the indoor humidity value used for the load calculation.

The latent cooling load value increases as the design value for indoor humidity decreases, and vice versa. If a blower Cfm adjustment cannot reconcile the difference in latent load vs. latent capacity, a new load calculation, based on a lower or higher humidity value is required (or investigate the performance of a different product, or change the relevant attributes of the structure and it's comfort system).

Also note that the indoor humidity value used for the load calculation affects the wet-bulb temperature of the air that enters the equipment, which affects the equipment's latent capacity. A lower indoor humidity value reduces the entering wet-bulb temperature and reduces latent capacity, and vice versa.

For example, 50% RH indoors is used for the load calculation, and the OEM's performance data shows excess latent capacity. If a new load calculation is made for a lower humidity value (say 48%RH), and if entering air wet-bulb and dry-bulb temperatures for 48% RH are used to extract a latent capacity value from the OEM's performance data, the amount of excess latent capacity will be reduced, eliminated, or deficient. If it is reduced, recalculate for an even lower indoor RH value, if deficient, recalculate for a higher indoor RH value, and so on until latent capacity equals latent load.

The upper curve for Figure 1-7 is for contemporary equipment. The lower curve is for equipment that is more than 30 years old. Notice that both curves settle to a steady-state condition after a period of time, but the pull-down time for contemporary equipment is much longer than for older equipment, and the steady state sensible heat ratio for new equipment can be significantly higher than for the older equipment. Stated differently, SEER ratings may have been improved at the expense of latent capacity for continuous compressor operation, and indoor humidity control when the compressor cycles.

- Figure 1-7 shows that effective latent capacity (i.e., indoor humidity control) improves with the length of compressor runtime. So anything that maximizes the equipment runtime fraction is desirable.

- The simplest way to achieve this goal is to have as little excess sensible cooling capacity for the summer design condition as possible.

The industry is very familiar with the performance of single-speed equipment, as summarized by the top curve for Figure 1-7. This generic curve shows a 15 minute pull-down time and a 0.80 steady-state sensible heat ratio. A similar curve for a specific product may have a shorter, or possibly longer, pull-down time, and may have a somewhat lower or higher sensible heat ratio (say plus or minus 0.01 to 0.05). Therefore, the over-size limit for a specific product depends on the details of it's pull-down curve.

- OEMs either do not have pull-down curves for their products, or if they do have them, they are not published in the engineering data for the product.

- Fine-tuning the equipment over-size limit for a specific pull-down curve is beyond the scope of a prescriptive procedure.

Staged or Modulating Compressor Speed

Two-speed and variable-speed equipment should improve indoor humidity control because the equipment provides a significant amount of latent capacity when the imposed cooling load is greater than the OEM's low-limit for compressor operation, which typically ranges from 40% to 60% of full capacity. However, the transient behavior for compressor cycling, as demonstrated by the top curve for Figure 1-7, applies when the imposed load is less than the OEM's low-limit for compressor operation.

Since compressor speed control increases effective latent capacity for the block of seasonal hours that produce a cooling load that exceeds the low-limit for compressor operation, the size limit for two-speed air-air and buried pipe-loop water-air equipment is increased from 1.15 to 1.20, and from 1.15 to 1.30 for variable-speed equipment. For once-through water (pump and dump) water-air equipment, the size limit for two-speed equipment is increased from 1.25 to 1.30, and from 1.15 to 1.35 for variable-speed equipment. Fine-tuning equipment size limits for differences in compressor design, refrigeration system design, and refrigeration cycle controls is beyond the scope of a prescriptive procedure.

- The increase in the excess capacity limit is cautious because the industry has inadequate knowledge of effective latent capacity when multi-speed or variable-speed equipment responds to part load conditions.

- Some products are not even supported by expanded performance data, or some products offer conditional performance data for total cooling capacity only.

- Two-speed equipment and some variable-speed products do offer expanded data for full compressor speed and minimum compressor speed. This data tends to show that minimum latent capacity is about half of full latent capacity.

- As previously noted, multi-speed and variable-speed equipment behaves like single-speed equipment when the imposed load is less than the OEM's low-limit for compressor operation (there is no latent capacity when the compressor does not operate).

- The concept of compressor speed control has been, and is being, abused. This technology is not a substitute for an accurate load calculation and proper use of performance data. For heat pumps, excessive cooling capacity must not be used to compensate for the lack of electric coil heat in a product.

- A conservative over-size limit maximizes hours of compressor use and maximizes the average compressor speed when in use, which maximizes indoor humidity control for thousands of part-load hours.

Low-Limit for Total Cooling Capacity

The maximum amount of total cooling capacity is carefully limited for applications that have a latent cooling load. This is done to provide the best possible control of indoor humidity for thousands of hours of part-load operation.

Because of steps in nominal size found in OEM product lines, the size limit window for total cooling capacity is expanded by setting the minimum sizing factor to 0.90.

- Lowering the minimum total capacity factor from 1.0 to 0.90 is compatible with the need for part-load humidity control. The alternative would be to raise the upper limit by 0.10, but this has an undesirable effect on part-load humidity control.

- A 0.90 low-limit for total cooling capacity and a 1.00 low-limit for latent cooling capacity cause a need for a 0.90 low-limit for sensible cooling capacity.

Load Calculation Sensible Heat Ratio

The amount of latent capacity needed for indoor humidity control depends on the attributes of the local climate, the attributes of the structure, and the attributes of the comfort system or comfort systems (the primary system may be supplemented by a separate ventilation system). In this regard, Figure A1-17 provides a simplified example for the effect of climate, infiltration, exposed duct loads, and engineered ventilation loads. However, the entire set of circumstantial and momentary issues is much larger (see Section 20-5).

The *Manual J* sensible heat ratio (the calculated sensible load divided by calculated total load) is the prescriptive proxy for evaluating the need for part-load humidity control. The threshold value for mandatory humidity control is relatively high (0.95 or greater), because what appears to be a small latent load for a few summer design hours, may be a significant latent load for a large number of part-load hours.

- Indoor humidity that exceeds 60% is a comfort issue, and may be a mold and mildew issue. The *Manual J* design value for indoor humidity is 50% RH when the Table 1A or Table 1B Gains Difference value for 50% RH is greater than zero. This allows for a ten percentage point drift from 50% RH to 60% RH. A load calculation based on 55% RH only allows a five percentage point drift.

- The alternative to the sensible heat ratio proxy is to calculate humidity excursion values for all possible part-load conditions on a case-by-case basis. In this regard two locations may have similar summer design conditions (dry-bulb temperature and coincident wet-bulb temperature), but significantly different hours of high humidity for the part-load temperature bins.

- Investigating part-load humidity excursions requires calculation tools that are not available to practitioners, and mandating such calculations is incompatible with the realities of the market place.

A20-4 Sizing for Heat Pump Energy Use

As previously explained, summer humidity control is the primary issue among a set of competing issues. The need for summer humidity control is determined by the 0.95 sensible heat ratio proxy, regardless of location.

Summer humidity control is not an issue for locations that have dry summer weather (when the load calculation sensible heat ratio is 0.95, or greater). So, the use of more compressor capacity for improved heating season efficiency depends on the distribution of the location's bin-hour data.

Load Calculation Sensible Heat Ratio vs. Energy, Comfort, and Air Quality

Any energy conservation measure that only reduces the sensible building envelope load, and/or sensible system load (typically for engineered ventilation and/or exposed duct runs) acerbates the indoor humidity control problem. It follows that any measure that only increases the latent building envelope load, and/or latent system load (typically for engineered ventilation and/or exposed duct runs) acerbates the indoor humidity control problem. In addition, continuous blower use for improved air distribution effectiveness tends to degrade indoor humidity control. To summarize, any measure that decreases the load calculation sensible heat ratio, or the sensible heat ratio for momentary loads, has an undesirable affect on indoor humidity control.

For example, Section A19-7 shows bin-hour graphs that are skewed toward heating hours (see Spokane, WA), skewed toward cooling hours (see Tucson, AZ), balanced over a large bin temperature range (see Aims, IA), and balanced over a relatively small bin temperature range (see Seattle and Tacoma, WA). These bar graphs indicate that a larger heat pump compressor may provide a useful reduction in energy use for Spokane, a negative benefit for Tucson, AZ, an unknown benefit for Aims, IA, (but Aims is disqualified by it's load calculation sensible heat ratio value), and no significant benefit or disadvantage for Seattle WA.

Performance Calculations

An industry-approved bin-hour calculation (see Figure A6-7), or hourly simulation determines the energy benefit of more compressor capacity for a housing scenario. In other words, the calculation is made for a specific location, a specific set of dwelling attributes, for a specific type of HVAC system, and for a specific set of equipment and controls attributes. However, there is no standard software tool for making such calculations, and a mandatory requirement for such an effort is not compatible with the realities of the market place. Therefore, prescriptive guidance is the preferred alternative to performance modeling.

Thermal Balance Point Indicator

In general, a larger compressor will provide little or no annual energy use (KWH) benefit if the thermal balance point diagram for a heat pump that has the correct amount of cooling capacity shows that the thermal balance point temperature for outdoor air is not significantly warmer than the winter design temperature for outdoor air. In other words, when there are no operating hours, or a modest number of operating hours, below the thermal balance point temperature, as determined by bin-hour data. This is because benefit of less electric coil power (KW) does not apply, or occurs for relatively small number of hours per season. In addition, over-sized equipment increases cooling season energy, and compressor heating energy when the compressor cycles for the operating hours that are above the thermal balance point.

- The penalty for more compressor capacity depends on the decrease in compressor runtime fraction for cooling and compressor-only heating.
- It also depends on how the cycling degradation coefficient varies with nominal equipment size.
- It also depends on difference in compressor heating performance for various products (based on the OEM's heating Btuh and COP values for the 17°F and 47°F rating tests, or water-air equivalent).
- It also depends on how heating and cooling Btuh output per KW input varies with a step in nominal equipment size, and on a difference in the cycling degradation coefficient vs. a step in size.

Degree Day Ratio Proxy

As the preceding discussion of bin-hour graphs explains, the distribution of bin heating hours and bin cooling hours determines the nature of the local climate, which may be heating dominate, balanced, or cooling dominate. In addition, the effect of beam radiation causes a need for cooling when the outdoor air temperature is less than the set-point of the thermostat.

- Depending on circumstances, cooling is required when the outdoor temperature is less than 65°F, and may be required when less than 60°F.
- Bin data only deals with outdoor dry-bulb and wet-bulb temperature. Beam radiation reduces the need for compressor heat and supplemental heat for many cold weather hours.
- A proper energy calculation considers these effects.

Investigations made by internal and external committee consultants versed in energy calculations determined that a degree day ratio based on heating degree days to the base 65°F, divided by cooling degree days to the base 50°F, serves as a reliable proxy for yes or no decisions pertaining to the use of more compressor capacity. An extra 15,000 Btuh of total cooling capacity is allowed when the HDD-65/CDD-50 value is 2.0, or more.

- The initial proposal for the limit for excess cooling capacity was 12,000 Btuh. However, an investigation of the consequences of available steps in nominal size caused this to be increase to 15,000 Btuh.
- The geographical consequence of the degree day proxy is summarized by Figure A20-1. This figure

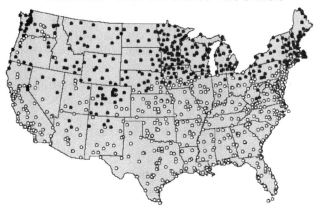

Courtesy of Jon Winkler; National Renewable Energy Laboratory

1) If the cooling load sensible heat ratio is less than 0.95 for a particular application, the sizing limits for a Condition A heat pump apply, regardless of the degree day ratio value.
2) The MJ8 sensible heat ratio is typically 0.95 or more for locations that are at 2,500 to 3,000 feet, and 1.0 above 3,000 feet.
3) Most upper mid-west locations and many northeast locations have a significant latent cooling load (cooling load sensible heat ratio less than 0.95).
4) For a given location, the size of the latent load depends on envelope construction details, duct loads, and engineered ventilation loads. An accurate load calculation determines the cooling load sensible heat ratio for a particular dwelling.

Figure A20-1

confirms behavior that would be predicted by a person that is well versed in energy-use calculations.

- Figure A20-1 shows where improved heating efficiency is possible, but it is not sensitivity to summer comfort. Some of the back dots on the figure will not pass the 0.95 sensible heat ratio test.

Examples

For the following examples, bear in mind that, for a given location, an energy calculation that estimates the effect of more compressor capacity for a specific set of construction and HVAC system circumstances does not establish a default value for the annual energy saving that may be expected for the location. This depends on too many interrelated variables, other than the attributes of the local climate.

Boise, Idaho with a One-Ton Step

The bin-hour graph that appears in Section 19-8 shows that Boise, Idaho has a lot of warm and mild weather. This is confirmed by a 2.01 degree day ratio (based on the NOAA data referenced in Section N1-5).

Note that Boise has a lot of bin-hours in the 35°F to 45°F range. This is important because adding one nominal ton of compressor capacity lowered the thermal balance point from about 42°F to about 37°F for the OEM-1 and OEM-2 products. This reduction in thermal balance point has a significant and desirable effect on reducing supplemental heat use.

Also note that the OEM-1 product has significantly better compressor heating performance than the OEM-2 product, regardless of size. In addition, the efficiency of the more efficient OEM product is relatively insensitive to a size step, while the efficiency of the less efficient product increases with a size step.

- Figure 1-5 shows solutions for the Smith House (see MJ8 Section 12 for construction details) served by a nominal 2-Ton heat pump and a nominal 3-Ton heat pump, provided by two different OEMs. Note that one-ton of extra cooling capacity saves 2,410 KWH to 5,130 KWH per year, depending on the heat pump product.

- The difference between these two values is mostly due to OEM data that shows a large difference in compressor heating efficiency at the 17°F and 47°F rating points. This difference would be even larger if the compressor heating efficiency of both products demonstrated the same output Btuh vs. input KW behavior for a one-ton step in nominal size, but in this case the efficiency of the less efficient product improved for a larger size, while the efficiency of the more efficient product was about the same for a larger size.

- Figure 1-5 also shows that use of continuous blower for continuous ventilation, and/or improved air distribution effectiveness, reduces annual energy savings by about 1,900 KWH (due to the difference in blower power for the larger equipment). This was about the same for both OEM products.

Akron, Minneapolis, Atlanta, and Tacoma, with a Half-Ton Step

Figure 2-6 footnotes summarize construction and equipment circumstances for a dwelling that is the same for four locations. Electricity is defaulted to 10 cents per KWH for these locations.

The NOAA degree day ratio for Akron, OH, is 2.14, and 3.62 for Minneapolis, MN, so annual energy use should be reduced by more compressor heating capacity. (These examples are academic, because both locations fail the sensible heat ratio test). Figure 2-6 shows that a half-ton of additional compressor capacity in Akron, OH, or Minneapolis, MN, saves about $80 per year.

The NOAA degree day ratio for Atlanta, GA, is 0.54, so annual energy use should not be reduced by more compressor heating capacity. (This example is academic, because this location fails the sensible heat ratio test).

Figure 2-6 also shows that more compressor capacity increases annual energy cost by a small amount. This is because cooling season penalties tend to cancel heating season benefits for this climate.

The NOAA degree day ratio for Tacoma, WA, is 2.19, so annual energy use should be reduced by more compressor heating capacity. (Tacoma passes the SHR test.) Figure 2-6 also shows that for Tacoma, one-half ton of additional compressor capacity has no significant effect on annual energy cost. This is because the climate is relatively mild during winter and summer, as summarized by the bin-hour graph provided by Section A19-7. (The benefit for this location may go positive, neutral, or negative, depending on the structure, the equipment, and using one-ton of additional capacity vs. a half-ton.)

Seattle, Washington with a One-Ton Step

The NOAA degree day ratio for Seattle, WA, is 2.14, so annual energy use should be reduced by more compressor heating capacity. (Seattle dwellings will probably pass the SHR test.) Figure A6-2 shows that for Seattle, one nominal ton of additional compressor capacity has no significant effect on annual energy cost. This is because the climate is relatively mild during winter and summer, as summarized by the bin-hour graph provided by Section A19-7. (The benefit for this location may go positive, neutral, or negative, depending on the structure, the equipment, and using one-ton of additional capacity vs. a half-ton).

Spokane, Washington with a One-Ton Step

The NOAA degree day ratio for Spokane, WA, is 3.31, so annual energy use should be reduced by more compressor heating capacity. (Spokane passes the SHR test.) Figure A6-4 shows that for Spokane, WA, one nominal ton of additional compressor capacity saves 600 to 800 KWH per year.

Denver, Colorado with a One-Ton Step

The NOAA degree day ratio for Denver, CO, is 2.24, so annual energy use should be reduced by more compressor heating capacity. (Denver passes the SHR test.) Figure A6-8 shows that for Denver, Co, one nominal ton of additional compressor capacity save 650 to 850 KWH per year.

A20-5 Performance Modeling for Cooling Equipment and Heat Pumps

For whole-house system performance modeling, the primary issues are indoor humidity control and energy use. When a dwelling has a latent cooling load, summer humidity control takes precedence, and energy use is optimized to the extent possible. When adequate control of indoor humidity is not an issue, energy use may be optimized to the fullest practical extent. However, adequate fresh air for occupants, and air distribution effectiveness are important issues for every dwelling.

The technical issues that effect occupant comfort and system efficiency are interrelated. Details pertaining to mathematical relationship between these issues is too extensive and complex to be discussed here. Brief comments on primary issues are provided below:

Indoor Humidity

For a particular latent-load climate, and a particular set of structural and HVAC system circumstances, the questions are; for each outdoor air temperature bin that applies to cooling, what are the magnitudes of the indoor humidity excursions (as affected by time-of-day differences in outdoor wet-bulb temperature, beam radiation, and internal loads), and what are the hours of occurrence values for these excursions.

- As explained by Section A20-3, conventional residential comfort systems do not control indoor humidity. The momentary relative humidity of the indoor air primary depends on the compressor duty cycle dictated by a dry-bulb thermostat.
- For part-load conditions, relative humidity excursions that peak at 55% RH, or less, are highly desirable, but this level of performance is typically beyond the capability of common equipment.
- For part-load conditions, relative humidity excursions that reach or exceed 60% RH, are undesirable, and this level of performance is often beyond the capability of common equipment.
- Calculations are significantly simplified if the investigation is limited to determining hours of occurrence for an indoor humidity of 60% RH or greater.
- Industry research shows that indoor humidity values of 60% RH, or more, occur for hundreds to thousands of hours per cooling season, depending on circumstances.
- High efficiency structures tend to have significantly more hours of high indoor humidity than a structure that is built to the basic HERS standard, or an equivalent code.
- The sidebar that begins on the previous page provides a basic list of issues that affect indoor humidity control.

Annual Energy Use

SEER and HSPF shall not be used for energy calculations because these ratings pertain to a special set of circumstances that generally do not apply to a particular application, except by uncommon coincidence.

- An hourly simulation, based on a mean standard year provides the most flexibility for modeling a particular set of structural details, a particular set

---

Humidity Excursion Modeling for Cooling

For comfort cooling, momentary indoor humidity depends on fixed circumstances which are, location, structural details, the type of comfort system and equipment, and the attributes of the equipment and controls; and variable circumstances, which are, the outdoor condition, the associated sensible and latent loads, and how the comfort system's equipment and controls react to these loads. There is a unique solution for each set of fixed circumstances.

- A location has a summer design condition, a winter design condition, and bin-hour data or hourly data that defines part-load conditions. If the structure, it's comfort system, and the system's equipment and controls are held constant, the number of solutions depends on local climate differences.
- For a given location, there tends to be some commonality for dwellings that have similar floor areas and floor plans, but the number of significantly different architectural designs is large (differences in fenestration loads and infiltration loads are especially important). In addition, comfort system details depend on the attributes of the architectural. The local climate may be a constant, but the number of solutions depends on the diversity of the local architecture, and the attributes of the comfort systems that serve these dwellings.
- Loads produced by duct runs in an unconditioned space are very important, as are outdoor air loads for engineered ventilation, and the use, or non-use of continuous blower. Cooling equipment performance varies with make and model, the method of compressor capacity control, the method for providing engineered ventilation, and the type and use of system controls. For a given architectural design, the building envelope and the local climate may be a constant, but the number of solutions depends on difference in the attributes of the comfort system and it's controls.

Compressor Runtime Fraction

Indoor humidity excursions occur when the compressor cycles on and off, and the size of a humidity excursion value increases as the compressor runtime fraction (RTF) decreases. The Compressor runtime fraction concept provides the basis for a humidity excursion model. The simplest form of the model uses monthly bin-hour data to determine momentary outdoor air dry-bulb and wet-bulb temperatures, and to calculate two RTF values for each outdoor air temperature bin;

of HVAC system features, applied to momentary weather circumstances.

- A bin-hour calculation based on bin weather data that has sensitivity to month-of-year and time-of-day can be manipulated to account for structural details, HVAC system features, and momentary weather circumstances.
- A model may be created from scratch, based on guidance provided by ASHRAE documents, and other industry resources, but the learning curve may be too steep for a person that is not familiar with energy calculation procedures.
- Software products provide energy use estimates. However, a person must be familiar with energy calculation procedures to decide if a product is the appropriate tool for the problem of interest.
- Appendix 6 provides entry level guidance that pertains to basic residential HVAC systems that do not have ancillary ventilation systems, or ancillary dehumidification systems.
- A proper energy calculation is decidedly complex because there are so many interrelated variables.

Outdoor Air

Industry standards provide guidance pertaining to engineered ventilation for dwellings. Various schemes may be used. Some have no heat recovery, others have sensible heat recovery, and others have enthalpy recovery. Some rely on the HVAC equipment blower, which may or may not operate continuously, others are self contained with a blower(s) or fan(s) that may, or may not, operate continuously.

The size of momentary indoor humidity excursions, the seasonal hours of indoor humidity above 60% RH, and annual energy use for cooling and heating are very sensitive to the type of engineered ventilation system, the amount of outdoor air Cfm provided when ventilation system is active, and the operation schedule of the ventilation system (continuous, or intermittent with compressor operation, or intermittent per an engineered schedule, or intermittent per an indoor air quality sensor).

At the simplest level, outdoor air may be ducted to the return side of the equipment. For this method, the use of continuous blower, or cycling the blower with the compressor, has a significant affect on indoor humidity excursions and energy use.

- Momentary blower use, or non use, affects the momentary latent cooling loads for infiltration, exposed duct leakage, and ventilation.
- Continuous blower may route two to three pounds of evaporator coil moisture to the conditioned space when the compressor is off.

which are, an RTF value for the beam radiation hours, and an RTF value for no beam radiation hours.

Momentary Runtime Fraction

The momentary runtime fraction equals the momentary sensible cooling load divided by the momentary sensible cooling capacity. For a bin-hour model, Figure 1-1 shows how load lines are used to evaluate momentary cooling loads, or perform an hourly load calculation.

Equipment Performance when the Compressor Cycles

A transient start-up curve similar to Figure 1-7 determines the effective sensible and latent capacity when the compressor cycles. Since capacity values change by the minute, the effective capacity for the on-cycle is the average value for the compressor operating time for the cycle.

Transient pull-down curves for industry products are not available. Figure 1-7 was provided by a contact that has access to OEM laboratory work. The upper curve shows a relatively long pull-down time to a 0.80 coil sensible heat ratio. This curve may, or may not, apply to a year 2000, or later, product. The pull-down time for products tested varied from about eight minutes, to more than 15 minutes, and the 0.80 coil sensible heat ratio is about average for products tested. The upper curve represents a worst-case possibility.

The lower curve is for older, relatively low SEER equipment. The lower curve shows a much shorter pull-down time to a 0.70 coil sensible heat ratio. The lower curve represents a best-case possibility.

Note that the slope of the pull-down curve has a significant effect on indoor humidity control sensitivity, vs. compressor runtime. The left side of the upper Figure 1-7 curve is relatively flat, so a few minutes difference in compressor runtime has little effect on the latent capacity for the cycle. The runtime effect increases as the slope of the pull-down curve increases.

Compressor Runtime per Cycle

A compressor runtime in minutes of operation per on-cycle is required to compute effective sensible and latent capacity, based on the Figure 1-7 curve. The NEMA thermostat model (see the equation at the end of this paragraph) provides compressor operating cycles per hour, based on the momentary runtime fraction (RTF) and the maximum number of cycles per hour (N_{max}), which may be set to three cycles per hour. Therefore, minutes of runtime per on-cycle equals $((60 \times RTF) / Cycles\ per\ Hour)$, and minutes of downtime per off-cycle equals $(Compressor\ Downtime\ per\ Hour / Cycles\ per\ Hour)$. Minutes of compressor downtime per cycle is used to compute space moisture gain for

- Annual energy use increases substantially when 500 Watts of blower power (or more), is used for thousands of hours per year.

Room Air Motion

A slight amount of air movement (about 25 Fpm) across a persons body is important for comfort. If the indoor blower cycles with the compressor, there is no air movement when the compressor is off.

Continuous blower operation improves air distribution effectiveness. However, the latent load produced by exposed duct leakage and engineered ventilation (as applicable) is undiminished when the compressor is off, and retained indoor coil moisture evaporates to supply air when the compressor is off. Therefore, continuous blower operation degrades indoor humidity control, compared to what happens when the blower cycles with the compressor. In addition:

- Continuous blower operation may significantly increase energy use and operating cost.
- Ceiling fans provide room air movement, or a dedicated air circulating system (blower, supply duct and grille, return duct and grille) provides room air motion. This increases installed cost, energy use and operating cost.
- For residential applications, there is no industry standard that specifies minimum blower runtime per hour, and there is no mathematical procedure that relates occupant comfort to blower runtime per hour.

Computational fluid mechanics (CDF) software may be used to investigate air distribution effectiveness of a particular set of circumstances.

For marketplace circumstances, all that can be said is that air distribution effectiveness should improve as blower runtime increases.

Continuous blower operation is standard practice for commercial applications, and is normally required by local code for commercial-use buildings.

Ancillary Dehumidification Equipment

Ancillary dehumidification equipment will provide excellent indoor humidity control, providing it is the correct size. Just set the control to the desired humidity level and enjoy the resulting comfort. The use of ancillary dehumidification equipment adds considerable complexity to annual energy calculations.

A20-6 Performance Method for Sizing Multi- and Variable-Speed Heat Pump Equipment

This section applies to air-air and water-air heat pump equipment that operates at two, or more, distinct speeds,

evaporation of residual indoor coil moisture when the blower operates while the compressor is off.

*Cycle/Hr = 4 * N_{max} * RTF * (1 – RTF)*

Initial and Final Values for Indoor RH

The momentary latent load, momentary entering wet-bulb temperature, and the momentary sensible and latent capacities depend on the indoor RH value when the compressor starts. Since this is the variable under investigation, a starting value for indoor RH is assumed, and the model calculates the amount of deficient or excessive latent capacity for this assumption. If latent capacity is deficient or excessive, a second calculation is made for a new RH guess. This process is repeated until momentary latent capacity equals momentary latent load.

The momentary entering wet-bulb temperature depends on the momentary condition of the indoor air, the momentary latent loads for infiltration, occupants and internal sources, the momentary latent load for a return duct in an unconditioned space, and the momentary latent load for engineered ventilation. As explained above, the calculations start with an assumed indoor RH value, and the model is iterated until momentary latent capacity equals momentary latent load.

Momentary Value for Total cooling Capacity

Use of the Figure 1-7 start-up curve requires a circumstantial steady state value for total cooling capacity. This value depends on the momentary values for the heat sink temperature, blower Cfm, and entering wet-bulb temperature, and is extracted from the OEM's expanded performance data. As explained above, the settled value for entering wet bulb temperature determines the momentary value for steady-state total capacity.

Indoor RH Excursion Hours

For a simple model, bin-hour data for a particular month is used to calculate sensible and latent loads and effective sensible and latent capacities, for beam radiation hours and for no beam radiation hours, or perform hourly calculations. As explained above, the circumstantial solution for indoor RH is the value that balances latent capacity and latent load. For a given month, there is a hours-of-occurrence value for the settled RH value for beam radiation, and a hours-of-occurrence value for the settled RH value for no beam radiation. If the same (approximately) RH value is determined for some other month, or months, the annual hours of occurrence for this RH value is the sum of the monthly hours.

or when the compressor speed is able to modulate between a minimum value and a maximum value. In both cases, the equipment cycles on-off when the momentary sensible cooling load is less than the momentary sensible capacity for the minimum compressor speed. This section does not apply to cooling-only equipment (Table N2-1 shall be used for cooling-only equipment).

Expanded Performance Data

The OEM's expanded performance for cooling, and for compressor heating, shall be used for equipment sizing, and for energy calculations. This data shall conform to Appendix 4 (of this manual) requirements.

Performance Data for Equipment Sizing

Condition A and Condition B heat pump equipment size is based on the cooling performance for minimum compressor speed. Expanded cooling performance data for the minimum compressor speed shall be used for this task. Heating performance data for full compressor speed is used for the thermal balance point diagram, and for sizing supplemental heat, if required.

Performance Data for Energy Calculations

Expanded cooling performance data for minimum compressor speed, and for full compressor speed (as defined in Section N1-1) shall be used for energy calculations. Expanded performance data for minimum-speed compressor heating, and for maximum-speed compressor heating shall be used for energy calculations.

Note: Per the Section N1 definitions, the maximum speed for compressor heating may be the 'Full Compressor Speed,' or the 'Enhanced Compressor Speed.' If enhanced speed data is used, this operating mode shall be available on a continuous basis for an unlimited amount of time.

Over-Size Limit for Cooling

Table N2-1 limits for single-speed cooling equipment establishes the maximum and minimum capacity rules for equipment sizing. These rules shall be applied to the *Manual J* cooling loads for the summer design condition, using the expanded performance data for minimum compressor speed. The sizing limit rules for applied cooling capacity are summarized here:

For Air-Air and Water-Air Pipe Loop Heat Pumps

- The over-size limit factor for total cooling capacity ranges from 0.90 to 1.15.
- Applied sensible capacity (after adjustment for excess latent capacity, where applicable) must not be less than 90% (0.90 factor) of the sensible load.
- The latent capacity value extracted from OEM data must be equal to, or greater than, the latent load.

Equipment Performance Issues

Inspection of OEM expanded performance data shows that some products have better latent capacity than other products. In other words, some products are designed for a high humidity climate, others are designed for a moderately humid climate, or dry climate. This depends on how the indoor equipment and controls, and blower Cfm/Ton are matched to the nominal capacity of the outdoor unit.

Effect of Excess Cooling Capacity

Excess cooling capacity for the summer design condition decreases the runtime fraction for all cooling season hours (including the 1% summer design condition hours, because the expanded performance data used to size equipment is steady-state data, which does not apply when cooling equipment cycles on during a summer design day). However, larger equipment has more latent capacity when the compressor operates.

In addition, the latent load for duct in an unconditioned space depends on blower operation, and if the blower is used for engineered ventilation, the latent load for ventilation depends on blower operation. If the blower cycles with the compressor, shorter runtime fractions reduce the average latent load per hour. A simplified model defaults to no duct or ventilation load when the compressor does not operate.

Effect of Continuous Blower

Evaporator coil moisture retention depends on the apparatus dew point, number of rows, coil circuiting, fins per inch, fin size, coil surface coating, coil face area and Cfm, coil mass, compressor cycles per hour and runtime per cycle. Depending on circumstances, something like 2.0 pounds to 3.0 pounds of moisture is added to the conditioned space when the compressor is off for a long time. The figure below shows the latent load transient for 2.5 pounds of water going to the space during a 26 minute time for coil dry-out. This

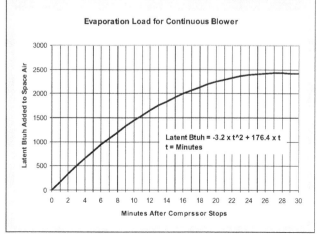

Evaporation Load for Continuous Blower

Latent Btuh = -3.2 x t^2 + 176.4 x t
t = Minutes

For Water-Air Open-Piping Heat Pump

- The over-size limit factor for total cooling capacity ranges from 0.90 to 1.25.
- Applied sensible capacity (after adjustment for excess latent capacity, where applicable) must not be less than 90% (0.90 factor) of the sensible load.
- The latent capacity value extracted from OEM data must be equal to, or greater than, the latent load.

The premise for this procedure is that minimum compressor capacity is used for summer cooling, and full compressor capacity is available for winter heating. This makes the indoor humidity control issue for multi-speed and variable-speed equipment identical to the indoor humidity control issue for single-speed equipment. In other words, the indoor humidity control provided by sophisticated equipment that cycles between minimum speed and off, is roughly equivalent to the indoor humidity control that is provided by properly sized single-speed equipment that cycles on and off.

Use of Cooling Performance Data for Equipment Sizing

The total, sensible and latent cooling capacity values extracted from the OEM's expanded performance data shall be for a blower Cfm value that is authorized by the OEM's performance data, for the actual entering wet-bulb and entering dry-bulb temperatures that apply to the project, and for the actual heat-sink temperatures that apply to the project.

- Appendix 2 procedures determine the entering wet-bulb and entering dry-bulb temperature values.
- For air-air equipment, the summer design condition for outdoor air, per the load calculation procedure, determines the heat-sink temperature.
- For water-air equipment, the maximum entering water temperature for the entire year determines the heat-sink temperature. Refer to Appendix 9 for more information.
- For water-air equipment that features a buried water piping loop, the capacity values from the expanded performance data shall be adjusted for the use of an antifreeze product, per the correction factors provided by the OEM's engineering data.

Base-Case Equipment for the Comparative Study

Energy and operation cost values for the candidate equipment shall be compared to a prescriptive design. For this comparison, the sizing limit values for the base-case (prescriptive) equipment are provided by Table N2-2. For the base-case design:

---

may add something like 2% RH to indoor humidity after ten minutes of compressor downtime, and increase indoor humidity by 4% RH after twenty five minutes of compressor downtime.

Using continuous blower for engineered ventilation may substantially increase part-load humidity excursions because the latent load for exposed duct surfaces and outdoor air Cfm are constant for every hour of the cooling season, and because a considerable amount moisture may be added to the conditioned space when the blower is off. A separate system may provide continuous ventilation with less affect on indoor humidity excursions.

Delaying Blower Start-Stop Time

Starting the compressor before starting the blower has a favorable affect on the evaporator pull-down curve, which may improve indoor humidity control somewhat. Operating the blower after the compressor stops has an unfavorable effect on indoor humidity control for the reasons that relate to continuous blower use. A simplified model just evaluates blower cycles with the compressor, and continuous blower.

Hygroscopic Materials Effect

Interior construction materials and furnishings absorb and release moisture as the moisture in the indoor air increases and decreases. This delays and buffers indoor humidity excursions. A simplified model assumes that all moisture is retained by the indoor air.

Staged and Variable Capacity Equipment

Compressors that are staged, or driven by a motor that has some type of speed control, have a minimum capacity value to protect the equipment. The runtime fraction model for single-speed equipment applies when such equipment cycles between minimum capacity and off.

When the momentary load exceeds the OEM's value for minimum capacity, two-speed equipment has some average set of cooling capacity values for cycling between high and low speeds. This also applies to variable-speed equipment, based on performance data for maximum speed and minimum speed, because data for intermediate speeds is not available.

- Table N2-2 limits for Condition A apply when the load calculation sensible heat ratio and degree day ratio indicate Condition A.
- Table N2-2 limits for Condition B apply when the load calculation sensible heat ratio and degree day ratio indicate Condition B.

- The base-case equipment uses the same compressor control technology, and the same heat-sink, heat-source fluid as the candidate equipment.
- It may be that a given product line does not offer a smaller size for base-case calculations. When this is the case, use some other product that has equivalent technology in a smaller size. The premise is that at some point, a given product line may not be suited for the application because the smallest size is not compatible with the application. When this is the case, search for a suitable product, and/or use some other technology.

Quantify the Efficiency Benefit

At the minimum, a simplified bin-hour calculation shall evaluate annual energy savings in KWH per year terms, and in operating cost per year terms.

- The annual efficiency of the candidate equipment shall be compared to the annual efficiency of the base-case equipment.
- A SEER value, HSPF value, cooling load hour value, or heating load hour value shall not be used in any part of the energy calculation procedure.
- A simplified bin-hour calculation, that is similar to the guidance provided by Appendix 6 of this document, is acceptable. See also:

  ASHRAE Handbook of Fundamentals (2013), Chapter 19.

  ASHRAE publication titled: Simplified Energy Analysis Using the Modified Bin Method.

  International Ground Source Heat Pump Association Design and Installation Guide, Oklahoma State University – Ground Source Heat Pump Residential and Light Commercial (2011).

- Bin-hour calculations shall be made for the base-case equipment, and for the candidate equipment.
- Temperature bins shall be for five degree increments.
- Use the sensible cooling load and the sensible cooling capacity for the balance point diagram for cooling. Use the sensible heating load and the sensible heating capacity for the balance point diagram for heating.
- The outdoor air temperature for no sensible cooling load, or sensible heating load shall be 65°F.
- For equipment that uses multi-speed or variable-speed technology, the Appendix 6 procedure shall be modified so that operating hours for each temperature bin are assigned to the three possible operating modes, which are:

> **Alternative Designs**
>
> Installation cost is a primary issue. A rigorous investigation of project economics would compare the candidate equipment with designs that use less sophisticated technology, and/or a different heat-sink, heat-source fluid. Such investigations are recommended, but not mandated by the Section 20-6 procedure. The premise is that the home owner has already decided to purchase the proposed technology.

  1) *The compressor cycles between off and low.*

  2) *The compressor cycles between minimum speed and maximum speed, or modulates between minimum speed and maximum speed.*

  3) *The compressor operates continuously.*

- OEM expanded performance data summarizes equipment performance for bin-hour calculations. This correlates output capacity and input power with heat-sink and heat-source temperatures.
- If the OEM's cycling degradation coefficient is known, it may be used to calculate part-load factors. If it is not known, 0.25 shall be used.
- For a buried water-loop heat pump, entering water temperature values shall be assigned to each air temperature bin per International Ground Source Heat Pump Association (IGSHPA) guidance.
- Bin energy calculations shall be for intermittent blower use. The indoor blower power draw (watts or KW) for a compressor operating mode shall be added to the compressor power draw.
- For air-air equipment, the outdoor fan power draw for a compressor operating mode shall be added to the compressor power draw.
- For water-air equipment, the water pump power draw or a compressor operating mode shall be added to the compressor power draw.
- For compressor heating, a thermal balance point diagram, with the OEM's defrost knee, if applicable, shall be used for the bin-hour calculation, shall determine the supplemental heat KW value for the winter design condition, and shall show the thermal balance point value for the combined house-equipment system.
- If the system has electric coil heat, the KHW used for the heating season shall be calculated.
- Total cooling energy shall be equal to the sum of the compressor energy, indoor blower energy, and outdoor fan energy, or the water pump energy for a water-air heat pump.

- Total heating energy shall be equal to the sum of the compressor energy, indoor blower energy, outdoor fan energy, or the water pump energy for a water-air heat pump, plus the electric coil energy.

- If continuous blower operation is used to improve air distribution effectiveness, the additional energy (KWH) used for this purpose shall be added to the cooling, and/or heating energy requirement.

- Current local utility rates, or rate schedules shall be used to convert cooling KWH to cooling dollars, and heating KWH to heating dollars.

Efficiency Benefit Report

An energy benefit report shall compare the performance attributes, KWH use, and the operating cost of the candidate equipment to the performance attributes, KWH use, and the operating cost of the base-case equipment. For each piece of equipment, evaluate performance for no blower operation when the compressor does not operate. Provide this information to the client:

- Blower Cfm values for cooling and heating, for minimum compressor speed, and for maximum compressor speed.

- The oversize factors (per Section N1-1 definitions) for total cooling capacity, sensible cooling capacity, and latent cooling capacity.

- The cycling degradation coefficients used for the bin calculations.

- The thermal balance point values for minimum compressor speed, and for maximum compressor speed.

- The supplemental heating load in Btuh and equivalent KW units, as read from the thermal balance point diagram for the outdoor air temperature used for the load calculation. The maximum compressor speed is used for these calculations.

- If an electric heating coil provides supplemental heat, list the standard KW size used for the design.

- The total KWH for the compressor and ancillary equipment required for the cooling season (refrigerant system energy for cooling).

- The total KWH required for the compressor and ancillary equipment for the heating season (refrigerant system energy for heating).

- If applicable, the total KWH required for electric coil heat for the heating season.

- The sum of the refrigerant system KWH for heating, and the electric coil KWH to obtain a value for the total KWH for the heating season.

- The sum of the KWH for the cooling season and the total KWH for the heating season to obtain a value for the annual KWH).

Air Distribution Effectiveness

Throw from supply air outlet that is designed for a constant supply air Cfm significantly decreases as supply air Cfm flowing through the outlet decreases. This is an issue for multi-speed and variable-speed equipment because the blower Cfm for minimum compressor capacity tends to be significantly less than for maximum compressor capacity. However, this is the same issue for the smaller, base-case equipment, and for the larger candidate equipment. Therefore, there is no requirement for comparing one to the other in this regard. The premise is that if one or more of the following measures are used, the comfort benefit and additional installation cost apply equally to the smaller equipment and the larger equipment.

- Room and space Cfm values shall be based on *Manual J* room and space loads, and the blower Cfm values that apply to operation during a summer design day and a winter design day.

- OEM engineering performance data for supply air outlets shall be used to select and size supply air hardware.

- Supply air outlet makes, models and sizes, shall be thoughtfully selected to obtain maximum throw for minimum blower Cfm without causing objectionable noise at maximum blower Cfm.

- Ceiling fans may provide air motion in the occupied space, which improves comfort.

- A separate air circulation system consisting of a relatively small blower, supply outlets, return grilles, and duct runs may provide air motion in the occupied space, which improves comfort.

- Two smaller outlets, vs. one larger outlet, for a room or space may be adjusted for seasonal blower Cfm. Close the damper for one outlet when blower Cfm is low, use both outlets when blower Cfm is high.

- Based on the utility rates that apply to the project, provide a cooling cost value, a compressor heating cost value, an electric heating coil cost value, a total heating cost value, and an annual cooling-heating cost value.

- Provide a KWH benefit value (subtract the annual KWH for the candidate equipment from the annual KWH for the base-case equipment).

- Provide an operating cost benefit value (subtract the annual operating cost for the candidate equipment from the annual operating cost for the base-case equipment).

Continuous Blower Report

If continuous blower operation is used to improve air distribution effectiveness, calculate the additional KWH values for the cooling season, the heating season , and for the entire year. Also do this for the additional operating cost values. Show calculations that compare two sets of energy use values, one for blower cycling, and one for continuous blower operation. Show calculations that compare two sets of operating cost values, one for blower cycling, and one for continuous blower operation.

Project Cost

The operating cost benefit for using the larger candidate equipment shall be compared to the difference in system owning cost. Provide an installed price for the candidate equipment, and an installed price for the base-case equipment.

A20-7 Furnace and Boiler Sizing

For heating provided by current products, excess furnace or boiler capacity has a minor effect on seasonal efficiency (see Appendix 11.). However, there is no rationale for installing excessive heating capacity. In deference to capacity steps in OEM product lines, the maximum heating capacity factor is 1.40, and the minimum heating capacity factor is 1.0

However, for a mild climate, the preferred furnace burner size may be incompatible with the blower Cfm and the blower power required for cooling. For this circumstances, the maximum heating capacity factor is increased to 2.0.

Appendx 20

This appendix is not part of the this standard. It is merely informative and does not contain requirements necessary for conformance to the standard. It has not been processed according to the ANSI requirements for a standard, and may contain material that has not been subject to public review or a consensus process. Unresolved objectors on informative material are not offered the right to appeal at ACCA or ANSI.

Appendix 21

Related Resources

This Appendix lists sources of information per the forts hal of Year 2014. Information pertaining to dwellings and their comfort systems is directly related to the procedures in this manual. Information pertaining to commercial buildings and their comfort systems may, in some cases, apply to the procedures in this manual.

AABC – Associated Air Balance Council

1518 K Street NW, Suite 503, Washington, DC, 20005; tel: 202/737-0202; *www.aabchq.org*.

- Commissioning Guideline, 2005.
- Test and Balance Procedures, 2002.

ACCA – Air Conditioning Contractors of America

2800 Shirlington Road, Suite 300, Arlington, VA, 22206; tel: 703/575-4477; *www.acca.org*.

Manuals and Standards

- Manual CS® Commercial Applications, Systems and Equipment, 1st ed., 1993.
- Manual D® Residential Duct Systems, 2014.
- Manual J® Residential Load Calculation, 8th ed., 2011.
- Manual N® Commercial Load Calculation, 5th ed., 2012.
- Manual RS® Comfort, Air Quality, and Efficiency by Design, 1997.
- Manual S® Residential Equipment Selection, 2004.
- Manual T® Air Distribution Basics for Residential and Small Commercial Buildings, 1992.
- Manual Q® Low Pressure, Low Velocity Duct System Design for Commercial Applications, 1990.
- Manual SPS® HVAC Design for Swimming Pools and Spas, 2010.
- Manual Zr® Residential zoning, 2012.
- ACCA 4 – 2013 (QM) Maintenance of Residential HVAC Systems in One- and Two-Family Dwellings Less Than Three Stories.
- ACCA 5 – 2010 (QI) HVAC Quality Installation Specification.
- ACCA 6 – 2007 (QR) Standard for Restoring the Cleanliness of HVAC Systems.
- ACCA 9 – 2011 (QIvp) HVAC Quality Installation Verification Protocols.
- ACCA 12 – 2012 (QH) Existing Homes Evaluation and Performance Improvement.

Other ACCA Documents

- Residential Duct Diagnostics and Repair, ACCA, 2003.
- Penney, Bradford A. J. D., Woods, James E. Ph. D. and Hourahan, Glenn C., Good HVAC Practices for Residential and Commercial Buildings: A Guide for Thermal, Moisture and Contaminant Control to Enhance System Performance and customer Satisfaction, 2003.

AHRI – Air Conditioning, Heating, and Refrigeration Institute

2111 Wilson Blvd. Suite 500, Arlington, VA, 22201; tel: 703/524-8800; *www.ahrinet.org*.

Standards and Guidelines

- Standard 210/240-2008 Performance Rating of Unitary Air Conditioning and Air-Source Heat Pump Equipment, 2008.
- ANSI/AHRI Standard 310/380-2004 Standard for Packaged Terminal Air-Conditioners and heat Pumps, 2004.
- Standard 320-98 1998 Standard for Water Source Heat Pumps.
- Standard 340/360-2007 Performance Rating of Commercial and Industrial Unitary Air Conditioning and Heat Pump Equipment, 2007.
- Standard 700-2012 Specification for Fluorocarbon Refrigerants, 2011.
- Standard 740-98 Refrigerant Recovery/Recycling Equipment, 1998.
- Standard 880-2011 Air Terminals, 1998.
- ANSI/AHRI Standard 1230 with Addendum 1, Standard for Performance Rating of Variable Refrigerant Flow (VRF) Multi-Split Air-Conditioning and Heat Pump Equipment, 2010.
- Guideline K-2009 Containers for Recovered Non-Flammable Fluorocarbon Refrigerants, 2009.
- Guideline N–2012 Assignment of Refrigerant Container Colors.
- Guideline Q-2010 Content Recovery and Proper Recycling of Refrigerant Cylinders, 2010.

Other AHRI Documents
- AHRI Product Certification directory/database: AHRI certification consists of manufacturers who voluntarily participate in independent testing to ensure that their product will perform according to published claims at specified controlled testing conditions. Go to:
  http://www.ari.org/standardscert/certprograms/directories/ for more information.
- Industry Recycling Guide (IRG-2), Handling and Reuse of Refrigerants in the US, 1994.

ASHRAE – American Society of Heating, Refrigerating and Air-Conditioning Engineers

1791 Tullie Circle, NE., Atlanta, GA; tel: 404/636-8400; *www.ashrae.org*.

Standards and Guidelines
- Standard 15-2013 Safety Standard for Refrigeration Systems.
- Standard 34-2013 Designation and Safety Classifications of Refrigerants.
- Standard 55-2013 Thermal Environmental Conditions for Human Occupancy.
- Standard 62.1-2013 Ventilation for Acceptable Indoor Air Quality.
- Standard 62.2-2013 Ventilation for Acceptable Indoor Air Quality in Low-Rise Residential Buildings, ANSI Approved.
- Standard 90.1-2013 Energy Standard for Buildings Except Low-Rise Residential Buildings.
- Standard 90.2-2007 Energy-Efficient Design of Low-Rise Residential Buildings.
- Standard 126-2008 Method of Testing HVAC Air Ducts.
- Standard 147-2013 Reducing the Release of Halogenated Refrigerants from Refrigerating and Air-Conditioning Equipment and Systems.
- Standard 152-2014 Method of Test for Determining the Design and Seasonal Efficiencies of Residential Thermal Distribution Systems.
- Standard 180-2012 Standard Practice for Inspection and Maintenance of Commercial HVAC Systems.
- Standard 183-2011 Peak Cooling and Heating Load Calculations in Buildings Except Low-Rise Residential Buildings.
- Standard 205P-Working Draft, Standard Representation of Performance Simulation Data for HVAC&R and Other Facility Equipment.
- Guideline 0-2013 The Commissioning Process.
- Guideline 1.1-2007 HVAC&R Technical Requirements for Commissioning Process.
- Guideline 4-2013 Preparation of Operating and Maintenance Documentation for Building Systems.

ASHRAE Books and Manuals
- Handbook of Fundamentals – 2013.
- HVAC Systems and Equipment – 2012.
- HVAC Applications – 2011.
- Refrigeration – 2010.
- Harriman, Lew, Geoffrey W. Brundrett, and Reinhold Kittler. Humidity Control Design Guide for Commercial and Institutional Buildings, 2001.

BCA – Building Commissioning Association

600 NW Compton Drive, Suite 200, Beverton, OR, 97006; tel: 877-666-2292; *www.bcxa.org*.

John A. Heinz & Rick Casault, The Building Commissioning Handbook, Second Edition.

CEE - Consortium for Energy Efficiency

98 North Washington St., Suite 101, Boston, MA, 02114-1918; tel: 617-589-3949; *www.cee1.org*.

The CEE/AHRI Verified Directory identifies a list of products (less than 65 Mbtuh) that the manufacturer represents as meeting energy performance tiers established by the Consortium for Energy Efficiency (CEE) as part of the Residential Air Conditioner and Heat Pump Initiative and the High-Efficiency Commercial Air Conditioning Initiative. These initiatives make use of tiers to differentiate equipment on the basis of energy performance with a higher tier representing a higher level of claimed performance. Go to: http://www.ceehvacdirectory.org/.

IAPMO – International Association of Plumbing and Mechanical Officials

4755 E. Philadelphia Street, Ontario, CA, 91761; tel: 909.472.4100; *www.iapmo.org).*

- Uniform Mechanical Code, 2012.
- Uniform Plumbing Code, 2012.

ICC – International Code Council

500 New Jersey Avenue, NW, 6th Floor, Washington, DC, 20001; tel: 888/422-7233; *www.iccsafe.org.*

- International Building Code, 2012.
- International Energy Conservation Code, 2012.

- International Fire Code, 2012.
- International Residential Code, 2012.
- International Mechanical Code, 2012.
- International Fuel Gas Code, 2012 (see Chapter 4, Tables 402.4(1) – 402.4 (33).

NAIMA – North American Insulation Manufacturers Association

44 Canal Center Plaza, Suite 310, Alexandria, VA 22314; tel 703/684-0084; *www.naima.org*.

- Fibrous Glass Duct Construction Manual, 1st edition, 1989.
- Fibrous Glass Duct Construction Standard, 2002.
- Fibrous Glass Duct Liner Standard, 2002.

NATE – North American Technician Excellence

2111 Wilson Blvd, Suite 510, Arlington, VA, 22201; tel: 703/276-7247; *www.natex.org*.

NATE offers certifications tests for service and installation technicians to highlight relevant applied knowledge. Separate 'service' and 'installation' tests are given in the following specialty categories: air conditioning, air distribution, air-to-air heat pump, gas heating (air), oil heating (air), hydronics gas, hydronics oil.

NEBB – National Environmental Balancing Bureau

8575 Grovemont Circle, Gaithersburg, Maryland 20877; tel: 301-977-3698; *www.nebb.org*).

- Procedural Standards for Testing, Adjusting, Balancing of Environmental Systems, 2005.
- Procedural Standards for Whole Building Systems Commissioning of New Construction, 2009.

NFPA – National Fire Protection Association

Batterymarch Park, Quincy, MA, 02169, tel: 617/770-300; www.nfpa.org.

- NFPA 31 Standard for Installation of Oil-Burning Equipment, 2011.
- NFPA 54 National Fuel Gas Code, 2012 (see Chapter 12, Tables 12.1 - 12.33).
- NFPA 70 National Electric Code, 2014.
- NFPA 90a Standard for the Installation of Conditioning and Ventilation Systems, 2015.
- NFPA 90b Standard for the Installation of Warm Air Heating and Air-Conditioning Systems, 2015.

PHCC – Plumbing-Heating-Cooling Contractors-National Association

180 S. Washington Street, Falls Church, VA, 22046; tel: (703) 237-8100; *www.phccweb.org*.

- Heating and Cooling Technical Manual.
- Variable Air Volume Systems.

RSES – Refrigeration Service Engineers Society

1911 Rohlwing Rd, Suite A, Rolling Meadows, IL, 60008; tel: 847-297-6464; *www.rses.org*.

Various training manuals, self-study courses, classes and CDs to enhance the professional development of practitioners within the refrigeration sector.

PECI – Portland Energy Conservation Inc.

100 SW Main St, Suite 1600, Portland, OR 97204; tel: 503/248-4636; *www.peci.org*.

- Model Commissioning Plan and Guide Specifications (v2.05); available for download.
- Operation and Maintenance Service Contracts: Guidelines for Obtaining Best-Practice Contracts for Commercial Buildings, available for download.
- Tudi Hassl and Terry Sharp, Practical Guide for Commissioning Existing Buildings, 1999.

SMACNA – Sheet Metal and Air Conditioning Contractors' National Association

4201 Lafayette Center Drive, Chantilly, VA, 20151; tel: 703/803-2980; *www.smacna.org*.

- Building Systems Analysis & Retrofit Manual, 2011.
- Fibrous Glass Duct Construction Standards, 2003.
- Fire, Smoke and Radiation Damper Installation Guide for HVAC Systems, 2002.
- HVAC Air Duct Leakage Test Manual, 2012.
- HVAC Duct Systems Inspection Guide, 2006.
- HVAC Duct Construction Standards, Metal and Flexible, 2005.
- HVAC Systems Commissioning Manual, 2013, 2nd Edition.
- HVAC Systems – Duct Design, 2006.
- HVAC Systems Testing, Adjusting & Balancing. 2002, 3rd Edition.
- IAQ Guidelines for Occupied Buildings Under Construction. 2007, 2nd Edition.
- Rectangular Industrial Duct Construction Standards, 2004.
- Round Industrial Duct Construction Standards, 1999.

Code Reference to ACCA Manuals

IAPMO - Uniform Mechanical Code (UMC).
Current edition: 2012.
Publishing cycle: 2012, 2009, 2006 (three years).
Refers to Manuals: J, D, N, Q, B, 4 QM.

ICC - International Energy Conservation Code (IECC).
Current edition: 2012.
Publishing cycle: 2012, 2009, 2006 (three years).
Refers to Manuals: J, S - RE: IRC §M1401.3.

ICC - International Fuel Gas Code (IFGC).
Current edition: 2012.
Publishing cycle: 2012, 2009, 2006 (three years).
Refers to Manuals: None.

ICC - International Mechanical Code (IMC).
Current edition: 2012.
Publishing cycle: 2012, 2009, 2006 (three years).
Refers to Manual: D.

ICC - International Residential Code (IRC).
Current edition: 2012.
Publishing cycle: 2012, 2009, 2006 (three years).
Refers to Manuals: J, S and D.

ICC - International Building Code (IBC).
Current edition: 2012.
Publishing cycle: 2012, 2009, 2006 (three years).
Refers to Manuals: D, RE: IBC §M2801.

International Association of Plumbing and Mechanical Officials; Uniform Mechanical Code, 2012.

Detailed Reference to ACCA Manuals, per April 2013.

2012 UMC §1106.1

Manual J8 Residential Load Calculation-8th Ed.
Manual N Commercial Load Calculations.

1106.1 Human Comfort (GENERAL REQUIREMENTS):

Cooling equipment used for human comfort in dwelling units shall be sized to satisfy the calculated loads determined in accordance with the reference standards in Chapter 17, or other approved methods.

2012 UMC §601.2

Manual D Residential Duct Systems.
Manual Q Low Pressure Low Velocity Duct Systems Design.

601.2 Sizing Requirements (DUCT SYSTEMS):

Duct systems used with blower-type equipment that are portions of a heating, cooling, absorption, evaporative cooling, or outdoor-air ventilation system shall be sized in accordance with Chapter 17, or by other approved methods.

Chapter 17 Standards | Table 17-1 Standards for Equipment and Materials.

Residential Load Calculation, ACCA Manual J, 2006.

Residential duct systems, ACCA Manual D, 2009.

Commercial Load calculation, ACCA Manual N, 2008.

Low Pressure Low Velocity Duct System Design, ACCA Manual Q, 2003.

Balancing and Testing Air and Hydronic Systems, ACCA Manual B, 2009.

Maintenance of Residential HVAC Systems, ACCA 4 QM-2007.

International Code Council; International Residential Code, 2009.

Detailed Reference to ACCA Manuals, per April 2013.

2012 IRC §M1401.3

Manual J Residential Load Calculation - 8th Ed.
Manual S Residential Equipment Selection.

M1401.3 - Sizing: Heating and cooling equipment shall be sized in accordance with ACCA Manual S based on building loads calculated in accordance with ACCA Manual J or other approved heating and cooling calculation methodologies.

2012 IRC §M1601.1; §M1601.2

Manual D Residential Duct Systems.

M1601.1 - Duct Design: Duct systems serving heating, cooling and ventilation equipment shall be fabricated in accordance with the provisions of this section and ACCA Manual D or other approved methods.

M1602.2 - Prohibited Sources: Outside or return air for a forced-air heating or cooling system shall not be taken from the following locations: ... 3. A room or space, the volume of which is less than 25 percent ... Where connected by a permanent opening having an area sized in accordance with ACCA Manual D, adjoining rooms ...

International Code Council; International Energy Conservation Code, 2009.

Detailed Reference to ACCA Manuals, per April 2013.

2012 IECC §403.6 and §404.6.1.2

Manual J8 Residential Load Calculation-8th Ed.

*403.6 Equipment sizing: Heating and cooling equipment shall be sized in accordance with Section 1401.3 of the International Residential Code. (**Manual J and S**).*

*404.6.1.2 Calculation software tools: Calculation of whole-building (as a single) sizing for the heating and cooling equipment in the standard reference design residence in accordance with Section 1401.3 of the International Residential Code. (**Manual J and S**).*

{2012 IRC §M1401.3}

Manual S Residential Equipment Selection.

International Code Council; International Mechanical Code, 2009.

Detailed Reference to ACCA Manuals, per April 2013.

2012 IMC §603.2

Manual D Residential Duct Systems.

603.2 Duct Sizing

Ducts installed within a single dwelling unit shall be sized in accordance with ACCA Manual D or other approved methods.

International Code Council; International Building Code, 2009.

Detailed Reference to ACCA Manuals, per April 2013.

2012 IBC §2801.1

Manual J8 Residential Load Calculation-8th Ed.
Manual D Residential Duct Systems.
Manual S Residential Equipment Selection.

2801.1 Scope. Mechanical appliances, equipment and systems shall be constructed, installed and maintained in accordance with the International Mechanical Code and the International Fuel Gas Code.

Related Papers and Reports

The following papers and electronic media were reviewed. Portions of the content may, or may not, applied to, or effected, the procedures in this manual.

1998 IGSHPA CLGS Heat Pump Systems Installation Guide (current 2009 has minor changes).

2008 ACEEE Summer Study on Energy Efficiency in Buildings, Measured Effect of Air Flow and Refrigerant Charge on a High Performance Heat Pump; Erin Kruse and Larry Palmiter, Ecotopr, inc.; Paul W. Francisco, Building Research Council, University of Illinois.

2008 ACEEE Summer Study on Energy Efficiency in Buildings, Field Monitoring of High Efficiency Residential Heat Pumps; Bob Davis, Ecotope, Inc. David Robson, Stellar Processes.

ASHRAE Journal, How to Properly Size Unitary Equipment, Glenn Hourahan, PE., Member ASHRAE, February 2004.

ASHRAE Paper 2010; Moving Ducts into Conditioned Space: Getting to Code in the Pacific Northwest, David Hales, David Baylon.

ASHRAE Paper AN-04-5-3, Heat Pump System, Performance in Northern Climates. Paul W. Francisco, David Baylon, Bob Davis, Larry Palmiter.

ASHRAE Systems and Equipment, 2008, Chapter 9; Design of Small Forced Air Heating and Cooling Systems.

Building Science Corporation; Final Task 3 Report: Identify Model development Needs, for: AHRAE RP-1449 Energy Efficiency and Cost Assessment of Humidity Control for Residential Buildings, (BSC, FSEC, Unv. Central FL., CDH Energy Corp).

Carrier Engineering Guide for Altitude Effects, Carrier Corporation 1967, Catalog No. 592-016.

Closing the Gap: Getting Full Performance from Residential central Air Conditioner. Simulation Results and Cost benefit Analysis; FSECCR-1716-07; April 27, 2007.

Ductless Heat Pump Impact & Process Evaluation: Field Metering Report; Report #E12-237; May 1, 2012; Prepared by: David Baylon, Ben Larson, Poppy Storm, Kevin Geraghty; Ecotope Inc.; 4056 9th Avenue NE; Seattle, WA 98105; Northwest Energy Efficiency Alliance.

EER & SEER as Predictors of Seasonal Cooling Performance;. Developed by: Southern California Edison Design & Engineering Services 6042 N. Irwindale Avenue, Suite B Irwindale, CA, 91702, Dec 2003.

Energy Efficient Requirements for Programmable Thermostats, Proposed Annex A for NEMA DC-3; Draft 5, June 28, 1009.

Final Report on Off — Design Performance of Residential Heat Pumps, Sponsored by ASHRAE. Submitted by, Jun-Hyeung, James E. Braun, and Echard A. Groll (Purdue Unv.); and Larry Palmiter (Ecotope, Inc.).

High Efficiency Heat Pump Heating and AC Monitoring Project, Ecotope, Inc., David Robison, Stellar Processes, Bob Davis, Ecotope, Inc., June 2008.

Laboratory Tests of the Impact of Variations of Refrigerant Charge and Airflow on Heat Pump Performance, Prepared by Larry Palmiter and Ben Larson, Ecotope, inc., Submitted to Ken Eklund, Idaho Offices of Energy Resources.

Manufactured Homes Installation manual Downflow/Upflow Electric Furnace, Johnson Controls Unitary Products 570929-BIM-A-0510.

Measured Impacts of Proper Air Conditioning Sizing in Four Florida Case Study Homes. STAC Solicitation #03-STAG-1; Final Report; FSEC-CR-1641-06; October 25, 2006.

National Energy Efficiency Alliance (neea), July 2011 Report No. E11-225; Ductless Heat Pump Impact & Process evaluation: Lab-Testing Report. Prepared by; Ecotope Inc. 4056 9th Avenue NE, Seattle, WA, 98105.

NREL/TP-5500-52791, December 2011; Laboratory Test Report for Six Energy Star® Dehumidifiers; Jon Winkler, Ph.D., Dane Christensen, Ph.D., and Jeff Tomerlin.

NREL/TP-5500-56354, Jan 2013; Improved Modeling of Residential Air Conditioners and Heat Pumps for Energy Calculations; D. Cutler, J. Winkler, N. Kruis, and C. Christensen (National Renewable Energy Laboratory);, M. Brandemuehl (Unv. Colorado).

Oak Ridge National Laboratory (ornl); Air-Source Heat pump: Field Measurements of Cycling, Frosting, and Defrosting Losses, 1981-83; V.D. Baxter, J.C Moyers.

Power Point Presentation: Ductless Heat Pumps "mini-splits" in PNW Cold and Marine Climates; Michael Lubliner, Luke Howard, David Hales, WSU Energy Program - Olympia, WA, Presented at ACI National Conference Baltimore, MD - March 2012.

Power Point Presentation, National Energy Efficiency Alliance (neea), NW Ductless Heat pump Project; Ductless Heat Pump Performance Results, David Baylon & Poppy Storm, Ecotope, Inc.

Power Point Presentation: Representing the Performance of Unitary Air Conditioning in Energy Models: Seven Hassles and Lessons Learned, ASHRAE winter Conference 2012, Chicago, IL; Dylan Cutler & Neal Kruis.

Power Point Presentation: Washington State Unv. Extension Energy Program, Heat Pump Commissioning Field Guide, May 2008.

Rating Water-Source Heat Pumps Using AHRI Standard 320 and ISO Standard 13256-1. W. Vance Payne and Piotr A. Domanski, National Institute of Standards and Technology Building and Fire Research Laboratory, Gaithersburg, MD, 20899-8230.

Sensitivity Analysis of Installation Faults On Heat Pump Performance. Piotr A. Domanski, Vance Payne, and Hugh Henderson; National Institute of Standards and Technology; Gaithersburg, MD, USA; CDH Energy Corporation, Cazenovia, NY, USA.

Simulating Seasonal Impact of Air Conditioner Faults. September 25, 2012; NIST - Gaithersburg, MD; Annex 36 Working Meeting; Hugh I. Henderson Jr.; CDH Energy Corp.

State Technology Advancement Collaborative, Residential Heat Pump and Air Conditioner Research, Demonstration, and Deployment Improving Pacific Northwest Utility and State HVAC Programs, Ken Eklund, Idaho Office of Energy Resources, September, 2008.

Trane Co. Effects of Altitude on Air Conditioning and Refrigeration Equipment, EB-MSCR28.

Understanding the Dehumidification Performance of Air-Conditioning Equipment at Part-Load Conditions. Final Report; FSEC-CR-1537-05; Shirey, Henderson, Raustad; January 2006.

U.S. Department of Energy, Building Technologies Program: Energy Savings and Peak Demand Reduction of a SEER 21 Heat Pump vs. a SEER 13 Heat Pump with Attic and Indoor Duct Systems; J. Cummings and C. Withers BA-PRIC, Dec 2001.

Weil-McLain, Boiler Replacement Guide; Step-by-Step Procedures for Properly Sizing Hot Water and Replacement Boilers for Homes and Small Commercial Buildings.

Software

Spreadsheet Software: Heating Fuel Comparison Calculator, Version HEAT-CALC-Vsn-D_1-09.xls, 3/15/2010; Florida Solar Energy Center, www.fsec.ucf.edu/en/publications/html/fsec-pf-413-04/

Spreadsheet Software: SEEM Bin-Hour Energy Calculation, Ecotope, Inc.

Appendix 22

Blank Forms

The appendix provides worksheets for calculating the return duct loads for heating, sensible cooling and latent cooling; and for calculating the condition of the air at the entrance to cooling and heating equipment. These worksheets supplement the equipment selection and sizing procedures provided by this manual. When a furnace is equipped with a cooling coil, the *Manual D* Friction Rate Worksheet is used to see if the furnace has enough blower power for cooling.

A22-1 Revised Version of *Manual J* Worksheet G

The exhibit of Worksheet G found in *Manual J*, Version 2.10, November 2011, page 515 (and all other occurrences) calculates duct load factors and a latent gain value for the entire duct system (supply-side, and return-side). The version of Worksheet G on the next page of this manual calculates duct load factors, and a latent gain value, for the entire duct system (left column), and duct load factors, and a latent gain value, for the return-side on the duct system (right column).

- Note that for lines 1 through 13, the right-column values are the same as the left-column values. Then, for lines 14, 15 and 16, the right column values are zero (i.e., no supply-side surface area). Then, for lines 17 through 20, 18, the right-column values are the same as the left-column values.

- On line 20, the SAA values for the entire duct system (left column) and the return-side of the system (right column) will be different, because the Rs value for the return-side is zero.

- Line 22 is a new item (does not appear on older versions of Worksheet G). This line calculates the latent gain for the return side of the duct system. The resulting value applies to the entire duct system (left column), and to the return-side of the system (right column). Where:

  Return-side leakage Cfm = Return-side area (SqFt from MJ8 Table 7) x Return-side leakage (Cfm/SqFt)

  Latent load Btuh = 0.68 x Return side leakage Cfm x Grains Difference value used for the Worksheet G calculation.

- On line 23, the LGA values for the entire duct system (left column) and the return-side of the system (right column) will be different, because the Rs value for the return-side is zero.

The adjusted latent gain (ALG) value on line 13 is for leakage scenarios that differ from the 0.12/0.24 default, per Table 7, MJ8.

The latent gain adjustment (LGA) on line 23 is for the installed duct surface area vs. the default duct surface area from Table 7, MJ8.

- The effective heat loss factor (line 24), sensible gain factor (line 25), and latent gain value (line 26) for the entire duct system (left column) and the return-side of the system (right column) will be different, because the Rs value for the return-side is zero.

A22-2 Entering Air Condition

The condition of the air that enters cooling-only equipment, or heat pump equipment, affects cooling performance, and compressor heating performance. For checking conformance for the maximum leaving air temperature allowed by OEM guidance, the dry-bulb temperature of air that enters a refrigerant coil, furnace, or electric heating coil, affects the temperature of the air leaving the equipment.

The entering air condition depends on the condition of the space air (typically the air at the return grill), the sensible and latent loads for the return duct (where applicable), and the sensible and latent loads for engineered ventilation (for mixing the air leaving the return duct with outdoor air, where applicable). Psychrometric procedures apply, and these must be adjusted for altitude, where applicable. The worksheets on the next page provide values for the condition of the air entering cooling and heating equipment. Appendix 2 provides detailed instructions for using these worksheets.

A22-3 Friction Rate Worksheet

The *Manual D* Friction Rate Worksheet determines if the blower has enough power to move the desired airflow rate (design Cfm value) through the supply-return path that produces the most resistance to airflow. Equipment that has adequate heating Btuh capacity, or cooling Btuh capacity, must not be used if blower power is inadequate. A copy of the *Manual D* Friction Rate Worksheet is provided two pages ahead.

Appendix 22

Worksheet G for *Manual S* Version 2.00
Duct Runs in Unconditioned Space

Location of duct runs: Levels served by duct runs (one or two):
Percent of duct system in this space: Floor area of primary level (SqFt):
Airway shape and configuration: Floor area of second level (SqFt):

Duct Table Number	Case Number	Look-Up Floor Area (SqFt)	SAT (°F) Heating	99% (°F) Dry-Bulb	1% (°F) Dry-Bulb	Table 1 ΔGrains

- Refer to MJ8, Section 23.6 for instructions pertaining to case number and look-up floor area.
- For multiple locations use a separate worksheet for each location. Then the Form J1 loss/gain factors and latent gain for the entire system equal the sum of the worksheet (Step 5) values. See MJ8, Section 23.7.

Step 1) Enter base-case load factors and latent heat value from Table 7 (eyeball interpolation is acceptable)

	Supply and Return Ducts			Return-Side Only	
	Base-case factors from duct table			Copy the base-case supply and return duct values	
1	Heat loss factor =			Heat loss factor =	
2	Sensible gain factor =			Sensible gain factor =	
3	Latent gain (Btuh) =			Latent gain (Btuh) =	

Step 2) R-Value Correction (WIF)   Copy the WIF supply and return duct values

	R-Value	For heat loss =			Heat loss =	
4						
5		For sensible gain =			Sensible gain =	
6		Adjusted heat loss factor =		< Line 1 factor x line 4 adjustment	Adj loss fact =	
7		Adjusted sensible gain factor =		< Line 2 factor x line 5 adjustment	Adj sens fact =	

Step 3) Leakage Rate Correction (LCF)   Copy the LCF supply and return duct values

	Cfm / SqFt		For heat loss =		Heat loss =	
8						
9		< SSL	Sensible gain =		Sensible gain =	
10		< RSL	Latent gain =		Latent gain =	
11			Adjusted heat loss factor =	< Line 6 factor x line 8 adjustment	Adj loss fact =	
12			Adjusted sensible gain factor =	< Line 7 factor x line 9 adjustment	Adj sens fact =	
13			Adjusted latent gain (ALG) =	< Line 3 value x line 10 adjustment	ALG =	

Step 4) Surface Area Adjustment (duct surface area units = SqFt; and Kr = 1 - Ks)

14	Installed supply area =		DSF for MJ8 Sect 23-18 shortcut	Installed supply area = Zero	0.00
15	Default (Table 7) supply area =			Default supply area = Zero	0.00
16	Rs = Installed area / default area =			Rs = Zero	0.00
17	Installed return area =			Copy the installed return area =	
18	Default (Table 7) return area (DFR) =			Copy the default return area (DFR) =	
19	Rr = Installed area / default area =			Copy the Rr value =	
20	Ks =		Kr =	Copy Ks =		Copy Kr =	
21	SAA (heating and sensible cooling) =		< Ks x Rs + Kr x Rr >		
22	RSL (default return-side latent gain) =		< 0.68 x DFR x RSL x ΔGrains >		
23	LGA (latent gain adjustment) =		< Rr x RSL / ALG + Rs x (ALG - RSL) / ALG >		
24	Effective heat loss factor (EHLF) =		< Line 11 Factor x Line 21 SAA value >		
25	Effective sensible gain factor (ESGF) =		< Line 12 Factor x Line 21 SAA value >		
26	Effective latent gain Btuh (ELG) =		< Line 13 gain x Line 22 LGA adjustment >		

Entering Air Worksheet

Entering Air Worksheet for Cooling

Outdoor Air (OA) and Altitude Correction Factor

Dry-Bulb (°F)	Wet-Bulb (°F)	A-Psych Grains	ACF Figure A5-1

Outdoor air values from MJ8, Table 1; or per code/utility value.
A-Psych grains from altitude sensitive psychrometrics.

Indoor Air at Return Grille

Dry-Bulb (°F)	RH (%)	A-Psych Wet-Bulb	A-Psych Grains

Indoor air per MJ8 default, or per code/utility value.
A-Psych values from altitude sensitive psychrometrics.

System Air Flow Values

Blower Cfm	OA Cfm	RA Cfm	OAF

Blower Cfm from OEM's expanded performance data.
OA Cfm per practitioner's design (observe code/utility guidance).
RAcfm = Bcfm - OAcfm
Outdoor air fraction = OAF = OAcfm / Bcfm

Return Duct Loads, Dry-Bulb Rise, and Grains Rise

Sensible Btuh	Latent Btuh	Dry-Bulb Rise (°F)	Grains Rise

Return duct loads from MJ8 Worksheet G (see Section A2-3).
Dry-Bulb rise = Sensible Btuh / (1.1 x ACF x RAcfm)
Grains rise = Latent Btuh / (0.68 x ACF x RAcfm)

Air Leaving Return Duct

Return DB RAdb (°F)	Return Grains RAgr	A-Psych WB (°F)	Return WB RAwb (°F)

RAdb = Indoor air DB + Return duct rise
RAgr = Indoor air A-Psych grains + Return duct rise
RAwb from altitude sensitive psychrometrics

Recovery Performance and Discharge Air (DA)

Sensible Effectiveness Seff	Latent Effectiveness Leff	Discharge Air Dry-Bulb DAdb (°F)	Discharge Air Grains DAgr

Effectiveness ratings from OEM performance data.
DAdb (°F) = OAdb - Seff x (OAdb - RAgr)
DAgr = OAgr - Leff x (OAgr - RAgr)

Air Entering the Equipment (read from A-Psych)

OAF	Entering DB EAdb (°F)	Entering WB EAwb (°F)	Entering Grains EAgr

Raw or processed outdoor air mixed with return duct air.
Use altitude sensitive psychrometrics for the outdoor air fraction.
Use the dry-bulb and wet-bulb values for air leaving return duct.
Use the dry-bulb and grains values for discharge air.

Entering Air Worksheet for Heating

Outdoor Air (OA) and Altitude Correction Factor

Dry-Bulb (°F)	Wet-Bulb (°F)	A-Psych Grains	ACF Figure A5-1

Outdoor air values from MJ8, Table 1; or per code/utility value.
A-Psych grains from altitude sensitive psychrometrics.

Indoor Air at Return Grille

Dry-Bulb (°F)	RH (%)	A-Psych Wet-Bulb	A-Psych Grains

Indoor air per MJ8 default, or per code/utility value.
A-Psych values from altitude sensitive psychrometrics.

System Air Flow Values

Blower Cfm	OA Cfm	RA Cfm	OAF

Blower Cfm from OEM's expanded performance data.
OA Cfm per practitioner's design (observe code/utility guidance).
RAcfm = Bcfm - OAcfm
Outdoor air fraction = OAF = OAcfm / Bcfm

Return Duct Loads, Dry-Bulb Rise, and Grains Rise

Sensible Btuh	Latent Btuh	Dry-Bulb Rise (°F)	Grains Rise

Return duct loads from MJ8 Worksheet G (see Section A2-3).
Dry-Bulb rise = Sensible Btuh / (1.1 x ACF x RAcfm)
Grains rise = Latent Btuh / (0.68 x ACF x RAcfm)

Air Leaving Return Duct

Return DB RAdb (°F)	Return Grains RAgr	A-Psych WB (°F)	Return WB RAwb (°F)

RAdb = Indoor air DB + Return duct rise
RAgr = Indoor air A-Psych grains + Return duct rise
RAwb from altitude sensitive psychrometrics

Recovery Performance and Discharge Air (DA)

Sensible Effectiveness Seff	Latent Effectiveness Leff	Discharge Air Dry-Bulb DAdb (°F)	Discharge Air Grains DAgr

Effectiveness ratings from OEM performance data.
DAdb (°F) = OAdb - Seff x (OAdb - RAgr)
DAgr = OAgr - Leff x (OAgr - RAgr)

Air Entering the Equipment (read from A-Psych)

OAF	Entering DB EAdb (°F)	Entering WB EAwb (°F)	Entering Grains EAgr

Raw or processed outdoor air mixed with return duct air.
Use altitude sensitive psychrometrics for the outdoor air fraction.
Use the dry-bulb and wet-bulb values for air leaving return duct.
Use the dry-bulb and grains values for discharge air.

Appendx 22

Manual D Friction Rate Worksheet

Step 1) Manufacturer's Blower Data

External static pressure (ESP) = _____ IWC   Cfm = _____

Step 2) Component Pressure Losses (CPL)

Direct expansion refrigerant coil _____
Electric resistance heating coil _____
Hot water coil _____
Heat exchanger _____
Low efficiency filter _____
High or mid-efficiency filter _____
Electronic filter _____
Humidifier _____
Supply outlet _____
Return grille _____
Balancing damper _____
UV lights or other component _____

Total component losses (CPL) _____ IWC

Step 3) Available Static Pressure (ASP)

ASP = (ESP - CPL) = (_____ - _____) = _____ IWC

Step 4) Total Effective Length (TEL)

Supply-side TEL + Return-side TEL = (_____ + _____) = _____ Feet

Step 5) Friction Rate Design Value (FR)

FR value from friction rate chart = _____ IWC/100 Feet

$$FR = \frac{ASP \times 100}{TEL}$$

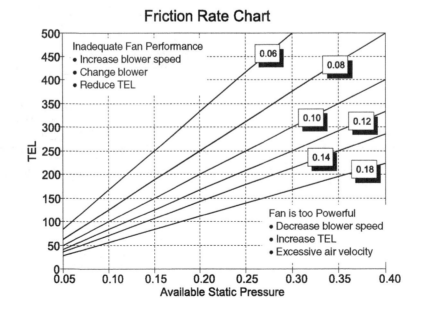

312

Index

A

Adjustable Defaults
  For load calculation tools.; 21

AHAM Appliances
  Definition; N1
  Size; 14
  Sizing rules and size limits; N18

AHRI Rating Data
  Must not be used to select equipment; N12, 181
  Narrative and issues pertaining to use; 181

AHRI Rating Speed
  Definition; N1
  For equipment sizing; 9

AHRI Rating Test
  For cooling equipment; N1
  For heat pump heating; N1

AHRI Ton
  Definition; 259

AHRI-Rated Equipment
  Cooling-only equipment
    Size limit table; N12
    Sizing rules and size limits; N12–N15
  Definition; N1, N8
  Heat pumps
    Size limit table; N13
    Sizing rules; N13

Air Changes per Hour
  Air change vs. air turnover; 167
  For engineered ventilation; 125, 185

Air Distribution
  Effectivness; 167
  Effectivness vs. continiuos blower; 296
  Issues; 1

Air Distribution Effectiveness
  Issues and discussion; 300

Air Temperature
  Entering a heat pump for heating; 85
  Entering, leaving, limits, rise
    Furnaces and electric heating coils; N12, 42, 87
  Equation for mixing outdoor and return air; 187
  Extreme values for outdoor air; 101
  For furnace discharge air, entering air, and temperature rise; 89
  High limit for indoor refrigerant coils and electric coils; 35
  In a dump zone may cause condensation; 219
  Indoor air temperature excursions for single zone and zoned systems; 17–18
  Limits; N7
  Limits for equipment and systems; 41
  Limits for zone damper systems; 23, 36, 41, 90
  Supply air temperature for air-air heat pump heating; 249
  See Also Entering Air Condition, Entering Air Calculations, and Default Conditions

Air Temperature Rise or Limit
  See Air Temperature

Air-Air Heat Pump
  Supply air temperature for heating; 249

Air-Side Component Data
  Pressure drop vs. Cfm; 180

Altitude
  Default threshold (2,500 Ft) for performance data adjustment; N7, 24
  Does not effect dew-point temperature; 219
  Effect on evaporative cooling psychrometrics; 54
  Effect on psychrometric calculations; 197
  Effects engineered ventilation loads; 23
  Effects entering air condition; 160, 162–163
  Effects equipment performance; 197
  Effects equipment performance models; 238
  Effects load calculations; 21
  Effects return duct load psychrometrics; 22
  Sea level performance data adjustment; 24, 42

Altitude Adjustment Factors
  For air-air cooling equipment; 199

Altitude Correction Factors
  For psychrometric equations; 197

Altitude Effect
  For air-air equipment; 198
  For combustion air; 200
  For electric heating coils; 199
  For gas burners; 200
  For heat pump compressor heating; 201
  For heat recovery equipment; 202
  For hot-gas coils; 200
  For hydronic equipment; 199
  For oil burners; 200
  For water-air equipment; 199
  On blower operating point; 201
  On blower performance; 201

Ancillary Dehumidification
  Conversion factors for dehumidification load; N16
  Equations for equipment performance; 255

Examples – ventilation dehumidifier; 53
Examples – whole house dehumidifier; 51
For new equipment, not used to control moisture for summer design conditions; N16
May convert Condition A to Condition B; 49
Moisture removal for part-load conditions; 253
No effect on load calculation; 15

Ancillary Dehumidification Equipment
Conditional performance data; N17
Efficiency; 50
Expanded performance data; 254
For improved summer humidity control; 296
Issues, sizing rules, and size limits, documentation; N9, N16, 49
OEM rating data; 49
Size and size limits; N17, 15, 50
See Also Whole House or Ventilation Dehumidifier

Applied Capacity
Definition; N1
Values
Determination; 26

B

Balance Point
See Economic Balance Point
See Thermal Balance Point

Ballpark Cfm Method
Searching OEM data for candidate equipment; 191

Bin Hour Calculation
Example for Boise heat pump; 4, 82
Example for Denver heat pump; 210
Example for four USA cities; 33
Example for Seattle heat pump; 206
Example for Spokane heat pump; 208
Monthly moisture removed by ancillary dehumidifcation; 253
Procedure and example; 209

Bin Hours
Below thermal balance point vs. energy savings; 206
See Glossary

Bin Temperature
See Glossary

Bin Weather Data; 283
Effect on direct evaporative cooling; 56
Outdoor moisture vs. climate type; 221

Blower
Adequate furnace blower pressure for air distribution; 44
With ECM motor; 5, 37, 44, 91, 93, 124, 177, 179
With PSC motor; 37, 44, 88, 90–93, 124–125, 172, 176–177
See Also Continuous Blower

Blower Cfm
Design value for cooling; 36
Design value for duct sizing; 36
Design value for evaporative cooling; 55
Design value for furnace selection; 43
Design value for heating; 36
Determination and use; N5
Effects cooling and heating performance; 7
Furnace blower issues; 87

Blower Data
For ductless single-split equipment; 134
For multi-split equipment; 147
For PSC and ECM motors; 176
Furnace; 44
Hydronic air handler; 124
Issues; 180
Issues and use; 36
PSC motor vs. ECM motor; 36

Blower Performance
Altitude effect; 201

Boiler
Over size effect on efficiency; 234
Part-load cycling effect on efficiency; 233
Sizing issues; 301
See Also Water Boilers

Break-Even COP
Dual fuel heating systems; 96
See Also Economic Balance Point

Buried Water Loop Design
For water-air heat pumps; 227
Loop design issues; 229
Piping geometry and pipe length; 228

Bypass Air
Temperature ramp issue; 237

Bypass Duct
Condensation; 215–216, 219

C

Capability
For load calculation tools.; 21

Climate
Climate Atlas of USA; 212
Design value for indoor relative humidity; 160–161
Effect on cooling Cfm per ton; 11
Effect on equipment selection and sizing
See Example problems
Effect on excess latent capacity; 11

Effect on heat pump defrost cycle; 173
Effect on latent cooling load; 11
Effects equipment size rules; N11

Climate types
Summarized on a psychrometric chart; 57

Combustion Air
Altitude effect; 200

Comfort
Capability of single zone system; 17
Capability of zoned system; 17
Expectations; 17
Indoor humidity effect; 215
Provided by a multi-zone system; 17
Provided by a single-zone system; 17
Temperature and humidity swing limits; 18

Comfort – Heat Pump Heating
Supply air temperature issues; 249

Comfort Chart
Target values for cooling and heating; 215

Compressor Speed
Enhanced speed
  Issues; 136, 149, 179
Equipment sizing limit effect; N11
Expanded cooling and heating data
  Must be for the speed used for the AHRI rating test; 194
Expanded cooling performance data
  For single-, multi-, and variable-speed equipment; 9–10
  For two-speed equipment; 70
  For variable-speed equipment; 70
For AHRI rating test; N1
For cooling-only equipment size limit; N12
For equipment sizing; N11
For heat pump equipment size limit; N13
For inverter (variable-speed equipment); N1
For single-, multi-, and variable-speed equipment; 179
For the thermal balance point diagram; 30, 77, 82–84, 175
For thermal balance point diagram; 71
Full speed definition; N2
Latent capacity and energy use issues; 72
Must be declared on the OEM's report for performance verification method; N21
Single speed performance issues; 289
Staged or modulating speed performance issues; 290
Use of minimum speed data; 85

Condensation
At outside of duct surfaces; 223
Calculations for summer issues; 216
Calculations for winter humidification; 215
Concealed in structural panels
  Summer; 222
  Winter; 221
Consequences; 225
Detailed calculation procedures; 219
Dew-point, surface temperature and R-value issues; 219
Duct system; 216
From winter humidification; 215
In a dump zone (zone damper system); 217
Inside of duct runs; 222
On duct insulation; 224
On glass and frames; 221
On surfaces during winter and summer; 219
Software; 225

Condensing Unit Performance
Depends on evaporator performance; 235

Condition A or Condition B Heat Pump; N3, 9, 62
Map shows possible locations for condition B heat pump; 292

Continuous Indoor Blower Operation
Equalizes room temperature differences, but creates other problems; 17
Increases seasonal energy use; 212
May negate benefit of balance point manipulation; 33
Space air motion and energy issues; 4
Space humidity and air motion, and energy issues; 1
Space humidity control issues; 217

Controls
Cooling equipment and heat pumps; 37
Ductless split equipment; 39
Fuel train and combustion; 46
Furnace and water boiler; 46
Zone damper systems; 39, 47

Conversion Factors
For dehumidification and humidification loads; N16, 50, 277

Cooling Capacity
Size limits for cooling-only equipment; N12, 61
Size limits for heat pump equipment; N12–N13, 62

Cooling Equipment
Operating conditions; 159

Cooling Equipment Selection and Size
Step-by-step procedure (for cooling only and heat pumps); 24
See Also Example Problems

Cooling Load
See Load Calculations

Index

Cooling-Only Equipment
Latent and sensible capacity limits; N13
Total capacity limits; N13

Cycling Degradation Coefficient
Default value; 33
Effects annual energy use; 33

D

Default
Coil temperature drop for ballpark cooling Cfm; 192
Conversion factors for dehumidification and humidification loads; N16
Fixed defaults and adjustable defaults for load calculation tools.; 21
For cycling degradation coefficient; 33
For entering Air Condition
See Entering Air Condition – Defaults
For heat content of fuels; 95
For heat pump emergency heat; 34, 78
For thermal balance point; 30
For zone system performance; 18
Frosting condition for AHRI compressor heating test; 173
Frosting condition, frost load, and frost knee; 31
Indoor air condition for load calculation; 15, 18, 22, 160, 192, 209, 219
Indoor humidity value for load calculation and equipment size; 18, 22, 61, 160–161, 215
Leaving air temperature for ballpark cooling Cfm; 192
Load line for thermal balance point diagram; 3, 31, 181
Outdoor air temperature for heating-cooling changeover; 31, 77
Pressure drop values for supply/return grilles and balancing damper; 44

Default Altitude Value
For applying altitude correction; 64
For equipment selection/sizing; 102

Default Conditions
For dehumidifier selection and sizing; 50
For equipment selection and sizing; 170
For indoor air; 51, 170
For load calculations; 41, 170

Default Effect on Entering Air Condition
For return duct load and outdoor air load; 162, 165

Default Entering Water Temperature
For water-air equipment selection and sizing; 34

Default Operating Mode
For ventilation dehumidifer; 53

Definitions; N1
See Also Glossary

Defrost Control
Issues and modeling considerations; 242

Defrost Cycle and Defrost Knee
Default shape; 31
For air-air heat pumps; 172–173
For thermal balance point diagram; 30
Frosting potential; 173

Degree Day Data
See Weather Data

Degree Day Ratio (HDD/CDD)
Ancillary dehumidification may allow Condition B heat pump; N16, 49
Determines excess cooling capacity for heat pumps; N13
Indicator for energy savings vs. excess heat pump cooling capacity; 208
Indicator superceded by bin-hour or hourly energy calculations; 208
Map shows possible locations for Condition B heat pump; 292
Map shows possible locations for Condition B sizing; 292
Proxy for heat pump sizing decisions; 292

Dehumidification
Ancillary equipment; 15, 49
For summer cooling; 5
Whole-house and ventilation dehumidifier equipment; N16
See Also Humidity Control

Dehumidification Equipment
See Ancillary Dehumidification

Design Conditions
For equipment selection; 135, 155
See Also Default, Indoor Design Conditions, Outdoor Design Conditions

Dew-Point Temperature
Condensation effect; 219
Not affected by altitude; 219

Direct Evaporative Cooling
Equipment performance; 54
Equipment size; 15
Psychrometrics, design issues, equipment selection; 54
Sizing rules and size limits; N10, N19

Direct Evaporative Cooling Equipment
Blower Cfm; 55
Economic issues and operating issues; 57
Efficiency; 55

Index

Equipment size limits; 57
Part-load performance; 56

Direct Saturation Efficiency
For evaporative cooling; 55

Documentation
For AHAM appliances; N10
For ancillary dehumidification equipment; N9
For cooling-only and heat pump equipment; N7
For electric heating coils; N9
For fossil fuel and electric furnaces; N8
For humidification equipment; N9
For load calculations; N7
For water boilers and coils; N9
Requirements for project design work; N7

Dry Cooling Coil
Entering wet-bulb value for cooling; 8, 27, 113, 172, 174, 178, 181, 186, 198

Dry-Bulb Temperature
See Temperature Control

Dual Fuel Heating Systems
Energy and economic issues; 95
Equipment size limits; 13
Equipment sizing rules and limits; N16
Furnace sizing; 97
Heat pump sizing; 97
Retrofit issues; 98
Return on investment; 97

Duct Airway Sizes
Manual D friction rate for airway sizing; 178
Not affected by altitude; 201

Duct Leakage
Table 7 leakage options; N8

Duct System
Condensation; 216, 219, 222–224

Duct System Operating Point
Altitude effect; 201

Duct System Performance
Altitude effect; 201

Ductless Multi-Split Equipment
Features, options and attributes; 138, 140
Refrigerant piping; 231

Ductless Multi-Split System; 137
Air distribution; 137–139, 141, 146
Applications; 137
Available static pressure for ducted fan coil; 139
Blower data for ducted fan coils; 147
Capacity range; 138
Cooling performance data; 141
Design goals; 138
Duct design for fan coil unit; 147
Engineered ventilation; 137, 139
Enhanced heating capacity; 139
Equipment capacity vs. load; 137–138
Equipment selection and sizing; 147
Heat recovery; 137
Heating performance data; 144
Indoor equipment features; 139
Noise ratings; 146
Nominal sizes
For indoor equipment; 139
For outdoor equipment; 138
Outdoor equipment features; 138
Performance and performance data; 174–175
Performance data; 138–139
Performance data requirement; 148
Power supply; 139
Simultaneous heating-cooling; 137, 139
Supplemental heat; 137, 139
Variable refrigerant flow; 137, 139
Zoning; 19

Ductless Single-Split Equipment; 129
Air distribution; 129–130, 133
Applications; 129
Available static pressure for ducted fan coil; 130
Blower data for ducted fan coils; 134
Capacity range; 130
Design goals; 129
Duct design for fan coil unit; 134
Engineered ventilation; 129
Enhanced heating capacity; 130
Equipment capacity vs. load; 129–130
Equipment selection and sizing; 135
Expanded cooling-heating performance data; 132
Features, options and attributes; 130–131
Indoor equipment features; 130
Noise ratings; 134
Nominal size
For indoor equipment; 130
For outdoor equipment; 130
Outdoor equipment features; 130
Performance and performance data; 174–175
Performance data; 131
For heating conditions; 133
Simultaneous heating-cooling; 129
Supplemental heat; 129

Dump Zone
Over cooling issues; 219
Over cooling vs. condensation issues; 217

E

ECM Blower; 5, 37, 44, 91, 93, 124, 177, 179
Does not affect size limits; N11

Economic Balance Point
Definition; N1
Determines control strategy; 13
Example problem; 97–99
For a dual fuel heating system; 95
For a dual fuel system; 13
Related to break-even COP; 96
See Also Break Even COP

Efficiency
Direct saturation efficiency; 55
Furnace or boiler cycling effect; 233

Electric Heating Coil
Air temperature limit; 23–24, 35
Altitude affect on leaving air temperature; 198–199
Control; 36
Defrost KW effects heat pump efficiency; 33
Effects heat pump efficency; 16
Heating load for size; 12
In a furnace or boiler; 41, 94
Lock out above thermal balance point; N14, 78
May not be in ductless split-coil equipment; 130, 136–137, 139, 149
May not be in single-package equipment; 151
Performance data; N12, 24, 36
Pressure drop (IWC); 37
Reducing use of supplemental heat; 205
Size limit table; N14
Sizing and/or staging; N14, 11, 34–35, 71, 78–79, 252
Supplemental and emergency for heat pump; 78
Temperature rise; 7
See Also Example problems, Sections 6 and 9

Emergency Heat for Heat Pumps
Sizing and issues; N14, 12, 34, 78, 252

Energy and Operating Cost
Heat pump sizing issues; 291
Thermal balance point indicates heat pump efficiency; 291

Energy and Operating Cost Calculations
Advanced energy calculation models and procedures; 211
Basic bin-hour calculation procedure and example; 209
Bin-hour and hourly simulation methods; 208
Effect of excess heat pump cooling capacity; 208
Effect of thermal balance point manipulation; 32–33
Example for dual fuel heating system; 96
Example investigates heat pump size issues; 4, 33
For water-air heat pumps; 229
Issues that effect supplemental heating energy; 32
Narrative and examples; 205
Performance data requirements; 297
Procedures and standards; 19
Reduce use of supplemental heat; 205
Thermal balance point diagram model; 205
Weather data sources; 212

Energy Factor
Entering air adjustment for ventilation dehumidifiers; N18
For ancillary dehumidification equipment; 50
For water heater appliance; 122

Energy Savings
See Energy and Operating Cost Calculations

Engineered Ventilation
ASHRAE 62.2; 23
Effects coil SHR and humidity control; 154
Effects equipment capacity; 22
Effects humidity control; 216
For ductless multi-spilt equipment; 137
For ductless single-split equipment; 129
For single package equipment; 152
Issues for hot water heating systems; 125–126
Load effects entering air condition
   Evaluated by Entering Air Worksheet; 188
   No heat recovery; 161
   With heat recovery; 163
Mixed air psychrometrics; 22
Outdoor air fraction; 185
Outdoor air vs. energy use and indoor humidity control; 295
See Also Entering Air Calculations and Entering Air Condition

Enhanced Compressor Speed
Definition; N1
For a balance point diagram; N14, 77, 82, 118
For heat pump heating; N14, 130, 136, 139–140, 149, 175, 194
For the thermal balance point diagram.; 71
OEM data for heat pump heating; 82

Entering Air Calculations
Circumstances at the return grille; 183
Comprehensive instruction; 183
Engineered ventilation (outdoor air, no recovery) effect; 185
Engineered ventilation (outdoor air, with recovery) effect; 186
For application circumstances; 183
Return duct effect; 183–184
Worksheet; 189
See Also Entering Air Condition and Air Temperature

Entering Air Condition
At indoor coil for heat pump heating; 164
At indoor cooling coil; 160, 162–163
Defaults for cooling

No return duct or ventilation load; 160
Return duct load effect; 162
Ventilation load effect – no recovery; 162
Ventilation load effect – with recovery; 163
Defaults for heat pump heating
Return duct load effect; 165
Ventilation load effect – no recovery; 165
Ventilation load effect – with recovery; 166
Effects cooling and heating performance; 8
Effects heat pump heating capacity; 165
Example shows calculation procedures; 187
For ancillary dehumidification equipment; 50
For cooling equipment and heat pumps; 22
For cooling season ventilation with no heat recovery; 161
For cooling season ventilation with recovery; 163
For equipment selection and sizing
Cooling equipment; N5
Heating equipment; N5
For heating season ventilation with and without recovery; 166
For no duct or ventilation load for cooling; 160
For no duct or ventilation load for heat pump heating; 165
For wet-coil cooling, and for dry-coil cooling; 8
Return duct effect for cooling; 161
Return duct effect for heating; 166
See Also Entering Air Calculations and Air Temperature

Entering Water Temperature
Default values for buried water loop systems; 101
For buried water-loop systems; 7
For water-air heat pump; 101
For water-air heat pumps; N6
Once-through or buried earth-loop heat pump; 159, 164, 227

Equipment
Altitude affects; 197
Ductless multi-split equipment; 137
Ductless single-split; 129
Operating limits; N12
Operating limits vs. intended use; 23, 41
Performance data
Single package; 153
Single package AC and heat pump; 151

Equipment Performance Models
Altitude effect; 238
Cooling-only and heat pump equipment; 237
For air-air cooling; 238
For air-air heating; 241
For water-air cooling; 242-243
For water-air heating; 246
Margin for error; 245
Modeling issues and caveats; 247
OEM data format issues; 247
Used to compensate for deficient data presentation; 243
Used to improve data presentation; 240
Uses; 237, 245

Equipment Selection and Sizing
AHAM appliances; N18, 14
AHRI cooling-only equipment; N12
AHRI heat pump equipment; N13
Ancillary dehumidification equipment; N16, 15, 49
Cooling and heat pump equipment; N11
Cooling-only and heat pump equipment; 21
Cooling-only equipment; 8, 24
Direct evaporative cooling equipment; N19, 15, 54
Dual fuel system equipment; N16, 13
Ductless multi-split systems; 137
Ductless single-split equipment; 129
Electric heating coils; N14, 11
Emergency electric coil heat; 34
Examples for central ducted furnace; 87
Examples for cooling-only and heat pump equipment; 61
Examples for dual fuel system equipment; 95
Examples for heat pump supplemental heat; 77
Examples for hydronic heating equipment; 119
Examples for water-air equipment; 101
Fossil fuel furnaces; N15, 13
Furnace and electric heating coils; N12
Furnaces and water boilers; 41, 44
Heat pump equipment; 9, 15, 28
Humidification equipment; 15
Hydronic heating equipment; 119
Issues and limits; 1, 287
Issues for all types of equipment; N12
Limits; N7
Metrics (rules and requirements); N11
Must not be based on standard sizes; N12
Must use expanded performance data; 23
OEM data method or performance verification path method; 8
Operating limits; 23, 41
Power disruption, start up and recovery issues; 16
Prerequisite tasks and information; 171
Rationale for sizing limits; 287
Searching through OEM data; 191
Seasonal efficiency rating; 23, 41
Single package AC and heat pump equipment; 151
Size limits for residential HVAC equipment; N11
Start up and set point recovery issues; 38, 47
Steps; N3
Supplemental electric coil heat; 34
Water boilers and water heaters; 13
Water heater for space heat; N15
See Also Set-Up and Set-Back

Index

Evaporative Cooling
See Direct Evaporative Cooling

Evaporator Performance
Effect of condensing unit performance; 235

Example Problems
Altitude adjustment
Blower operating point; 201
Cooling capacity for air-air equipment; 198
Cooling capacity for water-air equipment; 199
For furnace performance; 200
Ancillary dehumidification equipment
Bin hour calculation for monthly moisture removal ; 253
Ventilation dehumidifer selection and size; 53
Whole house dehumidifer selection and size; 51
Compare one-speed, two-speed, variable speed equipment performance
Boise, ID; 74
Brunswick, GA; 73
Fayetteville, AR; 72
Condensation on surfaces
Concealed condensation in structural panels; 221–222
Condensation on duct wrap; 223
Duct condensation; 222–223
Fenestration glass and frames; 220
Interior and exterior structural surfaces; 220
Dual fuel heating systems
Economic balance point
Boise, ID; 99
Brunswick, GA; 98
Fayetteville, AR; 98
Dual fuel heating system design
See Sections 8-11 to 8-13
Energy and Operating Cost
See Section 3 and Appendix 3
Enegry saving provided by larger heat pump; 292
Entering air condition
Circumstantial values; 187
For a ventilation dehumidifier; 53
For a whole house dehumidifier; 51
For central ducted furnaces; 89–90
For direct evaporative cooling equipment; 54
See Also Central Ducted Air-Air Cooling Examples – Section 5
See Also Central Ducted Air-Air Heat Pump Heating Examples – Section 7
See Also Entering Air Calculations – Appendix 2
See Also Hydronic Heating Equipment Examples – Section 10
See Also Water-Air Equipment Examples – Section 9
Heat pump efficiency
Bin hour calculation for Denver; 209
Bin hour calculation for Seattle; 206
Bin hour calculation for Spokane; 207
Excess cooling capacity vs. heating Kwh savings; 4, 33, 82
Hydronic heating equipment selection and sizing
See Sections 10-6 through 10-10
Latent load and JSHR vs. infiltration, duct leakage and location, outdoor air Cfm; 168
Modeling equipment performance
Air-air cooling equipment; 239
Water-air cooling equipment; 245
Select and size cooling-only and heat pump equipment
See Sections 5-8 through 5-19
Size heat pump supplemental heat, air-air equipment
See Sections 6-3 through 6-9
Size heat pump supplemental heat, water-air equipment
See Sections 9-3 through 9-5
Thermal balance point for air-air heat pump
See Sections 6-3 through 6-9
Thermal balance point for water-air heat pump
See Sections 9-3 through 9-5
Water-air heat pump selection and sizing
See Sections 9-3 through 9-5

Excess Cooling Capacity
Effect on cooling and heat pump heating performance; 3–5

Excess Latent Capacity; N13, 11
Definition; N1
Explaination; 289

Expanded Performance Data
Accuracy of OEM data; 247
Altitude Effect; 24
Definition; N1
Ductless single-split cooling-heating; 132
See Also Equipment Performance Models
For AHAM Equipment; 24
For air-air cooling; 171
For air-air heat pump compressor heating; 172
For compressor heating; 10
For cooling; 9
For cooling and compressor heating; 24
For cooling, graph shows Cfm, EWB, EDB, OAT/EWT effects; 248
For ductless equipment; 174–175
For ductless multi-split equipment; 141
For performance method sizing; 297–298
For water-air equipment; 173
Graphs show circumstantial behivor; 248
Heating data for multi-split equipment; 144
Mandatory requirement for equipment sizing; N11

Minimum reporting and presentation requirements
   Air-air and water-air equipment; 193
Must be used for equipment selection; 23
Narrative; 171
Research for ancillary dehumidification equipment; 254
Single package equipment; 154
See Also Performance Data

F

Fenestration Issues
   Condensation; 220

Fixed Defaults
   For load calculation tools.; 21

Fossil Fuel
   Fuel train and combustion controls; 46
   Furnace burner size vs. adequate blower power; 13
   Furnace size limit table; N15
   Furnace sizing rules and size limits; N15

Freeze Protection
   For hot water heating equipment; 125

Full Capacity
   Definition; N2

Full Compressor Speed
   Definition; N2
   OEM data for the balance point diagram; 82

Furnace
   Air temperature rise and temperature limits; 87
   Blower Cfm issues; 87
   Blower data; 44
   Design value for blower Cfm; 43
   Efficiency - part load cycling effect; 233
   Electric; 94
   Minimum and maximum capacity; 87
   Oil or propane; 94
   Over size effect on efficiency; 234
   Selection and sizing examples; 87
   Selection and sizing, step-by-step; 44
   Size for a dual fuel heating system; 97
   Sizing issues; 301

G

Gpm
   Water pump GPM
     For water-air heat pumps; N6

H

Heat Pump
   Air-air and water-air equipment
     Is sized for cooling; 28, 77, 82, 101, 135, 146, 148, 155, 171, 201
     Must be sized for cooling; N3, N13
     Must not be sized for an arbitrary balance point; 30
   Efficiency vs. equipment size
     Reduce use of electric coil heat; N13, 1, 3-4, 9, 32, 87, 205
     See Also Sections 5 and 6, example problems
   Equipment selection and sizing, step-by-step; 28
   Excess cooling capacity vs. heating efficiency
     Governing authority; 15
   Latent and sensible cooling capacity limits; N14
   Operating conditions for air-air and water-air equipment; 164
   Size vs. energy use; 291
   Sizing condition (A or B); N3
   Sizing for use in a dual fuel heating system; 97
   Supply air temperature for heating; 249
   Total cooling capacity limits; N13
   Use for dual fuel heating system; 95

Heat Recovery
   Effectiveness for air-air heat equipment; 186
   For engineered ventilation
     Effect on entering air condition examples; 187, 189
     See Also Example problems in Sections 8 through 9
     Effects entering air condition; 163, 166
   For ventilation (outdoor) air; 186

Heat Sink and Heat Source Temperature
   For air-air and water-air equipment; 7, 159, 164
   For water-air equipment; 227

Heating Load
   Definition for equipment selection and sizing; N2
   See Load Calculations

High Limit
   For blower Cfm; 43
   For boiler or water heater water temperature, and temperature rise; 41, 43
   For equipment air and water temperatures, and blower Cfm; 23–24
   For furnace air temperature, and temperature rise; 41–42
   For leaving air temperature; N12
   Leaving water temperature and temperature rise; 119
   Temperature for refrigerant and electric heating coils; 35

Hot Tub
Indoor humidity issues; 217

Hot Water Coil
Equations for air-side and water-side performance; 121
Freeze protection; 125
In hydronic air handler; 124
Performance Data; 121, 123
Performance vs. altitude; 198–199
Performance vs. Cfm, GPM, and entering air condition; 7
Pressure drop for Manual D calculations; 121
Selection and size example; 120, 122

Humidification Equipment
Condensation, mold and mildew issues; 15
Sizing rules and size limits; N17, 15
Winter humidification; 57

Humidification Load
Winter humidification; 15, 57, 166

Humidity
See Indoor Humidity

Humidity Control
Ancillary dehumidification equipment; N9, N16, 49
Depends on coil sensible heat ratio; 133, 142, 144, 154
Design issues and considerations; 217
Exhaust fans and vents vs. infiltration of moist air; 216
For comfort, health and safety; 18
For part load cooling hours; 5
Indoor humidity for cooling; 288
Latent internal and envelope loads; 217
Minimize moisture gains; 216
Monthly moisture removed by ancillary dehumidifcation; 253
Vs. maximum cooling capacity; 61
Winter humidification; 5
See Also Condensation
See Also Dehumidification
See Also Indoor Humidity
See Also Pull-Down Transient
See Section 1 procedures

Hydronic Heating Equipment
Engineered ventilation and freeze protection; 125
Example problems; 120, 122
Heating Capacity; 119
Hydronic Air Handler; 123
Selection and sizing examples; 119
Water heaters; N15

I

Indoor Air Quality
Engineered ventilation produces outdoor air loads; 22
Filters; 131, 139
Outdoor air Cfm for engineered ventilation; 185
See Also Condensation
See Also Engineered Ventilation and Indoor Humidity
See Also Moisture and Condensation Issues – Appendix 7

Indoor Design Conditions
Determines dry-bulb and wet-bulb temperatures at return grille; 183
For summer comfort, winter heating, and winter humidification; 215
Humidity issues; 5
Multi-zone performance; 17
RH design value effects latent load and JSHR; 169
Single-zone performance; 17
With ancillary dehumidification equipment; 51

Indoor Humidity
Continuous blower effect for summer cooling; 217
Depends on evaporator performance vs. condensing unit performance; 235
Design for 45% RH for dry climate cooling; 161
Excursions for part-load cooling; 294
For health and comfort; 215, 225
Hot tub moisture issues; 217
Optimum range condensation and mold-mildew issues; 5
Summer and winter issues and control; 5

Indoor Temperature
Design values for summer cooling and winter heating; 215
Multi-zone performance; 17
Single-zone performance; 17

Infiltration
Effects humidity control; 216
Examples show effect on latent load and JSHR; 168
Loads depend on altitude; 21

Interpolation and Extrapolation
Follow OEM guidance; 241
Of expanded performance data; N7
Requirements; 10, 195

L

Large Homes; 137

Latent Cooling Capacity
- Blower Cfm and leaving air temperature must be compatible with the latent load; 192
- Dehumidifier moisture removal performance; N16
- Enhancement; 38
- Graph shows Cfm, EWB, EDB, OAT/EWT effects; 248
- Indoor air condition for dehumidifier sizing; N17
- Limits; 10, 288
- Limits for cooling-only equipment; N13
- Limits for heat pump equipment; N14
- Select equipment that is designed for the latent load; 169

Latent Cooling Load
- For month of year; 254
- Indoor air condition for dehumidifier sizing; N17
- Issues; 2, 61

Leaving Air Temperature
- Evaporative cooling equipment; 55
- Momentary dry-bulb leaving direct evaporation equipment; 56
- *See Also* Air Temperature
- *See Also* High Limit and Low Limit

Load Calculation
- Altitude effect; 21
- Definition; N2
- Design condition loads; 2
- Engineered ventilation loads; 22
- For cooling-only and heat pump equipment; 21
- For dehumidifier sizing; 50
- For direct evaporative cooling equipmnet; 56
- For ductless multi-split systems; 138, 148
- For ductless single-split equipment; 129, 135
- For equipment sizing values; N3
- For furnace sizing; 87
- For furnaces and water boilers; 41
- For hot water heating equipment; 119
- For primary equipment with ancillary dehumidification; 51
- Load values effect condition of entering air; 21
- Momentary, circumstantial cooling and heating loads (part-load); 2
- Not adjusted for dehumidifier use; N3
- Procedure – proper use and issues; 21
- Required for equipment selection and sizing; 159
- Return duct loads; 22
- Sensible heat ratio issues; 291
- Tools; 21
- Total cooling load and heating load for equipment selection and sizing; N1
- Winter humidification load; 166

Low Limit
- Entering water temperature; 119
- For blower Cfm; 43
- For blower Cfm and leaving air temperature for cooling; 36
- For boiler and water heater water temperature; 41
- For equipment air and water temperatures, and blower Cfm; 23–24
- For water temperature entering boiler; 41

M

Maximum and Minimum Capacity
- For AHAM appliances; N18
- For ancillary dehumidification equipment; N16
- For cooling-only equipment; N12, 61
- For direct evaporative cooling equipment; N2, N19
- For dual fuel heating system equipment; N16
- For electric heating coils; N14
- For fossil fuel furnaces; N15
- For heat pumps; N13, 62
- For staged and variable speed equipment; N2
- For water boilers and water heaters; N16

Mixed Air Temperature
- For engineered ventilation; 185

Moisture Issues
- For winter and summer; 215
- *See Also* Condensation, and Mold and Mildew

Mold and Mildew
- Conditions for; 216
- *See Also* Condensation calculations
- *See Also* Humidity

Multi-Speed Equipment
- Compressor heating performance for two-speed compressor; 82
- Cooling performance for two speed compressor; 70
- Cooling-heating performance for water-air equipment; 118
- Performance data for reduced speed compressor; 71
- Selection; 82

Multi-Split Systems
- *See* Ductless multi-split systems

Multi-Zone Systems
- Temperature and humidity goals for comfort; 18
- *See Also* Zone Damper Systems and Zoning

Index

N

Noise
  Ductless multi-split equipment; 146
  Ductless single-split equipment; 134
  NC curve; 134–135, 146–147
  Single package air distribution; 154

O

OEM Performance Data; 6
  See Also Expanded Performance Data
  Extract capacity values
    Air to air cooling equipment; N6
    Air to air heat pump - compressor heating; N6
    Water to air cooling equipment; N6
    Water to air heat pump - compressor heating; N6
  Minimum requirements for cooling-only, heat pumps, electric coils, furnaces, water boilers, and blowers; N4
  See Also Expanded Performance Data
  See Also Performance Data

OEM Verification Path; N5
  Requirements, procedures, and reports; N21

Operating Conditions
  For air-air and water-air cooling equipment
    At the condenser; 159
    At the indoor coil; 160
  For air-air and water-air heating equipment
    At the evaporator; 164
    At the indoor coil; 164
  For Furances; 167
  For heat pump heating
    Air-air and water-air equipment; 164

Operating Cost
  See Energy and Operating Cost Calculations

Operating Limits
  Conform to OEM guidance; N12
  Must be compatible with intended use
    AHAM equipment; 153
    Cooling-only and heat pump equipment; 23
    Ductless multi-split equipment; 139
    Ductless single-split equipment; 131
    Furnace and boiler equipment; 41
    Hydronic heating equipment; 119
    PTAC and PTHP equipment; 153
  See Also High Limit and Low Limit

Outdoor Air
  See Engineered Ventilation

Outdoor Air Fraction
  Default values for application scenarios; 184
  Definition and equation; 185
  Determination and issues; 185–186
  For mixing outdoor air and return air; 50
  Maximum outdoor air Cfm for ventilation dehumidifer; N17

Outdoor Air Moisture
  Bin-hour values for dry, moist, and humid climates; 57
  Effect on direct evaporative cooling equipment performance; 54
  Rainy season effect ; 56

Outdoor Air Temperature
  Default value for heating-cooling changeover; 31

Over Size Factor
  Definition; N2

Over Size Limit
  Definition; N2
  Depends on climate; N11

P

Packaged Terminal Air Conditioners
  See Single-package equipment

Packaged Terminal heat Pumps
  See Single-package equipment

Part-Load
  Ancillary dehumidification improves part load humidity control; 49
  Cooling pull down transient; 6
  Cycling effect on furnace or boiler efficiency; 233

Performance Data
  AHRI certification (rating) values; 181
  AHTR cooling and heat pump equipment; N4
  Air-side component pressure drop; 180
  Altitude Effect for furnaces and boilers; 42
  Ancillary dehumidification equipment; 49
  Blower data issues; 180
  Cooling data issues; 178
  Ductless multi-split equipment; 139
  Electric heating coils; N4, 24
  For air-side components; 177
  Formats; 178
  Fossil fuel furnaces; N5
  Furnaces and boilers; 41
  Heating data issues; 179
  Indoor air blowers; N5
  Issues for cooling data; 178
  Issues for heating data; 179
  See Also OEM Performance Data
  Single package equipment; 154
  Standard Formats; 180, 193
  Water boilers; N5

Performance Data Exhibits
    Air-air single-speed compressor heat; 79-80, 172, 201
    Air-air single-speed cooling; 64, 171, 198, 238
    Air-air two-speed compressor heat; 83
    Air-air two-speed cooling; 70
    Air-air variable speed compressor heat; 84
    Air-air variable-speed cooling; 71
    Air-side component pressure drop; 44
    Ancillary dehumidification equipment; N17, 50
    Ductless multi-split cooling-heating equipment; 141–144, 175–176
    Ductless single-split cooling-heating equipment; 133
    ECM blower; 177
    Furnace; 42, 88
    Furnace PSC blower; 43, 89
    Heating capacity for enhanced compressor speed; 131, 139
    Hot water coil; 121, 123
    PSC blower; 125, 176
    PSC blower for ductless-split indoor unit; 135
    PTAC and PTHP equipment; 154
    Supply air grille for ductless indoor unit; 134, 146
    Tankless water heater; 125
    Water boiler; 42, 120
    Water heater; 122
    Water-air heat pump cooling-heating capacity; 103, 108, 113
    Water-air single-speed cooling; 244
    Water-air single-speed cooling-heating; 174

Performance Method
    Base case for comparitive study; 298
    Energy benifit report; 300-301
    For sizing multi- and variable-speed heat pumps; N13, 296
    Quantify energy benifit; 299
    Vs. Prescriptive size limits; 287

Performance Modeling
    Annual energy use; 294
    For cooling and heat pump equipment; 293
    Indoor humidity excursions for cooling; 294

Performance Verification Path; 180
    Equipment sizing method; 8

Potable Water Heat
    Refer to other guidance; N15, 14, 41

Power Disruptions – Intentional or Programmed
    Not compatible with equipment sizing rules; 16

Prescriptive Sizing Limits
    Rationale; 287
        Vs. Performance Procedure; 287

Pressure Drop Data
    For air-side components; 37, 44, 177

PSC Blower; 37, 44, 91, 93, 124–125, 172–173, 176–177

Psychrometric Calculations
    Chart shows humid, moist, and dry climate.; 57
    Direct evaporative cooling; 54
    Equations for sensible and latent heat; 189
    See Also Altitude

Pull-Down Transient
    Diagram; 6
    Latent cooling capacity after start-up; 6
    Special controls improve latent capacity; 38

R

Radiant Heat
    Refer to other guidance; N15, 14

Rainy Season
    Effect on evaporative cooling; 56
    Produces a short term latent load for a dry climate; 161

Refrigerant Piping
    Ductless multi-split equipment; 231

Return Air
    Provide dedicated path; 19

Return Duct Load
    Effects entering air condition for cooling; 161
    Effects entering air condition for heat pump heating; 166
    Effects equipment capacity; 22
    Evaluated by Entering Air Worksheet; 188

Rounding Rules; N3

Run Time Fraction; 3–4, 6, 71

S

Sensible Capacity
    Limits; 11
    Limits for cooling-only equipment; N13
    Limits for heat pump equipment; N14

Sensible Cooling Capacity
    Graph shows Cfm, EWB, EDB, OAT/EWT effects; 248

Sensible Heat Ratio
    For load calculation and cooling coil; 168
    Issues; 52, 61, 291
    Sensitivity to circumstances; 168
    See Glossary

Index

Sensitivity
   For load calculation tools.; 21

Set Point Recovery
   After start up, or set-up, or set-back; 38, 47

Set-Up or Set-Back
   Recovery Issues; 16, 38, 47
   Recovery issues for hot water heat; 13
   Recovery vs. programmed or intentional power disruptions; 16
   Vs. energy use; 16
   Vs. equipment sizing rules; 17

Simultaneous Heating-Cooling; 17
   For ductless single-split equipment; 129
   Multi-split equipment piping issues; 231
   See Also Ductless multi-split equipment
   See Also Single-package equipment
   Single Speed equipment
   Performance Data and data use; 179

Single-Package Equipment; 151
   Air distribution; 152, 154
   Applications; 151
   Available static pressure for duct run; 152
   Capacity range; 153
   Design Goals; 152
   Engineered Ventilation; 152
   Equipment capacity vs. load; 151–152
   Equipment selection and sizing; 155
   Expanded cooling performance data; 154
   Features, options and attributes; 152–153
   Noise; 154
   Nominal size; 153
   Performance data
      For heating conditions; 154
      For PTAC and PTHP; 153
      For window units and through wall units; 153
   PTAC and PTHP; 151
   Simultaneous Heating-Cooling; 151
   Supplemental heat; 151

Single-Zone Systems
   Temperature and humidity goals for comfort; 18

Size limits
   Compliance; N11
   For air-air and water-air heat pumps; 297
   For cooling equipment; 297
   For cooling-only equipment; N12
   For direct evaporative cooling equipment; N2, N19
   For electric heating coils; N14
   For equipment; N7, 287
   For fossil fuel furnaces; N15
   For heat pump equipment; N13
   For humidification equipment; N17
   For water boilers and water heaters; N16
   Normative requirements; N11

Sizing
   Effect on heat pump energy use; 291

Sizing Procedure
   Requirements; 8

Sizing Value
   For AHAM Equipment; N18
   For cooling and heat pump equipment; 14
   For dehumidification equipment; 15
   For dehumidifier sizing; N16
   For direct evaporative cooling; N2, N19, 15
   For electric heating coils; 12
   For emergency heat; N14
   For fossil fuel furnaces; 13
   For furnace burner capacity; N15
   For heat pumps; 9
   For heating-only equipment ; N14
   For humidification equipment; N17, 15
   For Supplemental Heat; N14
   For total capacity; N13
   For total cooling capacity; N12
   For total cooling load; 8
   For water boilers; N15, 14

Snow Melting
   Refer to other guidance; N15, 14, 41

Software
   Building Science; 226
   Condensation; 225
   See Also Equipment Performance Models
   For buried water-loop design; 229

Steady State Efficiency
   For furnaces and boilers; 42

Supplemental Heat
   Electric coil capacity control; 35
   For heat pumps; 78
   Issues; 34
   Issues that effect energy use; 32
   Lock out electric coil above thermal balance point; 35
   Reducing use for energy savings; 205
   Sizing and staging for comfort; 252
   Sizing rules; N14
   See Also Electric Heating Coils

Supply Air Cfm
   Cooling Cfm determination; 169
   Equations for heating and cooling Cfm; 167

T

Target Value
   Definition; N2

Index

Temperature
See Air Temperature, Water Temperature

Temperature Bin
See Glossary

Temperature Contorl
For heating and cooling dry-bulb; 287

Temperature Swing
Acceptable performance for single-zone and multi-zone systems; 18
Multi-zone performance; 17
Room to room; 17
Single zone performance; 17

Thermal Balance Point
Bin hours below TBP vs. energy savings; 206
Default value; 30
Definition; N2
Depends on heating-cooling load ratio; 31
Depends on momentary circumstances; 2, 31
Depends on momentary defrost effect; 30
For PTHP and other single-package equipment; 155
For water-air heat pumps
  Depends on entering water temperature; 31
Issues and caveats; 33, 77
Lock out supplemental heat; 35
Must not be dictated by arbitrary mandate; 33
Must not be used to size equipment; 30
Proper use
  Size supplemental heat, make control decisions; 33

Thermal Balance Point Diagram
Air-air examples
  See Sections 6-3 through 6-9
Compressor speed effect; 71
Construction; N14, 30, 77, 101
Deffinition; N2
Defrost and defrost knee issues; 30, 173
Energy and operating cost examples
  See Appendix 6
Excess cooling capacity effect; 3
For AHAM equipment; 24
For energy calculations; 205
For enhanced compressor speed; 175–176
For multi-speed and variable speed equipment; 82–83
For single-package equipment; 155
For staging supplemental heat; 249
Heat pump heating energy issues; 32
OEM compressor heating data is mandatory; N21
Used to size supplemental heat; N14, 12
Water-air examples
  See Sections 9-3 through 9-5

Thermal Balance Point Manipulation
Effect on energy and operating cost
  See Appendix 6
Example of energy and op-cost effect; 33
Methods, issues, energy use; 32
Vs. humidity control, air distribution, blower power, and other issues; 33

Thermostat
Location vs. room-room temperature differances; 17

Through Wall Units
See Single-package equipment

Total Cooling Capacity
Graph shows Cfm, EWB, EDB, OAT/EWT effects; 248, 253
High limit vs. compressor speed control; 289
Limits for cooling-only equipment; N13
Limits for heat pump equipment; N13
Low limit vs. compressor speed control; 290
Method for searching OEM data for candidate equipment; 191

Total Cooling Load
Definition for equipment selection and sizing; N2

Two Speed Equipment
Performance data and data use; 179

Two-Speed Equipment
See Also Compressor Speed

V

Vapor Retarding Membrane
For duct runs; 223
  USA map shows when required; 224
Placement vs. climate; 221

Variable Refrigerant Flow
See Ductless multi-split systems

Variable-Speed Equipment
Compressor heating performance for variable-speed compressor; 83
Cooling performance for variable speed compressor; 70
Cooling-heating performance for water-air equipment; 118
Performance data and data use; 179
Performance data for reduced speed compressor; 71
Selection; 82
See Also Compressor Speed

Ventilation
See Engineered ventilation

Index

Ventilation Dehumidifier
 Definition; N2
 Maximum outdoor air fraction; N17
 Performance adjustment for entering air condition; N18
 Sizing rules and size limits; N16

Venting
 Furnace or water boiler; 46

W

Water Boiler
 Selection and size example; 120
 Size limit table; N16
 Sizing rules and size limits; N15
 Sizing rules are for space heating only; N16
 Used for potable water heating; N16
 Used for radiant heat; N16
 Used for snow melting; N16

Water Boiler and Water Heater
 Size; 13

Water Gpm
 Effects water-air cooling and heating performance; 7

Water Heater
 Used for space heat; N15–N16

Water Pump
 Gpm for water-air heat pumps; N6

Water Temperature
 For water-air heat pumps; N6
 Limits; N7

Water Temperature Limits
 For hydronic heating equipment; 119
 For water boilers and heaters; 43

Water Temperature Rise
 For water boilers and heaters; 43

Water-Air Heat Pumps
 Buried horizontal or vertical loop design; 227
 Energy calculations; 229
 Software for water-loop design; 229

Weather Data
 ASHRAE; N4, 182
 ASHRAE degree day data; N4
 Degree day data, ASHRAE and NOAA; 182
 For energy calculations; 212
 NOAA; 182
 NOAA degree day data; N4

Weather Data Use
 Proximity Issues; 213

Whole-House Dehumidifier
 Definition; N3
 Sizing rules and size limits; N16

Window Units
 See Single-package equipment

Winter Humidification
 Equipment; 57

Worksheet
 For entering air calculations; 189, 309
 Manual D Friction Rate Worksheet; 44, 46, 87, 89, 92–93, 97–98, 121, 123, 177, 309

Z

Zone Damper Systems
 Minimize excess cooling and heating capacity; N12–N15
 See Also Multi-Zone Systems and Zoning

Zoned Systems
 Goals for comfort and safety; 18
 Simultaneous heating and cooling; 19

Zoning
 Air zoning controls; 39
 Benefits and issues; 17

Zoning Decisions
 Issues to consider; 17, 19